Jill Liddington was born in Manchester in 1946 and returned to live in the area in 1974. For the past ten years she has taught women's studies and local history classes, especially for the Workers' Educational Association (WEA). Since 1982 she has been at Leeds University Department of Adult Education; she was one of the contributors to *Over Our Dead Bodies: Women Against the Bomb* (Virago). She lives in Halifax, West Yorkshire.

In 1978 Jill Liddington co-authored with Jill Norris the highly acclaimed *One Hand Tied Behind Us: The Rise of the Women's Suffrage Movement*. In *The Life and Times of a Respectable Rebel* she takes up another forgotten strand of women's history, told through the eyes of Selina Cooper (1864–1946), a Lancashire working-class woman who was at the forefront of all the progressive movements of her time. But this is much more than the biography of one woman: using oral testimony, unpublished letters, diaries, contemporary documents and photographs, Jill Liddington provides a unique history of those turbulent years.

THE LIFE AND TIMES OF A RESPECTABLE REBEL

SELINA COOPER
(1864-1946)

JILL LIDDINGTON

Published by VIRAGO PRESS Limited 1984
41 William IV Street, London WC2N 4DB

Copyright © Jill Liddington 1984

British Library Cataloguing in Publication Data
Liddington, Jill
    The life and times of a respectable rebel.
    1. Cooper, Selina
    2. Feminists–Great Britain–Biography
    I. Title
    305.4'2'0924   HQ1593

    ISBN 0-86068-418-0

Printed in Great Britain by litho at
The Anchor Press, Tiptree, Essex

CONTENTS

ACKNOWLEDGEMENTS

This biography could never have been written without the generous support and encouragement of Selina Cooper's daughter, Mary. I knew Mary for seven years and during that period, whenever I visited her to talk about her mother, she always made me warmly welcome. At each visit she opened up to me her rich reserve of memories and of family papers: I seldom left the house without a lengthy taped interview and an armful of letters and photographs for deposit in the local record office. To the very end of her life, Mary seemed to be *willing* me to produce a book that would at last do justice to her remarkable mother. This biography is as much a tribute to Mary as it is to Selina Cooper; yet tragically, Mary died, aged eighty-three, just a year before it was published.

The most valuable documentary and oral evidence about Selina naturally stemmed from Mary herself, an only child. However, Selina had six brothers and, from their descendants, I have been able to draw upon other family history. I would like to thank John Coombe's son, Billy, as well as Richard Coombe's grandchildren, Harold and Thomas; and Robert Cooper's niece, Jenny Cranfield, who helped me sort through the remaining family papers after Mary's death.

I am enormously grateful to all the people of Nelson who have shown me hospitality over the years and have helped me understand what life in their town used to be like earlier this century. I am particularly indebted to Stan and Ivy Iveson who showed me their records of the Nelson ILP branch; Len and Betty Dole who let me see their local Labour Party material; the late Bessie Dickinson and her husband Harold Dickinson, both centrally involved in the 'more looms' dispute of the 1930s; the late Henry Foulds, weaver and local historian; Jane Summersgill, the first woman on the Nelson Weavers' Committee; Eva Ingham whose mother-in-law led the Women's Peace demonstration with Selina Cooper in 1917; and Maggie Chapman who in 1934 brought Selina her invitation to visit Nazi Germany.

The Life and Times of a Respectable Rebel is the story of a forgotten strand of women's history, told here through the eyes of one woman, Selina Cooper. But it also tells of the experience of other radical suffragists who worked closely with her during and after the women's suffrage campaign. I would therefore like particularly to thank Doris Chew, only daughter of Ada Nield Chew; Helen Wilson, only surviving daughter of Annot Robinson; Alice Hartley, niece of Margaret Aldersley; and Gwen Coleman who is, as far as either of us knows, the only surviving organiser of the National Union of Women's Suffrage Societies.

I have had considerable help from librarians and archivists, especially Susan Byrne at Nelson Library who never failed to respond to my many requests; Stephen Bird at the Labour Party Archive; David Doughan at the Fawcett Library who gave me valuable advice on the treasures lurking there; the staff of the Nelson Weavers' office for their kindliness and many cups of tea; and the staff, both past and present, of the Lancashire Record Office who calendared the original deposits and who have patiently received the trickle of subsequent additions to the Cooper papers. I also thank the Twenty Seven Foundation for a grant towards some of the costs incurred in research.

Selina Cooper's active life stretched over more than half a century. In finding out about these years I have been lucky enough to be able to talk to friends expert on particular aspects of this history. I am grateful to Sue Bruley for our conversations about women in the Communist Party and about Women Against War and Fascism; Stuart Rawnsley for discussions on the 1930s; and Alan Fowler for joining me to form a two-person Nelson History Workshop. Many of the ideas about Nelson politics stem from arguments with Alan.

I would also like to thank Jane Cousins, Deedee Glass and John Slater who shared in the original discovery of the Cooper papers; Anne Moseley, Diana Kealey and the late Gloden Dallas for their sisterly comments on early chapters; and Pete and Gaby for help towards an electric typewriter. Many people have commented on the final draft of this biography, and I am grateful to Jane Lewis, Logie Barrow, Miriam Zukas, Dick Taylor, Ruthie Petrie, Stuart Rawnsley, Jill Norris, Penny Shimmin and Jean McCrindle.

There are four people to whom special thanks are due; they each read and commented on an early – and therefore lengthy – draft as it slowly emerged from the typewriter. First Karen Hunt of the Manchester Women's History Group; second Ursula Owen at Virago who watched patiently as this book swelled from a slim biography into something much larger; third Jo Vellacott in Montreal, whose encouragement and scholarly comments on the suffrage sections were of enormous value; and lastly Julian Harber, a fellow historian. Although my fiercest critic, Julian was always genuinely interested to hear of the small nuggets of gold I believed I had dug up at the end of each day's research. Without Julian, this biography would have been started, but possibly might never have been completed – and certainly would not have been so enjoyable to write.

MAIN CHARACTERS IN ORDER OF APPEARANCE

PART ONE: GROWING UP VICTORIAN 1864–1899

THE COOMBE FAMILY

(see Coombe family tree on p 6)

THE EARLY SOCIALIST MOVEMENT

Deborah Smith, weaver and secretary of Nelson Women's Co-operative Guild
Henry Hyndman, leader of Social Democratic Federation
Mrs Grocott, Guildswoman and wife of a Burnley shoemaker
Mary Brown, doctor's wife and friend of Olive Schreiner
Margaret McMillan, ILP member of Bradford School Board
Dan Irving, Social Democratic Federation organiser, Burnley
Reverend Leonard, socialist minister at Colne
Ben Smith and Abel Latham, weavers and Brierfield Labour councillors
Tom Mann, secretary of Independent Labour Party
Mrs Holt, cook at Co-operative Holiday Association, Keld
Mary Robb, doctor's wife and Poor Law Guardian

PART TWO: VOTES FOR WOMEN 1899–1918

EARLY SUFFRAGISTS

Mrs Fawcett, President of National Union of Women's Suffrage

Societies
Caroline Martyn, Enid Stacy and Catharine Conway, ILP
speakers
Helen Phillip, Manchester suffragist
Lady O'Hagan of Townley Hall, Guardian
Isabella Ford, Leeds Quaker, member of Independent Labour
Party
Mrs Pankhurst and Christabel, leaders of Women's Social and
Political Union
Esther Roper and Eva Gore-Booth, Manchester suffragists
Annie Heaton, Burnley cotton worker
Sarah Reddish, Guildswoman and member of Bolton School
Board
Eleanor Rathbone, secretary of Liverpool Suffrage Society, later
an MP
Lady Frances and Lady Betty Balfour, leading Tory suffragists

THE EARLY LABOUR MOVEMENT

John Thornton, socialist Poor Law Guardian
Ramsay MacDonald, secretary of Labour Representation Com-
mittee, later Prime Minister
Philip Snowden, Cowling councillor, later Chancellor of
Exchequer
William Rickard, councillor and Nelson's first Labour mayor
David Shackleton, MP for Clitheroe
Albert Smith, Overlookers' Secretary, later an MP
Harriette Beanland, dressmaker and Poor Law Guardian

NELSON SUFFRAGE SOCIETY

Sarah Thomas, temperance worker and Liberal
Margaret Aldersley, ILP member and Poor Law Guardian
Ula Blackburn, Emily Murgatroyd, Nancy Shimbles, Florence
Shuttleworth, weavers
Mary Ann Coombe, chain beamer, Selina's sister-in-law
Clara Myers, widow of schoolteacher
Miss Moser, French teacher at grammar school
Mr and Mrs Kershaw, Clara Baldwin, Miss Cliff and Miss Todd,
other members

SUFFRAGISTS AND SUFFRAGETTES

Sylvia Pankhurst, founder of East London Federation of Suffragettes

Dora Montefiore, tax resister

Charlotte Despard, a leader of Women's Freedom League

Helena Swanwick, Manchester suffragist and writer

Fenner Brockway, member of Independent Labour Party

Kate Courtney, secretary of National Union of Women's Suffrage Societies

Catherine Marshall, secretary of Election Fighting Fund

Margaret Ashton, Manchester city councillor

Ray Strachey, parliamentary secretary of National Union of Women's Suffrage Societies

NATIONAL UNION OF WOMEN'S SUFFRAGE SOCIETIES ORGANISERS

Emilie Gardner, Birmingham suffragist

Margaret Robertson, Manchester (later Election Fighting Fund) organiser

Annot Robinson, suffragette who joined National Union of Women's Suffrage Societies

Ada Nield Chew, organiser for Women's Trade Union League

Ellen Wilkinson, Manchester suffragist, later Cabinet Minister

PART THREE: WOMEN BETWEEN THE WARS 1918-1939

THE INTER - WAR WOMEN'S MOVEMENT

Marion Phillips, Chief Woman Officer of Labour Party

Jennie Baker, Dora Russell and Stella Browne, birth control campaigners

Eva Hubback, parliamentary secretary of NUSEC

Monica Whately, member of deputation to Nazi Germany

Lady Astor, first woman to sit in House of Commons

Elizabeth Abbott, organiser of Open Door Council

LABOUR COUNCILLORS IN NELSON

Alec Campbell, tailor, Guardian and friend of Coopers
Richard Bland, weaver and pacifist
Andrew Smith JP, mayor
Pat Quinn, plumber, first Irish mayor
Willie John Throup, Guardian, Labour Party agent and playwright
Richard Winterbottom, jobbing gardener, mayor

OTHER SOCIALISTS

Alex Ingham, weaver and Conscientious Objector
Gertrude Ingham, a leader of Women's Peace Crusade
Dan Caradice, Labourers' Union secretary and Conscientious Objector
Carey Hargreaves, secretary of Nelson Weavers
Jane McCall, first woman on Nelson Weavers' committee
Arthur Greenwood MP, Minister of Health 1929–31

MEMBERS OF THE COMMUNIST PARTY

Seth Sagar, Elliot Ratcliffe, Bessie and Harold Dickinson, weavers
Rose Smith, Women's Organiser in Burnley
Maggie Chapman, weaver, shared house with Rose Smith
Elizabeth Stanworth, secretary of the local Anti-War Group

MEMBERS OF THE MAGISTRATES' BENCH

Dr Jackson, former mayor
Sir Amos Nelson, cotton manufacturer at Valley Mills

MEMBERS OF THE PEOPLE'S CONVENTION

D.N. Pritt, MP, barrister and propagandist
Arthur Mantel and Alan Fisher
Joe Bracewell, chairman of local General and Municipal Workers' Union

CHRONOLOGY

1850	Marriage of Jane Uren and Charles Coombe
1864	Birth of Selina Coombe
1876	Death of Charles Coombe
1889	Death of Jane Coombe
1892	Nelson Independent Labour Party branch formed
1893	Robert Cooper sails to America
1896	Marriage of Selina Coombe and Robert Cooper
1897	Birth of John Ruskin Cooper
	National Union of Women's Suffrage Societies formed
1899	Selina and Robert Cooper spend summer in Swaledale
1900	Birth of Mary Cooper
1901–2	Selina Cooper to Westminster with textile workers' petitions. Elected Poor Law Guardian
1902	David Shackleton becomes the Coopers' Labour MP
1903	Selina Cooper forms Nelson and Colne Suffrage Committee
1904	Selina Cooper and Harriette Beanland elected Guardians
1905–7	Selina Cooper urges women's suffrage at Labour Party Conferences
1906	Formation of Nelson and District Suffrage Society
from 1906	Selina Cooper employed as suffrage organiser
1912	Election Fighting Fund formed
1913	Suffrage Pilgrimage to London
1914	Outbreak of war
1917	Russian revolutions; Nelson women's peace demon-

PREFACE

This biography tells the story of one working woman's experience from her mid-Victorian childhood, through her long years in Lancashire, to her death in 1946. Selina Cooper's life, till recently almost forgotten, spans the most crucial half-century of the history of the women's movement.

Her tale is traced here from her parents' ill-fated marriage in 1850, through her involvement in the socialist and feminist crusade of the 1890s, to the rise of the Labour Party and of the suffrage movement. At the turn of the century Selina Cooper was suddenly converted by the logic of suffrage. From then on she campaigned unceasingly as a suffragist* right up to the victory of 1918. Once women won the vote, Selina worked for birth control and for the right of married women to work – and against those three evils that so soured 'the devil's decade' of the 1930s: unemployment, fascism and war.

Everything described in these pages is narrated through Selina Cooper's own sharp eyes. This particular woman's experience is faithfully traced in detail over a fifty-year period: no aspect of her life story has been omitted. Yet *The Life and Times of a Respectable Rebel* emerges as something broader than a single-focus biography. Each section fits Selina's own experiences into the wider history of the time. The first part, 'Growing Up Victorian',

---

* The suffragists differed from the suffragettes in that they did not agree with using militant tactics to win the vote. The major group of militant suffragettes was the Women's Social and Political Union (WSPU), formed in 1903 and led by Mrs Pankhurst and her daughter Christabel. The major non-militant group was the National Union of Women's Suffrage Societies, formed in 1897 and led by Mrs Fawcett.

takes the story back to the half-forgotten childhood world of dame schools and infant deaths, of railway navvies and child labourers. Very little is known about the lives of working-class girls of this generation. But despite the scarcity of sources, Selina's childhood is reconstructed here in as great detail as possible; where the narrative is still tentative and doubts remain, these are noted in the text or the footnotes. The second part, 'Votes for Women', tells of the suffrage years from 1900 to 1918, tracing Selina Cooper's tale as she emerges as a talented organiser and speaker. Her experience throws considerable light on these troubled years. For instance, her day-to-day story during 1912–14 clearly confirms the importance of the political alliance forged between the suffrage and labour movements. Finally, the third part, 'Women between the Wars', recounts what happened to suffragists like Selina once the vote was won. It records the experience of working women in the depressed industrial north who campaigned against the Means Test and for married women's right to work. And it reveals the sustained campaign by suffragists like Selina against war, first in 1914–18, then for disarmament in the 1920s, later against war and fascism, and even (in Selina's own case) against the Second World War.

Tracing these detailed connections and continuities through Selina Cooper's own experience has been possible only because of the loyal support and encouragement of Selina's only surviving child, Mary, born in 1900.

I first came across Mary in March 1976, introduced to her through a friend of a friend. With my fellow interviewer, Jill Norris, I visited Mary twice that year. On both occasions we made a tape recording of Mary's memories of her mother's suffrage work and other campaigns, and afterwards we transcribed these interviews.[1]

When I met Mary Cooper, she had just had her seventy-sixth birthday. She had short, straight grey hair and was still energetically involved in local socialist politics – as secretary of the local Labour Party Women's Section and as a member of the party's executive. Without a second's hesitation, Mary welcomed us into her small terraced house, and immediately proceeded to regale us with an intoxicating string of anecdotes about her mother's life.

The two women had shared the house together for nearly fifty years, Mary happily devoting her life to caring for her mother. Thirty years after Selina's death, Mary still remained fiercely loyal to everything her mother had stood for. 'The story went that I was neglected, because my mother was away,' working for women's suffrage; but Mary stoutly denied such rumours. 'I sort of missed her, because I worshipped my mother. Up to dying we were always pals.'[2]

I remember reeling out of the house onto the cold stone Nelson streets after the visit, punch-drunk from Mary's rapid succession of tales about her mother. Memories had tumbled out one on top of another, and Mary sometimes left half-sentences dangling in her eagerness to recount Selina's stories.* These memories raced breathlessly from Mary's having recently thrown away some of the rusted chains that were carried by the Cradley Heath chain-makers when, it turned out, Selina shepherded them down from the Black Country for a women's suffrage procession in London in 1909 to Mary's description of how her mother had spoken in Central Hall, Westminster on married women's right to work in, I later discovered, 1933. Minutes later Mary was explaining how her mother coped as the only socialist woman elected to the Burnley Board of Guardians at the turn of the century; and then the conversation swooped with scarcely a pause to Lancashire's violent industrial struggles during the Depression when Mary's mother sitting (again as the only socialist woman) on the Nelson magistrates' bench, took a courageous stand when demonstrators were hauled up by the police.[3]

It was all too much to digest at one sitting. Mary Cooper was quite rightly hardly going to provide us, two keen but innocent historians, with a precise chronology for the tales of her mother. And so it was unclear to us in which year between the 1880s and 1940s particular events took place. I found the second interview recorded a few months later equally bewildering. However much we tried to read as widely as possible to puzzle out Mary's stories, some seemed to remain obstinately unrelated to events described in history books. For instance, Mary told of how her mother

---

* Where incomplete sentences are quoted from the taped interviews, the missing words have been added in brackets.

travelled with two other women to Nazi Germany in 1934, supposedly to interview Hitler about his treatment of imprisoned
women hostages. The search to discover how on earth this
unlikely deputation was organised seemed fruitless.

Then in May 1977 I decided to record a third and final interview with Mary Cooper in order to check a few factual details for
One Hand Tied Behind Us.* When I arrived in Nelson, Mary welcomed me with her characteristically forthright hospitality. But
the visit turned out to be by no means the final one. Now finding
she had more spare time on her hands, Mary had begun rooting
around her house and had stumbled across some of her mother's
papers that she had carefully stored away in stout wooden boxes
after Selina's death in 1946, and subsequently forgotten about.
To my great surprise, Mary presented me with an armful of
letters, photographs and pamphlets that she and her mother had
kept and whose existence Mary had long ago pushed to the back of
her mind. No one except Mary knew such papers existed; and I
staggered out of the house and up to Nelson station clutching a
carrier bag full of intriguing documents – all on their way to be
safely deposited in the county record office.

Subsequent visits to Nelson to see Mary and record further
interviews produced yet more material. Over the next few years it
grew into a splendid family archive. By the end of 1981, ten
successive deposits embraced over 250 letters, sheaves of press
cuttings and about a hundred photographs (some of them taken
long before Selina was born and dating back to her father's mid-
nineteenth century youth). A diary Selina kept during 1908–9
was unearthed: it gives a brisk day-by-day account of the hectic
doings of a suffrage organiser. Although a political rather than a
personal record, it tells of the daily life of a woman activist at a
time when direct testimony from working women remains very,
very rare. Later visits also produced an autograph book begun in
1899 by Selina and her husband Robert, a weaver, and a small
but interesting collection of late nineteenth-century birth control
tracts.[4]

Documents such as these allowed me to check the accuracy of

---

* Liddington, J. and Norris, J., *One Hand Tied Behind Us: the Rise of the Women's Suffrage
Movement* (Virago, London 1978)

Mary's oral testimony which had so dazzled me a year or two earlier. Mary's detailed recall of her mother's activities was shown to be reliable historical evidence. How could I wonder any more about the deputation to Nazi Germany with the papers spread out before me of an organisation called Women Against War and Fascism? Even tales about Selina's early life that had been passed down to Mary as a child were borne out. Mary had told of how her mother's railway-navvy father had died in his prime; and here indeed were photographs of him working building bridges and of his grim widow in deep mourning.

However, even this powerful combination of oral evidence and family papers could not tell the complete story of Selina Cooper's life. The job of filling in the gaps turned out to be time-consuming and often frustrating. I had originally believed that someone who bequeathed such a wealth of memories and documents must surely have left her mark in a number of other places. I began to search through library catalogues and through archive listings. I doggedly pursued every minute clue, every pathetic shred of evidence, but was constantly rebuffed by silences and stonewalls. Sometimes there seemed to be yawning omissions, in particular the absence of letters that Selina wrote to other people. Surely, I told myself, the hundreds of letters written *to* her must have spawned at least a few replies. But I have so far been unable to trace any letters *from* her: perhaps those few written by Selina which have survived are still lying forgotten in tin trunks, under spare beds and up in attics.[5] Another area of noticeable silence were the precious few clues that Selina, like so many other working women of her generation, left about her childhood and her early years. And, again like so many others among her contemporaries, Selina preferred to draw a proud veil over her relationship with her husband. Robert Cooper is scarcely ever referred to. This silence is particularly noticeable in the 1908–9 suffrage diary. Selina's brisk entries note the meetings she addressed, the time she spent with Mary – but never referred even once to Robert.

After a further visit to Mary in 1978 (which alone produced over 300 new documents), I began to feel that here at last was sufficient evidence to be able to narrate the life of at least one of the radical suffragists* whom Jill Norris and I briefly described in *One Hand Tied Behind Us*. I found myself increasingly committed to telling the story of this woman's remarkable life and I began systematically sifting through the tape transcripts and reading the minute books of those organisations, such as the Burnley Weavers' Association and the 1930s Lancashire Public Assistance Committee, that Selina Cooper became involved in.

Before long I realised that my plan for a slim biography was getting out of hand. Whatever I read seemed always to lead on to something else, which itself then needed urgent following up. I recognised that Selina Cooper's story could only be understood if it was placed in a wide historical context and that therefore the book would take far longer to research than envisaged. This was particularly true for the most time-consuming task: reading through Nelson's weekly newspapers. The prospect of reading the entire run of papers from 1893 to 1935 (and for certain episodes it was necessary to compare three or four papers to get a balanced view) was daunting. But by the end I was glad to have done it. For instance, the mid-1920s papers, which I had originally thought of leaving out, told of Selina in the middle of a blazing row in the Nelson Town Council Chamber, which sprang from the controversy over access to birth control information; it represented a key episode in her life which had otherwise been forgotten.

By 1981 most of the research was complete. All that remained was for the 1881 household census to be made available the following spring. When, at long last, sitting in the Record Office in London, I stumbled across sixteen-year-old Selina listed as a 'Cotton Operative' living with her widowed mother ('Dressmaker Formerly'), grandmother ('Formerly Laundress') and three brothers ('Bootmaker', 'Cotton Weaver' and 'Scholar') in an isolated textile town on the Lancashire-Yorkshire border, I was overcome with delight.

Writing was also a slow process and I'm grateful to Ursula Owen at Virago for reading the chapters as they gradually took

---

* 'Radical suffragist' was the name we coined to describe the women who came to the suffrage campaign through the labour and socialist movements, who later on grew concerned about the suffragettes' use of militant tactics, and who afterwards opposed the First World War.

shape. On the other hand, Mary Cooper will sadly never read what I have written about her mother – just because it *has* been such a slow process. Three years ago, in 1980, Mary celebrated her eightieth birthday with a party and received a national merit award for her services to the Labour Party during her sixty-seven years of membership. But by 1981 the infirmities of old age had begun to tighten their grip. Before long it became clear to friends, neighbours and her few remaining relatives that Mary, though physically fit, was no longer able to remain living by herself in her own home. She needed help and, for the last fifteen months of her life, was carefully looked after in a local hospital. Mary died peacefully in her sleep in July 1983.[6]

Mary's house, the Coopers' home since 1901, has now been sold: with no living descendants, Selina Cooper's saga had finally come to an end. Yet, as Mary's cousin and I were clearing out the house after the funeral, still more family papers were unearthed. The first known portrait of Selina, dating from the early 1890s, came to light. And at the bottom of the cellar steps were dis-covered two lengths of stout, hand-beaten chain which had lain in 59 St Marys Street since 1909 when Selina escorted the Cradley Heath chainmakers down to London.

This biography is written in memory of, not just Selina Cooper, but also Mary. Were it not for her help and encourage-ment, scarcely a line of it would exist; for, by the 1970s, only a dwindling handful of people could remember Selina as anything but an elderly lady. (Even Fenner Brockway, now in his nineties, who had worked with her in 1913 for the labour-suffrage alliance, admitted that, over the intervening seventy years, his memory of this particular suffragist had understandably grown dim.[7])

Mary's own memories, on the other hand, remained vivid to the end. 'My mother never dictated any of this history,' she explained disarmingly. 'I picked it up – it clung to me. Because my mother and father were always head-over-heels in the current affairs that were going on.' But if there was no time for reminiscing while her mother was alive, Mary afterwards proudly cherished her memories of her mother. And it was this resilient memory that sent me scouring dusty library cellars and pestering local people who might have known Selina in the hope that I could eventually fit all the pieces of the jigsaw together.

As Selina Cooper's suffragist generation faded further and further away in people's memories, so Mary's stories of her childhood were increasingly dismissed as rambling fairy tales by impatient listeners. The 1950s and 1960s were years when few people wanted to remember women's suffrage. Luckily, for seven years, from March 1976 when I was first introduced to Mary, to her death in July 1983, I was able to visit Selina's daughter regularly and got to know her very well. Gradually I puzzled out what Mary's long and colourful stories of the past were about, and I came to believe them to be true. You, the reader, must decide for yourself.

Halifax
October 1983

PART ONE:
GROWING UP VICTORIAN

CHAPTER ONE

A WEST COUNTRY CHILDHOOD:
1864-1876

The garden, wedged at the end of a tight row of terraced houses, was sheltered from the chill winds blowing off the Cornish coast. Between its walls wild hydrangeas and fuchsias bloomed. Selina, six years old, had grown fond of these brightly coloured flowers. But her real favourite in the garden was the big tree. Each summer it bore a rich crop of fine black cherries; and each summer, as they played together in the garden, she and her younger brother Alf would hang the cherries over their ears pretending they were earrings.[1]

On such days there was no one to disturb their game. Selina and Alf Coombe were the youngest of seven children, and their elder brothers were busy and seldom bothered them. Charles, a religious boy, was ten and spent most of his day at school. Richard, a year older, had already left home to become apprenticed as a carpenter in a neighbouring village. William was twelve and was kept busy running errands for shopkeepers in Callington. And their two eldest brothers were thoroughly grown up, for Harry worked as a carter and John was already well on the way to becoming a skilled bootmaker.[2]

The only person who might interrupt their game was their mother. On such occasions Jane Coombe would rush into the garden, flustered and angry. She was a small, careworn woman in her forties whose sharp eyes missed little. Before marriage she had worked as a tailoress, and she still kept a small sewing machine by her so that she could make clothes for her fast-growing family. Now, with seven children to bring up virtually single-handedly, she had little enough time for sewing. Selina was too small to be any real help in the house, while Jane Coombe's wastrel husband

3

was seldom home long enough to notice what a wearisome task it was bringing up a large family.

Selina was beginning to realise at such moments that her mother's fury spelt another family crisis. She and Alf were propelled unceremoniously out of the garden and into the jingle, as the little Cornish carts were called. Their mother hastily adjusted the donkey's harness, squeezed into the driving seat and grabbed the reins. The three of them set off on their urgent journey, the donkey trotting through Callington and out into the high-banked lanes of the Cornish countryside.

Alf was too young to understand. Selina herself was only just beginning to puzzle out what caused her mother's rage. Jane Coombe must have received another hateful anonymous letter – a letter which told her, as if she needed to be reminded again, that her husband was about to desert her. Building the iron rails up and down the coast of Devon and Cornwall for new 'railway trains' to run on kept Charles Coombe away from home for weeks on end. Recently his absences had lengthened suspiciously. Then a well-informed person living near the railway gang's shanty town had written to tell Jane what had happened: that Charles Coombe was having another affair with a local woman.

After the last few bumpy rides in the jingle Jane Coombe had discovered that the woman concerned was the tall and strikingly handsome daughter of a publican who lived near the navvies' camp. Jane might be able to see why this young woman had caught her husband's eye; but she also knew that she and the younger children depended on Charles Coombe's wages coming directly to her rather than to his mistress. Unless she intervened, the family would be destitute.

Jane Coombe arrived at the navvies' camp with this grim thought uppermost in her mind. Selina and Alf had also been to the shanty town before and began to recognise some of its familiar sights. There were always other children there who seemed forever to tag around with the navvies from camp to camp; and there were particular men, one with a distinctive way of turning up the brim of his hat, another of keeping up his moleskin trousers. They had odd names too: Streaky Dick, Hedgehog or Rainbow Peg. After the familiarities of Callington, their father's railway life seemed foreign and exciting.

Selina and Alf amused themselves while their mother somehow completed the more important business: ensuring that a family crisis was once again averted. The job done, the three of them clambered back into the jingle and let the donkey jog them back to the safety of Callington. Their childhood life was shaped by their harassed mother and her domestic routines: their exotic father remained a remote and towering figure for both of them.[3]

The anonymous letters, the trips in the jingle, her mother's bitter humiliation over Charles Coombe's mistress – these remained Selina's most powerful recollections of her West Country childhood. These ugly memories never faded, and years later she in turn was to pass them on to *her* daughter.

As she grew older Selina began to appreciate how painful her parents' marriage was for her mother. From the very beginning it seemed there had been a disturbing tension between the stay-at-home dressmaker and her roaming husband. It had hardly been a promising match even before the wedding. The two families, the Urens and the Coombes, lived only a mile from each other, among the tiny hamlets that dotted the rolling Cornish countryside north of Callington. Charles Coombe's family, like so many in that isolated area, worked on the land; his father, Sampson Coombe, was an agricultural labourer while his mother, Catherine, looked after the children and took in occasional bundles of washing from neighbouring farming families to supplement her husband's low wage.

Jane Uren's family, on the other hand, was rather different. Her father, Simon Uren, was an expert tailor, and he carefully passed on his skills to his three daughters and one of his sons. Similarly, Jane's mother was proud to be descended from a family of notable Quaker radicals; she could claim among her ancestors John Littlejohn who in 1688 led an army of defiant Cornishmen to Bodmin Castle to rescue Bishop Trelawney, reputedly singing:

And shall Trelawney die, and shall Trelawney die?
Then thirty thousand Cornish boys will know the reason why.

Charles Coombe and Jane Uren grew up in neighbouring farming hamlets during the 1830s. By the 1840s Jane was learning the family trade of dressmaking and before long she and her sisters

THE COOMBE FAMILY TREE

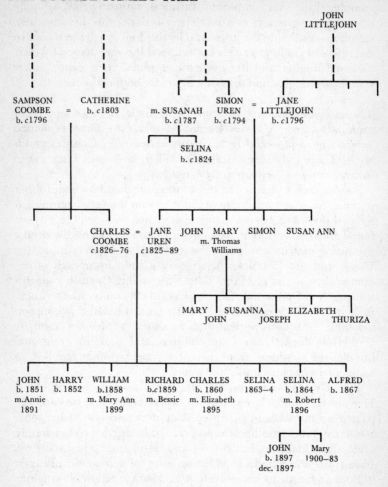

were packed off for a week or a fortnight at a time to stay with well-to-do Cornish families to do their sewing. Meanwhile Charles Coombe had also grown old enough to leave home: he followed in his father's footsteps and found a farm labouring job not too far away.[4]

The plodding life of a landless labourer did not hold Charles Coombe's attention for long. An energetic and capable man, he became interested in intriguing new developments only a dozen miles away that were opening up the timeless countryside of his boyhood. He heard stories of how tin and copper miners around Callington earned wages far higher than a poor farm labourer could ever dream of. Even more fascinating, he began to hear tales of how the newly-formed 'railway companies' were looking out for labourers, young men just like himself.

He certainly had the right physique for navvying and he was drawn to the idea of bettering himself in the world and being constantly on the move, working wherever the railways needed to be built. Better still, he came to hear of a brilliant young engineer with the memorable name of Isambard Kingdom Brunel, who planned to extend the Great Western Railway network (which already stretched from London to Bristol) down to Exeter and Plymouth and even into sleepy Cornwall. A railway link all the way from London to Cornwall still seemed an impossible fantasy to young Charles Coombe. After all, the county was effectively cut off from the rest of England by the River Tamar, and people still joked that it was easier to emigrate across the Atlantic than to cross the forbidding Tamar estuary into Devon.

Brunel's genius soared above such traditional obstacles. As engineer to the South Devon, Cornwall and West Cornwall Companies, he began to forge a railway line along the inhospitable south Cornish coast. To the amazement of doubting bystanders, he proceeded to span the innumerable creeks and inlets with his distinctive wooden viaducts. Under him Brunel appointed agents responsible for a section of railway line, and they in turn let out parcels of work to sub-contractors. The sub-contractors then hired gangers, the corporals of railway building, who employed as many navvies as they needed. And the navvies built the railways, toiling long hours at tunnelling and cutting, moving mountains of soil, all to ensure one vital objective: that the railway engine ran effortlessly along the smallest possible gradient.

So in the late 1840s Charles Coombe became one of Brunel's navvies. Still in his early twenties, he was a man of immense energy and considerable ambition. He was prepared to work very hard and seemed to have become a popular figure among the gangs with their peculiar rough freemasonry. A heavy drinker and popular with the women who invariably followed them from camp to camp, he soon felt at home among the navvies.[5]

Occasionally he used to wander back to see his family; while he was there he would sometimes go an extra mile to visit the Urens. He must have beguiled young Jane Uren, now in her mid-twenties, with entrancing stories of faraway places and of the railway companies' exploits. Charles Coombe's tales would have seemed wonderful to her, tied as she was to her home patch by her long hours of dressmaking. Her parents, on the other hand, can have been none too happy that their eldest daughter spent so much time with a foot-loose navvy, fearing that all he really coveted was the social standing he so visibly lacked.

Jane Uren was completely entranced by her towering suitor. Indeed, so entranced was she that one summer, in 1850, twenty-four-year-old Jane found she was pregnant. Her parents came to hear of this, and wondered how best to smooth over the situation for their eldest daughter. The couple must get married without delay – though not in the local parish church where their Coombe and Littlejohn ancestors were so respectably buried. Harmful gossip would spread for miles across the county within days. A far better plan was for Jane and Charles to leave Cornwall, cross over into Devon and stay with her father's sister-in-law, aunt Susannah Uren who lived in Plymouth.

The plan unfolded. Susannah Uren, a widow in her sixties, lived in one of the crowded streets behind Plymouth's docks. Mount Street, Devonport was a most convenient place for a distressed young couple to lodge while the banns were rushed through. Down by the dockside, the anonymous streets were full of strangers passing through: soldiers from the neighbouring barracks, paupers from Devonport's massive workhouse, and carpenters and shipwrights attracted by dockyard jobs. Among such crowds Jane and Charles could pass without notice.

Luckily Aunt Susannah was used to taking in dockside lodgers and agreed to put up the young couple for a few weeks, for, of her children, only her youngest daughter still remained at home, Selina Jane, a twenty-seven-year-old milliner and straw-bonnet-maker.

The wedding duly took place in Devonport's parish church on 22 September 1850. Selina Jane obligingly acted as one of the witnesses; and Jane Uren, four months pregnant and doubtless nervous about the awkward situation she found herself in, signed a wobbly maiden signature for the last time. Afterwards, with little reason to remain in Devonport, they returned as Mr and Mrs Coombe over the Tamar River and back into Cornwall. Fortunately Jane's parents took pity on their daughter and her newly-acquired husband. So that they should not be homeless with a baby on the way, Simon Uren and his wife invited the young couple to live with them and their younger children. In such cramped surroundings Jane Coombe gave birth to John Henry, the first of her many sons, in February 1851.[6]

Life was hard for the young mother. Her husband was seldom at home. Too ambitious to remain a navvy for long, he rose to become a railway ganger within the sprawling Brunel empire, and was soon hard at work helping construct a railway link through southern Cornwall that was planned – and this was Brunel at his most visionary – to cross the Tamar estuary at Plymouth. Charles Coombe thrived on such adventures. Photographs of his gang of navvies that have survived, apparently from the late 1850s, show him to be a well-built, good looking man in his thirties with a neat black beard and a jaunty cap.

Charles Coombe did make his way back to the Urens' house frequently enough to ensure that his wife regularly bore him another child. Harry was born in 1852, William in 1858, with Richard and Charles following shortly after. Even before William arrived it was becoming quite clear that the Urens' house could no longer accommodate so many small and noisy children. So Jane and Charles Coombe moved from their rural isolation to the small mining town of Callington, a few miles south. Here at least Jane Coombe would be nearer the railway and could keep a close eye on her elusive husband; and in a town she could more easily find work for herself and, when the time came, apprenticeships for her growing sons. And so in the mid-1850s the Coombe family moved in among the tin and copper miners of Callington. There Jane Coombe found herself a convenient job, with a house attached, as a toll collector at the town's northern entrance. She could now supplement her husband's growing, but sadly irregular, wages with money collected as she swung open the town's toll gate for passing carriages.[7]

Repeated pregnancies and childbirths coupled with long hours of exhausting housework had sapped Jane's body of its earlier vitality. At the same time she knew, like other Victorian women of her generation, that not every baby she bore would necessarily survive its first perilous years for infant mortality rates were still frighteningly high. After her fifth son Charles, she gave birth at last to a daughter, in 1863. Probably in honour of her Devonport cousin who had stood witness for her at the hasty wedding a dozen years previously, she named the baby girl Selina Jane. Yet her infant daughter's life was to be brutally short: she hardly survived her first birthday and in July 1864 was buried in the graveyard of Callington parish church.

By this time Jane Coombe was pregnant once again and, on 4 December 1864, gave birth to a second daughter. The baby's arrival in the middle of winter was duly registered in Callington by her father, just three days before Christmas. The second Selina Jane Coombe did live and even survived her second Cornish winter, the harsh chill of 1866–7. Then in November 1867 Jane gave birth to her eighth and last child, a boy called Alfred.[8]

Selina and Alf grew up surrounded by the hardship experienced by the Callington miners. One by one Cornwall's tin and copper mines were closing down. Foreign competition coupled with financial panic turned a mining recession into a catastrophe. During the bitter stormy winter of 1866–7 some of the mines flooded and by spring half the miners in Cornwall were on the verge of starvation. Tens of thousands of men were thrown out of work. Many emigrated, either to the more promising mines of Chile, Australia and America, or else north to Scotland, Yorkshire and Lancashire. Within three years over six hundred families left Cornwall for the north of England; indeed so many of the poor emigrants made for the cotton mills and coal mines of

Burnley that part of this Lancashire town became known as 'Little Cornwall'.

It became a common sight in the Coombes' part of Cornwall to see miners' wives and children, whose breadwinners were out of work or had emigrated, trudging to the next workhouse, hoping to apply for relief of their desperate hunger and poverty.[9] The Coombe family itself was protected from these icy blasts. Charles Coombe's job was unaffected by the Cornish mining slump; indeed, he had risen so high in the railway world that he was fast on his way to becoming a sub-contractor. He was even in a sufficiently influential position to offer employment to his relatives. His wife's brother Simon, a carpenter, was contracted to provide him with planking for railway sleepers; and his wife's brother-in-law, Thomas Williams, a lead miner who had fallen on hard times and had six children to support, was taken on as the foreman of one of his gangs of navvies. Charles Coombe even found jobs for one or two of his sons, hoping that they would study the necessary engineering textbooks and follow equally successfully in his footsteps.

In the 1870s the family entered a period of prosperity and Charles Coombe began to dress the part of self-made Victorian respectability. His beard, now grey, grew to dignified bushiness; his suits were tailored to fit his massive frame, and an impressive watch dangled on a chain over his expansive double-breasted waistcoat. Mrs Coombe gave up her toll-keeping job and, as befitted the wife of a local businessman, became a full-time housewife. The family moved into a house that could comfortably accommodate all the children, the end of terrace house not far from the centre of Callington, with its garden bearing wild hydrangeas, fuchsias and, of course, the cherry tree. The Coombes even acquired a jingle and pony.[10]

This was the house where Selina spent the greater part of her childhood, where her memory of her early years was most firmly rooted. Her mother's anonymous letters and the urgent trips in the jingle were, of course, the incidents most fiercely etched in her mind; but she also remembered more routine events too. She could recall how her mother had taught her to read and write – for this was before the days of compulsory elementary education, when the standard of teaching in local dame schools seldom went beyond the 'G-O, go' rote chanting; and how later the rector of Callington had taught her sums in return for a few pence a week. (Selina was not brought up Church of England though; her father took little interest in religion, her mother was a Quaker, and none of the children, apart from Charles, cared a great deal about church or chapel.[11]) Selina also remembered how she and her brothers would be off to play in the thick woods that still covered the valley slopes in that part of Cornwall. On other occasions they would entertain themselves with tales of Cornish smugglers, of dramatic shipwrecks off the rocky coast, and of local people struggling out to sea to try and salvage booty from the wrecks.[12]

By the mid-1870s when Selina was ten years old, there were signs that her West Country childhood could not last forever. Charles Coombe remained a successful contractor, but had to shift from railways to road-building. Perhaps because of these changes, or perhaps because they found their father an irascible taskmaster, his elder sons seemed to drift away from railway work. They could see there were far better prospects out of Cornwall, up in areas like north-east Lancashire where the cotton industry was rapidly expanding. By 1875 seventeen-year-old Richard had left Callington and moved north to Burnley to work in one of the town's many mills. John, the eldest son, drifted north about this time too. With so many miners out of work, the prospects for skilled bootmakers looked far better up in Lancashire than they did in Cornwall.[13]

Back in Callington, Selina, Alf and their mother were left alone in the echoing house. Cornwall seemed rather desolate now. Behind the town, looking down over Callington and the low-lying countryside around, rose a hill whose gentle slopes were covered with scrubland, gorse and heather. It was known as Kit Hill. If the two children set out to scramble to the top they found they could see for miles across the melancholy Cornish countryside in every direction. From the top of Kit Hill it seemed as if their family history over the last few generations was spread out before them like a picture book. To the north the children could make out quite clearly the farming hamlets where their parents came from, and where their Uren and Coombe grandparents, aunts and uncles still lived. Looking much further north, they could imagine the long journeys their elder brothers had taken up to Lancashire in search of good trades. Turning to the south-west, they could look down on Callington itself and marvel how under their very feet men still burrowed like moles to get at the tin and copper hidden underground. To the south-east they could, if they strained their eyes against the sun, just make out the glimmering shape of the great Saltash Bridge across the Tamar which their father and Mr Brunel had constructed together long before the children were born.

From the top of Kit Hill, the two children could marvel at the changes their father and the navvies of his generation had made to the Cornish landscape. Thanks to them, fresh fruit and vegetables from Penzance now sped across Cornwall and up to London without days of delay. There were even plans to bring a single-track railway to Callington itself, skirting round the bottom of Kit Hill.[14]

Selina and Alf never saw the railway that was to link Callington with the outside world. One autumn day in 1876 their childhood world of jingles and cherry trees was brought to an abrupt and tragic end. Overnight everything changed. Charles Coombe died of typhoid fever a few months before Selina's twelfth birthday.

During that autumn Charles Coombe and his gang, including his wife's brother-in-law Thomas Williams, had been working on a construction job near the coast. The temporary shanties the navvies lived in, a huddle of insanitary makeshift huts, offered scant protection against dirt and disease. Epidemics such as smallpox periodically ran through gangs, killing some and leaving others weakened and wretched. Even in towns, haphazard sewage systems still permitted disease to spread. Typhus was particularly feared locally: only a year earlier a Liverpool man arriving in that part of Cornwall had brought the fatal disease with him; eight people died within a few months and over a hundred more were infected.

This time Charles Coombe's gang joined the list of fatalities. The navvies succumbed to the lethal typhoid fever. Only Thomas Williams survived, his badly pock-marked skin always a reminder of his narrow escape. Charles Coombe's intestines became badly affected and he was rushed back home. His wife and young daughter did their best for him and an illiterate woman, perhaps a self-taught local healer, came in to help nurse him; but they were no match for the fever. Charles Coombe, only fifty years old, died on 25 September 1876 and was buried three days later in the Callington parish churchyard.[15]

Jane Coombe was left destitute. Overnight the widow and her two youngest children found themselves stranded and penniless. Charles Coombe had been in the middle of a construction job that he had not yet been paid for, and now there was little likelihood that he ever would be. Worse still, he apparently owed Jane's brother Simon for timber he had bought but not paid for. Shop-keepers in Callington would begin to demand she paid their bills promptly. From being a favoured customer, married to a suc-cessful contractor, Jane Coombe was reduced overnight to a pauper, the widow of a bankrupt.

The lot of an impoverished widow in mid-Victorian England was unenviable, for convention still held women to be the depend-ants of men, whether fathers, husbands or brothers. Laws to pro-tect the property rights of married women remained highly controversial, and still waited for effective backing from Westminster. Women like Jane Coombe who had given up paid work for years of pregnancy and childbirth, only to be widowed in their fifties, were particularly luckless.

As she looked desperately around her, Jane could see only too clearly how few occupations were available to her in a small town like Callington. The jobs that local women performed – as washerwoman, domestic servant, dressmaker – brought in only a few shillings a week, hardly enough to feed herself and the two children. The Cornish mining slump made the position even more desperate. It conjured up the nightmare image of workless miners' wives trudging to the workhouse with their half-starved children. There seemed little to save her from such a calamitous fate. She could hardly go and throw herself on the mercy of her relations in Cornwall: her parents were elderly, and her two unmarried sisters, still working as dressmakers, could not be expected to feed three extra mouths on their limited earnings.[16]

It became clear that Jane Coombe must leave Cornwall. She would have to go north as her elder sons had done. Already Thomas Williams, having escaped the deadly typhoid epidemic, had fled from Cornwall with his wife Mary and their six children, and sped up to a small Pennine textile town on the Lancashire-Yorkshire border called Barnoldswick. Here the children had found jobs in the new steam-powered cotton mills; and two of Jane Coombe's elder sons, Richard and Charles, were also working in mills not far away, while John the bootmaker was in the neighbourhood too.

How sensible it would be for her to take Selina and Alf up to join them all in Barnoldswick! Were there not already cotton manufacturers' agents conveniently placed in Callington, only too happy to explain the advantages of factory life? They told how children in Lancashire could earn far more pennies in the mills than they could by venturing down a tin mine. And northern working conditions were less hazardous: children were kept safely above ground in the warm and dry factory; they were given only simple tasks to do in a cotton mill, and their young lives were regulated by successive factory acts in an orderly and responsible manner. Most important, the manufacturers were kind enough to ensure that their factory children received a proper education for a few hours every day. It was certainly a beneficent system compared to sending little Cornish boys down the mines or girls away into service. Selina's education would not be neglected, and she would be able to contribute her small wage to the household each week.

Jane Coombe became convinced that this was the right thing to do. And, although she could claim to be no more than a distant relation of the Williams family, she was delighted when she heard that they were prepared to share their home with a poor widow and her two children.

There must be no delay. Packing up all the belongings they could carry, they boarded the train. Their journey was a long one, taking them over Charles Coombe's Saltash Bridge, past Dartmoor and the wide Severn valley, through the Midlands and Lancashire, and up into the great Pennine uplands alongside the Leeds-Liverpool canal with its series of rising locks.

At one time Selina had found a trip through the high-banked Cornish lanes to visit the navvies' camp a thrilling expedition. Now all those familiar landmarks were wrenched away. Once the train crossed the Tamar she discovered people no longer spoke with the familiar Cornish accent she was used to. As she looked out of the window, she could see they were speeding past blackened Lancashire towns sprouting dozens of tall mill chimneys: row upon row of cramped terraced houses went by, and vast green-brown hills far higher than she had seen before. As they changed trains from the mainline to a small branch line and the train chugged into Barnoldswick's small station, she knew that her childhood years in the West Country had ended forever.[17]

CHAPTER TWO

THE SILENCE OF A DUTIFUL DAUGHTER: 1876-1891

Long, long after Selina Coombe had fled from Cornwall with her mother and brother, she used to entertain her own daughter with tales of her West Country childhood. Of the darker years in Barnoldswick, Selina's daughter learnt very little. 'I never remember her working at Barnoldswick,' she admitted. 'No, she never mentioned that.' Selina preferred not to reminisce about her early years in the mill, and so she emerges from this period as a shadowy, imprecise figure. Little evidence has survived which allows a glimpse of her girlhood.

One of the few stories that Selina did relate to her daughter was how warmly the Williams family welcomed the widow and her two children when they arrived in Barnoldswick. There was certainly never any question of their having to pay rent; and Jane Coombe, despite feeling an unwelcome rheumaticky stiffness in her joints, busied herself at her little chain sewing machine, tailoring suits and dresses for the family. Her two children were soon treated like an extra sister and brother rather than distant cousins; for Elizabeth and Thuriza Williams, the two youngest, were exactly the same age as Selina and Alf.[1]

Alf, who had just had his ninth birthday, went off to school each day. But for Selina, though not yet twelve, there was no such smooth transition from Cornwall to this new life. Unlike Callington where there had been so few jobs available for women, Selina now found that girls of ten and over were expected to work in one of the town's cotton mills, spending half the day in the factory and the other half at school. It dawned on Selina that she would have to follow the example of the Williams girls and

17

contribute her few shillings a week to the household budget. There was no alternative: once you reached your tenth birthday you joined the local army of half-timers in the mill.

Entrance qualifications for joining up were hardly demanding. Children merely had to demonstrate either that their reading, writing and arithmetic had reached a certain basic level or that they had put in the requisite number of attendances at school during the previous five years. It is unlikely that Selina, tutored as she had been by her mother and the rector, found the required standard exacting. So, armed with this modest qualification and given a perfunctory medical inspection at the mill, Selina entered the adult world of work.[2]

How she got through her first day in the mill is not recorded. In later years she drew a firm veil of silence over this part of her life. Unlike other Barnoldswick children, she had been catapulted into the mill without warning, and the initial shock for Selina must have been severe. She would have been rudely startled by the dust in the mill, by the incessant pounding of the machines and by the rigid timing of the work. When steam power was introduced into cotton manufacture, each mill worker's routine became ruled by an inflexible god: the mill engine. When the wheels started turning at six o'clock in the morning, everything in the mill started. An idle spinning mule or powerloom was losing money for the owner.

From occasional references she let drop in later years, it is certain that Selina was first set to work in the cardroom. The cardroom of a mill was where the raw cotton was first processed (before it made its way to the spinning section and then the weaving shed, finally leaving the mill as rolls of finished woven cloth) and it was a notoriously dusty place to work, full of big noisy machines. The cotton passed through a series of card-frames: a drawing frame which straightened out the loose cotton fibres, three speed frames, and then finally a jack frame for pro-ducing very fine cotton yarns. All these frames were minded by women cardframe tenters and their young assistants, known as creelers.

Selina's first job was as a half-time creeler, and as such she had to ensure a constant supply of fresh bobbins for the fleecy strands of cotton emerging from the card frames to be wound on to. It was lowly, monotonous work, demanding of the creeler negligible skill or training: Selina could learn all she needed to know from an older girl in a matter of hours. All that was necessary was unflagging attention and speed. Speed was essential in avoiding the accidents caused by the cardroom's terrifyingly fast machinery. The frames were driven by long leather belts suspended from the ceiling which brought the power from the steam engine; becoming caught in a belt invariably meant a serious injury – or death. On the frames themselves rows of countless bobbins whirled round at breathtaking speeds; and it was not unknown for a creeler's hand to get caught among them and her finger ripped off.

Selina managed to escape these cardroom horrors, though like everyone else, she inhaled cotton fluff into her lungs with every breath she took – cardroom workers were particularly susceptible to byssinosis or cardroom asthma, a malignant industrial disease. Like everyone else, she worked barefooted in the mill, and this gave rise to the only hint that Selina ever let drop in later years about how she got on with the other girls she worked with. 'Many years ago,' she confessed,

> when I was working in a cardroom as a creeler, and because of the greasiness of the floor we girls had to work bare-footed, I became very jealous of my partner, who had very tiny feet. My jealousy reached a climax when one day I jumped on them, after many previous attempts at pinching them. She wept bitterly, but I made no amends.[3]

With the monotony broken only occasionally by incidents such as this, Selina's day as a half-timer wore on. After two hours of filling and refilling the rows of countless bobbins, breakfast time at last came round. Tea had to be brewed quickly and drunk in the narrow alleyways between the now-silent cardframes before the relentless engine started up again. Afterwards there were more bobbins waiting for her, and Selina repeated the same movements that she had already done a thousand times that morning. With another four hours to dinner time, the grey drudgery stretched ahead relentlessly. At last the engine stopped for the midday break. Selina could burst out of the mill, rush round the corner and gobble down her dinner with her family. There was no time to be lost, for she was due any moment for the afternoon session at school.

The half-time system imposed a brutal timetable on children. It involved a long, exhausting day, with much breathless running to avoid penalties for lateness. And once at school, an exhausted half-timer, still trying to digest a hastily swallowed meal, found it hard to stay awake. Despite the recent education act, classes were still large, teachers over-worked and under-trained, with lessons seldom consisting of more than rote chantings. Although her spelling was sometimes shaky, Selina could write reasonably well and used to read a lot (though she admitted years later that when she was young she read mainly 'rubbish'). Yet it is unlikely she was able to learn much from the education half-timers in Barnoldswick were offered. Such children, teachers would complain, could even take forty winks while standing up.

Extraordinary as it might seem, the half-time system in the 1870s was stoutly defended by all concerned. 'It was a system,' one journalist explained, 'ordained by Providence, sanctified by custom, justified by utility, and calculated to exist for all time.' Certainly, when Selina was a half-timer no voices were raised in protest against it. After all, it was argued, the system allowed tens of thousands of Lancashire and Yorkshire children to continue their schooling up to thirteen, unlike the pitiful pauper children of the London slums, out on the streets selling newspapers in all weathers, or the children of farmworkers, called out whenever an extra pair of hands was needed.

Certainly the children themselves looked forward to the day when they could enter the mill and then, at the end of the week, 'tip up' their first wage for their mother. And since they were given back a penny pocket-money for every shilling they earned, they would not have thanked interfering busybodies who wanted to keep them cooped up at school reciting pointless lessons. Manufacturers and trade unionists defended the half-time system too, arguing that only workers who started young were able to master the intricacies of spinning or weaving; and that without inexpensive child labour to perform the simpler tasks in the mill, the cotton industry would be ruined by foreign competitors undercutting the price of Lancashire cloth. Leading Liberal trade unionists like David Holmes of the Burnley Weavers always stoutly defended the system. Most importantly, so did parents who relied on the two or three shillings their half-timers brought home each week. Certainly for Jane Coombe, a widow struggling to support two children on the pennies earned from dressmaking, her daughter's small but regular wage was a great boon.[4]

Any protest against child labour still lay well in the future. On 4 December 1877 Selina Coombe reached her thirteenth birthday. Her formal schooling now ended forever, and she could work full-time – fifty-six and a half hours a week in the mill. With this adult status came promotion from humble creeler. 'I worked my way up,' she later recalled, 'until in time I had charge of a [carding] machine.' Promotion meant a welcome rise too: girls in the cardroom could earn eight or nine shillings a week, with the prospect of wages rising eventually to sixteen or seventeen shillings. Selina could therefore rely on at least eightpence pocket-money a week, with the chance of a whole shilling before too long. Mill work might be hard and monotonous, but it did have some compensations.

Beyond such impersonal information about jobs and wages, it is still extremely difficult to sense what kind of person Selina Coombe was becoming during her adolescent years. When the Barnoldswick census enumerator went round from house to house in 1881, he recorded on his form the regulation information about her: her age, her occupation, where she was born; but sadly his census is unable to shed more light on what she was like. All it tells us is that by the time Selina was sixteen, the Coombe family had been able to move out of the cramped Williams house, round the corner to Wellhouse Square (named after the big Wellhouse Mill nearby) in the centre of Barnoldswick. Into this house was squeezed Jane Coombe, now fifty-five and sufficiently rheumaticky to give her occupation as 'Dressmaker Formerly'. Two of her elder sons still lived with her as well: John the bootmaker, aged thirty, and twenty-year-old Charles, a cotton weaver. Alf, now thirteen, was recorded as a 'scholar': it was obviously the privilege of the youngest son to stay on at school much longer than his sister. Old Catherine Coombe, Jane Coombe's widowed mother-in-law, now aged seventy-eight and given as 'Formerly Laundress', had also come up from Cornwall to live with them. And in the middle of this list, Selina J. Coombe is modestly recorded as 'Cotton Operative'. (Round the corner in lodgings lived Richard Coombe and his Cornish wife, both cardroom workers like Selina.)[5]

However, the picture depicted by the census enumerator was soon to change. As she neared sixty, Jane Coombe's rheumatism grew worse. Her joints so stiffened that she could barely move about. Before long she became a bed-ridden invalid. Luckily she retained the use of her hands so a board was fixed to her bed to carry her little sewing machine, and in this way she was able to continue tailoring her children's clothes.

Although Jane Coombe's hands were kept busy, she still needed someone to nurse her. In Victorian families this duty naturally fell to the unmarried daughter. Selina, a strong capable girl of about seventeen, was perfect for the task. (Alf was already planning to escape the drudgery of the mill town by enlisting as a regular soldier as soon as he could.) Although Selina's wages would be sorely missed, she must leave the cardroom and stay at home. So, following the example of numberless other obedient Victorian daughters, Selina dutifully left her job and began to nurse her mother. In her spare time, perhaps tutored by her grandmother Coombe, she began to take in washing. For a few pennies, she would wash and starch, mangle and iron bundles of soiled clothes for Barnoldswick's more comfortably-off families.

Selina Coombe had spent her first six years since she fled from Cornwall, from 1876 till about 1882, working in the cardroom. She was to spend the next seven years as part-time nurse, part-time washerwoman. Sadly she has left no record of what she felt about exchanging her mill job for this domestic drudgery. We shall never know whether she quietly resented her loss of independence or whether she was only too glad to give up her monotonous job in order to make the life of her long-suffering mother more comfortable. All we can gather from the silence she later preserved over these years is that she preferred to forget what was a dark and painful period.[6]

In 1883, when Selina Coombe was eighteen, she and her mother moved from the rural isolation of Barnoldswick to Brierfield, about seven or eight miles further south. Brierfield was squashed in a narrow valley between two fast-growing Lancashire textile towns, Nelson and Burnley. Here weaving mills went up almost overnight, taking advantage of the Leeds-Liverpool canal and the mainline railway, both of which threaded along the valley bottom. Tens of thousands of people flocked to Brierfield, Nelson and Burnley to find jobs as weavers in the new factories, some of them coming from the Pennine countryside and others from further afield.

John Coombe, Selina's eldest brother, was amongst those attracted by the bustle of industrialisation. There were more opportunities for a skilled bootmaker to set up in business on his own in Brierfield than in sleepy Barnoldswick. With houses going up all the time to accommodate the newly-arrived weavers, John was assured of ready business making new shoes, cobbling old ones, mending wooden clogs. Before long he established himself as 'John Coombe, boot and shoemaker, 67 Colne Road, Brierfield'.

With him came two of his brothers. Bill, who had worked as an errand boy in distant Callington, was now a giant of a man in his mid-twenties, an expert wrestler. He too found there were plenty of jobs in Brierfield, and got work looking after the massive steam engine at the biggest local mill, Tunstills', which was just across the road from John's shop. Charles, who had learnt to weave in Barnoldswick, also found a mill job in Brierfield, minding four looms probably in one of Tunstills' many weaving sheds.[7] With three wage-earning brothers working in Brierfield, it obviously made sense for Selina and her mother to leave Barnoldswick too and join the household at 67 Colne Road. It was, after all, highly convenient for John, Bill and Charles to have an unmarried sister living at home who could run the house and prepare the meals. Like so many other Victorian women of her generation, Selina found she was expected to work as an unpaid skivvy. 'My mother had all the washing, cleaning and cooking to do,' her daughter later explained. 'And there was Uncle Jack, and Uncle Bill, and this soldier [Uncle Alf] coming home whenever he wanted to. And she'd cook for all of them and wash for all of them.'

That was not all. At the back of John's small shop was a living room and above it two bedrooms. Into one of the bedrooms the three brothers must have squeezed, plus Alf when he came home on leave. The other would be for Mrs Coombe and her daughter; and it was in this room that Selina spent endless hours looking after her mother, now semi-paralysed. Her tiring job as nurse-maid did, as she explained years later, have its compensations: 'By the time they got to Brierfield,' Jane Coombe's grand-daughter recalled,

[my grandmother] was just about crippled up with rheumatism. And yet she sewed all my uncles' clothes . . . And my mother's clothes . . . She had a board on the bed and a little chain machine that she could work for the long seams . . .

You never saw such beautiful stitching in all your life . . . And the window overlooked the main road in Brierfield. And she'd look out – look at a costume, and sit down and cut it out on this board – she couldn't move her legs. And my mother had to lift her out of the bed; she used to tell us, she lifted her out of bed onto a blanket . . . And my uncle [John], with having this business, would look in at her . . . he could lift her.[8]

Well dressed she might be; but Selina Coombe was still taking in washing. Those were back-breaking years of boiling water, scrubbing, mangling, heating the irons by the fire, all done in cramped and primitive conditions. A washerwoman's lot was not enviable; its only virtue was that it offered a house-bound Victorian woman the chance of a small though unreliable wage of her own.

Selina's home life was one of domestic drudgery. There were only occasional interruptions. Elizabeth and Thuriza Williams (also having left Barnoldswick for nearby Nelson) would descend on the Coombe family, hoping to meet Alf, now resplendent in his dashing soldier's uniform.[9] And every Saturday evening she would go with her brothers on a tram into Burnley to watch a play or operetta there. On such outings she would be smartly dressed, wearing one of her mother's expertly tailored suits. Before long Selina became known as the 'Belle of Brierfield' and, according to the stories she passed on to her own daughter years later, attracted a number of young suitors. Among them was the organist of the local Primitive Methodist chapel which she sometimes attended (not because she was a strong Methodist, but because 'there wasn't much else to get connected with in those days'). Certainly, one of the rare books containing the signature 'Selina Coombe

Brierfield' that has survived is her weighty *Primitive Methodist Hymnal* full of lugubrious hymns of temptation and repentance. 'How sad our state by nature is!' Selina would have humbly sung in chapel on Sundays,

> Our sin how deep it stains!
> And Satan binds our captive minds
> Fast in his slavish chains.
>
> But there's a voice of sovereign grace
> Sounds from the sacred word, –
> Ho! ye despairing sinners, come,
> And trust upon the Lord.[9]

Selina Coombe's years as part-time washerwoman and part-time nurse must at times have seemed endless. Then, when she twenty-four, her domestic skivvying came to an abrupt end. On 27 August 1889 her mother, aged sixty-four, died. The funeral marked the end of an era for Selina just as her father's had done thirteen years before. How she felt about her mother's death is unclear. There is no clue whether it came as a tragic shock, or whether Selina felt a sense of relief that her long-suffering mother had at last been released from her pain, and perhaps even that she herself would be relieved of her back-breaking nursing duties.

There was no longer any pressing reason why Selina should be confined to the house. She could escape if she chose, and find a job. Yet, as she soon discovered, there was little besides mill work in Brierfield, just as there had been little choice in Barnoldswick. Her bothers may have been put into useful trades and learned how to become cobblers and engine-tenters and soldiers; but these were all options firmly closed to Victorian women. Clearly she must go back into the mill. That was the only job open to women who wanted to earn a reasonable wage in north-east Lancashire.

So shortly after her mother's death Selina began to work in Tunstills' cotton factory. The mill was conveniently jammed between the Leeds-Liverpool canal and the railway line: water lapped against its stone walls. Grim and menacing, the mill sprawled over most of the spare ground in the middle of Brierfield, and in size was certainly the most imposing building in the town. Its high grey walls and row upon row of faceless windows hid the sunlight from the terraced houses that crouched around its base. It was here, in one of Tunstills' winding rooms, that Selina worked for the next seven years.

Women who worked as winders were responsible for taking the spun yarn from the spinners and winding it onto larger cones ready for the weavers' looms. Although Selina's wages were far higher than when she had worked in the cardroom, winders were not well paid compared to others in the mill. When she entered Tunstills, Selina would have barely earned sixteen shillings (80p) a week, compared to twenty-one shillings (£1.05p) for a four-loom weaver (and at least thirty-six shilling (£1.80p) for the tacklers, the elite men who tuned the weavers' looms). Her wages might still be modest, but they were of course considerably higher than the pennies she had earned as a washerwoman and were – most importantly – paid regularly. In addition, Selina found the winding room much more congenial than her monotonous cardroom job. Much of the work was still repetitive, but the winding room did offer more dignity and autonomy than before. The machinery was quieter and, rather than having to lip-read as the weavers did, winders could chat amongst themselves while they worked. It was this sociable atmosphere at work that was to make such a difference to Selina's life.[10]

Shortly after she began work at Tunstills, Selina joined the local cotton union. There was no separate organisation for the winders, so she joined the large Burnley Weavers' Association, which incorporated small groups like the winders, and stretched north up the valley to Brierfield. Formed in 1870 by men like David Holmes, the union had successfully recruited among both men and women weavers by the time Selina joined. Its membership had swelled to nearly 10,000, with women probably just outnumbering men. Of the new members, Selina would hardly have been a reluctant recruit: she was already developing an interest in trade unionism, and this would have been strengthened by the general social pressure on young workers to join up in a textile town like Brierfield.

The Burnley Weavers employed thirty-five house-to-house collectors, men who would scurry up and down the cobbled streets, collecting the weekly pennies from members on their 'round'. The collector responsible for the north part of Brierfield would bustle up Colne Road and knock on the door of John Coombe's shop. Selina would fetch her contribution card (kept in an old leather-bound book once belonging to her father) and hand him the card and her money. Since collectors were paid on a commission basis, they were loathe to waste time chatting to their members. 'If anyone dared to raise any issues with him,' one weaver recalled, 'the questioner was brusquely bidden to "Tak' it tu't club." '

It is unlikely that Selina, whatever her grumbles, would have taken a complaint 'tu't club' when she first joined the Burnley Weavers. In 1890 it was still a rare sight indeed for women members to take any kind of active role in union affairs. Women might comprise the majority of the membership, but the union was still run by men. Prominent still were Liberals like David Holmes, men of an earlier generation of union pioneers, whose attitude to women members had scarcely changed over the years. Women were encouraged to join, but then to remain invisible; and when Selina Coombe became a member, there was little choice for her but to swell this silent battalion of women.[11]

Between 1876 when she fled from Cornwall northwards, to the early 1890s when, aged about twenty-eight, she began to emerge from obscurity, Selina Coombe remains a near-invisible figure. Only rarely do glimpses of her emerge from the records that have survived. The census enumerator gives a few formal clues, but his schedule naturally filters out most personal information. A handful of Victorian books inscribed 'Selina Coombe Barnoldswick' or 'Selina Coombe Brierfield' offer rare pinpoints of light on Selina's interests as she grew up: lengthy romantic novels and moralising handbooks on *Female Improvement*. Beyond this, documentary sources say nothing about this young woman. Mill records of when and where she worked in the factory are hard to come by. Selina kept no diary, apparently wrote or received no letters, preserved no scraps of paper.

The silence of the contemporary documents is scarcely lifted by later sources. Interviews she gave to newspapers years afterwards help breathe more life into the official documents, but still say little about this shadowy fifteen-year period. Similarly, when Selina passed stories about her youth on to her daughter Mary, these anecdotes focused far more on the drama of Selina's Cornish childhood, and remained obstinately silent on the years in Barnoldswick and in Tunstills' winding rooms. To lift this veil and see Selina Coombe clearly beneath it remains almost impossible.

Perhaps the saddest loss of all is not knowing what she looked like. At least twenty early photographs, identifiable as picturing the Coombes, have survived. But it seems that no picture of Selina was taken before the early 1890s or, if taken, has not survived. The family photographs from these early years depict aspects of Victorian life in which a girl like Selina could take no part. They show men in action: her father making railway history with his viaducts and cuttings, and later reflecting on his self-made success. They show her young brother Alf, the gallant soldier, posing proudly in his uniform in the distant British empire where military duty had dispatched him. The only surviving photograph of Jane Coombe reveals her as a humble Victorian widow. Her mouth seems set into a bitter line of resignation by her late husband's years of infidelity, her body prematurely bowed by constant child-bearing and now swathed in widow's weeds to mark her dependent position in a hostile world.[12]

Compared to her father, her brothers and even her mother, Selina Coombe remains shrouded in mystery. Here she experienced the same fate as other working-class women of her generation. Unlike their menfolk and unlike their better educated sisters, such women remain barely represented in the surviving documents. In Victorian England, the daughters of poor families were the lowest of the low. Their prime value was to help in the house, especially during their mothers' frequent confinements. Their education was given the lowest priority: every experience seemed to confirm their unimportance. 'Women of her time and sort . . .,' wrote a farm labourer's daughter about her mother, 'took seriously, if not literally, the story of Eve's creation from Adam's rib; they accepted their lessness.' Such women remained isolated at home and were strongly dissuaded from taking part in any wider activities, except church or temperance work. This particular farm labourer, for instance, supported local women's public efforts to curb one husband's drunkenness, but, his daughter recorded, 'would certainly have frowned on even a "silent organized league" of women except against the one enemy of drink'.

It is unsurprising then that Selina Coombe emerges from these

years as a dutiful but silent daughter. Her youth was shaped by
the demands of her mother and brothers. Even if a young woman
like Selina did go out to work, she still remains shrouded from the
historian's gaze, her voice muted and her feelings hidden.

By the early 1890s there were signs that this blanket of silence
was beginning to lift. A few working women's voices began to be
heard. Equally, the distinctive nature of Nelson and Brierfield
was emerging clearly. Selina Coombe was to spend the rest of her
life in this corner of Pennine Lancashire, and the particular form
of radicalism that emerged there was crucial in shaping the way
she now developed.[13]

CHAPTER THREE

FRONTIER TOWN

The windows of John Coombe's cobbler's shop looked directly onto Colne Road with the horses plodding past pulling lorry-loads of cotton bales. The busy road was the main link between Nelson and Colne to the north and Burnley and the rest of industrial Lancashire to the south. Beyond it, the land dropped away steeply to the railway line and to another of Brierfield's new weaving mills, its name set out boldly in white bricks at the top of its tall chimney. Nearby sprawled the buildings of Tunstills' flourishing textile factory. Behind lay the Leeds and Liverpool canal, and beyond it the winding river, Pendle Water, meandering down to Burnley and eventually joining the River Ribble. The far side of the valley was dotted with farms and hamlets, still untouched by the local weaving revolution. Further away still loomed the dark and unmistakable silhouette of Pendle Hill, once feared as the hiding place of local witches.

Barnoldswick, tucked away beyond the northern slopes of Pendle Hill, was cut off from the valley's booming industrial-isation. The small town had been Selina Coombe's first taste of life in a textile community, helping to soften the stark contrast between Cornwall and her new urban life in Brierfield and Nelson. Even during Selina's stay in Barnoldswick it was clear that such an isolated town was becoming a backwater, and would have to give way to places more in touch with the demands of late Victorian industrialisation.

The perfecting of the Blackburn loom in the 1840s meant that the weaving section of cotton manufacturing could expand as rapidly as the cotton spinning section had previously done. To take advantage of this new technical development, easy access to

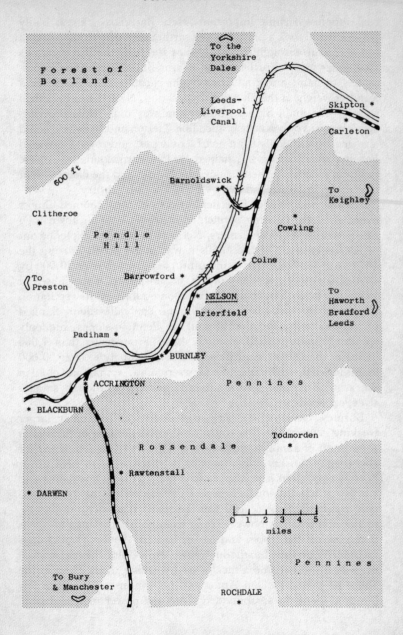

Forest of Bowland

To the Yorkshire Dales

Leeds-Liverpool Canal

Skipton *

Carleton *

600 ft

Barnoldswick *

To Keighley

Clitheroe *

Pendle Hill

Cowling *

Barrowford *

Colne *

To Preston

NELSON

Brierfield *

To Haworth Bradford Leeds

Padiham *

BURNLEY *

ACCRINGTON *

Pennines

BLACKBURN *

Todmorden *

Rossendale

Rawtenstall *

DARWEN *

0 1 2 3 4 5
miles

Pennines

To Bury & Manchester

ROCHDALE *

coal supplies became important. Here Barnoldswick was badly placed: it still took a pair of heavy carthorses a whole day to pull a ton of coal up through six canal lock-gates from the Brierfield pits nine miles away. Further south nearer Burnley coal was immediately to hand and could be bought cheaply: only fivepence a hundredweight at the pit head. In addition, Nelson and Brierfield were on the main Skipton-Burnley railway line, while Barnoldswick boasted only a little branch line. Nelson and Brierfield could also get stone cheaply from nearby quarries, and rows of terraced housing soon sprang up, helped by long-term loans from local building societies – the Burnley, the Nelson and the Colne – that opened up in the second half of the nineteenth century.

Nelson, and smaller Brierfield next to it, mushroomed almost overnight from farming hamlets into sizable weaving towns. To the incredulity of local farmers, Nelson's population exploded out of all recognition. In the 1860s it was under 4,000; during the 1870s and 1880s it more than quintupled to reach over 20,000 by 1890. Like other towns in north-east Lancashire, it specialised in weaving rather than spinning and soon established its reputation for producing very fine quality cotton. The valley floor, flanked on either side by Pendle Hill and the Pennine slopes, suddenly sprouted tightly-packed weaving sheds. From fewer than 4,000 looms in the 1860s, it mushroomed astonishingly to over 20,000 looms in 1890 – a loom apiece for every man, woman and child in the area. Brierfield saw a similarly successful, though smaller scale, expansion.

Burnley, Nelson and Brierfield were distinct from older, larger weaving centres like Blackburn or Preston because of their high proportion of small manufacturers. The area was renowned for encouraging an ambitious tackler or shopkeeper to save up or borrow enough to rent a space in a mill, set up a few looms and employ a handful of weavers. This was called the room-and-power system, since crucial was the small manufacturer's access to the mill's steam power. None exemplified the rags-to-riches potential of the room-and-power system better than James Nelson. A one-time handloom weaver from Colne, he had worked his way up to become a tackler in a weaving shed. Then in the 1880s he joined his son Amos and his son-in-law to run a few hundred looms in a subdivided room-and-power mill; and from that moment onwards the Nelson family never looked back.

The unusually high proportion of newly-arrived small manufacturers, so different from the great patrician employers of Blackburn or Preston, gave the area a distinctive feel. However there
were two or three major factory owners in the area whose mills
predated the era of phenomenal growth. Two are of particular
importance to this story. The Ecroyd family, the older of the two,
were Quakers whose Lomeshaye Mill on the outskirts of Nelson
dated back to the 1780s. They installed a steam engine, and so
Lomeshaye was well placed to exploit the new weaving revolution. One of the largest cotton manufacturers in the country, the
philanthropic Ecroyds built a model village to house their
weavers, and wielded considerable political power, both in Parliament and on the magistrates' bench.

By contrast, William Tunstill's father had, like James Nelson,
been a handloom weaver. He did not build his mill till the 1830s,
but from then on it expanded rapidly until it contained thousands
of looms. After the Brierfield coalpits closed in the 1870s, the
Tunstills became the only major employer in the small town. The
family owned the houses, controlled the gas supplies, and retained
interests in both the Burnley collieries and in the railways. They
chaired the Brierfield local government board and, ardent Methodists, contributed substantially to the Wesleyan chapel. The
Tunstills, in truth, ran Brierfield. Certainly it seemed only
natural that when the Nelson Local Board was first established in
the 1860s to run local affairs, William Ecroyd and William
Tunstill became the first two chairmen.[1]

When Selina Coombe arrived in Brierfield in the early 1880s
she was moving into an area of rapid, tumultuous social change.
One or two old families still retained considerable control, but
new entrepreneurs were springing up all the time, calling into
question the idea of paternalistic employers who knew what was
best for their mill workers – and kept a distinct distance from
them.

In the rough-and-tumble of the times, Nelson and Brierfield
came to resemble frontier towns of the American west. Tradition
was thrown to the winds. Newness was everything. Thousands of
migrant workers arrived, sucked in by the new weaving revolution which had created a mass of factory jobs where none had

previously existed. Tales spread of the fabulous wages that could be earned minding four looms at Tunstills, Lomeshaye or one of the room-and-power mills. Farm workers from distant East Anglia gave up the struggle to make a living from the land and set out on the long trek north, trusting that their labourers' hands would be supple enough for the fine threads they were to weave. Ecroyds brought up unemployed tin miners with strange Cornish names to work at Lomeshaye. Others came from neighbouring cotton towns, Blackburn or Rawtenstall-in-Rossendale, hearing tell that conditions in the new Nelson mills were far better than those in the older factories. Cornish accents were soon mingling with East Anglian ones, Rossendale folk settling down next door to Scots or Irish families.

There was one group of immigrants who played a particularly crucial role in shaping the character of the area. They came from the Pennine uplands just over the Yorkshire border, from the Dales and from the windswept moorlands of Brontë country. Impoverished tin miners and farm labourers came down in their hundreds from the hills of Swaledale and Wensleydale, some even selling their furniture to pay their rail fares. A great number travelled from the small weaving towns only a day's walk from Nelson. Cowling, lying between Colne and Keighley, was one such hillside handloom community. Like Barnoldswick, Cowling now found itself cut off from the new technical developments: it was miles from the nearest railway line and coal cost threepence a ton to carry up the road from the canal. Hard-pressed Cowling families began to look enviously at the fabulous wages they heard were offered over the border in Nelson.[2]

Immigrants made towns like Nelson and Brierfield. The textile communities stretching up the valley from Burnley to Colne all came to boast the same kind of pioneering roughness of far-flung frontier towns. This abrasive newness, coupled with the scarcity of large-scale paternalistic mill owners, became grafted on to existing democratic traditions that flourished locally.

Nelson and the nearby towns inherited considerable reputations for radicalism. After the Peterloo Massacre in 1819, a crowd of ten or fifteen thousand attended a protest demonstration, despite warnings from magistrates. Later, Chartist clubs flourished. When Fergus O'Connor, who published the Chartist *Northern*

Star, came to visit the collection of hamlets that was to become Nelson, he was given a warm welcome. Even after Chartist enthusiasm began to flag, the local struggle for wide-ranging democratic reforms continued. One key witness who has left us a graphic account of this radical tradition is Philip Snowden, who went on to become a leading Labour propagandist and politician.

Philip Snowden was one of those Cowling people who migrated to Nelson in search of a better way of life. In 1879, when he was fifteen, the mill where his family all worked went bankrupt and they trekked over the Pennines to find work. Philip, who had been able to stay on at school longer than his sisters, found a job as an insurance clerk and remained in Nelson for about seven years. This was a time when controversy raged over the 1884 Reform Bill. It was to give the vote to rural working-class men, but was firmly opposed by the House of Lords. 'Nelson was a hot-bed of Radicalism,' Philip Snowden recalled. 'Although still in my teens, I never missed a meeting in the district. I remember, when the House of Lords suspended the County Franchise Bill, walking in a procession holding aloft a banner with the words: "Down with the House of Lords" inscribed upon it.'

Religious nonconformity was an extremely powerful force in the area, with feeling running high against the Church of England and its archaic privileges. 'The Disestablishment question was a very lively issue in those days,' Philip Snowden added. 'The Liberation Society held many meetings in the district, and they aroused intense interest. I never missed one of them.'[3]

Nonconformity, and particularly Methodism, was the key to the growth of local socialism. Methodism had a passing influence on Selina Coombe, was of considerable concern to Philip Snowden (his father had been a Sunday School superintendent in Cowling), and was central to numberless other immigrants who flocked to the Nelson area. When they arrived they found that there existed a thriving Methodist congregation which supported at least seven chapels; by the turn of the century a further five had been built. The different emphases of these rival chapels is worth unravelling for they help explain how Nelson's radicalism developed.

There were three distinct strands. Nearest to the Church of England in terms of respectability stood Wesleyanism. Its six chapels attracted workers from the surrounding mills, but were dominated by local manufacturers, especially the Tunstills. The Tunstill family, the local newspaper explained, 'nursed and tended the tender sapling of Wesleyan Methodism in this district'. Like so many other employers of their generation, they demanded absolute obedience from their workers, but combined this with ritual philanthropy on ceremonial occasions. 'Mr Robert' was always vigilant about latecomers at the mill, threatening them with locked gates and the dreaded penny hole (a side entrance where people were charged a penny for being late). Yet, when a Tunstill son married, the 1,140 mill workers each received a new shilling, the men a packet of tobacco and the women and children a box of chocolates. By the conventions of Victorian Wesley-anism, the Tunstills were indeed model employers.[4]

At the other extreme were the smaller Primitive Methodists who had long ago broken away from the stuffiness of Wesleyanism. Their chapels, one in Nelson and another in Brierfield, offered working people like Selina Coombe strict temperance, a simple revivalist theology and a chance to sing the doleful hymns in the *Primitive Methodist Hymnal*. But particularly important was the Primitive Methodists' dislike of professional clerics: they pre-ferred to run their own chapels with their own lay preachers and trustees. Selina Coombe, with her desultory interest in chapel life, was not among those who benefited most from this opportunity for self-help and self-government. A far better example from Nelson's growing labour movement was a Cornish migrant called William Rickard. When he was nine William, following in his father's footsteps, became a tin and lead miner in Cornwall. Even at such an early age he was immersed in the culture of Primitive Methodism, and remembered how, as the miners descended the iron ladder down into the mine each day,

> they step to the rhythmic chanting of some popular hymn tune. It used to be that when the men of a shift had collected at the bottom of the mine, they would hold a short prayer meeting. Though only a youth at the time, I took an active part in those religious services . . . At the age of ten I was a teacher of the infants' class; and when I was twelve I went out with the lay preachers on circuit, helping in the service . . .

Not long afterwards, hearing that in Nelson 'the streets were paved with gold', William's father moved his family up north out

of Cornwall. William was put to work in the warehouse at
Lomeshaye Mill and became prominent in the Nelson Weavers'
Association and Labour Party. He always remained a staunch
Primitive and to the end of his days was proud to claim, 'I have
held every office there is in a Sunday School up to superin-
tendent.'[5]

Yet it was neither the Wesleyans nor the Primitives who provided the key ingredient to Nelson's radicalism. It was the Independent Methodists, an early breakaway sect from the Primitives.
They flourished in Nelson and Colne where, by the turn of the
century, they had over 1,300 members. Particularly impressive
was the giant Salem Chapel built in the 1850s which loomed
darkly over the centre of Nelson. The Independents emphasised
chapel democracy, self-government and temperance too, but
combined it with an intellectual concern for self-education and for
politics in the broadest sense. Attracted to Salem's Young Men's
Mutual Improvement Association classes were people who, at the
turn of the century, would lead Nelson's growing socialist groups.
Three brothers, Dan, William and Harrison Carradice, were
typical Salem members. They came from Kirkby Malham, a
Dales village near the magnificent limestone waterfall and tarn.
One man who knew the Carradice brothers well recalls their
egalitarian instincts, instincts which Salem and Nelson emphasised all the more strongly. 'They was brought up around
Malham Tarn,' he explained,

> . . . They worked in the lime quarries. But they were Liberals in
> those days . . . They went to the Methodist church, and the squire
> was Tory and High Church. But they didn't conform. Not only
> did they not conform in religion, they didn't conform in many
> ways.
>
> And Dan used to tell me the story about how they used to come
> down the lane, and they were expected to touch their cap to
> t'squire. And they wouldn't. But if the road sweeper . . . if he was
> about and the squire was there, they used to touch their hat to the
> road sweeper, bid him 'good morning' and call him 'sir'.
>
> And, knowing Dan Carradice, that was typical. He would enjoy
> doing that; and he would have done it with a straight face. He
> used to tell me about that . . .

It therefore seemed only natural that the Carradice brothers

and other like-minded people should eventually shift their allegiances from the Salem Chapel to a newer socialist group; they
moved to join the recently-formed Independent Labour Party
(ILP) which, as we shall see, was so crucial to Nelson's development. 'The movement sprang out of non-conformist church,'
continued the Carradices' friend.

> The ILP sprang out of Salem Chapel . . . Jack Robinson . . .
> originally, as a young man, was Secretary at Young Men's Class
> at Salem. And they were getting that many socialist speakers
> coming, and listening to them, and out of the ILP, that Jack
> thought he might as well be in the ILP. So he dropped the Salem
> side. It wasn't what they required. It wasn't supplying the needs of
> what they wanted, wasn't religion. And they thought the ILP and
> socialism were – or would do – and they left. And Dan Carradice,
> were brought up Methodist – came over into ILP.[6]

The popularity of Methodism – especially Independent
Methodism – in the Nelson area helped shape the town into a
socialist stronghold. This Nonconformist tradition, fed by the
waves of immigrants from Cornwall or Yorkshire, combined
magically with the other local ingredients: the high proportion of
small manufacturers and the very newness and roughness of the
place. In all this, it was doubtless the Yorkshire immigrants who
had the greatest impact. They strengthened the existing traditions
of temperance, of thrift, of egalitarianism – and of married
women's work. Women had always worked in places like Cowling:
Philip Snowden's mother, for instance, had returned to the mill
after her children were born. And in 1895 her son, now a parish
councillor back in Cowling, noted how 70 per cent of married
women there went out to work in the mill, it being

> a reproach for a young married woman with only a house to
> follow, and herself, a husband and one or two children to wait
> upon to stay away from the mill. The gospel of thrift as taught
> here tells her it would be better to be trying to do her share
> towards putting something by for a rainy day.[7]

The proportion of married women going out to work in the
mills would doubtless be lower in the Nelson area: in nearby
Burnley only one in three married women worked. Still, women's
work in the weaving sheds of north-east Lancashire was crucial to

the growth of socialism there. It produced a generation of women who had been wage earners for almost all their adult life. The distressing story of Deborah Smith, born in the 1850s among the stone-quarrying hamlets above Brierfield, can speak for many, many other women. She left school at thirteen to become a full-time weaver in one of the Nelson mills: here she was to spend much of her adult life:

> I got married young; I had to go to the mill to earn money, and when you've three young childer to bring up, feed and fend for, you haven't much time [for anything else] . . .
>   My first husband died at the age of twenty-six leaving me with three little childer . . . On top of that came another trouble. I buried my youngest child when he were four years old. That were a big trouble; he'd been such a comfort to me. He used to come to the top of the street when the factory were closing, and when he met me he'd say, 'Come to meet you again, mammy.'

Deborah Smith married again, began a second family but still continued to work as a weaver. 'I wove on,' she explained stoically, 'till the two oldest boys could run my looms.'[8]

Deborah Smith, Philip Snowden, the Carradice brothers, William Rickard and Selina Coombe, along with all the other immigrants pouring into this busy valley, found when they arrived that old-style party politics still held sway. Philip Snowden might remember Nelson as 'a hot-bed of Radicalism' in the 1880s, but it was still a radicalism that was contained within the broad embrace of Gladstone's Liberal Party. Right up to the end of the century local Liberals remained in control of both parliamentary and municipal politics. For instance, Nelson lay within the sprawling Clitheroe constituency that took in much of the old-fashioned farming country around Pendle: here a progressive Liberal and influential member of Gladstone's government, Sir Ughtred Kay-Shuttleworth, remained MP for seventeen years virtually without opposition. And as Nelson itself mushroomed from a cluster of hamlets into a town with its own Borough Council and its own mayor, its local government continued to be run by Liberal Nonconformist manufacturers such as Amos Nelson, risen far from his father's power-and-loom days to become mayor. In Burnley itself, the pattern was similar: two-thirds of the councillors were Liberals, while Liberal MPs were regularly returned to Westminster.

This all-pervasive Liberalism shaped the textile trade unions locally too. The Burnley Weavers, for instance, was still dominated by the Liberal old guard, notably David Holmes. Holmes' political influence was considerable: he was not only Burnley president and president of the great regional union federation (the Northern Counties' Amalgamated Association of Weavers, formed in 1884), but also chairman of the Trade Union Congress's powerful Parliamentary Committee, which liaised between trade unionists and Westminster. He also dominated politics in Burnley, not only as a magistrate and a councillor, but also as a member of the local School Board and the Board of Guardians (which administered education and the poor law respectively).

Few subjects illustrated David Holmes' zeal for blindly defending the status quo better than the half-timer question. In 1891 it was proposed to raise the minimum age for half-timers from ten to eleven years old. Under Holmes' guidance, the Burnley Weavers opposed this legislation and in 1894 again opposed efforts to raise the age to twelve. Holmes steadfastly refused to bend to the new progressive winds of the 1890s. 'Mr Holmes is a type of the old trade unionist,' noted one of the new socialist newspapers. 'His walls are hung with illuminated addresses; he has filled every important office to which the union could call him; and he still retains the esteem and affection of his constituents.'[9]

Around 1890, such old-fashioned ways began to be challenged. The complacent assumption that each generation of Liberals could forever hand the mayoral chain of office from one to another became open to question. This challenge came not from the right (the Conservatives had failed to woo local cotton weavers from Liberalism) but from the left. The Liberal leadership suddenly found itself being sniped at by socialists on every occasion – parliamentary elections, municipal elections, elections for School Boards and Boards of Guardians, for control of the major unions of miners and weavers, even for the otherwise unenviable post of municipal auditor. Harassed Liberals could no longer relax between elections: tireless socialist orators would be stumping the valley, from Burnley to Brierfield, from Nelson to Colne, speaking at every piece of waste ground and every street corner, taking disrespectful swipes at harmless Liberal dignitaries, and trying to persuade working men to vote for a *worker* rather than the traditional gentleman manufacturers.

Two socialist groups, both with a strong local presence, were responsible for upsetting local Liberals' time-honoured way of life; one was the Social Democratic Federation (SDF) and the other the Independent Labour Party (ILP), and both reflected the upsurge of a new socialism in the 1890s.

The older of the two groups, the Democratic Federation was formed in 1881, adopting the title 'Social Democratic Federation' three years later. Improbable as it might seem, the SDF was led by a wealthy businessman called Henry Hyndman. Hyndman himself had quarrelled with Karl Marx (and Marx's friend Engels rated him as little more than 'a pretty unscrupulous careerist'). Yet Hyndman managed to absorb Marx's analysis of capitalism and, under his leadership, the SDF set out a bold programme that was to sweep away the economic and social ills of nineteenth-century industrialism.

In its first few years the SDF remained largely London-based: as late as 1890 three-quarters of its membership was in London. Yet Hyndman developed the knack – though again it sounds improbable – of taking the SDF message to groups of industrial workers in Britain's expanding towns and cities. His speeches, wrote one socialist who heard Hyndman speak, were 'a hustings masterpiece . . . There was in his protagonism a fiery and even fanatical zeal. He appealed for better things – for justice and democracy – for a new system of politics and economics.' Certainly, Hyndman's brisk denunciations of capitalism gave him a growing following in the factory towns of north-east Lancashire. Though he invariably appeared formally dressed, he is still recalled fondly by older local people who 'can remember him coming into Burnley in that tall hat, frock coat . . . As a child I took to him, yes. I can remember him now in the Mechanics' [Institute], shaking hands as we all came through.'[10]

However much his detractors might snipe at him, Hyndman found a warm reception locally. Between 1891 and 1894 SDF membership in Lancashire blossomed from under a hundred to well over a thousand, far outnumbering even the London membership. Although not the earliest in Lancashire, the Burnley branch, formed in 1891, was soon the most important, boasting a membership of about 400 and over a thousand SDF sympathisers. It managed to recruit a number of hard-pressed coal miners during the mining lock-out of 1893, for instance: feeling ran so high against rich coal-owning Tories who were prepared to starve miners into submission that the Burnley SDF branch found it a golden opportunity for recruiting angry colliers. Henceforth, the Burnley Miners became a staunch supporter of Hyndman.

The SDF also made inroads into the smaller textile unions in the town: two of the earliest SDF town councillors were officials of the Burnley Twisters and the Burnley Miners. More resistant to change was the giant Burnley Weavers; as early as 1890, David Holmes had thundered at the Trades Union Congress against 'socialists who go up and down the country making a noise at other people's expense . . . Their object is not trade unionism but red-handed revolution.'[11]

Holmes did have good reason to feel perturbed. Moves to oust him from the leadership of the Burnley Weavers had not been entirely ineffective. By 1893 a socialist, already elected to the Weavers' committee, stood successfully for the union vice-presidency (though Holmes himself still remained president). At the same time, the Burnley SDF began to publish a weekly penny newspaper, the *Socialist and North-East Lancashire News*, with the daring slogan 'The World for the Workers'. Similarly, old-style Liberals were doubtless worried to learn that the SDF branch, watching the efficient house-to-house union collectors, had taken a leaf out of the Burnley Weavers' book:

A committee of 36 members was appointed; and this committee was divided into 12 threes, each for each ward of the town. The duty of these three members is to go to the private address of each in the party in the particular ward to collect his weekly subscription and leave his copy of *Justice* [the national SDF paper]. Incidentally a great deal of information is obtained. Each collector is provided with a book in which he notes whether the subscribing member is also a member of the Weavers' Association or the Co-operative Society. By this information and by judiciously whipping up the members, the SDF have been able to place socialists upon

the Committee of the Weavers' Association and upon the
committee of the Co-operative Society.[12]

If such impeccable organisation was to lead to some of his
members causing trouble, Holmes indeed had reason to worry.
Moreover, a similar story, though on a smaller scale, could be told
of successful SDF branches in Colne, Blackburn and, of course,
Nelson. Yet in Nelson it was the other new socialist group, the
Independent Labour Party, that was to emerge particularly
strongly.

The Independent Labour Party (ILP) was formed at a conference in Bradford in the West Riding of Yorkshire in January
1893. It was led by the Ayrshire Miners' Secretary, Keir Hardie,
a firm teetotaller with a genius for propaganda and for relating
socialist ideas to ordinary people's everyday experience. A warm-
hearted man, he won many ILP converts in the Pennine uplands
where the strength of temperance and of Independent Methodism
ensured his popularity. Certainly men like the Carradice brothers
quickly warmed to the ILP's brand of socialism. It spoke an
idealistic language, demanding a new 'co-operative common-
wealth' that would offer a radical change in the quality of
everyday life. At the same time the ILP was practical: it wanted
direct parliamentary representation of working-class people,
independent of both the Liberal and Tory parties. This combination of almost religious idealism and down-to-earth practicality
dovetailed in well with the pioneer roughness of a new frontier
town like Nelson. A Nelson branch of the ILP sprang up even
before the national ILP was formed, and no fewer than three local
men travelled over the Pennines to Bradford to attend the
founding conference.[13]

The atmosphere of a frontier society impatiently bursting out of
its old-fashioned Liberal strait-jacket which had bound it for too
long, shaped the lives of young immigrants like Selina Coombe.
She was amongst those growing up in this rapidly-changing
industrial valley who found events in the early 1890s happening
almost too fast to make clear sense at the time. But they were
events which, it is clear, moulded her adult life and the lives of
those closest to her.

CHAPTER FOUR

ROBERT COOPER AND THE GREAT CRUSADE: 1891-1896

Old John Cooper was an obstinate man who did nothing by halves. Born in 1839, he combined small-scale farming with lead mining in the wilds of Swaledale, high up in the North Riding. He married the daughter of a neighbouring farmer and together they produced no fewer than fourteen children. When he was twenty-seven he was converted to Primitive Methodism and from then on this became his ruling passion. He devoted his days to supporting the chapel and preaching on the local circuit. An unwavering opponent of both drinking and smoking, he lived out the revivalist simplicities of the Primitives' creed. Even while he was tramping each day the six miles from home to the entrance to the Swaledale lead mines, his hands were busy knitting socks for his family, his mind preparing his simple heart-felt sermons for the coming Sunday.

Old John Cooper's eldest son John also went into farming and by the time he was an adolescent he was busy milking cows and clipping sheep seven days a week in return for the mighty wage of ten pounds a year. As a poor farm labourer in an area where mining was in sad decline, John naturally pricked up his ears when he heard tell of a new Lancashire town called Nelson. There, looms were made of gold and weavers, so they said, received fabulous wages for no more work a week than he usually did in three days. So in the late 1880s, when he was nineteen or twenty, young John Cooper left his lowly farm job, said goodbye to his family and set off on the journey down through the Pennines to Nelson.

When he arrived, he found life far harder than the travellers' tales had led him to believe. Even weaving seemed difficult to master for someone brought up on the land. 'I did my twelve months' weaving at Lomeshaye,' he later recounted. 'I never had more than three looms . . . and I don't think I ever earned over a pound a week off them. I was too old to learn weaving . . . A pound a week was not enough for me, so I left weaving and joined the Post Office.' In 1889 John Cooper became one of Nelson's half-dozen postmen and, having settled into a secure job he liked, summoned his parents and some of his many brothers and sisters down from Swaledale. Old John Cooper got a job as a railway porter, while his children found work in Ecroyds' Mill, a few minutes walk from their house in Lomeshaye Road.

Before long the Cooper family emerged as active supporters of the Primitive Methodist Chapel in Nelson. Mrs Cooper, according to the Chapel leaders' minute book, used to beg fruit from local greengrocers and clean and polish it for the Harvest Festival. (Her granddaughter, however, was rather scathing about her grandmother's piety: she 'used to sit and read her Bible on Sunday; she reckoned she was right religious'.) All her children were involved in chapel life too; but it was her husband for whom it remained an all-consuming passion. When he was fifty-five, Brother Mr Cooper, according to the minutes for 1894, was to 'be recommended to the Quarterly meeting as a candidate for the Lay ministry'. The recommendation must have gone through for John Cooper did indeed become a lay preacher – though his granddaughter remembers how his 'ranting' embarrassed his children:

> My grandfather Cooper was a wonderful allelulia preacher. And some of my aunts and uncles used to have to go to chapel . . . and they used to be so ashamed of his ranting, they used to sneak out. But, to give him his due, he did it all for free . . . and he tramped at weekends as far as Earby and Barnoldswick . . . to preach.[1]

The second of Grandfather Cooper's sons, a young man who is to play a central role in this story, was called Robert. Robert Cooper, born in Swaledale in 1869, was a serious-minded boy. At the tiny village school, with its stone-mullioned windows, he excelled at both sums and writing. Yet in the Yorkshire Dales there were few opportunities for a working-class boy like him either to continue his schooling or to search out a clerical job. Instead, Robert left school as soon as possible and followed his brother John on to the land. He took to farming instinctively and never lost his love of the Dales countryside; but Robert realised there was little future in staying a labourer. So when his family decided to join his eldest brother in Nelson, he went with them.

Robert was about eighteen years old when he left Swaledale: life in a town seemed to offer him opportunities only dreamed of in the Dales. He followed his brother John into the Post Office and was soon delivering letters and heavy parcels up and down Nelson's steep cobbled streets. Like the rest of his family, he took part in chapel affairs: in 1890 the chapel leaders agreed that Robert Cooper, who had apparently gone back to the Dales for a summer holiday, 'be written to and kindly asked to secure some Barley Oats Wheat and Rye for the decorations, and if he is not coming home he forward some by luggage' for the chapel's autumn 'Fruit Banquet'. But already Robert was developing ambitions that neither the Post Office nor Methodism could fulfil.

Robert Cooper wanted to enter the Civil Service. The Civil Service, however, demanded exacting educational standards. Robert was undaunted. He determined to improve the rudimentary skills he had learnt at school by applying himself diligently to his education in the evenings once his postman's round was over. He set to, patiently polishing his reading, writing and arithmetic, and soon progressed to tackling the vulgar fractions and compound multiplication demanded by the Civil Service examinations.[2]

Unsatisfied by these accomplishments, Robert Cooper went further. He resolved to learn a rarer but seemingly valuable skill: writing in short-hand. From his modest wages, he acquired a number of Pitman's shorthand text books and was soon practising taking down speech verbatim to try and increase his speeds. He must have mastered Pitman's phonetic squiggles and dashes easily for, in May 1889 when he was still only nineteen, Robert earned one of Pitman's decorated 'Certificates of Proficiency in Phonography' which entitled him to membership of the Phonetic Society. There can have been few in Nelson who could have matched his secretarial skills, and Robert Cooper had good reason to feel that his ambition to enter the Civil Service and to put his hard-won education to use would soon be realised.[3]

He could hardly have foreseen the turn of events which was to undermine his careful plans. About 1890, just as he reached his twentieth birthday, Robert Cooper found himself caught up in a wave of trade union militancy which spread across the country to touch even the postmen of distant Nelson.

Since the 1880s there had been unrest amongst semi-skilled and unskilled workers previously outside trade union organisation. The strikes of the London dockworkers and of the Bryant and May matchgirls became renowned. Similarly, between 1889 and 1891 there was a wave of strikes in Bradford and Leeds like that of the Manningham mill workers. Nearer home there was even a strike of Nelson weavers. However, the new unionism had far less impact on the weavers, already well organised into mass unions, than on smaller groups of workers – like the postmen – outside the cotton factories. Inspired by the militancy of the East London postmen (who themselves seemed fired by the example set by nearby dockers and gasworkers), local postmen began to meet together to protest against the harsh conditions they worked under and to demand an eight-hour day. Robert Cooper was just the kind of young immigrant worker who was attracted to the campaign. He was immediately drawn in, as the postmen huddled together debating if – and then how – to form a branch of the postal workers' union in Nelson. When it was eventually agreed that a branch *should* be formed, who should naturally be appointed union secretary if not Robert Cooper? The young Dalesman could write a better letter than the other postmen and, in addition, could put his new shorthand skills to excellent use at branch meetings.

Rather recklessly Robert agreed to become union secretary. The opposition was fierce: both his own brother and, more importantly, the Post Office itself, took a dim view of such trouble-making. Robert did not last long in his new post, according to the tales he later passed on to his daughter:

> He did come as a postman, and his brother was head postman; his brother was anti-union – friction in the family for ages. They were . . . having postmen taking huge parcels on their backs, as well as letters. And my father saw this – and my uncle used to walk about [bent] double carrying [parcels].

> And my father got the others to form a union. And they [the
> Post Office] objected to this . . . and he got sacked. Anyhow, so
> then he learned to weave, because some of his sisters were
> weavers. There was a big mill down here [Ecroyds], and he
> learned to weave.[4]

All Robert's plans and ambitions were dashed overnight. The
chances of completing his training for the Civil Service once he
became a mill worker were slim indeed. He could of course continue his education in the evenings, but he was unlikely to find a
job outside the mill now. Worse still, Robert never took to
weaving and resented being confined within four factory walls. In
his early twenties, he found he was too old to learn the skills so
easily acquired by young half-timers, of knotting the fine warp
threads when they broke and of understanding the moods of his
looms. He yearned to return to the countryside, to the healthier
life of Swaledale, and he began to search for ways to understand
the sorry predicament he now found himself in. In radical Nelson,
crammed with the newest wave of immigrants, help was to hand.

Within months of his Post Office sacking, Robert came across a
political group which seemed to offer answers to his growing
questions. In June 1891 a London socialist called Herbert Burrows, a key supporter of the matchgirls' strike and now treasurer
of their trade union, came up to Nelson to inaugurate a local
branch of the SDF. Robert Cooper was among those working
men who went along to hear what Burrows had to say. Burrows
spoke to them on 'The Meaning of Socialism', adapting his
radical message to the traditional concerns of the Liberal textile
workers in his audience. Neither teetotalism nor trade union
could solve the labour question, he explained, for both recognised
the existence of capitalism. Rather, workers must demand both
manhood suffrage (i.e. the parliamentary vote for all men) and
the eight-hour day. He understood that some Lancashire weavers
opposed an eight-hour day because they were fearful of the cotton
trade being undercut by foreign competition. If they believed
that, thundered Burrows, they did not yet understand the nature
of international capitalism, for 'the mill owners of India are the
capitalists of the north of England'. At this, some of his audience
grew angry. 'When foreign socialists reduce *their* working day,'

protested one, 'then the Lancashire weaver will be prepared to do the same.'

Burrows' meeting was a tumultuous one, and many Liberals must have left muttering furiously about the speaker. But to Robert Cooper, Herbert Burrows' message came as a revelation. It helped make sense of both his recent sacking and his low-paid drudgery in the mill. Afterwards, the local newspaper report noted, 'a considerable number of persons remained behind to join the Branch'. One of them was Robert Cooper.

Along with thirty others, he helped organise the Nelson SDF branch. The following week five officers were duly elected, including a librarian: books were donated to start the branch library. The branch was to meet twice a week, on Sundays and Wednesdays, and invitations to come up and speak were dispatched to Henry Hyndman himself, as well as to Annie Besant who, like Herbert Burrows, had played a prominent part in the matchgirls' strike.[5]

The SDF branch activities came to mean a great deal to Robert Cooper as he struggled to master the art of cotton weaving. Yet his troubles were far from over. They were compounded when, after two years in the mill, the cotton industry was hit by one of its periodic slumps. Local unemployment rose. The Nelson SDF, already involved in tussles with the police over 'free speech' and the right to hold open-air political meetings, took up the challenge. An SDF member thrust his way into the room in Nelson Town Hall where the Poor Law Guardians' relief committee was sitting. 'Evidently speaking under emotion and excitement,' noted the *Nelson Chronicle* report, the intruder 'condemned the committee for not providing work for the unemployed'. They did not want charity and food tickets, he told the startled Guardians – until a police constable was summoned and he had to withdraw. Robert Cooper would have been closely involved in such agitation: a new and indifferent weaver, he seems to have been among those who lost their looms. If he was unemployed for any length of time, he too would have to go begging to the Guardians for food tickets.

His prospects looked grim. This final blow seemed to persuade him that factory work in Lancashire was not for him. Like so many other young Victorian men faced with hard times, he decided to emigrate across the Atlantic. His parents must have been greatly distressed to see him go; to help soften the blow of his departure and to keep their son on the right track in a foreign country, old John Cooper gave his son a copy of the King James Bible, carefully inscribed, 'A Present from John Cooper to his Son Robert on his departure from England to America April 6th 1893'.

It seems Robert had a hard time on the other side of the Atlantic Ocean, although the details have unfortunately been long forgotten. His daughter was later told stories of what her father got up to there, but over the years these faded from memory. All she was able to say about this distant era was that:

> He went out to America first. He learnt to weave here, but he didn't – he came from a farm and he didn't like weaving a bit. He was always off into the country . . . I think he must have been just in his twenties – twenty-three or -four. And he went to Massachusetts . . . He talked a lot about Massachusetts . . . He didn't stay long. I don't think he stayed above two years. Then he came back.[6]

Even before Robert Cooper set sail for America, Selina Coombe also found herself touched by the changes now affecting Burnley and Nelson. In 1891, two years after her mother died and Selina returned to work in a cotton mill, her eldest brother John got married. His new wife, Annie, the daughter of a Cornish miner, had worked as a cook-housekeeper and, once married, naturally wanted to run the Coombe household herself. So Selina, now twenty-six years old, moved out of her brother's house and into lodgings. 'She left because this young woman came,' her daughter explained. '. . . I think my mother realised that two women in the kitchen might quarrel. You see, my mother was a good cook, and she was one . . . Anyhow, she moved across, because I think she thought it would be better if they were left alone.'

Selina Coombe did not move far: she went to live with a family called Dugdale, just four doors up from her brother's shop. How long she lodged there, and how she adjusted to this break from the tight-knit Coombe family, is unknown. All that is clear is that Selina's new independence coincided with a welling up of the new political and industrial militancy in the area. The Nelson SDF had got off to a flying start a few months earlier, and a Burnley branch soon followed suit. Then, in December 1891 Selina witnessed a major textile dispute, initiated by a woman weaver, that had considerable local impact.[7]

What happened was this. Working conditions in the Lancashire cotton mills were notoriously poor, certainly by twentieth-century standards. By the early 1890s one or two progressive voices were at last being raised in protest against the barbarities of factory life. In 1893 a woman factory inspector reported with horror how in Lancashire, 'lavatories, opening from the shed in which men and women work together, are unprovided with doors'; and she noted that instances of 'immorality' occurred more frequently in Lancashire than in Yorkshire mills, and began to link this to the poorer sanitary accommodation. Likewise, complaints, occasionally from groups of women winders, would come before the Burnley Weavers' committee: the secretary would then be instructed to write to the sanitary inspector protesting about a particular mill's closets. Other, more strident voices were raised too. 'The loose sanitary arrangements in most mills,' thundered the socialist author of *The Effects of the Factory System*, 'produce loose conduct. The conveniences are often in a place exposed to the gaze of all operatives.' And he went on to attack the 'coarse home and factory environment – much indecent talk, as well as rude Phallic diversions, in the factories and weaving sheds'.[8]

Linked to this protest, there was also a growing number of complaints from women weavers against bullying by tacklers (i.e. overlookers) who tuned their looms. Some women objected to the way unscrupulous tacklers would 'drive' their weavers to finish more cloth by marking up on a slate how much each weaver produced and then publicly displaying this list. 'It were all put down on a slate and hung on th' shed door,' complained Deborah Smith, the weaver who worked till her sons were old enough to take over her looms. '. . . Of course everybody could tell what everybody else addled [earned].' On other occasions an overbearing tackler might resort to the kind of bullying which would now be termed sexual harassment. Certainly this explained the conflict in Nelson in 1891–2. A tackler was accused of using offensive language to women at work, and of making immoral propositions to one of the married women. Although the Nelson

Weavers' committee was run by men, the union actively supported the women's accusations. The weavers went out on strike
in protest and five hundred blacklegs, guarded by a large number
of constables, were ferried in from outside. So popular did the
strike become that three local ministers were invited to act as
arbitrators. They found the tackler guilty of the charges. He was
dismissed and the weavers out on strike were taken on again.[9]

The remarkable success of this Nelson strike seems to have
inspired other local women to express their own deep resentments
against male overlookers too. A few months later, the Burnley
Weavers' Association, which had received complaints of 'baiting'
[tormenting] from weavers at Tunstills, took up the case of a
Brierfield tackler who lived round the corner from Selina
Coombe. Local feeling against him ran so high that the union
collector undertook to go round and compile a dossier of complaints against this man (though in the end the case was dropped).
Despite Victorian women's reluctance to bring such matters
before the all-male committee, complaints still came in. Another
local tackler, probably also from Tunstills, was accused of behaving so foully to his women weavers that they demanded that they
give evidence against him anonymously and in private, and it was
eventually stipulated that:

> Wilson Fletcher be not allowed in the Room while the Females are
> giving their evidence against him: but that the same be taken
> down in writing and a Copy supplied to him without the names of
> the said Witnesses also that Mr Fletcher be in the Room while the
> men are giving their evidence against him.

Wilson Fletcher was found guilty of such gross behaviour that
he was fined fifty shillings (a week and a half's wage for him) and
reprimanded by his Overlookers' lodge.[10]

Working in the smaller, quieter winding room, Selina Coombe
never came up directly against such odious tacklers. There *were*
occasional complaints from women winders against the men who
worked near them, though none of these can be definitely traced
back to Selina's winding room at Tunstills. But whether or not she
had personal experience of such harassment herself, she was
becoming only too conscious of the kinds of humiliations suffered
by the women she worked with in the winding room. As she grew

older, nearing thirty, she became increasingly saddened by the way her fellow winders seemed to accept their demeaning conditions: the degrading lavatory provision, the jokes and bullying. Although she would laugh along with everyone else, she began to recognize that beneath the women's good-natured ribaldry lay a pitiful lack of self-respect. The rudiments of home nursing, first-aid and laundry work that Selina had picked up when she looked after her mother, taught her to question some of the unhygienic behaviour other winders took for granted. Eventually the slovenly acceptance of such degrading conditions made her speak out – though, as she later recounted to her own daughter, it nearly cost Selina her job:

> Women in those days didn't wear any sanitary protection; all their petticoats would be covered in blood every month. And my mother made some towelling . . . for a woman she worked with, a girl she worked with.
>
> And in those days skirts were down to the floor. In the winding room they talked a lot, did winders, because it wasn't noisy like the mill . . . used to talk and chat all the time they were working . . .
>
> Anyhow this [girl's] mother came back and played pop at the mill with the manager, because my mother had given this girl [some towels]. She said how was her daughter ever going to get off if they didn't know about this smell?
>
> Like an animal! [My mother said there] used to be blood on the floor of the winding room . . . Of course, they wore sort of drawers, and they were just legs up to here and all open at the – and of course it went straight down on to the floor, or on to the petticoats. It was an attraction. This woman played pop with the manager. My mother nearly got sacked for making her [daughter] some sanitary towels.[11]

Such pieces of myth-making, linking menstrual bleeding to fertility and sexual attraction, were perhaps coming to be disbelieved by the end of the nineteenth century. But what is certainly true is that once Selina Coombe had dared to raise her voice and had broken the silence surrounding such behaviour, she became whirled up in a series of new activities both inside and outside the mill. Having the courage to speak up on behalf of the other girls in the winding room signalled the beginning of a new era in Selina's life.

She was becoming increasingly conscious, for instance, of the importance of medical knowledge and of understanding how the human reproductive system works. If women of her generation were to avoid the suffering experienced by their mothers, then they must organise their own education on a self-help basis. A local St John Ambulance group had recently been formed in Brierfield, and it offered working people a proper training in first aid and ambulance work, regulated by examination. After her years of untrained nursing and her more recent experiences in the mill, Selina naturally warmed to the idea of mastering such valuable practical skills. She started the course in 1893, and did well: the following April she proudly received her decorated certificate for passing the first year examination in 'first aid to the injured'. (She had hardly finished the course before she was given tragic confirmation of the importance of such skills: her four-year-old niece, the daughter of her brother Richard and also called Selina Jane, was standing near the fireplace one evening when her nightdress caught fire. The doctor was called in, but within two days she had died. The verdict was accidental death.)

In such dire emergencies, the local St John Ambulance Corps played a crucial role. Reports in local newspapers bore this out: a cardroom worker at Tunstills would get her hand caught in a carding frame while she was cleaning it and, with a member of the ambulance corps, she would be rushed off to hospital for her thumb to be amputated. Unions like the Burnley Weavers had little hesitation about helping the St John Ambulance to organise collections in the mills to swell its funds. And Selina was increasingly willing to devote much of her spare time to supporting the corps. In May 1895 she passed an exam in nursing and hygiene; the same year she was invited on to the local St John Ambulance Committee and attended the Brierfield Ambulance Corps ball in the local assembly rooms.

Years later, Selina used to tell her own daughter how important such self-help groups were. My mother, Mary proudly explained, 'started the Ambulance in Brierfield. And in those days people daren't go to the doctor. Used to set arms and all sorts of things.' Not content with first aid and nursing, Selina set about mastering other useful skills. She began to read one or two textbooks about how the human body works; and she even took a course in the

principles of laundry work (something again she had been forced
to pick up by trial and error before) and later earned herself a
decorated certificate, this time from the Nelson Technical
School.[12]

Selina Coombe's search for self-education did not develop in a
vacuum. As early as 1883 the Women's Co-operative Guild was
formed as an offshoot of the main co-operative movement. It soon
established itself as the only organisation that brought working
women out of their kitchens to discuss matters beyond the narrow
confines of their domestic lives. Both nationally and locally, however, the impetus often came from upper-middle-class women.
Margaret Llewelyn Davies, who became General Secretary of the
Guild in 1889, was educated at Girton College, Cambridge,
recently founded by her aunt, Emily Davies. In the Burnley area
the lead was taken by a tireless reformer called Mary Brown, the
wife of an eminent local doctor. She taught a Sunday School class
for 'factory girls', was a pillar of the influential British Women's
Temperance Association, and helped found a local Rescue Home
for Friendless Girls.

One day, after the Guild had been growing nationally for a few
years, Mary Brown received a visit from three 'hard-working,
earnest, diffident and yet hopeful' women. One was a weaver,
another called Mrs Grocott the wife of a socialist shoemaker, and
the third was probably a housewife. They wanted, they told Mrs
Brown, to start a Guild branch in Burnley. After all, Burnley
Co-operative Society already had over six thousand members and
sales well over £200,000. The problem, they explained, lay with
the men. The custom was for 3 per cent of profits from the stores
to go to education – reading rooms, a fine library and lectures –
hitherto only accessible to men. Married women like themselves
seldom went to the quarterly meetings where such matters were
discussed. They insisted it was now time for women's voices to be
heard. After all, they argued, it was women who did the shopping
and therefore made the society's profits. Why should they not
have some say in how they were spent?

Eventually it was agreed that twelve women shareholders
should attend the quarterly meeting, and Mrs Brown should
accompany them to help state their case. 'We women sat in the
front row,' she recalled;

Towards the end of the meeting came our proposal 'that a Women's Guild be formed for the benefit of the women co-operators, with similar educational advantages to those given to men'. There was a stir and a hubbub. 'Education for women!' 'Let them sat at whoam!' 'Who's to mind the chidder?' etc. The chairman quieted the audience, and I rose and faced the lot. There was a lull, a scuffle of clogs, a few remarks, but I spoke out . . . I pointed out the injustice; said women did the actual buying . . . and on them depended the profits made by the stores . . . If it came to a strike, we women would leave the men to do the buying in . . . In spite of the interruptions I held my ground and then got one of the working women to say a few words. We carried our measure, and in spite of some dissension more than half the audience voted for us.[13]

In this way, a thriving Guild branch was formed in Burnley in 1889 with Mrs Brown as its President. (A few years later a branch also sprang up in Nelson, again with the help of the local doctor's wife, Mrs Robb.) With Mrs Brown's encouragement, the Burnley Guild was soon organising an excellent programme of meetings. Mrs Grocott the shoemaker's wife gave an ambulance demonstration, showing bed-making for invalids and first aid for broken limbs. Mrs Robb offered a laundry lecture on the 'best mode of getting up linen', and on another occasion talked on 'Should the Poor Marry?', a subject which unsurprisingly was followed by an animated discussion (and perhaps touched on the taboo subject of birth control). Another set of lectures was on 'Health' and 'the Human Body'; 'young persons' (i.e. girls) were specifically invited to come and listen, and life-size coloured plates of the body were shown.[14]

Quite possibly Selina Coombe would go from her Brierfield lodgings down into Burnley to listen to Mrs Grocott and the other Guild lecturers. It was by such means that she came to know Mary Brown, and so became introduced to a range of new people and ideas. The Browns used to offer hospitality to travelling speakers: Margaret Llewelyn Davies of the Guild, Karl Marx's daughter Eleanor, and other socialist, Liberal or temperance organisers. Among Mary Brown's closest friends who came to stay was a woman from distant South Africa. Her name was Olive Schreiner, the writer whose *Story of an African Farm* had caused such a public outcry when it was first published (thanks to help from the Browns) in 1883.

On Sunday afternoon, when Doctor Brown was at his surgery and 'the proper maid was out', Mrs Brown used to invite a group of men 'from loom or workshop' to spend an hour or two with her among her books. Her invitations to young working women must have been on a more informal basis but, by one means or another, certainly came to include Selina Coombe about 1893. 'Mrs Dr Brown was kind enough to introduce me to her friend Olive Schreiner when she came to Burnley,' Selina told a journalist years later. 'I had the pleasure of taking tea with her.'[15]

Selina was then about twenty-eight. A winder at Tunstills' mill, she must have been rather awed as she approached the doctor's grand house to meet such a celebrated author, a woman in touch with progressive thinkers and writers both in England and abroad. Yet Selina's outspokenness in the winding room had already helped to bring her into a far wider world than she had previously experienced. About this time, she plucked up her courage and ventured inside one of Burnley's 'instantaneous por-trait' studios to pose beside the rustic fence provided. The resulting photograph, taken about 1893 and the first known por-trait of Selina, reveals a neatly tailored and corseted young woman holding a respectable umbrella. Her face combines both the self-conscious diffidence of her earlier years and a hint of the rebellion beginning to stir within.

At the same time, Selina acquired a French conversation reader and books on English literature and history that she had never had a chance to read at school. Her life in the mill changed too. From the moment she got into trouble for daring to speak out, she found herself pushed to the front by the other winders she worked with – especially when someone was needed to confront the managers or the union officials. Long afterwards, she mentioned to her daughter a little of what happened. 'She worked as a winder, and she used to get into bother,' Mary explained. '. . . She'd been fighting, my mother . . . because she made [a girl] some sanitary towels. But she soon got – she was soon on the winders' com-mittee, and she began to speak, you see.'

This was the autumn of 1893.[16] Olive Schreiner was setting sail back to South Africa. The House of Lords had just thrown out

Gladstone's second Irish Home Rule Bill, leaving his Liberal Government in disarray. The slump in the cotton trade was still causing distress among mill workers. The Burnley Weavers continued their battle against the hated 'slate' system and against poor sanitary facilities in the mills. Then, into this familiar pattern, broke a new voice: the women winders'.

The winders, including those at Tunstills' mill, began to protest about their poor rates of pay. Well they might. They could look around at other departments in Tunstills and notice their piecework rates were low compared to those of other groups of workers. They saw that the weavers, far more numerous and easily organised, had recently managed to establish a Uniform List, that is, a list of piece-work rates for various kinds of cloth, which applied to all weaving mills. This was a major trade union victory which naturally spurred on smaller groups like the winders to follow suit.

Even though the winders were all women and the Burnley Weavers' officials all men, the winders' grumbles were listened to seriously. The union committee even agreed there should be 'district meetings of Winders with regard to complaints and the formation of a List'. Handbills were duly printed advertising a series of shop (i.e. mill) meetings towards the end of November 1893 – including one at Brierfield. We shall never know what took place at these meetings: the local newspapers refused to print the accounts the union officials sent in. We do know, though, that out of these meetings came an acknowledgement that many women winders were not even union members.

As a first step to tackling this, a special recruiting drive was launched. Collectors, always the vital link between factory and home, were instructed to gather information on all winders in their districts. This is exactly where a forthright woman like Selina Coombe would have come into her own. She could give the Brierfield collector the names and addresses of the non-union women she worked with at Tunstills. Equally importantly, she could talk to the women in the quietness of the winding room, encouraging them at least to think about joining the union.

Further shop meetings were organised for the winders. This canvassing turned out to be extremely successful, and by January 1894 there were sufficient winders in membership for union officials to feel confident enough 'to wait upon all firms regarding the Winders' List' – that is, for the union to go on the offensive over wages. Handbills were printed to publicise the proposed list (though again, no copies of the bill appear to have survived) and a series of deputations by union officials kept up the pressure on Tunstills and other local employers. Finally, in April 1894, it was agreed that the winders should be paid at the same rate as a three-loom weaver, and in August copies of the agreed Winders' List of Prices (i.e. wages) were printed. The battle over the women's wage rates had been won.[17]

The winders' battle was brief but successful. Its success was due to the system of local collectors; but it was also due to the enthusiasm of women like Selina Coombe working at the grass-roots. It is virtually impossible to gauge precisely what role she played in the union during these early years: the documentary evidence is unhelpful. However, oral testimony suggests very clearly that she was one of the key women activists locally. 'She never was a trade union official,' her daughter stressed, 'but she was in the trade union movement. I rather think she got those winders to join the trade union movement, because she worked with them a lot.'

Energetic and capable though she was, there was no way Selina could follow up the agitation she had begun among the Tunstill winders by being elected from the quarterly members' meeting to the main Weavers' committee in Burnley. In one or two towns further south in Lancashire where women dominated weaving to the virtual exclusion of men, it might have been possible. In Burnley or Nelson the strong presence of male weavers meant that women were not elected as officials. It was one of the many areas where Victorian women were expected to remain silent. Local conventions still inhibited any attempt to draw aside the veil. Once women had paid their weekly dues to the collector, they were to be screened away out of sight from the main business. These conventions were particularly obvious when a big public meeting was held. Thus when the Nelson, Colne, Brierfield and District Textile Trades Federation (to which Selina Coombe would be affiliated) invited one of the new independent Labour MPs to address them on 'trade unionism and how we can best improve our organisations', the federation booked the enormous Salem Chapel schoolroom in Nelson, but women were actively discouraged from sitting in the main body of the hall. 'Five forms,' the federation decreed, 'be reserved for ladies in the gallery and five men attend to same.'[18] It is clear how much of a snub such conventions were to an outspoken young woman like Selina Coombe. She paid her union dues, was entitled to attend meetings, only to find that she and the other women had no right to take part in politics and were relegated to a shadowy row of seats out of sight up in the gallery.

There were other aspects of textile trade unionism, too, that she felt increasingly dissatisfied with. She was finding it difficult to accept the traditional justification of men like David Holmes for a factory system which so exploited and stunted local children. As her anger against the half-time system grew, she determined to do something to help bring it to an end. With progressive reforms in mind, she began to collect information on the size and weight of young people who, like herself, had been half-timers; she forwarded her research to Sir Ughtred Kay-Shuttleworth, her MP and an influential member of Gladstone's ailing government. (Kay-Shuttleworth was a close friend of the Browns, and quite possibly it had been Mary Brown who brought together this seemingly unlikely pair: a great philanthropist whose family had been land-owners since the fifteenth century, and a factory winder, the daughter of railway navvy.)[19]

Improbable as this partnership was, it was valuable. The MP's views on the half-time question were well in advance of most parents and trade unionists in his constituency. Selina Coombe, with her growing conviction that the half-time system must be ended as soon as possible, must have felt at odds with most of her neighbours and relations, too. Luckily she came across the ideas of Margaret McMillan, a socialist from Bradford who, although the youngest member of the city's School Board, had led a deputation to Asquith, the Home Secretary, about the half-time system. Margaret McMillan occasionally spoke on education in the Brierfield area and, perhaps by going along to one of these lectures, Selina acquired a copy of her pamphlet published in 1895 called *Child Labour & the Half-time System*. It was an impassioned appeal against a system which still exacted its crippling price on 140,000 children, and which stunted their physical growth by three or four inches.[20]

Selina Coombe was able to clarify her thoughts on this particular issue. Other doubts and conflicting feelings remained: her
lack of formal education still seemed to hamper her struggle to
make sense of what she saw happening around her. About 1895
she was beginning to edge towards the socialists in the local SDF,
and was beginning to drop even her few remaining links with the
Primitive Methodist chapel. But she seemed to remain a little
uncertain about which direction her life might go. And perhaps
these uncertainties were felt more keenly because Selina, now in
her thirties, was susceptible to Victorian taunts about becoming
an 'old maid'.

Robert Cooper returned from Massachusetts, probably in the
spring of 1895, back to his thankless set of looms at Lomeshaye.
Precisely how Selina and he met remains unclear. Perhaps it was
at one of the social events organised by the Primitive Methodists.
Their daughter, however, had a hazy recollection that they met
shortly after her father arrived back from America through the
socialist movement. Certainly there was opportunity enough:
their paths were bound to cross sooner or later. A socialist group
in Brierfield used to mount smoking concerts; the Nelson, Colne,
Brierfield and District Textile Trades Federation would organise
'Annual Convivials' with a proper tea and concert; Burnley SDF
boasted a 'Socialist Band' which played at branch teas and
dances, and even the Nelson ILP had its own soberly-named
'Temperance Band'.[21]

It is easy to see why Selina and Robert were attracted to each
other. Both felt distanced from their unrewarding mill jobs. Both
lived surrounded by relations (and Robert apparently still lived
with his family, in a small house overlooking the canal at
Lomeshaye), but both had cut these links somewhat by their trade
union activity and interest in socialism. Naturally they found in
each other very welcome companionship and support, plus an
opportunity to escape from their cramped living quarters.

Beyond this, the similarity ended. Although five years younger
than her, Robert was far more cosmopolitan and sophisticated
than Selina. He had already spent several years in America
and – like Charles Coombe a generation earlier – must have
entertained his future wife with tales of distant lands across the

ocean which she could never dream of visiting. His foray into trade unionism too was so much more dramatic than her own more humdrum experience. And Robert already possessed a far more studious, intellectual approach to life than Selina's down-to-earth perspective. Not only was he proficient at shorthand, but he was also more committed than Selina to continuing his education in the evenings after a day in the mill. We can sense that, during their courtship, Robert was the person who largely took the lead, introducing Selina to new ideas, new books and new people. Certainly it seems that it was Robert, a founder-member of Nelson SDF, who convinced Selina to abandon any earlier doubts and join the socialists. Robert, already an enthusiastic supporter of the SDF candidate standing in Burnley at the 1895 general election, must have fired Selina's imagination for this campaign too.

Their courtship took place at a time when the Burnley branch of the SDF was growing from strength to strength. It had recently acquired a full-time organiser called Dan Irving. Irving was a railwayman from Bristol who had been Secretary of the Gasworkers' Union there; an irascible socialist who had lost his leg in a railway accident, he had led a colourful life as an itinerant socialist speaker and seemed an ideal man to help win the Burnley seat for the SDF. Henry Hyndman himself had agreed to stand against the sitting Liberal MP and Tory candidate; socialists in the Burnley area soon became infected by a millennial conviction that the longed-for revolution was at hand and that Hyndman would easily trounce the other two candidates. The SDF branch was by now organising no fewer than ten lecture-meetings on Sundays, drawing on such well-known names as Keir Hardie, Eleanor Marx and the Mayor of the Paris Commune. Money arrived from all quarters for Hyndman's election fund: some donations were large (Walter Crane the artist gave forty shillings), but many were small – the Mayor of the Paris Commune gave five, and Robert Cooper managed to save up 1s 6d from his weekly wage to donate. (Selina Coombe, being unable to vote for either Hyndman or any other parliamentary candidate, did not feel inclined to contribute to the fund.) Excitement rose to fever pitch as the July election drew nearer. ' "Oh, when will it [the socialist world] come?" do you cry?' a penny pamphlet demanded apocalyptically. ' "When would you have it come" is my reply . . . God is ready, nature is ready . . . When will you, the producers of wealth . . . stretch out your hands . . . and *will* this thing? Then – then – that very minute, it shall come . . .'[22]

However, the SDF's attack on 'sham' trade unions failed to convince working-class Burnley men. Hyndman never became the MP. Although the Liberals suffered badly elsewhere (they lost nearly a hundred seats overall and the victorious Tories formed the new government), they held Burnley – though with a reduced majority. Hyndman polled a respectable 1,500 votes (but the Tory won four times that number). This failure he put down to the Liberal MP's wealthy Russian wife and the use of a three-year-old electoral register which allowed 'dead' Liberal electors to cast their votes. 'I therefore declare,' Hyndman later reminisced bitterly, 'that the election had been won by Russian roubles and Radical resurrectionists.'[23]

For socialists like Selina Coombe and Robert Cooper the election results were a bitter disappointment. Even Keir Hardie lost the seat he had won three years earlier. In Burnley the heady days of Hyndman's election campaign soon faded: a SDF councillor was hounded out of the town, and the *Socialist* newspaper collapsed. In the Clitheroe constituency Sir Ughtred Kay-Shuttleworth was once again returned unopposed: the Nelson Trades Council had lobbied the ILP branch about putting up a Labour candidate at the election, but nothing came of this. Yet in the midst of these setbacks, Selina Coombe found that a successful campaign for independent labour representation was springing up on her own doorstep and demanded her support.

Sandwiched between Burnley and Nelson, Brierfield always had to struggle to preserve its separate identity. It had its own chapels, co-operative stores and St John Ambulance, but seemed too small to support an SDF, ILP or Women's Co-operative Guild branch of its own. Then, in the mid-1890s, up sprang a succession of energetic but short-lived groups, going under a variety of titles. First came the Brierfield Literary and Debating Society which took to ignoring literature and inviting instead socialist speakers. One such was the Reverend Leonard, an early member of Colne SDF and a Nonconformist minister there, who spoke on 'Darkest England: the way in and the way out', drawing parallels between Stanley's 'Darkest Africa' and General Booth's findings of 'Darkest England'.

Among the active members was a socialist weaver called Ben Smith: he took part in the society's debates on 'Labour and the production of wealth' and grew increasingly impatient that local trade unionists still lacked independent labour representation. When he learnt that even the Burnley Weavers' committee had agreed to support 'Labour' candidates at council elections, Ben Smith and other like-minded Brierfield weavers promptly organised a local meeting to select Labour candidates for the newly-formed Urban District Council. One hundred weavers (and possibly a sprinkling of winders like Selina Coombe as well) attended and voted for Ben Smith, plus a weaver called Abel Latham who was Brierfield's representative on the Burnley Weavers. Shortly afterwards a Brierfield branch was formed of the Labour Electoral Association, (a body started by the TUC in 1886 to encourage moderate trade unionists to stand for local council elections), at which point the Literary and Debating Society, having served its purpose, conveniently faded away.[24]

So under the rather cautious banner of the Labour Electoral Association, Ben Smith stood as a Labour candidate in Brierfield's north ward, the area around John Coombe's shop and the Dugdales' house. He told an election meeting how he had worked in a factory for thirty-five years and urged his audience to make sure more working-class men like himself were elected to public bodies. Although Ben Smith was unsuccessful, Abel Latham won in another Brierfield ward and this encouraged the socialists to become rather more forthright. The Labour Electoral Association was jettisoned and, in late 1895, a new and more ambitious group was launched. It was given a catch-all title obviously designed to appeal to everyone from progressive Liberals to SDF members: Brierfield United Labour Party Club. It was committed to both independent labour representation and also to an educational programme of political lectures and public meetings. Certainly it seems to have been effective, for it was about this time that Selina Coombe became drawn into active involvement with local socialists. 'It was in this town [Brierfield] I first embraced the idea of a collective state,' she later explained. 'It was while working in a cotton mill that I realised the only salvation for the worker was the collective state.' She too became excited by the electoral potential of the new organisation. When Ben Smith again stood in Brierfield's north ward in spring 1896 as a Labour candidate, she joined in the canvass, knocking on doors to drum up support for him. 'I threw in my lot with Brierfield Labour Party. That was the time Ben Smith put up for the Council.' Thanks to such efforts, Ben Smith *did* become councillor – though only by six votes. Indeed, Selina Coombe herself might have been entitled to cast her own vote at the Brierfield Urban District Council election: if she paid at least four shillings a week rent for her room in the Dugdales' house, she may well have been registered as a local government elector.[25]

Against this political backdrop, Robert and Selina's courtship flourished. By the summer of 1896 the two of them had grown very close. They began to talk of marriage. As they drew affectionately towards each other, planning a wedding and discussing where to live, they began to shape their lives in a common direction. Robert, despite his father's zeal and his own previous commitment, withdrew from the Primitive Methodist chapel: in June the Chapel leaders' minute book records 'that Robert Cooper be taken off the Class Book at his own request'. Methodism was no longer a faith that made much sense to Selina and Robert. At the same time, Selina had become more involved in SDF activities. Doubtless urged on by Robert's enthusiasm, she agreed to give a talk in the autumn to the Mutual Improvement Class run by his branch, the Nelson SDF.

The class boasted a weekly attendance of seventy members and Selina, who had had little opportunity to test her skills as a public speaker, must have approached the audience sitting before her in Nelson's Socialist Hall with considerable trepidation. Not only was this her debut: she also found she was the only woman listed as a speaker among an array of far more experienced men. However, she had chosen to speak on her experiences of a trip to the Lake District, entitled 'My Visit to Westmorland', and she plunged ahead bravely with this talk.

How she was received by the Mutual Improvement Class is not recorded. The lecture was not reported in the newspapers, and is only known about through the chance survival over almost ninety years of a copy of the class's 'Syllabus' for 1896–7. This rare local document, although formal in what it says, symbolises another important turning point in Selina Coombe's life. From 1896 onwards she begins to emerge, with her new name 'Mrs Cooper', a more confident and determined married woman.[26]

CHAPTER FIVE

THE REVOLT OF THE DAUGHTERS:
1896-1899

Selina Coombe, a thirty-one-year-old cotton winder, and Robert Cooper, a twenty-six-year-old cotton weaver, were married on 24 October 1896. Breaking with family tradition, their wedding was not held in a nearby Methodist chapel; instead, the couple decided to be married four miles away, up at Colne.

They had become friendly with the Colne Independent Chapel's socialist minister, Reverend Leonard. A supporter of Hyndman and a friend of Kelr Hardie, this rebellious clergyman was a key figure in the development of the local socialist culture. How the three of them originally met is unclear: Selina may have heard Leonard speak at the Brierfield Literary and Debating Society, or Robert may have listened to him at the Nelson SDF. Certainly, Leonard's chapel was an obvious choice for their wedding.

Possibly Selina and Robert had an additional reason for preferring Colne to Brierfield. Like both their parents before them, the bride had already discovered she was pregnant and so perhaps had reason to press for an early wedding date, away from her home town. However, unlike their own parents' rather flurried weddings (Selina's parents had, in effect, eloped to Devonport, while Robert's mother had caused great upset by marrying a humble labourer and then producing a baby a few months later), the occasion seems to have gone off smoothly. Leonard officiated, Selina's evangelical brother Charles acted as one witness, one of Robert's cousins as the other, and notices reporting the marriage duly appeared the following week in the local papers.[1]

Once married, Selina determined that, from then on, she would avoid all the troubles that her own hard-pressed mother had suffered. She determined that they should no longer live in other people's homes as lodgers. Luckily they managed to find a house to rent on the Nelson side of Brierfield, only about a half-mile walk for Robert along the towpath to Lomeshaye. Understandably Selina herself seems not to have returned to Tunstills' winding room – though the precise date when she gave up mill work remains cloudy, and she may possibly have kept working, as so many women did, during the earlier months of her pregnancy.[2]

On 21 May 1897, Selina gave birth to a baby son. We shall never know whether it was an easy birth – though other accounts of working-class women's experience of childbirth at the turn of the century suggests how little help was available if problems arose. Doctors were a costly luxury, trained midwives a rarity. One contemporary wrote that her baby was born only 'after twenty-four hours of intense suffering which an ignorant attendant did little to alleviate . . . my baby was brought into the world with instruments and without an anaesthetic. This operation was sheer barbarism.' Whether Selina Cooper's experience was as bitter as this or not, it is certain that, armed with her St John Ambulance training and guildswoman knowledge, she took the greatest care of this first small baby. She would be mindful of her brother Richard's little daughter and the frequency of tragic infant deaths. Small coffins were not an uncommon sight at the turn of the century.[3]

Selina and Robert decided to call their baby John Ruskin – John after Selina's eldest brother and Robert's own father, and Ruskin in honour of the writer who had had such an immense influence on socialists of their generation. (Robert Cooper had even written an essay for a class he was attending titled 'A short essay on John Ruskin and the New Political Economy'.)

Spring turned to summer. John Ruskin grew bigger as each month passed and Selina began to be able to take an interest again in what was going on around her. A Brierfield branch of the SDF was formed, and Selina became a founder member, helping organise its open-air and indoor meetings. It was also the time of Queen Victoria's Diamond Jubilee; of local socialist lectures on 'the Jubilee of cant'; and of Tom Mann from the engineers' union and Secretary of the ILP, announcing to a crowded ILP meeting in Nelson that 'there was nothing to jubilate about'. Tom Mann was one of the Coopers' favourite orators, and it seems they went along to hear him speak on this occasion: he denounced Lancashire's half-time system, urged people to support a socialist candidate at the next parliamentary election, and to 'chuck out' the local councillors since the local authority was currently harassing SDF speakers over free speech. All this was meat and drink to Robert and Selina Cooper, and they bought copies of two of Mann's pamphlets: *What the ILP is Driving At* and *A Socialist's View of Religion and the Churches*. Such an inspired speaker as Tom Mann (the collection at this meeting raised £4.16.4½d for the 'Free Speech Fund', a phenomenal amount compared to most sums raised by the Nelson ILP branch) helped awaken the Coopers' interest in ILP socialism, so much more tolerant of trade unionism than the SDF.[4]

Summer faded into autumn. John Ruskin, perhaps because he may have been premature, perhaps for other reasons, seemed to remain a frail baby. Certainly his chances of growing up fit and strong were hardly enhanced by his environment. Brierfield had a damp and smoky atmosphere, with many of its grimy streets jutting right onto the railway or Tunstills' mill. Further down the valley towards Burnley, hazards to children's health were even greater: cellar dwellings, back-to-back slums and one-room tenements were common and one child in four died before the age of one. Indeed, Burnley's appalling infant mortality rates were then as high as in India, and higher than in Mexico and Latin America.[5]

Robert and Selina Cooper still lived with their family within easy reach. Particularly near were John and Annie Coombe and their children, living above the cobbler's shop on the corner of Colne Road. Their eldest son was now five years old and was occasionally entrusted to wheel out his baby cousin, down past the railway, over the canal, and out towards the Pendle countryside.

One such jaunt that autumn – according to a tale related to Robert and Selina's daughter years later – ended in tragic disaster. John Ruskin

> must have been in a go-cart. My mother said, 'Look after him,' and he took him right down that Clitheroe Road, where the station is and that bridge. And it came on a thunderstorm. He [the baby] got soaked . . .

> And he was only little, was my cousin, and he couldn't pull the
> pram cover down. And he'd got him right down Quaker Bridge.
> And thunderstorms! My mother was frantic and the police
> looking – and then the police fetched him back. Crying, he was.
> She'd told him to stop in the sunshine, but it was a typical thun-
> dery hot day, and the baby was in a pool of water . . .[6]

John Ruskin caught severe bronchitis. Only four months old,
he died from acute bronchitic convulsions. His mother witnessed
his final violent spasms, just as her brother Richard had helplessly
watched his own daughter's last hours three years before. Like so
many other Victorian children – including Selina's own elder
sister and namesake – John Ruskin had been unable to survive
infancy.

The following day the distraught mother made her way to
Nelson to notify the deputy registrar of the sudden death of her
baby son – though so commonplace were infant deaths that no
inquest was ordered. The tiny coffin must have lain in the
Coopers' front room while the funeral arrangements were made.
Then, three days after his death, on 27 September 1897, John
Ruskin was buried in a little chapel graveyard out towards Pendle
Hill.

The effect on Selina Cooper of this tragedy was incalculable.
The death came as a terrible shock, and even years afterwards it
remained something she preferred never to talk about. Like other
women of her generation, whose lives were so often marked by
pregnancy followed by miscarriage, still birth or infant death, she
kept her grief private. Her sorrow was borne inwardly, never
publicly acknowledged. Yet, as Selina's daughter accidentally
discovered long afterwards, it remained a deeply wounding
memory that her mother found impossible to shake off:

> I never saw her nursing any babies – after she'd lost my brother as
> a little baby. And I opened a book – a right old book . . . And it
> was full of pictures of babies she cut out of newspapers. Young
> babies. And Evelyn [a friend of mine] claims that probably my
> mother nursed this . . .
> But she never said anything about this to me . . . I knew I had a
> brother . . . She never dwelt on it . . . And it must have been a
> very sore topic . . .
> I never saw her cutting out [the pictures] . . . She must have

been gradually cutting them out all the time. Oh, there must have
been about twenty. And all babies, not young children.[7]

Since Selina Cooper seems to given up her job as a winder at
Tunstills before John Ruskin was born, she could hardly be
accused of having neglected her baby by going out to work in a
factory. Yet conventional wisdom maintained that it was this kind
of neglect, plus maternal ignorance, that led to high infant mortality rates in working-class communities: the 'feckless' mother,
especially if she went out to work, became a convenient scapegoat,
rather than poor health, inadequate sanitation and widespread
poverty.

Yet Selina Cooper never fell – as many socialists in the SDF
and ILP did – for the arguments which favoured banning married women's work: she could see that Lancashire mothers were
just as good as those in parts of the country where married women
seldom worked. Nor, of course, would she accuse mothers –
women exactly like herself, suffering through a tragedy – of
fecklessness. Rather, the practical effect of her son's death was
to strengthen her belief in the importance of women's self-
education: working women like herself must acquire the knowledge and self-confidence to fight for better conditions, to avoid
such tragedies.[8]

Selina apparently went back to her job in the mill after her son
died (though the available evidence remains unclear here) and
used the next few years to read, to think, to explore new ideas and
settle her own opinions. It seems this was the last period in her life
that the luxury of free time was available to her, and she exploited
it to the full. The energy now welling up inside her becomes
almost visible, for the late 1890s were Selina Cooper's seed-time.[9]

By the mid-1890s some of the Victorian conventions shrouding
middle-class women's lives were being challenged: access to
higher education and the professions was being fought for. In the
midst of this debate an energetic series of articles entitled 'The
Revolt of the Daughters' appeared, which captured this mood.
'The revolt of the daughters is not, if I understand it, a revolt
against mere surface conventionalities,' railed one angry young
woman, '. . . but it is a revolt against a bondage that enslaves her

whole life. In the past she has belonged to other people, now she demands to belong to herself . . .' A copy of these articles made its way up to the doctor's house in Burnley, and Mary Brown pronounced herself most impressed by them – especially one by Mrs Fawcett, the women's suffrage leader.[10] It is less likely they found their way to Brierfield and to the Coopers' house, published as they were in a learned journal. But a similar spirit of rebellion was also animating working-class women like Selina Cooper. The direction was different – it sprang from their industrial experience – and the emphases were different. But the effect in the end was similar.

Robert Cooper, being a more serious student than his wife, seems to have introduced Selina to the habit of attending education evening classes and of undertaking the written work that was required. The only one of Selina's essays which appears to have survived, and which was probably written about 1898, was entitled 'The Lancashire Factory Girl'. It throws a valuable shaft of light on the bubbling up of Selina's anger at the way women like her were treated so shabbily:

> I have often heard the 'sarcastic' remark applied to the factory worker oh she [is] only a Factory girl; thus giving the impression to the World . . . that we have no right to aspire to any other society but our own. I am sorry to say that we are not fully awaken to the facts that we contribute largely to the nations wealth, and therefore demand respect, and not insult.
>
> For in many a Lancashire home are to be found heroines whose names will never be handed down to posterity; yet it is consoling to know that we as a class contribute to the World . . .
>
> In conclusion I hope that I have not impress[ed] the idea that we are claiming a superior position in the industrial world. But I do demand in the name of a Lancashire factory girl to be place[d] in the same social scale as all who earn their living, wether it be by the labour of the hand or the brains . . . Selina Cooper[11]

This essay, eight pages long and obviously the result of a considerable struggle to place her rebellious thoughts on paper in the orthodox way, is a rare example of Selina's writing. Already she was far happier reading (and talking) than writing. Robert certainly seems to have introduced Selina to a range of books that she had not previously known, books that suggested that their married life was very different from their parents'. One such book (dog-eared and minus its cover, as if it had been frequently passed from hand to hand) was *The Law of Population* by Annie Besant, originally published in 1877. Besant, secularist, freethinker and matchgirls' champion, had had to stand trial in 1877 for publishing an inexpensive edition of a pamphlet about birth control. Although found guilty, she produced *The Law of Population*, another birth-control tract, in which the value of various 'preventative checks' (pessaries, sponges, the use of quinine and of a syringe) were assessed. At the back of the booklet were printed advertisements from two suppliers, W.J. Rendell and E. Lambert, each giving a list of prices and their address in London.

Annie Besant withdrew *The Law of Population* in 1890, but not before it had sold 175,000 copies. At what date Robert and Selina acquired their copy is unclear. Quite possibly Robert came across it in the Nelson SDF branch in the early 1890s: perhaps it was even brought up to Nelson by Herbert Burrows for the inaugural meeting in 1891. Probably Selina knew of such birth-control texts before her marriage, and certainly her concern to inform herself on such matters remained strong. Among the Coopers' other books were two self-help manuals, both by a Doctor Allinson. *Medical Essays*, published in 1897, was full of hints for healthier living and advertisements for 'Dr Allinson's Natural Food for Babies'. His *Book for Married Women*, published two years later, helpfully described the nature of menstruation, various signs of pregnancy, the causes of miscarriage and how best to organise childbirth. Although far less direct than Annie Besant's controversial tract, it was still outspoken for its time:

> Women have rights as well as men, and to force a woman to have more children than her constitution will bear, or is her desire to have, is an act of cruelty that no upright man would sanction. It is against the true dignity of a woman to become a mere child-bearing drudge. From a health standpoint, it is better to use preventative means . . .

Yet Allinson's brave statement was accompanied neither by descriptions of appliances nor by details of stockists: in the 1890s those who advocated birth control remained in fear of prosecution.[12] (Far more discreet still were the various textbooks on human physiology that the Coopers had begun to acquire. They offered exhaustive descriptions of the digestive and muscle systems, but remained firmly silent about reproduction.[13]) Overall, it is difficult to gauge exactly what access a couple like the Coopers had to birth control at this time. However, their knowledge of the writings of Besant and Allinson suggests that it was quite possibly because they *could* rely on contraceptive supplies that Selina did not find herself pregnant again. Like the middle-class 'daughters' revolt' against the suffocations of marriage, a mill worker like Selina determined not to repeat the tribulations of her mother and mother-in-law, who between them had given birth to no fewer than twenty-two children.

But such decisions about family size were not taken in isolation. Both the Burnley and Nelson Guilds were well established by the late 1890s and together boasted over 650 members. Members may well have discussed birth control among themselves; certainly in nearby Accrington, at least one Guildswoman tried publicly to raise the issue of fertility control. However ignorance still remained widespread. Among members of the SDF, ignorance was combined with a theoretical opposition to any suggestion that there was an individualist solution (family limitation rather than the socialists' collective state) to working-class poverty.[14]

Selina Cooper, already active in the Brierfield SDF branch which she had helped form, realised the small town really needed a Guild branch of its own, too. So in October 1898 Selina, along with one or two other like-minded women, persuaded (just as Mary Brown and Mrs Grocott had done ten years earlier) the Brierfield Co-operative Education Committee to start a local Guild branch by putting on a concert in the Wesleyan Methodist schoolroom one Saturday night.

Mrs Grocott, the shoemaker's wife, came up from Burnley to preside over the crowded gathering, and the entertainment was followed by an address on Guild work by the president of the thriving Darwen branch not far away. Certainly Selina Cooper had good reason to feel proud at the evening's success: the following week no fewer than twenty members of the new Brierfield branch attended the Women's Co-operative Guild's regional conference.

Selina, with her experience of recruiting women into the

Weavers' Association and of addressing local SDF meetings, was an obvious choice for branch president. And as a recently-married wife of a weaver, with years of experience of mill work herself, she was an ideal person to take the lead. 'I helped form the Brierfield Women's Co-operative Guild, of which I was made President,' she later explained. 'That position necessitated a certain amount of public speaking on my part and so helped bring me out as a public speaker . . . I also prepared two papers, one on "poets" and one on "Good Behaviour" '.[15]

It might seem surprising that Selina Cooper's talks to the Guild were on literary subjects when five years previously even the Brierfield Literary and Debating Society was discussing 'Darkest England' and 'Labour and the production of wealth'. Her choice perhaps highlights the distance between men's public sphere and women's traditionally private one: in the late 1890s the Guild still remained the only organisation offering working-class women a forum for discussion beyond the traditional female areas of church work and temperance. So Selina Cooper ensured that the Brierfield Guild proceeded cautiously, wary of frightening away any member by too radical a programme. Instead, a Nelson woman gave a talk on 'My visit to California', an Accrington Guildswoman spoke on 'Co-operative work', and the branch opened its winter session in 1899 with a meat tea and social in a local schoolroom to which 'all lady friends' over the age of sixteen were cordially invited. Selina's approach paid dividends: by summer 1900 the branch had grown to fifty members, and together they drove in a wagonette over the Pennines to take part in a Guild conference at Hebden Bridge.[16]

Selina Cooper was elected Brierfield Guild president twice running, in 1898 and again in 1899. Here again the Guild seemed unique: it offered working women the rare responsibility of presiding at meetings, speaking before large audiences, organising agendas, taking minutes, planning next session's programme. For Selina Cooper it provided invaluable experience; it prevented her from dwelling morbidly on her own personal tragedy and gave her a real sense of her speaking and organising skills. The Women's Co-operative Guild helped make her name well-known locally, and acted as the springboard for much that she went on to do.

Selina Cooper continued to use these fruitful years to read more widely than she had in the past. 'I have not been as big a reader as people imagine,' she later acknowledged. 'At one period I read a lot of rubbish, but with age came discretion,' and she went on to say how she liked H.G. Wells, Charlotte Brontë, George Eliot, Robert Burns and other writers. Perhaps with Robert's encouragement, she began to tackle some of the leading socialist writers, too. The Coopers had shilling paperback editions of both Tom Paine's *Rights of Man* (reprinted in 1893), and of August Bebel's *Woman in the Past, Present and Future*. Bebel's book, originally published in 1883 in German and shortly afterwards in English, stressed the economic basis of women's inequality, an inequality that could not be removed merely by tinkering with the system:

> By a complete solution I understand not only the equality of men and women before the law, but their economic freedom and material independence, and, so far as possible, equality in mental development. This complete solution of the Women's Question is as unobtainable as the solution of the Labour Question under the existing social and political institutions.[17]

As she turned over the pages of Bebel, Selina Cooper found her mind whirling round to catch up with these new ideas. She could see around her labour as a rising force: Brierfield SDF attracted acclaimed orators like councillor Philip Snowden of Cowling. Both Ben Smith and Abel Latham were now on Brierfield Urban District Council as 'Labour' men; in Burnley Dan Irving was, with the support of Eleanor Marx who came up to help him, elected to the School Board; and in Nelson an SDF member had even become one of the two 'burgess auditors', elected to root out municipal extravagance and embezzlement.[18] Yet women seemed to remain powerless, unable to demand economic equality with men, let alone cast a vote at parliamentary elections.

Selina began to wonder whether trade unionism and the socialist ideal of a collective state, both of which she held dear, would be sufficient to guarantee women economic equality. Luckily, as she tried to unravel these conundrums, she was helped by a number of talented young women who came up to the Brierfield area to speak, and who cast quite a spell over her. The women were all about her age, though all far better educated;

their magical mix of practical day-to-day socialism with an appeal for sexual equality left an indelible impression on Selina.

Margaret McMillan, the Bradford educationalist, was one. Another was Caroline Martyn, tall, ethereal and hard-working. She conveyed an intensely religious vision of socialism which made her a popular speaker in the Nelson area. She died young. In 1896 she went up to help Tom Mann who was standing as an ILP parliamentary candidate in Aberdeen. The election campaign involved chilly open-air meetings, many of them in local stonemasons' yards, with Caroline Martyn speaking perched on top of granite blocks intended for tombstones. The cold she had grew worse and soon proved fatal. Selina Cooper was among those who were deeply moved by such selflessness; and to commemorate her death, Nelson ILP (whose members had listened to her speak only a few months before) set aside 3s 3d from their limited funds for a memorial photograph of her.[19]

Enid Stacy was another martyr to the gruelling cause. But before her death in 1903 she acted as a vital bridge, linking socialist ideas to feminist ones. A recent university graduate, she devoted her short life to open-air speaking and travelling. 'Miss Stacy is a bird of passage,' lamented a local writer struggling to catch up with her for an interview in the short-lived *Socialist* newspaper, 'and flits from city to city with a rapidity which I vainly endeavoured to cope with.' Her favourite audiences included those in north-east Lancashire and early in 1897 (shortly after the Coopers' wedding when Selina was some months pregnant) Enid Stacy undertook a fortnight's speaking tour for the Lancashire and Cheshire Socialist Societies' Federation. The tour included at least two meetings in Nelson and here she attracted outsize crowds (up to three or four thousand) of the kind matched by only one or two leading orators – Philip Snowden with his 'Come to Jesus' semi-religious appeal, or Tom Mann and his anti-jubilee 'Socialist Crusade'. Yet Enid Stacy also succeeded in dovetailing socialist propaganda with a deeply-felt concern for ordinary women. She contributed a seminal essay on 'A Century of Women's Rights' to an anthology, *Forecasts of the Coming Century* published in 1897. Here she reviewed the considerable progress the women's movement had made, but argued that women still needed to win their full legal and political rights, including the right to vote at all local and parliamentary elections.[20] From this time onwards, Selina Cooper was beginning to find such arguments compelling.

By the turn of the century Nelson ILP had over seventy paid-up members, and this placed it in the same league as other ILP strongholds: Blackburn, Bradford, and West Ham in London. Selina Cooper was now one of these seventy socialists (Brierfield had as yet no ILP branch of its own). The ILP made increasing good sense to her: it was prepared to work with trade unions, was committed to labour representation, and had an unusually sympathetic approach to the needs of its women members.[21]

As the old century drew to a close, Selina Cooper was able to survey her married life over the last three years. After their wedding it had been largely shaped by pregnancy, childbirth and caring for her new baby. John Ruskin's sudden tragic death the following autumn had devastated all Selina's careful hopes. She became thrust in upon herself, brooding privately on her sorrow.

These were fallow years for Selina. She apparently returned to working in the mill but much of her energy, we can sense, was turned inwards. It was a time for reading and thinking. Largely thanks to Robert, she grew familiar with some of the socialist classics, with literature and with self-help medical handbooks. Robert also encouraged his wife to become active in local politics, speaking to the SDF and joining the ILP. Their shared excitement in what was happening helped bond their marriage. 'My mother and father,' their daughter explained, 'were both soaked in that advanced community in those days.'

Yet there were already hints that the original balance of the marriage – Robert, the more wordly-wise and scholarly, encouraging his less sophisticated wife to take up new challenges – might be beginning to shift. It was almost as if some of Robert's earlier energy and drive now began to flow to Selina. He remained shackled to his daily looms in the mill, while she seemed to be increasingly opening up to new and exciting possibilities.

Selina's nephew, one of the few people able to recall the Coopers during the first years of their marriage, certainly confirmed this impression. The two of them looked different and indeed were different. 'He were a little inoffensive fellow . . .,' he explained candidly. 'Different' between chalk and cheese. Aunt Selina – a big bustling woman, she was. She was a big bustling woman once over, aye'.[22]

This shift of balance in the Coopers' relationship was to become more pronounced in the next year or two. It seemed almost as though Selina's star waxed as Robert's waned.

CHAPTER SIX

THE NEW LIFE:
1899-1900

The Coopers longed to leave Brierfield. Selina remained haunted by sad memories she would have preferred to forget. Only four months after John Ruskin had died, there was a local outbreak of typhoid because milk cans from a nearby Pendle farm had been washed out with polluted water. She felt the chance of ever bringing up a healthy baby in the small town remained depressingly remote. For Robert too there seemed little to look forward to: he was unlikely to be able to give up his factory job and return to his beloved Dales.

The Coopers were not alone in their despair. There was an important strand in socialist thinking which looked back to earlier centuries for the rural ideal which would provide the vision of the future. A radical transformation of the smoky cities and dank factories of the industrial north was a first step towards this dream. This socialism, which encouraged working people to escape from the towns out into the clean countryside, began to take practical shape during the 1890s. Cycling clubs sprang up; the best known of these were associated with the popular socialist newspaper, the *Clarion* founded in 1891. It was regular reading for the Coopers and thousands of other working people, and soon spawned Clarion Cycling Clubs and Clarion Vans to help bring socialist propaganda to remote country villages, along with Clarion Club Houses where working people were offered holidays at prices they could afford.

The Nelson area did not acquire its own Clarion house till the 1900s and so, during the 1890s, it was other less celebrated organisations which locally pioneered the return to the simple country life. Particularly important here was a now-forgotten group called the National Home Reading Union, formed in 1889. The union's appeal was to the kind of person who read the *Clarion*, but unlike the newspaper it offered anyone, however brief their schooling, the opportunity for adult education, regarding itself as 'the People's University'.

The union flourished particularly strongly in Lancashire. Informal 'home reading circles' grew up in Nelson, Burnley and elsewhere. The Coopers' friend, the Reverend Leonard, strongly championed it. 'Individual members can join and read the course indicated by the Union,' Leonard wrote enthusiastically in the *Colne and Nelson Times*, 'but by far the better way is to gather a circle of either the members of one's own household, neighbours, or those connected with any society or church to which one may happen to belong.' It is likely that Robert and Selina Cooper joined one of the study circles in Nelson for they were certainly precisely the kind of people, forced to leave school early yet with a burning curiosity to read and learn, that Leonard was appealing to.[1]

Leonard, seeing local mill workers crowd onto trains heading for Blackpool or Morecambe each Wakes Week, was keen to offer working people inexpensive holidays in the country. In 1891 he took over thirty members of his Colne church's Young Men's Guild on a short holiday to the Lake District. Many had never slept away from home before, but Leonard reassured them that it could be done – and for twenty-one shillings. 'We were all very enthusiastic over the preparations,' one young man wrote. 'One member of the party, a weaver, sought out his best loom and called it his holiday loom. He took great care that it was kept running whether the others ran or not so that his funds should be quite safe.'[2]

The idea spread and such holidays became regular events. When Leonard came up to talk to the Nelson branch of the National Home Reading Union the group decided to form a Nelson Working Men's Holiday Association: all members would pay 2s 6d on joining and then a shilling a week until the holiday started. Such experiments became so successful that Leonard decided to organise things on a more permanent footing and to open them to women as well. So, in 1893, the Co-operative Holiday Association was formed under the auspices of the

National Home Reading Union. This mix of high-minded idealism and Leonard's inspiring energy proved popular: in the first year three hundred people went on holiday this way and in 1894 no fewer than eight hundred. For a modest 31s 6d Leonard offered them,

> a week of glorious tramps over rock and heather, coach-rides, merry benches by the mountain streams, field chats about the 'ologies', and the art and literature of the district, with an 'off' day or two for rest and do-as-you-please purposes . . . And lest there be any misgivings on the part of the ladies joining our parties, they may be assured that the comfort of their sex is especially looked after by our hostesses.[3]

The Co-operative Holiday Association began to develop further afield, but the Lake District remained the most popular resort, with centres at both Keswick in Cumberland and Ambleside in Westmorland. It is difficult to document the Coopers' links with the Association prior to 1899; yet it must surely have been through such a holiday organisation that Selina was able to talk on 'My visit to Westmorland' to the Nelson SDF Mutual Improvement Class in 1896. Without such support it is unlikely that a winder from Tunstills could have ventured so far from home. And in her lecture she would have conveyed to her audience, not just pretty lantern slides, but Leonard's idealistic enthusiasm for the countryside, plus some of the 'ologies' she had learnt from the National Home Reading Union lecturers there.

The Co-operative Holiday Association had by then grown so rapidly that, in 1897, it was formed into a legally recognised company. Leonard became General Secretary, resigning from his church at Colne (Selina and Robert must have been among the last couples whose marriage he conducted). Isolated country houses were bought for conversion into guest houses, an ambitious gamble which paid off. 'Of course the money came. It always did,' Leonard wrote confidently. 'Folk tumbled over each other to lend us cash, for we all had boundless faith in each other and in the work.'

Staff were now needed to help run the centres who would share the Co-operative Holiday Association ideals. Leonard began to look around him for suitable people to manage a new centre that was to be opened in the Dales in 1899. Luckily he had kept in touch with the Coopers since the wedding; he must have sympathised with them over their own personal tragedy, and shared their current misgivings about life in Brierfield. It was therefore Robert and Selina Cooper he invited to come and work with him at this new Co-operative Holiday Association centre, at Keld in the wilds of Swaledale, the valley that the Cooper family had come from. Keld, as Robert remembered well, was an isolated hamlet of a dozen houses; the only way of reaching it was by walking from Hawes eight miles away, over Buttertubs Pass, on a rough road rising to over 1,600 feet. The Keld holiday centre, surrounded by giant grey hills and wide distant moors, would be spartan indeed.[4]

Leonard's offer of the job managing the Keld centre was timely. Selina had just discovered she was pregnant again, and had good reason to prefer to spend the next few months out in the fresh air of the Dales' countryside. Robert too welcomed the prospect of a change from the factory. Leonard of course benefited substantially from his side of the bargain:Selina possessed all the needed domestic skills while Robert could boast his childhood knowledge of Swaledale. So, with little to-do, the Coopers threw convention to the winds and handed in their notice at the mill. About June 1899 they packed up their belongings and set off from Brierfield on their Pennine journey northwards.

When they arrived at Keld, they realised that they would have their hands full to prepare for the first batch of guests due to arrive at the end of July. The tiny hamlet, miles from the shops, might be picturesque but was poorly equipped to offer hospitality to so many people. Everything, Selina and Robert recognised, would have to be done the hard way. Keld's tiny Literary Institute, built in 1861, was magically transformed into the dining-room. Below it was a makeshift kitchen where Selina and Mrs Holt, who came to do the cooking, toiled over giant roasts and baked countless loaves. Years later Selina and Robert used to regale their daughter with tales of how they coped in such spartan conditions. 'Seventy people to cater for and nothing to buy from the shops,' Mary Cooper explained. 'All the bread to be baked . . . They baked every day . . . only two of them to do it. Some girls came in from the village and cleaned and that sort of thing.'[5]

The Coopers found they were indeed dependent upon the

goodwill of the Keld people if the holiday centre was to succeed. Selina had to haggle with local housewives when she needed beds for extra visitors, and with their husbands when she wanted bacon and ham, lamb or eggs. The Keld schoolroom was shared with villagers who would join in the singing in the evenings, and guests were somehow put up in local cottages and in the disused post office, rented for a few shillings a week. 'My father had a lot of cousins out in the village,' Mary Cooper remembered, and visitors 'were parked out to sleep' in these homes. Yet even with all this local co-operation, Selina Cooper still had to face heavy routine chores each day:

> They'd four toilets – buckets, like lime toilets. And they had to be cleaned out every day, with all these people. And my mother did it. Well, they used to come up from Richmond to collect it . . . And they took those away and then – and my mother used to clean out, and put some clean ones in these four toilets. Because my father had a ticklish stomach, and she used to do it. And of course Mrs Holt was bothering with the food, that sort of thing. My mother did it . . .

Keld was hard physical labour, though Selina was well used to that. What made the summer different from being a washer-woman or a mill worker was that both she and Robert shared the work and took a full part in what was going on:

> It was a sort of joint job, because my father knew the Dales. He was the courier. And he also did a lot of the work . . . all the teatowels were taken to the River Swale, and my father used to dam the river and the force of the fall . . . he used to put some soap powder into the river and he washed the towels . . .
>
> You see, they could sort of fill the bill, and this friend of my mother's [Mrs Holt], had been cook for the Co-op, and my mother was an all-round cook . . .
>
> They [the guests] liked the baking, the northern baking – pastry – my mother was a lovely pastry-maker. And they used to get a right big breakfast, and then at dinner time there was always a lot of lamb – Dales lamb . . . And they'd go – my father took them out – several pictures of him – he took them out walking, and showing them the Dales, walking about. And then they'd come back to a late dinner, which my mother and Mrs Holt would have made for seventy people.[6]

Selina Cooper might spend much of her time that summer down in the kitchen working alongside Mrs Holt, but Keld still offered her something of a taste of true equality with the guests. 'Our "domestic helpers" are sensible, and in many cases, cultured women who,' Leonard urged, 'undertake to do the ordinary drudgery of the houses on the understanding that they have fixed hours of leisure and service, a fair wage, and – most important of all – are enabled to share in all the pleasures and advantages of the guesthouse while they are off duty.'[7]

At last, here at Keld, at the ripe age of thirty-four, Selina could feel the blackness of her earlier years receding. Exciting possibilities for her own future seemed now within reach. For the first time in her life she was not at the beck and call of either her family or the mill managers. As the thick shroud of past silence began to lift, a glimpse of the grown woman Selina had become is at last possible.

Her Keld summer was the very first episode that Selina Cooper was happy to reminisce to her daughter about afterwards. For the period from 1899 onwards, oral testimony suddenly blossoms forth. Selina's life also begins to become visually documented too. About half a dozen photographs taken at Keld during the summer have survived among the Cooper papers; these reveal – at long last – Selina as a tall, strong-featured woman, her dark brown hair drawn away from her face in a knot at the back of her head. She leans against the doorpost in a spotless white apron looking quite as if Swaledale had become her natural home, Robert and the other helpers posed either side of her. The contrast with the self-consciously demure young woman captured by the studio photographer half a dozen years earlier is dramatic.

As revealing as this new surge of oral and photographic evidence is the autograph book that Robert and Selina now kept. They began the book in May 1899, just the point at which they decided to take up Leonard's offer. The survival of this book underlines how much the Keld summer symbolised for them, for it seems inconceivable that either of them would have had the self-confidence to embark upon such a lasting document earlier on.

The first page is signed by Robert and Selina together (though it looks as if Robert, whose copperplate handwriting was neater than his wife's, signed for both of them); and below follow the signatures of various friends and relations living around Brierfield. Then, from 21 July onwards, once the Coopers had arrived in Swaledale and the first batch of guests arrived, the entries seem to be written by holiday guests newly arrived from London, Liverpool, Burnley, Keighley and elsewhere. At Selina's request each person added their 'favourite "Golden Maxim" ', and these remain eloquent testimony to the high-minded, almost religious strand of socialism that the Holiday Association fostered. The 'golden maxims' are a far cry from the secular Marxism of the Social Democratic Federation: the emphasis lay on how, in the eyes of God, all people are created equal and the world is indeed a thing of beauty. Keld visitors borrowed from Victorian poets – Wordsworth, Longfellow, Tennyson – verses that captured their simple and optimistic faith. Ruskin's prose was naturally a favourite:

> He who loves not God nor his brother, cannot love the grass
> beneath his feet, nor the creatures which live not for his uses,
> filling those spaces in the universe which he needs not; while none
> can love God, nor his human brother, without loving all things
> which his Father loves.[8]

It is also clear from the autographs – about 140 in all – that many of those drawn to the wilds of Swaledale that summer were educated people with an intellectual commitment to the Co-operative Holiday ideal. One such was a woman called Mary Champness who was, Selina Cooper explained some years later,

> Mr Leonard's 'right-hand man'. She was a grand woman . . . On
> sex matters she was as pure as an angel. She was a most
> unconventional woman, and her ways gave many a shock to the
> natives. She was fond of open-air bathing, and of a morning,
> robed in a swimming costume and raincoat would, to the conster-
> nation of the villagers, walk down to the river for her dip . . . This
> remarkable woman and I became the best of pals.

Mary Champness signed the autograph book with a suitably uplifting verse ('It is good to be last not first . . .') by Christina Rossetti. Another intellectual who befriended Selina Cooper at Keld was Dr T. Lewis Paton, high master of Manchester Grammar School, progressive educationalist and another keen champion of the National Home Reading Union. 'When he learned that I had worked in the mill,' Selina Cooper recalled, 'he sought my company to chat with me and ask questions about factory work and life.' Paton too signed the book with an exhortatory maxim – 'Blessed is the man who has learned to help himself . . .'[9]

It was a blow to Leonard that the middle-class visitors from the south so outnumbered northern factory workers. Of course factory owners did not pay their employees if they took a week's holiday yet; however, the more expensive attractions at Blackpool and Morecambe still lured people away from Swaledale. Some northern people did come, of course, (and there are signatories from Bolton, Bradford, Colne and elsewhere) but never in the numbers Leonard had dreamed of. Indeed, the Co-operative Holiday Association domestic committee, casting a stern eye on conditions at Keld, decreed it was too spartan for a proper guesthouse. The Swaledale experiment was sadly closed down after three summers. 'Many of us have since wandered disconsolately over the old haunts,' Leonard lamented, but 'the way was never opened for a return there of the jolly old parties.'

Keld had set itself such high ideals that it proved impracticable to meet them. Yet for the Coopers it provided one glorious summer. Selina, finding herself surrounded by so many serious and idealistic visitors, had to sharpen her socialist arguments in support of the collective state or else she would have been worsted in discussion. 'I came into contact with many intellectual people . . .,' she recalled. 'Keld was a wonderful experience for me and also for many of the southern middle-class people. I was up against them every time on account of my Labour principles.'[10]

The Coopers left Keld in the early autumn of 1899 after the first holiday season was over with Selina about four months pregnant. Swaledale, miles from any midwife, was hardly an ideal place for her to remain in the depths of winter. So the two of them travelled down to Brierfield again, invigorated by their long summer break.

Rather than going back to their old lodgings again, with all its unhappy associations, they managed to find another house not far from John Coombe's cobbler's shop. Selina's pregnancy continued through the winter and, on 8 March 1900, she gave birth to a baby daughter. Sadly, there is again no record of whether it was an easy or difficult birth, or how Selina coped with a second tiny baby to look after. All that is certain is that Selina never returned to the mill after this; and that, relying on Robert's wage as a weaver – still under twenty-five shillings a week – she must have been hard-pressed to feed and clothe two adults and one child.

In these straitened circumstances Mary Cooper spent the first ten or eleven months of her life. Then, about New Year 1901, her parents decided to move up the valley to Nelson, first into a house near Robert's parents at Lomeshaye, and then, a few months later, renting another house immediately behind it. After their gypsy-like existence over the past few years the three Coopers were to stay put in 59 St Mary's Street for the rest of their lives, and Mary herself was to live there for eighty years.[12]

PART TWO:
VOTES FOR WOMEN

CHAPTER SEVEN

THE POWER OF THE BALLOT BOX:
1894-1901

One of the many photographs preserved among the Cooper papers is a circular portrait of a Victorian lady with the bold signature of Helen E. Phillip in one corner. Usually such photographs can be readily identified as a friend or relation of Selina Cooper. Helen Phillip poses more of a problem: no clues among the family documents hint at who she was. Yet the distinctive signature suggests that Helen Phillip presented the portrait to Selina as a sign of their friendship.

However, clues to Helen Phillip's identity do lie elsewhere. It seems that Mrs Phillip was a member of the Manchester National Society for Women's Suffrage, which co-ordinated suffrage activity in the Lancashire area. The Society's annual report for 1894 records that a Mrs Phillip addressed a suffrage meeting in Accrington Town Hall; and the *Burnley Co-operative Record* for late 1897 notes that a Mrs Phillip from Manchester gave a talk to the local Women's Co-operative Guild on Women's Franchise. Selina Cooper was certainly actively involved in the Guild by then (she helped form the Brierfield branch shortly after), and although we do not know if she attended this meeting in Burnley, it is quite possible that she met Helen Phillip on one such occasion, and that the friendship between the two women grew as Selina Cooper became increasingly interested in votes for women.[1]

Helen Phillip had a difficult job trying to convince her audiences in Accrington and Burnley of the urgency of her cause. Although many of her listeners would be prepared to support her views, few saw women's suffrage as a priority for House of Commons legislation. The existing suffrage societies had made only sporadic attempts to interest working women; and even their

91

traditional basis of support – among progressive middle-class Liberals – had become sapped of much of its earlier fervour. By the 1890s suffrage was at a low ebb.

Yet the campaign had begun with great flourish in the 1860s. John Stuart Mill's amendment to the 1867 Reform Bill proposed that the vote should be extended, not just to men who met the new property qualifications, but to suitably qualified women as well. Mill spoke eloquently but was soundly defeated. Despite this, supporters organised a series of regional suffrage societies, including the one based in Manchester.

The Manchester Society was energetic: it even dispatched its secretary up to Colne in 1878 for a meeting in the Cloth Hall there, to press for the enfranchising of women householders. Another active Manchester member was the young Liberal barrister, Richard Pankhurst; he tried to defend the traditional claims of local women ratepayers to vote in parliamentary elections but – despite his erudite citing of judicial history – was brusquely dismissed. Instead, suffragists had to rely on conventional lobbying of sympathetic MPs, persuading them to introduce private member's bills.

Further disappointments lay in store in the 1880s. Suffragists became bitterly divided over whether they ought to include married women's rights in their demands: older suffragists thought this would be diversionary, while some 'progressive' women split away to fight the marriage conventions separately. A major blow was the 1884 Reform Bill, which extended the parliamentary franchise to a total two-thirds of adult men. The Act left so few working-class men disenfranchised that it numbed any effective pressure for further widening the suffrage for men during the next quarter of a century. The 1884 Act, by ignoring women completely, isolated women suffragists still further, and all but a handful of dedicated campaigners ceased to agitate about the issue.[2]

Women's suffrage, it seemed, could be easily caricatured by its political opponents' citing specious objections or lampooning its supporters. This clearly was what happened in Burnley at the 1885 general election. The previous year the Trades Union Congress had decided to support giving women the vote on the same basis as men. So, in the run-up to the election, a deputation from the newly-formed Burnley Trades Council visited the two candidates to find out their views. The sitting Liberal MP confidently deflected the deputation's impetus by dredging up a few salacious red herrings. What would happen, he demanded to know, if a man split up his property and got votes for his wife and daughters on the basis of pocket-handkerchief properties (the so-called 'faggot votes')? And, worse still, he speculated, 'if women lodgers had votes you would have sixty or seventy thousand women in London . . . of a class which I need not particularly describe, who in this case would become voters'. No mention was made of how women's pitiful wages might force them into prostitution. His lurid speculations allowed him to support merely a franchise limited to women householders; and David Holmes, already influential in Burnley, went along with this conservative view.[3]

By the early 1890s, innumerable private member's bills designed to enfranchise those few women who satisfied the existing property qualifications in their own right, had disappeared without trace. Women who wanted to play a part in public affairs were instead encouraged to channel their energies into local government. Particularly after legislation passed in 1894, it became easier for women to become parish councillors and members of the School Boards or Boards of Guardians. Helping run local affairs – whether overseeing parish affairs, bolstering reading standards in the local board school, or caring for pauper inmates of the workhouse – all this was seen to be Victorian women's rightful sphere. But to want to take part in the hurly-burly of parliamentary politics – defending Britain's distant empire, raising taxes to pay for wars they could not take part in, the niceties of diplomatic intrigue – was damned as unwomanly and unseemly.

Parliamentary votes for women, then, had precious few supporters in the early 1890s. Certainly none of the organisations that Selina Cooper* was involved in – Holmes' Burnley Weavers, Hyndman's Social Democratic Federation, the Independent Labour Party, or the Women's Co-operative Guild – gave active support to the women's suffrage campaigns. They were either

---

* Selina Cooper's married name is used throughout this chapter, even though some of the events occurred before her wedding.

nominally supportive (but equivocal or apathetic) or else down-right antagonistic. As a result, Selina Cooper and those like her did not take the demand for the vote at all seriously until the turn of the century. To them it was still more important to win the winders' uniform price list, to get 'labour' men onto the local council, and to form new Guild branches where none existed.

David Holmes, alarmed by the prospect of 'faggot voting' and vote-toting prostitutes, was quite content to keep the female half of his Burnley Weavers' members without a political voice (for only a paltry handful of his women members would have qualified on the basis of being householders, and these mainly widows). Certainly Holmes would not have wanted to bestow the parliamentary vote on Selina Cooper when she became a lodger in 1891. Indeed, so low had women's suffrage sunk in the eyes of the Burnley Weavers that in 1892 the union committee decided no longer to ask prospective parliamentary candidates whether they supported adult suffrage (including, of course, votes for adult women) but merely whether they supported 'manhood suffrage' – the enfranchisement of all adult men but only men, a position loathed and feared by suffragists like Richard Pankhurst and Helen Phillip. It was not till much later, when Holmes' long and illustrious career was drawing to a close (he died in 1906), that the Burnley Weavers eventually began to look more sympathetically on its thousands of disenfranchised women members.[4]

Almost as unhelpful, though for more complex reasons, was the Social Democratic Federation (SDF). In the 1890s SDF members were caught up (for instance in the debate about birth control) in a series of wide-ranging discussions on 'the women question'. These centred on the nature of women's position under capitalism, and thus women's economic dependence on their husbands within marriage. How would socialism do away with a wife's dependent status? Some writers and speakers advocated doing away with marriage and instead practising 'free love'. *Justice* ridiculed the rigid Victorian marriage laws, but sternly cautioned that 'socialists cannot effectively enter our protest against capitalism by individual anarchist action or personal revolt'. The solution had to be sought within the conventional framework and on a more collective basis. In this way, schemes for the 'free maintenance of children' and 'the endowment of motherhood' were widely discussed whereby traditional dependants within the family would be given financial 'support by the state (an early version of what later became known as 'family allowances').[5]

At least one of the SDF leaders took a decidedly misogynist stance; but when he tried to argue that marriage laws placed a weighty millstone round men's necks and operated entirely in women's favour, he was sharply taken to task by local SDF members. 'Man collectively treats woman as the capitalist treats both,' wrote someone signing herself 'L.B.' in *Justice*,

> by withholding the means of subsistence as far as possible and so forcing the weaker party to accept what terms are offered. As a rule he is as much opposed to the emancipation of women from his domination as the capitalist is to the emancipation of labour from the domination of capital.[6]

The debate continued. Some argued that women were naturally reactionary creatures, resentful of their husbands' attending Sunday SDF meetings since their late return home meant that roast dinners were inevitably ruined. Other readers of *Justice* objected to such stereotyping, and one even dared to suggest that the conventional division of labour, whereby women automatically cooked the Sunday roast, *was* open to change:

> I see no reason why men should not fit themselves better than they do for home duties, to the relief of their wives, so that they may have reasonable opportunities for taking part in public affairs and learning to better understand how men's material privilege and social domination have been guaranteed them for so long.[7]

Birth control, 'free love', 'the endowment of motherhood', the sexual division of labour – all these were hotly debated in the pages of *Justice* at exactly the time that Selina Cooper was becoming active in the SDF. Often the arguments seemed to be conducted between the more rigid anti-women SDF leaders and grassroots members who demanded a more imaginative approach to socialism.

Over the question of women's suffrage the SDF leadership – men like Henry Hyndman and the editor of *Justice*, Harry Quelch – put up a persuasive case against giving any priority to women's votes. They argued that the franchise was a class issue. Until the electoral register was reformed and the right to vote was dissociated from the ownership of property, the enfranchisement of women would merely strengthen the influence of reactionary propertied women, the enemies of socialism. And since adult suffrage was explicitly inscribed into the SDF programme, there was no need at all for any special pleading for votes for women. In the millennial excitement that accompanied, say, Hyndman's candidacy at Burnley in 1895, it did indeed seem a plausible argument. Those arguments for adult suffrage were so generally accepted within the SDF that when a private member's bill to enfranchise women on the same property basis as men voters passed its second reading in 1897, it was quickly damned by *Justice* as ridiculous, a parody of proper women's suffrage, designed merely to give the vote to 'eccentric spinsters' and the like. Certainly one of the reasons why Selina Cooper remained cool for so long towards women's suffrage, convinced it would merely give even more influence to 'fine ladies', was her involvement in the SDF.[8]

The local Women's Co-operative Guild was likewise reluctant to lend its influential support to votes for women. The pages of the *Burnley Co-operative Record* were full of homilies encouraging newly-married brides to keep their homes neat and pleasing to deter their husbands from sloping off to the pub ('Heaw Jimmy Thrifty and Sarah Savewell geet Sattl't') and sentimental tales of little Maggie and her drunken father, whose family was saved only by the useful habit of shopping at the co-op store. Guildswomen were to exert a moral, not a political influence, and suffragists were derided for pathetically trying to ape men:

> We have no sympathy . . . with the goggle-eyed human ostrich, the exponent of women's rights who dresses as men and whose bearing so nearly resembles that of a man. Who speaks with a sneer and a high-flown manner that sends a man home with a sneaking gladness in his heart that he was her auditor and not her husband.[9]

Yet the local Women's Co-operative Guild, while stressing women's special moral influence in the home, also genuinely encouraged working-class wives to develop wider interests. Particularly after 1894, Guildswomen were consistently urged to take up these new opportunities. Selina Cooper's friend, Mary Brown, played a vital role here locally. She told the Burnley Guild how important it was for mothers to teach their daughters how to make their homes into pleasant places from which men go out into the world strengthened; but, Mary Brown added significantly, while rocking the cradle, stooping over the washtub, baking the family bread or darning the stockings, 'the wise woman will with tact and ingenuity acquaint herself with what lies outside the home'.[10]

Elections for Poor Law Guardians occurred every three years and were due again in 1894. Nationally the Guild urged members to put themselves forward: forty-five Guildswomen did stand and no fewer than twenty-two were successful, including one or two working-class women. The Burnley Board (which covered not only the town itself, but also the valley up to Nelson and Colne, plus outlying Pendle hamlets with quaint rural names) now included two Guildswomen Guardians, both doctors' wives: Mary Brown in Burnley and Mary Robb in Nelson. The men on the Board tried to complain that if Mrs Brown were elected they would have to 'mind their language'. 'A good thing too, for the poor women and girls who come before you,' Mary Brown retorted briskly. Horrified by workhouse conditions (she came across a girl of fourteen, wasting away with consumption, who had been set to work sewing shrouds), she was soon demanding separate toothbrushes for each workhouse child and arranging for elderly pauper couples at least to share a room together.[11]

At the next Guardians' election two local women were again elected. Mary Brown was on her way to see Olive Schreiner in South Africa; but Mary Robb stood again with firm pledges of support from the Nelson Guild. The second woman was Burnley's aristocrat, Lady Alice O'Hagan. She was a delightful eccentric, who sported lorgnette and cigarettes, and whose progressive and unconventional views (she was a Catholic turned Unitarian) were to bring Selina Cooper and her together. Lady O'Hagan, widow of a Lord Chancellor of Ireland, lived in impoverished splendour in Townley Hall on the outskirts of Burnley, but went out of her way, like Mary Brown, to urge Guildswomen to develop wider interests. 'We have not got Parliamentary votes yet, it is true, though the time is coming,' she wrote in the *Burnley Co-operative Record* in 1897, 'but we can take a part in the work of many public bodies.' She was as good as her word, becoming a Guardian and later a member of the Burnley

School Board. (An old-fashioned member from one of the out-lying hamlets objected to her presence, but the Clerk of the Board laconically pointed out that he was not aware that women *per se* were disqualified from sitting on the Board.[12])

Selina Cooper watched these pioneering elections of women into local government. She could hardly fail to notice that Mary Brown, Mary Robb and Lady O'Hagan were no average Guildswomen; and that, moving as they did within the orbit of Sir Ughtred Kay-Shuttleworth's progressive Liberalism, none of them shared her socialist views. Yet they courageously paved the way for ordinary Guildswomen like Selina to stand for local election as the new century dawned. This was surely the Guild's greatest achievement in its early years: first it introduced working women to running their own organisation, then to participating in local government; and from that firm base it became just a short step for Selina Cooper and other like-minded Guildswomen to join the 'goggle-eyed human ostriches' previously derided, and put their considerable weight behind women's suffrage.[13]

The Guild gradually took up the cause for votes for women, but could hardly be said to have led the suffrage renaissance in the 1890s. Much of the credit for that lies with middle-class women Liberals and – of more direct interest to Selina Cooper – with Keir Hardie's Independent Labour Party.

There were always sufficient influential men and women in the ILP both locally and nationally to commit it to women's suffrage and the ILP was arguably the fairest of the new socialist groups in its attitude to women. Like the Guild, it led the way for women to become involved in local government: Isabella Ford, the Leeds Quaker, was on Adel Parish Council; Margaret McMillan, of course, on Bradford School Board; and Mrs Pankhurst, wife of the great barrister and suffragist, on one of the Manchester Boards of Guardians.

Yet staunch and faithful suffragists like Keir Hardie, Dr Pankhurst and Isabella Ford, always had to convince those in the ILP who argued, as did their counterparts in the SDF, that women's problems would be automatically solved once socialism was achieved. The belief still prevailed that until the electoral register was reformed and the right to vote dissociated from property, then women's suffrage was not a socialist demand. Influential ILP men like Philip Snowden felt that including adult suffrage in the ILP programme was a sufficient gesture.[14]

This ambivalence towards women was apparent in the ILP from the beginning. At the first ILP conference in 1893, a motion to abolish married women's work 'as one of the greatest curses in the country' was only just defeated – amidst great jocularity among delegates who wondered if it included widows. The following year young Enid Stacy made an impassioned plea on behalf of women ('so much shut up in the house' with often 'so little sympathy between husbands and wives') that they be encouraged to play an active part in the ILP. Her impact was somewhat muted by the late arrival of the editor of the *Clarion*, an ex-soldier called Robert Blatchford who sported a cavalier attitude to women's suffrage. He was ushered on to the platform and 'spoke playfully' to the delegates of the movement 'being captured by the ladies'.[15]

Such a danger was extremely remote. From 1895 onwards, the issue of women and their lack of political voice virtually disappeared from ILP conference debates. It did not re-emerge until the 1902 conference when Mrs Pankhurst, recently widowed, finally grew impatient with the shilly-shallying and moved a women's suffrage resolution. She demanded that 'immediate steps' be taken to grant 'the suffrage to women on the same terms on which it is, or may be, granted to men'. Mrs Pankhurst's historic resolution was adopted without a murmur of dissent. Minutes later, however, another resolution was passed demanding that the ILP should draft a bill to enfranchise all adults, both men and women, and that Keir Hardie should introduce it into the Commons as soon as he could. On the face of it, these two resolutions were perfectly compatible: yet it was becoming clear that a political organisation like the ILP would have to decide which demand was the more urgent – whether to give priority to women's suffrage *or* to adult suffrage. Any proposed bill would have to ask Parliament to support one or the other, either the moderate demand to give women satisfying the property qualifications the vote, or the uncompromising demand of abolishing both the sex qualification and the property qualification in one dramatic sweep. Yet, as late as 1902, the ILP did not recognise this and blithely voted to support both demands.[16] In doing this, it was ignoring a new groundswell of women's suffrage agitation that had been growing over the last eight or nine years.

The women's suffrage campaign, which had reached the doldrums by 1890, began over the next few years to show signs of revival. A women's suffrage bill was lost in the Commons again – but this time by only twenty-three votes. Loyal suffragists like Mrs Fawcett and Isabella Ford determined to build on this strength with a mass suffrage petition, and in 1893 the 'Special Appeal' was launched to be signed by 'Women of all Parties and All Classes'. This met with considerable success (even the Women's Co-operative Guild recommended the Special Appeal to its members) and over a quarter of a million signatures were collected. The north-west became particularly active: the Manchester Suffrage Society acquired an energetic new secretary, Esther Roper, a young university graduate. She threw herself into the job of publicising the Special Appeal and organising meetings with Mrs Fawcett, Dr and Mrs Pankhurst and Enid Stacy on the platform.

Esther Roper had the knack of promoting the campaign among both Liberals and socialists simultaneously. In this way, when she appointed two working women to take the Special Appeal out to the cotton towns, she chose a member of the Lancashire and Cheshire Women's Liberal Union who could happily speak alongside Helen Phillip, and Annie Heaton, a cotton worker from Burnley who already had experience of trade union organising. During 1894 Annie Heaton busied herself collecting signatures for the Appeal among women in Burnley and Nelson, Accrington and Bolton.[17]

It is unlikely that Selina Cooper was willing to oblige Annie Heaton and add her signature to the list. The arguments for women's suffrage still meant little to her. However persistently Annie Heaton knocked on doors and lobbied outside the mill gates, she would find a cool response from women like Selina.

Only gradually did this begin to change. By the end of 1897 another private member's bill had passed its second reading with a reasonable majority. The suffrage compaign grew in strength. A National Union of Women's Suffrage Societies had been formed, led by Mrs Fawcett, to co-ordinate this new activity. The Women's Co-operative Guild became more enthusiastic. And in Manchester Esther Roper was joined by Eva Gore-Booth, an aristocratic Irish poet; the two of them became life-long companions, Eva Gore-Booth's ethereal presence enhancing the northern suffrage campaign.

By late 1897, then, Selina Cooper may well have been in the right mood to drink in Helen Phillip's suffrage message when she came up to address the Burnley Women's Co-operative Guild. The memory of John Ruskin's death still loomed very large, and Selina was ready to respond to anything that promised to increase women's say in improving poor housing conditions and guaranteeing children a healthy start in life. She was growing increasingly irritated with being told that women did not need the vote because their interests were already represented in Parliament by men of their own class – their fathers, husbands or trade union leaders. She also grew exasperated with hearing at SDF or weavers' union meetings that women's suffrage was not in the interests of working women. It was easy for Hyndman or Holmes to take such a view: they already had the vote. Selina began to think that if they were still unenfranchised they might be a little less complacent.

So, as she came to know Helen Phillip, her doubts about the adult suffrage demand began to grow. She realised that her earlier faith in 'collectivism' was too simple on its own. A socialist collective state would not automatically give women the power to run their own lives; she came to see how powerless working-class women would remain if they had no voice in Parliament. Later she described how her change of mind had come about:

> I carefully watched the proceedings and policy pursued by such great unions as the Miners, Cotton Spinners and Engineers, who all pressed for State interference with the object of improving their industrial conditions. I was compelled to recognise the power of Parliament – a power that can and ought to be utilised for the public good. Those well-organised industries had the ballot-box as a lever to raise their standard of life, but the women workers, however well they combined, had no such lever to help them in their demand for the redressing of their grievances.[18]

After her return from Keld in 1899, Selina Cooper became

actively involved in the growing women's suffrage campaign. This was exactly the moment that Esther Roper and Eva Gore-Booth were busy planning a new and exciting suffrage campaign geared especially to the needs of women cotton workers. Such women had their lives regulated by successive factory acts (one of which even stipulated that a woman must take at least four weeks unpaid leave from work after childbirth) which were passed by male MPs whom they could neither choose nor vote for. Surely, argued the suffragists, politicians *must* respond to the claim to the vote by tens of thousands of women cotton workers whose long hours in the mills contributed so significantly to Britain's exports and therefore British prosperity.

So, as part of a new strategy to link the growing suffrage and labour movements, Esther Roper and others in the North of England Society for Women's Suffrage decided to launch a petition to be signed only by women working in the Lancashire cotton mills. It read:

> To the Right Honourable the Commons of Great Britain and Ireland, in Parliament assembled. The HUMBLE PETITION of the undersigned women workers in the cotton factories of Lancashire:
> *Sheweth:*
> That in the opinion of your petitioners the continued denial of the franchise to women is unjust and inexpedient.
> In the home, their position is lowered by such an exclusion from the responsibilities of national life.
> In the factory, their unrepresented condition places the regulation of their work in the hands of men who are often their rivals as well as their fellow workers . . .[19]

The petition was ceremoniously launched on May Day, 1900. Soon North of England Society petition workers were scurrying up and down Lancashire with their forms, visiting even the most remote textile hamlet. In the evenings they knocked on doors, hoping to catch the woman of the house between feeding the baby or cooking the supper and persuade her to break off for a moment and add her signature. Some sympathetic mill owners even allowed canvassing in the yards of their great cotton mills; the women would spread out their petition sheets on tables so that the weavers, winders or cardroom workers could be conveniently approached as they passed in or out of the yard.

Sometimes the petition workers addressed special meetings of the Guild or ILP women, persuading them of the importance of the vote to working women like themselves. One suffragist, a Manchester Guildswoman called Mrs Bayfield, came up to address the Burnley Guild at the end of May, and by the beginning of July was back again, speaking at two open air meetings in Nelson and another in Burnley.

Selina Cooper was just the kind of recruit Mrs Bayfield was looking for. Although she had recently given up her job in the mill, Selina had fourteen or fifteen years' experience of cotton factory work, and was in addition the wife of a weaver. Selina was already convinced by the suffrage arguments put forward by Helen Phillip, but had not yet committed herself actively to the campaign.

Whether Selina Cooper went along to listen to Mrs Bayfield that summer is not recorded. It certainly seems likely. Her daughter Mary was now four months old, and Selina could easily have made her way up from Brierfield to the open ground in Nelson (only half a mile away) with her baby in her arms. She would have been intrigued to find out exactly what the Manchester woman was speaking about.

It is clear that from the inspiration of one such meeting Selina Cooper found herself suddenly catapulted into the suffrage campaign. From this moment onwards, for the next fourteen years, women's suffrage took priority over virtually everything else. Selina Cooper's life became changed beyond all recognition. 'It was in the interests of the [suffrage] movement that I began my real public career,' she reminisced later.

> I took an active part in collecting signatures for the great petition. Up to that time the suffrage movement had been a purely academic one. It was through [Miss] Roper that this great petition started. I went about with petition forms, visiting thousands of doors . . .[20]

Annie Heaton apparently co-ordinated the canvassing of support for the petition in the Burnley area, and must have been delighted to win the support of such a valuable recruit. Selina was, after all, President of the Brierfield Women's Co-operative Guild and a woman with experience of union organising. Her local contacts in Burnley and up the valley would be invaluable: indeed, one of the first things Selina Cooper must have done was to introduce Annie Heaton to the women she used to work with because by October Annie was addressing a meeting in Burnley of women winders on women's suffrage.

Once she offered her services, Selina was promptly dispatched up to Colne and Barrowford to collect signatures. We can imagine her leaving Mary for a few hours with Robert's mother or with one of her sisters-in-law, catching the tram or train up to Colne, perhaps calling in at the Weavers' Association office there or at the home of a suffrage sympathiser to check names and addresses, and then making her careful way up and down the town's steep cobbled streets, knocking on door after door along cramped terraces (for Colne, a much older town than Nelson, still possessed overcrowded slums).

It was a busy time for her, with Mary not yet a year old. Mrs Bayfield came up to talk to the Nelson Women's Co-operative Guild in November, and Selina would have been involved in helping organise this. And, by dint of a lot of hard work, she collected over 800 signatures by spring 1901 – 500 in Colne and 300 in Barrowford. These were all from women working in the mills whom, as the local paper phrased it, 'she has brought over to seeing eye to eye with her on this subject'. She now subscribed a shilling annually to the North of England Society funds and, so persuasive had she become in this cause, she also collected subscriptions totalling three shillings from other local sympathisers.[21]

By spring 1901 the number of signatures collected reached 29,359. Esther Roper felt ready to confront the law-makers of Westminster with the results of her efforts. She selected fifteen of the Lancashire suffragists with long experience of the cotton mills to travel down to London. On Monday 18 March they would address the Lancashire MPs who were to receive the deputation.[22] Among the fifteen were Annie Heaton from Burnley; Sarah Reddish, influential president of the Bolton Women's Co-operative Guild and member of the town's School Board; and, quite naturally, Annie Heaton's hard-working new recruit from Nelson, Selina Cooper.

Even before her invitation to London arrived, the news of her involvement in the deputation caused quite a stir locally. The *Nelson Chronicle* depicted her . 'expecting to be summoned to London almost any day now'. The excitement is easily understood. It was not only a visit to Westminster, but also her first long journey since she had travelled up from Cornwall twenty-five years earlier.

We can imagine the little knot of Lancashire women approaching the formidable-looking Houses of Parliament that all the fuss was about. Clutching their enormous petition (Selina Cooper described the roll of signatures as being 'as big as a beer barrel'), they were ushered through endless Westminster corridors to Committee Room 18 where they would meet the MPs. Sarah Reddish as senior member introduced the deputation, explaining that it consisted entirely of past or present women cotton workers from Lancashire. They spoke on behalf of the 29,359 signatories, all of whom felt bitterly about Parliament's continued refusal to grant women the vote. Annie Heaton and three of the others spoke up too, stressing the 'utmost readiness' they had found among the women asked to sign the petition.

Then it was Selina Cooper's turn. Here was her chance to put to good use her experience of chairing Brierfield Guild meetings, addressing the SDF class and arguing with high-minded guests at Keld. Mary had had her first birthday only a few days previously, and Selina decided to argue the right to vote on the duties of motherhood. Women, she pointed out to the MPs, have 'to educate their children, but if they are not interested in national life, how,' she asked, 'could they impart to their children a knowledge of true citizenship?'

The MPs' spokesman suggested helpfully that the women might read books. This notion did not go down well. Selina Cooper, bitterly conscious of the struggle she and her husband had to acquire even a few inexpensive paperbacks and then to find the leisure time to read them, had her reply ready. She crisply rebuked the MPs by reminding them that women cotton workers, 'have ten hours in the factory every day, and, when they have done their daily labour, they have little energy left for reading severe classical books or studying economics', but if Parliament granted them the vote they could at least become directly interested in national life. She had come straight from the workers in

the mill, Selina told them, and had for many years been earning
her living as a textile worker. She was well acquainted with
women cotton workers' hopes and ideals. She told the MPs that
she had collected over 800 signatures, and stressed to these men
the great importance of the vote for children's elementary
education. 'If mothers are given an interest in national life, such
as the franchise would confer,' she stated, 'it will be all the better
for the upbringing of their children in the ideas of citizenship.'[23]

The MPs all nodded blandly and appeared sympathetic
towards the women's demands. Yet this was not entirely the case:
one of the Liberal MPs was currently steering through Parliament
an adult suffrage bill which, although it had little chance of success
under a Tory government, would deflect attention away from
women's claims. He and three other MPs agreed to sign a memo-
randum to the government asking for time to discuss women's
suffrage, but reserved the right to oppose the third reading of a
women's suffrage bill, since they really preferred to press for an
all-or-nothing adult suffrage bill.[24]

Such crafty evasions opened Selina Cooper's eyes to the compromises and half-truths of Liberal MPs that would so infuriate
suffragists in the years to come. There was little chance of full
adult suffrage, yet that was always a convenient pretext for not
supporting votes for women bills. Worse still, many diehard MPs
in the ruling Tory Party vehemently opposed even the principle of
women's suffrage; and without government support, private
members' bills always floundered hopelessly. A sympathetic
Labour MP like Keir Hardie, now representing Merthyr Tydfil,
could hardly exert much influence in the Commons in the face of
the great party machines.

Despite these formidable obstacles, the Lancashire women
could rely on the sisterly support from the National Union of
Women's Suffrage Societies. In the evening, having been shown
round the Houses of Parliament that otherwise remained out of
bounds to them, they were entertained to dinner at a continental
restaurant, the Florence, by Mrs Fawcett. Selina Cooper, Annie
Heaton, Sarah Reddish and the others suddenly found themselves thrust into a new and unfamiliar world. Seldom having
eaten away from home, they were now confronted by a lavish
dinner menu. Similarly, they had hardly encountered titled

women before (though Selina might have caught an occasional glimpse of eccentric Lady O'Hagan or Lady Kay-Shuttleworth, the MP's wife). Yet here she was sitting down to share 'sole à la ravigote' and 'pigeon en casserole' with Lady Frances Balfour, influential National Union member who had connections in the highest Tory places. She found herself eating alongside well-educated and often wealthy women who ran the National Union, including Mrs Fawcett and Isabella Ford.

Selina Cooper's encounter with Helen Phillip, symbolised by the signed circular portrait, and her subsequent collecting of suffrage signatures opened up the new direction that her life was now to take. It also introduced her to a different social world. One of the factors on which the success of the women's suffrage movement would ultimately depend was whether women from such different class backgrounds as Selina Cooper's and Lady Frances Balfour's could find a community of interest in their demand for the vote.

CHAPTER EIGHT

SOCIALISM INTO LABOUR:
1901-1907

St Mary's Street sloped straight from Nelson's main road down towards the canal and, beyond it, to the river and Lomeshaye's model mill village. The stone terraced houses flanking either side ran in two unbroken lines – door, window, door, window – right down to the mill at the bottom. The neighbouring streets, laid out at strict right angles, had been pushed up hastily twenty years earlier to house the immigrants pouring into Nelson in search of work.

Robert and Selina Cooper moved into their new house, 59 St Mary's Street, in spring 1901. It was the time of Mary's first birthday; and her memory of these early childhood years helps recreate what her parents' house looked like when she was a small child eighty years earlier. It was

> very sparse . . . We had oil cloth [on the floor], and then a little
> rug – sometimes a pegged rug . . . Very sparse [furniture]. Very
> poor . . .
> It [the fireplace] was sort of iron . . . and it had to be black-leaded
> . . . If you wanted to bake, you scooped all your red hot
> cinders under the oven to bake with. Then when you wanted a
> bath, you scooped all the fire under there, and it boiled [the
> water].

To fill the bath, water had to be ladled out of the boiler, a canful at a time. Inevitably such Edwardian households, lacking gas ovens and hot running water, revolved round the time-consuming coal fire; Mary can still recall how 'you had to rake all the coals out every morning – and my father was a marvellous maker of fires'.

But with Robert Cooper out of the house most of the day,

working at his Lomeshaye looms, it naturally fell to Selina to be responsible for the housework, then a back-breaking job. 'My father . . . didn't get down and do a proper clean. My mother would turn things out wholesale. If she was washing, sheets'd be coming down the steps. They'd all go in . . . She was a wholesale worker, was my mother.'[1]

Mary often watched her mother laboriously blackleading the stove, kneading the dough, washing the family clothes in a dolly tub and then hanging them up to dry in the steamy back kitchen. But Mary's earliest recollections of 59 St Mary's Street were also of politics. For Selina Cooper had a good reason to rush through her domestic chores. The house soon became a local meeting place, with people constantly coming and going, and Mary shooed off to her grandmother's house when her parents were busy.

> Meetings is my earliest memory – memories of this house. Because
> my father was secretary [of the ward Labour Party] . . . My
> earliest memories, I'll tell you, are of meetings in this house. They
> stand out. And my grandmother's. Going to my grand-
> mother's – she lived across the back street. And I had an aunt
> lived over there. I was everybody's child.[2]

For by the time she moved from Brierfield to Nelson, Selina brought with her a growing reputation as founder-president of the Brierfield Women's Co-operative Guild and as a skilled public speaker. Her study of the working conditions of women mill workers had established her as someone who knew what she was talking about. Her strong conviction about women's suffrage and her efficient collection of 800 signatures for the petition also marked her out as a determined campaigner. And her experience of canvassing for Labour candidates like Ben Smith, addressing the Nelson Mutual Improvement Class, and founding the Brierfield SDF branch, all combined to ensure that she would be taken seriously by both the ILP and the SDF once she settled in Nelson.

In February 1901, just before Selina took the suffrage petition down to Westminster, the three-yearly elections of Poor Law Guardians came round once again. Lady O'Hagan was again a candidate for Burnley, as was Mary Brown, recently returned from South Africa. But no working woman had yet been elected, and local socialists cast around for a suitable candidate to represent their views on the Board – and alighted on Selina Cooper.

The Nelson SDF and ILP branches agreed to adopt her as their joint candidate for the Guardianship election. They saw in her someone who could push forward their socialist policies. Equally important, they offered to pay her election costs and even her travel expenses to Burnley for the Guardian meetings. They were conscious that working people were hardly encouraged to stand for election, and that Boards were traditionally organised for the personal convenience of men with private incomes or their own businesses, not for the wives of Lomeshaye weavers.[3]

Selina Cooper readily agreed to run as a joint SDF-ILP candidate. It seems she had decided to put her political life before her personal concerns: this was just the opportunity she had been waiting for. But she soon found she was not the only woman hoping to win one of the seats allocated to Nelson on the Burnley Board. There was also a woman called Sarah Thomas, who had come to Nelson from Philip Snowden's village of Cowling nearly fifty years earlier and, like Snowden, had been brought up a Liberal. But unlike him, she never shook off these beliefs; indeed her father, also a Liberal, became first Mayor of Nelson, while she put her energies into the temperance campaign and the battle against the demon drink.[4]

The two women, one standing as a socialist and the other for temperance, had precious little in common. All they shared was their femaleness. But such were the rigid Victorian notions of chivalry and gallantry that still stamped public relations between the sexes that a fierce battle now erupted between the women's supporters and those of the men. In the heat of the fight, many of the political subtleties dividing candidates into 'rate-spenders' and 'rate-savers' were abandoned. It became virtually a sex war.

Reports in the local newspapers during the four-week run-up to the election revealed the righteous indignation of men who now found themselves being sniped at by creatures whose natural sphere was at home by the fireside. While the two newer papers, the *Nelson Chronicle* and the *Nelson Leader* looked sympathetically upon the prospects of 'lady Guardians', the older Liberal paper, the *Colne and Nelson Times*, frothed with angry abuse:

> At the risk of being described ungallant, we have to ask the elec-
> tors of Nelson to see to it that the three men candidates are elected
> Guardians . . . We hold that the interests of women are not
> neglected by administrative bodies consisting entirely of men . . .
> In the men candidates the ratepayers have . . . guardians who are
> lovers of their work and have the leisure – without the domestic
> ties which embarrass women – to perform the duties they are
> willing to undertake . . . Whatever happens to Mrs Thomas or
> Mrs Cooper, we venture to say that it is the duty of electors of
> Nelson to vote for Messrs Hudson, Horsfall and Thornton.

The following week, after Selina Cooper returned from petitioning Westminster, the anxious *Times* redoubled its attack on
women candidates:

> The contest is practically one of sex representation . . . In all prob-
> ability Lady O'Hagan and Mrs Brown will be elected to the Board
> for other townships, and we hold that these two ladies and one
> from Nelson are a sufficient representation of the female sex on the
> Union Authority . . . The presence of too many women on a
> public body could actually embarrass the men in their very essen-
> tial duties. After all, there is, we think, very little danger of such
> an event occurring. Women are, as a whole, too indifferent to
> what happens outside their domestic life to take a too prominent
> part in public work. This we say with a full appreciation of the
> value of the petition which Mrs Cooper and other ladies presented
> to several members of Parliament last Monday.[5]

Three days later the Nelson electors went to the polls. The three
men came top of the poll, headed by a heavily-bearded Liberal,
Alderman Hudson, with 839 votes and closely followed by the
other two, one Liberal and one Tory. But, to the Liberals' consternation, Selina Cooper came fourth with a respectable 679
votes and so was also elected. Sarah Thomas came an unsuccessful fifth.

Bitter recriminations followed. The sympathetic *Nelson
Chronicle*, noting that the three men had issued a joint address
despite their party differences, levelled accusations of 'electoral
conspiracy' against the two women. 'As the age of chivalry is
gone,' it suggested, 'it is not surprising to find the three candidates of the opposite sex combining against the two ladies.' And,
even though victorious, the *Colne and Nelson Times* complained

how unromantic the election contest had been compared to 'those classic conflicts when men fought ABOUT, and not AGAINST, women'. A closer parallel, the paper suggested fancifully, was 'to be found in the plains of Western Africa, where the King of Dahomy's amazons engage in conflict with either man or woman'. Mrs Cooper's amazonian daring went even further, alleged *The Times*: it attributed her success at the polls to 'a triumph of the electioneering expedient of distributing the lady's photograph, and in this way securing the fourth vote of many "mere men" who . . . were not insusceptible to the mute appeal of the lady's picture'.[6]

During these few weeks Selina Cooper had been brought face to face with the entrenched hostility of male politicians – whether MPs at Westminster or diehard Liberals in Nelson – sharing their power with voteless women. But, on the suffrage deputation, she had also experienced a sense of solidarity with the other women textile workers and with the suffragist leaders who had welcomed them so hospitably. Suddenly to find herself lionised by aristocratic ladies down in London, while opposed by local working-class men at the polls, felt odd to Selina who, after all, had till recently seen in the socialists' programme of 'collectivism' the cure for all political ills. She had only just begun to catch up with the significance of these recent events when she was suddenly hurtled into a new and unknown battleground: the meetings of the Burnley Board of Guardians.

Mary was again left with nearby relations, and Selina Cooper, her fare paid for her by the Nelson socialists, travelled down into Burnley town centre, wondering what she might encounter when, as the only working woman Guardian, she walked into the meeting. The only experienced Guardian she knew was Mary Brown. Yet, however much she admired the doctor's wife, Selina Cooper already recognised that she would not always find herself voting the same way as Mrs Brown; the fact that she was backed by the SDF, so disliked by staunch Burnley Liberals like the Browns, already suggested this. The other woman Guardian, Lady O'Hagan from Townley Hall, Selina Cooper soon warmed to; there was something unpretentious and direct about this impoverished aristocrat (standing as an independent and coming top of the Burnley poll), which drew Selina Cooper to her.

But, in contrast to the Nelson election, it was among the male Guardians on the Board that she immediately found most in common. Elected for Burnley, also on an SDF ticket, was fiery Dan Irving, and his socialist running-mate John Thornton. Surrounded as she now was by Tory gentleman-farmers from Pendle, 'progressive' Liberal businessmen and respectable Methodist ministers, Selina Cooper naturally sided with these two lone socialists. Certainly her years in the SDF had taught her to admire Dan Irving's tireless efforts as local branch organiser. He could sometimes be an embarrassing ally, with his habit of addressing individuals as if they were public meetings and of losing his temper with his opponents. But in the face of the hard-faced rate-cutting majority under the chairmanship of a Tory Anglican cotton manufacturer from Brierfield, Selina Cooper knew that Irving's foibles would have to be tolerated. At all costs the sorry lot of Burnley's paupers, both inside and outside the workhouse, must be improved.

As Selina Cooper entered the solemn Board Room in which the Guardians held their meetings, she could pick out little beyond a sea of men's faces: the three dozen men blurred into a dark grey-brown pattern of Edwardian respectability, hair brushed neatly back from foreheads, moustaches trim, fob watches resting comfortably against waistcoated stomachs (just as her father's had done so many years ago), an occasional face distinguished by a high stiff collar, or (again reminiscent of her father) a generous grey beard. The pattern was broken only by Mary Brown's long thin face and Lady O'Hagan's plumper one.

As she gradually got the measure of her fellow Guardians, she recognised that not only did the men outnumber the women, and the rural Guardians those representing the factory workers, but also that precious little power lay with the full Guardians' meetings. These were essentially rubber-stamping occasions. Rather, the important decisions were taken by smaller sub-committees, and it was for a place on these that the various factions now competed vigorously.

At that first meeting Guardians were allocated to the small local relief committees, each one responsible for administering out-relief (that is, small payments to people still living in their own homes who had so far been able to keep out of Burnley's dreaded workhouse). So Selina Cooper was placed on the Marsden (as Nelson was still archaically called) Relief Committee, alongside the other Nelson Guardians. She also found herself along with Dan Irving on the Vaccination Committee (at the time the focus of bitter controversy over the right of individuals to object to compulsory vaccination). Mrs Brown, Lady O'Hagan and others were allocated places on the crucial Visiting Committee which had responsibility for running the workhouse and for the well-being of its voiceless inmates.

A week later the horse-trading began as each faction lobbied the other over sub-committee places. First, Mrs Brown proposed Selina Cooper for the Visiting Committee: her experience in the St John Ambulance Brigade and as a Co-operative Guild president Mary Brown could, after all, vouch for personally. The assembled Guardians mulled this over, but sensed that allowing Selina within the workhouse would lead to more trouble than it was worth. So they voted to keep her off the Visiting Committee by twenty-six votes to six. Then socialist John Thornton proposed, even more rashly, that Dan Irving's name also be added to the committee; such an extreme suggestion was defeated by twenty-eight votes to five.[8]

Dan Irving was merely limbering up. At the next meeting, when the Visiting Committee asked the full Guardians' meeting formally to accept its minutes, he moved that they should be rejected – but was completely crushed: twenty-eight votes to one. On such occasions even Selina Cooper felt that Dan Irving was being a little absurd, and found herself siding with Mary Brown, Lady O'Hagan and the voice of moderation. After all, she was keenly aware that this was her first publicly elected post and she must appear dignified rather than becoming immediately embroiled in petty squabbles. Yet she often found herself agreeing with Irving's criticisms of the Machiavellian manoeuvrings of the right-wing; shortly after the Visiting Committee skirmish, she seconded his resolution condemning the way the Board had excluded them both from joining the Visiting Committee. Although their criticisms were rejected, it did lead to a vigorous debate with many Guardians taking their side.

Buoyed up by this, Dan Irving a few days later held a public meeting on Burnley market ground about the manipulation of the Guardians. Here local ratepayers – mainly SDF supporters – protested 'against the unjust and arbitrary conduct of the Chairman and other members of the Board', demanding the right of members of the public to attend Guardians' meetings occasionally. This Selina Cooper happily backed: her years in the SDF had made her value free speech and open political dealing. So, along with one or two others, she lent Dan Irving her support at the next meeting when he proposed 'that all Ordinary and Special Meetings of the Board shall be open to the public, and that the Building Committee be instructed to make provision for their attendance'. However the Building Committee had no need to brace itself for this new challenge: the resolution was heavily defeated. Undaunted, the socialists straightaway proposed that the Visiting Committee provide extra accommodation in the Men's Tramp Ward in the workhouse to halt 'the continual and disgraceful overcrowding therein, which under present conditions must be a dangerous means of disseminating filthy and loathsome diseases' – though this too was decisively rejected. They also suggested – and here at last they managed to touch a soft spot among the majority of Guardians – that elderly people in the workhouse 'who have lived decent lives, who can be trusted in regard to sobriety and general moral character', should be free to go in and out of the workhouse, so long as they returned at the times requested by the Workhouse Master. Such elderly people, the last generation to dread the workhouse before the introduction of old age pensions, were so obviously the 'deserving' rather than the 'undeserving poor'. The Guardians responded to their mute appeal and the Master was ordered to carry out the terms of the resolution.[9]

This was one small step towards humanising the harsh workhouse regime, but the socialists had so far failed to have Guardian meetings thrown open to the public. Yet to Dan Irving, this remained a crucial issue. He had been elected as a socialist to represent working people's interests, yet Board meetings remained behind firmly closed doors. Irving realised he had little hope of swaying many of the Guardians to his point of view, so he opted instead for direct action – tactics that would point a public spotlight at the Guardians' private cabals.

So one night in July 1901, in the SDF rooms in Burnley, the plot was laid. (It is unlikely that Selina Cooper was directly involved, though she doubtless had an inkling of what was afoot.) The next morning, six socialists somehow made their way into the building and into the Board Room. When the Guardians arrived they found the intruders occupying their chairs. The chairman asked them to leave. Immediately Dan Irving jumped up to protest. No one moved. The chairman summoned the police. Dan Irving bellowed that the public had a right to be present. Two burly policemen materialised and pushed the intruders out the door. The chairman tried to call the meeting to order, but Dan Irving and John Thornton continued their noisy heckling. Before long both Guardians were forcibly thrown out by the police, Dan Irving struggling with his captors all the way. As soon as the door closed on him he beat on it loudly, causing tremendous commotion. The police eventually allowed him back into the meeting – after all, he was an elected Guardian.[10]

Selina Cooper had not witnessed this drama; possibly she had been quietly warned to stay away that day. Nevertheless, such extreme tactics, attracting adverse publicity, left her in a difficult position. She wholly shared Dan Irving's aims of opening up meetings and making the Poor Law more humane. But she had doubts about his unrespectable tactics, and used to arrive home from Guardian meetings and tell her daughter stories about Irving's head-on collisions:

> When she became a Guardian, oh, she used to have such rows. They had to literally fight – the Tories used to fight rather than give sixpence . . . Dan Irving, he'd a wooden leg . . . like a peg-leg, like Treasure Island. Well, anyhow, he used to get so worked up, did Dan – he'd take his leg off and start hitting people with it! Start fighting! Yes!

Although the details of this anecdote have perhaps been embroidered over the years, the myths that grew up around Irving's behaviour seemed to be solidly based. He *was* intolerant of even the moderate Guardians. Yet it was amongst them that Selina Cooper realised that an effective alliance had to be built. She felt that an 'independent' like Lady O'Hagan must not be antagonised, but brought round gently to the socialists' point of view. Irving was intolerant of Selina's bid to woo even the middle ground. Mary Cooper recalled what a

> terrible temper he had. He used to get very vexed because my mother used to talk to Lady O'Hagan, and she was far more radical and she was more Labour – as she left the Catholic faith and went into the Unitarian [Church]. My mother was friendly with her . . .
>
> And he used to get wild – said she was hob-nobbing with the rich people, and they [the O'Hagans] were as poor as church crows. It's Townley Hall, the famous Townley Hall. And my mother used to take me there as a baby.[11]

Yet Irving's tactics did have effect. At the following Guardians' meeting there was again a small crowd outside and the headline, 'More Obstruction by Socialists' in the local press. Irving's shock tactics had at least woken up some of the sleepy Guardians: a month later they agreed to a motion, seconded by Selina Cooper, to set up a committee to revise the Board's Standing Orders, and that Dan Irving be included on it.

Overall, though, the socialists could count only pitifully few practical gains. When the Standing Orders committee reported back, all Irving's amendments had been defeated. Similarly, when Selina Cooper backed a resolution to abolish the ugly uniforms that workhouse paupers were forced to wear, she won little support. The following year she tried to put a stop to the practice of making people who lived in the workhouse do corn grinding, a degrading task for the paupers; this too was crushingly defeated. She also supported Dan Irving when he suggested an increase in the money given to the few paupers entitled to receive relief outside the workhouse. In her experience, she told the Guardians, 12s 6d was the absolute minimum that a family could live on; but this proposal was again defeated. Nor did the stalemate between left and right soften over the next year or two. In spring 1904, when Board members were facing election again, Dan Irving proposed that the constitution of the key committees should be made more democratic; Selina Cooper backed him up but their suggestion was rejected by twenty-five votes to two.

Selina Cooper's first three years' experience on the Burnley Board of Guardians was chequered. So long as the socialists' proposals involved no increase in the rates, they were allowed to wrest one or two small concessions from the Guardians. In this way, elderly people in the workhouse won some freedom of movement; and Selina Cooper, by behaving herself at meetings, was eventually allowed a seat on the Visiting Committee. (Among her family papers, a small printed invitation has survived, requesting 'the pleasure of the company of Mrs Cooper at the Workhouse on Thursday February 26, 1903. Tea at 5.30 pm.') But the old Victorian distinction between the deserving and undeserving poor still lay entrenched in the minds of most Guardians; they felt it was essential to stigmatise paupers because otherwise demands for poor relief would soar. Dan Irving, John Thornton and Selina Cooper kicked hard at these rock-like values, but hardly managed to shift them at all.[12]

Though also sponsored by the SDF, Selina Cooper found herself increasingly distanced from Irving and Thornton. Not only was she still the only working woman on the Board; she was also the only representative of the newer, more tolerant form of socialism that now flourished in Nelson and many other places. Both locally and nationally the ILP was seeking more practical alternatives to the SDF's confrontational tactics and Marxist creed. It was beginning to build links locally with the organised cotton workers to try and forge a broad-based alliance between socialists and trade unionists. Springing from the Salem Independent Methodist Chapel, and the radical traditions of the Yorkshire immigrants, Nelson's influential ILP branch was already giving shape to a strong labour group in the town. It was this group that pointed the way ahead for Selina Cooper, and made her second term as a Guardian rather different from her first.

Selina Cooper's difficulties on the Burnley Board of Guardians between 1901 and 1904 were a reflection of the wider problems faced nationally by Keir Hardie, Philip Snowden and others. They wanted to form an effective labour party, but the existing socialist groups – the SDF, ILP and others – seemed distanced from the great mass of trade unionists who still kept faith with their old party loyalties and time-honoured system of parliamentary lobbying. In the Coopers' corner of north-east Lancashire, the influence of old-style trade unionists like David

Holmes remained formidable. Liberalism seemed unshakeable: working men were apparently content for members of the landed gentry like Sir Ughtred Kay-Shuttleworth to represent their interests at Westminster.

Elsewhere in Britain progressive trade unionists began to support the new Labour Representation Committee (as the fledgling Labour Party was originally called), formed in 1900 under the leadership of Ramsay MacDonald. Its aim was to put up independent Labour candidates at elections, and in the general election that year chalked up two successes, Keir Hardie for Merthyr Tydfil, and a trade unionist MP. Yet the giant Lancashire cotton unions were still loathe to affiliate to Labour. Even the Nelson Weavers, despite socialist members like Robert Cooper, remained wary of taking this mighty step. [13]

Such was the situation in spring 1901 when Selina Cooper was elected a Guardian: she had to be sponsored by the local SDF and ILP because as yet no other labour group existed in Nelson. Yet even during her first year on the Burnley Board, rumblings began to signal discontent with the old order. And as the scenario began to unfold, both the Coopers found themselves in the thick of the drama.

Early warning signs heralding the change were already visible. The Nelson Weavers, the Colne Weavers and the Nelson, Colne, Brierfield and District Textile Trades Federation had grown keenly interested in the idea of labour representation. And there were growing doubts about whether Sir Ughtred was the ideal MP for the swelling army of industrial workers in his constituency. After all, he had failed to stop the 1899 bill raising the minimum half-timer age from eleven to twelve. Local parents wondered whether an MP who had been in the mill like themselves might not have fought harder against these new-fangled laws to keep their children penned in at school. Additionally Sir Ughtred tactlessly blotted his copybook by excusing himself from a local Textile Trades Federation conference on pretext that he had 'a previous engagement of special importance in London'. The trade union delegates present took a dim view of their MP's political priorities.

However, at the 1900 general election which returned the Tory Government to power, Sir Ughtred was returned unopposed as

Clitheroe's MP. Yet within months an historic judgement by the House of Lords upturned this apple cart. In 1901 the Lords decided that the railway workers' union was liable to pay the Taff Vale Railway Company £20,000 worth of damages incurred in a recent strike. Robert Cooper and other Lomeshaye weavers were currently involved in strike action and realised they too might find themselves liable for damages if their employer exercised this dangerous new right. Local weavers' fears deepened when they learned that nearby the big Blackburn Weavers' Association was also found liable for £11,000 for peaceful picketing during a strike.

Local trade unionists asked themselves whether Sir Ughtred was the right MP to campaign against the catastrophic Taff Vale judgement. Philip Snowden, now on Keighley Town Council, further fuelled this disgruntlement when he came to speak to the local Textile Trades Federation on Labour Representation. And at the 1901 municipal elections in Nelson, Labour emerged triumphant: William Rickard from Cornwall and a Weavers' candidate both became Labour councillors, along with a joint ILP-SDF candidate.

The Coopers would know William Rickard and they had also become friendly with Philip Snowden, offering him hospitality when he came to Nelson. 'These big people that came would only stay one night . . . ,' Mary explained. 'Even such as MacDonald and Snowden had nowhere else to go; they couldn't afford to stay in hotels.'[14] Perhaps urged on by Snowden's persuasive oratory, Robert Cooper began to take a lead in the battle to challenge the Liberals' power. Early in 1902, he issued a fighting statement to the *Nelson Chronicle*, threatening that: 'we fully intend to go against Liberalism on all occasions, and to practise or to utilise every legitimate method for the overthrowing of Liberalism, unless the Liberal Party are prepared to come forward and recognise the Labour Party.'

Robert also warned local socialists to 'employ a little diplomacy in their endeavours to wrest the seat from Sir Ughtred'.[15] His sober warning must have had some effect. Joint meetings of socialists and trade unionists were amicable, and before long Keir Hardie himself was invited up to address delegates on plans to put up an independent Labour candidate in Clitheroe. Support for the Labour Representation Committee was offered and local unions were urged to affiliate to it.

By the summer of 1902 the debate on whether to field a Labour candidate at the next election had been won. This was clear when the Nelson Weavers' members were balloted. Thanks to the lobbying of Robert Cooper and others, the vote was eight to one for affiliation, and five to one for their union to give financial support to a Labour candidate. And there the matter might have rested comfortably till the next general election. But within days of the ballot being announced, the constituency was plunged into unexpected electioneering frenzy. On 26 June Sir Ughtred was awarded a peerage. With their traditional MP elevated to the Lords, Clitheroe faced its first election contest for a decade.

The announcement caught all parties unawares. The Liberals had grown fat and complacent during the Sir Ughtred years: local Liberal clubs had degenerated into clubs for billiards and cards. Labour was even less prepared: although the recent union ballots had offered financial support, no levies of union members had yet been organised, and so there were no election funds available. Local Liberal papers, confident of infant Labour's weakness, suggested optimistically that Liberal and Labour might unite to prevent a Tory getting in. In fact the Tories had not contested the seat since 1892 and decided it was too hopeless to fight. In addition, there were rapid developments in the fast-growing Labour camp. Keir Hardie and Ramsay MacDonald both raced up to this key constituency, and it was hurriedly agreed that Labour would fight completely independent of the Liberals. The names of Philip Snowden and a local textile trade unionist, David Shackleton, were floated as possible Labour candidates. By 5 July, only days after the peerage was announced, the election had been settled. Philip Snowden, despite his local popularity as an ILP speaker, generously stood down. Councillor David Shackleton, JP, Secretary of the nearby Darwen Weavers' Association was selected instead. A figure of weighty municipal respectability – over sixteen stone – he was the ideal choice to allay the fears of moderate trade unionists. A one-time half-timer and temperance advocate, he had all the attributes to appease the middle ground. Indeed, so much of a Liberal was this 'Labour' candidate, that in the end the Liberal Party gave up any thought of running a candidate against him. So during these hurried midsummer days, it was decided to levy 6d per trade union member in order to raise £450 for Shackleton's election. A constituency-based Labour Representation Association was formed and whirled into action for the four-week run-up to the uncontested election. Sixpences were levied on all the thousands of trade unionists in Clitheroe through the effective system of house-to-house collectors.[16]

When Selina heard the news of the local by-election she was immediately in touch with her Manchester suffrage friends who had organised the women textile workers' petition. Within days, messages were flying up and down between 59 St Mary's Street and the headquarters of the North of England Society for Women's Suffrage. Overnight Selina Cooper, in her far-flung Nelson outpost, became the hub of the suffragists' new campaign.

Manchester suffragists like Esther Roper and Eva Gore-Booth leapt at the opportunity of using Shackleton's election to publicise their cause. They had already taken independent labour representation to its logical conclusion, and argued that women workers needed to be included in the new system as well as men. Esther Roper had even written to Ramsay MacDonald, secretary of the Labour Representation Committee, asking him to receive a deputation of these voteless working women. During the summer she bombarded him with requests for his influential attention. But Ramsay MacDonald impatiently brushed aside this irritating fly buzzing on his great political coatsleeve. 'We can claim *directly* to represent 68,000 women textile workers,' Esther Roper insisted in her letters. 'We speak in their name.' She even threatened to come and call on him uninvited. But MacDonald seemingly held all the cards in his hand. Certainly, no meeting took place.[17]

The Clitheroe by-election was therefore a godsend. To the Labour Representation Committee's embarrassment, it high-lighted one glaring anomaly: that disenfranchised women trade unionists in the Clitheroe constituency were being asked to con-tribute substantially to Shackleton's campaign but were still barred from electing him. Besides the Labour Representation Committee's annual levy of a penny per member to maintain Labour MPs in Parliament, there was now the extra six pence for Shackleton himself. This seemed the final straw to the suffragists.

Nelson, where the Weavers' Association had 3,515 women members to only 2,762 men, was the natural focus of the campaign. Selina Cooper, incensed by this blatant injustice to local women trade unionists, began to work fast. She used all the contacts she had made collecting suffrage signatures, people she met through the ILP or SDF, sympathetic neighbours, even trade union friends of her husband's. Within five days of Kay-Shuttleworth's peerage being announced – even before David Shackleton's name had been tossed into the ring – suffragists were busy addressing a string of small cottage meetings of local women trade unionists, pointing out the iniquity of Shackleton's salary.

Sarah Reddish, the Guildswoman who had accompanied Selina Cooper down to Westminster, travelled up to Nelson for this crucial campaign. (The two women were already co-operating together to collect information about local employment conditions and so had become close friends. 'This work has enabled me and you to see and learn more of each other,' wrote Sarah to Selina, 'and as a result let me say – your friendship is a pleasure to me which I hope long to share and enjoy.'[18]) Other suffragists who made their intrepid way north were, of course, Esther Roper and aristocratic Eva Gore-Booth. Such an other-worldly presence must have caused quite a stir down St Mary's Street, but Eva Gore-Booth and Selina Cooper became firm friends; among the family papers have survived a handful of slim blue volumes of Eva Gore-Booth's fay poetry, inscribed 'Mrs Cooper with love from Eva G.B.'[19]

Christabel, the Pankhursts' talented eldest daughter, also arrived in Nelson. An impressionable twenty-two-year-old, she had fallen under the spell of the enchanting Eva Gore-Booth and so became drawn into the day-by-day campaigning in the North of England Society. With her was her mother, Mrs Pankhurst, increasingly frustrated by the ILP's ambivalent attitude to women's suffrage. She too became drawn to Mrs Cooper and must have been pleased to discover such a talented ILP speaker tucked away up in Nelson, and to share with her their common problems as lone socialist women on Boards of Guardians. A friendship between these two remarkable suffragists grew up; and, again, among the Cooper papers has survived a portrait photograph of Mrs Pankhurst that dates from this period.

By the time Shackleton was selected on 5 July, Selina Cooper's constituency was fairly buzzing with suffragists and the campaign was well under way. Eva Gore-Booth promptly dispatched a letter to the *Manchester Guardian*, which pointedly dug at how Ramsay MacDonald had chosen to ignore working women's claims to representation:

> In reckoning the number of labour votes in the Clitheroe division, it is stated . . . that 60 per cent of the members of the Weavers Union are women and girls and therefore not entitled to parliamentary representation.
>
> This disqualification which entirely cuts off the majority of weavers from the political work of their own union, not only causes their special trade interest to be neglected in legislation, but cripples the power of the whole organisation in political matters. That the women are alive to the importance of this question is proved by the large petitions and repeated deputations they have sent to the House of Commons during the past eighteen months. After the object lesson of Clitheroe will Labour leaders be content to regard the enfranchisement of women as a middle-class fad?[20]

At the same time, the suffragists organised a deputation of women from all over the constituency. Shackleton saw them (he was, of course, being lobbied by every conceivable pressure group from the local Protestant League to the Nelson Butchers' Association) and dutifully pledged himself to seek the immediate enfranchisement of women on the same terms as men, doubtlessly thinking that he would now hear no more from these troublesome women.

Not so. The suffragists had only just begun. Sarah Reddish was soon telling a nearby Women's Co-operative Guild that 'women as a class must be the best judges of their own interest', and not have to rely upon an elected figurehead they had no power to choose. Selina Cooper chaired a big open air meeting in Nelson; still rather inexperienced at having to introduce speakers like Mrs Pankhurst to such a large crowd, she just said a few formal words and then stepped back. Sarah Reddish came forward, cogently reasoning for women's enfranchisement. Then Mrs Pankhurst spoke up, pleading for the rights of the disenfranchised women trade unionists of Clitheroe and drawing a telling parallel with the

Boer War. She took the argument about working men's votes and turned it on its head:

> Many of you recently became very enthusiastic about the griev-
> ances of the poor outlanders of South Africa, and yet here in
> England – in the Clitheroe Parliamentary Division – supposed to
> be the home of the free, the majority of the adult population has
> no vote, and no say as to what laws should be passed by the Gov-
> ernment . . . Mr Shackleton has already expressed himself in
> favour of it [enfranchising women], but we want him to do some-
> thing more than this . . . we want him to pledge himself to intro-
> duce a Bill in Parliament on the subject . . . The enfranchisement
> of women is a labour question, and women look to their Parlia-
> mentary representatives to advance it.

Eva Gore-Booth seconded Mrs Pankhurst's resolution, adding, 'it is to the women of the Clitheroe Division that the women of the world are looking to make this matter their particular war cry'. Christabel Pankhurst spoke too. 'Those who paid the piper ought to call the tune,' she declared, 'and as 60 per cent of the trade unionist members of the Clitheroe Division are women they ought to have something to do with calling the tune.' Her impeccable logic was not lost on the meeting, and her mother's resolution was carried almost unanimously – with a lone heckler voting against.[21]

Meanwhile the Shackleton campaign was gathering momentum in respectable trade union quarters, so vital for winning the support of Liberal working men. Even the venerable David Holmes (who, by comparison, made Shackleton seem almost a wild revolutionary) came to grace the by-election platforms in his capacity as Northern Counties' Weavers' Amalgamation president.

And so it happened, as Shackleton circulated with due dignity round his constituency, Selina Cooper took part two days before the election in a rather remarkable public meeting. It was one of those rare moments when people who had previously been sworn enemies, or were soon to fall out bitterly with each other, congre-gated together on the platform of Brierfield's local Primitive Methodist schoolroom, a room which Selina must have remem-bered from her youth. At the extreme left was Abel Latham, Brierfield's first Labour councillor, whom Selina Cooper knew from her Burnley Weavers days. Well to the right sat David Holmes and Lady Dilke, progressive reformer, there to console unhappy Liberals. In the midst was wedged the great bulk of Shackleton himself. And then amongst these dignitaries on the platform sat Selina Cooper and Christabel Pankhurst, their very presence a certain tribute to the serious effect the women's suffrage campaign was having in the constituency. Christabel was even allowed to make a short and optimistic speech

> in the name of those weavers who a short time ago sent a petition and a deputation to the House of Commons. We support Mr Shackleton because we believe he is going to the House of Commons to work for women's questions. Mr Shackleton's future career depends on the consent and acquiescence of the women, and I feel certain that he is going to earn that goodwill.[22]

Two days later, on 1 August 1902 Shackleton was returned unopposed, Labour MP for Clitheroe and third Labour man in Parliament. It had all happened so quietly with none of the usual boisterous rivalry of election hustings. But that did not disguise the historic importance of the change that had taken place. If one of the Lancashire textile constituencies could so readily swing to Labour, surely the propects for the Labour Representation Committee nationally must be rosy indeed?

Sarah Reddish went back to Bolton; Esther Roper, Eva Gore-Booth and the Pankhursts to Manchester. The Cooper household returned to normal, and Selina resumed her routine of housework and Guardians' meetings. But she could hardly fail to notice that Labour's parliamentary success had changed local politics out of all recognition. The old gulf separating the ILP from many Liberal trade unionists was now disappearing. Instead, the ILP had joined with the unions to support Shackleton, and this new and important alliance increasingly left the confrontationist SDF out on a limb. Robert and Selina Cooper still retained their connections with the SDF (after all, the local branch still contributed to her Guardian expenses), but over the years grew increasingly aware of the limitations of SDF dogma.[23] Generally, local events were reflecting the larger national pattern.

What people like the Coopers, so involved in local politics, now desperately needed was a group, like the big Clitheroe Labour

Representation Association, which could organise the *municipal* elections. After all, the principle of labour representation was as important in the Town Hall as it was in Westminster. Indeed in Edwardian England, Parliament had far less influence on people's lives than it does today, for so many decisions were still taken at a local level. So, only a few weeks after Shackleton's success, a Nelson Labour Representation Committee sprang up to put up its own candidates for council elections. The Weavers affiliated to it, and the committee liaised efficiently between the Nelson ILP branch and the various trade unions in the town.

Supported by this local party machine, the Coopers were pleased to see Labour beginning to blossom in Nelson. Within a couple of months, the ILP started a successful newspaper, the *Nelson Workers' Guide*: 4,000 copies of each monthly issue were given away free to local householders.[24] ILP branches were also formed at Colne and, with the help of Philip Snowden and Selina Cooper, even at Brierfield. In this new and confident mood, the Labour councillors became more ambitious, William Rickard even daring to propose that local aldermen (a quaint sounding archaism today, but then a powerful clique of senior councillors) should have to stand for re-selection. Such a radical suggestion sent shudders down many a conservative spine.

At the next local elections, in November 1902, the Nelson Labour Representation Committee successfully put up two more councillors of their own – including Albert Smith, Secretary of the Overlookers' Association, for the Coopers' own Whitefield ward. Labour appeared to be unstoppable, and the Coopers were delighted. It was a wonderful tribute to their laborious years' work. They both lent their support wherever they could: in the 1903 muncipal elections, Selina Cooper chaired a boisterous meeting in Nelson's Co-operative Hall for one of the Labour candidates, with Dan Irving now a socialist councillor in Burnley also on the platform. Labour was even more successful at the polls this time, achieving an indisputable majority by winning ten of the eighteen council seats. By early 1904, the national press was alarming its readers with stories of how Nelson Town Council was the first in Lancashire with a Labour majority. Nelson could not claim to be the first Labour Council in the country: that honour went to West Ham in London. But it had certainly given its

Liberal ratepayers a great deal to worry over. Had they opened
their copy of the *Nelson Workers' Guide*, for instance, they would
have read how the workers 'desire the dawn of Democracy – the
day of the Sovereign People – the Public Control of Public
Necessities. That is surely coming, [as] the Collectivist trend of
events . . . amply show'.[25] Such rebellious rhetoric was one thing
if it came from a small political sect: quite another from the ruling
group on the Town Council.

Labour's spectacular triumph on the Nelson Town Council coincided with the three-yearly elections to the Burnley Board of
Guardians. But the presence of a vigorous Labour Representation Committee in the town had radically altered the way the
Guardians' elections would run in future. There was no need any
longer for Selina Cooper's candidacy to be supported merely by
two small socialist groups. Now she could be put forward by
Nelson's influential Labour Representation Committee, which
could boast both parliamentary and municipal election successes.

There was another significant change, too. Women who were
put up could no longer be so easily ridiculed and isolated by
'chivalrous' male rivals. The presence of the suffragists at
Shackleton's election had helped see to that. Women's right to
claim the parliamentary vote and take part in local elections was
now more firmly established.

So when the Nelson Labour Representation Committee met in
February 1904 to select its Poor Law candidates, it seemed perfectly natural they should choose two ILP women: Selina Cooper,
of course, for she had served working people's interests well in her
first three years; and her friend, Harriette Beanland, a skilled
dressmaker.

Harriette Beanland was an unusual woman. Unlike other
Nelson immigrants who could merely claim to have come from
Callington or Cowling, Miss Beanland had grown up in
Gibraltar and became something of a local celebrity, giving talks
on her early life abroad. She was also not a mill worker, but a
self-employed dressmaker, and already a strong feminist. Her
great-nephew testified how his great-aunt Harriette was 'one of
the elite, shall we say, in the town'. When he was taken as a small
boy to visit her and her sister Emily, he was instructed before-

hand, ' "Now thee behave theeself, young fellow, these's Spanish is these." ' Mary Cooper also recalls Harriette Beanland, dignified and well-dressed, having qualities that complemented her mother's; Harriette had 'a much better education than my mother, because her father had been an army man in Spain. And she was very well read; but she wasn't a very good speaker. My mother was a natural born speaker, beautiful speaker.'[26]

Meeting together at the ILP, Selina Cooper and Harriette Beanland had fast become friends, and before long Harriette had become something of an additional aunt to Mary. Certainly the two women made a formidable election pair as together they sat down to work out their manifesto.

Selina's first draft, carefully copied out by her husband in his distinctive copperplate hand, has survived. So also has the final version, the printed manifesto, which she and Harriette Beanland jointly presented to the Nelson electors. The chance preservation of the earlier handwritten draft allows us to penetrate for a rare moment into the mind of a working woman candidate of eighty years ago. It is clear from reading this first draft (which she must have composed with her husband's help) that Selina Cooper chose to present herself to the electors essentially as a socialist candidate. The Coopers' prose is generously larded with slogans about 'the Workers . . . taking . . . into their own hands the administration of the Poor Law', and references to how 'Nelson is an essentially working-class Town [whose] people are mainly those who produce wealth'. With little reference at all to the appropriateness of *women* candidates standing as Guardians, the draft reads as if written before Selina's women's suffrage conversion, with a Hyndman or Irving prompting the Coopers' thoughts.

When it was agreed to present a *joint* manifesto, and when Harriette Beanland began to amend the handwritten draft, much of the language of class conflict was firmly deleted. We can imagine the feminist Miss Beanland arguing long and hard with her socialist friend over what would win support and what would alienate electors. In addition, the Labour Representation Committee officials in Nelson, who were after all backing their candidacies, were hardly likely to agree to a manifesto unacceptable to moderate trade unionists. So out from the final printed version went all references to the wealth-producing workers and how 'our industrial system does not secure to every person the means of earning a bare livelihood'. In instead came a new emphasis on the two candidates being not only Labour candidates but also women. 'It is almost imperative,' the re-drafted manifesto urged, 'that women should be on the Board in order to administer acts and receive confidences that could not be extended to men in the same capacity.' In this way the revised version was modified and tightened and, signed by both women, was soon on its way to the local printers.[27]

Selina Cooper and Harriette Beanland found they were fighting four other candidates (a Liberal alderman, Mrs Robb, a Catholic priest, and a man standing as an independent) for Nelson's four places on the Board of Guardians. This time Selina's candidature was proposed by William Rickard, the leading Labour councillor, and seconded by the chairman of the Nelson Labour Representation Committee, both men of unimpeachable working-class respectability. But in canvassing public support for the election both women also made sure they appealed to people outside the Labour circle. Even before copies of the manifesto were back from the printers, Selina Cooper raced off to talk to the Nelson Guild on 'Poor Law Guardian Work', and Harriette Beanland to entertain a local discussion group with 'Gibraltar up-to-date'.

Polling date was Monday, 28 March 1904. It was a bitterly cold day, with a keen east wind whipping mercilessly along the Nelson streets. To make matters worse, last-minute voters were met by a sudden torrential rainstorm in the evening. Everything seemed set to keep Labour voters at home. Even so, the prospect of no fewer than three women candidates contesting the election apparently kept the polling booths busy.

As soon as eight o'clock struck, the ballot boxes from Lomeshaye school at the bottom of St Mary's Street and from the five other polling stations were carried up to the Town Hall. Here the voting papers were counted under the watchful eye of the Town Clerk. Of the six candidates, only Selina Cooper and Harriette Beanland, on tenterhooks to find out if they had won, remained for the count, as it took nearly an hour to tot up the votes. And then, at nine o'clock, the results were announced. Selina Cooper had risen from near the bottom right up to top the poll, beating

even the Liberal Alderman by four votes. Harriette Beanland
came third, well ahead of the other three. Neither the Catholic
priest nor Mrs Robb was elected. It was a symbolic victory,
echoing Shackleton's 1902 election and Labour's growing
strength in the Town Hall.

The two women Guardians and their jubilant Labour supporters celebrated this splendid result with a victory meeting in
the ILP rooms. Despite the miserable weather, all their friends
turned up. Selina Cooper, buoyed up by her triumph, spoke more
confidently and passionately than she had ever done in her life.
We can hear her new eloquence even through the stilted prose of
the local newspaper reporter's transcription:

> There is a feeling abroad that women should not enter [Guardians'
> elections]. Their mission, people say, is to scrub floors; and I have
> had many insults to take during this fight. I shall, however, con-
> tinue to devote a portion of my time to the Labour movement and
> at the same time do the scrubbing of floors. The longer I continue
> in the [Labour] movement, the more pleased I am that I belong to
> the masses and not to the classes.
>
> I am pleased to have here with me tonight Miss Beanland, and
> although I may not be able to help her in anything pertaining to
> educational matters, yet I shall be able to help her in the work of
> the Guardians so far as my past experience will allow. I hope in
> the future to be true to the Labour Representation Committee . . .
> I thank you for the support you have given to me and to the cause
> we love this day.

She sat down amid applause, and was followed by Harriette
Beanland who made a similar speech:

> We are all working people, and although some people think that
> working folks are only fit to work, we have come to show that we
> are able to think as well. All wealth comes from labour – (hear,
> hear) – but in the past labour has not been represented as it ought
> to have been – (hear, hear) . . . We must claim our rights in the
> government of the country, for poverty is often the misfortune and
> not the fault of some people.[28]

The new Burnley Board of Guardians met in April, and Selina
noted some changes from the familiar faces. Dan Irving and John
Thornton had not been re-elected, much to the glee of the buoyant
Burnley Liberals. The backwoodsmen from the Pendle villages

were still well represented: the Guardians from the Nelson area included Tom Ridehalgh a Tory 'gentleman' from the Blacko hamlet, a farmer called Emmott from equally small Roughlee, and two Nelson Liberals: Alderman Smith Hudson and a Robert Thornton. The conservative rate-savers were still in the majority. But with Harriette Beanland by her side, Selina Cooper no longer felt isolated as the only working woman on the Board.

As the Guardians were again parcelled off to the appropriate local relief committees, Harriette found to her dismay that she was sent, not to the Nelson Committee that Selina sat on, but to Burnley Number Three Committee, miles away and of no interest to her. It outraged Selina that the two women should be forbidden to sit together, and she immediately tabled a protest amendment that Harriette Beanland be transferred back to Nelson, but this was narrowly rejected. A few weeks later Harriette herself tried, but most Guardians seemed to treat this blatant anomaly jocularly ('I object to Miss Beanland being made a laughing stock,' Selina had to reprimand) and the resolution was again defeated.

Worse was to come. The following year, in spring 1905, the same mean trick was played on Selina Cooper. She was removed quite against her wishes from the Nelson Relief Committee to the Padiham one. Furious at this second snub, she complained to the Nelson Representation Committee which promptly passed a resolution, on behalf of its eight thousand members, 'that Mrs Cooper be not asked to sit on any other relief committee but Nelson', and this was forwarded to the next Board meeting. Burnley's leading Liberal minister immediately pooh-poohed any allegation that Selina Cooper had been victimised. But it was suspicious: neither of the women Guardians representing the Labour-dominated town of Nelson was allowed to administer relief to those who elected them. The Liberal *Colne and Nelson Times* further rubbed salt into the wound with a leader backing the Guardians' decision and denying that Selina Cooper had any grounds at all for complaint.[29]

So Nelson might have a Labour MP down in Westminster and might be poised to win a Labour majority on the Town Council, but the Burnley Board of Guardians was still in the hands of Liberal manufacturers and Tory 'gentlemen'. In the face of this, the two Nelson women had to fight very hard to achieve their few small victories. They did manage to enlarge the crucial Visiting Committee and to include Harriette Beanland on it. But their reasonable suggestion that butter rather than unhealthy margarine should be used in the workhouse infirmary was defeated by twenty-one votes to ten.

Often they returned to Nelson from the Burnley Guardians' meeting smarting under the rebuffs they had to endure. They were furious that hard-hearted men who cared only to keep their ratepayers happy should still rule the Poor Law roost. Only years later was Selina Cooper able to look back wryly at these early battles:

> I was a member of the Burnley Board of Guardians for six years, and I was a very quiet member, always obedient to the authority of the chair. But I was the first working woman elected on the Board, [and] the wise men of the East who were there said that as a working woman I was too closely in touch with working people, and instead of putting me on the Nelson Relief Committee – though I was elected from Nelson – they put me on the Padiham committee. That was where my rebel spirit came in. For twelve months I refused to attend the Padiham Committee, and took my place where the electors of Nelson had sent me. For twelve months I did that, and then the Local Government Board came down and persuaded the wiseacres to put me back in my place – and they did so.[30]

While Selina was being helped by Whitehall's timely rescue, she was also playing a central role in the growth of Nelson's Labour movement. Local trade unions now solidly backed it, and the Nelson ILP – Labour's socialist arm – continued to expand, almost doubling its membership between 1903 and 1906. And after the 1905 municipal elections, Labour again triumphed at the polls and could boast six ILP councillors – not as many as big towns like Bradford or Woolwich (which already had an ILP Mayor), but certainly as many as West Ham.

The following January David Shackleton was returned at the 1906 general election with a impressive majority of over eight thousand. And only a few months later Nelson gained its first Labour Mayor, William Rickard, the Cornish pit-boy who, at fifteen, had come up to Nelson to weave at Lomeshaye. This was another major symbolic victory. In Edwardian politics a mayor was no toy-town figure, weighed down by a foolish tricorn hat and heavy chain: he held considerable power as the town's elected leader and, until more recently deprived of the right, sat *ex officio* on the magistrates' bench as chief Justice of the Peace. Small wonder then that socialists like Selina Cooper looked so respectfully on Rickard's mayoralty. 'In the past we have worked too much as iconoclasts,' she suggested at the celebration meeting in the Weavers' Institute, perhaps mindful of her early days in the SDF. 'While it is necessary that we should pull down, we must also show that we can construct' – and a Labour mayor presiding over a forward-looking Labour council was surely one of the best ways of bringing about real municipal socialism.

Mayor Rickard personified for Nelson what few other towns had so far been able to achieve: an effective coalition of trade unions and socialists. And Labour in Nelson did not merely flower at elections and then wither away in between. It kept alive, week in and week out, a vigorous socialist culture, largely based in the ILP, which offered people a genuine social alternative to classes at Salem Chapel or Band of Hope lantern lectures.

Nelson ILP membership expanded so fast that it soon needed larger premises than the rooms traditionally used. A plan for a great new ILP Hall was dreamed of and gradually took shape. And at last, on Saturday, 27 July 1907, a ceremonial laying of the foundation stone took place. Selina Cooper, probably accompanied by both Robert and seven-year-old Mary, walked along from St Mary's Street to join a large crowd congregated at the Co-operative Hall. With them, the Coopers marched behind the local brass band as it struck up with the hymn 'Onward, Christian Soldiers', proceeding up the road to the new site, singing:

> Toilers of the nations,
>   Thinkers of the time,
> Sound the note of battle
>   Loud thro' every clime.
> March ye 'gainst the tyrants,
>   Heedless of their steel,
> Be a band of brothers,
>   Speed the common weal!

> Onward, friends of Freedom,
> Onward for the strife,
> Each for all we struggle,
> One in death and life.

The crowd watched as one of the first ILP women speakers, Katharine Conway (or Katharine Bruce Glasier as she had become since her marriage), laid one of the two foundation stones for the new ILP Hall in honour of two early socialist pioneers, William Morris and one of the *Clarion*'s popular contributors. Then it was the turn of a local ILP member chosen to represent the branch. Selina Cooper stepped forward to lay the second stone. She was, after all, one of its most gifted speakers and influential members.

Selina Cooper told the assembled crowd that she laid the foundation stone in memory of two great women whose work would survive long after their tragic deaths: Caroline Martyn, so beloved of Nelson ILP, whose short life was brought to an untimely end in the service of the movement; and Enid Stacy, the feminist who helped bridge the gulf between the socialist and suffragist campaigns but who never lived to see the full fruit of her work.[32]

After the ILP Hall was opened in 1908, it offered a spacious home to Nelson's many socialist groupings. One of the liveliest of these was the Socialist Sunday School which each week offered its pupils an alternative ceremony to the Sunday School services of the town's many chapels and churches. Selina Cooper felt that this kind of socialist education was vitally important, and used to give occasional talks at the school. One ILP member, then a young boy, can still recall the tales she would tell them on Sunday mornings: of how she had walked up one of Nelson's residential roads, past the big manufacturers' houses with their long drives and notices marked 'private', and just peeked round one of the gates to admire the flowers. She was soon stopped and told this was private land. 'And she spoke of how this beauty was for everyone, surely,' he reminisced, 'and not just to be considered for one or two people who lived in this home. She weren't doing any damage . . . Those are the kind of things that people had a right to – to the beauty in this world, and not all the drabness.'[33]

The Coopers were naturally keen that Mary should benefit

from this alternative education, so lacking in their own child-
hoods. So every Sunday morning Mary would make her way up
to the ILP Hall, clutching her copy of *The Socialist Sunday School
Hymn Book*; at the front of it she had inscribed in her wobbly
child's handwriting 'Mary Cooper 59 St Mary's Street Nelson'.
Certainly among her childhood memories, those of the Socialist
Sunday School stand out particularly vividly:

> It was a good school, a lot of people, good classes. And we didn't
> used to start with religious prayers or anything like that. We used
> to march. The piano were playing, and we did figures – like you
> do at school – figures of eight. And then we settled into our classes
> . . . and sit in a little circle round our teachers . . .
>
>   I tell you what they used to do. They used to . . . have bap-
> tisms – but done by a prominent – Keir Hardie, or something,
> would come down . . . We'd have a middle name like 'Bruce
> Glasier' . . .
>
>   I remember these baptisms . . . quite big affairs. We
> didn't used to have our classes. There'd be a little service . . .
> We'd sing hymns, and 'The Red Flag' . . . I can remember
> these things. Yes, they stand out in my mind.[34]

There was one particular Sunday when Mary was a few years
older that she had particular reason to remember. She played the
central role in a naming ceremony which was reported in the
Nelson Leader:

> Mr Keir Hardie MP, who performed the ceremony, was welcomed
> to the school in a neat little speech by Miss M Cooper, a scholar . . .
> who said that the three chief reasons why they welcomed him were,
> first, because of his championship of the working classes in the
> House of Commons; second because he was in favour of Adult Suf-
> frage which included votes for women; and third, because of his life
> of unselfish devotion to the uplifting of the down-trodden humanity.

Mary and the other scholars sang, Hardie gave a short address
and then, the newspaper adds, he performed the dedication ceremony being 'especially pleased with the baby named Keir
Hardie Clegg and hoped that the infant would be greater than his
namer'. Selina Cooper, who would have gone along to hear her
daughter's welcoming speech to Hardie, must have sat in the ILP
Hall rejoicing that her years on the Burnley Guardians, the rise of
the local Labour Party, and her laying of the ILP stone, had all
borne such rich fruit.[35]

CHAPTER NINE

WOMEN ORGANISE TOGETHER:
1903-1911

Before Selina Cooper laid the foundation stone of the ILP Hall, and even before William Rickard became Nelson's first Labour mayor, there had already sprung up in the town a vigorous women's suffrage group. Selina Cooper was, without doubt, its original inspiration and remained one of its key members right to the very end. Encouraged by Nelson's strong radicalism and by the tradition of women's trade unionism, it also drew in two or three dozen other women in the area, many of them weavers, some of them schoolteachers, at least two of them Guardians. Together they shaped the local Women's Suffrage Society into one of the longest-lived groups in the country.

Suffrage historians have long had to make do without this important local perspective. Although the national tale is often retold, such grassroots experiences have till recently been sadly neglected. Yet it is difficult to understand fully the impact of the suffrage movement unless the feelings of ordinary women up and down the country are taken into some account. Luckily among the Coopers' papers have survived some of this particular local society's records and these, studied alongside oral testimony, local newspaper reports and other documentary evidence, help us imagine something of what an Edwardian suffrage society in a northern industrial town was like.

The suffrage group came about this way. As we have seen, David Shackleton became Labour MP for Clitheroe in August 1902, on the backs – or so argued the suffragists – of thousands of disenfranchised women trade unionists. And, with Shackleton now sitting complacently in the House of Commons, the North of

England Society for Women's Suffrage continued pestering Ramsay MacDonald, reminding him of the embarrassing anomaly of Shackleton's salary depending on the dues of voteless women. The Labour Representation Committee in London steadfastly ignored this northern sniping. Esther Roper grew increasingly impatient. 'I should very much like to know,' she wrote tetchily,

> whether your Committee are aware that . . . the Nelson and District Weavers' Association [which] has affiliated to your Committee [has a membership of] 2,762 men and 3,515 women.
>
> Does your Committee think it can be considered fair to these 3,515 women that they should decline to meet and discuss a Labour question as important as the enfranchisement of women workers?[1]

Labour remained impervious to these pinprick criticisms; so two weeks later Esther Roper wrote again, this time on a more imperious note:

> I should like to put a question, *by word of mouth*, to your Committee, viz.,
>
> 'Do the Committee advocate representation of both male and female labour, and what practical steps are being taken to secure the representation of female labour in view of the fact that women labourers who have no vote cannot be represented?'[2]

The Labour Representation Committee ducked this direct challenge and the unhappy correspondence trickled to a close. But the suffragists did not give up easily. Esther Roper composed a propaganda leaflet, 'The Cotton Trade Unions and the Enfranchisement of Women', which directly attacked what she saw to be Labour's hypocrisy. And signatures from the disenfranchised women members of the textile unions in Shackleton's constituency were again painstakingly collected; Sarah Reddish came up again from Bolton to talk to local women weavers, and once more the Coopers' house buzzed with activity. 'She'd go all over,' said Mary, then a young child for whom her mother's petition sheets soon became part of domestic routine:

> round to the mill gates and on to the streets, and anywhere, up to the houses – backwards and forwards to the houses. Oh, I don't know how she used to do it, because she'd come home and wash

and clean. She was never a lady . . . She was never [stuck] up.[3]

By now Selina Cooper knew every mill and factory gate in the area. By early 1903, 5,500 signatures had been collected – nearly two-thirds of those eligible to sign. A deputation of women trade unionists met Shackleton in the Nelson Weavers' Institute, demanding he introduce women's suffrage during that parliamentary session and reminding him gently that it was their sixpences that enabled him to go down to Westminster in the first place. Shackleton, unable to slide out of it as MacDonald had done, promised to introduce a Women's Franchise Resolution next session. But even at this stage, Selina Cooper must have known that Shackleton was a broken reed. He might nominally be Labour's third MP, but he showed none of Keir Hardie's heartfelt commitment to the women's cause.[4]

So the suffragists turned their attention instead to the tactic used successfully over labour representation: they would ask individual textile trade unions to ballot their members on the question of women's suffrage. Sarah Reddish and Esther Roper raced up and down the region addressing union branch meetings. Selina undertook the job of persuading the unions in the Nelson area. Three-year-old Mary was either left with Grandma Cooper or else taken along too, and in this way Selina managed to address four meetings of local women in the Weavers' Association.

Her efforts were soon rewarded. The Nelson Weavers agreed to ballot its members on women's suffrage being made 'a Trade Union question in the same way that Labour Representation has been made a Trade Union question'. Even better, when the results of the ballot were announced she discovered 4,594 members had voted in favour and a mere 881 against. So the major union in the town had endorsed her claim that women's suffrage was centrally important to the labour movement; and this success was echoed by similar results throughout Lancashire.[5]

As the summer of 1903 slipped into autumn, Selina Cooper and the other suffragists took stock of the situation. Shackleton's behaviour in the Commons was disappointing: he seemingly had not moved a finger to help. Yet, they agreed, they badly needed someone inside Parliament who would single-mindedly press their demands. Selina Cooper, Sarah Reddish, Esther Roper and

Eva Gore-Booth discussed the problem from every angle.[6] Together they devised a daring strategy: they would put up their *own* independent women's suffrage candidate for election in a textile constituency. They knew it would be difficult to do that through the ordinary North of England Women's Suffrage Society; so they decided to form their own separate group, and cast around for a name that would faithfully reflect their political aims. Eventually they plumped for a name which, although awkwardly cumbersome, was at least accurate: the Lancashire and Cheshire Women Textile and Other Workers' Representation Committee. They looked for a suitable constituency, quickly settled on Wigan, drafted a circular 'To the Trade Unions and Working Men of Wigan' and then sat back to wait for the Tory government to resign and call a general election.[7]

While Selina Cooper was involved in launching this new political committee a second suffrage group was being formed in Manchester: the Pankhursts' Women's Social and Political Union. Since the Shackleton election the previous year, Selina had kept in close contact with the Pankhurst family and had a copy of Christabel's penny pamphlet, *The Parliamentary Vote for Women*. Subtitled, 'Political Power Must Precede Social Regeneration', it was a strong plea for breaking down 'the oldest and strongest of tyrannies – the tyranny of sex'. Christabel boldly took up the cudgels on behalf both of the disenfranchised women cotton workers and of middle-class daughters forced to 'choose between a state of dependence with comfort and one of independence with poverty'.

As she read this pamphlet Selina Cooper could see the seeds of Christabel's impatience with the Labour movement. Before long Christabel did indeed begin to criticise publicly both the Labour Representation Committee's apathy towards women and the timidity of the ILP. Mrs Pankhurst still retained her old faith in the ILP, but recognised too the need for an independent pressure group which could niggle away at Labour. Thus was formed the Women's Social and Political Union (WSPU) at the Pankhursts' house in October 1903. To exert pressure, Mrs Pankhurst planned to bring up the women's suffrage issue again at the next ILP Conference; and Christabel continued to taunt Labour politicians for their complacency on the suffrage issue in the

Commons. 'Even Mr Shackleton,' Christabel wrote accusingly in the *Nelson Leader*, 'who . . . is financially dependent to a greater extent on women than on men, was silent.' Shackleton replied that he *had* tried to catch the Speaker's eye, rose three times in the debate, but was not called. 'As to the personal reference to myself being "financially dependent",' Shackleton replied pompously, 'I had hoped for better things from the quarter from which it came.'[8]

With the formation of these two new groups in 1903, the suffrage campaign in the north moved into a higher gear. Up to now most of the activity had centred either on Manchester or on Nelson. This new energy rippled outwards to touch the lives of women further afield. Under the broad umbrella of the North of England Society (and therefore linked to Mrs Fawcett's giant National Union of Women's Suffrage Societies) seventeen small suffrage committees were formed in various northern towns such as Bolton and Burnley, Keighley and Wakefield. One of the smallest communities to boast its own suffrage committee by the end of the year was, of course, Nelson and Colne, with Selina Cooper as its founding secretary.[9]

Urged on by her suffrage friends in Manchester, Selina Cooper undertook the formidable task of building up the local group from nothing. From the beginning Selina Cooper recognised that merely to rely on the handful of individual women whom she had already won over to active support of suffrage would no longer be sufficient. Instead she must seek backing from existing political groups in Nelson. In these early days Liberalism was still predominant in the town. So Selina naturally turned to Nelson's strong Women's Liberal Association when she took her first tentative steps to recruit potential suffragists. Selina had scant sympathy for Liberals, but she recognised that the Association had already shown an active interest in women's suffrage and even contributed to the North of England Society funds.

In about October 1903, shortly after helping launch the Lancashire Women Textile Workers' Representation Committee, Selina began to plan the Nelson women's 'representation committee'; and she asked Sarah Thomas, the unsuccessful temperance candidate in the Guardians' election, to be president. Sarah Thomas' Liberal Nonconformist background made her an ideal figurehead and she successfully presided at the inaugural meeting of the 'representation committee' held under the auspices of the Nelson Women's Liberal Association. A Manchester suffragist came up for this crucial meeting and explained about the election plans for Wigan, appealing to every woman textile worker to give sixpence (the amount, after all, that took Shackleton to Westminster) to help the campaign.

Over the next few years Nelson's political balance shifted dramatically. As the Labour Representation Committee began to flourish, Labour women became drawn into the suffrage committee. Sarah Thomas found herself almost swamped by Labour women who saw Liberalism as stuffy and old-fashioned. 'I were connected with the Women's Suffrage Movement,' she reminisced later, 'and elected to the committee. They were very near all Labour, but one, that were on that committee.' Still, she took all this in good part, and was soon busy collecting signatures for yet a further suffrage petition.[10]

One of the first Labour women Selina Cooper persuaded to join the suffrage committee was, of course, Harriette Beanland. The elegant dressmaker was so incensed by the shabby way she was being treated on the Board of Guardians, and so convinced a feminist, she needed little persuasion to throw her lot in with the suffrage movement.

By the end of 1904, the two women Guardians were busy organising an impressive suffrage meeting in the great Salem Chapel school hall. Helped by Eva Gore-Booth and Sarah Reddish, they persuaded David Shackleton to chair the meeting. Indeed, they demonstrated publicly that the local labour movement *did* endorse the women's cause: up on the platform was the Nelson Labour Representation Committee chairman while on the floor of the hall in the audience sat most of the Labour councillors, and the meeting was opened by the ILP choir singing 'Hail, Bounteous May'. Shackleton, obviously primed by Selina Cooper and others beforehand, gave a worthy speech urging that women's suffrage be made a test question for the next election. Selina then proposed that the Tory government should introduce a bill to enfranchise women, and dealt smartly with some anti-suffragist arguments about stay-at-home women who didn't go out to work.

It all went according to plan. Both in Nelson and elsewhere the suffrage campaign gained valuable converts in the labour movement. In her secretary's *Annual Report* 1904–5 for the North of England Society, Esther Roper was able to report how

> such a stir has been made during the last twelve months and the question has become so prominent amongst labour people of all shades of opinion, that there is no doubt that the pressure of working-class feeling, and especially of the claims of the women cotton workers, are beginning to force the attentions of practical politicians . . .[11]

Selina Cooper had by now established herself as a central figure in these stirring times. She was invited to speak further afield and, with Mary now at Lomeshaye elementary school, she was able to go. She addressed meetings in Burnley with Sarah Reddish and Esther Roper, and a large audience in Blackburn, with Sarah Reddish again and with a valuable new ally, the recently-converted ILP orator, Philip Snowden. It was all most encouraging. But there was a world of difference, Selina reminded herself grimly, between the soothing words of a politician like Shackleton and his practical deeds.

Among this widening support, the suffragists won a crucial ally: the Women's Co-operative Guild. When suffrage had been discussed at its last Annual conference, some Guildswomen had voiced genuine worries as to whether the proposed women's suffrage legislation would really give the vote to working women like themselves, whose husbands paid the rent or mortgage on their homes. But although they entertained such doubts, in the end they voted emphatically in favour of women's suffrage. This was an extremely encouraging victory for, as Selina Cooper knew, it meant winning the support of the only national organisation that could speak for married working-class women. She could now ask Nelson Guildswomen to join the suffrage committee, confident that she could quote national policy decisions.

But she remained anxious about Guildswomen's doubts. Some of them had even written to 'Women's Corner' in the *Co-operative News* alleging that the bill currently being considered would only enfranchise wealthy women with property in their own names and so leave ordinary Guildswomen out. This was a vital argument that the suffragists must win. And the only way to win was by producing figures to back up their case.

So a series of investigations was begun to show what a high proportion of working women would indeed benefit from the current bill. Keir Hardie, always the most loyal suffrage champion, initiated a survey carried out by ILP branches; and at the same time the Women's Co-operative Guild and the Lancashire Women Textile Workers' Representation Committee began another, investigating specific wards in the country and entrusting Robert and Selina with the major responsibility.

The Coopers' task was to select a typical ward in Nelson, and then to go round house-to-house, counting up how many women would be enfranchised under the bill, and what proportion of them were 'working women'. It was a time-consuming job, and one that could really only be done in the evenings, after Robert and other mill workers were home. But they were able to publish their joint survey in the *Co-operative News* in early 1905, the results of which they interpreted very optimistically. Selina and Robert calculated that if the existing household and lodger franchise were extended to women, nearly five hundred women in the ward would become parliamentary voters. Of these, only two were 'rich women householders' and five teachers. Of the rest, half were weavers while the remainder worked as winders, dressmakers, charwomen, as well as a tripe dealer, corset-maker, midwife and so on. Doing their sums when they got home (presumably Robert's responsibility for he was better at figures than his wife) the Coopers calculated that in this ward 95 per cent of the new voters would be 'working women'. And, just to be absolutely certain of their claim, Robert and Selina spent laborious hours tracing the occupation of every single woman listed in Nelson's municipal register; and so were able to confirm that for the whole town no fewer than 93 per cent of women enfranchised as house holders in local government elections were indeed 'working women'.

Similarly, investigations by Guildswomen in Leeds, Cambridge and elsewhere (coupled with Keir Hardie's ILP survey) seemed to show that well over 80 per cent of women who would benefit from the bill were 'working women'. Selina, Robert, their friend Keir Hardie and the other suffragists, must have drawn comfort from this brave show of statistics. But in fact the figures were of doubtful worth. The areas covered were by no means representative of the whole country: certainly Nelson had an usually high proportion of married women who did waged work outside the home. In addition, the phrase 'working women' was so vague as to be almost meaningless. Certainly the opponents of women's suffrage remained unconvinced that many married women had much hope of benefiting from the bill.

Yet we must accept that Selina Cooper saw the figures as genuine. The fight for women's suffrage she now knew had to take precedence over everything else. The campaign was accelerating far too fast to allow time for pedantic reservations or nagging doubts. During the summer of 1905 Selina was busy organising and addressing meetings, especially for the Lancashire Women Textile Workers' Representation Committee. Even Robert became caught up: at a meeting on Brierfield's market ground he was persuaded to join his wife on the makeshift platform and give a speech even though he knew he had none of her eloquence. Then for the general election in January 1906, Selina raced across to campaign for their suffrage candidate in Wigan. Introduced to the crowd as a member of the Burnley Board of Guardians, she made a powerful speech to quieten the fears of working-class men that to give women the vote would hinder Labour's progress. 'Every woman in England is longing for her political freedom,' she told the Wigan electors, 'in order to make the lot of the worker pleasanter and to bring about reforms that are wanted. We do not want it as a mere plaything,' she said to a round of applause from the crowd.[13] When the Wigan election results were announced she learnt that their suffrage candidate had lost to the Tory; but at least he had beaten the Liberal, so Selina could count her midwinter trip across to Wigan a reasonable success. (Overall, of course, the Liberals emerged triumphant from the general election and formed a government with an unshakeable majority.)

By the summer of 1906 the Nelson Suffrage Committee had established itself in the town. Selina Cooper saw the time was ripe to launch it more publicly as a proper Women's Suffrage Society. She was confident that this was the right thing to do, for she could now draw on the active support of two valuable new recruits:

Margaret Aldersley and Ula Blackburn.

Margaret Aldersley was older than Selina Cooper. The daughter of a miner and mother of four children, with many years experience of mill work, she possessed the reassuring solidity of comfortable middle-age. She was active in both the Co-operative movement and the ILP and was soon to become Nelson's third woman Guardian. Unlike Harriette Beanland she was already an accomplished public speaker, happy to climb upon a soap-box and take on the crowd. Therefore, at the first public meeting of the newly-launched Nelson and District Suffrage Society that summer, it was Mrs Aldersley who chaired the meeting and who first stepped forward to speak her mind:

> We have been ruled by men long enough . . . Although in Nelson we are in a good position so far as the textile trade is concerned, there are many parts [of the country] where it is thought that women should not have the same wages as men. This is an injustice, and all we want is . . . not . . . to have to look up to the men for all we want. We as women are oppressed in many ways by being ruled by men only.

The second new recruit was related to Harriette Beanland. Ula Blackburn was a mill worker and keen Guildswoman from Burnley. About the same age as Selina Cooper, she too had been a half-timer and used to tell her nephew tales of the bad old days when mothers brought their babies to work and left them in a weft can. 'And at feeding time,' he recalled her saying, 'the other ladies'd gather round and run her looms while she went out to the toilet to feed.'

Ula Blackburn, a strong character and, according to her nephew, 'Mrs Cooper again in looks', was another ideal speaker for the inaugural meeting. After Margaret Aldersley had stepped back, and after Selina Cooper had put the women's key argument ('No sex can legislate for another sex, no more than one class can legislate for another'), it was Ula Blackburn's turn. She put paid to some of the anti-suffrage arguments being floated, even in a town like Nelson, that women's place was in the home. 'We are not anti-men, but want to work with him . . . Women are good enough . . . to help pay off debts, but when it comes to voting, we are not considered good enough for that.'

At the end of the meeting, Margaret Aldersley moved a resolution demanding women workers' political rights, protesting 'with indignation and alarm against the indifferent and dilatory attitude of the government,' and urging it to introduce a bill immediately to give women the vote. Selina Cooper seconded the resolution and it was carried. This public launching of the new Suffrage Society in 1906 marked the flowering of the women's campaign in Nelson.[14]

Other women joined too. One was Emily Murgatroyd, a young weaver from Brierfield whose family originally came from Yorkshire. She heard about the Society, contacted Selina Cooper, and so became drawn in. Another was Nancy Shimbles, also a young weaver and active in the Nelson Weavers' Association. The Coopers knew her because she was in the ILP and taught Mary 'physical culture' and drill each week at the Socialist Sunday school.

Now was the time to attract all local women to the society, and Selina Cooper never let possible new members slip through her fingers. She even tried to persuade her relations. She had no luck with Grandma Cooper, now a widow and still a dour Primitive Methodist; Grandma Cooper used to threaten to use the household mangle to tie her erring daughter-in-law down to her house and family. ' "I'm going to put your mother –" ' she would threaten Mary ' "– your mother's skirt – and wind her in there." ' Robert's brother and sisters were less antagonistic, but Selina still had a hard job interesting them in her new-fangled notions. It was much the same story with her own Coombe relations. With Alf in the army, they tended to take a dim view of women's demand for a voice in national politics. After all, it was men, not women, who risked their lives defending Britain's empire around the world. In fact, the only one of her sisters-in-law Selina managed to recruit was Bill's wife, Mary Ann Coombe, who lived in Brierfield.

Mary knew her aunt Mary Ann very well for each weekend, after Socialist Sunday School, Mary recalls, 'My father used to take me on, on Sunday morning. You could get along by the river . . . And my aunt Mary Ann would be making the dinner.' Uncle Bill was the engineer at Tunstills, and his wife 'was a chain beamer.* Yes. A woman chain beamer. And she was very proud of her home and that. Because she earned money.' Mary Ann Coombe had emigrated from Ireland, though she dropped her Catholicism afterwards. 'She was a very strong socialist,' Mary Cooper explained, 'and she worshipped my mother.' Certainly Mary Ann became a keen member of the Suffrage Society. Another valuable recruit was Mary Ann's next door neighbour, Florence Shuttleworth. These two friends 'trotted about together', according to Mary. She and her husband, both weavers, had come to Nelson from the radical Pennine villages around Skipton and Keighley. Florence Shuttleworth was a keen ILP member and became president of the Nelson Guild; she had eight children and would return to the mill between babies. The Coombe and Shuttleworth families, keen *Clarion* readers, set off together at weekends to the nearby Clarion House. 'And there'd be Aunt Mary Ann and Mrs Shuttleworth – not my Uncle [Bill], but Mr Shuttleworth, and my aunt Mary Ann's two sons, and a whole crowd of kids from the street,' Mary recalled.[15]

Based on the support of such women – Ula Blackburn, Mary Ann Coombe, Florence Shuttleworth and the others – the Nelson Suffrage Society now began to hold regular members' meetings in the Coopers' small front room. Mary was just six when the society started, and was a fascinated eye-witness to everything that occurred. Years later she still retained her child-hood impressions of all these people squashed into her house:

> I can remember making the coffee. And I thought I was doing great . . . I was about eight, and there was a crowd of women in here . . . There were minutes taken and all that sort of thing . . . And my father kept the books – the cash, the accountancy.

Sadly the Nelson Suffrage Society minute books appear not to have survived. But one of Robert Cooper's account books dating from 1912 (the earlier ones are missing) has been preserved and bears out the accuracy of his daughter's recollections. From Robert's scrupulously kept notebook the members of the society spring to life. Here are inscribed the names of Emily Murgatroyd, with her sister and her mother, who each sub-

---

* A chain beamer took the warp threads and drew these ends on to a long cylindrical beam ready for the weavers' looms.

scribed sixpence to funds; of Selina and Robert Cooper; and of Mary Ann Coombe and Florence Shuttleworth who could each only manage to contribute threepence.

Clearly none could afford to give the society more than a shilling each year. Members were apparently supposed to pay threepence a quarter, but for many this was impossible to find from their weavers' wages. Certainly Nancy Shimbles and Margaret Aldersley could only contribute their threepences irregularly. Others could not even do that. Some were so poor, Mary Cooper explained, that all they could afford to pay was an occasional penny or two towards the coffee.[16]

Robert Cooper's meticulous entries also tell us a considerable amount about the Nelson Suffrage Society which even Mary's childhood memories and a careful reading of the local newspapers fail to reveal. It gives us the name of each of the three dozen subscribing members of the society and allows us to trace the links between this membership and that of other groups in the town. What soon becomes clear is the number of Guildswomen who became suffragists: Selina Cooper, of course, Margaret Aldersley and Florence Shuttleworth, but others as well: Clara Myers, a schoolteacher's widow, ILP member and Nelson Guild president; Deborah Smith, the daughter of illiterate parents, who first attended school when she became a half-timer aged ten and who gained her education through the Guild (for she had helped form the Nelson branch in 1892 and subsequently became its secretary); and a Mrs Kershaw, an ILP member who was on the Guild committee, but about whom little else is known.[17]

Indeed, the account book reminds us how little is recorded of the lives of grass-roots suffragists. Names appear among the subscribers of women who otherwise seem to disappear from history. Who, we might wonder, was Miss Rickard, who subscribed her threepence to society funds? Was she perhaps the sister or daughter of the mayor, William Rickard? How was Nurse Duckworth able to subscribe a whole shilling? And how did the elusive Miss Walton or Miss Green become involved in the campaign? What we can be certain of is that the Nelson Suffrage Society was run on a shoestring. Its annual income totalled no more than a pound or two. Yet Robert Cooper's accounts make it vividly clear that shortage of funds never hampered the enthusiasm of the members. This little group, tucked away in north-east Lancashire, still managed to pay its five shilling affiliation fee to Mrs Fawcett's National Union of Women's Suffrage Societies, hire meeting rooms, buy suffrage literature plus buns and milk for refreshments, have handbills printed – and still have enough left over to tip the postman sixpence at Christmas (well deserved, for the Nelson suffragists were prolific letter writers). Mary Cooper distinctly remembers how busy meetings were when she was small:

> They used to stick to business. Then they'd have, you know, any other business and coffee and a chat. But they always went through business, you see. There was always something. 'Cos I remember listening at the keyhole, you know what I mean, listening at the door. I was puzzled by it, couldn't understand it. But – there was always some resolution going before a trade union, or they were going to go and march somewhere, or go and help – they used to help candidates that were suffrage.[18]

As the battle intensified, and the new Liberal Government still remained deaf to suffragists' reason, fighting elections and helping sympathetic candidates became increasingly important to the strategy of the National Union. But the local suffrage societies which had sprung up around the country wherever women decided to organise together had evolved spontaneously with little regard for parliamentary boundaries.

In 1909–10, in recognition of this problem, the National Union reorganised its many small societies on constituency lines. It was a daunting task for just as the Nelson Suffrage Society had mushroomed over the last few years, so had the National Union itself. In 1906 it boasted only thirty-one branch societies; but by 1910 this had mushroomed to over two hundred.

So the Nelson Women's Suffrage Society, along with the others, fell in with this new National Union directive. It was renamed the Clitheroe Society and tried to cover the whole of Shackleton's sprawling constituency. Here it was aided by another imaginative National Union innovation: the forming of regional federations. These great federations were invaluable in co-ordinating campaigning activity in their areas and offering local societies a link with the London headquarters. The Clitheroe

Society became part of the strong Manchester and District Federation, which was soon encouraging new branches to be formed in Accrington, Burnley and elsewhere.[19]

The new Clitheroe Society was launched with due ceremony on Tuesday evening, 18 May 1909, at a 'drawing room meeting at Mrs Moser's residence, Laurel Villas'. (Mr and Mrs Moser and their daughter were active members of the society and, compared with the Coopers, lived in a spacious house fronted by a small garden; Miss Moser was the French mistress at Nelson's grammar school.) Robert Cooper outlined the political workings of the constituency. Then Selina explained how the National Union worked and what it hoped to achieve. Fifteen or sixteen people immediately signed up to join and the officers were elected: Mrs Aldersley, now a Poor Law Guardian, as president; Miss Moser, the elusive Miss Walton, Ula Blackburn and Deborah Smith as vice-presidents; an ILP member called Clara Baldwin as secretary; and Clara Myers as treasurer. Meanwhile Selina, particularly adept at lobbying, undertook the house-to-house visiting necessary to convince the half-hearted of the urgency of women's suffrage. This inaugural gathering also planned a big public meeting in Nelson and decided that, of all the nationally-known suffrage speakers, they would invite Charlotte Despard to address them.[20]

It was a revealing choice. Mrs Despard, wealthy Irish eccentric, was a remarkable woman. After her husband's death in 1890, she gave up her comfortable widow's life and went to live in Battersea in south London. She became a Poor Law Guardian and an active socialist and, helped by Keir Hardie's arguments, was finally won over to the suffrage campaign. She joined the Pankhursts' Women's Social and Political Union (which had recently moved from Manchester to London) and threw herself impetuously into the suffrage struggle, eventually getting imprisoned. But Mrs Despard grew disenchanted with what she saw as the WSPU's autocratic structure and its misguided militant tactics. Then, about the time she came up to Nelson, she chanced to meet a young Indian lawyer called Gandhi whose ideas about passive resistance struck a ready chord with her. It was a form of resistance that also appealed directly to Nelson's radical tradition. Little wonder, then, that its big Weavers' Institute was packed with people curious to find out what this majestic white-haired suffragette, in her black lace mantilla and open sandals, had to say.[21]

Ula Blackburn opened the meeting with a rousing speech. 'People after people, and class after class,' she cried, 'have won their freedom, but through it all woman has been a slave . . . Women do not intend to give up this fight until they have won it.' Then Margaret Aldersley spoke from her own experiences: 'As mothers and citizens we cannot do our full duty until we are enfranchised.' Finally Clara Baldwin, as Society secretary, introduced Mrs Despard.

That afternoon Selina Cooper had gone round to Mrs Moser's house to meet Mrs Despard, and now was sitting in the audience to listen to her speak on 'Women as Citizens'. She heard Charlotte Despard soberly recount the tale of her imprisonment at the hands of the Liberal Government, and hint at the shift in her ideas towards Gandhian passive resistance:

> the militant tactics have made the question into a living question . . . The suffragettes . . . [tried to] present a petition . . . We simply went to the House of Commons in February last to assert our citizens' rights. We did not obstruct anybody, but the police obstructed us. I was given a month in the second division . . . We went again and again and we were not arrested, which shows that we have gained some ground. We were going to try and prove that we have a constitutional right to present petitions . . . Women are actually citizens. The proper basis of citizenship is 'No right without duty, and no duty without right'. . . . We are asking for the vote so that we might get our proper place, for at present we are slaves, as slavery is to have to obey laws over which we have no control.[22]

Mrs Despard, who was developing plans for women to resist paying tax and to boycott the census, made it all sound so easy. Winning the vote, she assured her audience, would bring about 'a better world, a holier, purer, and more beautiful world for men, women and children.' But even Mrs Despard's eloquence could not smooth away all the little bumps and irritations that suffragists – men, women and children – encountered regularly in a small northern town like Nelson.

Selina Cooper had by now become adept at dealing with anti-women prejudice. She never took it personally and so managed to rise serenely above it. Mary had a harder time. Until she was twelve, she went to Lomeshaye elementary school whose hard-pressed teachers, facing unwieldly classes of sleepy half-timers, had scant sympathy for 'suffragettes'. Mary recalls how she was

> teased when I was very little . . . going to this school down here . . . I used to have papers pinned on my back, and I never knew what people'd be laughing at until I got home. 'Suffragette'. And people'd pass and laugh. I'd get back and say, 'What's the matter?' My mother'd turn round and say, '[They've] put another paper on you'. You see, pinned on: 'Suffragette', 'Socialist'. And I used to walk jauntily home, and . . . my mother says, 'You're not upset?' I says, 'No.' She says, 'Well, you won't have to be.' She says, 'You can't be a suffragette and get upset.' And they gave over after a bit.

Mary robustly survived the classroom jibes and her mother's sharp tongue, and when she was twelve won a scholarship that would keep her at grammar school for four years. Here she found the atmosphere more tolerant: the children might still tease her, but at least some of the teachers were suffragists and friends of her mother:

> I remember at grammar school once . . . and I remember that they did pin things on my back. And one of the teachers who was suffragette-inclined and knew my mother, and says, 'Who's put that on Mary? Come out here! Who's put it on?' And none of them spoke – it was a big class.
>   'That's done it again,' [the teacher said, all you lot can go] 'into the schoolmaster, and you know what sort of cane he's got'. And [all the time] I didn't know there was anything on my back.
>   She [the teacher] was quite friendly with my mother. She was called Miss Moser, and she spoke French beautifully . . . And a teacher at school called Miss Cliff – and she was friendly too. They were all friendly, were the suffrage movement, and they used to come here for meetings. So they stuck up for me.[23]

On the whole, carefree Mary thrived on having a mother who was a suffragist, and when she was fifteen she too began to contribute her shilling to Suffrage Society funds. For Robert it was less easy. By Edwardian standards, a woman's demanding the vote somehow emasculated her husband. It undermined all the traditional notions of his rightful control over his wife. An especially sorry figure, people thought, was the husband of a suffragist: while his wife was gadding about preaching women's rights, who would cook his tea when he came home tired from work? A man who sympathised with the cause for which his wife campaigned must be entirely soft.

Certainly, local gossip had it that Robert Cooper was henpecked by his formidable wife. He and Selina, for one reason or another, now slept in separate beds. 'He was a very meek-looking little man, nice fellow,' explained one local weaver. 'I never spoke to him, and like I just knew he was Mrs Cooper's husband.' Indeed, as his wife's star rose, Robert seemed to shrink further back inside himself, a lonely and introverted man. Robert spent his Sundays out walking, either on his own, with a friend or with Mary. He must have grown wistful that he and Selina could no longer enjoy trips like their long-ago Keld summer. Instead he would set out with Mary on the tram to Colne, walking over to Skipton to watch the sheep dog trials or travelling further north up into the Dales in summertime to help with the harvest. In the autumn, though, Robert would have to leave farming for his dreary set of looms. He hated it and the damp atmosphere of the weaving shed seemed only to make his poor health worse. He went away to convalesce at one stage, but despaired of real change. Selina was increasingly caught up in the suffrage campaign; but for Robert there was no way forward. All his painfully-acquired education at evening classes would never transform him into a magnetic speaker like his wife. Everything seemed to conspire to alienate Robert Cooper from Selina's heartfelt commitment to women's suffrage. Yet this was not the case. For Robert was a fair man and a logical thinker: he could see no way round the suffragists' argument that if men needed independent labour representation so, even more urgently, did women. Unlike many other Edwardian husbands, he gave his wife all the help she needed. He became a key member of the Suffrage Society, often the only man present. He undertook the door-to-door survey, he kept the accounts and helped his wife out with her correspondence, knowing that writing and arithmetic were not her strong points. He joined the Men's League for Women's Suffrage and, according to one postcard, was sometimes in urgent demand at meetings:

> Mr Cooper could you come to Brierfield tomorrow night and try
> to get Mr Moser to come along as their [sic] is a lecture at the
> liberal club open to anyone we have approached the committee but
> they wont have women speaker[s] they say it would create a uproar
> so we thought if you could come along and ask a question . . .

Whether or not Robert agreed to confront the Brierfield
Liberals, he must at times have felt remorse as he saw his talented
wife grow away from him. Yet, even during his illness, he never
seems to have stood in her path.[24]

Much of Robert Cooper's experience was the lowly humdrum
stuff of suffrage politics: collecting subscriptions, writing to politicians, finding speakers for meetings and putting them up for the
night. All his entries in his account book testify to that. But one
particular summer's day when Mary was eleven, the society
members – including all three Coopers – were involved in something different.

In mid-1911, after futile years of suffrage bills passing their
second readings and then disappearing for good, it seemed to the
weary women that perhaps the vote was at last within reach. A
Conciliation Bill, designed to appease all parties, had recently
passed its second reading with a strong majority; and the Liberal
Government had promised adequate parliamentary time for the
third reading. This was good news indeed. A spirit of optimism
and reconciliation washed over the various suffrage groups. So
when the WSPU organised a 'Women's Coronation Procession'
in London for mid-June, the National Union of Women's
Suffrage Societies agreed to take part.

Selina Cooper quickly got to work. She was in touch with the
Manchester Federation suffragists, and it was agreed to organise
a special train down to London from Colne and Nelson. Selina's
job was to fill it, so she rushed a small advertisement into the local
paper:

A GREAT WOMEN'S SUFFRAGE PROCESSION
IN LONDON ON SATURDAY JUNE 17th

On the above date a special train will leave Colne and Nelson to
Euston; Colne 8.25, Nelson 8.30 am. Return fare 11/-
Tickets and further information may be obtained from Mrs
Cooper, 59 St Mary's St, Nelson

Eleven shillings was a forbidding sum for a weaver to raise. Luckily, the resourceful Manchester Federation raised money to pay for 300 'assisted tickets' so that working people could join the procession. Some of these tickets were allocated to Nelson, and in this way Selina Cooper managed to persuade her brother John's wife, Annie Coombe, who had previously 'thought they were all daft' to join in. 'There was hundreds went down,' Annie's son explained. 'They got paid for – their railway fares . . . else they'd have to walk it.'

In all, about sixty people from the Clitheroe Society said they would go. The society banner, newly made and bearing emblems of a cotton plant and a red rose of Lancashire, was carefully rolled up and two labels attached in preparation for its long journey south. Summer clothes were brought out of closets and spruced up for the occasion. Straw hats were decorated with flowers, and picnics were packed in small baskets to keep the travellers going through the long day.

At last the suffragists gathered early in the morning on the station platform, everyone dressed in their best clothes; and, as the steam train chugged into sight, the *Nelson Leader* photographer captured the moment with a picture of the group posing on the platform under a gas lamp.

Eleven-year-old Mary, wearing a sash in the suffragist colours – red, green and white – over her shoulder, had made her way to the front of the group: she was after all the youngest person present. To the right of her stands her father clutching an umbrella in one hand and the banner in the other. Beyond him, Margaret Aldersley's daughter, a few years older than Mary, also sports a suffrage sash. Beyond her, at the right-hand end of the front row is Mrs Aldersley, now the Clitheroe Society president as well as a Guardian, in a dark suit, white blouse and black-and-white hat. Tucked behind her to the left is Nancy Shimbles in a large dark hat. To Mary Cooper's immediate left, stands Mrs Todd, an ILP member and Socialist Sunday School teacher with her stiff panama. Beyond her is Selina Cooper herself, looking sunny and relaxed, resplendent in a long pale dress and wide-brimmed straw hat decorated with flowers. Towards the back stands Harriette Beanland wearing a grand dark-coloured hat, its generous brim swept upwards away from her face (though slightly obscured in the photograph by the pole of the banner). Tucked away modestly at the very back are the two other men, Mr Moser and the Society's auditor, Mr Kershaw. And among the group, though not immediately identifiable, stand suffragists like founder-member Sarah Thomas.

The Colne train drew into the station and they all clambered on. Reinforcements also joined them at Burnley, Accrington, Blackburn, Darwen and Bolton, arriving at Manchester's grand Victoria Station nearly two hours later. Altogether 630 members of the Federation joined the special train, and, as an eye-witness from Nelson later described, at Victoria,

> enthusiasm reached its height, where hundreds of women, many in University robes, and all wearing the colours of the different suffrage societies, boarded us. We did not know our train again, for it seemed to mysteriously expand to an enormous length, and at Stockport and Crewe we had further additions, till in a train over half a mile long corridored from end to end, and carrying nearly 1,000 suffragists, we rushed and roared over the metals at express speed to London.
>
> It was a unique experience in British railway travelling . . . It rather seemed like being in a merry beehive. A peep into one compartment found busy fingers making up rosettes and sashes for those who had failed to supply themselves with these emblems; in the corridors pretty girls sold badges and suffrage papers. In the saloons, secretaries wrote industriously, regardless of the sixty miles an hour pace of the swaying train! Committee meetings were held and a scratch choir was formed by an energetic lady to go round and teach the occupants of every compartment the marching song!

At Euston wagonettes carried the Clitheroe contingent through London to Whitehall. Here they unfurled their banner and lined up neatly to form a five-abreast column with the other Manchester Federation societies. The procession, a triumph of organisation, comprised about 40,000 women and was seven miles long. It took no less than three hours to pass and poor Mary had to wait a full hour before she could move off. 'At last our turn came,' the eye-witness report continued,

> we got our order to march, and . . . away we went, through dense crowds of spectators. Many and various were the remarks we over-

heard en route: 'Good old Clitheroe!' . . . 'Play up, Nelson'.
'Hurrah for the Lancashire weavers!' Trafalgar Square greeted us
with tremendous cheers from its packed multitudes.[25]

The Coopers were particularly amused when they walked
through the West End. 'We pass through Pall Mall where all the
clubs are,' Selina Cooper scribbled down later, 'at one of the clubs
a young blood call from one of the windows to the Lancashire
section, "Who washes your old man shirt". The pat reply went
over to him '."Ho! We keeps Maid to do that" '. Among the
marchers were suffragettes who had been to prison, each one
dressed in white and carrying a small silver pennant. Young
Sylvia Pankhurst, already haunted by personal doubts about the
direction the WSPU was heading under her elder sister's leadership, stood on the steps of the Albert Hall, 'to watch the mighty
procession roll on, feeling sadly aloof from all this jubilation,
convinced that the end was not yet'.[26]

Mary Cooper was far too wrapped up in all the pageantry and
excitement to share Sylvia's adult anxieties, and soon found it was
time to wend her way back to Euston. This was where Mary's
problems began. She found herself with her Socialist Sunday
School drill teacher, Nancy Shimbles, separated from the rest of
the Clitheroe group. The two of them tried to make their way back
together through the crowd to the station. But Nancy Shimbles
had lost her sense of direction and began to panic:

> She got hysterical . . . She'd never been to London before. And it
> was midnight, and we asked one or two people and they seemed to
> purposely mislead us. And we were wandering about these places.
> We only wanted to get to Euston Station. And neither of us had a
> penny . . . I was only at school. So cheeky me went and got a taxi.
> And my mother and father going quite loopy – hunting all over for
> we'd wandered quite a long way into London.
>
>   It was quite a heavy fare . . . At Euston Station . . . I'm run-
> ning round and the taxi driver's after me and saying – I said, 'I'll
> find my mother and father. If I don't, somebody'd pay.' And the
> train was in to go back. And she was still hysterical, was Miss
> Shimbles . . .
>
>   Anyhow, I saw my father first, and I spotted him and – I think
> he'd to see my mother first before he'd enough to pay. And we
> paid this man, and then – I don't think she calmed down till we
> were well on the way back to Nelson.[27]

CHAPTER TEN

THE LABOUR PARTY DESERTS WOMEN:
1905-1907

The Suffrage Society in Nelson survived through the long years, putting most of its energies into local campaigns. During this early period, the only member involved nationally was Selina Cooper. Until 1907 she pinned many of her hopes for women's suffrage on the Labour Party, which now had about thirty MPs at Westminster. After all, she had helped form the party locally and was a Labour-nominated Guardian. Her faith, it turned out, was misplaced. Between 1905 and 1907 the Labour Party decided to desert her and to desert her cause. This chapter tells the tale of this desertion, and therefore opens up Selina's story from the local focus it has so far occupied and shifts it to the national story. The story unfolds against a background of Selina's friendship with Mrs Pankhurst, of the growth of the National Union, and of the escalation of suffragette militancy.

Selina Cooper was beginning to find the anti-woman spirit in the Labour Party disconcertingly vigorous. By adopting the word 'Labour' in its title, the party firmly stressed waged work outside the home and gave a commanding voice to the big battalions of organised workers, the trade unions. Many of the socialist ideas about women and the family such as the endowment of motherhood or birth control that had interested Selina Cooper were set aside by the Labour Party, keen to woo great trade unions like the miners and textile workers away from their Liberal allegiances. As a result, the Labour Party preferred women not to assert their demand for the vote too loudly, for otherwise its carefully constructed party unity might be upset and its programme of social reform set back for years. Although it was the only major party to feel real concern for the lives of working women, even so, Labour politicians like Ramsay MacDonald and David Shackleton still shilly-shallied over women's suffrage, never denying the women's claims but never exerting themselves about it.[1]

Adult suffragists had, as we have seen, slumbered quietly since the 1884 Reform Act extended the vote to about two-thirds of all adult men. Occasional flickers of wakefulness soon faded. As Selina Cooper's first Guardian election showed, the main opposition at the turn of the century to women's rights came from old-fashioned Tories (and Liberals) who still believed the sexes' separate spheres were ordained from on high. Indeed, as the Lancashire Women Textile Workers' Representation Committee and Mrs Pankhurst's WSPU began their campaigns in 1903, women's suffrage did at least seem to be able to rely on gathering Labour support.[2]

Yet it was just such signs of activity that stirred the long-dormant adult suffragists into furious opposition. During the winter of 1904–05, as the Coopers were collecting their evidence in Nelson and Keir Hardie's survey of women voters elsewhere was underway, the opponents of women's suffrage suddenly exploded into action.

The touch paper was lit by a surprising hand. Ada Nield Chew was one of that remarkable generation of northern women who sprang from anonymity as a result of her industrial experiences. As early as 1894, when she was working as a tailoress in Crewe, she had written an extraordinary series of letters to the local newspaper, protesting at the appalling conditions and merely signing herself 'A Crewe Factory Girl'. 'Why, because we are weak women, without pluck and grit enough to stand up for our rights,' she had demanded, 'should we be ground down to this miserable wage?' She went on to join the ILP and become a local Guardian, later moving up to Rochdale with her husband and small daughter.

Ada Nield Chew worked as an organiser for the Women's Trade Union League in the 1900s, encouraging other low paid women to join trade unions. She grew perturbed at the way working women were being duped – as she saw it – by suffragists into believing that they would be enfranchised by the current legislation, when in fact they had no hope of satisfying the property qualifications. Ada Nield Chew, though no more formally educated than Selina Cooper, was a talented and prolific writer. She took it upon herself to confront publicly the northern suffragists and their energetic campaign among working women. She skirmished angrily with Christabel Pankhurst in the pages of the *Clarion*, neither side prepared to concede an inch. At the same time, she did battle with the Coopers in the *Nelson Leader*; she was furious, she wrote, that women cotton workers were being gulled into believing that they would be enfranchised by the current bill. She believed they would be left out for, she wanted to know, 'how many, even of the well-to-do cotton workers pay four shillings per week for an unfurnished room?'

The Coopers were alarmed to read such a forceful attack on their cause in the *Leader*, especially in the midst of their survey. Selina was particularly dismayed that the critic was neither an enfranchised man nor a well-to-do lady, but a working woman like herself. Horrified, she immediately wrote off a reply, defending her interpretation of the bill. The next week the *Leader* published Ada Nield Chew's forthright retort:

> Even amongst the aristocrats – the organised cotton
> workers – only here and there one would be able to vote under this
> bill. How much less the great army of women who have not half
> the income of cotton workers? . . . All we ask is that the facts shall
> be placed before all working women. We are not afraid of their
> judgement. Mrs Cooper's own remarks about the bill only tend to
> strengthen my position . . .
>   The Labour party can rightly and logically support adult
> suffrage, and at the same time oppose a class and property
> measure, which would benefit well-to-do women at the expense of
> working women though this is a fact which these zealous women
> suffragists seem quite unable to grasp.

By now, mid-January 1905, Selina was away from Nelson on suffrage business, and it was Robert who replied. He had already developed a good line in undermining even the fiercest opponents:

> Judging by Mrs Chew's careless misrepresentations, I am not at
> all surprised to learn from her own pen that she has failed to grasp
> the objects of the Women's Suffrage Movement. The movement
> has arisen out of the fact that simply because women are women

they are disenfranchised, and they have no voice, politically
speaking in the affairs of this country. It was this fact which
induced the Nelson Weavers' Union – with a membership of
6,000, half of whom are female – to almost unanimously pass the
resolution that the Parliamentary vote should be granted to women
on the same terms as it is or may be granted to men. Nelson
women could easily perceive, without the aid of Mrs Chew's phi-
losophy, that what was good for the gander should also be good for
the goose . . .

Robert Cooper then went on to expose the major weakness of
the adultist argument. Their demand for total all-or-nothing
adult suffrage was unlikely to be supported either by Tory or even
Liberal governments. By demanding everything, the adultists
would end up with nothing.

Much as Mrs Chew and myself may desire that Parliament should
move quickly, it seems that we are either going to accept reform
little by little or no reform at all. But by all means let us keep up
the agitation for Adult Suffrage as well as the immediate
enfranchisement of women going; nay, I go further and say let us
never rest satisfied until we have nationalised all the means of production, distribution and exchange.

Robert Cooper showed he was every bit as much a socialist as
Ada Nield Chew – and also a suffragist. She hit back furiously.
His 'letter has so evidently been written in an excited state of mind
that it is inevitably rather mixed and difficult to unravel'.
Women's suffrage, she still maintained, was a middle-class
movement. There was nothing wrong in that, she allowed, but:

what I do oppose is the notion that this Bill is a working woman's
Bill, and what I protest against is that these middle-class women
should take advantage of the ignorance of women by telling them
what is untrue – that this Bill would help to raise their status as
workers . . . It is the duty of other women who cannot be gulled
by such nonsense to speak out against it.

And she was unimpressed by the Coopers' survey of working
women in Nelson, and of those done elsewhere. 'If your correspondent's statements . . . are true, then it means that most of the
householders in those towns are women, and if that be so, I would
ask if any men live there at all?' Ada Nield Chew heaped ridicule

on the suffragists' statistics, and on this discordant note the letters fizzled out, each side still convinced that its interpretation of the bill's controversial small print was correct.[3]

Who was right in predicting the bill's practical effects – suffragists or adultists? Since the legislation was never enacted it is difficult to judge. What is clear is that the suffragists' figures *were* questionable but that the adultists' revolutionary purity made far less practical political sense than the suffragists' equal rights demand. Equally clear is that Ada Nield Chew's outbursts had helped unleash and legitimise the adultist opposition to women's suffrage within the Labour movement. From now on, suffragists had to argue not merely against diehard Tories and shifty Liberals, but also against Labour supporters accusing them of duping working women with false hopes and empty promises.

Meanwhile Selina Cooper had begun to attract the attention of ILP leaders as a skilled public speaker. She seemed the ideal woman to grace Labour platforms; she was, after all, an experienced mill worker, a socialist Guardian and a signatory to the Lancashire Women Textile Workers' Representation Committee manifesto. Certainly Mrs Pankhurst had been highly impressed by Selina during the Shackleton election, and she began to wonder whether Mrs Cooper might not be just the person to push a strong women's suffrage resolution through the next Labour Party Conference. She would help quieten the growing adultist opposition; and she would not irritate men like MacDonald in the way Esther Roper and Eva Gore-Booth had done. MacDonald too warmed to the idea of Mrs Cooper's speaking; Mrs Pankhurst wrote to him in mid-January 1905 to finalise the conference arrangements. 'I have written to Mr Snowden as you suggest re Mrs Cooper. She would be most valuable. She speaks well, and is very nice and pleasing too, a charmingly simple style.' Mrs Pankhurst already had an inkling that the adultists were preparing to do battle, and so she added:

> Mr Hardie suggests getting Standing Orders Committee to recommend a composite resolution, and so enable delegates to vote for a.s. and w.s. [adult suffrage and women's suffrage] . . .
> When I think of the handful of people who are trying to defeat

our fifty years of work for women just as victory is in sight, I
understand how sometimes only physical violence meets the case.[4]

So it was arranged. Selina Cooper would be Nelson ILP delegate to the 1905 Labour Party Conference in Liverpool, and
would second the women's suffrage resolution. Philip Snowden
wrote to her with directions to the conference hall; and Selina,
leaving Mary with relations, made her way up St Mary's Street to
Nelson station, and boarded a train that would take her across
Lancashire to Liverpool.

The conference was one of the largest gatherings Selina had
ever attended. The massed ranks of dark-suited union delegates
were daunting; but at least she could rely on the support of ILP
women like Mrs Pankhurst. And the suffrage resolution, so
worded to placate any prickly adult suffragist, was proposed by
the Scottish delegate of the powerful Engineers' union:

> this conference heartily approves of adult suffrage and the com-
> plete enfranchisement of both sexes, and endorses the Women's
> Enfranchisement Bill introduced into Parliament last session,
> believing it to be an important step towards adult suffrage.

The Engineers' delegate sat down. It was now Selina Cooper's
turn. She had every reason to feel nervous: she was one of the very
few working-class women present in the hall, and certainly the
first working woman to speak on suffrage at a Labour Party Conference. She was aware that opposition to her cause was now
spreading like wildfire among Labour supporters; but she hoped
that the careful wording of the resolution, coupled with her own
sincerity, might win sufficient votes to get it passed. She had to
persuade delegates that to support the resolution *was* to support
Labour – not to undermine it.

Gathering up her courage, she rose from her chair and began to
speak. But, she recalled some years later, she had hardly got out
her first few words before 'my supporters pressed me to go on the
platform – I had been speaking from the body of the hall – and
address the conference on the suffrage movement. It was no easy
task for me to mount the platform and face the vast audience of
delegates.' But she managed it; and she explained to conference
that she held the views that she did

because I am a working woman and because I recognise that it is only by the means mentioned in the resolution that we can take a practical step towards complete enfranchisement. I speak on behalf of thousands of women engaged in the textile trades, to whose class I belong . . . In the Clitheroe Division alone, 5,500 women have signed a petition in favour of women having the vote on the same terms as men, and I would impress upon you not to think that women want the vote merely as women. We are as keenly alive to the needs of the people as anyone, and if we have the vote we will be able to use it in the interests of reform.

No sooner had she finished than up sprang Harry Quelch, delegate from the London Trades Council, an SDF leader and an implacable opponent of women's suffrage. Quelch was familiar with the Nelson area and must have known that Selina Cooper did indeed speak on behalf of thousands of disenfranchised women trade unionists. But he remained unmoved by her appeal and held obstinately to the SDF line that votes for women was anti-socialist because it would only benefit propertied ladies. Like Ada Nield Chew, he was a fervent believer in adult suffrage – but unlike her he was prepared to resort to every sly rhetorical trick to undermine the suffragists. 'Mrs Cooper,' he claimed

has appealed to the sentiment of sex, but I repudiate that there is any sex antagonism. Mrs Cooper has placed sex first; but it is not the place of the [Labour] party to place sex first; we have to put Labour first in every case

and he moved an adult suffrage amendment that ran diametrically against Selina Cooper's resolution.

Philip Snowden defended women's suffrage. The bill might not be perfect, he admitted; but at least it conceded to women the vital principle of equal political rights and was practical politics. 'No sensible man,' he told the delegates, 'can fail to realise that there is no likelihood in the imminent future of any House of Commons taking the important step of granting adult suffrage.' Other speakers backed Quelch up. Then Mrs Pankhurst came forward to support Selina Cooper, quoting the suffragists' surveys to prove that about 90 per cent of potential voters were working-class women. 'I am appealing to you to discard sex prejudice,' she said, neatly turning Quelch's jibe on its head; for otherwise manhood suffrage would be introduced and votes for women would become a lost cause.

Selina Cooper and the others had worked hard to build up support for the current bill, while admitting that it was only the first step to full adult suffrage. But Quelch and his supporters had raised the bogey of 'sex prejudice' versus 'class prejudice', and this fuelled doubts about women's suffrage already entertained by the listening trades union delegates. Quelch's jibe about 'the sentiment of sex' was effective, and as a result his amendment was carried by a large majority, 483 votes to 270. It was then put as a substantive motion and adopted. The Labour Party was now set resolutely on its adultist course of opposition to women's suffrage.[5]

Bitterly disappointed, Selina Cooper made her way back to Nelson. The conference vote made hollow mockery of her last five years' work. She felt deeply resentful towards SDF men like Harry Quelch and wondered forlornly how suffragists could ever win over trade unionists from parts of the country lacking Lancashire's experience of working women. Mrs Pankhurst felt equally gloomy. 'I feel deeply grieved at our defeat,' she wrote to Philip Snowden,

> for I felt so confident we should carry the composite resolution . . .
> I had not sufficiently realised the forces working against us . . . I
> am so weary of it and the long years of struggle first against ridi-
> cule and contempt and now of indifference and apathy. Still I feel
> more hopeful than I have ever been for the defeat at Liverpool has
> aroused much interest among men and women alike . . .

The same day she also dashed off an encouraging letter to Mrs Cooper, full of suggestions for continuing the campaign.

> Dear Mrs Cooper
> I hope you feel more cheerful than when we parted at Liverpool
> and ready to renew the fight.
>   What are you intending to do with the Textile men to make
> them truer to w[omen's] s[uffrage]? I think Mr Shackleton should
> be told that Mr Hardie means to reintroduce the Bill next Session
> and should be asked to back it and ballot for a place.
>   Can you not work to get women on the executives of the Unions
> and begin to agitate to get women sent as delegates to next year's
> Conference . . .

If I can be of any use to you in getting the textile women to
assert themselves let me know and I will do all I can
With Kind regards
sincerely yours
E. Pankhurst.[6]

It is not known how Selina Cooper replied to this friendly letter.
Better recorded is Keir Hardie's ill luck in the balloting: he failed
to win a place to reintroduce the bill. But Mrs Pankhurst
managed to persuade another backbencher, who *had* drawn a
place, to take up the women's cause and introduce the bill in May
1905. With victory in sight, a mood of optimism softened the blow
of the Labour Party conference vote. Great suffrage meetings
were held in London, Manchester and elsewhere, with Selina
Cooper joining Philip Snowden and Sarah Reddish at a large
meeting in Blackburn.

Suffragists recognised that it was now even more crucial for the
ILP, the most progressive group in the Labour Party, to commit
itself to supporting the bill. The previous year the ILP Conference
had once more casually passed *both* Mrs Pankhurst's resolution
and the adult suffrage one. Selina Cooper, among others, determined that this year there would be no such woolly-minded
ambivalence. Nelson ILP agreed to send her as one of their delegates to the ILP's Easter conference, contributing – the branch
account book tells us – £1 from its limited funds for her trip down
to Manchester.

Seated with the other delegates in the Free Trade Hall, Selina
Cooper watched as a Woolwich delegate moved the women's
suffrage resolution, as carefully worded as the Labour Party one.
It committed the ILP, as a step towards adult suffrage, to giving
women the vote on the same terms as men enjoyed. Christabel
Pankhurst from the Manchester Central ILP seconded it. 'The
Labour Party,' she warned ominously, 'cannot afford to neglect
the appeal of their sisters in their hour of need.' Up leapt two
adultists with the usual objections about propertied women, flourishing a contrary amendment. Another WSPU member spoke
defending the bill, quoting how 90 per cent of those enfranchised
would be working women. 'Legal opinion,' she claimed daringly,
'had decided that under the bill married women will also be
enfranchised.' Selina Cooper listened as the debate grew so

heated that its timetable had to be specially extended to allow
everyone to speak. She heard Keir Hardie himself wind up,
quoting the survey of municipal registers. 'In the face of these
figures it is nonsense to say that this is a middle class measure,'
Hardie told them. '. . . It opens the door by which every woman
in England can enter into citizenship.' Most delegates agreed with
Hardie: when the vote was taken only six or seven opposed the
women's suffrage resolution. The ILP had come out decisively in
favour of the bill – even though this flew in the face of the recent
Labour Party decision.[7]

The Pankhursts held a reception for delegates at their home in
south Manchester, and so Selina Cooper had the opportunity to
discuss these serious matters with Mrs Pankhurst. A few days
later the two women, buoyed up by the ILP's support, travelled
over the Pennines for a meeting in Halifax. They each explained
to the audience in the local schoolroom how they had become
involved in the campaign. Selina, speaking first, told of her years'
work in a cotton factory, and how she had learned that trade
unionism could never be effective unless coupled with political
power. Mrs Pankhurst traced her association with the suffrage
movement further back. 'For nearly fifty years women in England
have been struggling to obtain their political emancipation,' she
said, adding as a swipe at the adultists: 'Now almost at the eleventh hour there are people who are trying to turn us from the
objective we are striving after.' Clearly the two women balanced
each other excellently: one able to speak for working women, the
other intimately linked to the half-century suffrage struggle.[8] Despite the support of suffrage groups and the ILP, the bill when it
came before the Commons in May 1905, was talked out by anti-
suffragist MPs. The suffragists were incensed that Westminster
should insult women in this way, certain that if adequate time had
been allowed the bill would have passed this vital second reading.
They returned north fired with new vigour: Selina Cooper spoke
at meetings almost daily, both in Nelson and further afield. And
when in the autumn she heard that Christabel and a new WSPU
recruit called Annie Kenney had demonstrated at the Liberals'
Free Trade Hall meeting, demanding votes for women, she was
naturally delighted at their courage. She and other local
suffragists were horrified to learn of Christabel and Annie's rough

handling and subsequent imprisonment. The Nelson Guild immediately dispatched a letter to Christabel, protesting strongly against the behaviour of the Liberal leaders. Selina and Robert, remembering Christabel from the Shackleton meeting in Brierfield and from the more recent ILP conference, also wrote a personal letter of congratulations on her bravery. They received a prompt and enthusiastic reply:

> Dear Mr and Mrs Cooper,
> Many thanks from Miss Kenney and myself for your kind letter of congratulations. I wish you had been at the meeting on Friday [held in the Free Trade Hall to protest against the imprisonments]. It was a great success and worth all the unpleasantness we have been through . . .
>   Could anything be done in your district? . . .
>   C. Pankhurst[9]

In January 1906 the general election confirmed the Liberals in power. It was therefore to the new Liberal Government that suffragists like Selina Cooper looked with greatest hope during the spring. The new Prime Minister, Campbell-Bannerman, had already shown sympathy towards the disenfranchised women textile workers, and was the obvious political leader to woo. He was approached by all groups to receive a suffrage deputation. But now he was in government, he grew noticeably bashful about these advances. Sylvia Pankhurst lobbied him on behalf of the WSPU, but was refused; WSPU members even tried sitting on his doorstep. Mrs Fawcett's National Union tried too but was brushed aside. 'Sir Henry C.B. has refused to see us,' Isabella Ford wrote to inform Selina Cooper. In the end, however, the Prime Minister came under such pressure that he relented and agreed to see a joint deputation of all suffrage groups on 19 May 1906.

This gave the Lancashire suffragists a long-awaited opportunity to show their grassroots strength to the government in London (for previously they had met only backbenchers like Shackleton and Hardie). Selina Cooper and the other members of the Lancashire Women Textile Workers' Representation Committee set about organising a massive deputation. Altogether about forty or fifty women, including Selina Cooper (wearing a hat of uncompromising proportions), travelled down to London.

They marched from the Embankment with their proud banners, proclaiming that '306,000 women in the cotton trade want votes' and 'Women produce the wealth of Lancashire'.[10]

In all, the deputation to Campbell-Bannerman represented over a quarter of a million voteless women, including 50,000 textile workers. The handful allowed to speak implored the Prime Minister to listen to their cause. Mrs Pankhurst appealed on behalf of the WSPU, Eva Gore-Booth for working women, and the current Guild president for tens of thousands of Guildswomen. But Campbell-Bannerman turned a deaf ear. He himself was sympathetic, he assured the women, but his Cabinet was generally opposed. He could offer them no pledges, but blithely advocated 'the virtue of patience'. Selina Cooper and the others were deeply disappointed to be so patronisingly dismissed in this way. They walked dispiritedly away.[11]

1906 was a difficult year for the suffrage campaign as hopes that the new Liberal Government would be true to women began to fade. Back home in Nelson, Selina Cooper kept an eye open to see what the brave WSPU women – now known as 'suffragettes' – were doing down in London. She was friendly with Dora Montefiore, a well-to-do widow who was a socialist and WSPU member as well as a keen supporter of the Lancashire suffragists and their candidate at Wigan. Now Mrs Montefiore was involved in a more direct challenge to the government. She had raised the old cry, 'Taxation without representation is tyranny!', had refused to pay her income tax and turned her Hammersmith house into a fortress at which the bailiffs hammered in vain. Hearing of this, Selina immediately wrote to support this 'siege', and received this prompt reply:

> Dear Mrs Cooper,
> I was indeed so glad to hear from you and know you were all so interested in Lancs. in my action. Indeed it has 'caught on' more than I ever dared [think] it would; and proves how much more valuable an action is in propaganda than oceans of the best reason and the wisest speeches . . .
> How I wish you could get some women in your part to follow my example: the weak joint in the whole matter is that no woman is making a sign of being willing to come out on the same lines.

Can you think of no *action* by which your Textile workers could
embarrass the government?

. . . Best remembrances to your husband a kiss to the little girl,
yrs in the cause,
D.B. Montefiore[12]

Tax resistance for Edwardian women was, of course, limited to
a few wealthy single or widowed women like Mrs Despard or Mrs
Montefiore. It was difficult for Selina Cooper to explain to supporters in London all the practical problems faced by women
textile trade unionists. However, at the same time, Selina was also
watching the WSPU begin to heckle Liberals like Asquith, the
anti-suffragist Chancellor of the Exchequer. Suffragettes soon
found themselves scuffling with the police and arrests and imprisonments added to their notoriety. Later, when Parliament was
opened in October, Mrs Pankhurst led a WSPU protest about
government inaction at Westminster which resulted in ten
suffragettes, including Mrs Montefiore and Mrs Pankhurst's
youngest daughter Adela, being sent to prison for two months.
That such women, some with influential connections, should be
incarcerated in Holloway like common felons roused widespread
anger. Mrs Fawcett was among those who stepped forward to
congratulate the suffragettes, as was the ILP. Selina Cooper and
other ILP women felt so strongly about what had happened that
they signed a manifesto of solidarity:

Manifesto to the Women's Social and Political Union

We, the undersigned women of the Independent Labour Party,
desire to place on record our warm appreciation and high admiration of the work done for Women's Suffrage by the Women of the
Social and Political Union. In particular do we admire and congratulate the brave women who have had the courage to suffer in
prison for their convictions, and we assert, with them, our profound belief that no real and lasting progress will ever be made,
apart from the complete enfranchisement of women.

There were over 500 signatures. Margaret McMillan and
Isabella Ford for the ILP's executive signed it as well as dozens of
members from ILP branches in Manchester, Halifax, Blackburn
and Liverpool, twenty women from Colne ILP and twenty-two
women from Nelson. A glance down the list of signatories reveals

many of the familiar names of local suffragists: Selina Cooper heading the list, followed by Harriette Beanland and her sister Emily, Florence Shuttleworth and others.[13] Selina Cooper would defend such WSPU courage to the end. But both she and other ILP members were growing anxious about another side to the suffragettes. They had noticed how Christabel Pankhurst and others in the WSPU at a recent by-election had refused to urge men to vote for the Labour candidate. Relationships between the WSPU and the ILP grew sourer in November 1906 when, at a by-election in Huddersfield, the suffragettes arrived in full force to attack the Liberal Government but did nothing to help the Labour candidate.

Mrs Pankhurst and Mrs Cooper were both present at this contest and, for the first time, found themselves campaigning on different sides. A contingent of released suffragettes appeared, and were soon driving round in a wagonette bearing a large placard, 'Oppose the Government that imprisons women, and vote against the Liberal candidate', without hinting whether the voters should then vote Labour or Tory. Selina Cooper, along with other members of the Lancashire Women Textile Workers' Representation Committee, watched all this with a sinking heart. The Labour candidate, she knew, was a staunch supporter of women's suffrage, and she and her friends were busy urging the men to vote Labour. It seemed that the two suffrage groups had developed contradictory policies. Despite her old friendship with Mrs Pankhurst, Selina grew irked by these suffragette attacks on Labour, and irritated that the imprisoned suffragettes, whom she had so willingly supported, should steal the limelight with their dubious political slogans. It all highlighted how fast the WSPU was losing its old faith in working women's organisations.[14]

But in the end, the suffragettes failed to keep the Liberal candidate out – and the suffragists failed to get Labour elected; a Liberal was returned, though his tiny majority over Labour was reduced to a few hundred votes. Selina Cooper must have wondered bitterly whether Labour might have won this marginal seat had it not been hindered by the suffragettes. She too was impatient with the Labour Party's lack of sympathy for women's suffrage; but she would never, even by default, encourage electors to support the Tory party. At the same time she was also growing aware that the suffrage campaign was now a national concern; small regional groups like the Lancashire Women Textile Workers' Representation Committee could not command sufficient resources to campaign up and down the country. What was needed was the backing of a strong national organisation – like the Labour Party. With the 1907 Party Conference drawing nearer, she decided to try once again to reverse the adult suffrage majorities of the last two years.

If anybody could undertake this near-impossible task it was Selina Cooper. Ramsay MacDonald had already written to her, urging her to press forward with women's suffrage:

> Dear Mrs Cooper,
> What I wanted to do was to advise you most strongly to try and get a resolution in favour of women's enfranchisement put upon our next Agenda in the name of the Textile Operatives. We really must upset that Liverpool decision and I do not see much hope in doing it yet, unless the cotton operatives take the lead . . .

and he suggested that the conference resolution might again be diplomatically worded, antagonising as few adultists as possible. Such a motion, demanding women be given the vote on the same basis as men, should be supported, he added,

> both as an act of justice to working women many of whom would be enfranchised by it, and also as a necessary preliminary to a more satisfactory measure dealing with adult suffrage.
>   If you agree to something like this being done, I think you had better set about it at once, as time will soon fly. You shd. instruct your executive to place the resolution on our next agenda.
>   With kindest regards
>   Yours very sincerely
>   J. Ramsay MacDonald[15]

Ramsay MacDonald, like so many of the others who wrote to Selina Cooper from London urging immediate action 'in the name of the Textile Operatives', failed to appreciate that this was utterly impossible. Women might outnumber men in the cotton industry, but, as Selina knew full well from her years in the Burnley Weavers' Association, the union committees were run entirely by men. Men continued to hold almost all the influential positions; they might make a show of support for women's suffrage occasionally, but they were hardly passionate advocates. The strongest lobby within the Labour Party for women was still the ILP – despite the ILP fracas with the WSPU. So it was arranged that a delegate from the ILP stronghold of Woolwich should propose the suffrage motion similar to the wording MacDonald had suggested; and that Selina Cooper should attend as one of the ILP delegates (for, as the ILP national secretary wrote to invite her, 'both Miss Ford and Mrs Pankhurst are unable to go and the appointment of a woman delegate is now being considered'). She was especially delighted to attend because this year's conference was to be held in Belfast (still part of a united Ireland under British rule); and as a tribute to the Home Rule fight, she asked her friend Harriette Beanland to make her a vivid emerald green velvet dress to take with her. Indeed, the occasion looked at first like becoming a celebration of Irish independence. Selina later scribbled in her notebook about:

> Joe Biggar [a Catholic MP] grave outside Belfast he was a Home Ruler he caused the Government of that day more all night sittings than any member
>   The Church Warden took me to see his grave . . .
>   When the Labour Party held their conference at Belfast a reception was held for delegates Jim Connolly [an Irish socialist] took the chair I had gote a green velvet frock in compliment to Ireland when I was introduced to him I told [him] about it.

She also pinned a spray of shamrock to her dress which appealed to the assembled delegates who greeted her with a round of applause.[16]

But it was not Ireland and Home Rule which provided the controversial centrepiece of the conference: it was women's suffrage. The battle began a few days beforehand. Christabel Pankhurst, 'with her characteristic faculty for flinging the apple of discord' (as her sister Sylvia put it), had issued a press statement announcing that the WSPU's attack on the government made no distinction between Tory and Labour parties. For Keir Hardie, Selina Cooper and the other suffragists in Belfast, her timing could not have been worse. Her provocative remark played perfectly into the adultist court, alienating undecided delegates from women's suffrage.

The people present in that great Belfast hall represented nearly a million Labour Party members. The overwhelming majority of them were, of course, trade union men and a photograph taken at the time shows Selina Cooper to be the only woman to be seen on the floor of the hall. The Labour Party, by stressing organised waged labour, still gave little voice to working women and therefore to women's suffrage. Clearly only a handful of delegates present would have personally benefited from supporting women's suffrage.

The delegate from Woolwich proposed the motion similar to that which MacDonald had suggested to Selina Cooper: that the conference supports adult suffrage and equality of the sexes, and urges the immediate enfranchisement of women on the same basis as men. He stressed, in an effort to counteract Christabel's pronouncement, that he supported the resolution as 'a revolutionary, class-conscious Socialist'. Then it was Selina Cooper's turn. She had the unenviable task of undermining the allegations of two formidable but distinct opponents: Harry Quelch and Christabel Pankhurst. Even as she mounted the platform in front of the rows of sober-suited men, she must have realised despondently how heavily Labour opinion was weighted against her. She could rely on only a minority of real friends among the delegates.

Her speech was more compact than at Liverpool in 1905. She spoke to the delegates, she said, as a cotton factory worker, and told them that giving women the vote would in no way harm Labour. Her opponents claimed that working women would not benefit from current legislation. Her answer to that was that in her own home town of Nelson, of the thousand women who would be enfranchised, 995 would be working class. Such women, she stressed, must be allowed to play their part in the reforms demanded by Labour; and she strongly advised the conference not to aim at the impossible ideal of adult suffrage, but to strive for the practical compromise in the resolution.

She must have sat down with a sense of foreboding about the direction the rest of the debate would take. And, true to form, up jumped Harry Quelch to move his adultist amendment, opposing as 'a retrograde step' any extension of the franchise on the existing property qualifications. The current bill would disenfranchise a woman once she got married, he alleged, but would 'give every wealthy man the power to create as many faggot voters as he has daughters'. He was seconded by a woman trade unionist representing the Telegraph Clerks. She claimed that the bill would be no benefit at all to working women, and she strengthened her argument by lunging out at the suffragettes:

> I protest against this artificial agitation, which is endeavouring to capture all grades of society towards its ends. Although I admire the women for their pluck and heroism they have shown, I cannot help thinking that . . . they have created a sex antagonism instead of a class antagonism, and it is contrary to the spirit of Socialism that this should be so.

Hers was, unfortunately, the voice of mainstream Labour opinion. Keir Hardie felt as gloomy as Selina Cooper as they listened to this speech and noted how well it was received by the delegates. He was now, as always, ready to champion the women's cause despite the growing opposition. 'Keir Hardie strongly supported me,' Selina explained later, 'in the face of the whole conference.' Indeed, this was a modest understatement of the drama that now unfolded. Hardie walked up to the platform and delivered one of his most passionate and effective attacks on the adultists who opposed the very principle of women's suffrage:

> If the bill were a property qualification bill I would not support it . . . What was the fact? Women today are classed with criminals and lunatics as being unfit to exercise the vote. There is no property qualification required for men – there might be a household one – and the bill does not propose to establish any new qualification, but it says that the qualification which men accept should also apply to women. So long as women are held to be inferior to men they cannot expect that comradeship in the great Labour movement which we all desire to see.

But even Hardie's heartfelt oratory failed to move the adultists. Their amendment was carried by a card vote, 605,000 to a paltry 268,000; then it was put as a substantive motion and carried by the conference.

It was a stinging defeat, even more wounding than the 1905 conference vote. Selina Cooper began to ask herself bitterly why she remained within an organisation that treated women so con-temptuously and where her voice counted for so very little. Not so Hardie, still the most influential of the left-Labour MPs. He shared her great sadness about the decision; while he outwardly remained calm during the rest of the day, he privately resolved to startle the delegates into recognising their shabby desertion of women. So, at the end of the conference as he was moving the vote of thanks, he electrified his audience with a brave and moving denunciation of the party he loved:

> Twenty-five years ago I cut myself adrift from every relationship, political or other, in order to assist in building up a workers' party. I thought the days of my pioneering were over; but of late I have felt, with increasing intensity, the injustice inflicted upon women by our present laws. The intimation I wish to make to the Confer-ence is this: if the resolution which has been carried today is intended to limit the action of the Party in the House of Com-mons, I shall have seriously to consider whether I can remain a member further. I make that announcement with great respect to the Conference, and with great feeling. The Party is largely my own child, and I cannot part from it lightly or without pain; but at the same time I cannot sever myself from the principles I hold. If it is necessary for me to separate myself from what has been my life's work, I do so in order to remove the stigma resting upon our wives, mothers and sisters of being accounted unfit for citizen-ship.[17]

Hardie's threat of resignation was received in stunned silence. Afterwards Labour MPs tried to smooth away this public embar-rassment; Shackleton blandly told the press that the majority in favour of the resolution 'was so great that we are bound to take it as more or less binding upon us . . . I do not think that the matter is sufficiently serious to cause Mr Hardie to resign'. And Hardie was indeed eventually persuaded to stay.

But the damage of Belfast was done. Women recognised beyond doubt that the Labour Party had deserted them. For the WSPU, and especially for Christabel, Belfast merely confirmed their low opinion of Labour's cowardice, and the militant suffragettes now broke their remaining ties with the party. For non-militant suffragists like Selina Cooper it was far less easy. Her loyalty to the party was no less fierce and passionate than

Hardie's. She too saw it almost as her child from whom she could never sever the links. But Belfast bitterly convinced her of one thing: she could no longer work to help the party's electoral prospects until it reversed its decision on women. She resolved to have no more to do with the local Women's Labour League, formed in 1906 to work for the party and to canvass for Labour candidates at elections. It was insulting to knock on doors and run fund-raising bazaars for a party that rejected the principle of equal rights for women. She was a founder-member of the Nelson Women's Labour League, and currently its president. In resigning, she apparently took with her all the other local women – like Harriette Beanland – who had joined. They agreed to suspend the local league until the party changed its mind. And, true to their word, Nelson heard no more of the Women's Labour League for many years, and therefore presumably lost these women's services at election time.[18]

Of course Selina Cooper, Harriette Beanland and many other suffragists, remained within the ILP. That Easter Selina attended the ILP Annual Conference as a delegate of the small but lively Brierfield branch. Coming only months after the Huddersfield by-election and Belfast defeat, it marked the final break between the WSPU and the ILP, and highlighted the growing coolness between the two ILP suffrage friends, Mrs Pankhurst and Mrs Cooper.

The suffrage debate at the 1907 conference went to and fro. 'There are today those in the socialist ranks,' claimed one suffrage supporter, 'who were political babes in the days when some of the women were warriors and heroes' – a sentiment which must have caused Selina Cooper, sitting quietly among the other delegates, to smile wryly. To her delight, Keir Hardie received a tremendous ovation when he finally stood up to speak. 'We are going to decide whether or not the ILP is to retain the services of some of its most valuable women workers,' he proclaimed. 'Were I a woman . . . I would feel ashamed to belong to a party that had turned its back upon women.' His humbling words had their effect: the ILP passed its women's suffrage resolution by 236 votes to a mere 24.

The conference then moved to more delicate matters. The ILP executive had already told the WSPU that its behaviour at by-elections was responsible for the defeat at Belfast; and this criticism of the suffragettes was now embodied in a resolution and open to debate. Before things could grow too heated, a conciliatory message was read from four leading ILP women (including Mrs Despard of the WSPU and Isabella Ford of the National Union of Women's Suffrage Societies) which stated that: 'We pledge ourselves never to go down to any constituency or take part in any election unless we go to help the Labour Party.' Selina Cooper might feel that, despite the numbing blow of Belfast, this was a valuable statement: the four ILP women were women she could trust. But Mrs Pankhurst was having none of it. She sprang to her feet and passionately repudiated this pledge, justifying the WSPU's independent stand. 'We are not going to wait until the Labour Party can give us a vote,' she declared. 'It is by putting pressure on the present government that we shall get it . . . If you think my conduct inconsistent with my membership I will resign. And if I am to go I will go alone.' She so won the sympathy of her audience, conscious of the debt the ILP owed her and her husband, that the motion of censure on the WSPU was dropped.

For Selina Cooper it was an uneasy conference. In the Labour Party, the divide was clearly between suffragists and adultists. Here in the ILP it seemed to be between those who supported the WSPU's independent stand at by-elections and those who did not. She did not, but found that this now distanced her from women like Mrs Pankhurst whom she admired.

Her dilemma was solved during the summer. It appeared that the ILP's tolerance towards the WSPU had been largely wasted, for shortly afterwards Mrs Pankhurst and Christabel both resigned from the ILP, so cutting their last formal links with socialism. Indeed, by October Christabel was even writing to the leader of the Conservatives inviting his party to support the suffragettes, and explaining how she had broken with Labour because, 'the working-class vote is now largely controlled and organised by Labour politicians and T.U. officials' who tried to limit working women's opportunities.[19]

By the end of 1907 a firm pattern of suffrage allegiances was beginning to emerge which would shape the campaign in the coming years. The WSPU continued its militant tactics against the Liberal Government, especially after Easter 1908 when the arch anti-suffragist Asquith became Prime Minister. It also grew noticeably autocratic under the Pankhursts' leadership (and, as a result, in 1907, suffragettes like Charlotte Despard left to form a separate and more democratic militant group, the Women's Freedom League).

At the other extreme, the Labour Party continued to vote down women's suffrage. At its 1908 conference Quelch, slipping in disparaging remarks about the suffragettes' 'Merry Andrew antics', again got his way; and subsequent conferences, caught up as they were by other 'urgent' electoral reforms, paid little attention to women. During these harsh years, every Labour woman who cared about equal rights had good cause to feel sorely betrayed by the party. Certainly, Selina Cooper did not return to party conferences after Belfast. For socialist women like herself, these were difficult years spent in the wilderness.

The ILP remained a true friend, of course. She continued to attend ILP conferences, one year taking Harriette Beanland along too; but even here she found that women's suffrage could easily be submerged by seemingly more pressing issues like unemployment. Indeed during these dark days it appeared that every politician – whether Liberal Cabinet Minister, Labour or ILP leader – had priorities more urgent than women's demands. Suffrage found itself competing for parliamentary attention with such weighty matters as Lloyd George's budget and reform of the House of Lords.

It seemed that women had only themselves to rely on. Yet Selina Cooper saw that there were now so many different suffrage groups, each pursuing its own line and often competing for attention with the others. There were the two militant groups: the Pankhursts' WSPU and Mrs Despard's Women's Freedom League. There was also the Lancashire Women Textile Workers' Representation Committee which she had helped form; but much as she loved women like Sarah Reddish and Eva Gore-Booth, she grew increasingly concerned that it was becoming isolated from the rest of the growing suffrage movement. She recognised that such a regional campaign, however dedicated and sincere, did not have the muscle of a national organisation and had made scarcely a dent in the male power structures of the cotton unions; and she worried about their urge to champion ever smaller groups of women workers – cigar-makers, barmaids, pit-brow lasses – easy targets for caricature by their Labour opponents.

Assessing the strengths of the various suffrage groups in this way, Selina Cooper, with her sure political instincts, found herself increasingly drawn towards Mrs Fawcett's National Union of Women's Suffrage Societies. It was by far the broadest-based of all the organisations and already had a countrywide network of local groups like the Nelson Society, as well as bigger societies in the cities and a national London headquarters. And it was expanding rapidly each year, attracting thousands of women to join its ranks. And because it was so large, it could afford to employ full-time organisers who could cover the country, campaigning in a particular area for a week or two whenever a local group needed professional help.

From autumn 1906 Selina Cooper became one of this small band of National Union organisers; and from spring 1907, after she had cast off her Guardian responsibilities, it became virtually a full-time commitment for her.

Precisely how Selina Cooper was contacted and engaged by the National Union in 1906–07 remains uncertain. What is clear is why Mrs Fawcett and the National Union officers should have wanted to include Selina in the first batch of organisers. She had impressed the London suffragists when she helped present the textile petition in 1901; since then she had served as a Guardian, organised the Nelson suffrage group, helped launch the Lancashire Women Textile Workers' Representation Committee, and made a very telling speech at Labour's 1905 Conference. A most likeable working-class woman, Selina got on well with most people (she presumably guarded her sharp tongue), and was an efficient organiser and inspired speaker. She was indeed an ideal choice for the National Union.

The job suited Selina perfectly. Disenchanted with the Labour Party, she saw that the National Union was the only organisation with effective muscle to campaign for women's votes up and down the country. It was run by well-to-do women, often Liberals, and clung firmly to its 'non-party' stance – but at least it did not attack Labour as the WSPU now did; and Selina must have hoped that perhaps the National Union could eventually be slowly shifted leftwards. She relished the prospect of stumping the country, speaking and organising with a wide range of different women; and she was pleased that the job did not entail much writing, still an unwelcome chore for her. With Mary growing up fast, she could more easily be left behind for a few days, cared for by Robert or by a close relation.

Selina Cooper knew her gifts and was ready to spread her political wings. The National Union was keen to employ her. So she now threw herself headlong into the fast-moving national suffrage campaign: until women eventually won the vote, she could not allow herself the luxury of thinking about much else.[20]

CHAPTER ELEVEN

REFLECTIONS OF A SUFFRAGIST:
1907-1908

The suffragists' straightforward demand for votes for working women could easily appear overshadowed by the WSPU's more dramatic appeal. Women like Selina Cooper might seem to pale beside the powerful pictures of imprisoned suffragettes. This imbalance lingered on. Years after women finally won the vote, the powerful images of suffragettes being carried off by policemen or posing in prison clothes remain etched in the mind. Still familiar seventy years later are photographs of Mrs Pankhurst's strikingly poignant face and of great WSPU 'from prison to citizenship' processions.

It is difficult to set this mesmerising succession of suffragette images into context, and to see the reflection of non-militant suffragists like Selina Cooper clearly once again across the intervening years. It would be easy to believe that suffragists were rarely photographed. Yet this was by no means so.[1] Certainly Selina's photograph appeared regularly in one way or another from 1907 to the outbreak of war. Luckily a rich hoard of these suffrage pictures has been preserved among the Cooper papers, offering a rare and vivid reflection of what life was like for a National Union organiser during these stirring years.

Among her suffrage photographs are series of small sepia snapshots which capture the fleeting moments of open-air organising and are obviously the work of sympathetic amateurs.[2] Others were by professional newspaper photographers, skilled at capturing every detail of the group Selina was with; one such was the picture of suffragists on Nelson station waiting for their London train. More formal still were the posed studio portraits, often taken for propaganda purposes and printed as postcards by the National Union.[3] Among the other photographs in the collection are blurry newspaper cuttings of Selina in action at by-elections, and portraits of Mary posing with her schoolfriends or with her mother.

From all these different pictures, we know what Selina Cooper looked like when she became a National Union organiser. We see reflected a striking woman in her forties, whose face has begun to fill out and soften the gaunter lines of the earlier Keld photographs. The stamp of her character has grown even stronger since the Guardian portraits of a few years previously. Scarcely beautiful, she obviously possessed a magnificent dignity, emphasised by the splendidly imposing hats she invariably wore. Her entry into a room would be hard to ignore; and when she appeared at rowdy open-air meetings it is easy to understand why her manner immediately quietened hecklers and moved hostile audiences to sympathy.

Luckily, in this period of her life we can peer beyond the photograph images, for this was a time when Selina was a frequent correspondent with other women up and down the country: between 1907 and 1912, over sixty letters written to her by suffragists have survived. These letters, though usually concerning matter-of-fact National Union business, reveal Selina not only as an energetic propagandist with a remarkable public presence, but also as someone who readily aroused in other women a warm affection. They might be slightly in awe of her, but they hoped that she was as fond of them as they were of her. 'I *would* so like to be campaigning with you again,' wrote veteran suffragist Isabella Ford humbly. '. . . For I do like you so much dear Mrs Cooper. Please try and like me.'[4]

The entries that Selina jotted down in her daily diary during 1908 and 1909 also help explain why others wanted to be liked by her. They read briskly, giving an almost impersonal glimpse into the life of a suffrage campaigner. Selina is revealed as a business-like organiser, with little room to spare in her life for time-wasting emotions or private introspection. During the years she kept her diary there is not one single reference to her husband Robert: although the two of them obviously still rubbed along well together as comrades, he figured less in her day-to-day life than her other friends. Mary is there in the diary, and so are other people Selina cared for: yet Robert remains absent from his wife's curt and busy entries for 1909:

20th July: Morning Chalked the Pavement Dinner hour meeting at the Dinting Dye Works Evening Glossop Market Place . . .

22nd July: Polling day High Peak Collected Signatures outside Polling Station Hadfield Had tea with an anti-Suffragist

23rd July: Left Glossop for Nelson Mary returns Home from Yorkshire

Selina Cooper's diary, despite its impersonal brusqueness, remains invaluable source material. It offers a rare cross-section through the busy suffrage years of a working-class organiser, opening up to view the closely-compressed layers of her hectic experiences. For instance, Selina's entries for just one week in April 1909 reveal her completing a month's propaganda campaign in Leicester, going to Birmingham and then to Stratford to address an open-air meeting, catching the midnight mail train back to Nelson, sleeping off her exhaustion at home, then travelling up to Edinburgh for the annual ILP Conference, more open-air speaking and then a meeting with the Edinburgh Suffrage Committee. Such had become the pace of a typical seven days for an organiser like Selina Cooper.

Her diary also reveals how smoothly efficient the suffragist propaganda and by-election campaigns were now becoming. The small-time regional campaigning of Wigan or Huddersfield was now well past: an organiser like Selina Cooper was increasingly able to work effectively in almost any corner of Britain at a moment's notice. This is confirmed by the growing newspaper reports of her campaigning, and by her meticulously kept organiser's account book, also fortunately preserved among her papers. With each credit and debit entry carefully noted from October 1908 to beyond the war, it is vivid testimony to the smooth running of the National Union machinery.[5]

As historical source material, Mary's oral testimony here is naturally less helpful, for she remained in Nelson, going to school each day. Her recollections of this aspect of her mother's life are therefore largely based on the stories Selina Cooper brought home to entertain her daughter, the postcards sent from the towns where her mother worked, and the presents given by kind-hearted suffragists who feared the little girl might pine for her mother. In practice, Mary was so caught up with her own friends and so surrounded by loving relatives, that she seemed to survive her mother's regular absences without great upset. Local people accused Selina of neglecting her daughter, but Mary always laughed away such notions, though she admitted: 'I pined for her . . . I was always wanting her to come [back].' Certainly she would grow very excited when her mother was expected to arrive back home after one of her suffrage trips. On such evenings, Mary would lull her long-suffering father into believing she was safely tucked up and asleep in bed, then creep down the stairs, run out of the house and up St Mary's Street to the station to meet her. She confessed this years later.

> She used to come off the London train at midnight, and all the porters knew me, because I'd be waiting. I was only little, but I'd be waiting for her to come home. [My father] wouldn't know where I'd gone! I'd get up from being in bed and go.[6]

The plentiful evidence from these years – photographs, letters, diary and account book, newspaper reports, National Union records and Mary's oral testimony – offers a telling reflection of Selina Cooper's experiences as a suffrage organiser. What makes this particularly interesting is that Selina was among the first of the dozens of organisers that the National Union eventually employed: her tale tells us therefore a great deal of how the National Union grew during these crucial years.

Selina Cooper had begun to work for the National Union in October 1906 when it decided to appoint three organisers. Its Executive Committee promptly dispatched Selina Cooper, Ethel Snowden (recently married to Philip Snowden, now an MP) and a third suffragist off to South Wales. They travelled down to Mid-Glamorgan, a constituency where over half the electors were miners, and where an autumn by-election had been called. Selina Cooper and the others were to go to the aid of that rarest of men: a Miners' Federation socialist who was hoping to stand as a Labour candidate and who was keenly in favour of women's suffrage. (In the event, it proved to be a false trail: the cautious South Wales

Miners' Federation refused to endorse him, and so the Liberal MP was returned unopposed.)[7] Still, the experience gave Selina Cooper her first taste of what life was like among the Welsh miners, and reminded her how difficult it would be to persuade a large Liberal-inclined union like the Miners' to support women's suffrage.

More successful was Selina Cooper's long campaign in Liverpool, though again she had to adapt her campaign to local problems. Women workers in the city were poorly paid and ill-organised and so were unable to establish a grassroots suffrage campaign like their sisters in eastern Lancashire. Instead, the Liverpool Women's Suffrage Society found its strength among well-to-do women; the driving force was the society's influential secretary, Eleanor Rathbone, the daughter of a Liberal MP, and a member of one of the city's leading political families.

Somehow an unlikely friendship grew between Selina Cooper and this eminent Liberal philanthropist. But in Liverpool such class differences became blurred by religion, for the city was savagely divided between Tory Protestants and Irish Nationalist Catholics. So when Selina Cooper was dispatched there in late autumn 1906, presumably at Eleanor Rathbone's request, she found the key people to lobby were the religious leaders. She soon set to work to visit ministers of all denominations trying to persuade them that votes for women was neither a dastardly Protestant nor a Catholic plot.[8]

It was a formidable, time-consuming task, organising canvasses and distributing leaflets. Eleanor Rathbone arranged for her to speak to unions like the Carpenters and Joiners, and she also visited British Women's Temperance Association groups and chapel Mothers' Meetings. For months she commuted between 59 St Mary's Street and Eleanor Rathbone's house in Liverpool. 'Dear Mary, I hope you have been a good girl,' she wrote on a picture postcard of St George's Hall. 'I am sending you a picture of a big Hall in Liverpool and there are lots of little children sat on the steps without any stockings on. I am coming home this week. S. Cooper.'[9]

However hard she worked, Selina Cooper could never forget that the city was riven by religious bigotry. The ritual Orange marches and St Patrick's Day celebrations were forcible reminders, as a note she later scribbled down suggests:

In Liverpool staying at Greenbank the Home of the Rathbone family one night on the 12th July Orange day Mr Rathbone told me not to stay out and get mixed up with the crowds in the Scotland R[oad] district in one street they were burning the Prince of Orange the other the Pope the police made an accoring [a cordon] at both ends of the street therefore I was a prisoner

Mary rounded off the tale, remembering what her mother said when she returned home again:

There was a cordon round. They hadn't to go – and my mother got under this cordon. She was taken – they had to come and bail her out. She got taken to prison. They rang Miss Rathbone up. She said she was staying there. They wouldn't believe her. They thought she was among this gang – this gang that had been fighting.[10]

This bitterness spilled over into her first Liverpool by-election in autumn 1907. The city's 'Orange' Kirkdale division was traditionally Tory territory, though Labour was now a strong challenge. Selina Cooper and the others addressed no fewer than thirty-five election meetings but could make little headway with the two candidates: neither seemed to offer support to suffrage, and the Tory won again.[11]

In mid-1910, one of Selina's later visits to Liverpool was photographed, and the picture reflects the respectable and well-clad world of the Liverpool suffragists. The occasion was another by-election, again in the Tory stronghold of Kirkdale. The Labour candidate this time was sponsored by the Carpenters and was a particularly strong champion of women's suffrage – perhaps partly due to Selina's earlier lobbying of his union. So both the Liverpool Women's Suffrage Society and the National Union decided on this occasion to offer Labour their warmest support. Selina helped open a suffrage shop with a 'Vote for Cameron' notice outside; and a six horsepower Rover was acquired to speed the suffragists' progress round the constituency. Yet all these efforts were to little avail. The by-election was as sectarian as ever. The Labour candidate, despite his impeccable credentials as an Ulsterman and a Presbyterian trade unionist, failed to wrest the seat from the ruling Tory group. Liverpool, with its religious rivalries and weak Labour Party, resisted Selina's persuasive appeal to enfranchise its lowly-paid women workers. Such a city made her job as a National Union organiser disheartening. But despite these problems, Selina retained a warm affection for Liverpool and her friendship with Eleanor Rathbone continued for the rest of their lives.[12]

After Easter 1907 Selina Cooper committed herself whole-heartedly to working for the National Union. Immediately she was dispatched off to another Tory stronghold, Wimbledon, to help Bertrand Russell. Russell, a rising young philosopher, had agreed to stand at the Wimbledon by-election as a National Union suffrage candidate, rather than let the diehard anti-suffrage Tory (who declared on the subject of votes for women, that 'he might be very old-fashioned, but he drew the line at that') be returned unopposed.

Selina found Wimbledon a breathless affair. Russell agreed to stand on 2 May; on 3 May he issued his election leaflet ('If elected I should urge the claims of women to enfranchisement at every opportunity'), and the day after a suffragist Election Committee was formed: it had only ten hasty days to persuade the suburban electors (nearly a quarter of whom lived outside the constituency and voted by courtesy of their business premises) to forsake their Tory ways and vote for a young Liberal who, preposterous as it must have sounded, was claiming that all political issues such as old age pensions and Free Trade were secondary to votes for women.

Even more daunting for Selina Cooper was that it was not the sort of area where she automatically felt most at home. 'The democracy of the future,' she used to declare, 'will be composed, not of one class, but the aristocracy of intellect and character from all classes.' Such socialist rhetoric, attacking the class structure of Edwardian society, had already provoked raised eyebrows in the Home Counties. A Tunbridge Wells suffragist had pleaded with her not to 'let that class-hatred and bitterness come into your heart again . . . *None* of us can help society being broken up into classes, and therefore . . . why hate each other for it.'[13] Selina had little time for such deterministic logic; but she does seem to have moderated her socialism for constituencies like Tory Wimbledon.

Campaigning alongside Selina for Russell were a number of other National Union women: a recent Cambridge graduate called Emilie Gardner, plus Ethel Snowden, a veteran Liberal suffragist, and Mrs Fawcett herself, always the epitome of respectability. But even their impeccable credentials were little protection against Wimbledon's hooligans, all longing to harass the suffragists who were, after all, as the Tory candidate had told them, only a 'few masculine women and a few feminine men'. Trouble erupted at Russell's first meeting. Tory rowdies released live rats into the crowded hall. 'Cowardly Cads Turn Rats Loose', ran the horrified headlines in the *Wimbledon Borough News*. 'Larrikins and Hooligans Yell Themselves Hoarse'. In fact the trick back-fired. 'The terrified animals,' reported the paper straightfacedly, 'instead of creating panic among the suffragists, showed more discrimination, and made for a little group of men in front of the platform, who appeared somewhat disturbed by the unwelcome apparitions.' Even after the rats were rounded up, the hecklers continued their hooting and whistling. Ethel Snowden could hardly make herself heard and gradually lost patience. Suddenly she stopped speaking and jabbed her finger at a particularly obstreperous Tory at the back of the hall. 'What are you paid? What are you paid?' she demanded. A wag in the audience immediately quipped, 'Four bob a nob.'

But the rowdiness grew worse. A few days later Russell's wife had a rotten egg hurled at her which hit her squarely between the eyes. On polling day, then, it came as little surprise when the anti-suffragist Tory was returned to Parliament with three times Russell's vote. (However, Russell graciously wrote to Selina, and presumably the others, thanking her for all her help during the turbulent contest: and Selina preserved the letter, little thinking Bertrand Russell would later become a household name.)[14]

Even someone as resilient as Selina Cooper might well feel cast down after her first probationary months of National Union by-elections. How difficult it seemed to place women's suffrage on the political agenda when there were so many other claims and divisions being thrust before the electors. The complex Edwardian franchise system, so weighted towards wealthy men, seemed designed to keep women voteless for as long as possible. Certainly very, very few MPs were prepared to agree that women's suffrage was more important than those other political issues – pensions, the House of Lords, Irish Home Rule – which so agitated Westminster in the 1900s. For Selina and a growing number of other women, though, the campaign for the vote *had* to take priority over all else – not that it promised everything they wanted, but without it so much else they were involved in was devalued. But the battle to convince those who held political power that women really did want the vote was obviously going to be an intense one; and before the end of 1907 Selina was back electioneering again, this time at West Hull, fighting to keep another anti-suffragist out of Parliament. She went to help the Labour candidate there, and the photograph the *Daily Mirror* published of her captures the tremendous energy with which she canvassed the electors' support.[15]

The following year, the National Union was involved in no fewer than sixteen by-elections, of which Selina Cooper took part in at least eight. The growing pace of the campaign meant that the time Selina Cooper could now spend at home with her family grew less and less, and she began to feel concerned about how Mary would cope with such frequent absences especially as Robert had occasional ill spells now. In fact, as we know, carefree Mary seemed to thrive among all her friends and relations; but Selina must have voiced her anxieties to the National Union officials who, loathe to lose one of their valuable organisers, decided to act. So it was arranged that the Coopers would have a living-in housekeeper, whose small salary the National Union was prepared to cover.

The Coopers' regular housekeeper seems to have been Mrs Holt, the cook from Keld, who had remained friends over the years. 'People said I was neglected, but,' Mary would explain carefully, 'we always had this [housekeeper]; we either had Mrs Holt or somebody else in to look after me. And the suffrage movement allowed my mother expenses for that.' Certainly Mrs Holt seems to have fitted easily into the household. Mary recalls how her parents, Harriette Beanland and Mrs Holt would go on long country walks together, always debating one subject or another as they went, and remembers that Mrs Holt 'was awful well read. Yes, soaked in books' – like her parents. (The other housekeeper, a more shadowy figure, seems to have been less of a success. A Scottish woman who tramped down to Nelson, arriving penniless, she was taken in by the kind-hearted Coopers, but drank all her wages whenever she was paid, filling Mary up with toffees to keep her quiet; she ended up in the Burnley work-house, and only after a pauper's death was discovered to be a wealthy – and highly eccentric – heiress.)

Selina Cooper's first by-election in 1908 – and therefore the first where she jotted a note each day in her new diary – was in Mid-Devon:

Jan 6th: Went to Newton Abbot, to Work in Mid Devon Election
Jan 7th: Spoke at Dinner hour meeting, Newton Abbot, Also in the Parish School Ho[use]
Jan 8th: Newton Abbot Market place meeting

It was also one of the first by-elections that Selina had fought as a National Union organiser at which she found she was directly competing with – and opposing the election policy of – Mrs Pankhurst and the WSPU. It revealed something of the coolness now growing between these two women.

The Mid-Devon contest, one of Liberalism's traditional strongholds, was a straight fight between the Liberal MP and his Tory rival. It was also a violent fight. Young Liberal hooligans rioted more viciously than even the Tories had done in Wimbledon. For Mrs Pankhurst it was a good constituency because the WSPU policy was still to oppose all Liberals (whether sympathetic or not) since they were the party of government and therefore, the WSPU held, responsible for blocking women's suffrage legislation. In effect, then, Mrs Pankhurst was urging the Mid-Devon electors to vote Tory – an act of some courage given local Liberals' brutally fierce loyalties and the rowdyism of clay-cutters from nearby pits.

Selina Cooper was there with Emilie Gardner and two others. Since both candidates claimed to agree with women's suffrage, the National Union, following its usual policy, decided not to support any one candidate but to do general propaganda work. But the Mid-Devon electors cared little for fine distinctions between anti-Liberal suffragettes and non-party suffragists. *All* women in their eyes were tarred with the same brush, and so Selina and the others found themselves manhandled and heckled in the same way. The Newton Abbot roughs were notorious, but Selina bravely held open-air meetings three days running in the local marketplace – although on one occasion a Liberal shoe-maker became so incensed that he smashed the stool he was sitting on and hurled the legs at the suffragists. Eventually he calmed down and listened to Selina's speech. 'His friends laughed at him saying you have lost your seat,' she noted later. 'I joined in and told him that the Liberal would lose his seat too' – a false predic-tion in this case. However the general irony of Mid-Devon was noticed by some: that women like Selina, who had done no more than peacefully ask for the vote, should be endangered by the rough anger of shoemakers or clay-cutters. One sympathiser, clipping a photograph of Selina and the others from the *Western Daily Mercury* for her cuttings book, wrote, 'I have put in the pic-ture of these magnificent looking outlawed women to show the types that may *not* go to the Polls while big drunken loafer latchkey lodger/male is enfranchised'.[18]

Selina Cooper emerged from Mid-Devon rubbing her bruises, yet all the more determined to continue the campaign. It was becoming clear that the National Union should further sharpen its organisation if it was to withstand not only the obduracy of male politicians but also the more dramatic tactics of the suffragettes, also competing for the hearts, minds and votes of the same elec-tors. Fortunately the National Union was now well equipped to switch its activities to a higher gear. Thousands of women, many of them first alerted to the cause by suffragette imprisonments, were now being drawn into the National Union's countrywide network of local groups. By 1909 membership had swollen to over 13,000. Money poured in too and the National Union's Central Fund swelled sufficiently for it to be able to employ its organisers on a more stable basis. So, by summer 1908, the National Union could proudly announce that it now had 'three permanent paid organisers' – Emilie Gardner, Margaret Robertson and Selina Cooper.[19]

The women made an impressive trio, complementing each other's skills well. Selina Cooper was the eldest and the only one without an Oxbridge degree. But she alone could claim any industrial experience; indeed, in these early years of her organising work Selina appeared a rarity among the well-educated National Union women. Margaret Robertson, with a literature degree and a small edition of Keats to her name, resigned her teaching post to become the organiser of the North of England Society for Women's Suffrage. With her dark wavy hair and classical features, she brought to the Manchester-based campaign an impressive Pre-Raphaelite quality, and quickly acquired the political skills needed in such a demanding job. She grew, according to Helena Swanwick, an influential Manchester suffragist, 'to become the best open-air speaker I have ever heard'. Margaret Robertson naturally saw a great deal of Selina and perhaps partly due to her influence, Margaret became drawn towards the socialist movement and seemed destined to rise within it. One of those she impressed was young Fenner (later Lord) Brockway, then editor of the *Labour Leader*; he recognised she 'had an exceptionally good political mind. She joined the ILP and I expected her to become leader of the Party.'[20]

Margaret Robertson and Selina Cooper both had a nose for politics. They tackled their organising problems with panache, and their contribution to the suffrage campaign was considerable. Emilie Gardner, on the other hand, seems to have lacked the instinctive confidence of the others. Head girl of her school, she graduated from Cambridge with a history degree in 1907, becoming secretary of the Birmingham Suffrage Society. She soon became a National Union organiser and worked closely with Selina Cooper, the two of them campaigning together at the tumultuous Mid-Devon by-election. But we can sense that Emilie would occasionally flounder in the muddied waters of Edwardian politics, and have to turn to the older woman for guidance and inspiration.[21]

The National Union also set about strengthening its organisational base. It issued a no-nonsense 'Election Leaflet', appealing for 'electors to extract a public pledge from the Candidates' and for 'voteless women to unite in demanding this great reform'. At the same time it printed an internal document for National Union workers headed 'General Instructions for By-election Work'; Selina Cooper, Margaret Robertson and Emilie Gardner would have studied the Executive Committee's brisk command that:

Immediately a vacancy occurs in a constituency an Organiser shall
go to the most important centre to make preliminary arrangements
. . . The Committee-room should be found before the best positions are already taken . . .

   The Organiser must keep in constant touch with the National
Union London Office . . . On receipt of the Organiser's preliminary report the Executive Committee will at once hold a Special
Meeting to consider it; and will decide whether one Candidate is
to be supported against another . . .

For it was certainly not up to the lowly organisers, mere paid
employees, to decide such things: their job was just to carry out
agreed National Union policy.

Selina Cooper found ample opportunities during 1908 to dem-
onstrate to her employers that she could meet the high standards
of efficiency demanded of her, such as at a particularly crucial
Manchester by-election. Campbell Bannerman had resigned at
Easter and Asquith became Prime Minister. In the ensuing
Cabinet reshuffle, many ministers had to stand for re-election.
Among these was Winston Churchill, MP for North-West
Manchester; he was up against not only a Tory, but also Selina
Cooper's old Guardian comrade, Dan Irving, the socialist candidate. The National Union, always so willing to look on the bright
side, marked all three candidates down as 'not unfavourable' to
women's suffrage, and so Selina was asked just to do general
'propaganda work'.

It turned out to be a hectic contest, with all political interests
jostling with each other. Christabel Pankhurst came up to North-
West Manchester, delighted to oppose a Liberal minister. Selina
Cooper's old friends from the Lancashire Women Textile
Workers' Representation Committee were also busy, defending
the rights of another tiny group of women workers (in this case
barmaids) whose jobs were threatened by Liberal legislation. Eva
Gore-Booth even persuaded her flamboyant Irish sister, Countess
Markievicz, to help publicise the case by driving a coach and four
white horses through the city crowds. Selina Cooper found herself
being whisked through the streets of Manchester alongside a
woman blowing a trumpet. She became so immersed in the
excitement that she had time to scribble only one brief entry in her
diary: 'April 22nd . . . Manchester Suffrage Cart Mob[b]ed

evening spoke at St John.' (In the event, Churchill, with everyone from Christabel and Countess Markievicz to the Tory brewers and the voteless barmaids ranged against him, lost his seat to the Tory).[22]

A week later Selina Cooper set off for a by-election in Wolverhampton with Emilie Gardner.[23] Afterwards she hurried home, spent a few days speaking in Bristol and then rushed straightaway off to Pudsey, a constituency squeezed in between Leeds and Bradford, where a by-election was fixed for mid-June, and where she was again to work with Emilie Gardner. The National Union had decided, since all three Pudsey candidates purported to support women's suffrage, again just to do 'propaganda work'. On this particular occasion, Selina Cooper must have felt irked by her employers' 'non-party' line, for the third candidate was a socialist. In fact, she stayed in Pudsey only for polling day, selling suffrage badges in the street, but then had to rush off to Wales (probably for another by-election) before the Tory candidate's victory was announced, leaving Emilie Gardner to tidy up the loose ends.

The two women wrote to each other over the next week or so and, although Selina's half of the correspondence has not come to light, Emilie's letters, preserved among the Cooper papers, reflect something of the relationship between the two organisers. Turning over the pages, it is clear how torn Selina Cooper sometimes became between her paid non-party suffrage job, and her support for Labour. And it is also clear how much Emilie Gardner wanted Selina's affection and admired her good political sense. The day after polling Emilie wrote:

> Dear Mrs Cooper,
>   You will have seen the dire result . . . I should have gone to bed in deepest blues but on my way home I met the socialist procession . . . singing 'We'll Keep the Red Flag Flying'. They waved their hats at me and I went home comforted.
>   Report is going round – they say with good authority – that the Tories paid for Benson's [the socialist candidate] nomination fee. Can you find out if this is true? . . . I cannot believe it . . . It makes me feel miserable to think of it – just when I have made socialism my own . . .
>   Remember our agreement that all women ought to work only for the vote till it is won! I shall be miserable if you decide the wrong way. I'd rather work with you than anybody because you

are not like an ordinary helper to me now. We have had so many conversations, and you have had so much influence in leading me into the red regions of socialism and I like you so much that I count you as one of my friends if you will let me, and when I say friend I don't mean acquaintance, and I do mean what I say sincerely. I always feel frightened that your dreadful jack-in-the-box 'class war' feelings will pop up! Please smother them or like me reserve them for Lady Dorothy Howard [who was in Pudsey to help the Liberals]!

Love from yours affectionately
Emilie M. Gardner

Selina, far away in Wales, must have decided the 'right way' for we hear no more of her being tempted away from 'working only for the vote till it is won'. She was still a firm socialist but recognised that the only way to alter the National Union's 'non-party' stance was to change the minds of its members, just as she had shifted Emilie Gardner's. It would take a long time but, it seems, Selina was prepared to be patient. Certainly, she replied encouragingly and, for once, at length, from Wales; a week later Emilie dispatched this second letter from Pudsey:

My dear Mrs Cooper,
I was so glad to get your jolly letter and would have answered it before if I had had time. It was nice of you to write like that.
I am very glad to hear what you say abt. Tory gold . . . I hope you are enjoying your Welsh trip. I often think of you . . .
Some day I will write a proper answer to your letter but I feel very stupid just now . . . I just wanted you to know how much I appreciated your letter. You have let me in to a world that I knew nothing about before I knew you.

Much love
Yours affly
Em. Gardner[24]

These few surviving pages from Selina Cooper's correspondence with another organiser are only a one-sided echo of her widening suffrage relationships. Yet the preservation of such letters allows us a rare glimpse of a side of Selina seldom revealed by the photographs, newspaper reports or even by her own diary. We see reflected a woman who commanded deep affection from those she worked with; whose business-like approach to the supreme demand for the vote cloaked the love she inspired in other women.

CHAPTER TWELVE

CAPTAIN TREMAIN'S FOLLY:
1909-1913

The shape of these hectic suffrage years is well known. The tale has often been told of monster processions, Liberal Government intransigence, spiralling suffragette militancy, hunger strikes in prison and the 'Cat-and-Mouse' Act. Selina Cooper's experience of rushing from by-election to by-election, of deputations to Downing Street, of keeping up the propaganda pressure week in week out, was shared by scores of other dedicated suffrage workers at the time. For this reason, this chapter does not recount her activities year by year but instead looks at key themes: relations with the suffragettes, with the aristocratic women Selina worked with, and the reasons behind the original demand for the vote.

In mid-1908 the WSPU organised an enormous procession to Hyde Park: here an immense throng (probably over a quarter of a million people) passed a resolution demanding that the government give women the vote immediately. This Asquith, as usual, ignored. Suffragette frustration mounted in the face of this studied Liberal deafness. WSPU members smashed Asquith's windows, and Christabel and her mother laid plans to 'rush the House of Commons'. Trials and imprisonments followed. In early 1909 the WSPU staged another march on Parliament and twenty-eight more suffragettes were given prison sentences.

Selina Cooper watched these events anxiously. Although she had welcomed the WSPU's original civil disobedience, she grew fearful that the key issue of votes for women would become overshadowed by the more dramatic, but less significant, issue of suffragette arrests and prison conditions. More disturbing still was the WSPU's marked shift from its ILP origins to an almost pro-Tory stance, and Selina would probably have gone along with Sylvia Pankhurst's judgement of her elder sister Christabel: 'I detested her incipient Toryism; I was wounded by her frequent ruthless casting out of trusty friends for a mere hair's-breadth difference of view; I often considered her policy mistaken either in conception or in application; but,' admitted Sylvia, 'her speaking always delighted me . . . I admired her.'[1]

This admiration for the suffragettes' stylish courage kept the relationship between the two major suffrage groups, militant and non-militant, reasonably friendly at the beginning of 1908. For instance, Selina Cooper travelled across Lancashire to speak to the small WSPU group in Preston in early spring. There was even talk of bringing the two wings together, though the WSPU's anti-Liberal policy made an alliance with the National Union unlikely.

But as premeditated violence grew later that year, even conciliatory Mrs Fawcett, who had earlier welcomed imprisoned suffragettes on their release, felt that enough was enough. 'In 1908 the NUWSS [National Union] made a definite break with the WSPU,' she wrote later, 'on account of the latter having finally abandoned the policy which they had at first adopted of suffering violence but using none.' As militancy escalated, the National Union line hardened and it openly condemned such tactics.[2]

While the outlines of this new National Union policy were taking shape, Selina Cooper travelled north with Margaret Robertson to Newcastle for another by-election. Mrs Pankhurst and the suffragettes were there too, again competing for the same crowds, and Selina noted later how:

> at an outdoor meeting in Newcastle I had Mrs Pankhurst as my competitor
> I could not get a crowd so I took my hat off and my hair
> tumbled down my back so I soon got a crowd.

To win her audience, Selina might resort to such below-the-belt tricks with her waist-length chestnut hair. But for the peaceable suffragists, now indiscriminately blamed for suffragette stone-throwing, by-elections had grown terrifyingly rough affairs. For instance, it was difficult for the women to find landladies when they arrived in a strange town, for everyone now believed that suffrage spelt violence. Selina later noted how,

> An Election at Newcastle on Tyne during the Suffrage day[s] we were turned out of our Hotel where we were staying into the streets, the only concession the Landlord gave us was to leave by the back door so that the crowd could not molest us
> whe[n] coming down the back street a very timid Curate came up to us saying he had a Taxi waiting for us he took four of us to his Home and [we] stayed there during the election
> he was very brave we were very grateful to him[3]

Over the coming months, Selina had her dress and coat badly torn at a mill meeting in Oldham, was pelted with rotten eggs in Pontefract market in Yorkshire and was jostled by a rowdy by-election crowd in mid-Essex. On this last occasion, Sylvia Pankhurst acknowledged, 'the constitutional suffragists fell victims to disorder, which might, more justly, have been directed against us. We saw them swept from the market place.'[4]

It seemed as though suffragette militancy, at first an excellent means of alerting public attention to the government's shabby treatment of women, was beginning to have ugly side effects. The WSPU tactics were used as an excuse for the disgraceful actions of anti-suffrage roughs. By-elections and political meetings, sometimes already rowdy, became fair game for the hecklers. Indeed there is even evidence of co-ordinated rowdyism among the anti-suffrage louts. As violence was met by violence, the arguments about women's right to take part in the political process often seemed drowned in the uproar.

Escalating militancy increasingly soured the relationship between the two suffrage camps. In February 1909 Selina Cooper again set off north, this time to organise a by-election campaign in Glasgow Central. Her diary depicts her bustling down to the docks for a meeting and hurriedly preparing a suffrage window, presumably in one of the city's shopping streets. Yet the WSPU was in Glasgow for the by-election too, and Selina's diary for 17 February ends cryptically, 'had an interview with Mrs Pankhurst in the Waverley Hotel Glasgow'. What transpired at the interview we shall sadly never know. We can only imagine the vexatious conversation that took place between these two dignified and impressive women, and the sadness both must have felt on realising how far apart they had recently grown. The different by-election strategies and Christabel's shift towards Toryism would have been discussed; so too would militant tactics, for the WSPU was planning to 'rush' the House of Commons again. Clearly the two women no longer shared the same point of view. They scarcely spoke the same language. By 1909 the chances of reconciliation had fast receded.

In her diary two days later Selina Cooper noted more revealingly, 'Spoke to Mrs Pankhurst in the Hotel. She was very Cold and not at all Fri[e]ndly.' Even from these two curt sentences we can glimpse Selina's forlorn regret at what was happening to the women's movement; and at what could, in other circumstances, have been a great united women's suffrage campaign, untouched by bitterness and divisions.[5]

Over the next two or three years WSPU militancy continued to spiral. There was widespread window-smashing and arson. Courageous suffragette prisoners went on hunger strike to shame the Liberal Government into changing its mind; but they were met only by brutal forced feeding by the authorities. The WSPU offices were raided by the police and Christabel fled across the Channel, to direct suffragette operations from safe exile in Paris. Increasingly, those who dared to question Christabel's policies were edged out of the WSPU: the organisation became pared down to a band of dedicated women who were prepared to act obediently on her command – even when that involved arson attempts and thus considerable personal danger. (The little that remained of the WSPU's early attempts to win popular working-class support now lay with Sylvia Pankhurst: she turned her considerable energies towards organising a campaign in the East End of London. The Cabinet could be persuaded, 'not by the secret militancy of a few enthusiasts but the rousing of the masses,' she later explained. 'The East End was the greatest homogenous working-class area accessible to the House of Commons by popular demonstration.')[6]

Escalating WSPU militancy still sent out far-reaching ripples, with anti-suffrage hostility swollen into malevolent violence. Suffragists were now at high risk as they addressed meetings around the country. Even someone like Selina Cooper, who seldom grew ruffled in public, found some of the crowds terrifying. At one election she went to work for the National Union in the nearby constituency of Darwen, and set off for where she was billed to speak:

> . . . arriving at the Station every house seem to be in darkness as I walked through the long streets on my way to the Square. I had ordered a lurry for a platform when I got to the meeting place there were thousands of People waiting the Police tryed to make way for me but the crowd Hustled me and the Police.
> The platform was upset and I had to escape for my life a number of sympathisers helped the Police to get me into the Liberal Club which was close by the crowd stoned the windows . . . [7]

Meanwhile Mary Cooper, now at Nelson grammar school, began to sense her mother's anxieties about the direction the suffrage campaign was taking.

> My mother, she joined with them all the time until they began to destroy. I suppose she might have been thinking it might have happened to me. It could have been. But they weren't bothering. They were going against anybody who spoke against them in Parliament, and they were destroying houses.

Both Mary and Selina, who kept in touch with Sylvia Pankhurst long afterwards, were convinced that most of the blame lay at Christabel's door. 'I must make this straight,' Mary stressed, trying to convey the complex emotions of these years.

> . . . I've nothing but admiration [for many of the suffragettes], and Mrs Pankhurst at first was all right, but she got obsessed with her eldest daughter . . . And she was a criminal, was Christabel. And she started . . . burning bins and art galleries . . . and then she dodged off to Paris.

Mary also felt it important to emphasise that her mother was not someone too cowardly to go to prison or undergo hunger strike. 'But my mother had left before then. It wasn't that she shirked it, but she saw what was coming.'[8]

Stone throwing and arson, hunger strikes and forced feeding: the chill at the pit of Selina's stomach grew colder and colder. She believed that the tactical violence practised by a small guerrilla band of women was not really the most effective way of wresting political concessions from a reluctant government. She felt that hunger strikes, though a brave and noble sacrifice, easily deflected the government's attention away from the central constitutional change women demanded and allowed it to legislate merely on the side issue of prison discipline. In 1913 the 'Cat and Mouse' Act was rushed through Parliament, giving the government power to rearrest hunger strikers given temporary discharge from prison so they could recover their health. In addition she, and others like her, recognised the irony of an undemocratic group like the WSPU, which now seldom permitted a dissident voice to be raised, fighting for women to be given the democratic right to vote. However crucial the ends, such means were not justified.

However terrifying the suffrage campaign became, Selina Cooper never forgot for whom she was demanding the vote. Although an employee of the National Union, she had ample opportunities to work with groups of working women in those parts of the country where the labour movement and suffrage campaign could best work together. In spring 1909, for instance, she set off for a month in Leicester. Leicester had elected as one of its two MPs none other than Ramsay MacDonald, and the city boasted both a strong ILP branch and a tradition of women's work in the local hosiery and boot-and-shoe industries. So Selina was kept busy, visiting the Secretary of the Women Boot and Shoe Operatives, chalking the pavements to advertise meetings, speaking outside the Co-operative Wheatsheaf works in the city and generally encouraging women to believe they were *worth* enfranchising. 'We are sometimes told that there are more pressing things than women's suffrage, but the men who say that have the vote,' she urged them. 'Women's suffrage is, to women, the most important thing in the world, and when we get it we will use it for the good of the world.'[9]

With such speeches did Selina draw other working women into the National Union, and help shape it into a more broadly-based organisation. She possessed the rare knack of being able to persuade working-class women that suffrage was something that touched their day-to-day lives and for which they too could actively campaign. Shortly after Leicester she was back in the Midlands again, this time at Cradley Heath. Here women and girls carried out their traditional ill-paid labour: forging heavy iron chains in ramshackle workshops near their homes. According to Mary, Selina long retained her memory of how keenly impressed she had been by these sturdy chainmakers:

> She saw the scars on those women's bodies . . . It burned through and they were scarred, through the corsets. Because they were hammering them hot . . . Oh, and she said what rough women they were. Because she'd worked among the fisherwomen, [but] she said she'd never seen such hard ones as the chainmakers. Oh, they could booze. She says they were like men . . . hard callouses on their hands . . . and bad language.

Her task was to organise a deputation of ten chainmakers to travel down to London for the great International Woman Suffrage Alliance (formed in the 1890s to link together voteless women across the world) procession to the Albert Hall on 27 April 1909. The National Union paid the fares, and Selina Cooper and the ten women – their ages ranging between sixteen and sixty-five – set off down to Euston. She shepherded them to their hotel and took them – with their heavy iron chains – to join the procession and to impress genteel London. 'It would be impossible to give a list of the groups' in the procession, the official report commented, 'but especially notable were the chainmakers from Cradley Heath, who toiled for about 4s per week of sixty hours.' The following day Selina took the chainmakers round Westminster Abbey and made sure they all got a good dinner before returning to their forges. Her kindness was not forgotten: the women presented her with a length of heavy chain that they had worked with their own hands, and this Selina treasured all her life.[10]

Later that year Selina's portrait appeared on the front page of *Common Cause* with a caption that stated, obviously without much exaggeration, that 'her direct and fearless nature makes her not only respected but loved by every audience she addresses'. The same photograph was used by the National Union as a signed propaganda postcard to help publicise the suffrage cause. On the back, Selina Cooper wrote 'Make no More Giants Oh Lord But elevate the Race at once', a democratic message confirming her beliefs. Indeed, her socialism helped take her into industrial communities where she found herself sucked into local tragedies caused by the Liberal Government's high-handedness. In 1910 she was working up on the Cumberland coast at Whitehaven; in this isolated little coalfield, mines ran fathoms deep under the sea and miners braved considerable dangers to get near these buried coal seams. While Selina was there an explosion occurred trapping over a hundred men underground. She was horrified by what she witnessed and afterwards jotted down her recollections of that tragic day:

> I stood on the Shore talking to the Women whose husbands were entombed
> I shall never forget the tragic look when the order was given out the crowd cried it is all over we shall never see our Men folk again.

One hundred and thirty-six men died at Whitehaven – and they represented only a small fraction of the miners involved each year in treacherous pit accidents. The Liberal Government seemed to do little to force the greedy coal owners to tighten mine safety, and only meagre compensation was paid out to miners' families. Feelings ran even higher later that year when Winston Churchill, the Home Secretary, called out the troops to Tonypandy in South Wales to use bayonets against miners on strike over wages.[11]

Such experiences further strengthened Selina Cooper's resolve to intensify pressure on the Liberals, deaf to the claims of both the miners and voteless women. The January 1910 General Election had weakened the Liberal Government's confidence, and with its majority in the Commons greatly reduced by the Tories, the balance of power now lay in the hands of about eighty Irish MPs' and about forty Labour members. Of these, the Irish MPs cared little for votes for women, anxious only about the long-awaited Home Rule Bill. Nor were the Labour MPs, with a few honourable exceptions like Keir Hardie and Philip Snowden, much concerned about women's suffrage; most of them (particularly the MPs from the Miners' Federation which had recently affiliated to the Labour Party) were content to tag submissively along on the Liberals' coat-tails, in support of such progressive measures as old age pensions or a national insurance scheme. In this, of course, Labour MPs were backed by party conference decisions favouring general franchise reform rather than specific measures for women's suffrage. To the right of the Liberal Party, the Tories still tended to support enfranchising only those few women who held property in their own right. Looming over all this was the House of Lords, whose traditional right to veto bills it did not like was currently being challenged by the Liberals. A women's suffrage bill that would scrape through the Lords would have to be narrow indeed.

So, shortly after the January election, an all-party Conciliation Committee was formed. It drew up a bill, narrowly conceived to enfranchise about a million women who were either occupiers or householders. This cautious initiative won the support of all the major suffrage groups and, as the second reading of this Conciliation Bill loomed nearer in mid-summer 1910, they organised a series of great demonstrations of public support for it.

Selina Cooper played a key role in the National Union's campaign that summer. She might have entertained personal doubts about whether such a narrow bill would benefit a married woman like herself at all; but she recognised that it was the principle of women's equal rights that was crucial, and that at least this cautious bill had a reasonable chance of success. But to achieve this the National Union had to convince Asquith that women really did want the vote; so they organised a deputation to see the Prime Minister at 10 Downing Street on 20 June 1910. Selina was invited to join, the only woman with industrial experience; the other twenty suffragists included Ethel Snowden, Isabella Ford and Eleanor Rathbone, now one of Liverpool's City Councillors. Four of the women were allowed to speak: Mrs Fawcett, of course, two other stalwart suffragists – and Selina Cooper. What she felt on confronting this arch-tormentor of women's suffrage we shall never know. Certainly she can have entertained few illusions about such an obstinate prime minister, but must have urged him not to ignore the tens of thousands of women textile workers for much longer.

Three days later Asquith announced that he would give time for the crucial second reading of the Conciliation Bill in July. The National Union stepped up its campaign with public demonstrations up and down the country. Two days before the bill was due to be debated, it organised a mass rally in Trafalgar Square, with no fewer than six platforms from which the crowd could be addressed. Selina Cooper, clutching her ticket admitting her to the plinth at the centre of Nelson's Column, mounted Platform One in the centre of the square. She had now firmly emerged as one of the National Union's foremost speakers.

With her on the platform were Mrs Fawcett, Ethel Snowden and an American suffragist. Selina's eye swept over the great crowd assembled before her; she could catch a glimpse here and there of many of her suffrage friends mounting the other platforms in distant parts of the square. It was almost like a roll–call of the past ten years of her life. On Platform Three over to the east were Eva Gore-Booth, Sarah Reddish and Esther Roper from the Lancashire Women Textile Workers' Representation Committee. There, too, was another Nelson woman, Margaret Aldersley, currently a Labour Guardian on the Burnley Board and increasingly caught up by the national suffrage campaign. On the parapet were ranged members of the Men's League for Women's Suffrage. Dotted round the square were bright red banners inscribed with a town, and the number of parliamentary electors who had signed the petition for women's suffrage. To the west she could distinguish some of the women she had come to know through the National Union: Eleanor Rathbone, Margaret Robertson from Manchester, Isabella Ford.[12] The sight of these Trafalgar Square crowds reminded Selina Cooper of how much of her recent life she had invested in the campaign. Victory seemed to be almost within reach as she watched the great crowd duly pass the resolution on the bill to be debated in three days' time.

Expectations ran high. The bill easily passed this second reading, despite the opposition of leading Liberals like Lloyd George and Winston Churchill who claimed it was 'anti-democratic' and would benefit only the Tories. The opposition of such Cabinet Ministers was worrying. Worse still, the Commons then voted to refer the bill, not to a small committee, but to a committee of the whole House – a clever device whereby the government could smother a bill while keeping its hands relatively clean. Afterwards Asquith and the Liberals kept the women dangling for the rest of the year, seemingly preoccupied with other more pressing questions. At the December 1910 general election, the Commons' almighty struggle over the power of the Lords came to the fore – not women's suffrage. Then during 1911 the government faced massive waves of industrial strikes. Surely, the Liberals could now argue, it was more urgent to guarantee miners a decent wage and introduce a progressive National Insurance scheme than to court disruptive constitutional changes by enfranchising a million or more unpredictable (and probably Tory) women voters.

Tens of thousands of women said no. Keen to add their voice to the campaign, they flocked to join the National Union. In 1911 membership rose to over 30,000 and in 1912 to over 42,000. The number of local suffrage societies mushroomed to over four hundred in 1912. As we have seen, the National Union responded to this grassroots strength by re-organising the societies on a constituency basis with great federations to link isolated groups in each region. The federations were an inspired idea and by 1911 no fewer than seventeen had sprung up: Manchester and District, South Wales and Monmouthshire, the West Riding and so on. The National Union Executive, which had been steadily increasing its organisers from the original three, quickly appreciated the value of employing ten of its trained organisers, each to work specifically in one of these federations. By 1912 it boasted a total of sixty-one organisers (with annual salaries and expenses exceeding £2,800).

Who were these newly recruited organisers? Responsible for the influential Manchester Federation was, of course, Margaret Robertson. Under her guidance suffrage societies were soon springing up in previously unpromising communities: Blackburn, Rawtenstall and Todmorden, for instance. A newer recruit was a splendid Scotswoman called Annot Robinson, a St Andrew's University graduate who had become an active member of the Manchester ILP and married the propaganda secretary of Manchester's central ILP branch. She had earlier been involved with the WSPU and had twice been imprisoned after suffragette scuffles with the police. But after the birth of her elder daughter in 1909, Annot began to move towards the National Union. The reasons why she chose to distance herself from the militant suffragettes seem to have been similar to Selina Cooper's. 'Oh, I can tell you about why [my mother turned to the non-militant National Union],' Annot Robinson's younger daughter stated. 'She couldn't stand it. When Mrs Pankhurst blew up Lloyd George's house, a lot of them left – she was endangering lives.' Annot was also dismayed by 'Mrs Pankhurst's imperious dictatorship' of the WSPU, and by suffragette attacks not only on the Labour Party but on the ILP as well.

So about 1910 Annot Robinson joined the National Union and began to work with the Manchester Federation. It was not easy for her, especially with two small daughters: a photograph of a Manchester suffrage meeting that has survived among the family papers shows a baby, Annot's elder daughter, perched on a table amidst a crowded room of women. An even more difficult problem for Annot was her husband's attitude to her suffrage activities. Although he was in the ILP and sympathetic in principle, he found being married to a suffragist impossible to accept, and on occasions would even heckle her at meetings. A friend of Annot's, her younger daughter recalled, 'said the first time she met my parents was at a meeting and my mother was speaking, and this man kept getting up. "Why aren't you at home looking after your husband? Why aren't you looking after your children?" He'd been drinking, you see. Jealousy. He would drink to get the courage.' This domestic strife was worsened by money problems, but Annot bravely carried on and before long her speaking talents were noticed. In 1911 the National Union appointed her as a temporary organiser, and within a year she had grown, like Selina Cooper and Margaret Robertson before her, to become a key organiser, helping to shift the great Manchester Federation away from its traditional Liberal loyalties.[13]

An equally valuable new recruit was Ada Nield Chew. Perhaps her conversion is particularly surprising since she had earlier been a vehement opponent of women's suffrage, arguing bitterly with both Christabel Pankhurst and the Coopers. Yet in 1911 she too became a National Union organiser. Ada Nield Chew, a woman of fiercely independent views, published her explanation for her dramatic conversion from uncompromising adultist to passionate suffragist in the *Common Cause*. Her candid letter reveals the troubled spirits of those women who changed sides in these tumultuous days. It also offers a more sophisticatedly phrased version of Selina's own change of mind from trade unionism to suffragism a dozen years earlier:

I have not changed my opinion as to the immediate value and wisdom of trade unionism for women workers, but it has been forced on my consciousness more and more that whilst women are at a political disadvantage trade unionism is necessarily limited (which does not detract from the value of trade unionism, but emphasises the importance of the vote): But I could not see that anything less than Adult Suffrage would be of any use to the working woman, and therefore opposed a limited measure as being reactionary. Now, after many months of anxious thinking, I have come to the conclusion that we cannot get on whilst women have *no* means of even presenting their point of view, and that we shall be at a standstill till this necessary 'first step' is taken; and that to be determined to wait until all women can vote is as reactionary and impracticable as to oppose all reform because it does not go as far on our way as we wish it to go . . .

So, to the 'first step'! The journey is indeed a long one, but that should make us all the more eager to start. I want to help the beginning, though I may never see the end, and as an earnest of this have become a member of the Rochdale branch of the National Union, and am prepared to 'stand my corner' as far as time and ability allow.[14]

Ada Nield Chew joined the National Union when she realised how hollow the adultist arguments came to sound. Annot Robinson joined as the suffragettes sped further and further away from her ILP beliefs. Other labour women became organisers without any such dramatic conversion: they merely accelerated their level of commitment. Another Nelson woman, Margaret Aldersley, the Poor Law Guardian, also became a National Union organiser, on a casual basis at first in 1911 and then with a more formal appointment in 1912.[15] A further recruit was Ellen Wilkinson (later an MP and Labour Government minister) who became an organiser in 1913 when she graduated from Manchester University aged twenty-one. She was soon rushing from meeting to meeting, giving unruly hecklers as good as they got. 'You do well to class me with criminals and lunatics for I can see that you are both,' she would shout. 'And you can't aim straight either.'[16]

By 1911–12, then, Selina Cooper found herself supported in the National Union by a new generation of radical organisers: not just

Emilie Gardner and Margaret Robertson, but also Annot Robinson, Ada Nield Chew, Margaret Aldersley, and later Ellen Wilkinson. These were stirring years when it would have been all too easy for such suffragists to forget *why* they were demanding the vote for women. But this was not so. Neither Selina Cooper nor the other radical suffragists forgot the reforms demanded by women at work and mothers at home that crucially underpinned the campaign for the vote.

The Liberal Government might turn a deaf ear to pleas for the vote, but did introduce a series of important welfare reforms into Britain. Selina followed the introduction of old age pensions and National Insurance very closely: her six years' experience on the Board of Guardians and her harrowing visits to the Burnley workhouse had taught her how vital it was to relieve working people of the terrors of old age and unemployment. Like Sylvia Pankhurst, she supported the 1911 National Insurance Act, despite women's powerlessness to shape such laws (other women objected strongly to the Act on the grounds of 'no taxation without representation'). Selina was even appointed one of the official National Insurance lecturers the following year, and went down to London for a month's training in what the act's different provisions, in particular the new maternity benefit, meant in practice. Her new skills were vital. Margaret Llewelyn Davies, General Secretary of the Women's Co-operative Guild, wrote to Selina about addressing a Guild conference with the object of enabling 'our members to obtain a clear knowledge of the Act as it affects women'. At the same time Selina Cooper used the act as suffrage propaganda. 'The Insurance Act affects women just as much as men,' she urged one by-election crowd, 'and they have to contribute 3d per week equally with men. But the men have the option of voting either for or against the Act, and the women have not.'[17]

Yet it was around mothers' experience of pregnancy, childbirth and motherhood that Selina Cooper felt women's votelessness most strongly. After her own bitter experiences of maternity, Selina knew only too well the daily struggle of an overburdened mother trying to preserve the frail life of a small baby during its first few months. In rows of poorly built terraced houses, inadequately heated and ventilated, housewives fought a harsh battle against poverty and dirt. Despite the Liberal Government's progressive measures, infant mortality still remained tragically high. A few imaginative local authorities had begun to take steps to prevent baby deaths: for instance, when Selina was working in Leicester, she recorded in her diary that she went 'to the Leicestershire Milk Depot to see the Babies weighed' – a progressive scheme to ensure daily supplies of special milk for young babies, and to make a weekly check on babies' weights. And about the same time Sarah Reddish and other Guildswomen sailed across the Channel to visit the pioneering 'Consultations for Mothers' in Ghent. Sarah Reddish brought back these ideas and started a similar School for Mothers in Bolton.

Particularly during 1913, a time when Christabel Pankhurst was publishing her alarmist *Great Scourge* articles warning women that three-quarters of all men were infected by venereal disease before marriage, the issues of motherhood, sexuality and their links to women's suffrage grew prominent. The Women's Co-operative Guild had managed to exert sufficient pressure for the National Insurance Act to be amended and for the maternity benefit to be made the legal property of the mother – a highly controversial notion. This helped highlight the whole issue of what was expected of Edwardian mothers and to revive the old bogey that infant mortality was caused, not by family poverty, but by mothers going out to work. Some even felt that working mothers should be prohibited by law. Selina Cooper, coming from a Lancashire town with so many women working in the mills, had always opposed such foolish ideas; in August 1913 she wrote a brisk letter to *Common Cause* making this point, and naturally linking it to the women's suffrage campaign:

> [Most] alarming is the fact that working women are voteless, and their power to check panic legislation, which may take the form of prohibiting married women from having the right to work without giving her other means whereby she can assert her own individuality is 'very limited indeed'.
>   . . . One reason why I am a convinced suffragist is that the mothers (even as wage-earners) take the greater share of the responsibility in the upbringing of their children; therefore, they ought to have the greater means, not the less, to enable them to do justice to the rising generation. The mothers of Lancashire are not

shirking their duty as parents any more than working-women of other counties . . .[18]

Suffragists like Selina also began to think seriously about issues like the financial independence of mothers. In the autumn the National Union branched out with an education campaign: local study circles were set up and provided with syllabuses focusing on the inadequacy of existing state provision for child welfare and the disabilities wives and mothers experienced. Whether such a study circle got under way in Nelson is unclear: Selina, of course, was away for much of the time, as was Margaret Aldersley. But Harriette Beanland, for one, cared deeply about such issues and was increasingly incensed at the indignities voteless women had to suffer at the hands of men. When a woman accused of conducting back-street abortions in Nelson was tried for manslaughter amidst much sensationalism, Harriette Beanland dispatched a blistering letter to the *Nelson Leader* which linked women's votelessness with the complex question of motherhood:

> The idea that women should not have motherhood forced on them against their will is regarded as strange . . . When a woman's death is the result of an illegal operation all the majesty of the law is invoked, wigs, robes, and all the solemn and awe-inspiring adjuncts of the court to crush the miserable creature who has committed the crime. But no one cares about the awful slaughter of mothers in childbirth. That is looked upon with callous indifference. It has been stated that during the Boer War more women died through childbirth in Great Britain than all the men who died from wounds or disease in that war. Yet women are told they ought not to vote because they do not sacrifice their lives for their country![19]

By 1913 the Nelson Women's Labour League had been revived and Harriette Beanland was its secretary. It was through the league, both in Nelson and nationally, that much of this pressure was now exerted for proper mother and baby clinics to be set up. A couple of days after her letter was published in the *Leader*, the Nelson Women's Labour League passed the following resolution and Harriette duly forwarded it to Labour Party headquarters:

> That in view of the high infantile death rate, and the large number of children who enter school suffering from physical defects, this

Branch of the Women's Labour League urges the Government to
encourage Local Authorities to establish Baby Clinics for the
medical treatment of Babies and Children under School age, and
to make grants to such Institutions from National Funds.

Although Selina was away from Nelson much of that autumn,
Harriette must have kept her friend informed on what was happening; and we can imagine Harriette, with no direct experience
of motherhood, turning to Selina for extra facts and arguments to
boost the campaign during her friend's brief spells at home. Certainly, a few weeks later Harriette forwarded another appeal to
the local paper which echoed Selina's own feelings on the matter.
In Nelson, despite all its new housing, 102 babies out of a thousand still died in their first year, Harriette wrote.

> Mothers know from their own experience how terrible it is to lose
> their little ones, and when we realise that . . . the chief cause of the
> high infantile death rate is poverty, we cannot help believing that
> the general public will no longer allow this sorrow to be the
> constant lot of the wage-earning class . . . Already we have the
> principle of school clinics as well as school medical inspection
> adopted. Now we see that it is too late to begin this work when the
> child goes to school. We must fill up the gap that comes before that
> time. We need, in fact, Baby Clinics . . .

Local councils did at last begin to move, faced by such arguments and statistics. Brierfield formed an Infant Aid Society
which planned a 'Babies Welcome' voluntary clinic. And Nelson
employed a woman health visitor to visit the mother in her own
home as soon as the Town Council was notified of a birth, to check
the baby's weight and to encourage the mother to breastfeed (or at
least to discourage feeding with unhygienic rubber tubes). In such
ways Nelson managed to reduce its infant mortality rate by 1914,
although it still remained a tragic ninety-one deaths per thousand
births. But provision of clinics remained patchy and dependent on
local goodwill; and, of course, every woman, mother or not,
remained voteless – powerless to improve the situation.[20]

The extraordinary thing about the Edwardian suffrage movement
was, because women were kept disenfranchised on the grounds of
their *sex* and for no other reason, it drew together women across

class boundaries in a way no other campaign could – not even the temperance movement. The WSPU attracted a number of wealthy and aristocratic supporters: among the best known was Lady Constance Lytton. Similarly the National Union always included a generous sprinkling of the rich and influential. One such was Lady Frances Balfour, among those with whom Selina Cooper had sat down to dinner on that long-ago deputation to Westminster. Lady Frances, highly connected in the Tory Party, was now a leader of an important right-wing pressure group, the Conservative and Unionist Women's Suffrage Association, as well as President of the London Society for Women's Suffrage. She was enthusiastic about the parliamentary franchise being entrusted to well-connected and reliable women like herself, but distinctly dubious about it being given to the rabble. 'I frankly hated this appeal to the mob,' she admitted, 'and always went with reluctance on suffrage marches and demonstrations.'

Lady Frances was apparently the sort of National Union leader who might appear snobbish and patronising to those suffrage organisers who received a wage for their work. 'Lady Frances Balfour,' Selina Cooper scribbled in her notebook years later, 'she belive [sic] that only the diplomats of the past can go forward and the masses were not fitted.' Selina, with her democratic faith in the 'masses' rather than the 'classes', found such arrogance highly irksome. But what was remarkable about the National Union was that its ponderous democratic structure was suffi- ciently elastic to allow the voices of titled ladies like Lady Frances, graduates like Emilie Gardner, and northern working women like Selina Cooper, all to be heard. There was of course friction between those who offered their services free to the National Union and those who had to work for a living. (Ada Nield Chew's daughter recalls her mother liked the upper-middle-class women who led the National Union, 'and she admired them, and she respected them. But she thought a few of them looked down on her because she had to be paid for what she did and she resented that very much.') It would have been impossible to run a mass organi- sation in Edwardian England in which no such class snobbery was present. What is unusual about the National Union is that it retained – without splits or public rows – all classes of women within its tolerant embrace.[21]

Selina Cooper spent a lot of time campaigning with women like Lady Frances Balfour, hostility between Labour and Tory temporarily forgotten. Indeed the suffrage campaign introduced Selina to the odd ways of local gentry in different parts of the country. One entry in her diary in 1909, for instance, reads 'Went to Truro, met at the Station with a Motor Car rode 7 miles through the snow . . . Stay at Captain Tremain's Hall . . . Children Danced in the Drawing [Room] 8 Oclock Dinner a grand array of Silver.' This brief description seems to have been the model of visitor's tact for only years and years later did Selina feel at liberty to record a more truthful report:

> Addressing a Meeting in Turo Town Hall After the Meeting
> was over a Lady was waiting to take me to her Home
> 2 Miles Snow
> about 7 Miles out of the City She introduced me to her
> Husband Captain Tremain He was drunk
> at the Hall a beautiful Granite Hall
> In the Bedroom there was a glorious Wood fire burning
> My Host dress for dinner
> he was still drunk he knock the top off a Bottle of win
> with as much grace as a King
> next morning he came with me to the station
> he was still drunk
> he saw me in the train bought me paper and bid me goodbye
> as if there was nothing the matter with him

But for the women's suffrage movement Selina would never have found common cause with aristocrats such as Lady Betty Balfour, sister-in-law of the last Conservative Prime Minister, now currently leader of the party. Selina also used to stay with the Cadburys, a big Quaker family; 'the Eiderdown with the Peacock work in silk made in India', she later wrote in her notebook; 'a Native woman 6 Months to work it. I could not sleep it was so beautiful'. And she became particularly friendly with Lady St Helier, a close relation of Winston Churchill's. 'The first drawing-room audience I addressed,' Selina later explained,

> was at Lady St Helier's. Lady St Helier took a great fancy to me
> . . . She was the only woman I came across who tried to carry on a
> political saloon . . . Occasionally she would give a dinner party,
> and around her table I met . . . Lord Robert Cecil [son of Lord

Salisbury, the late Prime Minister, and a member of the leading
Tory dynasty], Winston Churchill, George Lansbury, H.M.
Hyndman and other well known politicians. The conversation at
table was most wonderful . . . The language, it was wonderful.[22]

Selina, mill worker from Nelson, took all this in her stride. The
demands of fashionable London never appeared to daunt her.
Although she can have had little to spend on her clothes she always
appeared, with Harriette Beanland's help, most elegantly
dressed. Her elaborate hats allowed her to sail through the most
formal of social gatherings. A graceful speaker, she delighted in
the glittering wit of the supper tables of Tory London. This was an
increasingly important asset. By 1911–12 the suffrage situation
had grown so unpromising and the Liberal and Labour Parties so
unhelpful, that Selina and other suffragists found themselves
looking increasingly to Tories like the Balfours and Cecils for
support. The National Union Executive therefore organised a
series of lavish suffrage dinner parties to give members of both
Houses of Parliament an opportunity to meet National Union suffragists. Selina was naturally one of those who could assure the
success of such delicate occasions. Present at these 'At Homes'
were men like Lord Robert Cecil, one of the few men in Parliament
to protest against the outrage of forced-feeding of imprisoned suffragettes. The occasional entries in Selina's diary at the time
suggest that she had become friendly with Cecil – and also that
she was still as keen a theatre-goer as she had been in her youth:

25th Lady St Helier Lunch with Lord Robert Cecil, Miss
[Eleanor] Glynn and Miss Braitwaite who took the Madona in the
Miracle
26th The guest of Lady St Helier 52 Portland Place London. Evening went to the Theatre Bunty Pulls the Strings
27th Spoke at the Conservative Franchise Society at the
Knightsbridge Palace Hotel with Lord Robert Cecil

Selina and Lady St Helier continued to correspond with each
other after this visit. But, it turned out, spring 1912 was not an
appropriate time to enjoy leisurely theatre trips. On 1 March, a
couple of days later, the WSPU began another rash of window
smashing. On the same day, nearly a million miners came out on
strike, demanding a national minimum wage. Tom Mann, the

labour leader who had so influenced Selina Cooper, was arrested. Nelson ILP passed an emergency resolution of strong protest 'against the arrests and convictions now being promulgated by the Government against members of the working class'. Lady St Helier was also perturbed by such events and wrote an affectionate letter to her friend up in Nelson:

> I often think of the nice times we had when you were here and how much I enjoyed it all. I hope you will be able to come again before very long.
>
> The strike is very horrible, and I trust things are clearing up a little, we do not feel it here as you do in the country, and it is *difficult* for us to gauge the suffering and want so far from the centre of it all.

For Selina Cooper there was no difficulty. She knew that the cotton mills that her husband and other cotton workers relied on would soon stop without coal. And she also knew, from her experiences in South Wales and on the Cumberland coast, how much the miners deserved better wages and working conditions. What she did not yet know was that over the next couple of years she would spend long days lobbying miners around the coalfields of Britain. For, in spring 1912, the women's suffrage campaign took off in a new and unforeseen direction, drawing Selina's talents as organiser and speaker right into the centre of events.[23]

CHAPTER THIRTEEN

THE ELECTION FIGHTING FUND: 1912-1913

The years before the Great War broke out were, histories of the period explain, peppered by outbursts of fierce militancy. The stability of Asquith's Liberal Government was under attack from three directions: from Ulster's aggressive campaign of protest against Irish Home Rule; from repeated industrial strikes, especially among key groups like the South Wales Miners; and from the spiralling militancy of the suffragettes. These three onslaughts on Liberal rule might have toppled the government had not a luckless archduke in a distant part of Europe been assassinated at the eleventh hour.

What is seldom mentioned is the close alliance between two of these troublesome groups: labour and suffrage. Mesmerised as historians have often been by more dramatic events of workers' strikes and suffragette arson, they have lost sight of the links forged between the national labour and suffrage groups. Historians usually nod in the direction of, say, Sylvia Pankhurst's East London Federation of Suffragettes or Labour MP George Lansbury's rebel suffrage by-election in nearby Bromley and Bow; but then scurry to the more familiar territory of Emily Wilding Davison's suffragette death on the Derby race course, or the effects of the cruel Cat-and-Mouse Act. By failing to follow the suffrage battle out beyond the maelstrom of London to the distant hustings and remote provincial meeting rooms, historians may easily miss the electoral alliance cemented between labour and suffrage in 1912 and subsequently strengthened in 1913–14.[1]

During the two-and-a-half years before war broke out, the big battalions of labour (the Labour Party, together with linked organisations like the Miners' Federation and the ILP) and the big battalions of suffrage (the National Union alone had over 53,000 members by the outbreak of war) went to the electors hand-in-hand. This alliance operated in no fewer than eight by-elections. It lent its considerable weight to pro-suffrage candidates, with the aim of nibbling away the Liberal Government's fragile command of the Commons. As a result, they prised four seats away from the Liberals and heavily reduced the Liberal majority in three others. (However, because of the oddities of three-cornered elections, they were unable to increase the number of Labour seats even though they significantly increased the Labour *vote*. The immediate beneficiary was ironically the Tory Party.)

The effect of this labour-suffrage alliance on Edwardian electoral arithmetic was worrying to Liberal politicians. But had such men cared to lift their eyes from their party political sums, they might have become even more alarmed by the long-term implications of the alliance. For the alliance did, it seems, spur the drift of many active women out of the Liberal Party and into the Labour Party, the ILP or into independence from party ties. It helped drive deeper the wedge between the Liberal Party and those women, brought up as faithful and loyal Liberals, who now began to entertain doubts about the integrity of a party whose treatment of voteless women was so cavalier.

The alliance also brought for the first time in English history the great weight of the labour and trade union movements, including eventually the might of the giant Miners' Federation, behind demands for women's political rights. It helped weaken the umbilical link between the infant Labour Party and its elderly Liberal parents. It assisted Labour to challenge traditional Liberal seats in a series of closely fought three-cornered by-elections; and in this way it weakened the secret electoral agreement that Labour had earlier struck with the Liberals for sharing out likely constituencies between them. For here was a highly contentious issue – women's suffrage – where the two parties from 1912 onwards apparently took diametrically different sides. Indeed, the labour-suffrage pact arguably threatened the Liberal Party on two fronts: the haemorrhage of able Liberal women out of the party and the electoral challenge by Labour to the Liberals in some key industrial constituencies.

The years of patient campaigning by Selina Cooper and other radical suffragists were triumphantly vindicated by the labour-suffrage alliance. Whether this aim had been part of their long-term strategy is not immediately clear. Had they been burrowing deep into the National Union's roots with labour propaganda during the last few years? Had Selina and other like-minded organisers ever discussed such tactics? We know she had considerable impact on Emilie Gardner, introducing her 'into the red regions of socialism'. But beyond this, there is unfortunately no evidence that she was directly involved in any attempt to shift National Union *policy* leftwards – and, as a lowly salaried organiser, she was hardly best placed to influence it.

But whether the alliance was something she worked towards or not, Selina must certainly have been delighted to find National Union suffragists now sharing the same platforms as mainstream labour leaders. Certainly, 1912–14 were triumphant years for such socialist suffragists as Selina, Margaret Aldersley, Margaret Robertson, Annot Robinson, Ada Nield Chew and Ellen Wilkinson. They were kept busy stumping the country in support of Labour candidates at by-elections and rallying labour support behind the women's demands. Alongside them stood their loyal male comrades, pioneers like Keir Hardie and ILP sprigs such as Fenner Brockway.

As we have seen, the Labour Party had spurned Selina Cooper's passionate appeal at the 1905 and 1907 conferences, voting instead for all-or-nothing adult suffrage. What had made Labour change its mind? How did such an unexpected alliance come about?

It was Asquith himself who unwittingly pushed this unlikely pair – the Labour Party and the National Union – towards each other. In November 1911 the obdurate Prime Minister unleashed a great fury by casually promising a government-backed Franchise Bill for the coming parliamentary session. The bill would include manhood suffrage and, Asquith added graciously, suffragists might, if they wanted, attach to it an amendment concerning women. He could hardly have devised a better way to infuriate so many women at one fell stroke. A government bill to give votes to *all* men (with the vague possibility of some small concessions to women tagged on untidily at the end) had of course always been the suffragists' greatest fear. It would mean, they believed, abandoning their patient hopes for the Conciliation Bill, and so setting back for decades the cause of votes for women and the principle of equal political rights. [2]

WSPU suffragettes responded to the grim news with window-smashing, heckling Cabinet Ministers and burning postboxes. Equally incensed were the Conservative women who, along with some of their parliamentary leaders, had so welcomed the narrow proposals of the Conciliation Bills, carefully designed to benefit only the 'right' class of woman. Now Ladies Frances and Betty Balfour faced the dread possibility that every Tom, Dick and gardener's boy in the great Tory households of the land would be able to vote – but not the lady of the house herself. The prospect sent shivers down Tory backbones: they blanched at the prospect of opening 'the gate of our sacred "polis" to a babble of illiterates'. [3] Liberal women were hardly happier; and the National Union was certainly furious, circulating a protest to all local societies. 'Even the mildest and most pacific of suffragists,' Mrs Fawcett wrote, 'felt that she had received from the Prime Minister a personal insult. If it had been his object to enrage every woman suffragist to the point of frenzy he could not have acted with greater perspicacity.' [4]

Times were desperate. Suffragists, seeing their hopes for even moderate gains fade, must need seek allies where they could. And so early in 1912, as we have seen, Selina Cooper and others found themselves working closely with leading Tories and even addressing meetings of the Conservative women's suffrage groups. At the back of Selina's mind must have been the despairing thought that perhaps a right-of-centre Tory-suffrage alliance might at least force through the *principle* of women's equal claims, from which all else would eventually follow.

This was not how things turned out. The political party that made the first practical protest against Asquith's betrayal was not the Tories, but a much smaller group well to the left of the Liberal Party – the Independent Labour Party. At recent ILP conferences Annot Robinson had firmly chided the executive for its dilatory attitude towards women, and, supported by Keir Hardie, she had renewed conference support for women's suffrage. So when Asquith let drop his manhood suffrage bombshell, the ILP executive responded briskly. It immediately passed an historic resolution urging 'that proposals for franchise extension which do not confer citizenship upon women should be definitely opposed'.

Ironically what Asquith had done was to help heal the differences between suffragists and adultists in the labour movement. If he was serious about introducing complete manhood suffrage (i.e., abolishing male property qualification), then suffragists could now respond with an 'equal rights for women' demand that would necessarily mean votes for *all* adult women. Thus the days of the divisive arguments about precisely how many working-class women would be enfranchised by 'equal rights' legislation were happily over. Those adultist men in the labour movement who had opposed votes for women as anti-socialist could now be called on to honour their beliefs and support a demand to include women as well as men in any proposed legislation.

The ILP, still very much the conscience of the Labour Party, was as good as its word. Within a month it had circulated a leaflet to sympathetic women:

POLITICAL EQUALITY CAMPAIGN

December 1911

Dear Madam,

The Independent Labour Party is about to inaugurate a great national campaign on the Suffrage question. This has been rendered imperative by the Government's intention to bring forward a Manhood Suffrage Bill next year . . . Equity can be established next year if working-class opinion is organised and brought to bear on the Government . . .

No movement is better qualified than ours to rouse working-class conviction. We have some 800 branches . . . We intend to set in operation the whole force and power of this vast machinery. We are part of the National Labour Party, which has 1,500,000 working-class adherents, and we are in close and friendly alliance with the great bodies of Organised Labour. It is our purpose to reach the Trade Unions and the workers generally, to distribute leaflets, broadcast, and to hold many hundreds of meetings in the industrial centres . . .

We hope to make our proposed campaign a striking crusade on behalf of political justice and freedom alike for men and women. We do not take up this question as a matter of party politics, but

as a matter of human right. The continued exclusion of women
from the rights and responsibilities of citizenship is a harsh and
intolerable wrong . . .

We confidently ask for your financial aid (irrespective of party
politics) so that our protest and plea may be effective.

> Wm. C. ANDERSON, Chairman
> T.D. BENSON, Treasurer
> FRANCIS JOHNSON, Secretary

The leaflet was couched in uncompromising language (and we
can imagine Keir Hardie leaning over the shoulders of the three
ILP officials, urging them on). With its campaign the ILP had
overnight breathed new life into the suffrage stalemate, and over
the next few months it organised about two hundred Political
Equality meetings. Selina Cooper, constrained from showing too
much public enthusiasm at this stage (for, of course, the National
Union attitude was still strictly 'non-party'), must have watched
the ILP lobbying Labour Party leaders with a mounting excitement difficult to disguise. At last, after years of waiting, the
women's suffrage campaign was moving in the direction she had
hoped for.[5]

She did not attend the Labour Party Conference in January
1912, but she would have read accounts of this momentous occasion. She would have heard how the influential Arthur Henderson
MP, Secretary of the Labour Party, had been present when
Asquith had chanced to announce his manhood suffrage plans,
and how his patience had finally snapped. The Labour Party had
previously committed itself to support adult suffrage; and so,
Henderson's resolution stated, the Parliamentary Labour Party
must make it clear that reform bills introduced by the government
which did *not* include adult women 'cannot be acceptable to the
Labour and Socialist Movement'. The ILP Chairman seconded
this. 'The Conference must stand for political equality between
men and women,' he said, 'and whilst leaving the Parliamentary
Party largely a free hand in Parliament, we must say that there is a
minimum and this minimum must include the political claims of
women.' Predictably the Miners' Federation of Great Britain
disagreed. 'We must fight for the women but,' argued its
spokesman, 'rather than lose Manhood Suffrage we are opposed
to the latter part of the resolution. In my opinion Manhood

Suffrage would not retard Women's Suffrage.' One of the most telling speeches came from Mary MacArthur, an ILP delegate and leading trade unionist. She had previously been an adultist, she told the conference, and (rather like Ada Nield Chew) had refused in the name of poorly-paid women trade unionists to support a limited property-based women's suffrage. But, she added, when she had said 'the men and women of the Labour Movement were going to stand together for full Adult Suffrage, I little thought that the men whom I stand by would come to this conference and desert women'. This strong appeal for the adultists to remain true to their earlier claims and not leave women out in the cold swung almost all the delegates – except the Miners – behind Henderson's resolution. The voting was 919,000 for and only 686,000 against.[6]

So, to Selina Cooper's great delight, her old ILP friends had at last won the support of the Labour Party, and had turned the Miners' opposition into a minority voice. But the wording of Henderson's resolution was loose and vague. In what way were Labour MPs 'to make it clear' that a bill excluding women was 'unacceptable'? Did it mean that all Labour MPs *must* vote against all readings of such a bill, or did it merely *encourage* them to vote against it at certain stages? Selina Cooper, busy with her lectures on the National Insurance Act, watched to see how the National Union leaders would react. Even the most diehard anti-socialist among them seems to have appreciated what possibilities the Labour decision opened up: Mrs Fawcett wrote to Ramsay MacDonald a few days later confessing, 'I wish you were double your present strength in the House of Commons.'

A fortnight later the ILP Political Equality Campaign and the Labour Party jointly organised a massive demonstration in the Albert Hall to demand the vote for all adult men and women; nearly 8,000 people attended and Ramsay MacDonald presided and rather rashly answered 'certainly' when asked whether he would actually turn the Liberal Government out if women were not included in the bill.

Despite this meeting, the cautious National Union was still wary of responding too fast. Later in February, it held its own mass meeting in the Albert Hall, chaired by Mrs Fawcett. Selina Cooper went along to it, preserving the copy of her programme which still proclaimed the National Union as 'non-party'. No great Labour figures were invited to adorn its platform, but merely Lloyd George (who was, of course, angrily heckled by militants).[7]

The following day Selina Cooper, still in London, attended the National Union's Annual Council Meeting: there she witnessed the beginning of a momentous turn in National Union policy. This historic meeting passed a resolution welcoming the Labour Party Conference decision, and noting that Labour MPs seemed to be promising to vote against the third reading of the bill unless it included women. But, with this expression of rather vague gratitude, matters were left for a while – until events suddenly forced the coyly reluctant suffragists to edge nearer their new Labour friends.[8]

At the end of March, amid great industrial disputes, the long-awaited second reading of the Conciliation Bill was defeated in the Commons. The defeat was close and was largely engineered by single-minded Irish Nationalist MPs who wanted at all costs to avoid any embarrassing defeat of the government (especially if followed by Asquith's rumoured resignation) that might jeopardise Irish Home Rule. But what did not escape the sharp-eyed suffragists was that of the two dozen Labour MPs present (the rest were away in their constituencies wrestling with the outbreak of industrial militancy) *none* voted against the bill, while many Liberals had been cowed into opposition for fear of Asquith's wrath. Such voting patterns, coupled with Labour's earlier declaration of loyalty, could not but soften the hearts of even the most staunchly Liberal suffragist.

Selina Cooper and her ILP friends waited as hesitant talks between the National Union and the Labour Party flowered into more formal negotiations during the spring. Gently, tactfully, Henderson from the Labour Party and Kate Courtney, as Secretary of the National Union, edged their bashful members towards each other. At last in mid-May, only six weeks since the Irish had wrecked hopes of a Conciliation Bill, a National Union Special Council meeting formally inaugurated the new policy of co-operation with the Labour Party.

The National Union argument ran like this: in the past its policy had been strictly non-party, supporting whomever was the most sympathetic to women's suffrage. Now candidates were not judged as individuals but, more realistically, as members of a political party. The Labour Party was so far the only one to support women's suffrage. Therefore the National Union would support Labour candidates at by-elections, and would support Labour as a means to put pressure on the Liberals.

The days were now over when the National Union's policy was determined by well-to-do ladies for whom the Labour Party was merely a group of down-at-heel agitators inhabiting dingy committee rooms. There were of course still those in the National Union who grumbled at this revolutionary turn of events. The organisation was a democratic one, and up and down the country the unhappy laments of Liberal (and Tory) members had to be patiently listened to. Indeed, the Clitheroe Society, the great majority of whose members were ILP sympathisers, must have been one of the few that found the transition wonderfully easy to make – though perhaps a handful of older Liberal women like Sarah Thomas had to be tactfully placated.[9]

Despite some foot-dragging here and there, the great virtue of the alliance was that the strengths and weaknesses of one side complemented the weaknesses and strengths of the other. The great majority of Labour Party members possessed votes and therefore had a direct voice in the Commons. The great majority of the National Union did not and badly needed the party's influence. But what the National Union increasingly had, and the Labour Party still possessed only patchily, was a country wide organisation which could efficiently run by-election campaigns anywhere. When it came to elections, many a local Labour Party badly needed the National Union's help.

There were currently forty-two Labour MPs in the Commons. And the party's membership, now the Miners' Federation had affiliated, had swollen to almost one and a half million members, though of course all but a handful of these – 35,000 – were trade union affiliations. The National Union membership, currently standing at 42,000, seemed tiny by comparison, though a very high proportion of these members would be actively involved. In addition, the National Union now had over 400 local societies while Labour Party organisation was still often weak. In only a handful of constituencies, like the Coopers' Clitheroe division and

Woolwich, did local parties work smoothly, combining strong union solidarity with individual membership. In cities like Liverpool, as Selina Cooper had found, sectarian rivalries left Labour weak. In mining constituencies, the Miners' Federations were now nominally Labour supporters, but seldom boasted electoral machinery independent of local Liberals. One of the reasons why the national Labour Party could not briskly lick itself into shape in these problem constituencies was that it still operated on a shoestring. Relying essentially on the support of working-class members, its head office budget for salaries and expenses was still below £2,500. This was a paltry sum compared to the National Union, which had always been able to rely on the donations of well-to-do – though still voteless – women. Its Central Fund had now reached over £10,000, and the income of the local societies exceeded £17,000: its total income could be estimated to be about £35,000. As a result it could well afford to pay the salaries of its sixty-one organisers.[10]

The weakness of many local Labour Party organisations meant that, when it came to elections, they were unable to call upon their supporters' votes; for in Edwardian elections, voters still had to go through the archaic process of registering, and an efficient local party soon acquainted itself with the laborious game of completing registration lists, chasing up elusive supporters falsely rumoured to have died or moved away, and checking whether lodgers were paying sufficient weekly rent to enfranchise them. In sorting out these time-consuming conundrums the National Union was able to give the Labour Party badly-needed aid. Its organisers could parachute into constituencies where a fledgling party boasted neither committee rooms nor a meeting hall, and help shape it into something which might effectively fight an election. And the National Union, through radical suffragists like Selina Cooper, could lobby recalcitrant trade unionists, particularly old-fashioned miners, to wean them away from their Liberal loyalties and – most difficult but most crucial – towards supporting women's suffrage.

The National Union might have funds, organisers, a network of supporters, but it still desperately needed Labour voters and MPs to put effective pressure on the government. To wrest some of the Liberals' traditional seats from them was a daunting task. How could it best be organised? The National Union sensibly decided to set up a separate campaigning organisation with its own funds, to be responsible for this vital political work. So in May-June 1912 it established the crucial Election Fighting Fund, run by a twenty-two member committee including some of the leading ILP women – Isabella Ford, Ethel Snowden and Margaret McMillan – along with many of the suffragists that Selina Cooper had long worked with, like Helena Swanwick and Margaret Ashton. Mrs Fawcett was in the chair, and in the key job of Secretary was Catherine Marshall from the Lake District, guiding spirit of the North West Federation.[11]

If Selina Cooper typified those energetic socialist working women who became National Union organisers, Catherine Marshall epitomised the middle-class women whose stars rose within the National Union, and whom suffrage forced to forsake their traditional Liberalism. The daughter of a housemaster at Harrow School, Catherine grew up in a Liberal family and after leaving school studied music and languages, travelled and helped her mother run the household. In 1908 she and her parents formed the Keswick Women's Suffrage Association, and Catherine began working on an almost full-time voluntary basis for the National Union, first locally through the North West Federation, and before long nationally – for her organising energy and political competence were soon recognised.

Ably guided by Catherine Marshall and Kate Courtney, the Election Fighting Fund was launched amid great enthusiasm. Nearly £2,000 was raised even before a special appeal was circulated. Money poured in from suffragists excited by the new alliance, and by the end of the year the fund totalled nearly £6,000. Ten Election Fighting Fund organisers were taken on, co-ordinated by Margaret Robertson (who left her Manchester post for this new and more important job).[12]

While these far-reaching plans were being laid, Selina Cooper set off for South Wales again: to Merthyr Tydfil where the 1912 ILP Conference was to be held. Once again she found the sessions on women's suffrage tempestuous; but this time the arguments were no longer between enthusiastic women and foot-dragging adultists but between the men themselves – between those who realised how far the Political Equality Campaign committed the

ILP to women's suffrage, and those who realised it but did *not* like it.

The National Union had prepared the ground well. Annot Robinson held an open-air meeting in Merthyr on Sunday, and Selina a very successful indoor one the following day. These helped influence the ensuing debate. Philip Snowden pointed out to the conference that the ILP was committing itself 'to oppose any reform bill which, in its final form, proposes to give more votes to men and refuses them to women'. Other delegates were far from happy. One local councillor protested angrily at being 'asked to sacrifice the cause of progress in the interests of women'. Up jumped George Lansbury, the volatile MP from Bromley and Bow, to attack such appeals to mere expediency. 'I do not want votes for women because they will vote for Socialism,' he urged. '. . . I demand votes for women because they are human beings.' But the implication of this principled stand remained unclear. Was the Labour Party really prepared to turn out the Liberal Government over the issue of women's suffrage, asked one bemused delegate? The small ILP could not speak for all forty-two Labour MPs, of course, but the vote at the end of the debate *did* commit the handful of ILP MPs to vote against the government if, in its final working, the bill left women out.

The following day the ILP's tough commitment to women was made even more uncompromising. Annot Robinson's husband Sam, a man keen on women's suffrage at least in the abstract, demanded that all Labour MPs vote against the third reading of the bill unless women were included. Keir Hardie, while noting the practical difficulties, backed up Sam Robinson. The ILP MPs would try 'irrespective of consequence', Hardie promised, to persuade Labour MPs to vote against the third reading even if it involved the fate of the bill. So, with Hardie's help, Sam Robinson's tough resolution was passed with a strong majority. The ILP was now committed to persuade the many half-hearted Labour MPs to vote against an unacceptable bill – even if it meant toppling Asquith's Government and thereby forcing yet another General Election.[13]

Coupled with the National Union's new policy, it was a significant victory. All that was needed now was a little extra lobbying to win over all Labour MPs (including ex-overlooker Albert Smith, the Coopers' new member) and a few by-election victories to show the Liberals that the new alliance really meant business. Selina arrived back home confident that victory was no longer beyond reach. With Robert, she immediately organised support among sympathetic councillors and managed to get a suffrage resolution passed by Nelson Town Council in early June – one more pressure point on Albert Smith MP.

But there was no time for leisurely rejoicing. With the Election Fighting Fund less than a week old, a by-election was suddenly announced for 20 June due to the resignation of the Liberal MP in Holmfirth on the West Riding Pennine slopes. The fund immediately plunged into hectic electioneering plans in support of the Labour candidate, an ILP founder-member and checkweighman at a nearby colliery. It seemed an ideal debut for the fund: a local ILP man standing in a three-cornered contest in a traditionally Liberal mining seat. An organiser must be sent immediately. But no Election Fighting Fund staff had been taken on yet. One of the National Union organisers would have to go instead, someone who could win over Holmfirth's miners and textile workers. Selina Cooper was the ideal choice.[14] So, with little more than a week to polling day, Selina again packed her bags and hurried across the Pennines, where she was joined by Annot Robinson, Margaret Ashton and Ada Nield Chew.

The situation Selina found in Holmfirth was sobering. Most of the stone-built villages across the straggling constituency seemed perversely situated on the tops of hills. And, with about one in four electors a coal miner, it was very much an instinctively Liberal seat: the last Labour candidate had won only a quarter the number of votes of the Liberal. This time, at least the powerful Yorkshire Miners' Association was backing a Labour miner. Even so, many older miners remained Liberal at heart, and the Liberal machine was still highly organised locally: it held over forty meetings before the Labour candidate even opened his hurried campaign.

Holmfirth hardly augured well for the brave new labour-suffrage alliance. The local Labour Party, faced with an uphill battle to establish itself in the minds of old-fashioned electors, had scant patience for fancy alliances cooked up by party leaders down in London – and seemingly little time for such trivial issues as women's suffrage. It was reluctant to share the same committee rooms as National Union organisers, and on this was backed up by advice from Arthur Henderson. When Ramsay MacDonald arrived for the election, he appeared to begin speaking for Labour without any consultation with the suffragists there – this despite the £100 promised by the Election Fighting Fund to help the Labour campaign.

Undaunted, Selina Cooper and the others quickly set to work, helped by the loan of a Manchester Federation motor car. Selina spoke at open-air meetings, telling the crowd about her long years as a textile trade unionist and how she was now lecturer for the National Insurance Commissioners, but that women had had no say in passing the act. Luckily Keir Hardie arrived for the end of the campaign. 'In this part of Yorkshire your fathers and grand-fathers were Radicals and Chartists fighting for the vote for working men,' he proclaimed, 'and working women are now fighting for the vote' in the same way. But this brave rhetoric failed to sway the electors. The Liberal candidate again headed the poll, with Labour coming only third. This new Election Fighting Fund, Selina concluded grimly as she travelled back over the Pennines, would take a bit of working on.

On reflection though, the result held out some hope for the future. 'Labour Vote Doubled in Holmfirth, Liberal Party Set-Back, Tory Party Stationary', the *Labour Leader* headline could proclaim. The by-election *had* shown that the Yorkshire miners had no qualms about supporting Labour; and pro-suffrage seeds had been sown among local Labour members that would before long bear fruit.[15]

And gradually the new Election Fighting Fund policy began to take practical shape. Two days after Holmfirth, Selina Cooper took part in a big suffrage demonstration on Manchester's Platt Fields, winning the crowd's approval when she explained how she was going door-to-door with a petition asking Asquith, if he brought in a minimum wage bill, to include women in it. 'Could any working man honestly say that women should not dabble in politics,' she demanded, 'when of the fourteen million workers who were brought in under the National Insurance Act nearly four million are women?' And alongside Selina spoke Margaret Ashton, a particularly significant addition to Election Fighting

Charles Coombe with one of his elder sons, probably Richard, early 1870s

Jane Coombe, recently widowed, with her youngest son, Alf, 1876-7

Charles Coombe second from right, with a group of railway navvies, probably late 1850s

Selina Coombe, the first known portrait, c. 1893

Signed portrait of Helen Philip, c. 1897

Co-operative Holiday Association workers at Keld, Swaledale, 1899. Selina Cooper second from left, Robert Cooper far right

Selina Cooper, *Nelson Workers' Guide*,
March 1903

Margaret Aldersley, date unknown

Nelson Relief Committee of the Burnley Board of Guardians, *c.* 1904. Selina Cooper
seated left, Harriette Beanland seated right

Clitheroe Women's Suffrage Society, Nelson Station, 17 June 1911. Centre front, Mary Cooper; immediately right, Selina Cooper; immediately left, Robert Cooper, *Nelson Leader*, 23 June 1911

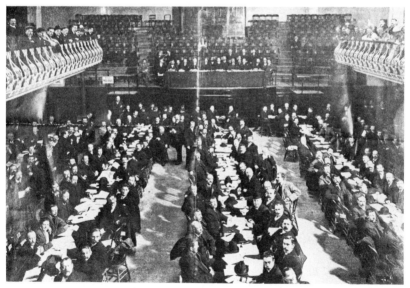

Labour Party Conference, Belfast, January 1907. Selina Cooper seated bottom left, *Black and White*, 2 February 1907

Selina Cooper campaigning at the Hull West by-election, *Daily Mirror*, 28 November 1907

Liverpool Women's Suffrage Society, Kirkdale by-election, July 1910. Selina Cooper seated far right

Mary and her mother, *c.* 1911

Selina Cooper's address, Nelson
Council elections, November 1923

A charabanc outing *c.* 1930. Selina Cooper seated centre front, Mary immediately right

Women Against War and Fascism delegation to Nazi Germany, October 1934. Selina Cooper, centre

Fund platforms. She used to chair the Lancashire and Cheshire Union of Women's Liberal Associations but she left the Liberal Party in 1906 when she discovered the new government had little intention of giving women the vote. A Manchester City Councillor, she wielded considerable influence. The disaffection of women like Margaret Ashton was to cost the Liberal Party dear.

The Election Fighting Fund fought four more by-elections that summer. Each highlighted some of the National Union's problems in trying to get Labour MPs elected to Parliament – especially in mining seats. The only by-election Selina Cooper went to after Holmfirth that summer reminded her of some of these difficulties. East Carmarthenshire was a Liberal stronghold where one in six voters was a miner. The regional suffrage federation there, still pinning its faith on Welsh Liberal MPs, had little time for the new-fangled election policy. And even though Catherine Marshall hurried to South Wales and sent Selina Cooper and other organisers over, in the end the local problems proved too deep-seated for the Election Fighting Fund to be able to do much. The Liberals retained the seat and Labour came a very poor third.[16]

There was then a convenient autumn lull in the by-election contests, an opportunity to assess the fund's success so far. Thanks in part to the suffragists' intervention, the Liberals had lost two seats, retained Holmfirth and East Carmarthenshire, but gained one seat from Labour in a freak mining contest. The frailty of Labour's electoral machinery, coupled with the Liberal instincts of many miners, was consuming a great deal of Election Fighting Fund energy. Moreover, Labour was proving a slippery ally: Catherine Marshall persistently tried to lobby MacDonald, was refused an interview, managed to corner him on a train only to be told that the 'time is not ripe yet' for the Labour Party to declare how it would vote on the Reform Bill to enfranchise all men if women were left out of it.[17]

Less wasteful of precious resources was a longer-term strategy based on key constituencies. These were calculated to be seats held by anti-suffragist ministers who could be toppled by Labour; seats already held by Labour MPs; and seats where a Labour candidate had already been supported. So Selina Cooper helped organise a deputation to Albert Smith, her own Labour MP. It was an influential group that visited him, including ex-Mayor

Rickard, various councillors and the Nelson ILP chairman. Margaret Aldersley was there too, and so were Harriette Beanland, Clara Myers, Nancy Shimbles and Miss Moser, Mary's French teacher. They showed him their distrust of the government. 'I cannot understand any Government leaving out women,' Selina told him bluntly, 'when it is extending the franchise to two and a half million men who have never asked for it, and when women have been working for it for the last forty years.' But like so many other Labour MPs, Albert Smith wriggled out of committing himself, merely making sympathetic noises about the injustices women bore. He commended to them the democratic nature of the bill (manhood suffrage without any property qualifications, abolition of the antiquated registration system, and so on) but refused to say he would vote against the third reading if women were not included. Such Labour men were the thorn in the side of the labour-suffrage alliance: however many working women they represented and however heavy the pressure from their constituencies, such MPs were not prepared either to jeopardise a chance to enfranchise more men, or to vote against the 'progressive' Liberals.[18]

At the same time, autumn 1912, the Election Fighting Fund as part of its long-term strategy began to dispatch its organisers to constituencies held by anti-suffragist ministers. Margaret Aldersley was sent to East Bristol, seat of the Chancellor of the Duchy of Lancaster, and later to Rossendale, the Lancashire seat held by a particularly hated Liberal minister. Ada Nield Chew was posted to Accrington where the MP, Financial Secretary to the Home Office, was an active anti-suffragist. And the National Union Executive arranged for Selina Cooper to spend two months working in the Potteries, an industrial area where Labour was still weak and women workers poorly paid. Help was even given to George Lansbury who, having resigned his seat of Bromley and Bow because he believed Labour Party support for women's suffrage was too half-hearted, stood for independent election there in November 1912 with the WSPU's help – though without success. By the end of the year the Election Fighting Fund was able to talk in terms of fighting the next general election, expected in 1915, in six ministerial seats including Accrington, Bristol East, Rossendale and North Monmouth (the constituency of the current

Home Secretary, Reginald McKenna, notorious for continuing his predecessor's brutal policy of forcible-feeding of suffragette hunger strikers); and the fund was to hold £2,000 in reserve for this election.[19]

To work in key constituencies to get Labour men elected in place of anti-suffragist Liberal Ministers was one plank of the Election Fighting Fund's long-term strategy. The other was to change the minds of hostile trade unionists, in particular of course the miners. There were signs that the giant Miners' Federation might be prepared to soften its opposition to women. In mid-1912 the 'old school' president had died, and Robert Smillie became leader. Smillie, founder-member of the ILP and good friend and disciple of Keir Hardie, symbolised a new generation of miners. There was a chance he might help shape the iron-hearted federation into a friend to women rather than a foe. So the Election Fighting Fund began to channel its energies into lobbying local miners. At its committee meeting at the end of the year, ambitious plans were laid to send an organiser to North Monmouthshire (where miners comprised over a third of the electorate); to Whitehaven, notorious for the under-the-sea mining accident Selina Cooper had witnessed; and to approach Mary MacArthur and Arthur Henderson to discuss launching a trade union campaign to influence the Miners' Federation decision about suffrage.

Such lobbying seemed to be effective – especially after a bombshell announcement early in 1913. In January the Speaker of the House of Commons suddenly ruled that no women's suffrage amendment could be added to the current Reform Bill. Suffragists' resolve stiffened overnight. The WSPU burnt slogans on golf courses and cut telephone wires. At the crucial Labour Party Conference, also in January, a general pro-women's suffrage resolution was proposed, to which the ILP added the controversial amendment that the conference 'further calls upon the Party in Parliament to oppose any Franchise Bill in which women are not included.' A Miners' delegate immediately opposed this amendment: were they, he demanded, to oppose a bill which would greatly benefit working men merely because it did nothing for women? Philip Snowden sprang to his feet from the back of the conference hall. Yes, he passionately proclaimed:

yes, yes, yes. And in his speech he turned on the miner, accusing him of being happy to allow Labour members 'to steal more votes for men at the expense of the women'. Snowden was a persuasive orator, and he sat down amidst overwhelming applause. The vote on the ILP amendment was taken by a card vote: 850,000 for with only 437,000 against, with the Miners this time significantly remaining neutral. Hearing the result, jubilant suffragist delegates sprang from their chairs; women in the gallery clapped and cheered. It was a big advance on last year: this year's resolution now committed Labour MPs more firmly to oppose manhood suffrage, and was no longer opposed by the Miners' Federation.[20]

Neutral miners were a big advance on antagonistic miners. But it was still essential to change their neutrality into active support. The Election Fighting Fund therefore spared no effort during 1913 to persuade miners that votes for women was no longer the old bogey of enfranchising 'propertied women', but was part of a much wider campaign for broader democratic rights. They aimed in this way to alter the Miners' vote at the TUC Congress in September, the Miners' Federation's own conference in October, and next year's Labour Party Conference the following January. For the National Union organisers, then, and especially for Selina Cooper, 1913 became the year of the miners.

CHAPTER FOURTEEN

WOMEN AND THE MIGHT
OF THE MINERS:
1913-14

It is very gratifying to find an organisation like the Miners'
Federation openly ranging itself on the side of the women in their
fight for political power. It is an indication that the opponents of
the extension of the franchise to women will, in the long run,
have to justify their actions to organised labour. When that
comes about the end is not far off.

> John Robertson, Vice-President of the Scottish
> Miners' Federation, *Common Cause* 3 October 1913

The Miners' Federation could wield immense influence in
Edwardian politics. When it eventually decided to affiliate to the
Labour Party in 1909 it brought no fewer than 550,000 new
members into the party overnight. Of these probably well over 50
per cent were voters, mainly in constituencies where the local
miners exercised considerable power. John Robertson perhaps
had a point when he suggested that once the miners decided to
back women's suffrage the campaign acquired an inevitability
about it. But the miners' crucial support had to be wooed before it
could be won.

Unfortunately the courtship took place in inauspicious circumstances. The political tension during spring 1913 grew almost
to breaking point. WSPU militancy after the Speaker's ruling
included an attempt to bomb Lloyd George's house. Mrs
Pankhurst was arrested, tried for incitement at the Old Bailey
and sentenced to three years. Sylvia Pankhurst in prison added
to her hunger strike a terrifying thirst and sleep strike. The
Home Secretary McKenna, as we know, rushed through Parliament his notorious 'Cat and Mouse' Act. During these months

the painstaking lobbying of miners up and down the country became increasingly difficult – but daily more urgent.

Robert Cooper, a diligent member of the Men's League for Women's Suffrage, was among those who early on appreciated the urgency. 'The miners' representatives in Parliament do not intend to allow the National Labour Conference to control them on the question of Women's Suffrage,' he lamented. 'They stand first of all for Manhood Suffrage, but some useful purpose may be served if our Suffrage Friends would write in their respective constituencies to the Labour MP and ask him if he is prepared to oppose every proposed extension of the Franchise unless it includes the enfranchisement of women.'

Catherine Marshall was another who understood precisely how pressure should be exerted on miners and other trade unionists. As Secretary of the Election Fighting Fund, her organising genius lent itself to the surreptitious politicking necessary, and later she described how:

> So far as possible the people who were sent to speak to the Trade Unionists were women who had themselves a grasp of Labour and Trade Union principles, and would therefore put the case for Women's Suffrage from the standpoint most likely to appeal to the men they addressed. Moreover many of them were women whose credentials, from the Labour standpoint, were such as to gain them admittance where the ordinary suffrage speaker might have knocked in vain.

And who better than Selina Cooper? Her credentials were impeccable. By early April 1913 she had begun lobbying the coalfield constituencies. Her first call came when the West Riding Federation organiser wrote to the Election Fighting Fund saying, 'Mrs Cooper we want very much . . . We should like her for as long as Manchester and District [Federation] could spare her.' This plan quickly took shape. 'The places we should like Mrs Cooper for are Doncaster, Dewsbury, Bradford, Leeds, and', the organiser added, 'for a little campaign in the Osgoldcross div [ision in which 40 per cent of the electors were miners] where we are now working – as I expect you know there are rumours of a Labour candidate . . . We really could keep Mrs Cooper going for some time in this Fed . . .' Again, in May the West Riding organiser wrote to Catherine Marshall suggesting that 'Mrs

Cooper might occupy the time visiting all the Miners' Lodges, do you think this would be a best plan?' And in June *Common Cause* reported Selina Cooper's week of open-air campaigning in the Dewsbury area – with working men, all sympathetic, attending meetings in their thousands.[1]

Although Selina's skills had long been recognised by the National Union, from 1912 – and more particularly from 1913 – she came into her own. Selina, along with the other radical suffragists employed as organisers, now found themselves in heavy demand. They received more requests for meetings than they could hope to cope with. 'I am afraid from your letter received this morning there is little likelihood of our having Mrs Cooper,' the organiser for the Liverpool area bemoaned. '. . . I had several times applied to Mrs Cooper, Mrs Annot Robinson, Mrs Chew etc – and always found them engaged – Open air meetings are very popular in Lancashire, and Mrs Cooper is most popular with Lancs. audiences.' But Liverpool, with its weak labour movement, had to take a back seat now. As summer slipped into autumn and the conference season loomed closer, Selina's single priority had become the Miners' vote on women's suffrage at the TUC in early September. All hopes were now pinned on that, and on the Miners' own conference at Scarborough the following month at which the Election Fighting Fund planned a big suffrage meeting.

Margaret Robertson took the responsibility for discreetly lobbying the miners' delegates at the TUC. The suffrage resolution there stated 'that this congress protests against the Prime Minister's failure to redeem his repeated pledges to women, and calls upon the Parliamentary Committee [of the TUC] to press for the immediate enfranchisement of women'. How would the miners, the biggest single block, vote? It turned out to be a knife-edge decision. 'Did I tell you the agonies at the TUC?' Margaret Robertson confided to Catherine Marshall afterwards. 'How the miners actually decided to vote *against* and I had to chase all round and see them individually and get them to meet and reverse it (deadly secret of course that I had anything to do with it) that sort of thing makes my grey hairs sprout.' Her grey hairs were worth it. The TUC supported the resolution almost unanimously. The Election Fighting Fund immediately decided to send a letter with the TUC resolution on it to every single Member of Parliament. Certainly this success augured well for Scarborough.

Even before the TUC Congress, Selina Cooper was busy working towards the Scarborough conference. On 1 September Margaret Robertson wrote to Catherine Marshall explaining, 'We must take the theatre which holds 1,500, and make a big thing of it. I want Mrs Cooper, who still has lodges to visit in Yorkshire, to spend the next month more or less working the meeting up. I have written telling her to go to N. & E. Ridings. I have great hopes of its political effect in binding the Miners to us . . .'

Such letters from Election Fighting Fund officials and occasional newspaper reports throw light on Selina's day-to-day organising work in Yorkshire that autumn. It was laborious, grass-roots lobbying. 'Approaching officials is not an easy matter,' ran one *Common Cause* report.

> A large part of the trade union business is transacted in the homes of the secretaries, and before a worker can be invited inside to interview the men, she has to get hold of the women. When she has succeeded in getting an interview, it must take the form of a friendly chat before touching on the vital question. Later an invitation to address the men on the Suffrage question may be received. The speaker, on arrival, is conducted to a private room to wait until the trade union business is over; she is then called in and asked by the chairman to state her case. Mrs Cooper, one of our most successful EFF organisers, has been working among the miners in the West Riding of Yorkshire for about two months, and she has already secured good results.

Selina appeared particularly adept in wooing local miners in this painstaking way. Fourteen branches of the Yorkshire Miners' Association whose membership totalled 20,000 – Grimethorpe and Featherstone Main, Hemsworth and Houghton Main, and others – had already passed resolutions demanding votes for women. Indeed, Selina was so good at her job that letters flew between Election Fighting Fund officers discussing where she should be dispatched next, and by the end of September she was off to the Midlands to work with the Nottinghamshire miners. There, in a constituency like Mansfield, almost every other voter was a miner and a Liberal miner at that and so Selina had her work cut out – especially when the miners grew angry at WSPU disruption of a meeting with their hero Lloyd George. However, even in this unpromising territory, she managed to wrest suffrage resolutions from two miners' branches.[2]

All this helped to ensure that the Scarborough demonstration on 8 October was a success. Certainly Selina spared no effort. Along with another suffragist she went from door to door in Scarborough, chatting to people as she did so, and distributing no fewer than five thousand handbills. She went down to the harbour and held open-air suffrage meetings there. She went along to Women's Co-operative Guild and Trades Council meetings. She visited trade union officials, and she ensured that Trades Council representatives, along with those from other important labour groups – Railwaymen, Printers, Painters, Tailors, Shop Assistants, Muncipal Employees, the ILP, the Guild and the Railway Women's Guild – all came to the demonstration.

Selina Cooper was there on 8 October too: long afterwards she treasured her ticket for the demonstration. At 8pm that evening she could at last sit back exhausted in the theatre audience, happy to watch the two great bodies – the National Union of Women's Suffrage Societies and the Miners' Federation of Great Britain – meeting together. Even a year ago such co-operation would have been impossible. Before her, Selina could see ranged up on the platform Isabella Ford who was chairing the meeting, along with a host of dark-suited Miners' leaders. And the miners did the women proud. 'I speak for myself, I speak for this mighty federation of nearly three-quarters of a million men,' urged one of the Staffordshire miners' MPs. 'I will work with you, and we will hail the day when woman has come into her own right.' Present too was Robert Smillie, Miners' Federation President. 'I am asked whether or not the miners will declare a general strike in order to secure votes for women,' he told the meeting. 'That would really be my own method; I question however whether we should secure a majority of that way of thinking. But I think the women will have all the power the Miners' Federation can bring to bear upon Parliament to bring this measure of justice.' And the suffrage resolution was passed almost without dissent.[3]

Selina Cooper left Scarborough jubilant. But within days she was off again, this time to South Wales where another Election Fighting Fund campaign was to be launched in McKenna's constituency, North Monmouthshire. There too were Ada Nield Chew, Margaret Aldersley, Fenner Brockway and Helena Swanwick. For North Monmouth, with its five or six thousand miners' votes and its 'Cat-and-Mouse' MP, was ideal Election Fighting Fund territory; and the organisers worked hard to encourage the local Labour Party to put up a good candidate for the coming general election. To strengthen Labour's chances, Selina and the others set to work organising meetings in the Abergavenny area (though on one occasion there, the crowd grew so hostile she had to take refuge in the cellar of the Town Hall – along with the eerie figure of a policeman that turned out to be part of a waxworks show).[4]

Hardly had she arrived in South Wales, than a terrible catastrophe occurred. She was visiting Senghenydd nearby, staying in a miner's cottage close to a mine shaft when there was a tremendous noise from deep below the earth's surface, and the whole village seemed to shudder violently. Everyone in Senghenydd knew instinctively what this signalled. But Selina Cooper's ear was not accustomed to catch this subterranean sound. 'I did not know what it meant,' she told a journalist afterwards,

> but women, old and young, all about knew only too dreadfully what that awful roar meant to them. They knew that behind that roar lurked death in its most awful and horrible form. Death from fire. The women started to run in the direction of the pit. I joined the crowd. I do not know how we did it, but we ran the whole of the two miles that lay between us and the pithead.

The terrible moment remained etched in Selina Cooper's memory forever. Years later she could jot down in her notebook how, 'I was allowed inside the enclosure. I saw bodies [piled] up just like a bone taken out of the fire . . . members dug rows of coffins alongside the enclosure.' Four hundred and thirty-nine miners lost their lives that day. Beside this horrific figure the earlier accident Selina witnessed at Whitehaven paled into insignificance. The whole community was touched by the tragedy. 'Scarcely a house without a drawn blind', mourned Ada Nield Chew in *Common Cause*. Only paltry fines were imposed on the colliery for breaches of the safety regulations. 'MINERS' LIVES', ran the headline in one local Labour paper, 'AT 1s 1¾d EACH.' Both the voteless women and unprotected miners had good reason to resent the Liberal Government with a mounting intensity. And this common cause led suffragists like Selina to value the miners' support of women's suffrage even more.

Mary was thirteen at the time of the Senghenydd disaster and years later could still clearly recall the incident. The miners, she recounted,

> were buried alive. And my mother's ambulance [training] came in handy. Well, she was working for suffrage down there . . . and my mother wrote and asked if she could do her ambulance work and help . . . Oh, it was terrible. And she'd been away six weeks. And she wrote [home] to say . . . she might get back – there was a train that got in to Nelson at midnight, and she might get back on it, but she wasn't sure, and we must go to bed . . . My father shooed me off to bed . . . I slipped out. I went up to station . . . And the porters got to know me . . . And my father was wild, because he was right vexed with me. And my mother wasn't vexed, but I wanted to see her so badly.[5]

That summer in 1913 Emily Wilding Davison threw herself under the King's horse at the Derby. The WSPU honoured its first suffragette martyr with a moving funeral procession through London. Also Sylvia Pankhurst, in and out of prison under the 'Cat-and-Mouse' Act, formed the East London Federation of the WSPU, despite the disapproval of her eldest sister in Paris. And during that summer, Christabel began her *Great Scourge* articles. With 'Cat-and-Mouse' police chases, martyrdom, the anti-men VD scare and the continued arson campaign, the militant movement entered its final and most extreme phase.

In the midst of all this, the National Union organised a national Suffrage Pilgrimage for July 1913. It still firmly believed that demanding women's suffrage was fruitless unless the majority of women backed that demand; and it still believed that its behind-the-scenes lobbying of key unions and key constituencies could only be effective if it was supported by widespread public opinion. The constitutional changes that the suffragists were demanding were, Selina and other National Union democrats believed, far too important to be left to a few activists or to the manipulations of politicians cut off from the experiences of the millions of voteless women.

So from all corners of the kingdom, by a spiderweb of routes converging on Hyde Park, women pilgrims trudged hundreds of weary miles with their banners. A few members of the Clitheroe Society were able to take time off work to walk part of the way, but their wages were sorely needed at home and they had to get back to Nelson after a day or two. The only woman among Selina Cooper's local friends who managed to cover the whole journey was Emily Murgatroyd, the Brierfield weaver who was one of Selina's early suffrage recruits in Nelson. An unmarried woman in her thirties, her wages – then about 23 shillings – would have been badly needed at home since she was one of the family's breadwinners. 'I had to save up money to leave with my mother,' she recalled, 'because she couldn't manage to get along without it. When I went away on suffrage work I always left a pound at home.' But brave Emily, setting out from Manchester with the hundreds of other pilgrims for the three-week march, soon found how difficult it was to demonstrate for the vote in 1913. The widespread publicity given to the pilgrimage made it even harder: even though the women were peaceful and non-militant, the meetings held along the route still attracted rowdyism and violence. People still did not distinguish between suffragists and suffragettes, Emily Murgatroyd explained, 'so we were all treated in the same way – things were thrown at us'.[6]

At last, on 26 July, the pilgrims reached London. Here they were joined by suffragists like Selina Cooper – twelve years older than her friend Emily, and a little less sprightly – who were not able to walk the whole way. Together this great mass of women surged towards Hyde Park, *Common Cause* posters fluttering everywhere. In the park nineteen platforms had been set up and people flocked to these. One of the biggest crowds gathered round the President's platform, presided over by Margaret Robertson, where Mrs Fawcett, Kate Courtney, an American suffragist and Selina Cooper were the speakers. Selina told her giant audience of the need for industrial women workers to have the power of the vote. 'We are fighting for the women in the slums, we are fighting for the women in the sweated dens,' Margaret Robertson added. 'We are here today to speak for the women who cannot speak for themselves.'[7]

The popular impact on the public imagination around the

country of this peaceful pilgrimage was tremendous; and in the autumn, as described earlier, the TUC and the Miners' Federation both swung round to support the suffragists against Asquith. With such newly-won public allies, it was time for the Election Fighting Fund to turn once again to fighting key constituencies.

One of the fund's priorities remained seats held by virulently anti-suffragist Liberal ministers, and here suffragists continued to help Labour Parties get their candidate adopted for the General Election – still expected for 1915. The Lancashire constituency of Accrington remained one such target. When its MP moved the rejection of a women's franchise bill, he hardly reckoned with the Manchester Federation and the fund. During late October, suffragists poured into this little textiles-cum-engineering town from all over the north of England for a joint labour-suffrage campaign. They included not only Selina Cooper, Ada Nield Chew, Margaret Ashton, Isabella Ford, Helena Swanwick, Fenner Brockway, Annot Robinson and Sarah Reddish, but now also young Ellen Wilkinson.

The campaign opened with a mass meeting addressed by Selina Cooper and others. Symbolically it was held in Accrington Town Hall, the very same building where Helen Phillip, whose photograph Selina still possessed, had spoken on suffrage thirty years previously. Local suffrage shops sprang up. Eighteen thousand leaflets were given out, encouraging Labour voters to ensure their names were on the electoral register. Ada Nield Chew published an excellent series of stories called 'Men, Women & the Vote' in the *Accrington Observer*, and afterwards wrote how it had been 'a week full of "crowded hours of glorious life" '. And all the suffragists' concerted effort proved worthwhile. By the end of the year, an Accrington ILP branch was formed; women began to organise a local Labour Party and, during the early years of the war, a Labour candidate was adopted. At least one leading anti-suffragist Minister had good cause to fret about this troublesome labour-suffrage alliance.[8]

Selina Cooper hurried from Accrington westwards across the Pennines to Keighley just over the Lancashire border, where a by-election was scheduled for early November. The sitting Liberal MP, Sir Stanley Buckmaster, had to stand for re-election because he had recently been promoted to become Solicitor

General. The idyllic hilltop village of Howarth fell within the constituency, and Selina went with Margaret Aldersley to address an open-air meeting from the market cross; but, as Mary Cooper recalls, the two women soon came under fire:

> Well, they threw rotten eggs and tomatoes and all sorts of things . . . they kept coming back into this cafe where they were sheltering . . . and then Mrs Aldersley went out and came back crying – oh, covered with egg and tomatoes and – so my mother – she's slow to rouse, but when my mother was roused I was scared stiff of her. She was right slow to rouse; my father was quick-tempered. Anyhow, my mother went out, and she stood on this cross, and she said, 'I'm stopping here, whatever you throw, so go and fetch all the stuff you've got to throw, because,' she says, 'I'm going to speak to you, I've come here to speak. And,' she says, 'this blooming village would never have been known about but for three women – the Brontës.'[9]

By the end of 1913 the labour-suffrage alliance was working smoothly. Just before Christmas it helped unseat the Liberal at a Scottish by-election; and in the new year it turned its attention to North West Durham.

North West Durham, with two out of every three electors a coal miner, was just the kind of constituency that Selina Cooper relished. She travelled north, along with Margaret Robertson, Annot Robinson and Ada Nield Chew, eager to meet the electors in their tiny pit-head villages. It was however a difficult election. The Liberal candidate was a known friend of suffrage, and this posed an agonizing dilemma for National Union stalwarts like Mrs Fawcett. But in the end, even she had to agree that the National Union must stand by its commitment to Labour, how-ever enticing an individual Liberal candidate might be. So four Election Fighting Fund organisers scurried north to act as sub-agents for the weak little Labour Party struggling to get off the ground there.

A vigorous campaign was launched to persuade local miners to vote Labour and support suffrage. Luckily, the Labour candi-date, though not a miner himself, was extremely sympathetic to the eager women suddenly swarming into his constituency. He was even prepared to oppose giving any further extensions of the franchise to men unless women were included. 'I see nothing but harm from withholding the vote from at least half the adult population,' he told the *Common Cause*. The suffragists were greatly cheered by his brave declaration. 'The [Labour] Party has risked their existence for women,' Margaret Robertson informed an election meeting in one of the local Co-operative Halls, 'and the women are going to stand by them for this reason.' Suffragists addressed Labour meetings chaired by local miners – a great advance on the uncertain situation at Holmfirth eighteen months previously. Selina Cooper even shared a platform with the Labour candidate himself at a crowded meeting in the Co-operative Hall in Consett. She told her audience how she had gone into a cotton mill when she was eleven, and about her long hard years as a winder and trade unionist.

Annot Robinson shared a platform with Keir Hardie and the candidate. 'If the wives have a vote then God have mercy on the Liberals and Tories,' Hardie told the meeting. 'We want votes for women . . . We are out for the full liberty of the working classes.' Indeed, so closely were Labour and suffrage now co-operating that the *Consett and Stanley Chronicle* perceptively commented that 'anybody going to any of the Labour meetings and listening to the speeches of the Suffragists might be forgiven for wondering if the suffrage organisation is, after all, a Labour organisation'. And *Common Cause* noted delightedly 'how the Labour men are encouraging their womenfolk to come out and take an interest in politics. "They scrub up too much!" the men say – and one of them has even shown his practical sympathy with the woman's lot by undertaking the scrubbing of the yard, that she may have more time!'

But this was part of the problem in this northern coalfield. Locally women had little tradition of waged work outside the home, and so were less in the habit of going out to meetings. Selina Cooper's usual appeal to the needs of women trade unionists would meet with less response in pit villages than elsewhere. Moreover, a combination of older miners (who were still suspicious of upstart Labour) plus pro-Home-Rule Irish voters ensured that a Liberal MP was again returned to Westminster. For Labour to win over five thousand votes for the first time it fought this seat, and to reduce the Liberal vote by two and a half thousand was excellent – but it was still not enough.

The 'old tradition has once more proved too strong,' lamented *Common Cause*, caricaturing the local Irish vote as 'a compact mass of nearly three thousand, controlled from headquarters and presented to the Liberal Party'. However smoothly the labour-suffrage electoral pact operated, the complex three-cornered elections of these pre-war years contained too many byzantine complications – like Home Rule and miners' Lib-Labism – to allow a strong electoral statement about voteless women's demands to be heard clearly down in the distant Houses of Parliament.[10]

It seemed virtually impossible to increase the number of Labour MPs in the Commons. Yet all the suffragists' patient lobbying of the Miners' Federation had some good effect. While electioneering in Durham was rising to a crescendo, the 1914 Labour Party Conference passed a strong women's suffrage resolution, condemning the Liberal Cabinet, and committing the Parliamentary Labour Party to raise women's suffrage at the earliest opportunity. And this time, at last, the Miners voted as solidly in support of the resolution as they had opposed it two years previously. Two weeks later the National Union organised a great suffrage meeting in the Albert Hall to which over three hundred trade unions sent delegates.

The Election Fighting Fund still did not slacken its efforts. That summer Selina Cooper returned to North Monmouth to help replace McKenna with the Labour candidate, an ILP and Miners' Federation man. Catherine Marshall sent brisk telegrams flying across the country, deploying her organisers as best she could to cover North Monmouth *and* a miners' by-election in North East Derbyshire. 'You can have . . . Cooper if wanted wire her . . . Pontnewydd she knows Derbyshire miners,' Catherine Marshall instructed the Election Fighting Fund's recently appointed by-election agent; and then she warned Selina, staying in lodgings in Pontnewydd, to be on the alert in case she was summoned elsewhere.

Selina was not summoned. In July 1914 she was speaking in the Abertillery area and in early August she was still in North Monmouth. Yet her attempts in South Wales to replace the callous Home Secretary with a Labour MP in the coming General

Election were cut brutally short. There was no Election. There was only war.[11]

What had Selina Cooper and the other Election Fighting Fund suffragists achieved during the last two and a quarter years? In strict parliamentary terms their impact was necessarily limited. There had been eight by-elections at which the Election Fighting Fund had supported Labour; and at two of these, Holmfirth and North West Durham, Selina had been actively involved. In four of these eight, the Liberal lost his seat – but, of course, to a Tory. In three – including Holmfirth and North West Durham – the Liberals' majority was badly dented. Although there were no Labour gains, there *were* four Liberal losses.

Equally important, the Labour vote shot up. At Holmfirth, Selina Cooper saw it double, and at North West Durham Labour won over five thousand votes though it was the first time it had put up a candidate. For at least seven of the contests the Election Fighting Fund could claim that the total loss to the Liberals was over 15,000 votes and the overall gain to Labour exceeded 16,000 votes – an average of 2,000 votes transferred from Liberal to Labour at each by-election. It is difficult to guess for how many of these votes the Election Fighting Fund itself was responsible, though estimates put it at between five hundred and a thousand. Certainly, fund organisers seem to have helped tip the balance against the Liberals, especially as so many of the constituencies were marginal ones: the Liberals lost one seat by only sixteen votes. Equally, suffrage organisers were crucial in constituencies where local Labour Party organisation was patchy or demoralised.

The Liberal Government had therefore lost four seats and had good reason to worry about three others. But more important than counting MPs' heads were the long-term trends which should have worried Asquith's party agents. They might have noticed the old Lib-Lab electoral agreement start to falter, as Labour boldly began to contest industrial seats previously 'claimed' by Liberals. Additionally, they might have become alarmed by the growing strength of Labour Party machinery in half-a-dozen constituencies held by anti-suffragist ministers – like North Monmouth and Accrington. It is a hazardous game guessing how Labour *would* have fared in a 1915 general election. But perhaps part of Labour's greatly increased electoral strength after the war might be traced back to these challenges in Liberal strongholds.

Yet arguably the Election Fighting Fund's historical significance lay not so much in this electoral arithmetic, but rather in bringing together two giants: women and labour. This was no localised alliance between a small women's organisation and a socialist splinter group. Rather, it linked two great national organisations whose joint membership was massive and whose combined networks stretched to all corners of the country. The alliance took time to shake down; but by 1913–14 the two organisations could exert considerable political pressure, the full realisation of which was cut short only by the war. 'The whole of the women's movement,' commented Beatrice Webb in the *New Statesman* early in 1914, 'finds itself side-slipping, almost unintentionally, into Labour and Socialist politics.' Catherine Marshall, writing just six weeks before war broke out, was even more forthright:

> The present state of things is creating a revolutionary spirit in the women's movement (quite apart from the militancy) which will inevitably . . . join hands with the revolutionary element in the labour movement . . . Women's suffrage is bound to come soon, Militancy or no Militancy, if for no other reason than because the Labour Party will insist upon it.[12]

The validity of Catherine Marshall's predictions is suggested in the next two chapters – though, of course, the impact of war radically reshaped the nature of this 'revolutionary spirit'.

Asquith's anti-suffragist obduracy and the ensuing Labour-suffrage pact also had profound repercussions upon the lives of a whole generation of suffragists. The drift of influential women out of the Liberal Party gathered speed. It had begun with Margaret Ashton. Margaret Robertson and even Emilie Gardner had shifted leftwards towards 'the red regions of socialism'. Now Catherine Marshall, who had grown up in the world of Women's Liberal Associations, also moved away and into the ILP. In 1913, in an effort to console another troubled Liberal woman, Catherine Marshall wrote how she had 'been an active Liberal woman myself until a few years ago when I realised that it was necessary to give all one's time and energy to suffrage work'. Sadly, the names of many other such Liberal women are unknown and their personal agonies of political conversion go unrecorded.

For another important group of women, already active in the socialist movement, the labour-suffrage alliance had less dramatic personal repercussions. Women like Selina Cooper and Ada Nield Chew, Annot Robinson and Margaret Aldersley, found that at long last the two parts of their life were united, each strengthening the other. After the long wilderness years of 1905 to 1912 when it had seemed Labour had deserted women, the alliance was a triumphant vindication of all they had ever worked for.[13]

CHAPTER FIFTEEN

SUFFRAGISTS FACE WAR:
1914-1916

On 28 June 1914 Archduke Franz Ferdinand of Austria was assassinated in distant Sarajevo. His death propelled Britain and the rest of Europe into 'a war to end all wars'. In early August Germany declared war on Russia and France, and invaded Belgium. Within days Britain had declared war on Germany. The suffrage campaign, after half a century of constant activity, juddered to halt. Britain was soon basking in a warm glow of patriotism. Recruiting offices thronged with eager young men: a hundred thousand volunteered within the first three weeks.

War changed everything. Suffragette prisoners were released. Christabel Pankhurst returned from her Paris exile and, with her mother and some WSPU followers, put her considerable energies into defeating the German Kaiser. The National Union, having refused to condone militancy in fighting for the vote, was less willing to support militarism so wholeheartedly. Instead, it turned its impressive organising skills to relief work, helping alleviate some of the immediate distress caused by the war.

The work of the Election Fighting Fund was suspended. Selina Cooper, away in the Abertillery area when war was declared, quickly made her way back home from South Wales. Sadly, Selina's personal reaction to the outbreak of war is unrecorded: her daily diary petered out after 1912 – and anyway she was not a woman given to committing her emotions to paper. We shall never know whether she welcomed the chance to recuperate at home after eight years of ceaseless campaigning. Or whether she felt deeply frustrated that the Election Fighting Fund work had halted just as it was beginning to bear fruit. Or whether, as an ILP internationalist, she caught a bleak glimpse of the spectre of death hovering over Europe. No doubt her response was something of all these. All we know is that Robert Cooper, within days of the outbreak of war (and doubtless having contacted his wife in North Monmouthshire) placed a short notice in the *Nelson Leader* on behalf of the Clitheroe Suffrage Society explaining that:

> owing to the terrible crisis caused by the War, the National Union . . . have ceased their propaganda . . . and, in consequence, they will devote their organisations for the present in co-operating with the local distress committee.

Arriving home, Selina was quick to see how badly the Lancashire towns were hit by war. The cotton industry which had thrived on importing raw cotton and exporting woven goods right round the world, now slumped. Local unemployment rose, and food prices spiralled by a third as the war forced up the cost of living. Worst hit were those weavers who lost their jobs; but even those who retained their looms felt the pinch.

In such desperate circumstances it was arranged that Selina should work part-time, her retainer fee of £1 a week still being paid by the Election Fighting Fund.[1] Her wage was welcome at home as Robert's earnings grew precarious. This part-time job also allowed her to contribute 10s immediately the local Relief Fund was set up by Nelson's mayor. A few months later she joined a local labour movement protest against the high price of food; she angrily demanded that the Liberal Government should control supplies and increase the number of ships bearing much-needed wheat from Argentina and Canada. And she was prepared to go further. 'I urge that we insist on the Government securing a complete monopoly which, I believe, would be a blessing for working people,' she added.

In 1915 a wartime coalition government was formed, still headed by Asquith. Its Cabinet included – for the first time ever – a Labour MP, Arthur Henderson. But the problems of poverty and high prices remained, and the need for local relief work continued. By spring that year Selina had, as she reported to *Common Cause*, 'been placed on all the Committees dealing with Relief Work in Nelson. I have also conducted fortnightly discussion classes on all kinds of social and war subjects.'[2]

These classes must have been fiery occasions, for Selina's repudiation of the war was as passionate as her feminism. Both she and Robert were convinced opponents, and this made the next four weary years an extremely bitter time for them. For, even in a town like Nelson where the traditions of radical ILP dissent were so strong, the Coopers' pacifism set them at violent odds with the patriotic emotion sweeping Britain at the time.

As Vera Brittain's *Testament of Youth* documents so movingly, the lives of a whole generation of young women were tragically affected by the war. Selina was forty-nine when war broke out: she was not personally scarred as a younger generation of women was by the insane slaughter of young men who went to their deaths in the trenches. Mary was still only a schoolgirl: and Selina had no sons to be seduced away to the battlefields of Flanders by Kitchener's admonishing finger. Perhaps for the first time in years, she felt relief that her beloved son John Ruskin had not survived to witness the horror beginning to devastate a continent. For, had he lived, John Ruskin would have been seventeen and would have soon caught the eye of the recruiting sergeant who inevitably materialised in Nelson at the outbreak of war. Nor was Robert, now forty-five years old, in any immediate danger. He had never quite recovered his health after his earlier illness, but even if he had his age would have protected him.

What the war did mean for the Coopers was that at last Selina returned home to stay. This forced her to confront some of the difficulties that were beginning to emerge in her relationship with Robert after nearly twenty years of marriage. It was not something she would ever talk about publicly (and Mary's deep loyalties to her parents forbade her recalling any quarrels between them), but at the back of her mind Selina must have increasingly recognised that she and Robert were growing in different directions. Life for Robert, despite his loyalties to his wife, seemed to grind on dismally and despairingly. Most of his earlier dreams and ambitions – to become a civil servant or help run a local union – had long ago faded away.

War also helped reshape other relationships in Selina's family. John, Bill and Richard Coombe were just the sort of men to revel in anti-Kaiser military pageantry, just as their father would have done were he still alive. John the cobbler was already in his sixties, but his twenty-year-old son joined up and was subsequently wounded in battle. And young Alf, now a dignified forty-six and still a professional soldier, was of course in his element. Working as a gunner, he was part of the regular British army's attempt to beat back the Germans.

So even within her immediate family, Selina had to defend her pacifist principles in bitter argument. The Coopers were pitted diametrically against Alf and the other Coombes. And they had to defend their unpopular views, not only among their own relatives and neighbours, but within the labour movement itself. And, if such pacifists felt they had their backs to the wall in August 1914, the opposition grew even more violent when conscription was introduced later on. Luckily Selina and Robert were not isolated in their beliefs. Out of Nelson's traditions of stubborn opposition to hierarchy and coercion sprang one of the strongest and proudest anti-war communities in the country.

These rebellious roots stretched back into the nineteenth century, to the Nelson immigrants who refused to touch their cap to the squire. During the Boer War socialists had objected to schools being closed to celebrate the Relief of Mafeking, since for children to associate 'rejoicing and holiday-making with war & bloodshed was distinctly immoral'. Then when the 1902 Education Act was introduced favouring Anglican and Catholic schools, local Nonconformists withheld part of their rates rather than 'pay for popery'. Some of these 'Passive Resisters' in Nelson were imprisoned, including the first Labour mayor, William Rickard. The Nelson Passive Resisters' League, defending the rights of these individuals whose consciences refused to allow them to obey Westminster's dictates, laid the foundation upon which wartime pacifists built.

This tradition flourished most strongly in Nelson's ILP branch, now with nearly eight hundred members and housed in its fine new hall. Earlier in 1914 it had protested against official celebrations for the king's visit to Nelson, impishly suggesting publicising instead the 'cost of the Royalty together with a comparison of a worker's budget'. And it also condemned the 'Cat and Mouse' Act because, 'whilst not condoning militant action', it saw the Act as one 'of murder, and murder by Act of Parliament.'[3] Even before the outbreak of war, Nelson ILP had been seriously alarmed at the dangerous growth of military spending,

demanding an enquiry into the world-wide influence of armament dealers. In contrast to the ILP, the SDF grew increasingly
jingoistic, urging extra battleships to repel the German foe. Selina
and Robert had been alarmed when the SDF had earlier isolated
itself from the mainstream Labour Party. Now, as war began,
they were aghast at the way SDF leaders, as their daughter put it,
'went round recruiting like Mrs Pankhurst'. They cut their last
links with the SDF and threw in their lot with the ILP. After all, it
was the ILP's Political Equality Campaign which had pioneered
the Labour-suffrage alliance in peacetime; and it was now the ILP
which obviously would spearhead local opposition to the war.

As soon as war was declared, then, local labour opinion was
immediately polarised, for and against. Many ILP members
resigned or let their subscriptions lapse, unwilling to belong to an
unpatriotic organisation. The Labour Party was split. At a
national level, Keir Hardie of course opposed the war and
Ramsay MacDonald resigned the leadership of the Parliamentary
Labour Party because of his anti-war views. But the bulk of the
trade unions backed the war, with Arthur Henderson even
joining the Cabinet. These savage divisions were mirrored locally
too. By October 1914 the Coopers' MP, Albert Smith, had joined
an all-party recruiting campaign, along with an available earl, a
handful of Liberals, and the chairman of the constituency Labour
Party. Local ILP members were aghast. What was their MP up
to, they demanded angrily? Albert Smith hastily explained that he
had no quarrel with the German people, only with 'its bellicose
Prussian Hun, whose sole ambition was to repeat the massacres of
Atilla a few centuries back'. Such vague historical allusions failed
to heal the rift. The constituency party chairman resigned, muttering angrily about the disproportionate influence of the pacifist
ILP. And the severity of the row was only slightly softened a few
months later by a note of bathos: Captain Albert Smith (for he had
joined the army himself) was reported to be in a military hospital
in Gibraltar – recovering from severe sunstroke caught at
Gallipoli.[4]

In the midst of all this, the other members of the Clitheroe
Suffrage Society repudiated the war too (except perhaps Sarah
Thomas, still a staunch Liberal). By far the most outspoken oppo-
nent was Harriette Beanland. She was furious that voteless

women were being dragged into a war about which they had never been consulted by a government that refused to enfranchise them. On 11 August 1914 she drafted an angry letter to the *Nelson Leader*, protesting against:

> the erroneous impression that this and other countries are at war with one another. They are not. Their governments, composed of men and responsible only to the men of each country, and backed by the majority of men who have caught the war and glory fever, have declared war on one another. The women of all these countries have not been consulted as to whether they would have war or not . . . If they [men] deliberately shut out women, the peace-loving sex, from their rightful share in ruling their countries and Churches, than all the appeals and sentiments and prayers will be of no avail in preventing hostilities . . .
>
> Yours, etc . . .
>
> H.M. BEANLAND[5]

Harriette's anger at how ordinary people – most especially voteless women – had become dupes of jingoistic propaganda intensified. 'How blind and foolish most Englishmen seem,' she told Selina Cooper. 'They are ranting and raving about German atrocities on the continent, but are quite indifferent to the atrocities committed by Britain.'[6] Before long she found the strains of war unbearable. Although it was years since she had left Gibraltar, she decided she could no longer remain in war-mongering Britain. She must emigrate, as far away as possible. So, one dark cold morning in January 1915, Selina and a small knot of Harriette's other friends gathered once again on Nelson station. This time they were not bound for a suffrage procession in London; they were there to wave goodbye to Harriette and see her off on her long journey – first by train to Blackburn and London, and then by ship via her native Gibraltar to Australia and New Zealand.

Selina said her final farewells with the forlorn feeling that a chapter in her life was drawing to a close. Harriette had been one of her closest friends since the heady days of their Guardian election eleven years earlier. Before she left Harriette had promised to write regularly from New Zealand but Selina must have walked home from the station bleakly conscious of the sister she had lost. Increasingly she turned to Mary, nearly fifteen, to fill the gap Harriette had left. Her bouncy and robust daughter would provide the close friendship that she needed, and which perhaps her husband could no longer offer.[7]

The war dragged on through 1915. The British army's traditional strategy for fighting across enemy lines of barbed wire to gain territory no longer seemed to be working. Horrific stories of young soldiers slowly dying, strung up on the German wire, began to filter through. The mud and deaths and hopelessness of trench warfare unleashed the passionate fury of people like Selina. Yet within weeks, Selina and her fellow pacifists were engulfed in a greater nightmare: conscription. Trench warfare was now mercilessly devouring thousands upon thousands of young men. Stirring the public conscience with recruiting posters was no longer enough. Men would have to be *ordered* into the army. Legislation was introduced and, by mid-1916, had so tightened up the loopholes that there was, in effect, universal conscription. The only concession made to dissenters from the war – such as members of the recently-formed No Conscription Fellowship – was that in certain cases men, 'on the ground of a conscientious objection to bearing arms', might be granted exemption through a system of tribunals.

From the beginning, Selina Cooper vehemently opposed both the principle and the practice of military conscription. The Nelson ILP branch had already urged Parliament 'to offer their utmost opposition to any proposal to impose upon the British people a yoke which is one of the chief curses of Prussian militarism'. But the yoke continued to be imposed. Feelings ran high against 'shirkers' and 'conchies'. Reports told of ILP and Quaker meetings being broken up. In Nelson in late 1915 a meeting was held in Salem School hall in protest against conscription being introduced – but was disrupted when a gang of Home Defence Corps men burst in, led by a local cotton manufacturer proclaiming, 'We are stopping this meeting.' Scuffling broke out. The chairwoman had to find refuge above the brawl by climbing on top of a piano. The police arrived but chose not to intervene. 'The Red Flag', a symbol of defiances, was struck up in an attempt to drown the Home Defence Corps' song, 'It's a Long Way to Tipperary'. The mood was ugly: the pacifists were routed.[8]

Such grim incidents reminded Selina how deep-seated was the opposition she faced. As conscription began to bite, she and her friends organised their protest. Early in 1916 Sylvia Pankhurst, sharing the same anti-war views as the radical suffragists, came up to talk to the Nelson ILP, and a branch of the No Conscription Fellowship was formed. Nelson ILP began to organise protection for those young men of military age likely to be called up; the No Conscription branch was given a room rent free in the ILP premises and ILP branch officials were authorised to let rooms to 'victimised anti-militarists for the purpose of sleeping accommodation'. As more and more young men were called up, women and older men stepped forward to fill their places as ILP branch officials and collectors-of-dues: Robert and Selina Cooper, Nancy Shimbles and others.

In spring 1916 Nelson's military tribunal, chaired by the Mayor and Captain Smith (happily recovered from his sunstroke), began its gruesome work. Among the dozens of cases heard, one was that of a leading member of the ILP and No Conscription Fellowship. 'I am against the Military Service Act and shall resist it by all spiritual and moral means,' he told the court. 'By doing that I shall be fighting Prussianism here.' When ILP members in the gallery heard his application had been refused, they booed and shouted angrily. The Mayor ordered the constables to clear the gallery. The ILP members struck up – as was now becoming customary – with 'The Red Flag'.

Throughout the dismal spring and summer of 1916 Selina Cooper watched a long procession of brave young men trail through the tribunals. She knew many of them as the children of her ILP friends, boys who had grown up through the Socialist Sunday School only a few years ahead of her own daughter. She could not but be deeply moved by this defiant procession of human misery.

Some of the young men were granted exemption, some recommended for non-combatant service, some were completely refused. A higher Appeal Tribunal began to examine difficult cases, and some local Conscientious Objectors – COs – had their exemption certificates cancelled. Mid-summer 1916 saw the first eight COs fined at Nelson magistrates' court for failing to report for military duty, and, watched by a crowd of about two thousand

women, they were 'escorted' to the station on their way to
Preston barracks. One was Dan Carradice, the Methodist who
joined the ILP. He was given a choice between seven days'
imprisonment or a 40s fine, and was then handed over to the
military authorities. 'What crime have I committed to be here?'
cried Dan Carradice's brother, a labourer, when it was his turn.
'Is it because I won't murder? I won't murder any man, neither
for you nor for anybody else.'[9]

   By now reports of tribunals were being edged out of the newspapers by countless pages of photographs of dead and wounded
soldiers. The horror of it was now inescapable. On 1 July 1916,
the first day of the Battle of the Somme, nearly twenty thousand
men were killed. At the same time stories filtered back – to those
who cared to listen – about the brutal treatment COs received at
the hands of the army. Sergeants would boast how they would
soon break in 'conchies'. They were knocked about and brutally
washed down with scrubbing brushes because they would not put
on army uniform. Local ILP members, desperately concerned
about the fate of their young comrades, began to write to them in
prison.

   One of these, a CO who came before the Nelson magistrates
that summer, was a weaver in his twenties called Alex Ingham.
Originally granted non-combatant service, this concession was
reversed by the higher Tribunal, and so his fate was the same as
Dan Carradice's: prison. Alex Ingham and others were 'escorted'
away by the police and by soldiers in khaki. Selina Cooper wrote
to Alex Ingham, for she was on friendly terms with his parents,
co-founders of the Nelson ILP. On 7 July, as the Somme battles
continued to rage, Selina sat down and carefully composed a letter
that would both cheer him up and also squeeze past the officials.
Mary, about to leave grammar school and already a far more
fluent writer than her mother, carefully copied it out in her neat
script:

> Dear Mr Ingham,
> I was pleased to hear from your father that you could receive let-
> ters, and therefore I am taking the opportunity of writing to you. I
> assure you that I fully appreciate your courage, in standing for
> conscience under very trying circumstances. It is well to know that

you are being treated better. I hope the terrible war will be over
soon and you will again be back into normal life.
I Remain
Yours fraternally,
Selina Cooper

Before long she received her original letter back, with this reply
in faint pencil written on the reverse:

Guard Room
117th Batt. Ches. Regt.
Preese Heath
Whitchurch
Salop

Dear Comrade,
Thank you for your letter. Letters from Nelson are the only gleams
of real sunshine that we get. You must excuse me writing back on
it, but I am doing this because I have nothing else to write on. We
are being as well treated as we can expect to be, now. In fact the
only hardships we have to suffer just now are the confinements and
the lack of seating accommodation. I suppose the next stage will be
worse. Well so be it. It's the path we have chosen. We are all in
good health and spirits. The fact that we have done what we are
convinced is right is a marvellous help. Please accept best wishes
for yourself and family.
Yours Fraternally
Alex. Ingham[10]

The Labour Party, hopelessly divided over the war, at least
remained intact to fight the post-war elections. The National
Union of Women's Suffrage Societies was not so lucky. From its
formation in 1897 right through to 1915, Mrs Fawcett's firm
diplomacy, combined with the Union's liberal–democratic
structure, had allowed it to flower into a mass movement without
splits or expulsions. But in 1915 it cracked right down the middle.
Pacifist internationalists became pitted headlong against pro-war
nationalists. It is perhaps one of the major tragedies in the history
of the women's movement that the giant National Union – it still
boasted over 50,000 members – never really recovered from this
crisis.
At the beginning of the war the National Union had been kept
busy organising relief work and tying up loose ends in key consti-

tuencies. Much of this work was undertaken by the dozen organisers who remained employees. One, of course, was Selina Cooper. Besides relief work, she found time to speak on women's suffrage at ILP or Guild meetings around north-east Lancashire. And her experience in the first year or two of war seems to have been typical of the other organisers. Annot Robinson also did relief work for the Manchester Federation, including running a centre for feeding nursing mothers and children under three. Her husband Sam was currently working as a soldiers' librarian in India, but the separation did nothing to improve their difficult relationship. Annot, working full-time and concerned about bringing up her two daughters, began to feel the strain; she had to swallow her pride and confide her growing troubles to her sister and to Margaret Ashton. Ada Nield Chew, also employed by the Manchester Federation but on a small retainer, was elected Rochdale Trades Council representative on the Mayor's Central Relief Committee, and was also involved in providing free meals to nursing mothers and young children. Like Annot, she was anxious to remain financially independent of her husband and she began to run her own small business. (Among the other organisers, Margaret Robertson married and eventually resigned her post).[11]

At the same time, Catherine Marshall as Election Fighting Fund Secretary kept in touch through local organisers with the political situation in the key constituencies. By mid-1915 she was able to give the National Union an impressive list of everything the Election Fighting Fund had achieved. Of six constituencies held by anti-suffragist ministers, four now had pro-suffrage Labour candidates ready to stand in the next General Election, including North Monmouth and Accrington. In a further ten constituencies, pro-suffrage Labour MPs, such as Philip Snowden and Arthur Henderson, had been promised election help by the Fund. And in another four constituencies, including Holmfirth and North West Durham, pro-suffrage Labour candidates had also been offered assistance. This impressive state of affairs, Catherine Marshall stressed, had only been achieved because of the organisers in the constituencies; and its importance was not merely that of electoral arithmetic, she argued but also that it brought 'the Women's Suffrage movement into friendly relations with the Democratic movement in the country'.

Catherine Marshall's work in co-ordinating organisers like Selina Cooper was still of course dependent upon support from the National Union as a whole. Yet the war was soon sending waves of tension right through the organisation. By 1915, it was clear to those involved in the day-to-day running of the giant Union that the old reflexes of compromise and reconciliation were now stretched to breaking point. On one side, Catherine Marshall and other anti-war members of the Executive strongly objected to the National Union's lending any support to the war effort. More important, they believed, was a broad education programme around ideas for a negotiated peace and internationalist links with women in other countries. Nonsense, retorted suffragists like Mrs Fawcett, Ray Strachey and Eleanor Rathbone. The first priority must be for Britain to win the war, to drive the Kaiser out of France and Belgium. All talk of education and internationalism must wait till then.

The internal quarrel grew more and more acute. Catherine Marshall and Mrs Fawcett were soon in public conflict, each keen to explain her own interpretation of National Union policy. Catherine Marshall, realising that Mrs Fawcett did not intend to soften her jingoistic stance, resigned from the Executive in February 1915 and fled to Holland. There, a group of British, Belgian, Dutch and German women were meeting to discuss peace proposals. They daringly planned to call a Congress of Women at The Hague for the end of April to cut across national enmities.

Invitations to the congress were issued. One was received by the National Union; the Executive decreed that local groups should be informed that because of the war National Union societies 'were not at liberty to send delegates to the conference'. At this, an immediate howl of protest rose up around the country. Resignations from the Executive flooded in – including those from such long-standing suffragists as Isabella Ford of Leeds and Margaret Ashton of Manchester. Many of them put their efforts into organising the conference at The Hague instead, forming the British Committee of the International Women's Congress (which included Margaret Ashton, Margaret Bondfield, Kate Courtney, Margaret Llewelyn Davies, Charlotte Despard, Isabella Ford, Eva Gore-Booth, Catherine Marshall, Sylvia

Pankhurst, Esther Roper, Ethel Snowden and many, many others). From groups of such women sprang the influential Women's International League for Peace and Freedom.[12]

The National Union was split in two by the resignations, and was led by the remaining conservative rump – Mrs Fawcett, Ray Strachey, Lady Frances Balfour, Eleanor Rathbone and a few others. Radical suffragists like Selina Cooper, far away from the maelstrom of London politics, witnessed this thunderclap with great alarm. Only days before the Hague Congress opened, she received a letter from an acquaintance in Manchester which revealed the full extent of the divisions:

> These are very trying days for suffragists and we in the N.U. are feeling the strain inside the organisation as well as outside. The cleavage of opinion has to my mind been apparent for some time, the war has brought it to a head. It is really the progressive section against the 'moderates' that is the dividing line, and unfortunately we have shed the ablest women in the NU . . . [13]

The question was whether Selina should resign too and put her energies into the international campaign. It was an impossible decision to make, and racked the waking hours of many a National Union activist. Of course, Selina saw herself on the side of the progressives rather than the patriots. Her years in the ILP had taught her to rebel against sham patriotism. And although she was not directly involved in the Hague Congress, Margaret Aldersley was among the 180 women in the British delegation (not that she ever got to The Hague: the British government refused passports to many of them, and in the end prevented any woman from leaving the country).

Of her own internationalism Selina Cooper had no doubts. But there were other arguments that made her hesitate before resigning from the National Union just because she could not immediately get her own way. Might not the National Union come round to her point of view, just as the Labour Party had done before the war? Perhaps Catherine Marshall, Kate Courtney and the others had been a little hasty. And after all, the National Union was still pledged, at least nominally, to lend its support to Labour candidates in the next election. That was a hard-won political victory that Selina could not afford to jettison lightly. And working under the conservative leadership of Ray Strachey and Lady Frances Balfour would hardly be ideal, but at least Selina knew from experience that she could rub along with such women; also the National Union remained sufficiently democratic under Mrs Fawcett's leadership for a leftward shift later on not to be ruled out. And would it not be silly for Selina to turn her back on suffrage just as the long-awaited victory seemed – war permitting – within reach? She was also aware that she was hardly an eminent Executive member of the National Union, but merely a half-time employee whose small weekly wage was much needed at home. If she did resign, there was little chance of finding other work locally. Earlier in the year, the National Union had agreed to keep its few remaining Election Fighting Fund organisers on, watching for the first signs of peace and a General Election. Even so, in these troubled times, an organiser's job was far from secure. Like Annot Robinson and Ada Nield Chew, Selina was keen to safeguard her independent income as long as she could.[14]

All these arguments weighed heavily with her during the summer of 1915. In the end she decided to remain with the suffrage movement and in her present post. At the same time she determined to keep in touch with the women who had initiated the Hague Congress and who went on to form the Women's International League at a meeting in Westminster in the autumn. Selina felt as desperately about the evils of militarism and trench warfare as they did and, a week before the Westminster meeting, she decided to take the only action that seemed open to her. On 22 September 1915 she wrote directly to the Secretary of the War Office, to Lord Kitchener himself, requesting permission to visit the war zone in France and explaining her motives. Needless to say, she received a firm rebuff from the Chief Permit Office in London who politely explained that,

> the Military authorities in France have received so many applica-
> tions based upon equally excellent claims that, although fully
> appreciating the motives which prompt such visits, they neverthe-
> less find it impossible to extend the limits of their sanction to visit
> the Zone of the Armies, beyond the bounds of actual necessity.[15]

CHAPTER SIXTEEN

PACIFISTS AND MOTHERS:
1915-1918

Selina might not be permitted to investigate the war-zone trenches in person, but no one could stop her from demanding improved maternity and infant welfare conditions in her own home town. At the outbreak of war, the Women's Labour League and the Women's Co-operative Guild along with other national pressure groups, were urging the government to help local authorities establish maternity clinics. And, just as events in distant Sarajevo were about to turn Europe on its head, the government began to respond. It recommended that local authorities set up centres and offered them a grant to cover half the costs. Ironically, the onset of war did not halt this welfare campaign: it accelerated it. For it soon became cruelly clear that trench warfare was an insatiable consumer of young men, of cannon fodder. Britain now more urgently than ever had to produce as many healthy children as possible if she was to perpetuate the 'imperial race' in the face of German or other alien threats. So, if the war elevated manhood as the noble defender of the British empire, it also raised up high motherhood as women's most sacred duty. Without the mothers' contribution, the future of the nation looked uncertain: the wartime emergency underlined the need for positive state intervention into this previously private 'family' area.

Selina Cooper was soon busy pressing for local facilities to be established, and by summer 1915 could report in *Common Cause* that she was 'now organising a Maternity Centre in Nelson'. Her efforts were given a powerful boost in September when the Women's Co-operative Guild published a collection of letters from Guildswomen, each recounting heart-rending stories of miscarriages and stillbirths, careless doctors and midwives, problems all made worse by poverty. Indeed some of the harrowing tales in *Maternity* closely reflected Selina's own experiences and those of her mother before her. 'My mother . . . brought fifteen little lives into the world; twelve are still living,' wrote one Guildswoman. 'I have seen my father strike my mother just before confinement, and known her to be up again at four days' end to look after us. You see, my mother . . . had been brought up to obey her husband.' Another woman, when she lost one of her two children, described how her 'interest in life seemed lost. I was nervous and hysterical; when I walked along the street I felt that the houses were falling on me, so I took to staying at home, which of course added to the trouble.'

The collective impact of these tales of mothers' and babies' wasted and maimed lives was considerable. *Maternity*, accompanied by Guild leaflets like 'Municipal Maternity Centres' and 'What Health Authorities can do', was highly effective propaganda. Local authorities began to respond by setting up maternity committees. 'We feel we can congratulate ourselves on the formation of these Municipal Committees', the Guild reported modestly. 'Work formerly done by voluntary societies is now being taken over by the municipality.' The Women's Co-operative Guild, justly proud of its local successes, reserved pride of place to Accrington, a local town that Selina had come to know so well. In October 1915 the Accrington and Church Guild invited her to come and speak at the opening of its Maternity and Child Welfare Week designed 'to promote Healthy Motherhood and to Save the Babies'. An exhibition 'of Hygienic Clothing for Children' was lent by the Women's Imperial Health Society, and generally the impact on Accrington seems to have been considerable. 'As a result,' the Guild's report explained,

the whole town was interested in the question, the deputation which went before the Health Committee was very well received, and a complete scheme is now being drawn up. It hoped that other Branches will take up this idea, and arrange similar exhibitions.

This they did. Not long after, in July 1916, Selina was invited to tiny Oswaldtwistle near Accrington by the local committee of the

Maternity and Child Welfare Centre to attend its opening ceremony. She determined that plans for a Maternity Centre in her *own* home town should be given the most urgent priority.[1]

During the first two years of the war Selina Cooper found for the first time for years that the pace of life slowed down. She had time enough to sit and write her friend Harriette Beanland chatty letters: about Billy the family cat, and his habit of lying on the Coopers' nasturtiums and going out on dark nights to lurk around pubs. 'I am shocked to hear he is on such friendly terms with the *brewers*,' Harriette replied. 'You really ought to read him a temperance tract.'

Towards the end of 1916 the tempo of Selina's life began to shift again. To begin with, the changes affected other members of her family. Because of the war, Robert had left the mill and, as Mary explained candidly,

> was transferred to the Post Office, because he never lost his knowledge of the streets . . . He'd be forty, in his later forties. But they were calling them up – transferring them to work [at different jobs] at that age. Well, he was then drafted back to the Post Office . . . and in those days there weren't raincoats and things like that . . . And it was a wet Christmas, there'd be coats dripping all round the kitchen. Pegged up round the kitchen, and every time they'd drip on you.

Mary had already begun to echo her mother's impatience with her long-suffering father. At the end of that summer term she left grammar school, armed with her commercial and shorthand certificates. Using her best schoolgirl copperplate, she drafted an application (on the back of an old piece of Suffrage Society paper that came to hand) to the Nelson Borough Treasurer for the coveted post of 'Lady Clerk' at a wage of sixteen shillings a week. Mary got the job, and it turned out to be a job for life. Robert and Selina's efforts to keep their daughter out of the mill to benefit from the education neither of them had been able to enjoy paid off.[2]

With both her husband and daughter in steady employment, Selina was under less pressure to hold on to her organiser's job. Ironically, it was just at this point that the suffrage campaign, after two years' virtual suspension, sprang into life again. Selina found herself thrust back into the hurly-burly of full-time politics. Early in 1917 she received a letter from what remained of the Election Fighting Fund, explaining how 'the EFF Committee yesterday decided to put you on full-time work and pay as you now appear to be able to manage whole time', and noting that her salary would now rise to £100 a year plus expenses. Selina was ready to fight what she trusted would be the final triumphant battle in the weary suffrage war.

Rumours had begun to circulate in 1916 that the Government was preparing a new Registration Bill designed to enfranchise soldiers fighting at the Front who otherwise would not qualify to vote under the old residential qualifications. Responses to this varied. At one extreme, jingoists like Mrs Pankhurst now relegated women's demands well below those of British soldiers. ('Could any woman,' she asked, 'face the possibility of the affairs of the country being settled by conscientious objectors, passive resisters and shirkers?') She even authorised a Conservative MP to state on her behalf in the Commons that the WSPU would not use the enfranchisement of soldiers and sailors as a pretext for agitating for women's votes. At the other extreme, ILP groups (like the Nelson branch), and Sylvia Pankhurst's Workers' Suffrage Federation (as her East London Federation of Suffragettes was now called) were not prepared to compromise on their demand for the vote for *all* adult men and women. In between stood the now-moderate National Union. It did not feel able to press women's claims too energetically in the midst of war, but it did not want them to be overlooked should the Registration Bill include any widening of the franchise. Selina Cooper as an organiser therefore busied herself with suffrage meetings in mid-1916. (Though as an ILP activist, she can hardly have agreed wholeheartedly with the moderate line that her National Union employers now adopted.)[3]

However, it was becoming increasingly clear that there *would* be a completely new Franchise Bill, and that there was considerable pressure on the government to include women in its proposals. Two influential Cabinet Ministers – Arthur Henderson for Labour and Lord Robert Cecil for the Tories – both hinted to Asquith that they might resign if women were left out. Asquith's Government, in its last days before Lloyd George took over, decided the only way to cope with this crisis in the midst of the disastrous war was to set up an all-party Conference under the House of Commons' Speaker, which could debate the tortuous issues in private and come back to the Commons with practical proposals. Between October 1916 and January 1917 this Conference therefore quietly indulged in some successful horse-trading. The Tories agreed on manhood suffrage (for they too were keen to give votes to all soldiers out in the trenches) in return for preserving certain plural voting anachronisms – for business premises and university graduates. But if the Conference accepted manhood suffrage, what should it do about women? The embarrassing thing about women was that there were so many of them. It would, after all, be fatal to allow such volatile creatures to form a majority of the electorate. Somehow a portion of them must remain unenfranchised.

It seems that the Conference valued more highly as a responsible voter the mature mother with a family rather than the flighty woman in her twenties, her head swollen by inflated earnings from a munitions factory. (One eminent politician even tried to urge the Speaker's Conference to give an additional vote to every married man and woman who had produced four children on the grounds that such people had 'an additional experience of life, and their vote is therefore of more value. Further they have rendered a service to the state without which the state could not continue to exist.') In the New Year the Conference reached a compromise that effectively kept disenfranchised so many of the young, single women who had temporarily taken over men's jobs during the war. It recommended giving the vote to about six million older women, leaving the Commons to impose an age limit to either thirty or thirty-five as it thought fit. In this unsensational way, thirty-two middle-aged and elderly politicians quietly settled the issue which had torn Edwardian England apart.[4]

Reactions to the Speaker's Conference Report varied. Arch-democrats like Sylvia Pankhurst and her Workers' Suffrage Federation were vehemently opposed to this arbitrary disenfranchising so many women wage-earners. The National Union, feeling the proposals were at least a workable compromise, tended to support them. But where did this leave Selina Cooper and the other radical suffragists? Selina had long based her campaign for women's suffrage on women wage-earners' right to a vote, and she could not casually abandon such a fiercely-held article of faith. Luckily she was not alone. At the beginning of New Year 1917 the West Riding Federation organiser mounted a campaign among women munition workers in Yorkshire, and suggested that Selina should help.

Selina once again packed her bags and travelled over the Pennines to start petitioning. The few clues she scribbled down in her notebook later suggest how dangerous her visit was:

> The Buff Girls wore Red hankerchiefs and buff Overalls and work in some kind of clay. I got a large number of them to sign a petition in favour of the vote we got 300 names one dinner time. I was in Sheffield when the German Zeplin came over the Pennines and drop bombs . . .
>
> When working at Wakefield getting the Petition for Suffrage at a place called BurnBow there was a great factory where high explosives were made there were 500 Women employed each shift there were a special station built no one were allowed to travel to it without a permit . . . I travelled up and down getting the women over 18 to sign a Petition in favour of the vote. The work was so dangerous that no women had to wear anything such as [metal] hairpins . . . [5]

The National Union agreed to extend this campaign wherever there were women munition workers, and that some of the remaining Election Fighting Fund organisers should spend three months on this. The Manchester Federation was particularly active, with both Selina Cooper and Annot Robinson working hard urging trades councils, trade unions and other political groups to put pressure on Lloyd George. However, even this campaigning among the Lancashire munition workers turned out to be a thankless task. Increasingly, all the influential suffrage groups came round to accepting the proposal that women under thirty *should* be left out of the bill. Even Labour Party women who had previously been unhappy about such unfairness were brought round by silver-tongued Labour MPs. 'A Memorial from Munition Workers was begun, but,' the Manchester Federation lamented afterwards, 'as the press of political work increased, this campaign had to be discontinued. Sufficient was however accomplished to show the annoyance of these women that they were not included by the provisions of this Bill.'

Such unfairness was a great blow to Selina Cooper. But she had to put this behind her, and concentrate instead on getting the bill as it stood through Parliament. She lobbied local women's groups and organised both a local Study Circle on the bill's proposals and a suffrage meeting with Annot Robinson, again in Accrington Town Hall.

With such energetic lobbying taking place up and down the country, suffragists began to feel cautiously optimistic. Indeed, in May 1917 the bill, including its long-awaited women's suffrage clause, passed its second reading in the Commons with a massive majority. Then, in mid-June the Commons debated the committee stage of the women's clause. There was naturally a great buzz of excitement in the Chamber. But it passed through easily, supported by seven out of every eight MPs. It looked as if at long last women might soon be able to vote.[6]

Selina Cooper missed no occasion to press home the women's suffrage case. But by mid-summer her interests had broadened far beyond the mechanics of parliamentary procedure and counting MPs' heads. 1917 was a year of worldwide unrest and rebellion. The repercussions of this were felt strongly up in Nelson and Selina was, as usual, to be found in the thick of it.

The war was going disastrously. That summer the Passchendaele campaign, fought over low-lying swamp, brought a quarter of a million casualties, yet only paltry gains. German submarines were hitting British shipping badly; in north-west England the cost of food more than doubled and food queues lengthened. Worse still, the army had grown so depleted that Lloyd George's government determined to 'comb out' yet more men for the Western Front. With so few men of military age left, it fell to women like Catherine Marshall to run the No Conscription Fellowship. To this daunting task she brought all her years' experience of suffrage campaigning.

Up in Nelson, Selina Cooper was only too conscious of the deepening crisis. The ILP and No Conscription Fellowship branches still remained firm opponents of militarism against all the odds: one of the town's leading pacifists had been courtmartialled and sentenced to two years' hard labour. But perhaps worst of all for Selina that summer was the death of Nancy Shimbles, aged only thirty-nine. A Poor Law Guardian, a member of the Weavers' Health Insurance Approved Society, the Nelson ILP Education Committee and the No Conscription Fellowship, she had passionately opposed the war till the very end. Shortly before she died she had protested, 'How can women sit still while men are dying in thousands on the battlefield?' At the Memorial Service for her in the ILP Hall she was likened to those two other pioneer women who had also died young: Carolyn Martyn and Enid Stacy. And Selina Cooper, remembering Nancy Shimbles' contribution to the Socialist Sunday School and her frantic panic when lost with Mary in London, paid a moving and affectionate tribute to her friend at the graveside.[7]

It was amid this mood of personal despair that socialists like Selina Cooper first welcomed the joyful news from Russia of the February Revolution and the downfall of the Czarist regime. As ILP members, both she and Robert had always been internationally minded and had early on contributed to Labour's Russian Fund. Now, the Nelson ILP decided to devote a special meeting to discussing events in Russia: the spirit of the Russian Revolution appealed directly to those anti-war rebels whose idealism had been pent up for so long.

In fact, the first tangible repercussion in Nelson of this revolutionary new spirit touched directly on the women's suffrage issue. Selina Cooper and other local suffragists had conscientiously toed the National Union line regarding the Speakers' Conference recommendations, giving no formal support to Sylvia Pankhurst's ultra-democratic demand for votes for every adult man and woman. But by summer 1917 their mood was changing. The suffrage victory was at last within reach. Confident of this, Selina Cooper and her friends felt free to welcome the events in Russia which seemed to open up long-awaited revolutionary changes in British politics. 'We desire to see achieved in this country what has been achieved in Russia,' boldly proclaimed Sylvia Pankhurst in her *Workers' Dreadnought* newspaper.

Our wish is to see the British Democracy taking strong and immediate steps to secure a stoppage of the War, and joining with the workers of Russia, Germany, and other nations, in establishing International Socialism, with equal rights for all men and women.

Such declarations touched the hearts and minds of the Nelson suffragists. In May 1917 a young Glasgow woman called Jessie Stephen came to address the Nelson ILP on the injustice to working women of the Speaker's Conference recommendations; Selina Cooper's group responded impulsively to her appeal and set up their own Workers' Suffrage Federation branch.

At the end of the year, the branch invited Sylvia Pankhurst herself up to address a meeting in the ILP Hall, with Margaret Aldersley in the chair. No fewer than six hundred people crowded into the building. Strong resolutions were passed demanding that the government accept Russia's proposed armistice, and calling on the Town Council to send a deputation to Westminster to urge this course. Another demanded 'the rejection of the Franchise Bill and the substitution of a complete adult suffrage measure'. And a third – rather provocatively – 'urged that the British housing problem should be solved as the Russian Bolsheviks have solved it, by giving municipalities power to commandeer empty houses and to install in them those who are living in insanitary and overcrowded dwellings'. Selina Cooper was thrilled with this new linking of Russia's proletarian uprising with the ILP's tradition of municipal socialism.

Perhaps it appears strange that Selina, an employee of the moderate National Union, should throw herself so fervently into this revolutionary activity. Certainly she must have been acutely conscious of the divide between the realisable demands of her paid suffrage work and the utopian visions of the Workers' Suffrage Federation. But then such tensions are familiar to any radical working for a middle-of-the-road organisation. Selina valued her regular wage, yet she did not allow her paid job to curb what she did in her free time, and she had no inhibitions about chairing a Workers' Suffrage Federation meeting on 'Women and Peace' a few months later. (But despite activity in Nelson and similar towns, Sylvia Pankhurst's Federation's national membership seems to have remained tiny. Certainly in Nelson, this particular revolutionary organisation appears to have flowered only briefly.)[8]

However, the feeling grew stronger that the British government was no longer a democratic government and no longer operated in the interests of working-class people. Inspired by Russia, local workers' and soldiers' councils were set up in Nelson and in other towns with a strong socialist presence. For Selina Cooper all such rebellious feeling came to a climax in one tumultuous summer month: August 1917. In these few stirring weeks, Selina found that the three strands of her wartime experiences – internationalism, women's rights, and maternity and infant welfare – became inextricably woven together in a strong web. This web was to shape the rest of her political life.

As more and more young men were winkled out of their homes and into army uniform, demands for peace-by-negotiation grew more urgent as each day passed. The Women's International League was among the organisations active here. But led as it was by highly educated women who 'had' languages, it sometimes seemed remote from, say, the members of a northern ILP branch. Instead such women put their efforts into the Women's Peace Crusade. Formed earlier in the war, the Crusade took off in 1917–18, bringing together radical anti-war women at the grassroots. In Glasgow, for instance, the Women's Peace Crusade mounted a demonstration of over 12,000 people in July 1917. Three days afterwards, Gertrude Ingham, mother of the imprisoned Alex, convened a public meeting; with women like Selina Cooper and Margaret Aldersley, she formed a local Women's Peace Crusade, loosely linked to the Women's International League. They set about organising a public demonstration on Nelson recreation ground for Saturday 11 August, and applied to the Town Council for permission. They placed an advertisement in the local papers for 'Nelson Women's Peace Crusade: Great Public Demonstration and Procession . . . Mothers, Wives, Sisters and Sweethearts are earnestly invited to join in the Procession'. But even before this advertisement appeared, Selina became caught up in another local event: Nelson Baby Week.

The Baby Week idea arose from the wartime campaign, so dear to Selina's heart, to improve maternity and child welfare. Now, thanks to the propaganda of the Women's Co-operative Guild and Women's Labour League, it had won official municipal backing. Organised locally by Nelson's Education Committee, the Week was opened by the Mayor who sat on the platform

flanked by the Chairman of the Town Council's Health Committee and by Nelson's deputy Medical Officer of Health. Nelson
was one of the most progressive boroughs in the country, the
speakers assured their audience: it had far fewer slums and back-
to-backs than older industrial towns, and ran both a school clinic
and school dentist. More recently – and doubtless spurred on by
civic pride to match Accrington and Oswaldtwistle – the Health
Committee had even set up a modest Infant Welfare Centre. It
was open every Wednesday afternoon, when a doctor gave a short
talk on how babies should be looked after and how mothers could
make suitable baby clothes. But, the deputy Medical Officer of
Health warned grimly, one baby in nine still died during its first
year of life. 'Motherhood is the most important feature of the
nation's life,' he added. 'The country that is not producing babies
is on the down grade and inevitably declines.' To help halt the
decline of the race (for the national birthrate was then spoken of as
a 'racial' problem) and to encourage mothers in their sacred duty,
a Liberal councillor promised a reward of a guinea for every child
born during Baby Week who reached its first birthday.

The irony of Nelson's Baby Week was that having been campaigned for by voteless women, it was now run by men with no
direct knowledge of the kind of experiences recorded in *Maternity*.
There were no local women councillors or medical officers of
health yet. Indeed the *only* woman invited to take an active part in
the week was Selina Cooper herself. She was already acquiring
something of a local reputation, and this meant that she, of all
women, could be less easily passed over. On the Wednesday of
Baby Week she gave a short talk to introduce the film 'Motherhood' which was being shown every night that week (the other
four speakers were, of course, male councillors and aldermen).
Sadly, the newspapers do not record what she said; but the film,
we are told, illustrated 'a mother's life from the expectant stage
until her child is well grown', and wound up 'with a baby show,
and the soldier-father's return from furlough in time to see his
baby win first prize'.[9]

In such ways, women were urged to look after their babies 'as
their most precious possession, and to put the welfare of their
babies and children before anything else'. The more babies
Nelson produced, the women were told, the better for Britain. Yet

the women heard nothing about how to use 'preventatives' in order to better space out their babies, a subject which *Maternity* had at least discreetly touched upon. Nor did they hear anything about greater financial security for women at childbirth, still often forced to get up and look after their other children before they were properly rested. Nor anything about bringing an end to the war rather than merely giving birth to the next generation of boys to grow up to become cannon fodder. The crucial issues of birth control and family allowances might have to wait a while; but mothers in Nelson took the issue of war and peace into their own hands in no uncertain way with their Women's Peace Crusade procession.

Even before the Saturday dawned, Selina recognised it was going to be a difficult day. The Council's reluctance to give them permission to use the recreation ground was a sure sign of that. Also, the women had wanted a band to lead the procession through the town, but so unpopular were pacifists – even women pacifists – that no local band would agree to play. So the women assembled just outside the town centre in silence. Selina Cooper and Gertrude Ingham courageously placed themselves at the head of the procession. In front of them were positioned mounted policemen, carefully keeping their horses reined in as thousands of noisy spectators, interspersed with police reinforcements, began to line the route. Behind Selina Cooper and Gertrude Ingham gathered the other women, including Margaret Aldersley and Margaret Bondfield (whom Selina had recently met opening the Accrington Welfare Week). They all bravely held up their banners – 'Peace our Hope', 'We demand a people's peace', 'Long live the International', 'Hail the Russian Revolution' and 'Workers' Suffrage Federation: We demand peace'. At the head of the crowds lined up a contingent of young girls, the ILP Girls' Guild and doubtless including seventeen-year-old Mary Cooper too. They were all dressed in white with green shoulder sashes proclaiming peace, and each bearing a wreath of leaves.

The sun was shining as Selina gave the signal for the procession to move off. The women, by now well over a thousand strong, marched slowly forward. But the crowd was hostile. 'Traitors! Murderers!' someone shouted, and women in the crowd tried to grab at the clothes of girls holding the banners. The booing and jeering grew louder and scuffling broke out. It was, as the nervous newspaper reporter covering the proceedings admitted, 'pandemonium let loose'.

Selina and her friends had arranged for two wagons to be set up for the speakers. But when they arrived at the recreation ground, the enormous crowd waiting for them looked far too menacing for that to be possible. So Selina and the others hastily made their way to the nearest wagon. (The hecklers of course took immediate advantage of the empty platform, and a group of discharged soldiers clambered on to it and conducted a noisy rival meeting.)

So antagonistic was the crowd, now swollen to fifteen thousand strong, that the woman who chaired the meeting had earth and lumps of grass thrown at her. Someone even threw a clinker, and the women's voices were drowned in the uproar. Margaret Bondfield tried to speak, but was audible only to those pressed right up to the wagon. She felt nothing but pity for the people making the noise, she said. 'I know there is not one member of this howling crowd that would willingly send their men-folk to an unnecessary death, but that is what you are doing by your attitude . . . Russia has shown us the way out, and has asked the people of this country to take our stand on the side of democracy and peace.' Another woman on the platform – possibly Selina herself – tried to mention Nelson Baby Week but was drowned by a rowdy rendering of 'Britons never shall be slaves'. 'You are all slaves,' she cried above the howling. 'The people who are asking us to save our children today because there is a war on are the people who have doomed us to live under conditions which cause our babies to die' – at which the crowd broke out rowdily with 'God Save The King'.

The eight mounted police positioned round the wagon along with extra constables stationed throughout the crowd had been able to prevent Selina and the other women from being physically mauled, but it would have been impossible for them to quieten the crowd sufficiently for the speakers to be heard. Margaret Bondfield, in memory of Nancy Shimbles, optimistically asked the crowd to maintain a minute's silence. Since this obviously did not work, she asked them to express their sympathy by holding up one hand. But the meeting had to be stopped after only forty minutes. Two hymns were sung and the historic occasion ended with 'Three cheers for the International'. (It had been intended to submit a resolution to the meeting that 'The women of Nelson call upon the Government to support the foreign policy of the new Government of Russia, and to express its agreement with the Russian proposal for world peace . . .' But of course it was never put; and Selina Cooper on the platform had to have a quick word with the newspaper reporters, explaining that 'it would have been dishonest to move a resolution and declare it carried when it could have been heard only by a small section of the crowd.')

People drifted away to the rival wagon where an ex-sergeant major waving a Union Jack was telling his audience amid great applause that the silly gullible women had of course been duped by male shirkers and conscientious objectors. They, the discharged soldiers, were prepared to fight in the trenches again. 'In destroying Germany,' he declared, 'we are destroying the vermin of the world.' The crowd was eventually dispersed by police. 'Later in the evening,' concluded the local newspaper report, true masters of unblinking understatement, 'a large crowd assembled in front of the ILP Institute, and a number of sods thrown and booing indulged in.'[10]

Selina Cooper and the others returned home on Saturday night badly shaken by their experiences. They had addressed enough suffrage meetings to know how unnerving it was to confront a rowdy audience amid a shower of insults and rotten vegetables. But the mood on Saturday had been far uglier. It demanded even greater courage to address a vast throng stretching as far as the eye could see, baying for blood and hurling earth and clinkers. It was a new and alarming sensation, even for as experienced a speaker as Selina. She would not forget the events of Saturday 11 August 1917 quickly.

Yet the women's determination to campaign for peace remained so strong that Selina helped organise another open meeting a fortnight later. It was held in the Salem School hall and again attracted a big audience, mainly of women. Up on the platform sat the speaker, ex-Nelsonian Ethel Snowden, along with Margaret Aldersley. Selina, chairing the meeting, opened with a moving and impassioned statement to rally the women's spirits during these most difficult times. 'I think that those who

took part in the procession did something wonderful,' she told
them:

> It is one thing to come to a meeting like this; it is another thing to
> march through the street to be jeered at and booed at. We will
> never forget that demonstration; I think it was something heroic
> . . . We women are in a different position from men, because the
> law doesn't allow us to fight, but we can go to the street corners
> and preach God's truth that this war should end . . . When the
> settlement comes, every woman who joined the crusade will be
> glad to be able to say, 'I joined the peace crusade'.

Margaret Aldersley followed her, demanding a negotiated
peace to end the war and explaining how her invitation to the 1915
Hague Congress had been withdrawn by the government. 'If you
are as determined as I am,' she cried, 'the present Government
will have to listen to what the women say; if they don't take
notice of our resolution, we must organise ourselves and march
until we reach London, and –', but her words were drowned in
jubilant cheering. Ethel Snowden rose to speak, again to enthusiastic applause, and seconded the resolution. 'Women do not want
their honour protecting at the expense of the life's blood of their
boys,' she urged them. 'I want neither a German peace, nor a
French peace, nor an English peace; I want a people's peace.' She
too was loudly applauded, the resolution carried unanimously,
and the meeting ended, as the *Nelson Leader* again euphemistically
reported, 'amid a tremendous demonstration of enthusiasm'.

On this euphoric note the Nelson Women's Peace Crusade
continued its active propaganda through the winter of 1917–18.
Linked to the Women's International League, it drew together
many of the women who had worked so closely during the peacetime suffrage years. Up to address the Nelson group travelled Eva
Gore-Booth and her friend Esther Roper, now both living in
London, Isabella Ford from Leeds and Margaret Ashton from
Manchester. And distrust had long disappeared between the
radical suffragists opposing the war and those courageous
suffragettes who, alarmed at WSPU elitism and jingoism, had
distanced themselves from Christabel Pankhurst and gone their
own way. Up to Nelson came Charlotte Despard of the Women's
Freedom League; Emmeline Pethick-Lawrence, one-time WSPU
leader; and a suffragette from Glasgow, now a Women's

International League organiser, Helen Crawfurd. Local suffragists – Selina Cooper, Margaret Aldersley, Clara Myers and others – developed links with the growing network of women's peace groups. Indeed, a week or two after the Salem School meeting, Selina received a letter from the chairman of the British Section of the Women's International League, Helena Swanwick, the Manchester suffragist:

> Dear Mrs Cooper,
> The WIL is holding a big meeting in London . . . when we hope to have a number of women speakers to tell Londoners how the Women's Peace Crusade has gone in the country during this year. We wondered whether you would come and tell us how you got on in Nelson. We have heard very glowing accounts and we would be very glad if you would tell your tale in person . . .
> > With warm regards
> > Ever sincerely yours
> > H.M. Swanwick

(In fact, Gertrude Ingham went to report on Nelson's tumultuous events, in place of Selina Cooper who was unable to attend.)

But despite the grass-roots strength of the Women's Peace Crusade, internationalists like Selina Cooper were still feared as dangerous and subversive people, an insidious threat to the nation's wartime security. The Defence of the Realm Act had increased the state's power to suppress unpatriotic newspapers (such as those of the ILP and No Conscription Fellowship) and to confiscate papers 'to prevent persons communicating with the enemy'. The local police seemed to view Selina's activities with increasing suspicion – though they certainly had no reason to believe she was a traitor in touch with the Germans. Mary, then seventeen, recalled years later in detail the bizarre scenario that now unfolded:

> I worked at the office with a boy called Sharman. And we were all pals in the office together. Anyway, his mother came one day to our house. And when I got home, she was just going . . . and her husband was the chief inspector at Nelson . . . Well, this Billy Sharman worked with me. Anyhow, they'd probably heard Billy Sharman talk about me. And his mother came to warn my mother that they were coming to search the house. And she [Mrs Sharman] didn't tell me why she'd called. My mother told me after she'd gone. And she [my mother] said, 'She told us that she

was pretty sure that I was doing nothing criminal, and she wanted me to know and be ready for whatever they could find.'

Well, my mother didn't bother, because we hadn't anything that they could find . . . They came, the police. The detectives came. And of course we didn't tell that she'd warned her [my mother]. They came – about four or five of them. And they searched every drawer – to see if we'd any anti-patriotic literature . . . I don't think there was anything they could've [taken away as evidence] . . .

And she [my mother] pretended like . . . She just said, 'What are you wanting?' . . . And they said, 'Oh, we're very sorry, Mrs Cooper; we have to search your house.' And she said, 'What for? Have we been stealing or something?' She didn't let on that this woman had been . . .

Anyhow they searched every room, they opened every drawer . . . They even searched in the oven. In the mangle, behind the mangle, in the clothes basket . . . They took away a few things away . . . And my mother wasn't bothered, because she'd spoken quite openly about it. There was no secret about it. So whether they thought she had a few Germans hidden away, I don't know.

From the summer of 1917 onwards Selina Cooper was caught up in a bewildering series of political battles. Everything occurred so fast that it became difficult to recall the exact sequence of events: introducing the 'Motherhood' film during Nelson Baby Week, leading the Women's Peace Crusade procession through the hostile crowds, watching detectives search her house for seditious literature, and chairing the Workers' Suffrage Federation meeting on 'Women and Peace'. Then, in addition, she began to hear news that there had not just been one Russian Revolution but two; in October the earlier government had been toppled by revolutionary Russians calling themselves Bolsheviks led by Lenin.[11]

Amid such confusion, Selina Cooper still kept a close watch on the slow progress of the Representation of the People Bill and its women's suffrage clause. Having passed through the Commons, it now went up to the Lords. The Lords had always been a bastion of anti-suffragism: the President of the League for Opposing Women's Suffrage was the Leader of the House. But by late 1917 even the most diehard 'antis' seemed to realise their days were numbered. Lloyd George had clipped their lordships' wings before the war; now they could ill afford to turn a deaf ear to the rumbles rising audibly from industrial workers and from unenfranchised women, both around the world and in Britain itself.

Already one of Selina Cooper's well-to-do suffrage friends (the wife of a judge, whose father chanced to be a friend of the Czar) had written to Selina anxiously about what would happen after the war. 'Do you think there will be revolutions and much discontent,' she asked, 'or do you think we shall understand each other better and class hatred be somewhat less?' Certainly such people had reason to fear the setting up of local workers' and soldiers' councils and Women's Peace Crusade propaganda. 'The shock to the foundations of existing social institutions already reverberating from Russia across Europe,' wrote Sylvia Pankhurst, 'made many old opponents [of women's suffrage] desire to enlist the new enthusiasm of women voters to stabilise the Parliamentary machine.'[12]

Indeed the House of Lords' debate on women's suffrage took place only months after the Bolshevik Revolution. Perhaps their lordships asked themselves anxiously whether it might not be expedient to enfranchise women over thirty in order to draw more people within the pale of parliamentary democracy and so ensure the stability of the British state. It might be inadvisable to anger key industrial workers like the miners who had already pledged their support to votes for women. As one earl remarked soberly, 'The vote is granted nowadays on no kind of fitness, but as a substitute for riot, revolution and the rifle.' One lord candidly urged support for a broad franchise to encourage the Labour Party to progress from being 'a mere class party' into 'a major agency for social stability', and reference during the key Lords' debate was made to events in Russia. Even the Leader of the House was realistic enough to urge his colleagues to abstain rather than oppose the women's clause, since rejection 'may involve us in a struggle from which the House of Commons is not likely to desist'. Violence must be avoided at all cost – for one of the first victims would be the House of Lords. And any combined uprising of unenfranchised women, disenchanted soldiers and industrial workers would surely threaten the state far more than the pre-war tactical violence of a few hundred suffragettes. Many of the Lords were still wary of entrusting the precious franchise to millions of propertyless, ignorant and unpredictable women; but, wisely choosing the lesser of two evils, their lordships at last took their historic vote. By 134 to a mere 71 the House of Lords endorsed women's suffrage.

In February 1918 the Representation of the People Bill received the Royal Assent and became law. And on 13 March, Selina Cooper was invited to attend a celebration where Mrs Fawcett, Arthur Henderson and others spoke of the great victory. One of the longest chapters in Selina's life had at last come to a successful conclusion. It had covered over seventeen years, from her friendship with Helen Phillip and from the textile workers' petition in 1900, through the Election Fighting Fund and her lobbying local miners' lodges, to the wartime campaign. Now it was only a matter of months before she could cast her first parliamentary vote in the post-war General Election.[13]

PART THREE:
WOMEN BETWEEN THE WARS

CHAPTER SEVENTEEN

WHAT DO YOU DO ONCE
YOU'VE WON THE VOTE?:
1918-1921

The suffrage campaign seemed like a long dark tunnel. Women found that once inside, marching forward took every last drop of their energy and commitment. At last they reached the end and emerged into the daylight blinking wearily: the various choices of direction that lay before them were bewildering. Worse still, it was difficult to get their bearings: the countryside looked so different from what they had been used to. The women stumbled forward hesitantly into the fierce dazzle.

Some suffragists had been committed to the one-issue fight for so long that they found the new post-war world hard to come to terms with. Mrs Fawcett had devoted over fifty years of her life to lobbying for just one cause. Her political reflexes had become so conditioned during the half-century that it was difficult for her to adapt to unfamiliar challenges. Younger women, immersing themselves in the suffrage campaign later, still emerged exhausted into the complex post-war world. Mrs Pankhurst, who had joined the fight over thirty years earlier, soon renounced politics to travel across Canada, denouncing the evils of venereal disease and unchastity. Christabel was a generation younger; but within a year of winning the vote, she too lost interest in politics and took up instead the cause of the Second Coming of Christ which the deteriorating inter-war situation convinced her was imminent.

Charlotte Despard had long been interested in theosophy, and its spiritual creed became enmeshed with her old millennarian socialism and her passionate support for Sinn Fein in Ireland. Other women too found theosophy's spiritual creed now offered the same certainties as votes for women had done. Others felt less need to alter dramatically the direction of their lives. Catherine

Marshall, for instance, remained closely involved in the Women's International League for Peace and Freedom, though after the war she never fully recovered her health nor her remarkable organising energy.

There was one group of women for whom entering the new post-war world was a particularly bruising experience. They were the radical suffragists who had been employed as organisers by the National Union of Women's Suffrage Societies but who had differed from Mrs Fawcett over the issue of internationalism versus patriotism. They now found themselves in an emotional and political vacuum, distanced from the majority of ordinary women by their pacifism. Worse still, they found they had worked themselves out of a job. The small but regular wage they had relied on during the suffrage years was drying up. Yet 1918 was hardly the best time to look for a job. Men were returning from the Front to claim back their positions: the shadow of unemployment that would darken the inter-war years was beginning to lengthen.

Ada Nield Chew, determined to preserve her financial independence, taught herself to type and do accounts so that she could be a more efficient businesswoman. 'For the next nine years she worked like one possessed,' her daughter wrote. 'All too soon she would be sixty; somehow she must make enough money from her business to keep her in retirement.' Annot Robinson found herself tormented by similar money worries and by the worsening relationship with her husband. After he returned home from the war he became morose, drunken and occasionally rough with his daughters. In a desperate attempt to keep herself and the two children, Annot took a succession of organising and speaking jobs, including organising secretary of the Manchester branch of the Women's International League for Peace and Freedom. This she enjoyed a great deal, but insoluble problems continued to press upon her. 'Which specialist in brain trouble,' she asked her sister in wry desperation, 'ought I to consult?'

Selina Cooper was affected less harshly by events than Annot Robinson. Yet 1918 also compounded some of her earlier problems. She was now in her early fifties and had devoted most of her adult life to women's suffrage. Looking around the new post-war world, she noticed how different it seemed from 1914. Some of her friends were gone. Harriette Beanland had emigrated; Nancy

Shimbles was dead; she was losing touch with her countrywide network of suffragist friends. Russia's revolutions had radically altered the meaning of the word 'socialism', Asquith's style of government had gone forever, and as the Liberals' star waned so that of Labour burned more brightly. Selina realised that the days of pre-war England were over.

If Selina had let her mind roam even further back to the turn of the century, she would have noticed even greater changes. She could recall the distant time when she and Robert had first met, and reflect on the magical summer they spent together at Keld – where socialism and science, literature and politics were lengthily debated. Some of their daring ideas had since become more generally accepted. Recently a scientist called Marie Stopes had even begun to challenge the silence shrouding the birth-control question.

At the same time, Selina had grown further apart from Robert during the suffrage years. The coolness between them had become almost visible. Selina was now majestically plump; by the early 1920s she was unashamedly stout. Robert by comparison seemed puny. Back again at his job in the weaving shed, he was increasingly pitied for allowing his seemingly formidable wife to rule the domestic roost. It was a problem that had no easy resolution for such married couples at that time. Annot Robinson considered consulting a magistrate about obtaining a separation order, though her pride would not let her do it. Ada Nield Chew moved house (and only later did her husband follow her). Possibly such thoughts went through Selina's mind too, though if they did she thrust them firmly to one side. It was rare in Nelson for couples to separate, and they would be the subject of gossip for years. None of the three Coopers could cock a snook at convention, for all were deeply rooted in the area. Mary apparently had no thought of leaving the area (though some ambitious boys from her grammar school did) and, eighteen years old when the war ended, began to grow into a dutiful spinster daughter, caring devotedly for her parents. So, over the coming difficult years, the three Coopers soldiered on together at 59 St Mary's Street.[1]

Selina Cooper's personal problems after the war were compounded by other wider ones. Selina had long ago developed a sure political instinct for assessing priorities and strategies; yet in the first three or four years of peace she found she had frequently to reassess the situation as the world changed about her. With the single-issue suffrage campaign virtually over, her political energy now turned to more varied forms of expression. So the coming pages follow her as, in rapid succession, she involved herself with the Labour Party and its new Women's Sections, with the 1918 general election, with the Communist Party, and with the National Union of Societies for Equal Citizenship. Only after she has led this brisk dance through the maze of post-war politics, is Selina able once again to feel confident of her political priorities and strategies.

Like so many other suffragists, Selina Cooper had spent most of her adult life hammering on the doors of Westminster, pleading to be let in. Now enfranchised, she became subject to all manner of offers and requests for favours, often from politicians who earlier had been loath to support women's suffrage. Party politics had suddenly changed: everyone wanted women's votes. Politicians eagerly pursued those whom they believed had sway over the millions of women voters. Early in 1918, while the Lords was still debating the issue, the Labour Party's chief agent wrote to Selina. He wanted to know whether she would allow her name to go forward to the Party's committee which was planning to appoint 'two women organisers for the purpose of touring the country and encouraging local Labour organisations in their work of enrolling women into the various constituency organisations'. Precisely how Selina replied is once again unclear. Certainly she does not seem to have taken up the suggestion. Possibly she felt the prospect of 'touring the country' again would be daunting, and that the job should go to a younger woman. The following year as well there was talk of Selina's helping the Miners' Federation propaganda campaign about nationalising the mines – though again nothing seems to have come of this suggestion.[2]

Perhaps one reason why Selina Cooper was disinclined to take up such proposals was because she had little interest in women merely being used as voting or propaganda fodder. That would make a complete nonsense of her long struggle for women's suffrage. She had fought for the vote so that working women could voice their *own* demands – not just perpetuate the old system.

The evidence available suggests she was far keener on ensuring that women voters were able to use their new political power wisely.

The word 'citizenship' has grown dowdy. It conjures up drab notions of 'civics' lessons drained of all passion. Yet this was far from the case in 1918. Had not Keir Hardie himself written a suffrage pamphlet called 'The Citizenship of Women'? And was not citizenship what Asquith's Government had so long denied women? Certainly this is what most suffragists believed. At the end of 1917, in preparation for enfranchisement, the National Union of Women's Suffrage Societies therefore dispatched its remaining half dozen organisers to all corners of the country. Selina Cooper was sent off to the South Wales area that she knew well: Cardiff, Swansea and Newport. Here she spent a few weeks organising and speaking on 'The Right of Citizenship'.[3]

It was convenient for Selina Cooper to remain a National Union organiser. She needed her wage; and in strategic terms, Selina recognised that the battle for suffrage might be virtually over, but women's real fight still lay ahead and the National Union remained a useful base to campaign from. Its leaders of course mainly came from the centre-right wing now; yet, oddly enough, when they decided early in 1918 which of their wartime organisers to retain, Selina was among the lucky few who were offered their old jobs. The National Union can hardly have agreed with her anti-patriotic pacifism, but they must have been prepared to swallow such traitorous qualities in order to secure Selina's valuable talents. As a result of this decision, Selina went to speak in Brighton, Northampton and elsewhere for the National Union in spring 1918. Most of her energies, however, were to be concentrated in the area covered by the old Manchester Federation (which had dissolved into a Women's Citizens' Association); in particular she now focused on her own home town of Nelson.[4]

The Representation of the People Act which finally became law in February 1918 not only gave women over thirty the vote but also redrew boundaries of parliamentary constituencies. The Coopers' old sprawling Clitheroe division became the Nelson and Colne constituency. At Easter 1918 women in this textile-dominated division also formed a local Women's Citizens'

Association, drawing upon local Guildswomen, as well as members of the Clitheroe Women's Suffrage Society.

Selina Cooper was not among the officials elected at the Association's founding conference, though she was certainly closely involved in setting it up. The little minute book preserved among her papers records that she booked a room belonging to the Co-operative Society for the Association's first meeting; and at this meeting it was arranged for a committee to meet three weeks later in the Coopers' front room at 59 St Mary's Street. On this occasion Selina gave the main talk, urging the need for such local citizens' associations. The group also demanded that Nelson's Health Committee form a voluntary committee (presumably of working-class mothers) to be elected to run the Maternity Clinic in line with Women's Co-operative Guild policy. But already Selina was growing anxious about the short-sightedness (resolutions about public lavatories in Colne) of some of her fellow members. At the next meeting she intervened and undertook to draft a leaflet that would be delivered to every woman in the constituency 'enlightening them as to the value and extent of their voting power'. Even still, she remained very worried about this fledgling group. Its members seemed to lack the purposefulness of the early suffrage days. The war was still dragging on and perhaps this deterred women from joining: they were still unsure of themselves and how to use their new powers. The members seemed too ready to look up to Selina Cooper, but Selina, a firm democrat, always resisted being pushed into such leadership roles.

During the summer the Women's Citizens' Association only just managed to keep going. In August, Selina Cooper took charge of the desperate situation. She again booked the Co-operative room and chaired the meeting at which the Association's failure was thrashed out. 'It was . . . decided after long discussion,' the minutes dismally record, 'that owing to the indifference of people caused by the war atmosphere, to suspend the meetings for a period of time. A resolution was passed to that effect by all present.' For the first time in her life, Selina Cooper had helped launch a group which had immediately foundered. In a fiercely radical town with a long tradition of women's organising, the attempt to run a post-suffrage group had fizzled out miserably. If that happened in Nelson, worse, Selina suspected, was no doubt occurring elsewhere.[5]

Certainly this failure seemed to hit Selina very hard. After the Association was wound up, she felt so despondent that she did very little over the next few months – an unusual hiatus for her. Only towards the end of 1918 after the Armistice was she able to put the problems of the war years behind her, and survey the wider scene.

It all seemed so confusing, so difficult to set priorities. Christabel Pankhurst and her mother were campaigning on behalf of their newly-formed Women's Party (as the Women's Social and Political Union became). It managed to combine a feminist programme, including support for nursing and expectant mothers, with racist conservatism (for instance ridding government departments of all officials with 'enemy blood'). On such a programme Christabel decided to stand in the December 1918 General Election, proclaiming that the Labour Party was 'entirely dominated by Bolshevism and Pacifism' and that electors must therefore chose between 'the Red Flag and the Union Jack'.

The National Union, still under Mrs Fawcett's presidency, steered clear of such extremes. It welcomed certain pieces of legislation passed during 1918. For instance, a new act allowed the Treasury to help local authorities set up maternity and child welfare services; another act was rushed through Parliament (and became law only shortly before the General Election) permitting women to stand for Parliament. But beyond tidying up the law here and there, the National Union was growing increasingly uncertain about the direction it should move in. Shorn of its radical women and now robbed of the one cause that had previously unified its members, the organisation began to divide within itself. One section wanted to keep faith with the old 'equalitarian' ideal of removing all obstacles hindering women's complete equality with men; the other hoped that women would now fight for the broader demands – such as family allowances – which had made them campaign for the vote in the first place. Selina Cooper, observing these tensions from Nelson, must have felt a certain impatience with such wrangles. To her it remained clear: both sets of demands must be pursued – equal rights *and* special needs.

The National Union was, moreover, rather at a disadvantage regarding the rights of working women. It was keen to protect women's right to a paid job against the growing threat of post-war female unemployment, but it no longer enjoyed close relationships with major trade unions and the labour movement. The National Union officers, it seems from a letter sent to Selina in summer 1918, had to rely on women like her to keep them informed:

> Dear Mrs Cooper,
> Thank you very much for your report about the skilled trades . . .
> Can you tell me who, if anyone, looks after the interests of the
> women in the General Labourers' Unions? . . . Will you . . . send
> me from time to time the names and addresses of men and women
> within different Unions who really take the same view that we take
> about the position of women [in] industry, I think it would be very
> helpful.
> > Yours sincerely,
> > Ray Strachey[6]

Selina Cooper was faced with such requests for information because clearly she still had close contact with the world of organised labour. Not only was her husband a member of the Nelson Weavers, and her daughter a member of the local government officers' union, but Selina herself remained active in the Labour Party and was watching with interest the changes in the party as it emerged strengthened after the war.

In keeping with the times, the Labour Party adopted a new constitution early in 1918. It now became committed to the socialist aim of securing for 'the producers by hand and by brain the full fruits of their industry' on the basis of 'the common ownership of the means of production'. It also adopted a new membership structure which included special provision for women. Local constituencies would be able to set up their own Women's Sections, because, explained Marion Phillips, the Party's new Chief Woman Officer, 'women are so newly come into political life that their development will be hindered . . . if the whole of their work is conducted in organisations including both sexes'. But at the same time party officials remained terrified lest the women in their Sections acquired too much power and took off in a separate direction from the rest of the party. Therefore the

Women's Sections would be no more than temporary expedients for, as Arthur Henderson chose to phrase it, 'the women of our movement have consistently opposed every development of the feminist agitation which tends to emphasise the unhappy sex-antagonism produced by the long and bitter struggle for the franchise'. Not only were the women's sections temporary, but they, and the regional and national structure above them, were given little direct say in determining party policy. For instance, women were allowed four seats on the party's powerful National Executive Committee, but these were to be elected neither by the women's conference nor by a women-only ballot, but by the Party Conference as a whole. Here of course the male union delegates could largely determine who those four women should be; for, despite its new constitution, the party remained as dominated by right-wing male trade unionists as it had been before the war.[7]

While Selina Cooper would not share Henderson's fear of 'feminist agitation', she was still keen to play her full part in the newly-formed Labour Party. She was elected to the Executive of the Nelson and Colne Constituency Labour Party at the inaugural conference early in 1918. Here, of course, she found herself the only woman out of twenty-two members. That was reason enough for Selina to join the new Nelson and Colne Women's Section – along with her old friend Florence Shuttleworth.[8]

And there her role in the Labour Party might have rested had not the act allowing women to stand for Parliament become law just three weeks before the December 1918 General Election. The National Union, surprised and delighted to see this bill sail through both Houses so effortlessly, sprang into action even before the law reached the statute books. Ray Strachey wrote Selina a letter, firmly marked 'private and confidential', on 28 October:

> Dear Mrs Cooper,
> I am proposing to the Executive Committee, and shall propose to the Council, that the National Union adopts the policy of running six women candidates at the next Election, two of each political Party . . .
> Would you yourself be willing to stand as one of our Labour candidates? If so, do you think that Nelson or Wigan would be

good constituencies, or do you know of any other places which would be better? We should hope, of course, first to get the official sanction of the Labour Party and second the approval of the Local Organisation. . . . I have not yet worked out in detail how the thing would be worked . . . Still, I feel sure that the thing could be worked out with sufficient care and I should much like your views both as to your own standing and as to suitable constituencies in Lancashire.

You will understand that neither the Committee nor, of course, the Council, have yet adopted the proposal, but, as far as I can judge, the Committee will endorse it; and Mrs Fawcett thinks that you would be a most excellent representative of the National Union.

                    Yours sincerely,
                    Ray Strachey

Selina must have written back to say she would be delighted to consider such a plan. Politics had become her life; she had long ago developed the knack of separating her own personal feelings from whatever political wrangle she was in, a knack that would stand her in good stead during the hurly-burly of an election. And she firmly believed that working women like herself should take their place at Westminster. The problem was time. Each precious day before the election was slipping away. Nelson ILP, for instance, had months ago decided to nominate a Manchester councillor for the constituency's Labour candidate. Few other organisations in the constituency would be prepared to nominate a known opponent of the war. Indeed, by the third week in November the Nelson and Colne Labour Party had selected Captain Albert Smith, ex-overlooker and sunburnt hero of Nelson's Military Tribunals, to be its candidate. With her own home constituency now out of the running, Selina began anxiously to look elsewhere in Lancashire. But in so many of the industrial seats, candidates nominated by the miners' or textile workers' unions were already firmly in place. Ray Strachey, herself standing as an Independent candidate, was only too aware of the sort of problems that Selina, searching for a seat at such short notice, was encountering:

Dear Mrs Cooper,
If we had more time and more workers and more money I should think Heywood and Radcliffe [between Manchester and Bury] a

very good fighting seat; but I rather feel that it would be too much for us at this late hour and that we should not get enough support to do the cause much good. If only I could come up and see you I should feel much happier, but I am hardly out of bed yet and my constituency is clamouring . . .

> Yours sincerely,
> Ray Strachey

Too little is known of the manoeuvrings that took place between women's organisations and the political parties during October and November 1918. All that has come to light of Selina's approaches to various labour groups, other than the two letters quoted, is a sad little note that she jotted down in her notebook years later:

> The NUWSuffage [Societies] sent my name a[s] a parliamtry Candidate for Berry [probably Bury], at that time the above Union was supporting the Labour Party I was not excepted

Selina seems not even to have mentioned this unhappy episode to her own daughter. Mary, fast becoming her mother's closest friend, had no memory of Selina's being considered as a parliamentary candidate. All she knew was that her mother often encountered anti-woman prejudice in the Labour Party, and that after the war her mother essentially ceased to be a national political figure. 'After the suffrage movement,' Mary explained stoically, 'she sort of shrank back into this area.'[9]

The Labour Party's preference for selecting men from the powerful trade unions (the miners alone put up over fifty candidates) meant that working-class women hoping to be chosen for one of the northern industrial seats had little chance of success. Indeed none of the radical suffragists, doubly disadvantaged by their known opposition to the war, became a parliamentary candidate. Certainly the 1918 General Election seemed to hit socialist women particularly hard. Of the seventeen women who eventually stood, only four were Labour candidates. And of these four none sprang from the National Union of Women's Suffrage Societies: Emmeline Pethick-Lawrence, for instance, had been in the WSPU, Charlotte Despard in the Women's Freedom League, and Mary MacArthur in the Women's Trade Union League.

Equally significantly, none of these four Labour women was standing in a northern textile or mining constituency.[10]

When the ballot boxes were emptied and the various returning officers announced their results, it became clear that only one of the seventeen women was elected. (Ironically she never took her seat in Parliament: Constance Markievicz, whom Selina had met when the flamboyant Countess drove her coach-and-four through Manchester's by-election crowds, was now a Dublin MP but as a Sinn Feiner refused to take her seat.) Christabel Pankhurst, standing as a Women's Party 'Coalition' candidate was narrowly beaten. Ray Strachey was unsuccessful. None of the four Labour women, not even Mary MacArthur on whom so many hopes were pinned, won a seat.

Despite their imaginative approach of uniting the labour and suffrage movements before the war, Labour women continued to do badly at the polls. The following year the first woman MP took her place in the Commons; but she was Lady Astor, who merely took over her husband's seat after he inherited his father's title and went to the Lords. Selina Cooper probably echoed Annot Robinson's ambivalent feelings about this. Before the by-election, Annot wrote to her sister, hoping that Lady Astor would be unsuccessful and adding, 'Do you think I should consider standing at the next General Election, if I am invited I mean. I am quite prepared to fight in public life even with the hardship of a drunken and degraded husband . . .'[11] But such hopes of socialist women were not to be fulfilled. At the 1922 Election, thirty-three women stood, ten of them Labour. Yet still no new woman MP was returned. Until 1923 there remained only two women in Parliament, Lady Astor a Conservative, and a Liberal who had also inherited her husband's seat.

If radical suffragists could not get selected to stand for Parliament, perhaps they could succeed at local elections. This is what Selina Cooper decided to do. The moment it became clear that becoming a parliamentary candidate was nigh impossible, she began to test out the idea. 'With regard to the question of your being a Town Councillor,' Ray Strachey wrote in reply to Selina's query, 'Would it preclude your doing other things as well? Because if not, it is always a good thing to have an official position behind you.' The following year, 1919, Selina was duly nominated by Nelson ILP for her own Whitefield ward – along with other ILP members for other wards: Alec Campbell a tailor, and an up-and-coming politician called Andrew Smith. But somehow, as the election drew near, Selina's name slipped from the list of candidates. She must have failed to be selected, lacking sufficient support for her nomination. Certainly her feminist and anti-war views would have told against her in the Whitefield ward, where the Labour vote was dominated by right-wing Catholics. Indeed, of the two or three Nelson women nominated that year, only one was successfully selected and stood in the November elections: Margaret Aldersley, radical suffragist and pacifist. Nevertheless even she was not a strong enough candidate to beat her Liberal opponent to the Council Chamber.[12]

Shortly afterwards, Margaret Aldersley, her four children grown up, decided to follow Harriette Beanland's example, and to emigrate to Australia, at least for a few years. Certainly Britain no longer seemed a friendly place for radical suffragists to remain. They seemed to be forever bumping up against hard brick walls. For instance, Selina Cooper put a proposal to the secretary of the Burnley Trades and Labour Council, only to receive this chilling reply:

Dear Madam,
I am in receipt of yours of the 22nd inst, and in reply thereto beg to state that the Burnley Trades and Labour Council have not discussed the question of the appointment of a Woman Organiser for Labour Propaganda in Burnley . . .
   I am indeed sorry if you have been inconvenienced by the statements you have heard, and if we are ever in a Financial position to consider the appointment of a Woman Organiser your enquiry shall be treated in the nature of an application for the post.
                    I Remain, Madam,
                         Yours faithfully,
                    J.W. Gradwell Sec-Agent

Faced with such rebuffs from supposed comrades, Selina's thoughts understandably turned to emigration too. Her correspondence with Harriette out in New Zealand during the immediate post-war years reveals that the Coopers were seriously considering emigrating as well. Harriette's letters were full of tips on how Robert might get farming work and Mary a job as a shop assistant; and of sympathy for Selina's feeling that she might give up political work. But in the end, Harriette painted too grim a picture of New Zealand's high prices, housing shortage and low wages to persuade the Coopers to go.

The hopes of the radical suffragists in the textile towns were very slow to bear fruit: it would be another fifteen years before Nelson, a town boasting one of the most active and long-lived suffrage societies, elected its first woman councillor. A little further south, the aspirations of Manchester suffragists were also being dashed for similar reasons. 'When in 1921 the ILP nominated me as municipal candidate for my ward,' revealed Hannah Mitchell, 'I was promptly turned down. I was too well known as a keen feminist, and, as they put it, "not amenable to discipline".' Elsewhere in the city, Annot Robinson was selected as the local Labour candidate but was beaten heavily by the Tory. She confided in her sister that this was partly because of the 'anti-woman cry', but partly because 'a very dead set was made against me – a Bolshevik, a German spy, a traitor . . .' In the early twenties the radical suffragists were too vulnerable to anti-woman, pro-war jibes to have much success – even with a local electorate which knew them well.[13]

Not only had socialist women had a hard time at the 1918 Election, but Labour generally had not done as well as hoped. It won only fifty-nine seats, of which nearly half were Miners' Federation MPs. Overall it was a decisive victory for Lloyd George and his conservative 'Coalition'. His electioneering taunt that 'the Labour Party is being run by the extreme pacifist, Bolshevist group' had not been ineffective, and the election heralded two decades of largely conservative rule. The small Parliamentary Labour Party was left virtually powerless to challenge the established order of things. Yet maybe, Selina Cooper mused, the lack of electoral influence on the part of socialist women and the Labour Party did not matter so much after all. The filling in of ballot papers and the totting up of votes was no longer all that socialists like her aspired to.

Selina could now look eastwards to Russia's model of socialism. If Westminster did not work in the interests of the working people who produced the wealth of the country then, some socialists argued, they must consider alternatives. These were years when it was conceivable that other European countries – and not just Russia – might be on the verge of revolution; and certain socialists, inspired by Lenin's ideas and achievements, began to draw up plans whereby the working class could seize power through direct action. Such feelings were particularly strong in industrial centres like Clydeside and in ILP towns like Nelson, where Conscientious Objectors still continued to be hounded and given punitive hard labour sentences, even though the war had ended.

In spring 1919 the Third (or Communist) International was formed in Moscow, based on Leninist principles of a Bolshevik Revolution (and in opposition to the earlier reformist Second International which, some socialists alleged, was now discredited because it had duped workers into fighting a war which was not in their interests). The Third International urged British socialists to join forces with it and during 1919, against a background of industrial discontent, heated arguments took place in Nelson and elsewhere, for and against affiliation to Lenin's Third International.[14]

At the same time, a newly-formed Nelson Workers' Committee invited John MacLean, an influential Clydeside socialist regarded by Russia as the 'Soviet Consul for Scotland', to speak on 'The Coming Revolution'. The seeds of rebellion had been sown. The Nelson Weavers, by far the largest labour grouping in the town, agreed after initial hesitation to support the Nelson Workers' Committee because, the union conceded, it was 'acting in the best interests of all workers by seeking to organise them on a class basis, through workshop committees, irrespective of the craft union they belong to ., . .' Moreover, the ILP let the Nelson Workers' Committee use its premises for its summer programme of education and propaganda.[15]

Meanwhile Selina Cooper and others grew increasingly anxious about the British government's attempts to crush the Bolshevik Revolution by invading Russian territory and co-operating with anti-Bolshevik forces. Feeling about the Soviet government's right to exist without outside interference ran high. In April 1919 both the Nelson Labour Party and the Nelson Weavers passed resolutions demanding the British government withdraw its troops from Russia. By June a meeting of the local

Labour Party organised in Salem school hall pledged to take industrial action if the government did not comply with its demands about Russia and the release of all Conscientious Objectors. For socialists like Selina, the plight of post-revolutionary Russia took on a symbolic importance. If necessary, she was prepared to use direct action to protect it from being crushed by foreign anti-Bolshevik armies.[16]

Selina Cooper watched the tumultuous events of 1919 flow past. It was all so bewildering. None of the old rules that she had grown up with seemed to apply any more. Yet no one seemed sure what the new rules were. Even with her sure political instincts she felt confused. Groups sprang up whose very names challenged the political institutions women had fought so long to enter. Motions threatening 'direct action' that would by-pass Parliament were agreed. Women, having just been handed the rule book, immediately had it wrenched from their grasp and had good reason to feel more confused than most. It seemed as if Selina's seventeen years of suffrage work were being derided as useless: even if she had been selected for Westminster or the Town Council, would it have meant anything now? She also noticed that the revolutionary talk seemed to make scant reference to women: class conflict and class actions were all stressed, but sex divisions and women's action were of little interest. Struggling to keep up with all the new developments, she must have found the worlds of Ray Strachey and of John MacLean hard to reconcile. The dovetailing of the feminism and socialism of the immediate pre-war years now seemed almost impossible. In the face of all these contradictory pressures, Selina Cooper kept a low political profile during 1919.

During 1920 she could discern a recognisable pattern begin to emerge as groups like the ILP aligned themselves more clearly for or against the Third International. In certain parts of the country, including Lancashire and Scotland, ILP members were keen to disaffiliate from the 'reformist' Second International and affiliate to the Third. In Nelson such feeling was particularly widespread, with Selina Cooper among the local ILP members whose emotional attachment to Russia was strong. Yet many of the ILP national leaders like Philip Snowden whom she had long admired felt increasingly hostile to Bolshevism, and to the notion that violent tactics which worked in Russia would necessarily work in

Britain. Indeed, when the ILP held its annual conference at Easter 1920, Ramsay MacDonald managed to persuade the delegates against immediate affiliation to the Third International. Similarly the Labour Party itself at its own Annual Conference a few months later also voted against joining by a massive majority. So, when the British Communist Party was formed a few weeks later, in July 1920, it lacked the support of any of the big battalions of labour. In organisational terms the new Leninist party could rely only on the minute socialist groups to the left of the ILP.

In individual towns, of course, the situation was far more fluid. Some socialists wanted to belong to the Labour Party *and* the Communist Party – and, as yet, there was nothing to prevent dual membership. (Indeed, when Ellen Wilkinson was elected as Labour councillor for one of the Manchester wards, she was still a member of the Communist Party.) Particularly among local ILP members there remained considerable ferment. A 'Left Wing Committee' was formed urging, despite the last Conference decision, immediate affiliation to the Third International. Among the Manchester members of this 'Committee' were two of Selina Cooper's old suffrage comrades, Ellen Wilkinson and Annot Robinson. In the Clydeside ILP too there were links between the old women's suffrage campaign and the new 'Left Wing Committee'. Certainly this seems to have been where Selina felt comfortably at home: keen to remain within the ILP which had such a good record on feminist issues, but also determined to defend the gains made in Russia.[17]

During 1920 Selina Cooper became increasingly caught up in the tragic plight of post-revolutionary Russia. Conflict between Russia and her neighbours continued and in the summer Russia's Bolshevik army moved into Poland. The British government ordered it to halt this advance and in August stated that military intervention might be necessary to 'save' Poland from Bolshevism. Immediately the whole British labour movement rose up in arms, so firm was its belief that the crucial principle of 'Hands Off Russia' was at stake. The socialist *Daily Herald*, appearing on a Sunday for the first time ever, bore the banner 'Not a Man, Not a Gun, Not a Sou!' The following day a special joint meeting of the TUC and Labour Party warned the government that 'the whole industrial power of the organised workers will be used to defeat this war', and that a Council of Action would be set up to organise this. Shortly after, a national Labour Conference met (attended by two Nelson Weavers representatives) and decided to empower the Council of Action to call a general strike to stop the war on Russia.

The challenge united the labour movement throughout the country as never before. Here was an issue that all socialists and trade unionists, whatever their views on importing Bolshevik tactics into Britain, could agree upon. Before long 350 local Councils of Action were springing up around the country. 'Never have we known,' reported a Home Office spy in Lancashire, 'such excitement and antagonism to be around against any project as has been around amongst the workers by the possibility of war with Russia.' Certainly, the 18,000-strong Nelson Weavers agreed to 'solemnly pledge ourselves to immediately carry into effect a Down Tools policy on receiving instruction to this effect'. It also asked the local Labour Party to call trade union committees together to consider setting up a local Council of Action, and this the party did. Selina Cooper's position on the Party Executive, coupled with her deep anxiety about Russia's future, thrust her to the forefront of these hasty planning sessions with local unionists. So when it was agreed that six delegates should be elected to represent the Labour Party wing on the Nelson Council of Action, it was natural that Selina should find herself among the half-dozen selected. She was prepared to go to any lengths to stop the Secretary of State for War, the virulent anti-Bolshevik Winston Churchill, from dragging Britain into war against socialist Russia.

In the event, neither she nor the other Council of Action delegates were called upon to co-ordinate any direct action. Sufficient pressure had apparently been exerted to persuade the government to stop threatening Russia. Certainly military intervention in Eastern Europe would have been impossible with such adamant opposition from the whole trade union movement. Some historians have since argued that the labour movement was pushing at an open door and the government's threats were never intended to be carried out. Possibly so; but this was by no means clear at the time, and for socialists like Selina Cooper the heady days of August 1920 acquired a symbolic importance. Labour, for the first time in its history, had threatened a political general strike to prevent a declaration of war, and this threat had apparently succeeded. Selina would never forget the lessons she learnt from the Councils of Action; nor would her hatred of Winston Churchill ever soften.[18]

On the defence of Russia, she stood shoulder to shoulder with the broad labour movement. During the troubled winter months of 1920–1, however, other political issues were less easily resolved. The post-war cotton boom had collapsed. Lancashire could no longer compete with the cheap goods produced by India, Japan and China where low labour costs kept prices right down. Unemployment began to soar, especially in towns specialising in exporting cloth. Nelson, producing for home consumption, was protected from the worst of these icy foreign gusts. Even so, as national unemployment crept up to two million in 1921, about five thousand women and men in Nelson were without jobs. There seemed no easy way to protect the livelihoods of families who depended on cotton.

At the same time, the discussion with the ILP for and against immediate affiliation to the Third International continued. The 'Left Wing Committee' remained committed to this, but many ILP members were beginning to realise that if the ILP did affiliate, it would forfeit its highly valued separate identity and just be merged into the new Communist Party. As these unwelcome implications grew clearer, regions like Lancashire and Scotland that had previously supported affiliation began to turn against it. It looked as if affiliation would again be defeated at the ILP's coming annual conference at Easter 1921.

The Nelson ILP chose as its two conference delegates Dan Carradice and Selina Cooper, perhaps thinking that the two of them represented a balance of views. Dan Carradice was a Conscientious Objector who had referred to Europe as 'a bloodstained carpet'. He was hardly likely to want to merge the ILP into a party based on violent revolution. Selina on the other hand was plagued by more doubts. She was a long-standing believer in the need to collectivise the means of production and a strong defender of Soviet Russia. Yet she too had been an ILP member for over a quarter of a century, and knew that on issues like women's suffrage and military conscription it was the only party to take the right line. She was loath to see all that the ILP represented sub-merged within the Communist Party. Affiliating to the Third International seemed to involve heavy sacrifice in return for rather hazy benefits. With such thoughts buzzing round her head, she set off to Southport with Dan Carradice for the conference.

It turned out to be a dramatic occasion. The crucial resolution demanded that 'this Conference . . . rejects the idea that this country must follow Russian methods . . . and, therefore, calls upon all workers and Socialists . . . to strengthen the Independent Labour Party, to capture the machinery of Government . . . and thus . . . transform the broken and bankrupt society of Capi-talism into Socialism'. The proposal was clear: the ILP's own brand of revolutionary socialism using non-violent means, rather than the Bolsheviks' civil war and bloodshed. Then a delegate immediately proposed an amendment *for* affiliation. The debate spilled over into the afternoon. Selina listened as her old hero Ramsay MacDonald lent his considerable weight against affiliation. He did not blame Lenin for some of the things he had had to do in Russia, MacDonald told the delegates. 'But let us think of the criminality of the men who come to ask us to create such a condition of things in our own country. It is a thing we have to fight tooth and nail and never tolerate until it is forced upon us by another class' – and he issued a strong appeal to support the resolution. The delegates responded. The amendment fell and the resolution against affiliation was carried overwhelmingly.

The Left Wing Committee had been crushed. Selina Cooper and Dan Carradice, travelling back from Southport to Nelson, must have felt a great sense of relief that the divisive issue had at last been settled. The ILP would never become part of the Com-munist International. A few hundred ILP members here and there, bitter about the Southport decision, decided to secede and join the Communist Party. But Nelson ILP seems to have been scarcely affected by such secessions. A local Labour Party member made a soothing statement to the *Nelson Leader* that although 'there were certainly many members with Communist leanings' he did not think they would want to isolate themselves from the local party. Local reformist socialist groups, he added blandly, were strong enough 'to combat adherents to the Moscow creed'.[19]

Selina Cooper could never see political activity in such cut-and-dried categories. However much she admired ILP leaders like MacDonald and Snowden, and however closely enmeshed she became in the local Labour Party, she still refused to sever all links with Communists. It was about this time that a small branch of the Communist Party started up in Nelson, and Selina must have been among those whom the founders hoped to recruit. Although it is unlikely she did join, she always made a point of keeping in close touch with her Communist comrades and of reading their newspaper. Indeed one of the Coopers' regular political activities in the early twenties (when links between individual Communist and Labour Party members remained fluid) was distributing the *Communist* locally. Mary's memory of this was a little hazy, but she recalls how copies of the paper were

> sent from headquarters. There must have been somebody fetched it round . . . Must have come to the station, and somebody must have lugged it down here. And they used to be on a chair, there, you see . . .
>
> [There] must have been about thirty [copies]. They weren't unpopular. You see at that time, Russia was popular then. [The Government] had had a bit of a dab at it [in 1920] . . .
>
> They were delivered here, and all the people came for them. And I can remember it: a pile used to stand up about so high. I can remember it must have been about twenty or thirty papers. And nobody'd believe you about that! No record of it . . . [20]

Selina's movements have been traced as she sped from the ill-fated Women's Citizens' Association and the Bury constituency selection procedures, to the Council of Action and the ILP furore over the Third International. By the early 1920s she had become clear in her own mind that her political loyalties lay with the ILP and, increasingly, with the growing Labour Party. The other tension – how to relate her socialism to her feminism – was less easy to resolve. There seemed to be no clear-cut guidelines. Women such as Selina, living in small communities like Nelson, had to struggle to link together two apparently divergent sets of ideas: for after the war, the National Union of Women's Suffrage Societies and its lobbying for piecemeal legislation seemed a world away from Councils of Action and talk of a general strike. Some women, we know, gave up trying to reconcile the two. Sylvia Pankhurst, for instance, dropped much of her concern about the specific oppression of women, believing that such problems would be solved by the revolutionary movement. On the other hand, members of the Women's International League for Peace and Freedom came to doubt the Russian Revolution they had originally welcomed in 1917, but which now seemed to promise violence and civil war.[21]

At the level of theory, the tension between feminism and socialism in the early 1920s was considerable. In practice, the struggle was to survive at all. At the grass-roots, the mood was against women-only groups unattached to a political party or the co-operative movement. The brief and unhappy life of the local Women's Citizens' Association testified to that. Against this background, the survival of the local Women's Suffrage Society after the war (and the account book records that it remained active up till autumn 1920) seems a remarkable achievement. The society was keenly aware that the vote for women under thirty still had to be fought for. To its end, it retained about sixteen paid-up members – including Emily Murgatroyd the pilgrim, Florence Shuttleworth the weaver, Selina and – a more recent recruit – Mary Cooper.

After the war the Women's Suffrage Society heard with sadness that Mrs Fawcett had finally decided to retire from the National Union, and Emily Murgatroyd and Selina wrote to her in fond appreciation of all she had done over the years.[22] In her stead as President came Eleanor Rathbone, whom Selina had long ago worked with in Liverpool; and the National Union changed its name to the National Union of Societies for Equal Citizenship. Both Mrs Fawcett and Eleanor Rathbone had grown up in the atmosphere of upper-middle-class Victorian Liberalism, and both had patriotically supported the war.[23] Yet there the similarity ended. On issues that were shortly to become crucial – such as the relationship between the state and the family – they opposed each other. Eleanor Rathbone supported the idea of family allowances to give hard-pressed mothers financial independence and ensure a family at least the basic necessities. Mrs Fawcett strongly disagreed. She believed such schemes would not be 'the charter of women's economic freedom, but rather . . . the ruin of family life'. She fought the proposals with all her might and main, but without success. Realising a new order now prevailed, Mrs Fawcett resigned her National Union membership altogether. Her resignation symbolized the end of the old suffrage era.

Eleanor Rathbone had early on developed her ideas about family allowances when she studied the women omitted from the benefits of Lloyd George's National Insurance scheme, and in 1913 published her report *The Condition of Widows under the Poor Law in Liverpool*. She began to evolve the theory of motherhood as a service to the community, and of a system of family allowance (called the endowment of motherhood) rather than having mothers and their children merely subsisting on the amount of money that the male breadwinner could – or chose to – pass on. Then in 1917 Eleanor Rathbone helped form a Family Endowment Committee, consisting of suffragists linked to the National Union plus socialists from the ILP. They were keen not only to eradicate child poverty, but also to raise women's low wages. One of the first pamphlets the group published was therefore *Equal Pay and the Family: A proposal for the National Endowment of Motherhood*.

Not all feminists agreed with such ideas. Ada Nield Chew, who disliked the notion of 'paying poor women to be wives', was one of those who objected, and she and Annot Robinson argued it out in the pages of *Common Cause*.[24] Certainly there was a side to Eleanor Rathbone's logic which was more concerned with the 'future of the race' than benefiting *all* mothers. She argued that the endowment of motherhood would put an end to the present system whereby 'the slum dwellers and mentally unfit continue to breed like rabbits, so that the national stock is recruited in increasing proportions from its least fit elements'. Selina Cooper however was among those quick to acknowledge that financial independence for mothers and children was essential, especially in large families where low wages were pitifully inadequate to feed all the mouths. She had seen too often working-class families where a mother would scrimp and starve herself so that the male 'breadwinner' would be fit enough to go out to work. Certainly she must have recognised that the years she spent bringing up Mary would have been easier with a system of family endowment.

Selina had remained in contact with Eleanor Rathbone since the suffrage campaign: she and Mary used to go and stay in the

Rathbone family's holiday house in the Lake District. These links were strengthened by the long years Selina worked for the National Union as a salaried organiser. So it is hardly surprising that, within a month of the formation of the Family Endowment Committee, Selina began to go round giving talks to local Women's Co-operative Guilds on 'State endowment of Motherhood'. Bradford, she chided the Guildswomen, was far ahead of Nelson in offering free meals to children; but it was just as important for mothers to be as well looked after as children; and mothers should begin thinking for themselves and voicing their own demands.

During the short life of the Nelson Women's Citizens' Association in 1918, it too took up the issue. 'The value of "State Maintenance of Motherhood" was also discussed,' the minute book records, 'and ardent supporters were found amongst those present.' Indeed at the public meeting of the Association at which it was wound up and which was chaired by Selina, 'an interesting discussion took place on the "State Maintenance of Motherhood", pointing out the great benefits which would result.'[25]

After 1919 Eleanor Rathbone's National Union of Societies for Equal Citizenship (NUSEC) worked energetically for both family allowances and equal pay for women. It is unclear what Selina Cooper's formal relationship with NUSEC was at this point; but it seems that she still worked as part-time organiser for a salary of about 30s a week.[26] In October that year Eleanor Rathbone came up to Nelson to help launch the Nelson branch of NUSEC, and clearly Selina Cooper was the local co-ordinator for this. Emily Murgatroyd chaired the meeting; and Eleanor Rathbone, billed as a Liverpool City Councillor and organiser of the scheme for civil widows' pensions, explained the objects of NUSEC to her audience. It wanted women under thirty to be able to vote and the civil service to be completely opened to women. She also outlined the campaign to give civil widows pensions on the same lines as soldiers' widows, and stressed the need for state aid as a right rather than as charity for fatherless children.

But for all Eleanor Rathbone's clear outline of the way forward, and for all Selina Cooper's behind-the-scenes organising, the Nelson branch of NUSEC went the way of the earlier Women's Citizens' Association – only rather more quickly. After only one meeting it collapsed and was never heard of again. Selina must have been bitterly disappointed by this second failure. Yet this was to be the pattern for many such branches in the twenties.[27]

Selina herself was more resilient. Throughout 1920 she continued her propaganda work for NUSEC, addressing local groups on both 'Widows' Pensions' and 'Mothers' Pensions'. She gave talks to the Nelson and Brierfield Women's Co-operative Guilds, as well as further afield, probably as part of NUSEC's scheme for local study circles on 'National Family Endowment' and equal pay. Certainly Mary, at home and busy with her job at the Town Hall, remembers clearly how hard her mother worked during these years:

> My mother continued after they got the vote, and did all sorts . . . My mother went all round the country districts . . . Well, my mother stayed a lot with Eleanor Rathbone . . . and she wanted this allowance for children . . . And my mother, she got, oh, heaps and heaps of petitions. She went speaking – all for nothing. Just her expenses, railway expenses – all over Lancashire and Yorkshire, speaking for this – Miss Rathbone's idea . . . My mother worked herself to death about this.

In making the remark about her mother's expenses, Mary was not merely protecting her mother's good name against allegations from local busy-bodies that Selina 'made money out of the movement'. She was reflecting the truth: the account book Selina kept from 1908 for her National Union work records that no more payments went into the account after late 1919. From that date Selina's work – on family endowment, equal pay or married women's right to work – does indeed seem to have been unpaid.

It was the end of a long era of Selina's suffrage work. By the end of 1920 even the long-lived local suffrage society dwindled to a halt: the final entry 'Sep 25 1921 To Balance of £1.5.2½ d' was entered into the society's account book. By autumn 1920 Selina Cooper's activity for NUSEC had also shrunk right down: during 1921 and 1922 she seems not to have addressed a single meeting. Finally, on 30 June 1923, she withdrew 15s 8d from the account, ruled a firm and final line across the debit and credit columns, and formally pulled down the curtain on one of the longest and most important eras of her life.[28]

Selina Cooper, the National Union's longest-serving organiser, had given up. With her track record, stretching from autumn 1906 right up to 1920, she could hardly be accused of dilettantism. She had, after all, already weathered the wartime storms, as well as the later change of name. But working as a paid organiser for a women's rights' organisation, basing herself in the industrial north of England, she was becoming an expensive anachronism: most of NUSEC's work was now done within lobbying distance of the House of Commons. With the beginning of the slump, staffing bills had to be pared down. (This was the tragedy that befell Annot Robinson when the Manchester branch of the Women's International League for Peace and Freedom decided in 1920 it could no longer employ her due to financial constraints. Annot somehow managed to struggle through the next few years with foreign lecture tours, temporary organising jobs and, eventually, by returning to Scotland as a teacher.[29])

There were of course reasons other than just finance for Selina Cooper's leaving NUSEC. She had reason to feel disenchanted with the organisation, despite her long-standing friendship with Eleanor Rathbone. One or two of the women who ran it seemed obsessed with detail and liable to lose the wood for the trees. For instance, NUSEC's Equal Moral Standard Special Committee urged the Ministry of Health not to put up notices in men's lavatories in Manchester about the prevention of Venereal Disease, since it was a direct incitement to prostitution and therefore to increased exploitation of women. Similarly, its dilatory Committee on the Employment of Married Women decided that 'as there is so much unemployment' and because women's organisations had so far adopted no definite policy on women's right to work, it would plan no public meetings on the subject.[30] Yet, with unemployment about two million, this was a time when groups like the ILP and the newly-formed National Unemployed Workers' Movement were campaigning actively. From Selina's perspective up in Nelson, some of NUSEC's lobbying down in London must have seemed time-wasting.

In addition, the old arguments within the National Union between old 'equalitarian' feminists and the new 'family allowance' feminists continued. Over the issue of protective legislation it proved divisive during the mid-1920s. Some argued that, for instance, women should be allowed to work night shifts since they should have equal rights with men; others said that women workers had special needs and should be protected by law from situations damaging to their health. Not only were there rifts within NUSEC, but there were also now a range of separate women's groups, each with a slightly different emphasis. Often the groups worked amicably together, but the fragmentation of women's efforts was depressing. For instance, both the old Women's Freedom League and the recently formed Open Door Council opposed family allowances. They saw it 'as no concern of the women's movement,' lamented Eleanor Rathbone, 'and above all as having no bearing on the demand for equal pay, except perhaps as a troublesome red herring drawn across the trail.' At the same time, the ILP, Labour women and even Liberal women were beginning to take up the idea of family allowances. In the light of such tensions, it became difficult to talk any more of a unified 'women's movement'.[31]

Selina Cooper had tried to support local independent women-only groups after the war, but they had failed. She had supported the Russian Revolution, but in the end come down firmly on the side of the ILP and the Labour Party. These first three post-war years were bewildering ones for Selina, but by about 1921 she began to recognise a clearer pattern. She saw that, outside London, the key issues like family endowment would be fought, not in separate women's groups, but within the political parties, the ILP, the Women's Co-operative Guild and – most importantly – the Labour Party. As Selina, in Mary's own phrasing, 'shrank back into this area', she quickly discovered that it was within these grass-roots organisations that she would put her energies in the coming years. This discovery served her well for the next controversy she plunged into: birth control.

CHAPTER EIGHTEEN

THE UNITED IRISH LEAGUE
AND THE BIRTH-CONTROL BATTLE:
1922-1925

Selina Cooper was becoming something of a local celebrity by the 1920s. An imposing woman, her hair magnificently coiled upon her head, she was in regular demand as a public speaker by the ILP, Women's Co-operative Guilds and Labour Party Women's Sections. This growing legendary quality owed much to her suffrage past and her anti-war campaigns. Then in November 1923 it was further enhanced when she finally stood, the only woman candidate that year, for the Town Council.

Selina stood for Whitefield Ward, in her part of town – but a difficult ward for Labour. At the previous year's Council elections in November 1922, Whitefield had been won by the chairman of the local United Irish League, a self-employed plumber called Patrick Quinn. The United Irish League was able to deliver Nelson's Catholic votes *en bloc* and – by understanding – usually to Labour. But on this occasion the influential Pat Quinn stood not as a Labour candidate but as an 'Independent', against a Conservative councillor. He had asked Selina, who only lived a few streets away from him, if she would be good enough to teach the Catholic women how to canvass for him on the doorstep. This Selina willingly did: it would after all help keep out the Tory. With the benefit of this open-handed help, Catholic 'Independent' Quinn had won Whitefield ward in November 1922.[1]

At the next Council elections in November 1923, the Labour Party put up Selina for Whitefield ward. She modestly put herself down on the election form as 'housewife', and she was described in the local paper just as 'a well-known Labour worker'. It would hardly have won her extra votes had she trailed clouds of suffrage glory in the election campaign.

Her opponent was a Conservative councillor. The *Colne and Nelson Times*, aware how marginal the ward was and fearful lest Labour might regain its majority on the Council, was in no doubt as to how right-minded Whitefield people should vote. In its 'Hints to Local Electors' it merely gave a token nod in Selina Cooper's direction and then commented placidly that 'as the electors of Nelson fight shy of sending women to the local Council Chamber and Councillor Lonsdale [the Conservative councillor] has served the ratepayers well, there is every prospect of [him] being sent back for another period of useful service'.

Selina might have predicted this newspaper's opposition to socialist women candidates. It was, after all, the position it had taken against her when she had first stood as a Poor Law Guardian, and it had obviously not seen fit to change its mind over twenty-two years. Less predictable and more bitter to swallow was the lack of co-operation from Pat Quinn, in whose hands lay the votes of Whitefield's Catholic electors. Selina Cooper, Mary remembered, asked him to sign her nomination form. He refused – on the grounds that he was now an 'Independent'. Worse still, he seemed unwilling to lend her election campaign his crucial support.

It was therefore hardly surprising that the Conservative candidate managed to hold on to his seat, winning by a majority of 120. Selina polled only 614 votes to his 734. According to Mary her mother even lost some of the Protestant votes on the grounds that she had helped Pat Quinn the year before, without gaining any Catholic votes. Never someone to bear a grudge over a near miss, Selina commented philosophically to a reporter afterwards, 'It was a very pleasant election; everybody – even my opponents – treated me with utmost courtesy.'[2]

Undeterred Selina decided to try again next year. The following spring in April 1924, she was nominated by the ILP for Whitefield ward. By the autumn she had again been selected by the local Labour Party as its Whitefield candidate. Perhaps this time she would be successful and Nelson would elect its first ever woman councillor? Such a prospect made Selina Cooper of particular interest to the local press; and about six weeks before the November elections were due she was visited by the *Nelson Leader*'s senior feature writer.

Joe Bates was a journalist currently writing an epic series of interviews with local people, published under the general title 'Men With A Mission'. In this series he portrayed those older inhabitants who had helped shape Nelson's strong labour traditions; among those interviewed for instance was a noted local pacifist who had been courtmartialled three times during the war. Under a suitably adapted title, he interviewed Deborah Smith, the half-timer who had become a founder-member of the Nelson Women's Co-operative Guild, and Sarah Thomas the Liberal who had supported Selina's fledgling suffrage committee. In September 1924, it was Selina Cooper's turn to be visited by the prolific Joe Bates.

Selina easily occupied Joe Bates' full-size pages in the *Leader* two weeks running. He had little difficulty persuading Selina to recount the story of her life. She told him about her navvy father who worked for Brunel. She even mentioned her childhood days as a half-time creeler in Barnoldswick and as a winder at Tunstills – memories she usually preferred to leave behind. Her suffrage days were recounted in detail. Few things were omitted (though the interview does not refer to her marriage, her husband or – even more surprisingly – her daughter). Joe Bates scribbled all this down in his notebook, and must have been hard pushed to keep pace with Selina's tales. 'Every minute,' he confessed in his article, 'she springs something new and startling upon me.' Perhaps to get a breathing space, Joe Bates gratefully took refuge in the Coopers' book case and surveyed its contents. 'When I enter a house the first thing my eyes look for is the bookcase,' he wrote chattily,

> . . . the kind of books in the case indicates the mental quality of those who live in the house . . . Here were books to my liking on many a shelf; books teeming with precious thoughts . . .
>
> We then exchanged ideas and thoughts on books and their writers . . . Mrs Cooper values very highly a copy of Tom Moore's poems given her by an old shoemaker. She likes Burns, has read Emerson and all Shakespeare . . .

Amidst all this literary chat, there was one category of book on the Coopers' shelves that was omitted from the survey. This was a set of books that either Selina had discreetly hidden, or that Joe Bates' gaze had hastily passed over.[3] These were her books on eugenics and human physiology. For when Joe Bates visited 59 St Mary's Street, the Coopers' shelves already contained about two dozen such books and pamphlets on eugenics, human physiology and sex education. The reason for this self-censorship seems clear: even in 1924 sex education remained a forbidden subject. A few of the taboos had been lifted since the war, especially in big cities, but in a small northern town like Nelson, with a strong Catholic population, the silence still hung heavy.

Selina Cooper remained as keenly interested in sex education as she had been in the 1890s, when she had first come across a dog-eared copy of Annie Besant's *The Law of Population*. From about the time of her marriage she had also begun to collect a series of textbooks on 'elementary physiology'. These meticulously detailed the workings of the muscle system and pulmonary arteries, but still preserved an uncanny silence about how the next generation of people – all perfectly equipped with smoothly-functioning retinas, kidneys and intestines – would be reproduced.

Selina Cooper's frustration at this dangerous censorship grew. How could working women have any control over their daily lives – vote or no vote – if they did not possess even the most rudimentary information about how their repeated pregnancies occurred? Right up to the First World War such elementary knowledge seems to have been virtually unobtainable in Nelson. For certainly, had there been books available, Selina Cooper would have nosed them out and passed them on to Mary. One of the few things she could find was a pamphlet, published in 1915, called *Parents' Guide to the Sex-Instruction of Sons and Daughters (Chiefly prepared for working-class readers)*. Selina had somehow acquired a copy of Part I, 'Conversation of a Mother and Daughter'. Though obviously well-intentioned, the pamphlet was exasperatingly coy. It told of white silk wedding-dresses, the virtue of chastity, and the sorrow of unmarried mothers. Human biology was explained with utmost modesty by the cunning device of two photographs, one of a Greek goddess and the other of the god Apollo. Overall it conveyed moral values rather than biological information. Selina – let alone young Mary – must have found it impossible to relate the *Parents' Guide* to the carefully drawn diagrams of organs in her physiology textbooks.[4]

It seemed as if sex education information was scarcely any more accessible than in the days of Selina's youth. What *had* grown since then was the serious attention given to eugenics. To traditional economic arguments for birth control (that unless the conception of additional children was prevented, the country would become over-populated and there would not be enough food for survival) was added new academic research on heredity, selective breeding and other ways of improving the race. Such eugenics research was pioneered by scientist Francis Galton, a cousin of Charles Darwin; and Selina was among those who early on became interested in Galton's ideas. (It is an area where contemporary feminists have difficulty in understanding why someone like Selina should have taken up such ideas. Nazi Germany has subsequently put such eugenicist notions into nightmare practice. But Selina's generation had no such knowledge. They saw that eugenicists were concerned about motherhood, childcare, and ensuring the quality of a healthy and pure race for the future – just as they themselves were.)

The Coopers' bookshelves contained a copy of *Essays in Eugenics*, an anthology of Galton's lectures published by the Eugenics Education Society in 1909. To us it makes alarming reading. To Edwardians, worried by the threat of 'race degeneration' after the Boer War had shown how few working-class men were fit enough to be soldiers, it sounded plausible. Galton believed human beings formed a natural hierarchy: eager or sluggish, intelligent or stupid. 'We each receive at our birth a definite endowment,' Galton argued; and these qualities 'go towards the making of civic worth in man'. His concern was to strengthen the qualities of 'civic worth' in the British race before it was swamped by 'inadequates'. He and many others were greatly alarmed that 'the less able and less energetic are more fertile than the better stocks' and that the birth-rate of the thrifty and provident was declining. Galton wanted such people – those with a high level of 'civic worth' in the nation – to be actively encouraged to breed:

> An enthusiasm to improve the race would probably express itself
> by granting diplomas to a select class of young men and women
> . . . and by provision for rearing children healthily. The means

that might be employed to compass these ends are dowries, especially for those to whom moderate sums are important, assured
help in emergencies during the early years of married life . . .
[and] the provision to exceptionally promising young couples of
healthy and convenient houses at low rentals.[5]

Selina Cooper must have wondered to which class Galton
would have consigned her. After all, her feckless father would
have been categorised as being of little 'civic worth'. However she
would have warmed to Galton's ideas of 'dowries' and 'healthy
homes'; they were not so very different from Eleanor Rathbone's
scheme for the state to offer an 'endowment of motherhood'.

Some of Galton's ideas were harder to swallow. He opposed
'indiscriminate charity', including out-relief by Boards of Guardians. Nor was he keen on higher education for women, whose
sacred task in life was solely motherhood. Selina Cooper's
bookshelves also contained a copy of a sixpenny paperback, *The
Methods of Race-Regeneration* published in 1911 and written by a
popularising eugenicist. He was another enthusiastic believer in
'the supremacy of motherhood', and argued that a woman who
did not breastfeed her children should be 'ashamed to look a tabby
cat in the face'. On married women's work and on girls' education he was particularly explicit:

In all times and places, women's primal and supreme function is
or should be that of choosing the fathers of the future. This great
idea should be recognised, implicitly and explicitly, in the
education of every girl.[6]

Although the fashion for eugenics was then at its height, Selina
somehow seemed to lose interest after this. Caught up in the last
hectic years of the suffrage campaign, she had little patience for
eugenicists who saw women primarily as breeding machines in
the service of the imperial race, and who lent their authority to the
attack on married women's right to work.

Selina Cooper saw that there was so much written encouraging
mothers to devote themselves to having babies, but still little
about how they might space out their pregnancies to prevent one
from relentlessly following another. Such information still had to
be gained surreptitiously – if at all. When the Guildswomen's
accounts were published in *Maternity*, it revealed how furtive

about birth control many women were. One mother of three told a friend that because of her miserable confinements she wanted her third baby to be her last. Her friend gave her advice but the Guildswoman confessed, 'I had to fight with my conscience before using a preventative.' Another bravely admitted that she had 'disgusted some of our Guild members by advocating restrictions'. Even the Introduction to *Maternity* explained that while some regarded a 'conscious check upon the growth of population' as a blessing, 'others see in it the suicide of a nation and the doom of a race'. As the war took its toll, there was even greater reason to fear 'the doom of the race'. At Nelson's Baby Week a guinea was offered for every baby reared, but there was still no public talk of limiting or even spacing pregnancies. Yet, even before the war ended, up sprang an eccentric scientist who, almost single-handedly, opened up birth control to public discussion.

Marie Stopes published her best seller *Married Love* in 1918. Overnight it changed everything. She took the campaign for birth control away from the economists' academic arguments about over-population, and instead provided a strong scientific justification for it. Although written in flowery language, it boldly placed women's sexual needs in central focus and did so without the coy imagery that *Parents' Guide* had used only a few years earlier. Dr Stopes' book was wildly successful, and she was soon publishing another, *Wise Parenthood*, offering contraceptive advice to married couples.

Marie Stopes dared to speak the unspeakable; but she was still steeped in the eugenicist values of her fellow Galtonian scientists. *Wise Parenthood* bemoaned 'the thriftless who breed so rapidly' that they give birth to children suffering from 'mental warping and weakness' and who needed to be supported by the thrifty. Indeed Dr Stopes' perspective was that of a conventional middle-class taxpayer who saw prisons and hospitals as places 'principally filled by inferior stock', and so expensive to support that the 'better classes' were deterred from having large families that they could ill-afford. Marie Stopes also shared the ruling class fear about the Russian Revolution. 'Most revolutionaries I have met,' she claimed, 'are people who have been warped or stunted in their personal growth.'[8]

It is unlikely that Selina Cooper had read Marie Stopes' books, for they were still expensively priced. More probable is that Selina came to hear of Dr Stopes' work as the controversy around her grew. It is clear however that the two women could not have been more dissimilar. One was an eminent palaeobotanist, whose international standing allowed her to cock her snook at any prurient gossip. The other, firmly rooted in Nelson's small town politics, enjoyed no such liberties. She could not ignore the disapproval of her conservative and Catholic neighbours. In addition, the two women's concern for spreading information about birth control was very differently motivated: Selina Cooper had no interest in stopping 'inferior stock' and 'stunted revolutionaries' from breeding. Rather, she wanted working women of her daughter's generation to have greater control over their pregnancies and so more say in shaping their own lives.

In doing this Selina not only had to combat those who had religious scruples about contraception. She also had to fight people within the labour movement who understandably resisted any eugenicist talk about contraception as something imposed on working people against their wishes. The old working-class fears about birth controllers stopping them from 'uncontrolled' breeding died hard. And Selina still had to fight the rule of silence imposed by frightened convention in a northern industrial town where everyone knew everyone else's business. Till the midtwenties, there was absolutely no public discussion at all in Nelson on the subject of birth control. Indeed Selina Cooper seems to have been one of the very few women in the town known to have an informed interest in such questions. She would go round to local Women's Co-operative Guilds giving talks, if not on birth control yet, on subjects like 'The Romance of the Human Body'. 'I feel,' she once confessed,

> I've got the gift of putting things to the average woman in a plain simple way, so that when they listen to me they will be able to understand the beating of the heart and the workings of the lungs. I was so interested in these subjects that I•took a course of training at Trinity College, Cambridge, on eugenics. I was the only working woman there. The professors who taught me were specialists in their particular subjects. One of the teachers was grandson of Charles Darwin. He used to wait for me after the class to have a chat on social subjects.

The date of this summer school on eugenics is unclear but Mary certainly recalled her mother coming back and telling her all about the new discoveries in heredity. 'A woman had come as a specimen, and they were talking about colour integration, and she was about six generations from an inter-marriage, and she had come out absolutely black,' Mary explained. Such technical information soon made Selina into a recognised expert on health questions among working women in Nelson. She was always in demand as something of a local 'wise woman'. Mary recalled that her mother used quietly to give advice to friends and neighbours, because birth control

> wasn't much talked about then, but my mother used to give a talk to the women that came here [to our house] about it . . . She used to meet with a lot of opposition, because there was quite a lot of Catholics. But she used to talk about those things – and elementary hygiene and elementary science and biology, and things we never got before.[9]

Certainly if the issue of birth-control information was to surface publicly in Nelson, Selina Cooper would be at the centre of the controversy.

From spring 1921, three years after the publication of *Married Love*, a national campaign began. In London Marie Stopes opened her Mothers' Clinic for Constructive Birth Control where women were examined by a qualified midwife and, if need be, the clinic's woman doctor; later that year she founded her Society for Constructive Birth Control and Racial Progress. Other more traditional birth controllers, jolted out of their academic discussions on the economics of population control, also opened a clinic, publicised by a campaign of open-air meetings – which met with a torrent of eggs and abuse.[10]

The agitation continued during 1922. Catholic pressure groups hit back and managed to get a question asked in the Commons of the Secretary of State, on 'what steps, in the way of criminal proceedings, he proposes to take in order to check the seriously increasing output of obscene literature having for its object the prevention of conception?' As the stakes rose, a general election was called for November 1922. It was an election in which

Labour, already establishing itself as the main opposition party to the Tories, felt that for the first time the power to put its social and economic policies into practice lay within its grasp. Marie Stopes saw the election differently. She circulated a questionnaire to all prospective parliamentary candidates demanding that they support her declaration that 'breeding chiefly from C3 population and burdening and discouraging the A1 is deplorable'; and promising that if elected they would 'press the Ministry of Health to give such scientific information through Ante-natal Clinics, Welfare Centres and other institutions in its control as will curtail the C3 and increase the A1'. Marie Stopes received only about 150 replies, largely from Labour candidates: on the whole they seemed doubtful that birth control was a key election issue.

In that sense her questionnaire failed. For instance, one of the 142 Labour MPs now returned to Westminster (for the party nationally had overnight managed to double its strength) was Arthur Greenwood, the Coopers' talented new MP. At the victory meeting held in Nelson's ILP Institute, the election was celebrated of the many ILP members (including early pioneers like Snowden and MacDonald, but also a cluster of new and fiery Clydesiders). Selina Cooper particularly praised Philip Snowden ('the Chancellor of the Exchequer in the Ideal State') and said she looked forward eagerly to the first Labour government. In none of these speeches – not even in Selina's – was birth control referred to. Indeed, if Arthur Greenwood *had* replied to Marie Stopes' questionnaire he would certainly have taken a dim view of her class-based eugenicist proposals which wanted to curtail the freedom of his Labour voters.[11]

But despite her reactionary views, Marie Stopes had put her finger on a key issue. Opening up birth-control clinics on a private, voluntary basis was all very well; but the crucial area lay within *state* provision. The 1918 Maternity and Child Welfare Act had enabled local authorities to set up clinics, staffed by midwives and health visitors. It was with these clinics, run by the local council through a specialist sub-committee, that women like Selina Cooper believed the answer now lay. For without such state provision, birth-control advice would remain the precarious privilege of wealthy and well-informed city-dwellers. Already Marie Stopes' approach had begun to involve her in litigation with a Catholic doctor.

In December, 1922, only weeks after the General Election, the issue of local council support for birth-control information suddenly exploded. Nurse Daniels, a health visitor employed by Edmonton Urban Council in London and a member of a birth-control league, was dismissed from her job for giving women who came to the municipal clinic the address of the Marie Stopes clinic. Despite a protest petition organised by local women, the Edmonton Maternity Committee backed the sacking.

This local decision was supported by the Ministry of Health: Maternity and Child Welfare Centres, it was agreed, were only for expectant and nursing mothers, not for those hoping to avoid pregnancy (unless – and very rarely – a case could be argued on medical grounds, and then a woman would be referred to a doctor or a hospital). Generally the medical profession jealously guarded access to birth-control information. The only alternative for most women in the early 1920s remained buying contraceptives furtively by mail order or, if she could stand the sniggers, in rubber goods shops. Yet the main method women used was the cervical cap and since so many mothers suffered internal injuries from previous childbirths, they badly needed medical assistance in having these fitted. Except in the handful of private clinics, this was not forthcoming.

Such was the political impasse at the beginning of 1923. The Ministry of Health was steadfast in its opposition. Marie Stopes' libel case came up in the High Court, amidst a flurry of newspaper reportage. Elsewhere in London, two anarchists were accused of selling an obscene publication, an inexpensive American pamphlet called *Family Limitation*. This case brought together a wide range of people concerned to campaign for birth-control information: Nurse Daniels, Emmeline Pethick-Lawrence, Bertrand Russell and his wife Dora. Unsurprisingly, the two defendants lost their case; and increasingly the birth-control campaign became less about individual propaganda initiatives, and more about persuading the increasingly influential Labour Party to support the demand for municipal welfare centres to be allowed to offer birth-control advice to those women who wanted it.[12]

Throughout 1923 birth control campaigners addressed Women's Co-operative Guilds, local Labour Parties, and women's sections of trade unions – mainly around London and South Wales. Battersea Labour Party even appointed a special sub-committee to press for a birth-control centre, though without winning any support from the Ministry of Health. In South Wales, one speaker reported how elderly women would come up and say, 'You've come too late to help me, Comrade, but give me some papers for my girls. I don't want them to have the life I've had.' But the cost of travel made it difficult for speakers to reach the north of England, and their efforts remained thinly scattered.

In Nelson women continued to pass information around informally amongst themselves. The Catholic community was alerted by reports in the *Catholic Times* about the evils of birth control, which was a conspiracy against the poor to reduce their numbers. Pat Quinn and the United Irish League would certainly have followed reports of Marie Stopes' long drawn out trial: she won, but the Catholic Church refused to accept defeat and appealed to the House of Lords.

It was at this inauspicious moment that Selina Cooper stood for election in November 1923. In the circumstances it is perhaps unsurprising that Pat Quinn decided he would not sign her nomination form or help her election campaign. Nor, in the circumstances, is it surprising that Selina Cooper's election address made no mention of birth control. The address merely noted that she had helped pioneer the Maternity Centre, and urged the election of women councillors so that they could help make decisions about 'Maternity and the care of children generally'. When writing it, Selina must have been uncomfortably aware that the United Irish League was this year particularly determined to let no known birth controller slip elected into the Council Chamber.[13]

Within a few weeks of Selina Cooper's defeat by the Tory in the Council elections, a row on this sensitive subject blew up in the Nelson Town Hall itself, and she found herself in the middle of it. The incident was a storm in a tea cup, a parochial episode compared to Marie Stopes' battles in the House of Lords. Yet it is worth investigating more closely because it reveals how bitterly the campaign was fought out in a tightly-knit northern community like Nelson.

Councillor Alec Campbell, the Scottish tailor and ILP member, was a good friend of the Coopers. He was keen to see working people involved in running their own affairs in the interests of their own class. 'Alec Campbell always treated people like human beings,' Mary recalled. He was, she added, a strong ally of her mother when Selina put up for council; he would go round to Labour supporters' houses, 'dragging them out to vote' for her. Mary dubbed him 'a real firebrand'. He was keen on taking direct action in defence of Russia, and, when he became councillor, he caused uproar by suggesting that councillors should travel by third – not first – class railway on official business. A particularly obstreperous member of the Burnley Board of Guardians, he was forever protesting against the appalling low scale of relief the Board offered poor families.

Selina Cooper, of course, agreed wholeheartedly with Campbell's politics. 'Alec Campbell'd come here and talk politics to my mother for hours on end,' Mary remembered. 'He'd always kept his friendship with my mother. Always stuck up for her.' Alec Campbell was sad that Selina had not become a councillor: she was just the kind of representative local working people needed; and he was particularly angry that her voice would not be heard on the Council's crucial Health Committee and its Maternity and Child Welfare Sub-Committee.

Councillor Campbell was prepared to fight for Selina. Presumably with her tacit agreement, he decided to try and make her one of the Sub-committee's two co-opted (i.e., non-councillor) members. A matter of political principle was at stake: the Women's Co-operative Guild and others had always insisted that working women should be represented on such bodies. Selina, a pioneer member of the St John Ambulance Association and of the local Guild, was an ideal figure. At the Council meeting on 4 December 1923 Alec Campbell therefore proposed that the name of Mrs Cooper be added to those of the two co-opted women members on the grounds that it would help the sub-committee to have someone of her experience present. The Mayor and Town Clerk ruled him out of order: the Council itself could not appoint co-opted members. Alec Campbell persisted; the Deputy Mayor protested at this interference in such matters. Other Labour councillors now became roused; Andrew Smith pointed out that neither of the co-opted women was a Labour member and that party politics had kept Selina Cooper out. 'There is no women who has done more for the working class in Nelson than has Mrs Cooper,' he went on. 'It might be true Mrs Cooper has not a CMB [Central Midwives Board] Certificate, but . . . it will be to the benefit of the Committee to have Mrs Cooper because she is in touch with the poorer women of the town, and it is these we are anxious to get into the Maternity Home.' Alec Campbell backed Andrew Smith up. 'It is not always individuals with high-flown titles behind them who are the most useful,' he said. On this note, the Labour councillors, riled by allegations of party bias, got their way and the Council voted – by ten votes to nine – to refer the matter back to the Health Committee for further consideration.[14]

So far so good: a fairly low-key debate between councillors, to be amiably resolved by the Health Committee in a fortnight's time. Yet when Nelson Town Council next met, on 8 January 1924, the storm exploded. The Health Committee again presented the list of people it would like appointed to the Maternity and Child Welfare Sub-committee – and again it did not include Selina Cooper. Alec Campbell immediately jumped up in the Council Chamber, protesting that the Committee's proposals went against Standing Order 71. The Town Clerk objected: Standing Order 71 did not apply in this case, he claimed. The Mayor hastily intervened: even though it *was* a breach of the Council's standing orders, he was going to permit discussion of the composition of this particular sub-committee to go ahead anyway. The Town Clerk was clearly put out: to waive standing orders in this casual way, he claimed, set dangerous precedents. Despite these legalisms and despite Liberal protests, the Mayor told Alec Campbell to proceed.

Councillor Campbell started his speech again. 'I wish to have included in this minute the name of an individual, proposed at the –' But again he was interrupted by further Liberal protest. The Mayor still insisted the Council accept his ruling, and at last Alec Campbell was able to proceed with his heartfelt defence of Selina Cooper:

> I wish to add, in place of one of the ladies co-opted to the Maternity and Child Welfare Committee, the name of Mrs Cooper, a name which has previously been moved in this Council, and also in committee. We have been told by several of those who are

opposed to that appointment that Mrs Cooper does not possess the qualifications necessary to fit her for a place on that committee. It may be true that some of the co-opted members of that committee do possess diplomas, but it is my contention that if a person does not possess such qualifications she ought not to be debarred . . .

In saying this I do not wish to decry people who possess qualifications. As a matter of fact, Mrs Cooper possesses many qualifications which fit her for service on such a committee. At the present moment she holds two very important positions in connection with the Lancashire County Council, for the welfare of children. Not only that but she has also had her home to maintain and a family to rear, both as a girl in her own home and as a married woman.

Furthermore, she has secured the highest credentials and diplomas from the St John Ambulance Association in Nelson itself. This ought to stand in her favour as being fitted for taking a place on a committee of this character.

She had also secured further honours in regard to hygiene, having made a special study of hygiene work under some of the most capable hygienists in the whole country . . .

Another matter has been raised, and in my opinion it is a very mean thing to do. It has been said that because Mrs Cooper has fought an election and had been turned down by the electorate, she ought not to be made a member of this committee. Even though she has been beaten Mrs Cooper has secured the distinction, not obtained by any other lady in Nelson, of having fought a municipal election. No other woman in the town has had the courage of her convictions to face the electorate –

A Liberal councillor, perhaps remembering Margaret Aldersley, interrupted the flow to challenge this claim. Undeterred, Alec Campbell ended his speech by moving that the name of Mrs Cooper be substituted for that of one of the other women, and sat down.

There was a short – and presumably embarrassing – silence. Labour men who a month before had been prepared to support Selina's claim to committee membership now fell silent. Andrew Smith who previously had defended her did not rise to second Alec Campbell. For whatever reason, the atmosphere had changed during the intervening weeks. Possibly Labour councillors, remembering the Catholic churches and mission halls dotted around the town, were embarrassed even by Alec Campbell's discreet reference to Selina's 'special study of hygiene work'. Possibly pressure had been quietly exerted on them over Christmas by leading Catholics.

The Mayor broke the silence. 'Is there no seconder?' he demanded. Only one other Labour councillor bravely offered to defend Selina. He was sure, he said, that there was nobody present who could honestly say that Mrs Cooper was not fitted to serve on the Maternity and Child Welfare sub-committee. 'She does a great deal of quiet work among the poor mothers of the town,' he added, 'and has their confidence.' Sadly, there were no other councillors prepared to back Alec Campbell in his crusade. The Mayor therefore put the matter to the vote and Alec Campbell's amendment was defeated. Only six councillors voted for it.

The effect on Selina Cooper personally must have been devastating. Not only had she failed at a parliamentary selection in Bury and failed to win a local election in Whitefield, she now had failed to win a Council co-option issue. And she knew that three Labour councillors – members of her own party – had changed their minds and voted against her. Worse still, the fight had been played out in full public gaze. 'Mayor Defies Town Clerk', blared the *Nelson Leader* headlines. 'Unprecedented scene in Council Chamber'. She had her name dragged through both the Town Council and through the local press, including her personal history from the time she looked after her bed-ridden mother to her recent election defeat.

Other women would have retired at this point, stung by such a humiliation – or at least would have grown bitter at the thanklessness of it all. But Selina was never one to concede defeat readily, nor to dwell overlong on her opponents' wily ways. Indeed Mary recalls how the next day her parents laughed about it at midday (Robert would come home from the mill for his dinner). Still loyally supporting Selina, Robert consoled his wife, according to Mary, saying that the whole matter was perfectly ridiculous since it was, beyond any shadow of doubt, Selina who had pioneered infant welfare in the town.[15]

National events were meanwhile moving fast in a very different direction. In December 1923 another General Election had been held. Arthur Greenwood was re-elected to Nelson and Colne with an even larger majority, and the number of women MPs suddenly quadrupled: of the eight, three were at long last Labour women, including Margaret Bondfield. In addition, the number of Labour seats rose by a third to 191 although the Tories still remained the largest party at Westminster.

What eventually emerged at the end of January 1924 from these confusing election results was a minority Labour government, headed by Ramsay MacDonald, with Philip Snowden as Chancellor of the Exchequer. Selina Cooper was overjoyed at the news: at last her years of hard work in the ILP were bearing fruit. 'Mr Ramsay MacDonald has been for twenty-three or -four years a member of the ILP and has been a pioneer in our great movement,' she informed a crowded open-air meeting in Nelson. 'We are proud of him as the second man in the Kingdom.'

Selina was naturally anxious to see who MacDonald would appoint as his Minister of Health. Her reaction must have been mixed. John Wheatley was an uncompromising socialist, one of the ILP's Clydeside brigade; his Housing Act, helping local authorities to provide inexpensive housing, was soon to become the most notable achievement of this precarious first Labour Government. Yet Wheatley was also a Roman Catholic, and Catholics were still in ferment over the saga of Marie Stopes' libel case. However, Arthur Greenwood was appointed as Parliamentary Secretary to Wheatley, which at least gave Selina and others in the local Labour Party Women's Section slightly easier access to this crucial ministry.

The public discussion of birth control in Nelson seemed opened up at last. Perhaps this was partly due to the liberating effect of the coming of Britain's first ever Labour Government; perhaps it was something to do with Arthur Greenwood's tacit encouragement to local Labour women; perhaps the row in the Council Chamber had the indirect effect of opening up the forbidden topic. Whatever the cause, the mood at the beginning of 1924 noticeably changed.[16]

At the beginning of February Selina Cooper addressed an ILP meeting for 'married ladies' – surely a talk about birth control, and therefore her first public address on the subject. Three weeks later, Nelson's Labour Party Women's Section organised a meeting on birth control, the first to be publicly advertised in the local press. The speaker was an elderly woman called Jennie Baker, a member of a north London Women's Section and of Marie Stopes' Constructive Birth Control Society; her credentials must have allayed any suspicions of local women that birth control was a eugenicist plot to stop the working class from breeding. Certainly Selina Cooper must have felt mightily relieved that there were at last other women willing to speak out in Nelson on this most highly charged subject. These seeds soon began to bear fruit; Nelson Labour Party Women's Section now joined a dozen other Sections in passing resolutions in favour of birth-control advice at welfare centres.[17]

Among those particularly active in trying to reverse the Ministry of Health's policy here was Dora Russell. With other Labour women, she began, as she explained in her autobiography,

> to sound out Members of Parliament, doctors and medical officers who were favourable . . . The Independent Labour Party was especially inclined towards us . . . [But] the Clydesiders accused us of wanting to throw the baby out with the bathwater: they were, naturally, resentful of the attitude of the Eugenicists, who implied that the working classes should not breed because they were of inferior stock.

Undeterred, in May 1924 Dora Russell and her comrades organised an influential deputation to interview Wheatley. It included Jennie Baker, H.G. Wells, one of the new women Labour MPs, and representatives of local Labour Women's Sections. They demanded that birth-control advice be made available at municipal welfare centres. This Wheatley rejected, as they knew he would; his explanation was that such an innovation would need to be sanctioned by Parliament.

'We saw our next steps clearly,' commented Dora Russell. 'Mr Wheatley had referred us to Parliament, to Parliament therefore we would go. But first of all we would obtain the verdict of the Labour Women's Conference.' This Conference was only a few days away, and already the Nelson Women's Section and the dozen other sections had sent in their resolutions. Jennie Baker was to move the birth-control amendment and Dora Russell to second it. (Though even before the debate began Marion Phillips, the Labour Party Woman Organiser, tried to pressurise her into withdrawing it. 'I cannot, Dr Phillips,' Dora Russell almost stammered, 'I am instructed by my Section to move it.' 'Sex should not be dragged into politics, you will split the Party from top to bottom,' Marion Phillips apparently retorted.) Despite the formidable official opposition, the amendment was given thundering support – one thousand votes to eight. It was made abundantly clear to Wheatley what Labour women felt on this matter.

Dora Russell and the others continued their energetic propaganda. 'Mr Wheatley had stirred a hornet's nest: all through 1924 we buzzed and stung,' she recorded. However, the autumn of that year was to be a difficult time for these feminists and socialists. At the Labour Party Conference the birth-control resolution was defeated by the predominantly male conference delegates, more attentive to Catholic votes than women's demands, however clearly voiced. Then a hasty General Election was called, the third in three years. The Labour Party, caught up in smears and scare stories about Russian plots, did badly, winning only about 150 seats compared to over 400 Conservative ones. Arthur Greenwood still held Nelson and Colne of course, but his majority over his Liberal opponent was narrowed. A few weeks later Marie Stopes' libel appeal was finally heard by five elderly Law Lords: they decided in favour of the Catholic doctor and against her birth-control campaign.[18]

The birth-control campaign had suffered severe setbacks; the election ushered in a period of conservative rule that was to govern the country with only one interruption for the next twenty years. In such unfavourable circumstances did Selina Cooper stand again in her Whitefield ward at the local elections in November 1924. Nominated once more by the ILP, she found herself pitted against a Liberal cotton manufacturer. Coming only days after the General Election debacle, it was a difficult contest for Labour. Selina's Russian sympathies would have told against her, and certainly the Catholic voters would be even more suspicious of her candidacy this year. Alec Campbell and her other ILP comrades canvassed for her unceasingly, but the opposition was too strong. Selina received 611 votes to the Liberal's 774.

Selina Cooper never stood again at another local election (though the ILP nominated her the following year). She certainly had good reason to feel discouraged. Although Whitefield was a marginal ward, it did seem there *was* a personal vote against her – partly because of her socialism, partly because of the Irish opposition, and partly because she was a woman. 'She tried for Council a few times, but they knew her. Aye, they knew her. Wouldn't entertain her,' her nephew, John Coombe's eldest son, reminisced cryptically; and he hinted that this judgement sprang from public disapproval of the way Selina supposedly dominated her meek husband. Mary certainly remained among those loyally convinced that there *were* some groups prejudiced against her mother:

> I used to get vexed, you see. She'd put up two or three times for the council . . . and she'd find spoiled papers of people who pretended to be working for her. And they deliberately spoiled the papers . . . and so she'd know they were not working for her. And I used to get vexed.
>
> They'd come the following day, . . . asking advice. And I'd say [to my mother] 'You know very well what they did to you.' She'd say, 'They can't help it. It's their loss.' She'd ask them to come in . . . She wasn't brought up particularly Christian, but she was a true Christian in that [way].[19]

At the 1925 local elections the Labour Party meekly agreed not to put up a candidate against Councillor Quinn in the Whitefield ward. Quinn was thus returned unopposed to the Town Hall and was on his way to becoming an alderman, a magistrate and Nelson's first Catholic Mayor.

Despite these setbacks, Labour women in Nelson did not give up their campaign. Selina Cooper gave a talk to one of the local Women's Co-operative Guilds on 'Married Women and the Law' – surely about access to birth-control information. At the end of 1925, Dora Russell came up to the Nelson Weavers' Institute to address a meeting organised by the Labour Women's Section. She explained what had been happening that year: in the summer the Women's Labour Party Conference had demanded that the party put pressure on the current Tory Minister of Health regarding birth control information being made available in welfare centres. But the women's demand – which, of course, carried no weight at all – had again been defeated at the Labour

Party Conference in the autumn. This Conference decided that birth control should not be made a party political issue, but be left to 'individual convictions'. This decision, made largely by Labour men, naturally infuriated Dora Russell. She told the Nelson meeting how deeply she regretted that the Labour Party should turn down women's appeal for birth-control advice. It was, she protested, grossly unfair that rich women should be able to buy access to such crucial information while it was denied to working women who desperately needed it. It was they who could least afford to have pregnancy followed by pregnancy in close succession. Unless a woman had an opportunity to rebuild her strength after childbirth the health of the whole family – and therefore the nation – was bound to suffer.[20]

The battle continued. Dora Russell and other Labour women managed to win support at the 1926 Labour Conference. But, Dora admitted, 'our victory was a hollow one. Labour was not in power, and the fear of the Catholic vote was a potent force.' The failure of the General Strike that year seemed to sap much of Labour's confidence. Despite all the efforts of women like Selina Cooper, winning the birth-control issue seemed to recede hopelessly in the late 1920s. Aged sixty-two, Selina attended a Labour Party Conference in Blackpool. It was the first time she had been since her defeat over women's suffrage in Belfast exactly twenty years earlier. Now, energetic Catholic lobbying of the trade union block votes again led to the defeat of the birth-control resolution. The following year Selina attended the Labour Women's Conference in Portsmouth, where the same thing occurred. Arthur Henderson came down and appealed to the women on behalf of the party leadership not to rock the boat over such a sensitive subject. It seemed that the Labour Party preferred not to hear the women's appeals. Instead, the campaign began to be fought more broadly, around the less contentious issue of reducing the high level of maternal mortality and winning the support of groups like NUSEC and the Women's Liberal Association.[21]

Despite these setbacks, birth control remained an issue on which Selina Cooper refused to give up. On May Day 1929, she chaired a public women-only meeting in the Weavers' Institute on 'Happy and Welcome Births'. The speaker was Stella Browne, a pioneer birth controller whom Selina introduced as 'a radical feminist . . . foremost in women's questions'. Stella Browne traced the movement's history back to Annie Besant, and included criticism of Arthur Greenwood as well, for the way he 'neglected to support' a recent birth-control bill in the Commons. Greenwood, like the Labour councillors in Nelson, must have been uncomfortably aware of Patrick Quinn and the United Irish League voters, whenever the issue of birth control was raised.

By the end of the 1920s there were still fewer than twenty birth-control clinics in the country. The one nearest to Nelson lay in Salford, over thirty miles away. It was open just for three and a half hours a week: only the most determined women from north-east Lancashire would have paid it a visit. Yet Selina would not be silenced. 'She used to talk at the Guilds about birth control, and get walloped for it,' Mary explained. 'You see, [there were] a lot of Catholics and there'd be a terrible row.' Certainly Selina seemed to be at odds with the local Catholic priest over such issues. One of the Coopers' neighbours was a Catholic and would, according to Mary, occasionally come round and see Selina and 'cry because she had very bad – she had babies at home, but she had very bad deliveries. Although she was a Catholic, her husband got very vexed and said, "There'll be no more bloody children here. Priest can have them!" Got so vexed, but mother . . . used to take food in.'[22]

Only slowly during the 1930s did a network of family-planning clinics in the big cities begin to emerge; but they still remained thin on the ground in Selina's own lifetime, especially in a northern industrial town with a significant Catholic electorate.[23]

The mid-1920s were difficult years for Selina Cooper. But the personal defeats she suffered were somewhat softened when she was appointed a magistrate at the end of 1924. She remained rather puzzled about who had nominated her. 'It was always a mystery about that,' Mary explained. 'But my mother got to the bottom of it. And it was the Weavers and the Labour Party Executive that had moved her.' Documentary evidence confirms that this was indeed the case. The Nelson Weavers, according to its minute book, decided in August 1924 that 'we nominate Mrs S Cooper to the position of JP'. Just to be absolutely safe, the union committee agreed a week later that 'Mr A Greenwood MP be written to, with a view to him using his influence to get Mrs Cooper appointed on the Borough Bench of Magistrates'. Whether or not Greenwood did have to intervene in this way, the Weavers' nomination was successful, and Selina duly became one of the newly-appointed JPs.[24]

From 1924 to 1944 when she finally retired from the magistracy, Selina Cooper sat on the local bench, hearing countless cases of wife-battering and drunkenness, petty thefts and defaulting on maintenance orders. As Hannah Mitchell, who also became a magistrate in the mid-1920s, recounts in *The Hard Way Up*, this first generation of women magistrates had paraded before them in the police courts 'unhappy marriages with all their attendant misery and hopeless future, wretched women and desperate men and, worst of all, unhappy children . . . Hardened girls [came] to seek justice for themselves and their helpless babies.' Selina certainly saw her fair share of all these. 'When she became a magistrate,' Mary recalled,

> they'd come for her to go to court at a minute's notice, because she was so near. And I'd come home, and there'd be a card on the table – 'Your dinner's in the oven' . . .
>
> And I remember once there was a woman – one or two women, when my mother's a magistrate – summoned for illegal operations. And one poor woman hadn't been doing it for a long time, and a girl came and pleaded with her to do it. And she died, and this woman went to prison. And I can remember my mother saying how tragic it was for this poor woman. Because she'd begged her to do it, and a lot of girls would keep the secret to their death rather than tell. But this girl told, and the woman went to prison for six years.[25]

Selina Cooper faced much else while on the magistrates' bench. As Nelson's industrial conflict began to erupt at the end of the twenties, she found herself once again in the midst of an epic and sometimes violent struggle.

CHAPTER NINETEEN

POVERTY AND POWER:
1926-1931

While Selina Cooper was thrust into the middle of the battle to save the local cotton industry, her husband was little more than one of its numberless victims. Robert had witnessed the industry's rise in Nelson and was now suffering its swift fall. A nineteen-year-old boy, he had been wrenched out of Swaledale by tales of a boom town where fabulous wages lay within the reach of every farm labourer. But the reality turned out sourer. Sacked from the Post Office for his trade unionism, he tried a spell in Lomeshaye Mill, only to find his job hit by one of the industry's cyclical slumps. He tested his luck in America, but life was no easier there. He had to return to Lomeshaye and his hated set of looms. Locally, jobs outside the mill that paid enough to support a wife and baby were hard to come by. The damp factory atmosphere continued to affect his poor health, and in despair Robert even toyed with the idea of emigrating to New Zealand and becoming a farmer again. Watching his life slip slowly away with so few of his earlier dreams realised, Robert had to resign himself to the daily grind. His only escape remained his beloved Swaledale: farming summers made the rest of the year more bearable.

The post-war cotton boom had collapsed in the early 1920s. Wages were cut and one cotton worker in twelve still remained without a job. In Nelson the slump was not as severe as elsewhere in Lancashire; but Robert was among those who found the bitter taste of unemployment difficult to get rid of. One of the earliest casualties of the Depression, by the mid-1920s it was clear he was unlikely ever to work again. An indifferent weaver in his mid-fifties, he would be the first to go.

Whether he was in fact given the sack or not is unclear; but

Mary recalls how he left his Nelson looms and returned to the Dales:

> When he finished – he finished ten years before he died, so he must have finished in 1924 . . . I remember he went to Carleton . . . near Skipton. He had cousins [who] had a farm there, and he got weaving at Carleton . . . And he lived with those cousins then, and came home at weekends . . .
>
> He couldn't get work round here, because he must have been – he died at 64. So he must have been 54. And he had been sick for about five years before that, so he must have started being sick about 1920. And he'd have this awful indigestion and pains. Well, they didn't operate for stomach ulcers then.

The small mill run by his cousins could hardly provide Robert with a secure job. With his health deteriorating badly, Robert Cooper faced the dreary prospect of long-term unemployment. Nor was he sure what his illness was. Possibly he was suffering from cancer, but no one seemed able to cure it. 'My father . . . was always sick and ailing,' Mary Cooper explained in her usual matter-of-fact way, 'and he'd go out and get fresh air – that seemed to keep him going, did walking out in the fresh air. When he was dieting and only living on milk, he'd walk miles. He kept having illnesses . . .'[1]

Since there was no National Health Service, Robert, desperate to cure himself, was ready to try any diet or remedy – however cranky. He got hold of booklets like *What Is the Root Cause of Cancer: Is it Excessive Consumption of Common Salt . . .?* and *The Diet Essential to Health: the Value of Vitamins*. But nothing seemed to do the trick.

If Robert Cooper had been a grey figure compared to his wife before the war, he became even more overshadowed now. Increasingly his illness and weakness stood in stark contrast to Selina's vigour. She became a magistrate through pressure exerted by *his* union, yet he himself found that there was little the Nelson Weavers could do to help his situation, so common among its older members. Records of the last ten years of Robert's life are pathetically scanty. Not a single photograph of him taken since the war has survived.

Both mother and daughter seemed to prefer to push the ailing man to the back of their minds. Selina never referred publicly to her husband – not even to the practical family problem of his long-term unemployment. She was always known as 'Mrs Cooper, the Guardian' or 'Mrs Cooper JP', *never* as Robert's wife or even Mary's mother. Obviously it was a trying period for the three of them, cooped up together in a small terraced house. Selina was understandably reluctant to devote another long period of her life to looking after an invalid; she had after all spent her youth caring for her bed-ridden mother. Mary, the dutiful spinster daughter, has revealed little about her parents' relationship, for she possessed a deep-rooted sense of family loyalty that perhaps made her bury certain family memories at times. Certainly Mary claimed that she never heard her parents raising their voices – except when they were heatedly discussing politics. This may well have been the case for any tensions felt by Selina and Robert by now lay so deep that perhaps the need for arguing had long passed.

In the meantime mother and daughter grew closer, often going on holidays together. They looked forward to these trips away from Nelson and in 1928 Mary was able to take her mother abroad for the first time for a holiday in France. Interestingly, when Selina applied for a passport, she put down her occupation as 'professional organiser' even though her work for the National Union had long since ceased, and her position as a local magistrate hardly fitted that particular description. And yet in a sense 'political organiser' was just what Selina Cooper had become once again, despite her sixty-three years. As the struggle to defend the rights of the local unemployed began, Selina was to be found right in the thick of it.

Lloyd George's pre-war National Insurance scheme had seemed progressive enough at the time: workers would pay weekly contributions and so be entitled to modest unemployment benefits to help tide them over till their next job. It was utterly inadequate, however, in dealing with the massive wave of long-term unemployment that hit people like Robert Cooper in the 1920s. An insured worker could only claim benefit for a limited number of weeks in any one year. Since the benefit itself was meagre, with nothing allowed for dependants or children, there were few families who could survive many weeks of unemployment. In 1921, as unemployment rose, protests against these starvation sums grew and the government conceded a few shillings extra for a dependent wife or child. Even so, unemployed workers facing long stretches of joblessness still suffered great hardship. As their carefully hoarded savings dwindled to nothing, they realised they had no alternative but to swallow their pride and admit they had become paupers who must appeal to the dreaded Guardians. From 1921 onwards the number of unemployed people and their dependants on Poor Relief mushroomed.

The Boards of Guardians had hardly changed since the days when Selina Cooper was elected to the Burnley Board twenty years previously. They still dispensed Dickensian 'relief' (either 'indoor' relief in the workhouse or 'outdoor' relief for those lucky enough to stay at home) and this was largely financed from local rates. Many conservative Guardians still believed that their mission was to keep ratepayers happy rather than to provide the new unemployed (many of whom were skilled workers who never dreamed they would be reduced to pauper status) with amounts that they and their family could subsist on.[2]

In northern industrial towns like Burnley, the Board now found itself swamped with out-relief applicants, but was still dominated by traditionally-minded Guardians who managed to keep down the scales of relief. Guardians from Nelson, the Labour stronghold in the Board's area, grew incensed that people should be asked to live on such paltry amounts of money. Alec Campbell protested vociferously at Board meetings. Such socialist Guardians were encouraged in summer 1921 to see that at Poplar in East London the local Board of Guardians (which had a Labour majority) was paying high rates of relief, despite a legal writ issued against them. Defiant Poplar organised a demonstration from the local Town Hall to the High Court, with banners proclaiming 'Poplar is paying £4,500 a week on Out-Relief' and 'Let Justice prevail though the Heavens Fall'. One Nelson Guardian, John Willie Throup, angrily informed the Burnley Board that more relief money *would* be forthcoming if the local Guardians unanimously exerted pressure as the Poplar Guardians had done. Local anger was further fuelled when cotton workers came out on strike, yet were denied the right to claim out-relief. The Nelson ILP organised a protest march to the Guardians' office in Burnley, and under this pressure the Board agreed to increase the out-relief.[3]

Yet the situation remained far from satisfactory. Unemployment hit areas like South Wales and north-east Lancashire far more heavily than non-industrial, suburban regions. Yet most of the support for the unemployed had to be found from local rates. It was if the old industrial areas were being doubly punished. Poor boroughs such as Poplar began to demand that the burden should be shared more equally across different areas, and this was an idea that appealed directly to the Nelson socialists. Selina Cooper chaired a meeting of the local Labour Party Women's Section when the contentious issue of rates was discussed. The Section demanded that central government should take some of the burden off the local ratepayers and spread it more widely, and that the Poplar councillors imprisoned over this issue should be released.

In Poplar the fight was between the left-wing Board of Guardians and the conservative London authorities, less enthusiastic about lavish spending on the poor. In Burnley it was still between different factions *within* the Board of Guardians. Before long friction between the conservative members and the Nelson Guardians blew up. The Board decided to sack the Nelson Relieving Officer (responsible for the day-to-day administration of relief) and his clerk on grounds of alleged maladministration, but really because these two employees co-operated with the Nelson Guardians to ensure unemployed people were given enough to live on. Selina Cooper and others were appalled by such high-handed action by Burnley. They organised a protest meeting in Salem School. Alec Campbell and Willie John Throup both spoke, deploring what had happened. Selina proposed that the two men be reinstated and won the unanimous support of the meeting.[4]

But Nelson's radical voice on the Burnley Board of Guardians could always be drowned by the conservative majority. The two men were not reinstated; nor did the meagre out-relief scales fixed by the Board satisfy Guardians like Alec Campbell. When the Board decided to reduce the maximum amount for a family, he cried out in desperation at the meeting, 'My God! You could not keep a kitten on that, never mind a human being.'

Selina Cooper observed these battles on the Board of Guardians with growing concern. (When the Guardians' elections came round in 1922 she considered putting up as one of the Labour

candidates, but for one reason or another withdrew her name.)
She recognised that it was on the local Boards of Guardians that
many of the most crucial political battles were now being fought.
These fights were taking place not only in Poplar and Nelson: in
South Wales, a group of miners locked up the Guardians in the
workhouse for eighteen hours as a protest against cuts in relief;
and in West Scotland, the unemployed marched to Glasgow and
forced their way into the committee room.[5]

This conflict deepened during the General Strike of May 1926,
and during the longer mining dispute that ran on to the end of the
year. The government tried to clamp down on over-generous
Guardians giving relief to miners who remained out on strike.
The Minister of Health, Neville Chamberlain, even introduced
legislation to replace rebellious Guardians with tame government
appointees. A textile town like Nelson was not directly involved
that tumultuous summer, but Burnley with its own local coal
miners was. So it was to Burnley that Selina Cooper JP hastened
in June 1926 to address a meeting of the Labour Party Women's
Sections. The collapse of the General Strike, and the courage of
the hard-pressed miners still holding out, moved Selina deeply.
Having spent so much of her suffrage years campaigning in coal
mining areas, she felt a deep loyalty for the miners and their
families. Like so many other working-class people, she recognised
no effort was too great so long as the miners won their long and
bitter struggle.

Introduced to the Burnley meeting as a magistrate from
Nelson, Selina Cooper made one of the most stirring speeches of
her life, and one that echoed back to her pre-war years. 'Working-
class women must put a greater value on their lives,' she urged the
women in the audience:

> We should think of our collective value . . . I feel that soon we
> shall have to think collectively. I think the time is fast approaching
> when the present social order breaks down. That time is coming
> perhaps more quickly than we think . . .
>   We are quite as good as the duchesses. It is foolish to think that
> one class has a monopoly of any quality. It is only the distribution
> of the wealth of the country that is wrong. It is because we are
> continually thinking that we are inferior that we are driven lower
> and lower . . .

The meeting ended with 'The Red Flag', but had little effect on the Burnley Board. In August it voted to reduce the relief granted to local miners' families, despite fierce opposition from Alec Campbell and Willie John Throup. Selina Cooper watched in anguish as the poverty facing miners grew daily more desperate. She knew they badly needed the practical help that a community like Nelson, untouched by the miners' strike, could readily supply. All over the country Labour Party Women's Sections were forming Distress Committees and alerting people to the horrors of miners' malnutrition and starvation. She therefore helped set up a Nelson Women's Miners' Relief Committee. In collaboration with the Burnley Relief Committee for Miners' Wives and Children run by the local Women's Sections, it organised soup kitchens, fed needy children and provided for the mothers. Special attention was given to pregnant wives of miners: it was found that there were 150 such women in Burnley alone. They were given a special allowance of 10s a day in the form of nourishing food.

With winter approaching the miners' plight grew ever more desperate. Selina Cooper knew that warm clothes would soon be in heavy demand. So she turned her front room into a collection centre. People were urged to bring their gifts of winter clothes, either to the Weavers' Institute in the town centre or to the ILP Institute, or down to the Coopers' house at 59 St Mary's Street.[6] People responded readily to such appeals, and before long Selina – helped by Mary – was bundling up parcels of clothes and clogs as fast as they arrived. Three of the earliest parcels she dispatched went straight to Abertillery in Monmouthshire for the South Wales Miners' Federation. Selina still retained haunting memories of working for suffrage in the Welsh constituencies there; the mining disaster at Senghenydd would remain a terrible memory till the end of her life. Had she not been speaking in Abertillery just as the Great War broke out? With these indelible memories of the miners' past sufferings, Selina parcelled up clothing and shoes for the destitute families. In return she received this touching thank-you letter from the President of the Abertillery Women's Section:

A further parcel of clothing has been handed to me for the Miners' office. Thank you very much for the same they are a real Godsend just when things are most hopeless. It makes one feel that someone thinks of the poor dispirited folks of the mining districts. Anyway, we still keep up our courage and hope for the best.[7]

Before long other parcels were on their way to Burnley and Bolton, to Leeds and to Durham. Throughout the autumn Selina Cooper and the others kept busy. It was not till the end of the year that the miners, support for their strike crumbling away, were finally forced back to work. Nelson women could at least take pride in having supported the miners and their families for all the months they had remained out. Among the Cooper papers has survived a small invitation card which poignantly commemorates this solidarity.

NELSON WOMEN'S SECTION
Dear Friend,
The above Section will hold a. . . .

GRAND FANCY DRESS CARNIVAL
in the Weavers' Institute, Nelson, on Friday October
22nd, 1926, at 8 p.m.   Admission: 6d

All Proceeds in Aid of Miners' Wives and Children

ALL ARE WELCOME[8]

The shape of the industrial war to be fought so bitterly in the early 1930s was growing clearer. In 1927 Neville Chamberlain, who had already replaced some London Guardians with his own appointees, now used his new powers in two mining districts: he went over the heads of the elected Guardians in Durham and in the South Wales coalfield. Of course, there was little danger that even Chamberlain would want to unseat the Burnley Guardians. The fiercest battles there still took place amongst the Guardians themselves, for Nelson could never quite muster sufficient votes to outnumber the gentlemen farmers from Pendle.

At the end of 1927 this stalemate at last began to dissolve. At the local elections in Nelson, Labour recaptured power with a victory reminiscent of 1905 when Labour first won its majority on the Council. The triumphant party wasted no time. In the election of aldermen and choice of mayor, Labour completely swept the board. The new mayor, Andrew Smith, was offered an annual salary of £300 to enable him to do his job without being hindered by financial worries – a principle of municipal socialism long held dear by Labour. It was also decided there would be no Mayor's procession, and that committee meetings would be held in the evening rather than during the working day, so that they were accessible to ordinary people in the town.

It was clear to the party that Selina Cooper's experience and skills were hardly fully stretched on the local magistrates' bench. Yet Andrew Smith and other leading councillors recognised it would still be impolitic to co-opt her onto the Maternity and Child Welfare Sub-committee: birth control was still a highly sensitive issue with Catholics. So it was decided instead to co-opt her onto the less controversial Education Committee. It made sense: Selina had, ever since the half-timers' campaign, always taken a keen interest in education, and was determined that younger people should not be deprived in the way her generation had been. So she now began to concern herself with local schools, urging proper nursery education and helping to found an open-air school for children suffering from the effects of poor housing and poor food.

The Labour Party did not stop there. Additional council elections were held to replace those councillors raised to aldermen. Again Labour triumphed at the polls: there were now twenty Labour councillors to only twelve Liberals, Tories and Independents. 'The Red Flag' was ritually sung to celebrate. The town acquired a reputation as 'Red Nelson' and 'Little Moscow' through actions like its progressive housing policy: even before the first Labour Government Nelson had begun to build municipal housing, pulling down back-to-back homes and offering tenants airy houses with gardens. Its renown as a citadel of local socialism was also based on the self-confident pride of grass-roots members of the Weavers' Association. 'It's very hard to convey to you what the strength of the socialist movement was,' said one Nelson weaver.

> . . . Least mention of a meeting – 'Right, let's go' . . . The men would jump on the bikes. Off they'd go to hear the speaker. It was such enthusiasm for it . . . Nelson was the centre of controversy then . . . They were fighting for something, instead of just lying down to the business. Oh no, they were fighters in Nelson.[9]

Now there was a major issue to fight about. In spring 1928 a long-standing Nelson Weavers' official was sacked after an argument over an alleged mistake in a piece of cloth he had woven. Hundreds of weavers at his mill came out on strike in sympathy. The employers, spoiling for a fight with the uppity Weavers, responded with a lock-out of ten thousand weavers in the town, and the conflict bore all the signs of becoming long and bitter. Members of the Communist Party arrived from outside the district and began chalking the pavements to announce their meetings, increasingly critical of the Labour Party and trade union leadership. Nelson families became involved: whether they would be entitled to out-relief from the Board of Guardians was crucial. Willie John Throup demanded that they must be entitled, but this the Guardians rejected – along with a more moderate proposal for out-relief to be given to the weavers' dependants. All that the Burnley Board would accept was a stingy suggestion for relief to be offered on loan and repaid after the lock-out ended.

Selina Cooper became closely involved in the battle with the Burnley Board for she could see that if the weavers and their families were starved into submission, the lock-out would end disastrously without the sacked weaver being reinstated. Equally angry with the tight-fisted Guardians was Nelson's Labour-controlled Town Council: it decided to organise a march down to Burnley to lodge a public protest. A small deputation – Selina Cooper, Willie John Throup, the Nelson Weavers' Secretary and one or two Labour aldermen and councillors – would meet the Guardians and put Nelson's point of view. A clear indication of the strong feeling in 'Red Nelson' was that not one single councillor dared to vote against this official protest march and it went straight through the Council without a murmur of opposition. By now additional looms had been stopped and more mills closed as local employers tightened their grip on the town. No fewer than sixteen thousand people were now locked out.

At eleven o'clock on Thursday, 21 June 1928 the demonstration set off in the rain. Selina Cooper was among those leading it, and behind her marched a few hundred Nelson people, mainly young women. The procession wound its way down to Burnley singing the 'Red Flag' and bearing its banners: 'Workers, why talk ye of wages, whose is the wealth of the country but yours?'

Mary Cooper recalled how, 'When things got very bad, they'd out-door relief and my mother got into a few scrapes about this, because they had a procession and she led it . . . And they'd to fight to get sixpence increase in relief. They'd to fight: and they gave it them on loan . . .'

In Burnley, Selina Cooper and the others went in to the building, only to be informed that the Board had voted to refuse entry into the Guardians' Board Room for the Nelson delegation. On hearing of this snub, Selina and everyone else moved off to the nearby Burnley cattle market for an impromptu protest meeting.

The mood of the meeting was one of intense resentment that the rate-paying weavers of Nelson – and the delegation representing them – had been so rudely rebuffed by the Guardians. One councillor told the crowd that the Board's offer of relief on loan was just an underhand way of ducking its legal responsibility of ensuring that no one starved. Another said how proud he felt to belong to a town that could muster such a demonstration in thirty-six hours. 'We are getting to feel that we can do anything at Nelson,' he proclaimed. But 'when we get to Burnley we learn something else. We learn that while in Nelson Labour rules, in Burnley it does not,' and he urged the Burnley workers to follow 'Red Nelson's' example next election.

Then it was Selina's turn. She climbed up on the platform precariously improvised by balancing a box on top of a wheelbarrow, and told the crowd about her six years on the pre-war Burnley Board, and how the Guardians had tried – unsuccessfully – to keep her off the Nelson Relief Committee. 'It is wicked,' she protested,

> that a number of people in Nelson should have the power to lock out thousands. And the very people who object to giving relief don't care a brass farthing what is spent when it comes to dealing with the effects of such a policy.

And she took the Guardians to task for their short-sightedness. Tens of thousands of pounds of rate-payers' money, she said, was being spent at a Lancashire country hospital where children suffering from rickets had to be sent, in part because of stingy relief policies whereby children ended up living on a diet of margarine and treacle. 'Every child in England ought to be fed, not on fourth

grade milk, but on first grade,' she urged. The crowd cheered
Selina for her speech, and a protest motion strongly condemning
'the inhuman attitude of the Liberal and Tory majority on the
Burnley Board of Guardians' was supported wholeheartedly. As
usual, a few verses of 'The Red Flag' were sung, and everyone
gave 'three cheers for the Nelson Section of the Burnley Board of
Guardians'.

The lock-out ended in July with the dismissed weaver being
offered a job in another mill. Members of the Communist Party,
who had been active throughout, bitterly attacked this as a sell-
out.[10] However the controversy over relief refused to disappear.
The Burnley Board obstinately stuck to giving the locked-out
weavers relief only on loan despite Nelson's protests. At least the
Board of Guardians did not prosecute weavers for not repaying
this loan, which was one small victory for the persistently rebellious Nelson Guardians. Yet the principle at stake remained.
Selina Cooper could see that, with the growth of long-term
unemployment, another industrial dispute could easily grow far
more bitter unless striking weavers were given proper relief. For
this reason, the Board's interpretation of the Ministry of Health
rulings could well determine the outcome of a dispute and thereby
the standard of living of working people in the town. The political
balance on the Guardians therefore became a crucial factor in
maintaining the local standard of living. Selina's earlier hesitation
about becoming a Guardian again disappeared. She knew she
must get back on the Burnley Board to champion the rights of
Nelson's weavers.

However, before the next Guardians' election came round,
Selina Cooper found herself in the thick of another contest: the
1929 General Election. The Election was important because for
the first time women in their twenties were entitled to enter the
polling booth. Twenty-nine-year-old Mary Cooper, for instance,
was now able to join women over thirty and men over twenty-one
in casting her vote. In the Coopers' constituency, Arthur Greenwood was hoping to retain his seat. Selina felt optimistic about
Labour's strength; she was determined that the new 'flapper'
voters should support Greenwood rather than his Conservative
rival. By now one of the veterans of the local labour movement
who could recall the days long before the party was formed, Selina

went along to the Women's Section to encourage the younger women to use their votes wisely. 'Now that the Labour cause is taking on a new lease of life with new voters,' she told them, 'I want the women to formulate their own opinions,' and she entertained the meeting with stories about the first trade union meeting she went to which ended in a physical fight.

Selina was not disappointed. Arthur Greenwood was returned with a majority of over 10,000; it seemed as if all the newly-enfranchised women had voted for him. Overall Labour had done extremely well and won more seats than either of the two other parties. However the election result was again ambiguous. Labour still lacked an outright majority in the Commons. Despite this, Ramsay MacDonald was asked to form a government. Philip Snowden became Chancellor of the Exchequer, with Arthur Greenwood as Minister of Health, and Margaret Bondfield Minister of Labour. Not only was there now Britain's first ever woman Cabinet Minister, but also the number of women MPs – many of them Labour – had overnight shot up to fourteen. They included Selina's friend Eleanor Rathbone, and Selina wrote to congratulate her, and to congratulate Arthur Greenwood on his appointment as Minister of Health. She then happily sat back to wait for her old comrades, MacDonald and Snowden, to unfold their new socialist programme. After all, if democratically elected socialists had been able to reshape local government in Nelson, so could socialists in Westminster.

As Britain slipped from the twenties into the grim thirties, Selina's optimism was to be sorely tested. Before the end of the summer, wage cuts for cotton workers were agreed. In the autumn the stock market on Wall Street crashed, and the financial crisis which engulfed the United States resounded round the world. By January 1930 the number of unemployed people in Britain topped 1,500,000. Many local weavers were again reduced to short-time working, or to living on the wages from just one or two looms. An ominous local dispute erupted in nearby Barrowford where, it appeared, one or two weavers were working not four or even six but eight or ten looms; the Nelson Weavers called a strike, extremely apprehensive in case this maverick experiment in 'more looms' might spread unchecked beyond Barrowford and so throw hundreds of their members out of work.

They were right to be concerned: the 'more looms' battle was soon to enflame the whole of Lancashire.

By April 1930 unemployment passed two million. Communists in Nelson were already telling the weavers that the Labour Government and trade union leadership was selling them down the river: only the Communist Party could lead the fight against the 'more looms' system. 'Mr Arthur Greenwood is not the Minister of Health,' they proclaimed angrily, 'but the Minister of Starvation.' Labour was being therefore attacked not only from the right, but also from the left. It was at such a difficult moment that Selina Cooper regained her place on the Burnley Board of Guardians after nearly quarter of a century.[11]

What Selina found was that the administration of the Poor Law had recently changed drastically. Under his 1929 Local Government Act, Neville Chamberlain abolished forever the old Boards of Guardians, including of course the Burnley Board. Their powers were now transferred to the counties – in this case to the Lancashire County Council based at Preston. County Hall (which also acquired other new powers – for instance, over maternity and child welfare) was to administer relief through its new Public Assistance Committees. By this measure the government hoped to avoid the problem of 'Poplarism' whereby rebellious local towns could defy Ministry of Health rulings about out-relief. The 1929 Act was a savage blow to the principle of democratic local government run by directly-elected local people. It invested in distant bureaucrats, only remotely accountable to a local community, crucial powers over people's lives.

Lancashire's powerful Public Assistance Committee began its work in April 1930. The county was divided into districts, one of which was Number Six and covered the Burnley area. Each of these districts was administered day-to-day by its own local Guardians' Committee. Despite the use of the old 'Guardian' name, these no longer consisted of people elected directly by ratepayers, but of a number of town councillors, county councillors – plus other people appointed by the Public Assistance Committee, of which at least three had to be women. On to the Burnley Guardians therefore went Councillors Andrew Smith, Pat Quinn, Willie John Throup and others; and Mrs Selina Cooper

JP was co-opted on as a statutory woman along with two other women magistrates.[12]

Selina no longer had to face a gruelling election to become a Guardian; but the reverse side of the coin was that she was no longer directly answerable to the Nelson ratepayers, but to the extremely conservative Public Assistance Committee in Preston more than twenty miles away. The cosy days of Dan Irving banging his wooden leg, or of marches down to the Burnley offices, were definitely over. Now every relief order given by local Guardians on the Burnley Committee could be 'countermanded' by faceless officials at County Hall. With unemployment rising above two million, the question of relief was becoming an ever more burning political issue.

Selina Cooper was put on the Nelson Relief Committee, and on the Boarding-out Committee which sought homes for orphans and deserted children. She tried to help the poor people who came to her as best she could, and found that the Burnley Guardians' Committee (which at long last now had a *Labour* majority) backed her up. But Preston increasingly challenged the decisions about relief that she and other socialist Guardians made. Within months of the Public Assistance Committee starting work, relationships between Burnley Guardians like Selina Cooper and the Preston officials began visibly to sour.

By mid-summer 1930 the battle lines were drawn. On the one side, the Burnley Guardians' Committee, chaired by Andrew Smith, was determined to offer relief to weavers who had been reduced just to one or two looms and whose weekly wage of, say, 25s had to support a wife and two growing children. On the other side, the Public Assistance Committee was keen to overturn (or 'disapprove') relief given to men in 'full-time employment'. The cases of poor Nelson weavers were particularly contentious, not just because Nelson Guardians were particularly radical but because in Nelson the rent paid for privately-owned accommodation was unusually high; yet Guardians were not supposed to take high rents into account when calculating relief.

Selina felt very strongly about this: she had only to go out of her own front door to see the effects of the Public Assistance Committee's tight-fisted policy. 'In a street near where I live,' she told a Guardians' meeting that summer, there are . . . houses where rents of 15s 6d are being demanded. Some of these houses are occupied by men who are at present only running two looms and have to keep a wife and family. These people are not getting enough food; the children will suffer from rickets and all sorts of diseases, and the burden will come back again on the rates.[13]

Burnley Guardians' Committee's recommendation that high rents should be taken into account in calculating relief was flatly rejected by the Public Assistance Committee. The Nelson Guardians protested strongly against this harsh decision. Willie John Throup was particularly incensed about the effect on old people who could hardly afford food and coal after they had paid their rents and rates. 'I will not impose starvation on the old folks for 50,000 County Councils,' he thundered. 'It is a disgrace in a civilised country,' added Selina Cooper, 'that old age pensioners should have to come for out-relief at all.' 'If they want a Poplar or a West Ham . . . they can have it,' concluded another defiantly.[14]

It was agreed that a deputation of Guardians should go to Preston and protest in person to the Public Assistance Committee. Yet all that happened when they got there was that Preston nodded its head sagely but refused to modify its decisions in any way. At the next Burnley Committee, the Guardians' anger had not subsided. 'Today I have been told of a man who owns ninety houses which became decontrolled [whose rents went up] as soon as there was a change of tenants,' Selina Cooper raged. 'It is fearful that any man in this country should have the right to charge 14s or 15s a week for rent.'

Meanwhile the Public Assistance Committee went on to 'disapprove' relief to more local people. Preston seemed to be turning local Guardians into mere automatons. The newly-formed labour newspaper, the *Nelson Gazette* run by Councillor Andrew Smith JP, railed against the difficulties being faced by the Guardians:

Each week their respective Relief Committee spends hours in considering the cases that come before them: but the ink is scarcely dry on the order sheets they fill in, before the orders are crossed out, and others filled in by paid officials of the County, without any consultation and without any reason given to the Guardians for the action.

Selina Cooper and others recognised that their chances of shifting the Public Assistance Committee were remote. It remained dominated by county councillors with no experience of industrial depression. There therefore remained only one avenue open to them: they must talk to Arthur Greenwood himself. After all, he was not only the MP of the key constituency involved, but also in charge of the key ministry, Health. Selina and the other Labour activists placed considerable faith in Greenwood, and agreed that a deputation should interview him when he was next in the constituency.[15]

Greenwood was a sufficiently astute politician to combine being a popular constituency MP with being an able Whitehall administrator. He and his wife Kate kept in close touch with the Coopers and were, for instance, anxious about Selina's well-being when she broke her arm. Now at the Ministry of Health, Greenwood had managed to steer through a Housing Act which speeded up slum clearance, had plans to improve pensions, and was also developing far-sighted ideas for a national health service, (like Selina, he was extremely anxious about the high levels of maternal mortality and the inadequate health care offered to pregnant and nursing mothers). Greenwood was also concerned about the unemployment levels devastating industrial areas like his own constituency. However, the Labour Government was already under attack from left-wing ILP MPs and others for not doing enough to help the unemployed. Indeed, when Arthur Greenwood came up to address a meeting in the Nelson Weavers' Institute towards the end of 1930, he was fiercely barracked by a small communist group which distributed leaflets entitled 'Greenwood's Humbug'. It accused him of being more reactionary than even Neville Chamberlain and of using workers' starvation as a strike-breaking weapon. Greenwood put up a good defence, explaining that he was 'not a Mussolini' who could 'suddenly sweep an Act of Parliament off the Statute Book'. The law was the law until it was altered, and he could not take precipitate action without jeopardising his proposed legislation on pensions and housing – which he had no intention of doing. After eighteen months at the Ministry of Health, Greenwood had become a likely target for attack from both left and right within his constituency.[16]

When Arthur Greenwood met the Guardians' deputation shortly before Christmas 1930, unemployment had reached two-and-a-half million. In such desperate circumstances, Greenwood was naturally sympathetic to the Guardians' complaints that they had been reduced to mere automatons. He saw that they had been treated shabbily by Preston, and also that the relief some old people were forced to live on was hardly adequate. His feelings of support were communicated from his Ministry to a rather resentful Public Assistance Committee at Preston which grumpily dispatched a special inspector to visit controversial cases in the Burnley area. Greenwood could do little more: the law was the law. Power had been invested in the county councils, and Lancashire – unlike Burnley or Nelson – was still dominated by Tory and Liberal councillors.[17]

Three months later, in spring 1931, a five-act play was staged in Nelson. The playwright was Selina Cooper's fellow Guardian, Willie John Throup, and it was provocatively called *Poverty and Power*. It portrayed all the problems that Selina faced week in week out on the Nelson Relief Committee, problems which even Arthur Greenwood seemed unable to solve. Dramatizing the small-print rulings of the Lancashire Public Assistance Committee was no easy task, and Throup's prose is sometimes leaden. However, many local Guardians and officials sat among the audience in the Weavers' Institute at the crowded first night, and Selina Cooper could hardly have remained unmoved during the performance. *Poverty and Power* included a scene in the Relief Office when an old-age pensioner's relief was being challenged. One callous Guardian asked him, 'Have you nothing put by for a rainy day?' The old man replied, 'Ah hed, but it's bin rainin' for years.' Another applicant was the wife of an unemployed weaver. Her humiliation in front of the officials must have particularly touched Selina:

Relieving Officer: What does your husband do? What's his occupation?

Woman: He's a weaver, but he can't get a job anywhere. He can't get four looms, never mind talking about eight.

Relieving Officer: That's nothing to do with me. Don't you work? You look young enough. Can't you get charring? What income will you have this week?

Woman: 29s this week for the five of us . . . My rent is 14s
   weekly . . .
Relieving Officer: We have nothing to do with the rent. It's
   income we count, not rent. You'll have to get through. Try and
   get some work – make an effort.[18]

Selina Cooper's perception of the Depression was not merely
from her official position. Every time she went out to a Guardians'
meeting she left behind at home an ailing man. Robert's chances
of ever finding work had long since faded, Selina had only been
able to avoid the humiliation of the poor weaver's wife in *Poverty
and Power* because of Mary's small wage from the Town Hall.

Robert had become very sick. None of the diets had helped
him; his incurable illness was cutting him off from his wife and
daughter, as well as his old friends. However, even in the early
1930s he still managed to keep up one or two of his old political
activities, notably on the committee of the Nelson Co-operative
Society. (Although almost no record of Robert's cheerless life
after the war survived among the Cooper papers, one rare exception was his treasurer's account book he kept for the various
departments – plumbing and dairy, boot and shoe – of the local
Co-op.) His name seldom appeared in the newspaper in the way
his wife's regularly did; however, one rare and significant exception occurred when Robert entered into furious correspondence
with a diehard socialist of the extreme left in loyal defence of
Arthur Greenwood. Robert leapt to defend Greenwood with
vigorous quotations from Marx and Edward Carpenter.[19] He also
remained a keen newspaper reader to the end of his days. Otherwise his last few years were lonely ones. Mary remembered how
he would set out on his own to walk miles around the Pendle
countryside. By now he was living almost entirely on a milk diet;
even so, what little food he did eat would be regularly vomited up
again. Often he would be sick after the family had gone to bed,
and have to spend the rest of the night awake downstairs on his
own. Mary recalls her father becoming 'quarrelsome' as he
fought his hopeless battle against the cancerous disease. Robert's
resentment about his illness seems to have been echoed by his
wife and daughter. 'I used to get vexed with him, because he used
to keep eating, and it'd come back,' Mary openly admitted.

Certainly one of John Coombe's sons described Robert's last few years as unhappy ones for the Cooper family. 'Aunt Selina . . . was a big bustling woman,' her nephew stated, and added frankly that regarding her husband,

> she used to be disgusted with him. By the time he died, I were back home [in Burnley] and I think I were doing nowt [ie unemployed]. And I used to go out every night. They used to pay me to go out and sit up i'bed – sit up with him . . . Aye, he'd be jaundiced. . . . Were yellow, and they couldn't bide looking at him. Used to pay me . . . Aye, were yellow. Yellow. Proper yellow like a Chinese.[20]

To many, Selina's behaviour must have appeared callous. Robert, ill and unemployed, was seemingly shunned by both his wife and daughter. He was indeed the classic victim of Nelson's short-lived industrial revolution, a revolution – it was now becoming clear – that was to last less than the span of a man's life.

While Robert's life was drawing to a close, and while Selina and the other Labour Guardians were busy putting up a fight against Preston's high-handedness, Ramsay MacDonald's Government was growing increasingly precarious. Labour Ministers like Arthur Greenwood now needed all the support they could possibly muster. For Britain's second Labour Government did not have much longer to live. It was unable to survive the historic crisis of 1931.

CHAPTER TWENTY

A BENCH SWARMING WITH MANUFACTURERS:
1931-2

1931 was the year when so many of Selina Cooper's dreams turned to ashes, when the political heroes she had revered since her youth toppled from their pedestals and crashed to the ground.

The year began badly with unemployment rising above 2,600,000. Few places were worse hit than the Lancashire cotton towns; here the proportion of unemployed had risen from one worker in eight to one in three. The whole region was rapidly becoming derelict. Nelson might not be as badly hit as cotton towns like Oldham and Blackburn, but even here there were no jobs to be had. One Nelson weaver, in recounting his story, paints a vivid picture of what thousands of other mill workers were then experiencing:

> There was mass unemployment throughout all Lancashire, and finding work – it was an impossibility. In fact, on one occasion, coming back from Valley Mills [in Nelson] – you'd know nothing about it and then weavers would start telling each other, 'They've just put a notice up.' And you'd go to mill door and look and see. 'This mill will close down on Friday night for three weeks owing to depression in trade.' So of course you've got to go and sign on then for three weeks. But there were other – happen ten or twelve mills that had all done the same thing, and they were all signing on at the same time.
>
> Well, it were no good like going for work anyway. But I was one of them, so I thought I will find something. And I got a lift with a lorry driver from Nelson to Colne – and Colne is two miles further on than Nelson . . .

Well, I got off this [lorry]. And every door of every mill, and joiner's shop, and engineer's shop – any door that was open – they all had on 'No Admittance – No Vacancies – No Hands Wanted', and all this. And I went walking in them anyway. I had two slices of bread in my pocket [which] I had taken for my breakfast if I had got work . . . And I walked from Colne – in all these openings. I couldn't get a job at all . . .

You just had to wait your three week. Now, when your three week were up, mill'd start again. That's when they'd emptied half their warehouse of cloth, and you could start [work again]. Well, as soon as the warehouse started filling up again, they'd put up a notice again – 'This mill will close for so and so'. . . .

This particular young man decided to give up the struggle and join the metropolitan police force – hardly a choice open to older people with families – however long-term their unemployment. 'Well, the metropolitan police was in London,' this weaver admitted, 'and London was that far away; to us it were a foreign country.' So most people remained in the Nelson area, searching for jobs and signing on as 'available for work'.[1]

'Red Nelson' was already well known as a rebellious cotton town which refused to accept the attack on cotton workers' standard of living. One Nelson weaver explained how local Tory businessmen 'said they'd been to London and been insulted by various officials there: "Do you come from that place up north called Little Moscow?" You see, these things get around.' The Labour mayors who ruled Nelson throughout the 1930s made sure the town's radical traditions were maintained. The socialist Richard Winterbottom, who followed Andrew Smith as mayor, caused consternation in local patriotic circles by refusing to perform the opening ceremony on Empire Day if nationalistic music was played. 'There must be no National Anthem,' he declared. 'But,' the worried bandsmen asked, 'what about *Rule, Britannia* or *God Bless the Prince of Wales?*' 'Cut them out as well,' the Mayor instructed. The band, which had been practising *Land of Hope and Glory* specially for the occasion had without warning to switch to playing jazz instead. A few months later, the Nelson Parks Committee even imposed a ban on military bands in local parks.

However, the reason for Nelson's growing notoriety was not just its municipal socialism, but also its industrial militancy. During 1931 and 1932 the fight against the 'more looms' system raged angrily, sometimes growing violent. Socialist 'agitators' were hauled up before the magistrates and Selina Cooper now found herself – the only working-class woman on the bench – in the middle of an epic political battle.[2]

It happened this way. Some employers, seeing what stiff foreign competition they were up against, saw a way of cutting labour costs and so reducing the price of finished cloth without much extra investment or costly new machinery. They would rearrange their weaving sheds so that each weaver would be required to mind *more* looms than in the past, even though this meant the number of weaving jobs available would be cut. The Communist Party, keen to prove its capacity to lead the workers' struggle, decided to focus on the 'more looms' issue of north-east Lancashire. The secretary of a Burnley unemployed workers' organisation was among those involved in the fight, and she gave her interpretation of why the 'more looms' system had to be opposed:

> We, the Communists, had resolved to intensify our agitation. We were encouraged in this by the actions of the cotton employers themselves, who had resolved on the introduction of the eight-loom system in the weaving – a piece of the most crude and vicious speeding-up. A Lancashire weaver normally operates four looms, quite sufficient for any woman on the particular type of machine usual in the Lancashire weaving-sheds. The idea was to provide the woman with a young assistant, raise her wage, which was then on average about 34s per week, to 56s, and double the amount of looms she operated. This increased her pay packet by 22s, but out of this she had to pay her assistant and of course endure tremendous additional labour. Meanwhile the number of four-loom weavers would be reduced by precisely half, and unemployment automatically increased.
>
> As unemployed cotton workers, it was to our disadvantage to see the unemployment figures rising, and we resolved, by no means merely because the Party instructed us to, but because we were absolutely and sincerely determined, to beat down this iniquitous attack.[3]

Selina Cooper watched this conflict unfold at the beginning of 1931. Opposition to the 'more looms' system grew. The Nelson Weavers held a mass meeting in a local cinema, pledging its every last penny to fight this new system. However, it was Burnley that now became the main industrial battlefield, because there 'more loom' experiments were continuing, despite trade union opposition. As a result of this Burnley dispute, the employers chose to lock out over 100,000 weavers around Lancashire in January 1931.

Would the locked-out weavers be entitled to out-relief? During the 1928 lock-out, when Neville Chamberlain had been Minister of Health, relief had only been offered on loan. Would Arthur Greenwood and the Labour Government be more generous? At the beginning of February, the Communist Party organised a small group of weavers to march to Preston to find out. The Clerk to the Lancashire County Council, sensing an impending crisis, drafted a hasty telegram to Greenwood:

DIRECTED BY LANCASHIRE PUBLIC ASSISTANCE COMMITTEE TO REQUEST RULING WHETHER PERSONS THROUGHOUT COUNTY AREA WHO ARE LOCKED OUT FROM EMPLOYMENT IN COTTON INDUSTRY MUST BE REGARDED AS INVOLVED IN TRADE DISPUTE, AND POOR LAW RELIEF ILLEGAL.

Whether or not the existing case law here was clear, Greenwood must have been certain of two things. Firstly that, as a Labour Minister, he should not on principle help the employers by starving the weavers into submission. Secondly, if he ruled as Neville Chamberlain had ruled, he would neither be permitted back into his own constituency in one piece, nor would he be able to keep his seat in the next election. The Nelson Weavers, after all, virtually ran the Labour Party and the Labour Party ran the town, and Arthur Greenwood was on good terms with these trade unionists. Greenwood therefore let Preston know that weavers who had been locked out of their mills due to 'some extraneous dispute' *were* eligible to claim relief. The punctilious Clerk to the County Council was taken aback; he wrote to the Minister requesting clarification. Greenwood replied that, despite the ambiguities, he did mean what he said. The Clerk, vexed at this unexpected turn of events, read out the Minister's new instructions at the next Public Assistance Committee meeting and – reluctantly – notified local Guardians' Committees of the new directive. Selina Cooper, giving a talk on 'Guardians Old and New' to one of the local Guilds the following week, must have relished telling the story of how Nelson had got the better of stuffy Preston – thanks to the intervention of the Labour Government and their local MP. When the employers decided to call off the lock-out after only four weeks, the weavers had Arthur Greenwood's interpretation of the relief rules to thank.[4]

During the spring more trouble erupted in Barrowford. Communist pickets were arrested at the mill which was running the maverick eight-loom experiment without the agreement of the Nelson Weavers. They put in a noisy appearance at the magistrates' court. When the mill threatened to introduce a two-shift system to lengthen the working day, the Nelson Weavers' patience finally snapped. Cotton workers, whose families had been used to working a single daytime shift for over five generations, were highly suspicious of this threat to their traditional way of life.

War was declared on this employer and his knobstick mill. There was a march down to Barrowford with protesters banging a drum and shouting 'Down with the Blacklegs' (strike-breakers) and 'Down with the Double Shift'. The Nelson and Barrowford local Councils met the employer and tried to dissuade him from his provocative action – but to no avail. (At this point a Communist group wanted to call out all local weavers on strike, but the Nelson Weavers refused to sanction this.)[5]

Tension grew. Dan Carradice, ILP trade unionist, asked the constituency Labour Party to condemn 'the . . . ineffective policy of the Government' on unemployment, declaring that 'no policy is acceptable to us that does not aim at a rapid improvement in working class conditions', and this the Party passed. Only ten days later, on 11 May 1931, the conflict exploded dramatically. The Nelson Weavers had organised another march, from the Weavers' Institute down to Barrowford. The intention was to 'visit' the homes of non-unionist weavers who were black-legging at this mill. It was to be a peaceful demonstration, and Selina Cooper was among the crowd of over two thousand outside the Institute. 'Follow your leader and keep your hands in your pockets,' commanded the Weavers' secretary, Carey Hargreaves, seeing the police numbers grow, and fearful of violence.

A jazz band with banners proclaiming 'Blacklegs are a public nuisance' and 'Blacklegs are cheap today' emerged from the Institute ready to head the procession. But at that moment the police intervened. Their numbers were increasing every minute and included the ominous presence of mounted policemen. They bundled the band back inside the building where, as might be expected, the musicians played their instruments loudly through the windows. Outside the Institute, Selina Cooper watched the swelling crowd – mainly women and children – cheer and boo. Pandemonium mounted.

Carey Hargreaves and other Weavers' officials somehow managed to escape the mêlée, though they were closely followed by police. The enormous crowd was already hemmed in by a police cordon formed by men drafted in from other parts of Lancashire. It seemed they were determined to stop the march. The mood of the crowd grew ugly. Pendle Street beside the Institute was being repaired at the time; soon loose stones were flying through the air. The police superintendent ordered his mounted police to charge. 'Horsemen rushed from street to street to cope with the surging mob,' testified one witness. Nelson had known nothing like it.[6] Mary Cooper certainly remembered the terrifying story her mother painted of 'the battle of Pendle Street' when she finally arrived home:

> There'd been riots . . . they brought the mounted police. And my mother was out in the crowd, and they were running – they were running, the women and the men, to the wall – running them with the horses right up against the wall . . .

Another eye-witness, a weaver in his twenties, confirms this picture of police brutality:

> We were stood outside the Weavers' [Institute] . . . There'd be a regular gang of us and they wouldn't let us in . . . Well, Cleal [the police superintendent] shouted 'Charge!' and down they came – mounted police – the lot of them – and started belting these lads. They were repairing Pendle Street at the time . . . The air was black with these stones flying over – that the mob – myself included, was throwing at the coppers . . .
> Anyhow this battle started, and so we scattered because you can't do much against a horse and a fellow swinging a baton . . . You scram. Well, what happened was . . . they wouldn't let the

lads out that were inside the Weavers' Institute. And consequently our ranks were somewhat, shall I say, disorganised. . . .

So it ended in farce – except two of them got arrested . . . Rammy [Ramsden Butterfield] walked round corner, and another lad holding this banner, 'Down with the More Looms System'. And he – believe me, he'd just – copper come [and] grabbed him, and grabbed another lad, and the others scattered . . .

Anyhow, they arrested him, so we marched on. Well, it was getting into an unruly mob. We left the Weavers' Institute, walked along . . . to outside the Police Station and shouted – shouted out, you know, 'Release Rammy'. Just all that kind of nonsense. And I think it was Alderman Winterbottom that was mayor then. He came out and asked us to go home. So we did do . . .

My sister ran home. She said, 'Our Henry's fighting police down there!' Well, we weren't fighting police. So when I got home – eleven o'clock – my mother says, 'Where's thou been?' I says, 'Oh, with lads, like.' 'Hast thou been causing some bother?' 'No, no, no, we haven't been causing any bother.' So she says, 'Thou doesn't go up yonder no more.' . . .[7]

In fact, the incident was far from over. 'Nelson Mob Stone Police', blared the headlines in the *Northern Daily Telegraph* the next day. 'Baton Charges on Eight-Loom Demonstrators. Wild Street Scenes'. The Town Council meeting, also the following day, heard fierce criticism of the Lancashire police. 'I was there the whole time and, in my opinion, the police were deliberately provocative,' one councillor protested. 'I saw a youngster batoned to the ground, and I saw the mad rush made by the police . . .' 'Police Invasion of Nelson', headlined the *Telegraph* afterwards. 'Attack in Town Council'. The Council determined to investigate the allegation that the Lancashire police had used brutal 'Prussian' methods to keep order. The Nelson Weavers' committee called an emergency meeting the same day to organise a protest demonstration through the town.[8]

All eyes in Nelson now turned to what would happen to the man arrested during the 'battle of Pendle Street'. The following morning, Wednesday 13 May, Selina Cooper was called to the police court in Nelson for the first hearing of what was to become a bitterly protracted case. The public gallery in the court was crowded. Mayor Winterbottom, who presided over the bench, Selina Cooper, and six other magistrates filed in. The eight JPs heard how twenty-five-year-old Ramsden Butterfield, an ex-weaver now working as a property repairer, was charged with assaulting three police constables and wilfully damaging the uniforms of two of them outside the Weavers' Institute. Butterfield asked for a week's adjournment so that at least he could talk to a solicitor and call witnesses; he protested that he had never had anything to do with the police before and was innocent of the proper court procedures. Selina Cooper and the other magistrates agreed to his request and the hearing was postponed for a week. The Nelson Weavers committee held another emergency meeting: a strongly worded protest about police activities was sent to the Home Secretary (J.R. Clynes, himself an ex-cotton worker) with a copy to Greenwood; and a solicitor to defend Butterfield was engaged.

The next evening, Thursday 14 May, a huge demonstration of three thousand people marched through the town to the recreation ground (where the Women's Peace Crusade had held their demonstration during the war) in protest against the Barrowford 'more looms' mill. The impressive procession was led by none other than the Mayor, with Willie John Throup, other Labour councillors, and prominent local people – including, of course, Selina Cooper, magistrate, member of the Guardians' Committee and of Nelson Education Committee. She boldly walked in front of a banner proclaiming 'Unemployed Can't Get 4 Looms – What About Eight Looms?'

Figures such as Selina Cooper JP or Mayor Winterbottom could hardly be dubbed irresponsible agitators. Yet the conservative *Nelson Leader* looked very disapprovingly on the Mayor, councillors and magistrates making so public their attitude to the 'more looms' dispute. 'In view of the police court proceeding this week,' it commented cryptically, 'in connection with an incident arising out of the eight loom dispute, this photograph of prominent Labour leaders who headed the procession in the recent demonstration is of special interest.'

By the time the march reached the recreation ground the crowd had swollen phenomenally. No fewer than 20,000 people had taken to the streets in protest. As Nelson's population was only 38,000, this meant that well over half the town had turned out after work. The meeting was bigger even than the Women's

Peace Crusade meeting (though without, of course, any of its undertow of violence). Everyone present voted to support the Nelson Weavers wholeheartedly in their fight against the 'more looms' system, and to condemn roundly the provocative behaviour of the county police. Nelson had been known for some time as 'Little Moscow', one councillor commented, but he intended to rechristen it 'Little Aldershot' instead. He added that local capitalists, seeing a Labour Town Council where capitalism was gradually breaking down, were merely clutching desperately at straws.

Ramsden Butterfield duly reappeared in the police court on Wednesday 27 May. By now speculation and rumour were rife. Police accusations against Butterfield had come to symbolise the right of a radical town to settle its own disputes without outside interference. The public gallery was again filled to overflowing and among the anxious spectators sat the Nelson Weavers' secretary, Carey Hargreaves. His union committee was now deeply involved in the case and had requested Butterfield's solicitor to ask for a further adjournment.

The magistrates filed into the court. This time the bench had been enlarged to include no fewer than nine JPs – the Mayor, Selina Cooper and seven others. The prosecution lawyer, acting for the police, began by warning the bench that since the case arose from an industrial conflict, any magistrate who had an interest in the dispute should retire. The Nelson Weavers' lawyer immediately disputed this, pointing out that the ruling only referred to JPs' financial interests – and indeed none of the magistrates did retire. But it was already perfectly clear to Selina Cooper that it was to be no ordinary trial. It was a momentous contest of strength between the numerically-strong Nelson labour movement and the legally-powerful Lancashire County Council. It was a battle between law and order, and the right of working people to resist oppression in the only way open to them.

Selina Cooper sat and listened to the prosecution describe how Ramsden Butterfield had come out of the Weavers' Institute carrying a banner. A police constable had asked him to take it down because it was causing an obstruction; the prisoner had then struck him over the right eye with his fist; a scuffle ensued, other policemen had come to assist, and the crowd had gathered round.

However, the Weavers' defence lawyer managed to undermine the prosecution's case by showing that the police witnesses who claimed to recognise the prisoner did not know one of the most striking things about Butterfield: that he was a cripple. It would have been impossible for the prisoner to have torn the police tunics, the lawyer said and added that the police had obviously arrested the wrong man. The prosecution then questioned Ramsden Butterfield closely about his politics, hoping to find him guilty by linking his name to the Communist Party. Had he read the *Daily Worker* that week? Was it true that he was a member of a communist group? The prisoner flatly denied all these allegations, and two witnesses – including a young Labour councillor – testified to his not being the man with the banner, and therefore to his being wrongly arrested by the police.

Selina Cooper and the other magistrates then retired from the court, and remained outside for an unusually long time. We shall never know what Selina said during these deliberations, but we can imagine she was forthright in insisting that it was a clear case of mistaken identity, and that the police had arrested an innocent disabled bystander. When the JPs eventually filed back into the court, it became clear why it had taken them so long. The nine of them remained divided and, the Mayor admitted to the court, were unable to return a verdict. Mayor Winterbottom, Selina Cooper and the two Labour aldermen must have argued the case for acquitting Butterfield, while the three Tories (one of whom was the son of Nelson's biggest manufacturer, the recently-knighted Sir Amos Nelson) and a prominent Liberal must have proposed that he be found guilty. The ninth magistrate, caught unenviably in the middle of the epic struggle between Labour and Capital, presumably declined to use his casting vote.

The defence lawyer was naturally furious that his hapless young client was being treated as a political football, tossed between the forces of left and right. Despite the stalemate, he tried to persuade the court that the prisoner had the right to be discharged. But this was not to be. The Mayor announced that the case would be reheard and the court would be adjourned for a further fourteen days.[9]

Ramsden Butterfield had to appear for a third time in the police court, this time on Thursday 4 June. Once again Mayor Winterbottom presided over a court crowded with spectators. Selina Cooper was still a member of the ten-strong bench, as was one Labour alderman, plus two additional Labour JPs (including William Rickard). The five conservative magistrates were all new to the case, and included a Liberal cotton manufacturer and an old-school barrister-turned-doctor, Doctor Jackson, who had also been a Nelson mayor at the turn of the century. Indeed, the bench now included not only the present mayor, but also no fewer than five former mayors of Nelson – an indication of the gravity this historic case had now assumed.

Once again the prosecuting lawyer stood up and requested any magistrate with an interest in the matter to withdraw. 'Is this all necessary?' queried Mayor Winterbottom testily. 'It is an advocate's privilege', chipped in Dr Jackson. 'Personally,' the Mayor replied, 'I do object to all these statements.' But the prosecuting lawyer was not going to give up so easily. He noticed, he said, that at least one magistrate was a member of the Nelson Town Council which already had made its feelings plain on the issue. The defence lawyer jumped up to object: his client was neither a councillor nor a Weavers' official, and all the bench was being asked to do was to decide whether his client was or was not guilty of the charges before them. Amidst this hubbub and confusion, the Magistrates' Clerk began solemnly quoting from the small print of his legal manual as to whether any of the JPs should retire. The Mayor grew impatient and interrupted him; turning to Selina Cooper and the others he asked if any of them did want to retire. Needless to say, none responded, and so in this rather tetchy atmosphere the case continued, Labour having effectively won the first round.

Police witnesses summoned from elsewhere in Lancashire were cross-questioned. The defence again claimed mistaken identity. Magistrates began to question the witnesses. Selina, trying to get to the bottom of this difficult matter, asked a constable from Rossendale precisely what had happened when the scuffle broke out, and was told that the police were trying to take the banner away from the prisoner when the alleged assault occurred. Again the prosecution tried to 'smear' the prisoner with the label of communism. Butterfield did admit that he had been involved in organising a food kitchen for the unemployed, but that as soon as

he realised a communist grouping was behind it he had withdrawn. Again the young socialist councillor stoutly maintained
that the prisoner was not the man who struck the policeman, and
claimed that the real culprit's name 'is on the tongue of everybody in the town' – but he would not name him.

Selina Cooper and the nine other magistrates once again withdrew to consider the case. This time they remained out of the
court for a full three-quarters of an hour, and it must have been an
anxious time for Selina. Yet when they returned to the court little
had apparently changed:

> The Mayor: I have to tell the Court that the justices have consid-
> ered the case presented to them and they have not been able to
> arrive at a decision. They are equally divided – five in favour of
> acquitting the prisoner and five in favour of pronouncing him
> guilty. There will have to be a re-hearing.
> Defending lawyer: I still press on this occasion for the prisoner to
> be given the benefit of the doubt. Surely there must be some doubt
> in the minds of some of you. The prisoner has already been tried
> twice.
> Magistrates' Clerk: I am bound by the rules and there will have
> to be a re-hearing.

By now Nelson was in uproar. Nationally, unemployment had
risen above 2,700,000 and threatened to go still higher. In Nelson
alone there were over nine hundred families forced to go to the
Guardians for out-relief; the 'more looms' situation threatened to
increase local unemployment still further. The Labour Government seemed to be unable to do much about it. Ramsden Butterfield's court case acted as a tinder box to local feeling. Protest
against the Barrowford 'more looms' mill continued, and the
increasingly desperate Nelson Weavers even considered a strike of
all local weavers on the issue. The *Nelson Leader* muttered darkly
about the town being plunged again into 'disastrous turmoil'.
Then, worse still, feeling was inflamed by further police proceedings taken out against some of the Nelson Weavers' officials after
the 'battle of Pendle Street'.[10]

On Wednesday 17 June the fourth hearing of the Ramsden
Butterfield case took place. The bench, which had swollen from
the original eight to nine and then ten magistrates, now comprised

no fewer than fourteen JPs. The sight of such a packed bench reminded the court of the seriousness of the decision to be reached. Mayor Winterbottom was still there and so was Selina Cooper, together with Andrew Smith and another Labour magistrate and one connected with the Co-operative Society. However the conservative presence on the bench seemed to have grown more weighty. Dr Jackson was still there, along with at least three Liberal aldermen, and a sprinkling of Conservative mill-owners.[11]

This was exactly the kind of bench Selina Cooper feared, for she was always suspicious that on such controversial cases the bench would be packed with anti-Labour JPs. Mary recalled how her mother used to describe the way this happened:

> Whenever there was anything – say, a manufacturer missing putting his [insurance] stamps . . . all the manufacturers would turn up . . . There was a rota . . . and they always kept it [so] that there was only one Labour person on this rota. They always made it like that. That was done by the high-ups. But, if there was a case against a manufacturer, [insurance] stamps or anything, it was swarm – the Bench was swarm[ing] with manufacturers – which were legally allowed to come to back their own.

In such unfavourable circumstances, with the bench seemingly weighted by the 'high-ups' against Butterfield, the case reopened. The evidence was rehearsed again, for and against the case of mistaken identity. Butterfield once more protested his innocence. The Clerk of the Court appealed that the man whose name 'was on everybody's tongue in Nelson' should step forward 'to protect an innocent man who is in peril of his liberty'. But for one reason or another no one in the court was prepared to point the finger of guilt.

The bench retired once again to deliberate, and we can sense that this time Selina Cooper, Richard Winterbottom and the other Labour JPs found themselves in a minority against those keen to uphold 'law and order', and who probably opposed the 'more looms' demonstration in the first place. Certainly when they returned to the court Mayor Winterbottom announced that Ramsden Butterfield had been found guilty of all charges brought against him. Yet his sentence – doubtless to avoid stirring up resentment among the 20,000 supporters by creating a martyr – was very light. Butterfield was bound over to keep the peace for six months for the sum of £10; he also had to pay legal costs of 20s, and 11s to cover the cost of damage to the policemen's uniforms.[12]

The case, which had dragged on for over a month, was at last over. A man whom Selina Cooper, Richard Winterbottom and other Labour people believed to be innocent had been found guilty – albeit with a light sentence. Selina's suspicions about how the bench had been 'swarming with manufacturers' at the crucial hearing grew. However she had hardly time to reflect upon the questionable justice of the decision before she found herself at the centre of a second court case of more serious dimensions.

On Saturday 20 June, only three days after the final Butterfield hearing, the case against the local trade unionists came up at the Nelson police court. The men were accused of contravening the 1927 Trades Disputes Act; they had 'visited' the houses of non-union 'blackleg' weavers in Barrowford on the evening of the 'battle of Pendle Street', and so were accused of 'watching and besetting' (i.e., unlawful intimidation). The accused were none other than Carey Hargreaves along with the Nelson Weavers' President, three committee members and a Labour alderman who was secretary of another local union. The remaining two were members of the Nelson Communist Party – Seth Sagar and Elliot Ratcliffe.

Selina Cooper, who had been hearing more routine cases in the court earlier that morning, expected this controversial case to come up and so waited on the bench to observe what took place. In the tense atmosphere, the magistrates filed into the court. Then a rather unusual thing happened: Mayor Winterbottom announced that the JPs had already privately discussed the matter of who should constitute the bench and had unanimously agreed amongst themselves that this case should be heard before just four magistrates. These were two Liberal JPs, elderly Dr Jackson, and – presumably by way of balance – a middle-of-the-road Labour JP of the older generation. Mayor Winterbottom was himself excluded from the list of names, as was Selina Cooper. Then the Mayor, presumably hoping to keep the hearing low-key and with a sinking feeling about how the case would now unfold, left the central chairman's seat on the magistrates' bench and stepped down into the well of the court.

Selina Cooper, however, was less susceptible to establishment pressure. She was incensed that local trade unionists should not be represented by at least one JP sympathetic to the industrial struggle they were engaged in, and so she refused to move. Defying court protocol, she remained sitting on the bench where she had heard cases that morning. Although she did not adjudicate, she did, complained the police afterwards, make 'remarks on the Bench which were audible to persons in Court'.

The Weavers' defence lawyer, who had already acted for Ramsden Butterfield, began by explaining to the court that six of the accused pleaded guilty to 'watching and besetting'. Only Sagar and Ratcliffe pleaded not guilty. Then the prosecution lawyer (again the same man as before) painted for the court an emotive picture of the terrified elderly relatives and young children in the homes of the 'blacklegs' visited by the weavers on that particular evening. The defence lawyer then begged the bench to deal leniently with his six clients since, he said, they had already admitted their guilt and were merely reflecting popular local fears about the spread of the 'more looms' system. 'They admit a breach of the law; their best advocates are their character,' he added. This time there was no long and agonising wait as the magistrates fought it out among themselves. Dr Jackson, now acting as presiding magistrate, seemed to have no difficulty in promptly announcing the JPs' decision. He merely explained that the bench had agreed that the six men would be bound over to keep the peace for twelve months for the sum of £20, plus very moderate costs; and he added that he was pleased that the hearing had ended so satisfactorily. 'We did not want to have a long trial with acrimony,' he stated.

Seth Sagar, a long-standing member of the Nelson Weavers' committee and a founder-member of the Nelson Communist Party, and Elliot Ratcliffe were more noisy and defiant. To the consternation of the Magistrates' Clerk, Sagar began by declaiming his political beliefs:

> Sagar: I want to make it clear to the Court and the workers present that this is a political case . . . We have not broken the law in the eyes of 90,000 workers in Lancashire.
> Clerk: . . . Have you broken the law as it stands?
> Sagar: As it stands under capitalism, yes. I claim my freedom of

this court to state my case. . . .

  Dr Jackson: We don't want a political speech here; will you sit down?

At this, the court adjourned for two days till Monday.[13]

Selina Cooper had the weekend to work out what her strategy should now be. She could not just meekly allow the four magistrates to conduct the case without making any public comment. She must put up at least some symbolic resistance. Possibly Seth Sagar or someone else involved in the case came round to her house to discuss precisely what should be done. (The Coopers did not yet have a telephone, and Selina once or twice got into trouble for this sort of thing.) Certainly Selina would know Seth Sagar reasonably well. Like her, he had been a half-timer in a local cotton mill and had been active in the SDF. In addition, Selina may well have begun to share a little of Seth Sagar's impatience with the way Ramsay MacDonald's Labour Government was handling unemployment. Only the previous week Margaret Bondfield as Minister of Labour had introduced a government plan – an Anomalies Bill – to cut spending on unemployment insurance by making it harder for married women and other groups to claim benefit. Selina Cooper of course knew Margaret Bondfield from the rowdy Women's Peace Crusade demonstration; even so, callous attacks on married women workers hardly endeared MacDonald's Government to the cotton workers of Lancashire. Selina might recoil from the harsh attacks of Communists like Seth Sagar on Arthur Greenwood and the Labour Party (accused of being 'the third capitalist party' and no better than the Tories or Liberals); she certainly had no intention of joining their tiny Communist branch and leaving the Labour mainstream. But she recognised that some of the Communists' taunts were fair. Over key issues like unemployment, the handful of Communists showed more energy and commitment than many Labour and trade union leaders. Seth Sagar, for instance, was local organiser of the communist-inspired National Unemployed Workers' Movement.

  Such thoughts strengthened Selina Cooper's determination to challenge the court's handling of this particular case. On Monday 22 June she walked up St Mary's Street once more and along to the court. The same four magistrates were again on the bench, and again Selina refused to obey court rules and to sit in the public gallery. She defiantly took her seat on the magistrates' bench – though apart from the four other JPs.

The case opened with Seth Sagar's objecting to Dr Jackson as presiding magistrate 'on the grounds of political bias against the working class'. 'I am not connected with any political party,' protested Dr Jackson – and Sagar eventually was forced to drop his objection. The prosecuting lawyer, acting on instructions from the Chief Constable of Lancashire, then began *his* attack. He brought to the court's attention the fact that Selina was still sitting on the bench. 'I have to perform an unpleasant duty,' he proclaimed.

> I must take objection to the constitution of the bench, and raise objection to a lady member. I am prepared to state my objection in specific terms.

Selina must have been expecting some such complaint. 'I am not taking part in the adjudication of the case,' she answered. Her reply took the wind out of the lawyer's sails. 'I do not mind Mrs Cooper staying on the Bench as a listener only,' he had to concede lamely, 'although the statute states she should not sit on the Bench.'

From her watchful position high in the court Selina therefore observed the rest of the hearing. The lawyer described the fear that Sagar and Ratcliffe allegedly aroused in the streets of Barrowford. They had, he claimed, shouted 'Come out, you knobsticks,' and encouraged the crowd to start booing and singing 'The Red Flag'. It was alleged that the father of a resident had become so agitated he had collapsed.

Sagar and Ratcliffe then conducted their own defence, questioning police witnesses closely. 'Do you consider it an offence to sing "The Red Flag"?' they demanded of a Chief Inspector. He had to admit he did not. 'Are you aware that the eight loom system will throw 35 per cent more weavers out of work in Lancashire?' they continued. The Clerk intervened. 'That is like asking the sergeant major what he thinks about the war,' he suggested sardonically. The court laughed, and Sagar continued his attack:

The Labour Government, the police force, and this court has been
on trial before the workers of Nelson. You have definitely proved
to be guilty of being enemies of the working class. No matter what
the court decides, we shall continue to fight.

Eventually the magistrates retired, leaving Selina Cooper alone
on the bench. When they returned Dr Jackson reported – predictably – that all four of them found the defendants guilty. If the
two men were willing, he said, the bench was prepared to treat
them in the same way the six defendants were treated on Saturday. Were they willing to be bound over to keep the peace for
twelve months? Sagar and Ratcliffe both said they were not. Dr
Jackson said that they would therefore be fined £5 including costs
or be sent to prison for a month. 'Will you give us a month to
pay?' demanded Sagar. 'No! You have had the whip hand long
enough, and it's time somebody else had,' replied Dr Jackson
querulously.

Seth Sagar, whose mill had recently closed down, was currently
working as a council labourer. Ratcliffe still had his small
weaver's wage. Still, in 1931, £5 was a heavy fine. Selina Cooper
was enraged at the injustice of it all. As the hearing drew to a
close, she summoned up her courage to enquire of the prosecuting
lawyer what his objection had been to her sitting on the bench that
day:

> Lawyer: I have withdrawn my objection, and it will not serve
>   any useful purpose to give any explanation.
> Selina Cooper: I want your objection in writing.
> Lawyer: Very well, if you wish it, I will give it you in writing.[14]

But she remained far from satisfied by this small concessionary
crumb tossed in her direction. She was indignant that working
people, already bearing the brunt of the Depression, should be
treated in this high-handed way. Mary Cooper remembered quite
clearly Selina's action on her way out of the court:

> There'd been riots . . . they brought the mounted police . . . and
> my mother protested, you see. So when they came up at
> court – the rioters came up at court – they objected to my mother
> sitting. And so she said – we have a local paper called the *Evening
> Star* . . . and she said, 'Well, I'll have to obey the magistrates'
> order, but I'm stopping here to give a statement to the Press, when

it's all finished.' And there was a great big heading . . . that Mrs Cooper objected, because all the manufacturers sat there. But my mother'd been [in the court]; they'd objected to her sitting.

Selina did not stop there. Three days later she drafted a letter of formal protest to the Chief Constable of Lancashire, asking him to cite his reasons for objecting to her sitting on the bench during the recent hearings. The Chief Constable's lengthy reply, which has only recently come to light among a forgotten bundle of other Cooper papers, illustrates the kind of establishment pressure socialist magistrates were likely to come under during such industrial conflicts. He had before him the press photograph of Selina among the leaders of the Weavers' procession and, he said, she had made 'audible' remarks in the court from the bench. 'In view of the forgoing facts,' he added testily, 'I think the reason must be obvious why I considered it my duty to take exception to your adjudicating in these cases.'[15]

Selina Cooper seems to have been the only Labour JP prepared to speak out in defence of the two Communists, even though she risked confrontation with the police authorities. Yet she was by no means the only Labour Party member to feel growing dissatisfaction with the way Ramsay MacDonald's Government was compromising on its policies. Already the local Labour Party had condemned 'all understandings and agreements with the Liberal Party' which could entail 'a surrender of our Socialist Policies'. It also condemned the 'ineffective policy of the Government' on unemployment, demanding a 'living income', family allowances, and weekly pensions of £1 for those over sixty.[16]

The Labour Government, struggling through the summer of 1931, was having to set its sights well below family allowances and pensions for all. It merely hoped to survive. The violent industrial strife in north-east Lancashire may not have been paralleled elsewhere in the country, but the government's time was running out. On both left and right disillusionment with Labour's ability to govern grew. Unemployment was heading for three million. Gloomy reports were produced, showing that wages and unemployment payments must both be cut. The Bank of England conferred anxiously with MacDonald. ILP criticism of the government loudened, especially over unemployment. After all, the ILP had some years earlier produced its own policy statement, *A Living Wage*, which had argued for positive measures like family allowances. The Nelson ILP was still influential (though Selina Cooper herself had now withdrawn from it, preferring to put her energies into the Labour Party and the immediate political battles) and, for instance, organised a local rally at which Fenner Brockway spoke, attacking Margaret Bondfield and the government over the Anomalies Bill.[17]

By August the financial crisis had deepened. Rumours flew around of Cabinet splits and a possible National Government. Ministers like Arthur Greenwood remained anxious to avoid cuts in unemployment payments that would beat down working people still further and betray the party's traditional supporters. At a crucial Cabinet meeting at the end of August, Greenwood therefore sided with those ministers opposing further cuts, but found himself up against leaders like MacDonald, Snowden and Bondfield. There was complete deadlock. The only way out was for the government to resign. MacDonald went to see the King. Yet the next day the Cabinet learned, not that MacDonald had resigned, but that he had offered to lead a new National – and largely Conservative – Government. Snowden went with him, but was joined by no more than a handful of other Labour MPs. Even Margaret Bondfield refused to join the new government. Arthur Greenwood certainly would not desert the Labour Party in such an opportunistic way, and so had to watch his Ministry of Health being scooped back again by Neville Chamberlain.

Socialists in the Labour Party could hardly believe their ears. 'Years later,' one history of the period suggests, 'ageing Labour supporters were still saying, "I remember the time when Ramsay MacDonald went over", as though nothing that had ever happened since had made an equal impression.' It is certainly impossible to underestimate the emotional impact MacDonald's treachery had upon grass-roots supporters like Selina Cooper. She had entertained such high hopes of the 1923 and 1929 General Elections. August 1931 represented one of the lowest moments of her life. Mary remembered her mother, a woman who normally kept her feelings under tight rein, being mortally wounded when she heard the news:

> She got very sad. I could hear my mother crying in bed at

night – if she'd been to a meeting and that sort of thing. You see,
in a way, Philip Snowden and MacDonald took place of a God in
those days. And when they tumbled, my mother used – just used
to come back to 59 St Mary's Street and start all over again.[18]

Only someone of Selina's formidable resilience could keep
going during the unsettled days of autumn 1931. Philip Snowden,
now in the new National Government, introduced proposals to
cut unemployment payments and teachers' salaries. Meanwhile
in Burnley picketing against the 'more looms' system continued;
three members of the Communist Party (a woman called Rose
Smith and a couple, Bessie and Harold Dickinson) were arrested
for 'watching and besetting' and each given three months in
prison. Arthur Greenwood came up to speak in his constituency;
he was, to the great delight of local anti-Labour papers, loudly
heckled by the far left who shouted 'Judas' and accused him of
colluding with Margaret Bondfield's Anomalies legislation.

A General Election was arranged for 27 October. The constituency Labour Party called a hasty meeting to adopt its candidate.
There was no doubt in anyone's mind whom they wanted. Greenwood was duly proposed by Carey Hargreaves, and seconded by
Selina Cooper, Andrew Smith, Dan Carradice and others. They
all threw themselves into energetic support of Greenwood,
fending off both barbs from the left and Conservative smears
about 'Bolshevism run mad' from the right. Selina and the candidate addressed a special women's meeting in the Weavers' Institute on how 'Labour's policy means better times for the woman
with the basket'.

The overall election results for Labour could not have been
more disastrous. Labour seats were slashed from nearly three
hundred to about fifty. All the women Labour MPs lost. National
Government candidates – mainly Conservatives – swept to
victory. In Nelson and Colne Greenwood lost his seat to a Conservative. The Coopers found themselves without a Labour
representative in Parliament for the first time for nearly thirty
years. Arthur Greenwood, Selina Cooper, Willie John Throup
and other dispirited Labour supporters trailed off to the Weavers'
Institute once the results were known, but they were so down-
hearted the gathering became more like a wake than a post-
election meeting.

The events of autumn 1931 numbed Selina Cooper, and the election set the pattern for the rest of the decade, with Labour largely on the defensive and socialism seldom more than a small minority voice. Labour's humiliation was so complete that, despite unemployment and the threat of fascism during the 1930s, it was not till the very end of her lifetime, in 1945, that Selina was able to celebrate another Labour government.[19]

MacDonald's betrayal and Labour's débâcle were hard to bear, but the full brunt of the Depression was still to hit working-class families like the Coopers. Part of the National Government's cuts were, of course, cuts in unemployment payments. From now on, unemployed people who had been out of work for more than twenty-six weeks had to apply for a special payment which was 'means tested' by the Public Assistance Committee and the local Guardians. The Means Test meant that all money coming into an unemployed person's household had to be taken into account when payment was calculated. If a son or a daughter in a family was earning, for instance, then the amount of benefit an unemployed person was entitled to would be duly knocked down. Workers who had never previously dreamt of going to the Guardians now found that long-term unemployment gave the Poor Law authorities the right to pry into every modest corner of the family economy. Families became split up, with sons and daughters moving into lodgings to ensure that their parents were not financially disadvantaged.

Mary Cooper came under some pressure to leave home too; after all, she was thirty-one and could support herself, while her parents, now in their sixties, applied for out-relief. One busybody, whom Mary and Selina knew only by sight, even came round to the house, explaining that she took in lodgers and wondering whether Mary had thought of going into lodgings. The Coopers apparently sent her packing. The result, Mary recalled, had repercussions for her infirm father:

> because I was at home, he couldn't get any outdoor relief. You had to leave home. Heaps of families were broken up. They couldn't get outdoor relief unless you went to live somewhere [else]. Well, I stopped [at home]. And although I hadn't a big wage I *was* there, you see.

Indeed during these hard times, Mary and her wage from the Council's rate office were the lynchpin of the Cooper household. Selina was always bustling off to court, the Guardians' Committee, and the Labour Party Executive or the Education Committee meetings; but she never forgot that it was Mary's monthly wage that kept the St Mary's Street household together:

> I only got paid every five weeks sometimes – with five-week months, you see. And she'd say – you'd come home [from work] – and she was a good cook – and she'd say, 'You're having your dinner out of the dishcloth today.' Boiled dishcloth! Because it was five – it was an extra week. And she used to have her calendar marked – my mother – when I was paid.[20]

Selina Cooper, wife of a long-term unemployed weaver, knew only too well what it felt like to be on the receiving end of this new assault on working people's standard of living. At the same time, as a member of the Burnley Guardians' Committee, she was also dragged into administering the hated Means Test.

The Burnley Guardians had already protested that locked-out weavers should be eligible for relief, and that applicants should have high rents taken into account. Now it objected to the ruling from the Public Assistance Committee at Preston requiring *all* household income to be taken into account when calculating relief. By early 1932, with unemployment just under three million, the number of long-term jobless who had to apply for the special payment, and therefore were subject to the humiliating Means Test, had risen beyond 900,000. The Public Assistance Committee in Lancashire, dominated still by rural county councillors, was notoriously stingy. Applications from one in three of the long-term unemployed in Lancashire were disallowed altogether under the Means Test. The Burnley Guardians, especially those in Nelson, were up in arms, and were soon joined by those in other hard-hit Lancashire towns such as Bolton and Leigh, near Wigan.[21]

In spring 1932 the Nelson Weavers debated a motion put by Seth Sagar that it should take strike action for the immediate abolition of the Means Test. Not enough votes were mustered for the motion, but at least it reflected the angry mood of the time. Selina Cooper found herself involved in a daily tussle to sort out the Means Test problems of friends and neighbours. She grew bitter about insensitive officials and bureaucrats who drafted such baffling regulations; they were not only attacking working-class standards of living, but also further undermining time-honoured local democracy. There were, she proclaimed at a Guardians' meeting,

> all sorts of diplomatic ways for defeating the workers, and person-
> ally, I think [the Means Test] is one. This is the way the
> machiavellians work . . . They come week after week with new
> regulations . . . and the [Guardians'] committees do not know
> what they mean.

By the summer the Guardians from Nelson were, like many others from Labour strongholds, in trouble with the Public Assistance authorities. After the general election the previous year, Nelson could no longer turn to either a sympathetic MP or a minister. Yet Nelson's voice of protest remained loud and clear. Matters came to a dramatic head around August 1932.

Nelson's Relief Committee refused to administer the Means Test any more. They objected to the way that Preston's definition of 'family income' meant that every adult under one roof counted as 'family'; but Preston kept on countermanding their decisions. Therefore the Nelson Relief Committee, seeing no alternative, dissolved itself. 'I have decided to cease of function,' Alderman Andrew Smith informed the Burnley Guardians.[22] And Nelson was by no means a lone voice. Protest against the Means Test continued to pour into Preston during 1932 from the Lancashire and Cheshire Miners' Federation, the United Textile Factory Workers' Association (the political arm of the cotton unions), local Guardians, and from the Town Clerks of Salford, Darwen, Leigh and many other Lancashire towns.

At the same time, the industrial situation in Burnley grew increasingly bitter as protracted opposition to 'more looms' exploded into a massive strike. About 3,000 people led by Communists marched from Burnley towards Nelson, but were stopped from crossing into the town by a cordon of constables and mounted police. The dispute soon exploded into a countywide strike with about 150,000 Lancashire weavers out. Those who thought mass unemployment had cowed industrial workers' determination were proved wrong. In Nelson, for instance, all mills closed and no fewer than 16,000 cotton workers went out on strike, three-quarters of them weavers. There was mass picketing of mills, with extra foot and mounted police drafted in to protect the blacklegs.

The problem facing Selina Cooper during this massive industrial conflict was, once again, whether the strikers would be eligible for relief. The Public Assistance Committee seemed to take a hard line, and bitterness grew concerning strikers who, because they were not in a union, were not eligible for strike pay and so were reduced to virtual destitution. 'We are not going to have it said,' thundered Willie John Throup, 'that this strike is either won or lost on the bellies of little children.' In protest against such an inhumane regime, Nelson Labour Party organised a demonstration led by the mayor, Selina Cooper and others, to march down to the recreation ground from the Weavers' Institute. With them went their banners: 'This is a Grand National Government', '1914–18 heroes – 1932 zeroes' and 'Down with the Means Test'. There, on the recreation ground once again, Selina addressed the crowd. She congratulated the workers of Lancashire on 'the magnificent display of determination and solidarity', and demanded 'the abolition of the Means Test, believing it to be . . . deliberately designed by the National Government to crush the workers into complete subjection'. This proposal was – needless to say – carried unanimously.

The Lancashire strike ended – largely in the employers' favour, with 'more looms' being allowed to be run under certain conditions. However, opposition to the Means Test continued. Nelson Town Council pressed the government for its abolition, and Selina Cooper and Willie John Throup took part in a local hunger march to Preston to lobby the Public Assistance Committee there. Selina probably walked no further than Burnley (she was after all sixty-eight, and had put on a considerable amount of weight). Yet she was proud to march under an enormously defiant banner announcing 'Lancashire Hunger Marchers: Nelson and Colne: More Looms Means More Means Test: Down with the Means Test'.[23]

The National Unemployed Workers' Movement organised hunger marches down to London. But despite all this pressure – both from Nelson and other hard-hit areas – it was not till 1934 that cuts in benefit rate began to be restored. At the same time, the long-term jobless, who since 1931 had been 'means tested' by the Public Assistance Committee and Guardians, were now transferred to a new centralised, independent body. It was called the Unemployed Assistance Board and was safely removed from any direct pressure by locally-elected councillors or MPs. Henceforth Selina Cooper, as a member of a Guardians' Committee, was kept out of the political hurly-burly of unemployment relief. She could return to her earlier quiet, though equally crucial, concerns: the sick, the aged, orphans who needed to be boarded out, and the inhabitants of the Burnley workhouse.

1931 was one of the most difficult years of Selina Cooper's life. During that year she saw her local magistrates' bench seemingly packed against working people guilty of no more than trying to protect their threatened standards of living; MacDonald and Snowden betrayed the labour movement they had helped to build; and the Guardians' Committee on which Selina sat was required to administer the degrading household Means Test to people who, through no fault of their own, were long-term unemployed. Then the general election replaced Labour with a right-wing National Government. 1932 was little better. The government seemed deaf to the appeals rising up from the near-derelict industrial regions.

In all this, Selina was in an unusually strong position for warding off attacks on working people. She might not have been selected as a parliamentary candidate, nor elected to the Council, but she was a borough magistrate, and on the constituency Labour Party Executive and Burnley Guardians' Committee. Few others in the town could speak with her authority: certainly no other woman could.

Yet Selina Cooper never distanced herself from the people who lived alongside her, whose livelihoods she tried so hard to defend. 'They'd come here, always come here, for wanting things doing,' Mary Cooper explained. 'They'd say to my mother, ''We go to other magistrates; they keep us in the lobby, or ask us to keep out in the rain.'' No wonder they worshipped her.'

Indeed, if there was a protest to be made at the local court, a meeting to be addressed, or a hunger march to be supported, Selina Cooper could always be relied on to be there. In 'Red Nelson' during the years of great industrial strife 1928–33, so many of those who sat on the magistrates' bench, ran the Council or wore the Mayor's heavy chain of office, were prepared to use every method that lay within the law to protect their own class whose living standards had become subject to such savage attack. Selina Cooper, according to the chief constable, was one of those whose protest only just kept within the rule of law.

'WHY CHAMPION MONEY-MAKING WIVES?':
1931-1933

By 1933, unemployment, though decreasing, was still about two-and-a-half million; and the rights of women – especially married women – to paid employment were coming under attack from all directions. The slump fuelled criticisms of married women who worked outside the home, but it did not create it. Those roots stretched right back to the nineteenth century.

Many a Victorian trade union leader believed, in the words of one of them, that it was men's duty to ensure their wives were kept 'in their proper sphere at home, instead of being dragged into competition for livelihood against the great and strong men of the world'. Similarly socialists at the turn of the century dreamt of a better world where married men would earn a family wage big enough to keep their wives out of the factories and sweatshops.

Selina Cooper never subscribed to the belief that socialism meant all married women being cooped up at home, endlessly cooking and cleaning, washing and ironing. During the 1900s she had given talks to local Women's Co-operative Guilds on 'Why women should be wage-earners'. Later, when men returned home from the war and reclaimed their jobs, and when the military casualties left over one million 'surplus' spinsters and widows, the attack on married women's work became formidable. The slump of the early 1920s greatly increased pressure on jobs and offered a further reason to encourage women to stay at home. Married women teachers, civil servants and local government employees found life particularly difficult.

The National Union of Societies for Equal Citizenship (NUSEC) eventually gathered support for its Married Women

(Employment) Bill in the mid-1920s. This aimed to prevent public authorities from sacking a woman merely because she was married. Though the bill had little chance of success, Selina Cooper was among its keenest supporters. 'It was such a pleasure to have you with us again,' wrote Eva Hubback, NUSEC's Parliamentary Secretary in 1926. 'You must have realised how real your welcome was . . . The Mass Meeting was a great success.'

Selina's public championing of married women's right to work provoked predictable fury. One irate person scrawled her an anonymous postcard (addressed merely to 'Mrs Cooper Magistrate Nelson'), congratulating her with savage irony 'on your advocacy of "wages for wives" . . . How delightful!'[1] Certainly Selina was only too aware of how deeply-rooted was the belief that women were not *really* waged workers in the same way that men were. Even in a town like Nelson, whose economy depended almost entirely on cotton weaving and where married women weavers were commonplace, men were seen to have an indisputably stronger claim to a job than women. And married men had by far the strongest claim, married women the weakest. In 1931 there were nearly 7,500 women weavers in the town, but under 5,500 men. Yet these 7,500 women remained almost as silent and invisible as when Selina had been a member of the Burnley Weavers thirty years earlier. Not one single woman sat on the Nelson Weavers' committee until 1930: it remained tightly controlled by men, especially married men. Nor was there a single woman councillor elected till 1931, despite the town's tradition of women's suffrage activity. Women, it was felt, were too preoccupied with family problems to give their mind to such serious tasks: that was the job of married men with the responsibility of earning a 'family wage' to keep their wife and children.

The Depression of the 1930s only made women workers more vulnerable: the desperate scramble for jobs further divided working people, men against women. The experience of one of Mary Cooper's friends – as girls they went to the Socialist Sunday School together – illustrates this point only too well. Jane MacCall's father was Secretary of the Nelson Clothlookers' Association, and she had been a weaver till her mill closed down in late 1929. In 1930 Jane had got on the Weavers' Committee, its first ever woman member:[2]

The only woman on the committee with eleven men. Oh, boy! It was a battle, was that. We'd some tough 'uns. We'd a few on that committee that had been on a long time . . .

On one occasion they were having to consider cutting down on the subscriptions. It was when – 1930 – and we were losing a lot of members who just couldn't afford to pay one penny a week, let alone anything else. And so we . . . agreed that something would have to be done about it – we couldn't lose members like that . . .

Then at the end of the discussion . . . the Secretary [Carey Hargreaves] said, 'Well, I'd like somebody to come and work in the office and go through all the books and pick up the scope of this job. Find out how many there are in this state.' And so they agreed to this. 'Oh, yes, leave it to the Secretary's discretion to appoint one of the committee to do this.'

And I was sat down at the bottom of the table, quite uncon-scious. You could hear the silence that fell, but [Carey] hadn't said anything to me. Anyhow when they were going out . . . he just whispered to me, 'I want you to come in in the morning.' 'Ee,' I said, 'they'll blow place up if I come in.' 'Never mind,' he said, 'It's the Secretary's discretion you're talking about.' I said, 'All right.'

Well, I got home and . . . told my father. I said, 'I don't know whether I dare go or not . . . They'll have my hair if I go in there like that. Last on that committee – and getting that job.' Because you got a wage with it, you see. He said, 'Look, Carey's asked you to go . . . he'll look after you.'

So I went next morning – got behind the counter in the general office. We hadn't opened the door hardly before one came in, looked at me, stood there – ever so long. Then one by one . . . all these fellows on this committee kept coming in. And they didn't say anything because I was standing there. But they were talking to the other men in the office . . .

And I worked there for the rest of the day, and when I got to the meeting that night . . . the chairman stood up. 'Well, Mr Secre-tary, I have to make a statement before this meeting begins. Yes,' he said, 'this matter of assistance in the office,' he said. 'We see there is a young woman with no responsibilities there in that office. And there's all of us have been on this committee all this time, done . . . similar jobs before – all left out.' Oh, they were very hurt . . .

And Carey was saying to me, 'Keep quiet,' so I did. I just sat there. So when they'd all finished, Carey Hargreaves . . . stood up and he said, 'Now, gentlemen, you're questioning my discretion

. . . That's what you're questioning isn't it?' 'Oh, no, we aren't.' He says, 'Oh, yes, you are . . .'

'Now,' he said, 'I saw there a young woman who's worked in her father's office, a similar office. She's helped me here . . .' He said, 'I know she'll get through this work quicker than any of you would,' he says. 'In fact, she's done as much today as any of you would have done in a week . . .' He said, 'I'm saving the union money. That's what the object of this thing is.'

Well, they couldn't say a word back. Had to put up with it after that. It didn't make me any friends though.[3]

Earlier it was described how the post-war women's movement – the Women's Freedom League, the newer Open Door Council and other groups – had grown too divided amongst themselves to effectively challenge such discrimination against women workers in industrial towns. NUSEC, having shed many of its earlier links with the trade union movement, now became savagely split down the middle over the thorny problem of protective legislation for industrial women workers. In 1927 the half of its executive which supported complete legal equality for women resigned in protest against the 'special needs' arguments of Eleanor Rathbone and others. Henceforth, the main 'equalitarian' pressure against protective legislation came from outside NUSEC, from the Open Door Council and a similar organisation, Lady Rhondda's Six Point Group.

Selina Cooper, isolated from such squabbling, was still unsure what all the fuss was about. Of course women had special needs; and for that reason she had fought hard, though not yet successfully, for family endowment and access to birth-control information. Equally, she believed that laws which hindered women workers from being treated exactly the same as men must be opposed. However some other women in Nelson were more ambivalent about protective legislation. Jane McCall was one. She remembers her reservations about opposing such legislation when in 1929 she was invited (through Selina Cooper who took a great interest in Jane's activities) to join a deputation to Labour's Home Secretary, the ex-mill worker J.R. Clynes:

Mrs Cooper sent for me one day. She says, 'There's a deputation going to see the Home Secretary' – who was then J.R. Clynes . . . And she said that it's the Open Door Council; and she told me all about it; they were what had been suffragettes, and they were now pressing for further advantages in equality as far as laws and whatnot were concerned in industry. And she said, 'They want a woman who works in industry to go and speak with them.' She said, 'Now, the chairman of this deputation is Lady Rhondda' . . .

And so I said I'd go. I studied for a day or two, because I don't agree with all they stand for. They were against having restricted measures against women and young persons lifting heavy weights and doing night work and so on. I said, 'I can't shout about that, Mrs Cooper.' I said, 'I don't think they should [do heavy work]; and anyhow,' I said, 'there are other things as well in it.' So she said, 'Well, you'll be expected to speak.'

So I went home. I discussed it with my dad, and he said, 'Well, I don't agree with all they stand for, but there's some points that I do. Stress the points that you do stand for.'

So I went. I went with a most stinking cold. Oh, I could hardly breathe . . . We went to the deputation at the Home Office . . . And when I'd said what I wanted to say I apologised for my awful voice, because I could hardly croak. I said, 'This, as Mr Clynes will understand, is the result of steaming in cotton mills. Working in steam and going out into the cold.' And he nodded his head, oh very emphatically. He knew what that meant . . .

And I came home again. Well, a few weeks after that, our mill had closed down and I was unemployed . . .[4]

Women's groups remained split over such crucial issues. Unemployment was throwing out of work women who might otherwise have raised their voices about, say, protective legislation in industry. (Jane McCall, for one, had to leave the weaving industry: she was luckily able to go to Ruskin College in Oxford, and later became a district nurse.) Worse still, by the late twenties suffragists and suffragettes seemed to have become some faded relic of history. Younger women, even feminists, took great delight in praising particular women as 'barely a voter, hardly over thirty'; they were urged to fight shy of so much the older generation of pioneers had represented – and still demanded. When Mrs Pankhurst died in 1928 her obituary in the *Manchester Guardian* mirrored this feeling that women's *real* battles had been fought and won long ago. The paper suggested that, however mistaken her tactics, Mrs Pankhurst had at least lived to 'see an economic and social freedom for women which is still the subject of a few croaks and complaints but is not seriously challenged'.[5]

It was in such a mood of demoralisation that the assault on the rights of women workers was mounted. The cotton industry was surely an ideal battleground. It was an old industry where thousands of jobs were being shed as foreign competition bit into Lancashire's traditional markets. It was an industry where, not only did women workers outnumber men two to one, but where generally men's wages were notoriously low. A four-loom man weaver still earned under 40s, only about 2s 6d more than his female equivalent. Such men might be only too glad to comb out the women weavers who 'dragged down' their wages. And cotton manufacturers were ready poised to expand the 'more looms' experiments whereby fewer weavers worked a greater number of looms. In addition there were no other jobs available for men locally: it was weaving or nothing.

In such a situation, with the families of unemployed male weavers having to scrape a meagre existence on the dole, how sensible that it should be only married men who were given the new plum jobs. Such men could mind six or eight looms apiece and earn up to 56s or more a week, enough to keep his wife and children on. Women, and especially married women, could therefore be encouraged to leave the weaving shed and return to their homes. Caring for their families was, after all, a more natural and healthy occupation for women than working in the damp and noisy weaving sheds.

In this way women's traditional weaving jobs came under concerted attack. Women might try to protest by, for example, citing their centuries-old tradition of weaving, but sadly they were not well placed to resist, being represented neither on the Weavers' committee nor on the Council. The minute book of the Nelson Weavers' Committee for this crucial period is noticeably silent on the fact that its women members were threatened with losing their jobs. The union, the minutes confirm, was run *by* men *for* men. Any opposition to the replacement of women weavers would obviously have to originate from the broader labour movement outside the formal trade union structure. In such a situation, Selina Cooper was to play an important role.[6]

Valley Mills was by far the largest factory in the town, and its progressive owner, Sir Amos Nelson JP, one of the most influential men. Seeing which way the wind was blowing, Sir Amos was keen to reach an amicable agreement with the Weavers' Association about the introduction of 'more looms'. He was also keen not to ruffle any trade union feathers unnecessarily: for instance, he based his plans on one shift per day rather than the hated double shift. Similarly he assured the Secretary of the Northern Counties' Amalgamated Weavers' Association that 'no heads of families would be stopped'. The sacking of women weavers was not even referred to. Sir Amos just placated any anxieties by mentioning that winding – preparing the spun thread for the weavers, just as Selina had done years before – 'would, I am sure, absorb all the young female weavers'. The older married women (about one in three of women weavers) did not even merit a mention.

During spring 1931 Sir Amos worked out the details of his new scheme; just as Ramsden Butterfield was coming up before the magistrates following the 'battle of Pendle Street', he canvassed local approval for his plans through the *Nelson Leader* letters columns:

> Sir, . . . my suggestion has been to get eight looms to a weaver, and we have proved that it can be done quite easily without any more work for the weaver. As far as women weavers are concerned, it would be very much easier, because all pieces [rolls of woven material] would be taken away [by ancillary workers], and weft carried to the weavers. We have about 37 per cent married women at our mills. We should fix the wages at such that a man could afford to keep his wife at home, and in the cases of married women working who had husbands working, these would be stopped first . . .
>
> If we dispensed with the 37 per cent married women, and taking into account the fact that we should require extra men and women for cleaning, oiling, carrying pieces and winding, we should be at least twelve to eighteen months before we threw anyone out of work with the exception of the married women. This is a solution if the Weavers' Association would agree to it . . . Yours, etc
> AMOS NELSON[7]

How did the weavers in the local union respond to Sir Amos' brainwave? It seems from the Nelson Weavers' minute book that the married women who were immediately to lose their jobs put up no opposition. They already worked an exhausting 'double shift': a long day at the mill followed by an evening of putting the children to bed and housework. They were the least well placed of all the Weavers' members to attend meetings to voice their protest. In addition, the social pressures *against* married women 'taking jobs' from unemployed men was now sufficiently formidable to discourage them from undertaking the daunting battle of defending their jobs.

In this way Sir Amos Nelson was able to reach an agreement with the union by July 1931. The only opposition to his ideas came from the local Communist Party, never more than a tiny minority among the weavers.

However, implementing the plan to give priority to married men was not as simple as it sounded. The union wanted the new 'more looms' jobs given to 'family men' who were union members; the mill manager was more concerned to employ the best weavers available irrespective of whether they were union members or a head-of-a-household. Conflict therefore immediately arose when an unmarried man in his early twenties was offered a job at Valley Mills running eight looms. His tale reveals the weighty influence of married men in the union:

> They brought me up into the top office and said, 'We've got permission to try on . . . eight looms . . . We are going to give you a chance of proving it's possible to run eight looms' . . .
>
> So I set to – and, well, at home . . . my mother . . . [had] rheumatic fever . . . My dad was still . . . on two or three looms, and I had one young brother came on ten years younger than me . . .
>
> For running these eight looms they paid £3. 3s. 0d. a week . . . Now, this £3 that I were fetching home to give my – oh, it made my mother feel like a millionaire . . . So, within one or two weeks my mother had been able to buy, happen, a sheet for their bed and a sheet for our bed, me and our Tom . . .
>
> But after three and a half weeks, there was some of these married men that were stood with two loom at Valley Mills. They found out that I were running them. I were making a success . . . They went down to union, and they said, 'We had this clause, and it's in the clause – that married men are the first to be put on eight looms. And this fellow you put on is only a single lad . . .'
>
> Anyhow, general manager fetched me up, and he said that

about a dozen of the married men had been down to the union
. . . and he said, 'They sent word to union that you're to come
off.' I said, 'But I can't afford to come off.' I said, 'There's my
mother and youngest brother and myself and my father and he's
only got two loom,' I said.

So I went to the Nelson Weavers' union, and in front of committee and Secretary, and discussed this problem. And . . . they
said, 'Now then, if you're not off by weekend, we'll stop the mill.
We'll bring all weavers out.'

So the general manager brought me up – by the way, there's
close on three thousand looms at Valley Mills – and he told me he
was very sorry, and they would try and make it up to me. But they
couldn't afford to have the mill stopped.

And so the young man signed on as unemployed until he eventually got back to running his set of four looms again.

By giving preference to one particular group, the 'more looms'
agreement between Sir Amos and the trade union discriminated
against other weavers whose wages were equally needed to support dependants at home, though they were not married men.[8]
Equally, the agreement ignored women's long experience of running looms: their nimble fingers were now casually sacrificed to
the neat theory of the 'family wage'. But theory and practice
refused to fit, and this produced an insuperable difficulty
according to a revealing memoir of Sir Amos written by his son:

> The biggest snag, though, proved to be implementing the under-
> taking that heads of families would be given the first chance of
> retraining onto the eight-loom setts. In practice, it was found that
> it was almost impossible to retrain male weavers over about fifty
> years of age to run this number of looms on the specialist sorts
> [yarns] that were in production and as the only weavers the union
> would allow to go on the scheme were, in practice, men over fifty,
> the experiment got bogged down for a period . . .

These were practical objections to Sir Amos' 'head-of-
household' criteria.[9] There were of course political objections too.
Who would protest about the way women workers – especially
married women workers – were being pushed back into the home
without being consulted? The trades unions and Labour Party
seemed sluggish and uninterested, more concerned about overall
unemployment totals than about the complex question of the

sexual division of labour. So the only group to step forward and
defend women's right to work was the Communist Party.

The Communist Party had decided as part of its new
recruitment campaign to give urgent priority to work among
women workers in troubled industries like cotton. As its Burnley-
based women's organiser, it appointed Rose Smith. Rose was an
energetic young school teacher who had stood as a Communist
candidate in local Nottinghamshire elections in the early 1920s,
then moved up to Burnley as a full-time party organiser, and was
subsequently sentenced to three months' imprisonment during
the noisy 'more looms' picketing in 1931. Another party activist
was Bessie Dickinson, who had also served a three months' sentence. Bessie had left school at twelve to become a weaver, had
recently stood as a party candidate in Blackburn and been sent by
the party on a course at the Lenin school in Moscow. Such local
women tried to alert others to the threat to women's jobs. About
1931 Bessie Dickinson wrote a pamphlet called *Women and the More
Looms System* in which she urged women to recognise that it was
they

> who will very possibly be the ones 'not required' later on, if the
> bosses can only get the more loom system in operation. This is
> actually the case in Earby [near Colne] where all women have
> been stopped and the men are now running the looms. The
> employers are stating that women will be better off at home with
> their husbands working . . . In this way the woman herself is to be
> allowed no say in the matter. She is to become dependent upon her
> husband's wage, and denied the right to work . . .
>
> Fellow women workers, think of it, women are in the majority
> in the union and yet there are very few women on the
> Committee . . .
>
> We women can lead the way . . . Let us working women of
> Lancashire show to the workers throughout the country that we
> are going forward prepared to fight against any worsening of our
> conditions, that we consider that these conditions are already
> intolerable . . .[10]

Selina Cooper could not help admiring the courage of women
like Bessie Dickinson and Rose Smith in the battles between
police and pickets. At the same time she grew increasingly
concerned about what the new weaving system meant for the

traditional women's skills, fearing that it could signal the end of the proud era of equal pay for women in the local weaving mills. There were no obvious channels through which Selina could express her concern. Her husband had long ago ceased to be an active member of the Weavers. She was getting to know local women militants like Bessie, yet had no inclination to join the small Communist Party still so critical of Labour. There seemed little that she could do. Worse still, she could see that married women's right to work was now coming under fierce attack from the Labour Government itself. But Selina Cooper was able to play an active role in opposing at least this particular assault.

In 1929 Margaret Bondfield had become Britain's first woman Cabinet Minister. But if women cotton workers had entertained high hopes of this new Minister of Labour, these were soon bitterly dashed. Margaret Bondfield, trade unionist though she had been, seemed to have grown less radical since the war. Now in office, she tactlessly suggested that young unemployed women mill workers might consider turning to domestic service – or else have their unemployment benefit withdrawn. This naturally provoked a storm of outrage. The Nelson Weavers might not be eager to protect the rights of its women members against those of men; but it was not prepared to see its women members insulted by Whitehall. It dispatched a furious letter to both Ramsay MacDonald and Arthur Greenwood:

> We have particular objection to well-organised trade unionists
> being compelled to enter the ranks of the least organised workers,
> where they have no protection against the conduct of individual
> employers . . . Our women and girls are entitled to live in their
> own homes and not be compelled to live in lodgings in other peo-
> ple's houses . . . Those who want domestic servants should, like
> the members of the working class, do their own domestic work.

Despite such protests, government 'Homecraft Centres' were opened locally and desperate unemployed women mill workers trained there for domestic service jobs. Again, the local Communist Party protested particularly loudly. 'All women are bitterly opposed to this measure which means sending young girls away from home to scrub for the idle rich for a few bob a week,' one of its pamphlets stated.[11]

Worse still, in 1931 Margaret Bondfield introduced – despite opposition from the ILP MPs and others – the Anomalies Bill designed to clear up unemployment insurance regulations. Unfortunately in this tidying process she happened to sweep away the insurance rights of many women. From now on a married woman had to have paid a certain number of contributions *since* marriage or else she could lose her benefit – irrespective of how many contributions she had paid *before* marriage. Such legislation, of course, particularly affected the hard-hit textile workers. Within weeks, fifty married women in Nelson had been disqualified under the Anomalies Act. The Town Council's General Purposes Committee promptly protested to Margaret Bondfield about the hardship she was causing. By the end of the year a total of no fewer than 134,000 married women in Britain had lost their benefit. Members of the local Communist Party were once again forthright in their criticisms, accusing Bondfield of insulting women workers by saying that unemployment benefit 'was not a marriage dowry'. The legislation seemingly reduced the Labour Government's popularity in Lancashire. 'It helps explain why Lancashire speaks through clenched teeth of the "wicked Act", and why Labour Party candidates received such severe defeats in the General Election of 1931,' claimed one socialist writer.[12]

At the time Selina Cooper was heavily involved in fighting the degrading effects of the Depression on the Guardians' Committee, the magistrates' bench and through the Labour Party. However, by the end of 1932 north-east Lancashire, bruised and battered, was beginning to emerge from the devastating industrial warfare of recent years. Selina increasingly had time to weigh up the effects of the Anomalies Act and to calculate how best it might be opposed. She had always firmly believed that in industry no distinction should be made between single and married women workers, and the act unashamedly discriminated against the latter. Shortly before Christmas 1932 when she went to give a talk to the Cambridge Women's Citizens' Association, she therefore made no bones about the act's attack on the rights of married women. In Nelson, she told the Cambridge women, the legislation

has caused a great deal of hardship to married women, because

men's wages are calculated on the basis of [a couple's] joint ability
to keep the home. I am glad to say that in my home town, where
half the weavers are men and half are women, the men have taken
the women's side in trying to secure the money which women have
lost.[13]

Selina Cooper saw that the Communist Party was far more ready
to defend the rights of married women workers than was the
Labour Party, still numbed by MacDonald's betrayal and its
crushing defeat of 1931. In addition, she saw that the political
climate was now changing under the suffocating parliamentary
majority of the National Government.

In 1932 the ILP decided to leave the Labour Party, sickened by
the betrayal of the previous year. It now became a small independent group ranged well to the left of the Labour Party – not unlike
the Communist Party. The Communist Party itself was changing
dramatically too. In Germany, Hitler and the Nazis were fast
gaining strength: one of their first targets was the German Communist Party, conveniently blamed for the burning of the
Reichstag in early 1933.

In Russia Stalin's government realised that such a catastrophe
demanded a new policy: communist parties must form alliances
with other socialists in a desperate bid to stop fascism from
spreading. In Britain therefore, the Communist Party duly shook
off its recent sectarian intolerance whereby it had damned the
Labour Party as no better than the Tories and Liberals. In spring
1933 it approached the Labour Party, TUC and tiny ILP, suggesting a 'united front' against the real enemy at home and the
threat of fascism abroad. The Labour Party, bitter about recent
Communist attacks, was highly suspicious of such overtures. It
responded brusquely with *The Communist Solar System*, a pamphlet
designed to alert unwary Labour Party members to Communists'
use of devious front organisations to mask their real purpose.
Even the left-wing Nelson Labour Party was unenthusiastic. In
May 1933 it received a letter from the 'United Front Committee
on War and Fascism', inviting it to join a 'united demonstration'
on the recreation ground. The offical Labour line was still that
German fascism was not much worse than Soviet totalitarianism.
Nelson's invitation was therefore 'left to lie on the table' – that is,
ignored.[14]

Selina Cooper was one of those on the left of the Labour Party
who were not convinced by the official line. Shaken by Hitler's
rise to power, she saw good reason to welcome united action. Her
friendship with Bessie Dickinson and the fight she had seen Communist women put up against 'more looms' and the Anomalies
Act made her doubt whether the stuffy Labour Party stance was
necessarily the right one. At the same time, the Communist
Party, its narrow anti-Labour and anti-union period at an end,
encouraged its women activists to make contact with sympathetic
women within the broader labour movement. Selina Cooper was
one such obvious person in north-east Lancashire: her
irreproachable, dark-coated figure was known to everyone in the
area. Rose Smith, as leading woman Communist organiser in the
Burnley area, recognised that an approach to Selina Cooper must
be made as soon as possible. On 16 July 1933, she sat down and
wrote Selina a letter:

> Dear Mrs Cooper,
> Although I have not had the pleasure of meeting you I feel that
> we are not entirely strangers to each other, for I have heard so
> much of your pioneer work from my friends. I am very anxious
> that we women, who are concerned with bettering the conditions
> of the workers, shall discuss together what can be done to prevent
> the appalling spread of undernourishment, sickness and misery
> amongst the women of North East Lancashire. [We] would there-
> fore like to talk with you on Monday (17th July) evening. We
> will call upon you about 7pm . . . I know that as an under-
> standing woman you will excuse what otherwise may appear a
> liberty. I trust that this arrangement will not interfere with any of
> your commitments but we will understand if it is impossible for
> you to see us.
>   Yours sincerely,
>   Rose Smith

Selina Cooper can only have received this letter on the Monday
morning. Whether she was able to receive these two impromptu
visitors that evening we will never know. But certainly Rose
Smith's letter signalled the moment when Selina began to work
more closely with militant women in the Communist Party. She
shared their concern with the terrible effects that mass
unemployment and malnutrition had on maternal mortality

figures, and found that Communist groups were far more active here than the Labour Party. Though always careful to sup with a long spoon, she now began to work with Rose Smith, Bessie Dickinson, Seth Sagar and the others.

Exactly a week after she received the letter, Selina Cooper took part in the hunger march to Preston mentioned earlier, to lobby the Public Assistance Committee about the Means Test. She was happy to be photographed alongside Seth Sagar and · Elliot Ratcliffe banging a drum, the two men she had tried to help two years previously. It seems very probable that the hunger march was just the sort of local event Rose Smith and Selina would have discussed when they met, with Rose encouraging Selina to take part.[15]

Similarly, Selina grew increasingly close to Bessie Dickinson and her husband. Mary remembered her mother saying that she would have liked Bessie for her daughter; for Bessie, with her agitating in the local mills and her 'more looms' imprisonment, represented everything that was finest about the local Communists. Mary too shared her mother's growing interest and recalls how they both grew critical of official Labour's lack of rigorous analysis of capitalism. 'Willie John Throup always talked a lot of very sentimental stuff about poor people,' Mary explained. 'It wasn't really sound . . . He's what I call a sentimental socialist.' At the same time, Selina remained on the Labour Party Executive but daringly shared public platforms with women like Rose Smith, despite the official Labour Party line. 'Rose Smith used to come here a lot,' Mary remembered:

> She used to want my mother to speak at things – and my mother always went . . . Oh, [they were] industrial meetings. And anything to do with the weaving industry – they weren't communist meetings. They were always widely – women's things. But my mother always went. And she talked hours to Rose Smith. She used to come here regularly.

With the major confrontations in the cotton industry now over, Selina Cooper had more free time to discuss political problems at length with Rose and Bessie; and she was able to raise her eyes above the problems of north-east Lancashire and renew some of her old links with feminists in other parts of the country. Already her Cambridge speech had deeply impressed the chairman of the Open Door Council, Elizabeth Abbott. At New Year 1933 she sent Selina a long letter marked 'Personal and Confidential':

> Your speech, and the knowledge that lay behind it, is having its reverberations! I have been asked to write to you privately to ask your own thoughts as to the possibility of your standing for Parliament . . . *Suppose* that women's organisations wanted you to stand and offered support, what would your own view be? Would it be a possible thing? Would the local women stand firmly by you? . . . You see the present situation is one of complete immunity from criticism of the Government and its supporters: and the complete ignoring of women's needs and rights by the other side. Would the very threat of an independent woman, who knows the ropes and won't have dust thrown in her eyes, be a good thing?
>
> There's no need for me to add how happy we should be if you were in Parliament. That you know. . . . Only you know the local circumstances well enough to tell us frankly whether we would be doing a wise thing in making further enquiries and in seeking to get you adopted.

The letter was flattering, but the proposal was sadly impracticable. Selina once again had to explain to her feminist sisters that, however inspiring her oratory, she was unlikely to succeed at a selection conference in her own constituency. Sympathisers outside Lancashire always found it difficult to understand why, if so many women worked in the mills, they held so little sway in local textile union and Labour Party politics. However, despite this, Selina kept in close touch with her friends at the Open Door Council.[16]

By the end of 1933 married women's rights needed most urgent defending. The attack now came from all directions. Locally, Sir Amos Nelson was planning to extend his 'more loom' experiment and, again promising that 'heads of families' would be given preference, he managed to win union approval. Further afield, the pace was being set by fascist countries in Europe. Now Chancellor of Germany, Hitler was urging married women to stay at home. Thus when a leading British industrialist wanted to give weight to his plan to turn all women out of his employment and replace them with men, he quoted Hitler as a shining example.

The Open Door Council was aghast at these fascist developments. It had organised an international conference in Prague in the summer; here British delegates heard how an energetic Norwegian press campaign had managed to stop councils discriminating against married women employees. What worked in Norway might possibly work in this country. The Open Door Council, Lady Rhondda's Six Point Group, and over two dozen other similar groups all got to work. The main organiser was an energetic woman called Monica Whately, who had stood twice as a parliamentary Labour candidate and was a firm believer in women's full equality with men.[17]

A public meeting was fixed for London's Central Hall on 14 November. This date was chosen to coincide with the debate in Parliament about new unemployment legislation, and the women hoped the meeting would remind the government to include the hated Anomalies Act in their proposals for reform. During the autumn Monica Whately began to draw up the list of speakers for the Central Hall platform, whose combined prestige was such that even the National Government could not ignore them. Emmeline Pethick-Lawrence, a staunch fighter for the rights of married women, agreed to chair the meeting. Rebecca West the writer agreed to speak, as did Lord Buckmaster, a peer sufficiently sympathetic to women's needs to have moved a birth-control recommendation in the House of Lords in the 1920s. Another valuable addition as a speaker was the new deputy leader of the Labour Party, Major Clement Attlee. This impressive list was topped by Lady Astor MP: she and her Cliveden friends might be sympathetic towards fascism, but she was still the first woman to take her seat in the House of Commons and therefore a valuable ally.[18]

The meeting still needed someone to put the point of view of northern women textile workers. It was their traditional working patterns that were particularly threatened by the Anomalies Act. Monica Whately seems to have learnt from Elizabeth Abbott of the Open Door what an inspiring speaker Selina was. She dispatched to Nelson the invitation to Central Hall. Selina replied she would be delighted to come as a speaker; it would give her an opportunity to put her views publicly. News of this ran through the town, and before long a local reporter was knocking on

Selina's door for an interview. She explained to him about the iniquities of the Anomalies Act and how she was going to try and lobby the National Government so it fully understood the anger people felt on this vexed question. 'Honour for Mrs Cooper,' trumpeted the proud headline over the interview. 'Nelson Citizen and Women's Rights'.

At the beginning of November, Monica Whately sent Selina a copy of the resolution that was to be put to the meeting:

> This Mass Meeting protests against the increasing practice of the Government, local authorities, and private employers, of making celibacy a condition of employment for women, and suggesting that the unemployment problem can be solved by turning married women out of industry. This Meeting demands for the married woman the same rights to engage in paid employment as those of married men and the single woman.

(However Monica Whately had hastily to alter this wording and post Selina an amended version: Lady Astor had objected to the reference to celibacy and to unemployment.) Despite this last minute flurry, the meeting was a tremendous success. With Emmeline Pethick-Lawrence in the chair (whom Selina had last met in 1918 at Women's Peace Crusade meetings), it must have reminded Selina of the earlier suffrage campaigns. In this she was not alone. Another eye witness later wrote that 'the crowds, the [Votes for Women] banners, the enthusiasm, echoed, faintly but unmistakably the spirit of pre-war suffrage meetings'.

Emmeline Pethick-Lawrence made no bones about the threat fascism posed to working women. 'German women, married and unmarried, have been dismissed from their posts and sent back to the home, and told that their one and only function is to exhaust themselves in child-bearing,' she warned the meeting. 'The triumph of such ideas means that we are heading back to the dark ages.' Lady Astor's defence of married women's rights was less incisive; she emphasised home as the natural place for married women – provided she had a comfortable home and a comfortable husband. (However, she did go on to offer criticism of sex discrimination in the existing insurance rulings.) Rebecca West, in her turn, was so moved by the enthusiasm of the crowd that she ended her speech in tears of emotion. The loud clapping resounded round the packed hall. Yet it was Selina Cooper's speech about life in the Lancashire cotton mills which seems especially to have won the hearts of the audience. Pushing away the microphone, confident that her clear voice would reach the furthest listener, Selina excelled herself that evening. Her recent years of intense local activity had not been wasted. 'Married women in the north have always worked side by side with their men in economic equality,' she told her Westminster audience.

And I can speak as a wage-earner for fifty years, and a married wage-earner for twenty years. The married women of the north beg their sisters in the south to help them face the 'new menace' which is threatening our position as women workers, worthy of equal pay for equal work.[19]

Selina Cooper was met with thunderous applause when she finally sat down. Lord Buckmaster then proposed the resolution which was passed overwhelmingly; and Dame Ethel Smyth, suffragette and composer, conducted the singing, despite her growing deafness. 'After the meeting,' Selina recorded in her notebook later, 'Dame Ethel Smythe came and shook hands with me and said I have not been able to hear you but I know you have spoken wonderful[ly] because I have watch[ed] the people's faces.' Dame Ethel was not alone; Selina also jotted down in her notebook how, 'I met Dame Laura Knight the artist she came to me after I made my speach she came to me and said that she would give a great deal if she could impress an audience like I [had] done that evening.' Emmeline Pethick-Lawrence too had been impressed. The next morning she sent a note congratulating Selina on the way her speech 'took the meeting by storm'. Monica Whately wrote as well, thanking Selina for her inspiring contribution.

Not every comment was praise of course. Married women's right to work was far too threatening to escape a backlash. In *John Bull*, popular journalist Hannen Swaffer's 'Open Letter to Lord Buckmaster: Why Champion Money-making wives?' was bitterly sarcastic about Selina's speech. 'Personally, I am in favour of abolishing all female labour in cotton mills,' he pontificated. 'Civilisation is coming to a pretty plight when that sort of female slavery is to be cheered.' He put in a strong plea for all the millions of unemployed men who could not find jobs: *their* claim was far higher than that of their wives.[20]

Despite the meeting, the threat to women's jobs continued. The government did nothing about the Anomalies Act, and women continued to be dismissed from their jobs on marriage. In the years that followed, Selina Cooper found much of her energy was taken up with anti-fascist and anti-war campaigns. Yet she never lost her concern for the rights of women working in the local weaving sheds, and in 1935 wrote an article for an anti-fascist paper in which she lamented how

> the women of Lancashire have suffered so much . . . Their independence which has been their chief asset is in grave danger of crumbling away . . . The introduction of the more looms system . . . has in many cases made the monopoly of men in the weaving trade . . . Because the young girls see no future in the mills, the craft of weaving is bound to leave the women's fingers, who have been the best weavers and done the finest work in the past . . . I see . . . that the girls choose positions where the pay is far from equal with that of the men, and in many cases of a sweated nature. This is a scandal in a county that has always paid equal wages and where the majority of operatives has always been women.

Selina knew she was now fighting a losing battle. Women teachers or civil servants might eventually abolish the marriage bar and win equal pay with men, but women weavers had little hope of preserving their traditional independence and relatively high wages, for so long the envy of other women workers. In that sense the thirties marked an end of an era, the end of the golden age of women weavers. In 1936 Selina contributed her local knowledge to a countrywide survey, *Women Who Work*. Her 'Report On The Life Of Married Women Textile Workers' is a final elegy lamenting this passing of an era and listing the grim problems women mill workers now had to face:

> A great reduction in the rate of pay . . .

> A definite scarcity in the work obtainable, which lessens the independence of the married women.

> The introduction of the six-loom system . . .

> The adoption by some employers of the night-shift system, legally closing the door to women for the night period.

The pressure of the Anomalies Act on the married woman textile worker.

My opionion is that considering all the above points, the married woman's position here in Lancashire is becoming secondary to that of men, in strong contrast to her pre-war independence and complete equality of status . . .

The Lancashire woman is still making ends meet. Her independent spirit makes her fight grimly to do this, but I am afraid that behind the scenes the family is going short of food though presenting a brave front . . . [21]

WOMEN AGAINST WAR AND FASCISM:
1934-1935

By early 1934 Robert Cooper had become critically ill. At Easter he collapsed and was confined to bed. Still keenly interested in politics, he would send Mary out to buy the newspapers. In the middle of May, in his daughter's presence, his frail life finally ebbed away completely. The cancer of his pancreas had proved fatal.

Even in death, husband was overshadowed by wife. 'Lady Magistrate Bereaved', announced one local paper (though its short obituary did note his post office workers' union about forty years earlier and the part he had played in running the local Co-op stores). 'A model rank-and-file member of the Labour Party, doing work in a quiet but efficient manner', summed up another paper politely. To the funeral with Selina and Mary came Robert's brothers and sisters, nephews and nieces, both from Nelson and from Swaledale. Selina's nephew from Burnley who used to sit by Robert's bedside during his last few years of illness came too, and so did her youngest brother Alf. Old suffrage friends attended as well: Margaret Aldersley, now back from Australia, and Mrs Todd who had taught Mary at the Socialist Sunday School. Flowers were sent by the Co-op, by the Labour Party Women's Section, and by Mary's closest friends, Elizabeth Stanworth and her sisters.

It is hard to gauge Selina's feelings on the death of her husband. Some people suggested that she and Mary felt a surge of relief when Robert died; relief that he was released from his lingering illness would certainly have been understandable. But was it only that? It is certainly true that her widowhood scarcely affected Selina. Unlike the tragic moment when she realised that her early labour heroes had 'tumbled', there now seemed little call for tears. The bonds of feeling between Robert and Selina had wasted away over the years: his death merely set the final seal on what had become a bleakly functional marriage.[1]

If Selina felt any lingering remorse, she was soon prevented from dwelling on her recent widowhood by demands made on her from a new direction: the anti-war movement.

Since her early links with the Women's International League for Peace and Freedom, Selina Cooper had continued to be a peace activist. In 1917 Russia had shown how ordinary people could say 'no' to war; and this had inspired her to join the Nelson Council of Action in August 1920 to plan industrial action in protest at war with Russia. Selina also joined the committee of the Nelson branch of the League of Nations, adding her name to the panel of league speakers willing to talk to local groups. The No More War Movement, a pacifist and largely socialist group, naturally thrived in Nelson; again, Selina was among its active members.

Women like Selina worked in the 1920s towards two specific aims: a programme of disarmament whereby the strong nations would give up their weapons of destruction, and an international arbitration system to which warring states could refer disputes and so avoid bloodshed. Both aims were extremely ambitious, and both needed maximum public pressure to be put on the British Government for it to take any notice. To capture the public imagination for these demands, the Women's International League for Peace and Freedom and over two dozen other organisations decided to stage a spectacular national women's pilgrimage in summer 1926. It would be modelled upon the National Union of Women's Suffrage Societies' successful pilgrimage in 1913. Like its predecessor, the Peacemakers' Pilgrimage would invite women from all four corners of the country to walk to London along certain major routes for a big rally in Hyde Park.

Selina Cooper had kept in touch with women like Kate Courtney who were closely involved in the Women's International League, and so became drawn in as one of the local pilgrimage organisers. Her first job was to outline the proposal to the Nelson Women's Section and to explain the pilgrimage motto:

'The road to peace – arbitration, security and disarmament.' She also chaired a rally in the Weavers' Institute with League of Nations speakers as well as two Conscientious Objectors: Dan Carradice and an ILP councillor who was a weaver at Valley Mills, Richard Bland. The message from the rally was clear: the last war had wreaked destruction and achieved nothing – yet war *could* be stopped.

Two weeks later, two Nelson women set off to join the last leg of the pilgrimage in the Midlands. One was the indefatigable Emily Murgatroyd, the weaver who had already walked to London in the suffrage pilgrimage.[2] Yet, as in 1913, few other Nelson women could spare the time to leave their jobs and their families for so long. For them, Selina Cooper arranged a visit down to Manchester for a pilgrimage service in the cathedral to coincide with the first batch of marchers reaching the outskirts of London. Selina and sixteen other Nelson women duly pinned blue and yellow rosettes on to their coats and clambered into a blue and yellow char-a-banc. Before they set off, they posed for a photograph, Selina standing proudly beside their defiant wartime 'Peace Our Hope' banner. After a crowded service in Manchester Cathedral, they marched through the city and joined a 2,500-strong demonstration. 'Law can be substituted for war,' Kate Courtney told the crowd, 'as law has been substituted for duelling.'

At the same time, the two Nelson pilgrims made their way via Oxford (where they posted Selina a letter to let her know how they were doing) and on to London. Then, on 19 June, along with ten thousand other women, they marched to Hyde Park in the brilliant summer sunshine, and listened to the speakers – including Mrs Fawcett and Emmeline Pethick-Lawrence – urging the government to support disarmament and international arbitration. The two Nelson pilgrims returned home; but during the autumn they went round to local groups telling their story of the Women's Peace Pilgrimage.[3]

An ill-fated Disarmament Conference eventually opened in Geneva in 1932. Selina was among those who had worked hard for this, badgering all her St Mary's Street neighbours to sign an 'International Declaration on World Disarmament', organised by the Women's International League for Peace and Freedom, and which was to be presented at Geneva. Industrial communities like Nelson were deeply involved in struggles against the 'Means Test' and 'more looms', but were still keenly interested in such international issues. The Town Council passed a disarmament motion to coincide with the opening of the conference. The local Labour Party found time to protest against Japan's recent invasion of Manchuria; then after Hitler came to power in Germany in 1933 it unanimously condemned 'the vicious and repressive action of Fascism directed against our comrades in the working class movements, especially in Germany'. Selina Cooper, still a member of the party's executive, was amongst those stressing the urgency of such issues.

By 1934 Selina had developed a clear-cut attitude towards fascism and towards war. She adopted a socialist position, shared by many in the Labour Party's left-wing, and by those in groups to the left of Labour. Her creed was shaped by an all-powerful revulsion against the Great War, and an admiration for Russia's response in 1917. Her faith was based firmly in the organised strength of the working class, and she remembered August 1920 and still believed that the threat of a general strike could again prevent governments from plunging people into the horrors of war again. She saw fascism creeping across Europe and even, thanks to Oswald Mosley's new British Union of Fascists, into Britain. But like others on the left, she believed both fascism and war-mongering were the work of capitalist profiteers and arms manufacturers, people who could not be trusted either at home or abroad. Among those sharing her point of view was the young Labour MP for Ebbw Vale, Aneurin Bevan. Bevan's biographer explains clearly the logic behind such socialists' thinking in the mid-1930s:

> How could they see the tormentors of their people suddenly translated into stout defenders of working-class liberties? For Bevan, that would have implied a betrayal of a whole lifetime's experience and struggle. British capitalism, not German Fascism, was the enemy on his doorstep, as ancient as the industrial revolution itself, as modern as the latest Means Test infamy.

Selina Cooper, still numbed by the Great War and the slump , sincerely held such views. With the wisdom of hindsight, we can perhaps see that idealistic socialists under-estimated the military aggression of Nazi Germany. In the mid-1930s, however, the nature of fascism was not yet clear and many on the left believed it was capitalism and profit that caused wars. These convictions took fierce hold of Selina as she grew more elderly, and shaped her actions during her remaining years.[4]

The idea of a United Front against war and fascism was, of course, still rejected by Labour Party officialdom. So when Selina Cooper and other women organised a No More War Conference in Nelson in August 1934 they had to look elsewhere for support. Margaret Aldersley presided at the conference held in the Weavers' Institute. Now in her eighties, her ideas about war had, like Selina's, been largely shaped by her 1914–18 experiences. The other speakers were Selina Cooper, Dan Carradice, Richard Bland, a Methodist minister speaking on behalf of the local League of Nations branch, and Mary's friend Elizabeth Stanworth who was in the Communist Party. The eighty people present – from various religious, co-operative and trade union groups – had no hesitation in pointing the finger of guilt at the warmongers. They unanimously condemned the 'frantic' war moves of the capitalist governments, and declared that 'all the organised forces of the workers must be united against both the National Government and the armament makers who prepare fresh slaughter for mere profit'. Selina Cooper made her own views perfectly plain:

> We must bring it home to the man in the street and the woman in the backyard the reality and grave danger of the present day tendency of governments . . . The effects of the last war are obvious to every thinking man and woman. What it meant is that it took away from the world the control of a generation . . . It is women's work to be the keepers of the young life in this country. We have a great ideal to live up to, and we must see to it that in the future our interests are more truly served through taking a greater part in the counsel of nations.[5]

'Women's Anti-War Conference', headlined one of the local papers, and 'Nelson Inaugurates Vigorous Campaign'. An Anti-War Committee was set up, seemingly consisting largely of women, and began organising a demonstration for a fortnight later. About five hundred people took part, led by a local band

and a lorry upon which small children proudly displayed placards inscribed 'Workers, Unite Against War'. Margaret Aldersley, Selina and Mary Cooper walked in front of the Nelson Anti-War banner, and behind them came other women bearing banners demanding 'Mothers of England, Shall Youth Be Slaughtered', 'Remember August, 1914' and – a relic from the war and the Peace Pilgrimage – 'Peace Our Hope'.

On the recreation ground the crowd gave its support to a statement which, by its very phrasing, revealed how strongly such socialists still saw the main enemy to be the government at home rather than German fascism abroad:

> this large gathering of workers of Nelson . . . repudiates the war and fascist policy of the National Government as shown in:
> The immense war expenditure
> The failure of the Disarmament Conference and open talk of war . . .
> The covert attempt to use Japan as a battering ram in the Far East against Soviet Russia.
> We believe that by united effort we can stop these provocative moves towards Fascism and war.
> We declare ourselves united in a close and unbreakable group against all these things and pledge ourselves to a continuous struggle against them . . .[6]

Elsewhere larger anti-fascist and anti-war groups were taking shape. In Nazi Germany, the brutal attack on Communists was now extended to Jews. A Committee for the Relief of the Victims of German Fascism was formed, some of its members Communists, some not. The Labour Party National Executive banned it, fearing it to be yet another Communist front organisation. One such group, formed in summer 1934, was the Women's World Committee Against War and Fascism. Its British sponsors included women in the Communist Party, and an impressive sprinkling of those outside: Charlotte Despard, Sylvia Pankhurst, writers Vera Brittain and Storm Jameson, Ellen Wilkinson, Dame Evelyn Sharp and actress Sybil Thorndike.

During the summer the British Section of Women Against War and Fascism drew up a 'Women's Charter' by which it hoped to appeal to as broad a range of women as possible. Its ambitious demands included not only the repeal of the Anomalies Act and

Means Test, and a rent exemption for the unemployed, but also the right of married women to work, free maternity hospitals, birth control to be available at local clinics, legalisation of abortion and – most daringly – release of all women imprisoned for abortion. Only the final section of the charter demanded the disbandment of all fascist organisations, support for Russia's demand for total disarmament, and the conversion of armament production to production for social use.[7]

Such an all-embracing programme was designed to appeal to women outside the Communist Party, both prestigious national names and local supporters like Selina and Mary Cooper. This 'united-front' tactic of a communist-inspired group, deliberately widening its appeal to reach out to other progressive women, seems to have worked. Women Against War and Fascism staged a world congress in France in August 1934. Its British delegation was over forty-strong and included Monica Whately and Charlotte Despard, as well as Rose Smith and other members of the Communist Party. Perhaps one or two of the less wordly-wise delegates were rather taken aback to find the hall in Paris draped with slogans like 'Sustain the Peace Policy of the Soviet Union – the Country of Liberated Women!' But however stage-managed it was, the congress was successful as a launching pad for Women Against War and Fascism. Rose Smith was able to tell a Nelson anti-war meeting later that she had just returned from Paris where, she claimed, over a thousand delegates from all over the world and of all shades of political opinion had pledged themselves to fight against war. 'I hope that this meeting in Nelson,' she added amidst applause, 'will be a lighted beacon and inspiration to the whole women of this country.'

A strongly-worded national publicity leaflet was issued. It urged women to unite and form local groups 'lest war sweeps us into its whirlpool and Fascism perpetuates its rule of iniquity and misery'. These must have been widely circulated, for the Coopers possessed at least half a dozen copies, presumably brought round by Rose Smith on one of her visits to St Mary's Street.[8] The British section of Women Against War and Fascism also acquired a small London office and began organising a British delegation to visit Nazi Germany to investigate the plight of women held in jails or concentration camps. It was especially anxious about particular women held in Munich and Berlin and wanted to secure their release. They were being held hostage for their husbands who, as prominent Communists, had been imprisoned by the Nazis, but had managed to escape. Of particular concern was Mrs Beimler who was being held in 'protective custody' in Stadelheim Prison near Munich, along with her nineteen-year-old sister, as hostages for Hans Beimler; he was a Communist deputy in the Reichstag, who had managed to escape from the concentration camp at Dachau. The Women Against War And Fascism organisers issued an appeal to cover the expenses of the three-women delegation, hoping for a mid-October departure.

Deciding who the delegates should be proved more troublesome. Monica Whately agreed to go: her credentials, both as an active feminist and as a prospective Labour candidate, were impeccable. An interpreter was also found who was willing to undertake the dangerous journey. Rose Smith planned to go, but dropped out for one reason or another: someone who could represent working-class women from the north of England was still required.[9]

It seems to have been at this point, early in September 1934, that Rose Smith (or possibly Monica Whately) had a word in the ear of the London organisers. Why not invite Selina Cooper? She could after all speak on behalf of women textile workers. The matter was urgent. Someone must go up to Nelson, for the Coopers still had no telephone and a letter was hardly appropriate. Rose Smith seemingly arranged for her friend Maggie Chapman, who shared a house with Rose and their respective children in Burnley, to scurry up to Nelson. Maggie, a weaver and a long-standing member of the Communist Party, did not know Selina Cooper well (though they had met long ago at SDF meetings). This was the first time she had been to the Coopers' house, and nearly half a century later Maggie could still recall the historic visit in detail:

> They sent me to interview her, did our Party – to see if she could go to Germany . . .
> And she was washing in her back kitchen. Now you'd think a woman like that . . . [She'd say to you] 'Oh, I want to get this done, and talk to you after.' No. Down with everything.

As soon as Selina heard the reason behind the impromptu visit, she immediately dropped her housework, put the kettle on and offered Maggie a cup of tea. Maggie was most impressed by this:

> Of course, that's how they used to talk about Selina. She didn't care for housework, and she didn't do this and that. But I can understand a militant woman – wanting to do things.
>
> And when I asked her to go and see [the women imprisoned in Nazi Germany], she said yes, she'd go. Of course we had to pay her fare. I say 'we' – I mean the Party . . .

How aware Selina was of Communist string-pulling behind the scenes we shall never know. Mary understandably retained only a vague memory of who organised the trip to Germany.[10] Anyway, perhaps a little background manipulation did not matter overmuch. Selina was always her own woman, even at the height of the suffrage campaign when she had resisted the enticements of women she did not trust. Now, she probably recognised that it *was* a Communist initiative, but she also recognised the urgency of combating the twin evils: war and fascism. In 1934 there was little time left for pedantic worries about labels and motives. For this reason, Selina did not hesitate to accept the invitation. Maggie Chapman relayed the good news back to the Women Against War and Fascism office in London, and the machinery whirred into action. Travel arrangements were made. It was agreed that Selina should carry with her two sets of credentials, one from the influential Amalgamated Weavers' Association and the other from the Nelson Weavers; these it was hoped would ensure she would be taken seriously by politicians in Munich. Her old comrade Carey Hargreaves, remembering Selina's solidarity during the 'more looms' struggles, did her proud:

> To whom it may concern:-
>
> Mrs Selina Cooper JP of 59 St Mary's Street Nelson is a very well known and highly respected citizen of this town . . . She has devoted her life to the service of the working people of this town and country and has won her way into the respect and confidence of the class to which she belongs and the public in general . . .
>
> She belongs to a working-class family and not only she, but her family also, have served the Trade Union, Labour and Co-operative Movements with ability and devotion.

She can undoubtedly be trusted to represent the workers of this country in any dealings she may have with our comrades in Germany in this very difficult time.

Signed
C. Hargreaves
Secretary

Armed with these letters, Selina Cooper caught the train down to London, met Monica Whately and the interpreter, and on 15 October the three of them sailed overnight to the Hook of Holland. They then boarded an express train which took them along the Rhine to Munich. Selina's memories of the journey were homely. 'Our breakfast on the train, consisting of coffee, rolls and butter, amounted to 3s 4d per person,' she wrote. 'Tuesday seems to be the national washing day, and along the journey there appeared to be miles of white clothes floating in the breeze.'

The three of them found the horrors of Nazi Germany chilling. They had originally intended to visit four women prisoners, two in Berlin and two in Munich. But they discovered that of the two in Berlin, one had died and the other was so ill she had been taken from her prison to a civil hospital. This sobering news speeded their efforts to reach the other two women before it was too late. 'On our arrival in Munich', they reported later,

> we found that the atmosphere of the new Germany is one of bravado on the part of the rulers, and terror on the part of the ruled. The ordinary citizen is afraid to speak. Even when friends meet in the street they look round them nervously as they carry on their conversation. Many, even now, are being shadowed by the secret police, and for that reason we had to exercise the greatest caution in making contact with those who are not in favour of the present regime.
>
> The fact that we were known to be seeking information in connection with the treatment of political prisoners necessitated our being doubly careful. It was known that we were gravely concerned that women were being held as prisoners, women who had never been brought to trial – nor had been proved guilty of any Anti-Government activity . . .[11]

Selina Cooper, now nearing her seventieth birthday, found this atmosphere of menace, fear and secrecy took its toll. She anxiously sent Mary postcards almost daily from Munich, assuring her daughter that no evil had yet befallen her. One post-card noted, with careful understatement, 'it is very hard work we have a lot of walking about'. Mary treasured her Munich post-cards, and always retained a vivid memory of what her mother had had to endure in Nazi Germany:

> There was this deputation . . . it was the year my father died . . . And they had these men chained and they got away; so they [the Nazi officials] took their wives . . . in as hostages – which is against all legal law. Well, my mother and [Monica Whately] interviewed [various officials] – and the Minister of Justice was quite brave, and said it *was* against all international law that hostages should be kept in prison . . .
>
> My mother lost – in a fortnight – she lost ten pounds. Fright. Followed all over the place . . . They never spoke direct to any-body . . . Do you know, her clothes just hung off her when she came back.
>
> And they went to see one relative; and they'd knock at the door and say they'd come about the boy's violin lessons. And then she [a woman] let them in. The neighbours spied on one another.

Selina can then take up the tale in her own words:

> Our request to each official we visited was that on behalf of the women of England we hoped they would release Mrs Beimler and her sister, now held as hostages for their husbands in Munich. The sister's husband has died in a concentration camp since her impris-onment, so that it meant that both women are being held for Mr Beimler who was Deputy in the Reichstag, and escaped from prison where he was in chains, and is now in Paris an exile.

The deputation was unable to get to see Mrs Beimler and her sister, and was refused permission to visit the women's concentra-tion camps. In that sense Selina Cooper's visit to Nazi Germany achieved very little. Yet indirectly it was not unsuccessful in that it managed to alert a wider circle of women to the grim realities of Nazism. 'She came back, and wrote, and she spoke to different organisations about her visit,' Mary explained. 'And she scat-tered this news about what was going on in Germany.'[12] Selina was interviewed by local and regional papers, while the *Daily Worker* and *Daily Herald* reported what Monica Whately said. They both began addressing public meetings; on Armistice Day, for instance, Monica Whately and Rose Smith talked at a Women Against War and Fascism meeting in London. Monica Whately, reported the *Daily Worker* enthusiastically, 'roused the audience to a high pitch of indignation, as she described the appalling conditions of women held there as hostages, without trial, particularly Mrs Beimler, whose case she had specially investigated'. A resolution, pledging active support, both individually and collectively, for peace and against fascism was passed unanimously.[13]

Further north Selina Cooper was busy too, and kept in close touch with London. Monica Whately sent her a copy of the resolution she used at *her* meetings, and Selina sent down news of her campaign in Lancashire to the Women Against War and Fascism office. 'It is splendid that you are managing so many meetings,' the secretary told Selina, 'We are hoping that when our committees get really organised in the north you will be able to visit some of them. I wish we could go quicker ahead than we are doing but it is difficult when you are a new movement with not many contacts, to organise on a national basis.' Such organisational hitches concerned Selina less than the fundamental problem of trying to shift public opinion. Outside certain socialist circles, people remained apathetic about the plight of German Communists and Jews and preferred to retain their illusions about Germany. The Labour Party, apparently more concerned about Communist 'front' organisations than about combating fascism, included Women against War and Fascism in its list of proscribed organisations. Despite these great difficulties, Selina Cooper determinedly worked her patch. 'She went to Guilds and told them what had happened,' Mary explained. 'And she thinks it paid off in the long run, because people got alarmed. If she'd gone and said, "Oh, things are all right out in Germany," they'd have been soothed into [complacency].'[14]

By the end of the year, Selina was beginning to plan meetings further afield in cities like Manchester, and was spending a lot of time helping to draft the official delegation report, and writing her own 'Report of My Impressions on the Women's Delegation to Germany by Mrs S.J. Cooper'. Neatly copied out by Mary, still her mother's faithful scribe, the report told how one German Selina had talked to in Munich had asked her how she would like

to live in a fascist country where those wanting to express themselves freely feared imprisonment or death:

> He must have seen my startled expression at his unexpected ques-
> tion for he said, perhaps you think, that with your constitutional
> government in England, you are far from such a possibility, but
> we too were well advanced in civilisation and government, but the
> work of years was swept away by the wave of a hand.

Selina urged people reading the report not to condone what was
going on in Germany. She warned about

> the apparent loyalty to the Nazi Government – about the streets
> the flag-waving and Hitler salutes – and in conversation the
> parrot-cry of 'Heil Hitler' and 'All for the Leader'. It was all like a
> circus, well-staged, but their faces wore a sad mask, and their
> thoughts were inscrutable. Hitler thinks that women don't make
> history but it is for women all over the world to teach him that
> women create life and it is their business to preserve it.

It was particularly through the fascist threat to women's hard-
won rights that Selina hoped to alert people to the true horrors of
Nazism. After all, when she and Margaret Aldersley organised
the Nelson Anti-War Movement protest against the 'fascist policy
of the National Government', what they partly had in mind was
the Anomalies Act, pushing married women out of jobs and back
into the home. So when the formal report 'A Visit to Germany'
was eventually produced it stressed how Hitler had tried to cope
with German unemployment by pressing women into domestic
roles and by opening up about three hundred labour camps for
unemployed women who could be trained in housekeeping and
mothercraft. Selina Cooper wanted to warn women that it could
happen here too. 'Up to the time of the Hitler regime,' the report
added,

> the Feminist Organisations in Germany played a very active part.
> There were more women in the German parliament than in any
> other country. Those organisations, like the trade unions, have
> now been made illegal, and everything relating to the interests of
> women has been placed in the hands of 'Frauenschaft' [Organisa-
> tion of Women], an officially controlled section of the Nazi Party.
>   Women are no longer allowed to take an active part in politics,
> but, to maintain their status in some small degree, must

> concentrate on welfare work and its various branches. Their
> unimportance, except as wives and mothers, was verbally
> expressed by some leading former feminists.

And it ended:

> The visit of the delegation was far from reassuring. We feel that it
> is essential that the people of this country should voice their protest
> in a very definite form. Is elementary justice to be flouted – and
> can women of England be silent, while their German sisters are
> being subjected to imprisonment, torture – and even death?[15]

Selina Cooper had been deeply moved by her visit to Germany,
and continued to work energetically for the anti-fascist campaign,
alerting people both to the horrors of the Nazis and the threat of
fascism in Britain. However, according to Mary, her mother
became vexed at the way Communist Party women from
Manchester came up to Nelson and tried to pressurise her into
slanting her reports of what she'd seen. Yet Selina, always quick
to recognise when she was being manipulated, seems to have
stood her ground. Monica Whately, a prospective Labour candidate in the coming 1935 General Election, found things less easy.
She 'very soon understood that she wasn't going to get any benefit,' the delegation secretary suggested, '– any political benefit.
Rather, it was going to be labelled as a Communist-inspired
thing, and so she got out of it fairly quickly.' Some of this earlier
broad support for Women Against War and Fascism did indeed
seem to drop away, and money problems prevented the organisation from expanding much beyond London as it had hoped.

Nevertheless Selina Cooper felt the issues it focused on were so
crucial that she kept in touch with the organisation during
1935 – even though it still lay well beyond the official Labour
pale. Luckily for Selina, the Nelson Labour Party seems to have
been tolerant of her activities, letting her remain on the constituency executive while she was at the same time sharing anti-war
and anti-fascist platforms with Communists.[16]

1935 was a year in which the threat of fascism, both at home and
abroad, began to grow horrifyingly clear. But when the new year
dawned many British people still believed there was little in

Germany to alarm them. So when Selina Cooper was invited by the *Colne and Nelson Times* as one of its local 'personalities' to compose a New Year message for its readers, she had little hesitation about what she should write:

> In Bavaria at the present time the country that once rang with fairy tales and romance now listens to the sound of marching armies: and instead of the sword being turned into a ploughshare, the ploughshare has been turned into a sword.

The fascist menace was already far closer to home than Bavaria. Early in 1935 Sir Oswald Mosley came up to Burnley for a British Union of Fascists rally, his uniformed blackshirts acting as 'stewards'. The Nelson Anti-War Group – doubtless including Selina Cooper – went along to monitor Mosley's bully-boy tactics, and subsequently protested loudly about the underlying violence of the meeting. The Nelson branch of the British Union of Fascists already had over a hundred members. Extremely perturbed at these developments, the Anti-War Group urged local people to write to Women Against War and Fascism in London for its literature which detailed 'horrible, but true, stories of what fascism means to women'; and, it added, 'We know that once you are aware of the twin evils Nelson will declare itself, in no uncertain terms, an anti-fascist and anti-war town.' The campaign was considerably strengthened when, in February 1935, Charlotte Despard came up to address a Nelson Anti-war Group meeting.

Ninety-one-year-old Charlotte Despard was, of course, no newcomer to Nelson. Selina Cooper had already heard her speak at the inaugural meeting of the local suffrage society and, later, for the Women's Peace Crusade. More recently, Mrs Despard had been one of the celebrities willing to add her name to the Women Against War and Fascism sponsorship list. Now seeming like 'a promise of immortality[,] impossibly ancient, and as frail as pressed petals', she returned to Nelson to give her unique inspiration to the campaign.[17]

Charlotte Despard and Selina Cooper both responded to the troubled times with a shared idealistic zeal. Though neither was formally a member of the Communist Party, both happily shared public platforms with those who were. Both were deeply concerned lest Russia should once again be threatened with war by the capitalist countries. Charlotte Despard had recently visited Russia, and both old ladies passionately believed that the socialist utopia so long prophesied had been achieved at least in this one brave country. Charlotte Despard swallowed all the tales Stalin's officials told her; and Selina Cooper, listening to the accounts of such well-travelled socialists, believed them too. Certainly both women were deeply impressed by Communist energy in opposing fascism and war, and were cynical about official Labour's sluggishness. Their beliefs were both feminist and socialist ones, shaped by their earlier suffrage years, by the war and by the events of August 1920. Passionately idealistic, they were at odds with the mood of the time which increasingly acknowledged that military action might become necessary to stop one nation attacking another.[18]

The platform of Mrs Despard's Anti-War meeting was indeed a visible tribute to the old suffrage era. On one side sat Selina Cooper, now a dignified seventy. The meeting was chaired by Margaret Aldersley, herself in her eighties, while Charlotte Despard was in her nineties. (The platform then seemed to skip a generation or two: the other speakers were Elizabeth Stanworth and Councillor Richard Bland.)

Mrs Despard was welcomed with loud applause; she told her audience how war was caused by the need of capitalists for new markets – in contrast to socialist Russia. 'If two or three nations joined together in an effort to outlaw war,' she suggested, 'then I think war will cease to be . . . If British workers were as determined as the Russians, we would not have a war.' Despite occasionally absent-mindedly wandering away from the microphone and so becoming inaudible, Charlotte Despard won the hearts of her audience. Then Selina Cooper moved the resolution that a 'united front' between socialist groups, rather than relying on the capitalist National Government or the League of Nations, was the only way to avoid war:

> This meeting of the people of Nelson . . . recognises the increased preparation for war being carried out by the National Government. We recognise furthermore that their Fascist policy as typified in their support for Mosley . . . and realise that the united action of all our organisations and people, no matter what

individual, political or religious views, will combat the
developments of Fascism and its resultant – war . . .

Selina Cooper warned that fascism in Germany – which she
could speak about as an eye-witness – had put back the position of
women a hundred years. Richard Bland then proposed that
workers around the world should, in the event of war, oppose it by
threatening a general strike. This resolution – impracticable
though it might sound to our ears, wise after the event – was
passed by the enthusiastic meeting without a single voice raised
against it.[19]

The timeless figure of Mrs Despard returned to Ireland. Afterwards, letters still spattered the local press, praising Mosley's
seductive plans for solving Lancashire's unemployment by banning cotton imports into Britain. 'Blackshirt Government alone
can save Lancashire', claimed some correspondents. The Nelson
branch of the British Union of Fascists, which attracted disillu-
sioned mill workers (as well as some cranks and Tory businessmen), served as a grim reminder to Selina Cooper of the
nearness of fascism. Further afield, too, Nazi Germany continued
to rearm – as did Japan – and re-introduced conscription. In
Italy Mussolini seemed to be eyeing Abyssinia covetously. In such
circumstances, the idealistic socialist belief that capitalism was the
root cause of war and a general strike was the answer to it, left
itself wide open to criticism. However, the group carried on, firm
in its opposition to rearmament which would benefit only 'finan-
cier warmongers'. Then, at mid-summer, Selina Cooper was
pleased to be involved in a more broadly-based meeting organised
by an adult education group and addressed by Sylvia Pankhurst.

Like Charlotte Despard before her, Sylvia Pankhurst was no
stranger to the town. She had come up during the war to talk to
the short-lived Workers' Suffrage Federation branch. More
recently she had, again like Charlotte Despard, allowed her name
to be used as a sponsor for Women Against War and Fascism. A
fortnight earlier, for instance, she had spoken with Ellen
Wilkinson and others at a London 'Women Call for Peace'
meeting organised by Women Against War and Fascism and ILP
and Guild branches. Now, speaking before the audience in the
Nelson Weavers' Institute, Sylvia imaginatively wove together
the threads of feminism and anti-fascism.[20]

Selina Cooper had long admired Sylvia Pankhurst – though she might not have agreed with her every political action. She was certainly delighted to chair the afternoon meeting at which Sylvia traced the history of women's struggle for the vote. Sylvia began with her sister Christabel's interrupting the Liberal meeting in the Free Trade Hall, and discussed the suffragettes' arson campaign, forcible feeding and the 'Cat and Mouse' Act. (What Selina Cooper made of this account is unclear. Since she thought so highly of Sylvia she may possibly have come across a copy of Sylvia's classic history, *The Suffragette Movement*, a cheap edition of which had recently been published. Nevertheless, Sylvia's account hardly bore out Selina's own suffragist experiences, nor those of other women in the audience.)[21]

In the evening, at a meeting chaired by one of Nelson's recently-elected (but still rare) women councillors, Sylvia Pankhurst went on to talk about 'The World Position of Women Today'. 'We must admit,' she said, 'that since we got the vote the fire has largely gone out of the women's movement, and it needs rekindling.' She noted women had gained important footholds in medicine, architecture, journalism and even – through Amy Johnson – aviation. Divorce had been made fairer, and women had successfully lobbied for improved insurance and pensions. 'But we have not got women into party leaderships,' she noted, and with so few women among party leaders, crucial reforms, like enabling childbirth to take place in hospitals, would be slow. 'It is an extraordinary thing,' Sylvia pointed out, 'that while other death rates have fallen, the death rate of mothers [at childbirth] has been rising. It has never fallen since the beginning of the century and latterly has been rising because of the pressure on mothers through needless unemployment.'

She went on from the high rates of maternal mortality to condemn fascism itself:

The fascist movement is the greatest enemy of every form of freedom, and particularly a setback to women, because they suffer most in their economic position, and in their position and rights as citizens . . . I have heard people in the Labour movement say that Fascism is bound to come here. I do not believe that. But whether we get it or not, the influence of the propaganda put forward by these people is 'Back to the kitchen:' for women, instead of us going on to a form of society in which domestic work and the material drudgery of life takes up a smaller part of our energy and time than at the present.

She urged women to remain vigilant towards insidious fascist propaganda and to raise their voices loudly against increased armaments and war preparations. She suggested forming a united women's party, not like that of her sister and mother but based within the labour movement, that would press for practical reforms such as free maternity beds and free school milk.

Sylvia Pankhurst had pointed to the links between feminist demands to reduce maternal mortality rates and the more general anti-fascism and anti-war campaign; these links had originally been listed in the Women Against War and Fascism 'Women's Charter' of the previous summer, but had since become submerged by other seemingly more urgent political issues.

This was again what happened in the late summer of 1935. Mussolini's designs on Abyssinia helped turn the attention of Nelson's Anti-War Group from Sylvia Pankhurst's feminist perspective to the threat of real war. A procession again wound its way round the town, Selina Cooper walking alongside young men whose heads were hidden beneath hideous poison-gas masks. Banners alerted passers-by to the dangers of air raids. 'Poison gases are the latest "cure" for unemployment' one proclaimed. Within weeks the Italian forces had begun their attack on Abyssinia. Before long Italian aeroplanes were spraying poison gas over Abyssinian villages, apparently without effective protest from the British Government. At the same time the Home Office began to distribute air raid circulars, warning British civilians, virtually immune from war before, of the horrors of aerial bombardments and gas attacks. Yet at the same time there remained a feeling among certain influential circles that Germany had been punished too harshly after the last war. 'A clear understanding with Germany,' urged *The Times*, 'would not solve all the problems of the world, but it would be a very strong foundation on which to build.' This policy of 'appeasement' as it became known was of course fiercely opposed by people like Selina Cooper. Yet theirs was never more than a small minority voice (and their anti-Nazism was always difficult to disentangle from their fierce opposition to military rearmament).

At the November 1935 general election the Conservatives emerged as by far the strongest party and the National Government continued in power. (However Labour won back many seats lost in 1931, and the Coopers' constituency went to a new Labour MP called Sydney Silverman.) The 'united front' hopes of those on the left continued, despite great hostility from the Labour Party. The small Women Against War and Fascism organisation, for instance, ran on until the late 1930s, though Selina seems to have had little contact with it after 1935.[22] The Spanish Civil War which began the following year challenged head-on those on the anti-war left who had previously opposed the use of all armaments as profit-mongering: the needs of the embattled Republicans in Spain undermined that belief. Indeed, 1936 and 1937 seemed to be years when Selina, growing increasingly elderly, quietly took stock of the wicked world in preparation for the last major battle of her lifetime: confrontation with Labour Party officialdom.[23]

KBO AND THE PEOPLE'S CONVENTION: 1936-1946

In the quiet years that followed her visit to Nazi Germany, Selina Cooper had time to reflect on the events of the past few years. She sensed an era was drawing to a close. North-east Lancashire, with its massive support for strike action, had witnessed the most bitter industrial conflict of the 1930s. Yet locally unemployment still remained high with wages well below the 1920s level and trade union membership falling year by year. Women cotton workers were especially hard hit; relative to other women in newer industries, their wages never recovered their strong pre-war position while social pressures continued to push married women out of jobs.

In general, conservatism seemed to retain its grip on the minds of the British people, especially when they came anywhere near a ballot box. There were only 154 Labour MPs, with just four ILP MPs and one Communist. Neville Chamberlain, the Tories' one-time Minister of Health, took over as Prime Minister in 1937 to head the National Government. Meanwhile appeasement of Nazi Germany still commanded influential support, and the German embassy in London remained the scene of lavish and fashionable parties.

Selina Cooper never allowed herself to brood for too long on these depressing developments. Even after she had sat through a particularly long and tiresome political meeting in Nelson she would, Mary recalled, just 'come back to St Mary's Street and start all over again. She said her motto was "Keep Buggering On". KBO.'

It would have been all too easy to have grown cynical or

despondent. Age was beginning to take its toll. Selina could no longer climb the steep stairs at home, and each year brought news of the deaths of suffrage and anti-war comrades. Harriette Beanland had died in 1922 and Annot Robinson in 1925. By the end of the 1930s Margaret Ashton, Helena Swanwick and ninety-five-year-old Charlotte Despard were no longer alive. With the passing of Margaret Aldersley, Selina seemed to lose her last strong link with the distant and almost-forgotten world of National Union suffrage organisers, the Election Fighting Fund and the Women's Peace Crusade.[1]

There still remained other friendships. Selina was as close to her devoted daughter as she had ever been. Mary seemed perfectly happy to live her adult life in the shadow of her celebrated mother, never resenting Selina's demands on her. The two of them often went on trips together to places especially significant to Selina. They even went down to Callington; there they traced the house where the Coombe family had once lived and the garden where Selina and Alf had played by the black cherry tree nearly a lifetime earlier.

There was the cinema, too. Like so many people in the 1930s, Selina Cooper became a film addict. However much scrimping it involved, she went to the Queen's Cinema twice a week, either with Mary or with one of her own friends. Her particular favourites were love stories and cowboy films. Thrillers, she used to complain, lost her in the middle of their byzantine plots. So regular was Selina's attendance at the Queen's that she even became something of an institution there – or so it seemed to one impressionable young lad:

> Mrs Cooper in my opinion was the Daddy of them all. Yes, she was indeed. She could keep us in order, when she used to relax and go to the cinema. Anyroads, rough lads [would] shuffle us feet. That were *it*. [She'd just give us one look], and if we didn't behave – Percy – [the Queen's] chucker-out – 'Percy! Quiet these boys'.[2]

After such a rebuke the Queen's lads would relapse into silence. Selina Cooper had over the years acquired almost legendary authority. An elderly lady of imposing proportions (in old age, Mary explained candidly, Selina 'ran to fat'), she could appear formidable to younger people. 'Frightened was the wrong word, but,' her great nephew admitted, 'you'd to behave yourself in her presence and you knew it.' Yet to the small children from nearby streets she remained to the end of her days a delightful person who would always let them come in and play. And whenever any of her neighbours were in trouble or needed a magistrate's signature, Selina always made herself available, even if she was in the middle of cooking. 'My mother went – always at everyone's beck-and-call – flour on her hands, and everything,' said Mary.

So much of Selina Cooper's early life faded from living memory as the years passed, but the imposing figure she cut in Nelson in the late 1930s and 1940s is still remembered by older local people – especially those' in the labour movement. She was always an impressive speaker, presenting what she had to say in a manner that held everyone's attention. 'When you saw Mrs Cooper coming,' explained one member of the local Women's Section, 'you thought, "Oh, there'll be some good discussion now." There are some people like that. You like to see them come in, because you know that the meeting will have a liveliness in it.' One young plumber who as a boy had listened to Selina's talks at the Socialist Sunday School and who was now active in the ILP, recalls what Selina had come to symbolise for him:

> I put a bath in for her – downstairs [as she could no longer get upstairs] . . . When I got there and I heard it was Selina Jane Cooper – well! She didn't know me . . . Now, when I said [to her] I knew her and started talking about the ILP and Socialist Sunday School – well, that's your introduction, isn't it?
> I were there a long time, talking to her. She was marvellous to listen to, because she used to – you see, she knew she'd got an audience who would be interested, didn't she? With me in the ILP and all the rest. And she told me about various trips of hers . . . She talked to me about the Board of Guardians . . .

So beguiled was this young plumber by Selina's reminiscences that he took an unusually long time to put her bath in. When he got back to his boss he had some very hard explaining to do. Yet he had no regrets: Selina was worth lingering for.[3]

Selina Cooper not only found it difficult to go up hills or steep stairs: her physical world had also shrunk and, except to visit Preston for an insurance committee, she seldom left Nelson any more. Yet within the confines of that small town she remained to the end of her life one of its most respected citizens. She was still one of Nelson's three women JPs. She was on the Burnley Guardians' Committee, and in 1938 she was elected its vice-chairman and two years later chairman – thirty-nine years after she first became a Guardian. She also remained a co-opted member of the Nelson Education Committee, and in addition sat on a local Appeal Tribunal as a 'workpeople's representative', sorting out complicated unemployment claims as humanely as possible. Likewise, when the Ministry of Labour asked her to collect information for an 'Enquiry into Working Class Expenditure', Selina went round local families, asking them for details of their household budgets. In between she still found time to keep in touch with Elizabeth Abbott and the Open Door Council over the losing battle of equal pay for *all* women cotton workers.[4]

All the while, Selina remained in constant demand as a speaker. For instance, during the winter months of 1938 she gave a talk near Halifax, headlined in the *Co-operative News* 'Probation the Best Way With Juvenile Crime – Magistrate Talks to Calderdale District'. A week later she was reported in the *Nelson Leader* protesting at the scandal of how, in a working class town the size of Burnley, there was not one single working woman magistrate. 'Modern Cinderellas – Young Nelson Girls Who Do Housework While Brothers Attend Evening School' ran another headline over a report of Selina's criticisms at an Education Committee meeting.[5]

This suggests that what Mrs Cooper said was taken seriously in the town. She was an influential member of bodies responsible for the quality of life of local people. Yet, lest readers become lulled into believing that Selina had in her old age lost her earlier rebelliousness and become merely respectable, it must be remembered that she had one other string to her bow. She was still an active member of the Labour Party and delegate to the constituency party's Executive. Indeed, the Labour Party was more than just a bowstring: it was the foundation upon which all her other responsibilities sprang. She was invited to sit on public bodies *because* she was a member of Nelson's powerful Labour Party. Yet that long-standing bond snapped in the early 1940s, as Selina defied the party's official attitude to the war and Russia's role in it.

This story begins back in the mid-1930s. The Labour Party's uncompromising attitude towards the Communist Party had not softened over the years. Communists continued to urge united action against war and fascism, to which some Labour members daringly responded. In tolerant constituencies like· Nelson and Colne, Selina Cooper and others were able to work openly with Communists; but officially the Labour Party still preferred to keep them at arm's length.

Enthusiasm for unity remained widespread on the left of the Labour Party. Sir Stafford Cripps, a leading Labour MP and great political barrister, came to personify this enthusiasm. In the mid-1930s Cripps' Socialist League took on the role of gadfly to the party, a role traditionally taken by the ILP. From the left of the party, the Socialist League buzzed and stung, criticising Labour for its timidity in combating fascism and for its fear of Communist affiliation.

Support for Cripps was strong among rank-and-file socialists like Selina Cooper in Nelson and Colne. In 1935 the local party voted for a workers' 'general strike' against war, and in 1936 for Communist affiliation because it was 'in the interests of the workers in their desire to obtain a united labour movement against capitalism'.[6] Nationally the party took a dim view of such ideas. Yet Cripps and the defiant Labour left continued to press for 'unity'. Talks opened between the Socialist League and the Communist Party and ILP. Early in 1937 a three-way Unity Manifesto was produced to give voice to the millions of people in the country who, it claimed, were unrepresented by the reactionary National Government. The manifesto included many of the socialist demands supported by Selina Cooper and her local party – opposition to rearmament and military recruiting, support for the fight against fascism, and pensions of £1 a week for all people over sixty.

The Labour Party's powerful National Executive Committee lost no time before stepping in to crush this socialist upstart. Within days the Socialist League as an organisation was disaffiliated. Yet party officials still remained deeply suspicious of pro-communist individuals lurking in deep crevices of the party's structure. There was even a move, claimed one of Labour's woman organisers, 'to get the wives of Communists to join the Women's Sections so that they can get their point home, and get Sections to send delegates to various conferences'.[7]

Cripps, a brilliant parliamentary orator, remained popular among local constituency parties and unions like the miners. Tens of thousands of people enthusiastically signed unity 'pledge cards' and among them was undoubtedly Selina Cooper. Yet the issue of 'unity' and of the Socialist League was to split a left-wing constituency like Nelson and Colne down the middle. In Nelson itself, Dan Carradice's motion condemning the league's expulsion was debated at length – and only narrowly defeated twenty-three votes to twenty-two.[8]

Days later the National Executive Committee took a step further and declared that *individual* league members would soon become ineligible for Labour Party membership. The Nelson and Colne constituency executive, on which Selina Cooper still sat, met and discussed this. The Nelson Weavers and another powerful local union protested at what happened and demanded support for the unity campaign. A protracted debate followed with presumably (the curt minutes give few details) Selina Cooper and others arguing furiously against the right wing. The left on the executive lost. And when the league's expulsion issue came up before a big constituency meeting a few weeks later, the right-wing opposition was even more formidable. It was led, of course, by the two giants of Nelson's Labour machine: Alderman Andrew Smith JP, the party treasurer, and Willie John Throup, the party agent. After what was obviously an extremely bitter debate, the left's resolution was defeated. Officialdom had won, both at this local level and nationally.[9]

The National Executive Committee, backed by the inevitable massive trade union block vote, had beaten the Socialist League. But the left was far from defeated. Communists, increasingly anxious about the threat of fascism on Russia's own doorstep, moved towards a strategy called the Popular Front. As Hitler's troops crossed over the Rhine and later, in 1938, invaded Austria, arguments for a broad anti-fascist alliance seemed to grow daily more urgent. So, unlike the earlier attempts at unity, the Popular Front was designed to include, not just working-class organisations, but also Liberals, the churches and even rebel Tories. The idea of this broad front against Chamberlain's National Government won enthusiastic support from some leading Labour MPs –

not just Stafford Cripps, but also Ellen Wilkinson, Aneurin Bevan, and from independents like Eleanor Rathbone – though it was very coolly received by party officials. In Nelson this tension between left-wing enthusiasm for the Popular Front and right-wing coolness showed itself in a squabble over the Left Book Club, a successful socialist publishing venture which vividly captured the heady Popular Front spirit of those years. Selina and Mary Cooper possessed one or two Left Book Club titles; but the local party requested Sydney Silverman as constituency MP never to appear on any Left Book Club platform.[10]

Selina Cooper felt there was no acceptable alternative to the Popular Front in the late 1930s. 'Maybe the Popular Front was always a desperate, forlorn bid,' summarised Aneurin Bevan's biographer. 'But what other card in the Socialist hand was there left to play? Better this than the infuriating inertia of official Labour in the face of calamity.' However, there were a few to the left of the Labour Party who felt increasingly cynical about what they saw as communist manipulation of Popular Front hopes. News was filtering through of Stalin's show trials and the liquidation of his opposition. One ILP activist, growing hardened against such Stalinist ruthlessness, in both Russia and Spain, had a jaundiced memory of Selina Cooper's political activities then. He had no time for anyone who flirted with communism while still clinging on to their Labour Party membership. 'No, I always thought she'd got on the fringe – what for want of a better name, or whatever people use, fellow traveller,' he explained. 'She was a fellow traveller. Or getting on that way.' What particularly irked this ILP man was the way that such people within the Labour Party were pushed forward from outside by Communist Party members. He said he far preferred honest and open Communists like Bessie Dickinson or Seth Sagar.

> The Popular Front caught on a bit. And you got some of the Methodists like Arthur Mantel who were a socialist as well, who were a Labour man. You'd your Selina Jane Coopers . . . Alan Fisher. They were all playing around [with Communism] . . .
>
> They use you. And, well, you know there was all the things like the United Front, and then there was the Unity Campaign. Well, you got certain people then linking up with the Communist Party . . .

> And, oh, so many people that you knew, like Mary and all them, they were on the fringe of the Communist Party. They would not join. Their loyalties were to Labour Party; but they . . . would have voted for Communist affiliation to Labour Party . . .
>
> Well, they started a stunt of moving everybody onto committees, the Popular Front line. If Mary's mother had been there, Selina – 'I move Selina Jane – '. The Communists would have moved her. Arthur Mantel, a Methodist, who played around with labour movement and Communists. 'Move Mr Mantel.'
>
> Well they moved a most timid, mild type onto these committees. They were tools in their hands. I mean, Bessie Dickinson . . . Seth Sagar – would go through fire and water, would the Dickinsons and Seth and that lot . . .[11]

Neville Chamberlain had recently returned from Munich, having apparently made his peace with Hitler. Yet those who opposed such appeasement were bitterly divided against each other. The ILP and Communist Party distrusted each other; and the Labour Party remained divided between the loyalist majority, and the rebels supporting the Popular Front. These tensions within the party were strained to breaking-point in January 1939 when the National Executive Committee expelled Stafford Cripps.

Cripps, now outside the party pale, retained the support of dissident politicians like Aneurin Bevan, plus some trade unions and local constituency parties. In defiance of officialdom, Cripps launched his National Petition Campaign, calling for support for his demands 'to drive the National Government from office'. The Labour Party became highly embarrassed as Cripps appeared on platforms up and down the country amidst cheering audiences. Selina Cooper was among those grass-roots members horrified by the expulsion who gave the petition energetic support. Cripps' expulsion cast a shadow over the safety of party rebels like herself. 'It started with Stafford Cripps,' Mary Cooper recalls. 'And my mother saw what was happening. And this petition came round that was headed by Stafford Cripps . . . and my mother got hundreds of signatures for it. And it was against the Labour Party policy, you see.'[12]

In Nelson the Labour Party seemed split down the middle on the issue. One local Popular Front supporter, Joe Bracewell, tried to protest about Cripps' expulsion but was out-voted by a weighty amendment from Andrew Smith.[13] Indeed most local Labour

Parties supported the National Executive, which was therefore able to go ahead and expel some of Cripps' supporters – including Aneurin Bevan. It seemed that, amidst threats of expulsions and reprisals, the Popular Front could only muster derisory support within the Labour Party. By mid-1939 Selina Cooper felt utterly disenchanted with the great socialist party she had helped to form so long ago. With the outbreak of war only weeks away, she was becoming increasingly alienated from all that Labour came to symbolise.

In August 1939, Soviet Russia signed a 'non-aggression' pact with Nazi Germany. Hitler promptly invaded Poland, and Chamberlain declared war on Germany. Britain was at last at war. People turned their minds to the blackout and barrage balloons, to evacuees and gasmasks. Yet despite these wartime conditions, little happened. These early months did indeed constitute a 'phoney war'.

Certainly up in Nelson the war against Germany seemed far away and very 'phoney' indeed. Among socialists there was precious little support for Chamberlain and his War Cabinet. The combined weight of the local anti-war left was now considerable. It included pacifist ILP members, like Alderman Richard Bland, many of whom had suffered badly as Conscientious Objectors in the previous war; members of the Communist Party who opposed the war now Russia had changed sides; and Russian sympathisers like Selina Cooper who remembered the last war as a needless imperial bloodbath and who deeply distrusted Neville Chamberlain. After the appeasement of Munich, they argued, how could such politicians be trusted to wage war against fascists? These anti-war feelings were further strengthened by suspicions that the military situation was being used by Chamberlain's Government to trespass on the democratic rights and welfare provisions of ordinary people. Sydney Silverman was summoned up to his constituency for a meeting 'to counter the present tendency to decrease democratic rights'. Anti-war socialists like Joe Bracewell and Dan Carradice grew incensed at the government's shabby proposals on pensions, damning them as an 'outrageous insult to the aged workers in this country'.

Nelson was, of course, an anti-war stronghold and such feelings were not automatically echoed throughout the rest of the country. Indeed, the isolation of those Nelson socialists opposing the war became even more marked after Hitler invaded Norway in April 1940 and the 'phoney war' phase came to an end. Henceforth even the local Labour Party had no patience for motions that war was 'not in the interests of the working classes', and that Chamberlain's Government should be replaced by a Labour one which would end the war and so allow 'the workers to commence to deal with their real work, the abolition of poverty'. Both motions were thrown out.[14]

Yet Selina Cooper would have supported both. As Chamberlain gave way to Winston Churchill and the real war in Europe unfolded, Selina found herself in a tiny rebellious minority. She was a Labour member who opposed the war and therefore found herself at complete odds with the official party, now taking part in Churchill's new War Cabinet. The evacuation at Dunkirk meant that Britain stood out alone against Hitler's armies. Fear of invasion became very real, while rumours of German parachutists and Nazi collaborators were rife. 'Enemy aliens' were rounded up. Sir Oswald Mosley was arrested, his British Union of Fascists dissolved, and Nelson's leading fascist sent to an internment camp on the Isle of Man. The Blitz began, with heavy bombing of London's East End and cities like Coventry. But such momentous events seem hardly to have impinged on elderly Mrs Cooper. Living in Nelson, she remained remote from the horrors of the German bombing raids. As a magistrate, she did intervene on behalf of two Bradford children evacuated to Nelson whom she feared had been abandoned by their father. But otherwise Selina's war experiences were at odds with those of the great majority of people.[15]

She held fast to her belief that Churchill's war could not be a genuine anti-fascist war. She remembered Winston Churchill from her suffrage days and the 1908 Manchester by-election. Later she had observed his attitude towards the miners' militancy, towards British intervention in post-revolutionary Russia, and towards the general strike in 1926. She had a long memory for imperialist wars fought by the workers in the interests of the ruling class, and she saw no more reason to trust Churchill's leadership now than she had before.

Selina Cooper found herself set apart from the patriotic millions who supported Churchill's fight against Hitler. Yet she was not entirely alone. From mid-1940 she became involved in a small dissident organisation called the People's Convention. It was this unorthodox allegiance that shaped the last few years of Selina's life.

The People's Convention opposed the war on socialist rather than pacifist grounds. It believed it to be an imperialist rather than a genuinely anti-fascist fight; its members shared a deep suspicion of the tired 'Men of Munich' and of the Labour Party's uncritical collaboration with Churchill. Since France's ruling class had capitulated to the Germans rather than mount popular resistance, they argued, might not the British ruling class capitulate as well?

The People's Convention was initiated by the Communist Party, and drew most of its strength from it. It was a time when the Communist Party was very isolated, open to taunts about the Nazi-Soviet Pact, Russia's attack on Finland, and the party's unblinking defence of Stalin's Russia. The heady days of broad Popular Front links were now a thing of the past. It was hardly the best moment for the Communist Party to suggest that war could be avoided if only Britain had a *real* People's Government. Yet the People's Convention did win a sprinkling of support from those outside the Communist Party. A number of idealist socialists were drawn in who remembered the restrictions on liberty of the last war and wanted to protect people's freedoms; who wanted to plan for a post-war society; and who wanted, despite the Nazi-Soviet Pact, closer friendship with Russia.

A leading supporter was a socialist barrister, D.N. Pritt KC, MP, a man who occupied a high position in the Labour Party not dissimilar to Cripps'. Pritt was fanatically and unquestioningly pro-Soviet. Even at the height of Stalin's terror, he returned from Russia and told people how 'I formed a favourable impression' of the Moscow show trials, since the rules governing Soviet criminal procedure were so *fair*; and later he went on to justify Russia's invasion of Poland and Finland. Yet all the while Pritt remained not only a Labour MP but also a member of its influential National Executive Committee. He was only finally expelled from the party in early 1940 – and even then he remained unrepentantly an MP. 'I felt,' he wrote, 'that I was . . . only being expelled by people who were betraying Socialism; and I felt sure that I was right about

Finland and the USSR.'[16]

Such whitewashing of Stalinism may seem implausible to readers wise in the knowledge of what has since happened in eastern Europe. But to a long-standing socialist like Selina Cooper, it was all too easy to believe the reports and propaganda of D.N. Pritt. For Selina to feel that socialism was working in at least one major state made the long struggle in Britain easier to maintain. In this way, a number of ordinary Labour Party members like Selina were persuaded that Russia's approach to the war was right, and that in Britain a left opposition should be mounted to Churchill.

In midsummer 1940, then, a People's Convention was set up. It called for vigilance to protect democratic rights, for friendship with Russia, and was against appeasement and the 'Men of Munich'. The response was good and when a meeting was called in London the hall was filled to overflowing. There was also a reasonable local response to the call for a 'People's Government'. For instance, a meeting organised by the National Council for Civil Liberties on the protection of democratic rights was held in the Nelson Weavers' Institute.[17]

Precisely how Selina Cooper was drawn into the People's Convention remains unclear. No family papers for late 1940 have survived, and Mary's testimony is understandably hazy. Possibly Selina heard Rose Smith, now on a *Daily Worker* speaking tour, talk on the 'People's Government'. Possibly Seth Sagar, Bessie Dickinson, or Elizabeth Stanworth came round for a chat about the People's Convention. Or Selina may have gone along to the 'People's Rally' in Nelson at which Bessie Dickinson spoke. In one way or another, Selina Cooper had by Christmas 1940 become firmly committed to the People's Convention.[18]

There remained one insoluble problem: the Labour Party. Selina had of course sailed close to the wind before. Since her trip to Nazi Germany six years earlier, she had been involved with campaigns such as Women Against War and Fascism or Cripps' Petition Campaign that were firmly opposed by party officialdom. Indeed, if her own constituency Labour Party had not been reasonably willing to turn a blind eye to individual communist sympathisers within its ranks, Selina Cooper might have found herself already on the expulsions list along with national leaders like Cripps and Pritt.[19]

This time the chance for tolerant local compromises had passed. Labour MPs in Churchill's Government were directly involved in the fight against Hitler. To have party members sniping at their war aims could not be tolerated. The National Executive Committee therefore hastily proscribed the People's Convention and expelled its leading members. By autumn 1940 local party members involved in such proscribed activities were being warned. Up in Nelson and Colne the pressure was certainly on. It is not clear how many local Labour Party members besides Selina Cooper, Joe Bracewell, Arthur Mantel and one or two others openly supported the People's Convention. Certainly there were at least nine people deeply involved in the constituency, two of them Labour councillors, and there were doubtless other less active members on the fringes. Andrew Smith, Willie John Throup and other officials must have spent anxious moments during the autumn toting up how many of their members were at risk, and how many might be eased back inside the party fold after a brisk talking-to.[20]

As 1940 drew to a close against a background of heavy bombing, talk of local expulsions was in the air. As the battle lines for and against the People's Convention grew clearer, Selina Cooper found herself under increasing pressure to decide which way to jump. Seventy-six years old, she was one of that dwindling band of pioneers who had helped form the Labour Party. There were few of her generation left. Chairman of the Guardians and an experienced magistrate, her credentials within the local labour movement were impeccable. Whether she stayed in the Labour Party or was expelled, the side which won her allegiance could claim a significant victory. Selina Cooper had come to symbolize so much that socialism traditionally stood for in England.

The issue was finally and dramatically fought out on New Year's Eve 1940 when Selina was interviewed by the constituency party's executive committee, a body to which she was of course still a delegate. It was an evening that was long to remain lodged in Mary Cooper's memory:

> She was hauled before the [Executive]. I'll never forget it because she had to go before this Executive to see whether she'd be thrown out . . . And she'd to . . . either take her name off this [People's Convention] or be thrown out.
>
> And somebody [Seth Sagar] came here, and was anxious to know

how my mother had gone on. And [he was here] waiting. And she didn't get home till about six. And she came in looking very white. And [Seth] . . . well, he was a . . . right old foundation-member of the Communist Party. And he was worried about this, that my mother was going to get slung out of the Labour Party because of this. And the Communists had backed [the People's Convention].

It was, Mary recalls, a dramatic moment when her mother finally staggered into the house after her gruelling interview:

They'd put her through such a grill[ing]. And she wouldn't withdraw [her support for the People's Convention]. They said they'd forgive her if she'd withdraw it, you see . . . It had been condemned.

Anyhow, she came home and . . . Seth said, 'Well, I waited to see.' She says, 'Well, I'm leaving. I'm not letting them [tell me what to do].'[21]

Selina Cooper's mind was clearly made up. She was a proud woman and she was determined to stay not a moment longer in the party she disagreed with over such crucial principles as the conduct of the war and friendship with Russia. Yet however adamant Selina was, she still found herself being lent on by the local Labour Party agent. He was desperate for her to reconsider her fatal decision:

Well, my mother decided. And the organiser was called Willie John Throup, and he came the next day for my mother's answer. I shall never forget it. It was New Year's Day, and the honours list was coming out. And we had a very primitive way of washing then, you see. We used to dry our clothes across this front room, sheets and what nots. And he came right early, because he were anxious – because she had a lot of power you see.

And he rang the bell of the door, and we'd only just got up and we'd had our breakfast. These clothes were still across the room . . . So we took them down. Anyway, he sat down and he said, 'What have you decided?' She said, 'I'm going to send my resignation in . . .'

She was a founder of the Labour Party in Nelson. And he tried to persuade her. He tried to tell her that if she'd wait a bit longer [things would change in the way she hoped].

Throughout all this pressure, Selina Cooper obstinately refused to modify her position. Despite her long-standing membership and her excellent anti-fascist record, her days in the Labour Party were now numbered. Four days after Willie John Throup's visit, the constituency executive met to debate once again the tiresome problem of the nine remaining supporters of the People's Convention. It was obviously keen to obey loyally the National Executive's ruling. Yet the People's Convention seemed unstoppable; local supporters were becoming organised; and, when a National Convention was held in London on 12 January, over two thousand delegates attended – including two from Nelson. So successful was this People's Convention meeting that the government even banned the *Daily Worker* which had helped publicize it.[22] A government with Labour members in it had seen fit to silence the communist press. Had any doubts lingered in Selina Cooper's mind, they were now banished.

Shortly afterwards, Sydney Silverman came up to address the constituency executive on the question. 'The action of certain members who had supported the People's Convention was discussed,' the minute book explains with its customary curtness, 'and the executive decided to support the action of the National Party on the matter.' Expulsions were agreed. Selina Cooper was therefore to be expelled from the Labour Party. This woman who in 1896, half a century earlier, had campaigned for Ben Smith as a Labour councillor, who had been elected an ILP-SDF Guardian in 1901, who had later laid the ILP foundation stone and had pressed for women's suffrage at two early Labour Party Conferences – this elderly woman was now thrown out of the party. Out with her went Joe Bracewell and four other members, including one of the councillors. (Arthur Mantel and two others decided to 'withdraw support and reaffirm loyalty' to the party instead.) When the National Executive Committee met on 26 February, it was reported that a total of well over a hundred members had been expelled. In the middle of the long list of individual expulsions was the name of 'Mrs J.S. Cooper, Nelson'.

Selina Cooper had been one of the six Nelson representatives on the constituency's executive for twenty-three years. Now her name was struck off and someone else was elected to occupy her seat. For the first time for half a century, she found herself thrust into the darkness, far outside the pale of mainstream labour politics. It was all a bitter blow to a proud old lady. 'The only time I ever remember her crying,' Mary Cooper said,

> and she didn't show me – I heard her crying in bed – when they
> threw her out of the Labour Party. Because she'd been mother of
> the Labour Party in Nelson, and they threw her out . . . She never
> let me see she was crying, but I heard her crying. And she said she
> wouldn't take her name off . . .[23]

The problem was made worse because, of course, Selina still had
to sit, both on the magistrates' bench and at Guardians' meetings,
alongside those very same Labour men who had expelled her.
Some of them, Mary explains, 'got quite nasty with her'.

> After my mother [was expelled] and she was . . . more than seventy
> then. And they used to have meetings at Reedley for the area, and
> my mother was chairman of the [Guardians] committee. And
> they'd come out; [the Labour men]'d have to come to a local
> meeting in Nelson. And they'd pass my mother in cars and leave
> her [so that] she got to the [next] meeting wet through. And she'd
> have to wait for the bus; and they'd go with cars empty past her.
>   Damned Tory people picked her up; and they used to say to my
> mother – well, you see, they'd see some fertile soil they could use.
> They'd say, 'If only you'd come over to us with your lovely voice,
> Mrs Cooper.' And my mother would say, 'I shall be no good
> because it would only be a voice. My principles wouldn't be right.'
> Used to send her letters inviting her to come into the Tory Party,
> after they knew she'd left [Labour].[24]

Selina Cooper might be out of the Labour Party, but she was by
no means out on her own. From amongst the Nelson supporters of
the People's Convention there emerged an organising committee.
Early on this group recognised not just Selina's symbolic value but
also her considerable skills as a public speaker, skills scarcely
dimmed by age. During 1941, therefore, Selina began to address
local People's Convention meetings, much to the gratitude of Joe
Bracewell, the secretary. 'The Committee are of the unanimous
opinion that the Meeting was a success and that much of this is due
to your co-operation . . .', he wrote in the spring. 'Literature sold
well & 24 copies of Mr Pritts latest book were sold as a result of the
Meeting.'[25]

However, within weeks the People's Convention Committee
was suddenly overtaken by far larger global event. On 22 June
1941, at four o'clock in the morning, Germany invaded Russia.

Hitler's troops were soon sweeping eastwards towards Moscow. Winston Churchill broadcast to the nation his change of policy. Although a long-standing anti-communist, now 'the cause of any Russian fighting for his hearth and home is the cause of free men and free people in every quarter of the globe'. An Anglo-Soviet Alliance set the seal on Britain's sudden friendship with Russia.[26]

Two days after Hitler's invasion, Selina Cooper was invited to comment on this new turn of events by an official of the Manchester People's Convention committee at a meeting of Lancashire delegates. 'We feel sure that the audience would be most interested to hear your position with regard to the Labour Party and appreciate the courageous stand which you have taken . . .', he wrote. How Selina responded is unclear. Possibly she told the Manchester delegates that the new alliance with Russia spelled, in the words of D.N. Pritt, 'the end of Hitler, and that it was now the duty of the British people to see that the existing war became a genuinely anti-Fascist war, with ourselves in alliance with the Soviet Union, as we should have been in 1939 to prevent war ever breaking out.'[27]

With Russia now on Britain's side in the war against fascism, the Communist Party switched its line on the war and began to urge increased war production to defeat Hitler. Along with others in the Communist Party and on the broad left, Selina Cooper now became caught up in the demand for a 'Second Front' in Europe. Russia's Red Army was bravely and stubbornly fighting Hitler on Germany's eastern front, the argument ran; and so Russia should have the pressure taken off her by opening up a western assault on Germany. Selina Cooper obtained a copy of a pamphlet published in October 1941 called *The People's Convention Says* . . . which spelt out these issues clearly: 'What are we waiting for? Why can we not attack Hitler in the west – now, when almost the whole of his forces are on the eastern front?'

Yet the opening up of a Second Front was endlessly delayed. It appeared to Selina Cooper almost as if Winston Churchill preferred to see the German and Russian armies annihilate each other, rather than the Soviet Union victorious. All her earlier doubts about Churchill hardened: his new-found 'friendship' with Russia seemed merely a temporary expedient. Mary Cooper can still recall the feelings of suspicion about Churchill she and her mother shared during these wartime years:

> I think it was true, that Churchill, although he reckoned to fight
> with Russia, was holding his Second Front back so that Russia'd
> get hammered . . . He was delaying because he wanted Russia to
> be absolutely wiped out . . . He always had this thing against
> Russia, really, did Churchill. Although he was the right man for
> that war position . . .[28]

There were other practical repercussions from the Anglo-Soviet
Alliance as well. Enthusiasm for Russia and for its Red Army now
seemed boundless. But with so much of the Communist Party
members' energy going into Anglo-Soviet committees or into
campaigning for the Second Front, the People's Convention itself
seemed squeezed by these newer, more popular movements
supporting Russia's war effort. The political room left for a
democratic movement demanding a 'People's Government' was
rapidly shrinking. Certainly Communist Party enthusiasm for an
independent People's Convention movement waned during
autumn 1941, and by the end of the year it became clear the convention was to be 'suspended'.

Pritt was among those outside the party who resented this high-
handed action. 'There were many among us who did not relish
the conclusion,' he confessed later, 'especially in some provincial
towns where our committees were still the only real sources of
active political thought and life.' The decision to disband was
finally taken in January 1942, and Selina Cooper duly received a
printed circular letter from convention officials. It explained why
the organisation was being wound up in favour of work 'on a
wider front', and pointed out the triumph of at least one of its
demands: friendship with the Soviet Union. A few weeks later
Selina Cooper also received a touching handwritten letter from
Joe Bracewell, secretary of the late Nelson People's Convention
Committee, telling her that the local group was being disbanded
too and noting that the remaining funds, twelve guineas in all,
would be responsibly disposed of, mainly to the Soviet Medical
Aid Fund. 'The Committee wishes me to convey their thanks to
you,' the letter poignantly concluded, 'for your support and to
express the hope that you will continue to keep a vigilant watch
upon events and to work for the establishment of a saner and more
equitable system in the World.'[29]

Did Selina Cooper share Pritt's resentment at the way the

People's Convention was killed off? Probably so. It was, after all, the political organisation for whose sake she had allowed herself to be drummed out of the Labour Party. However fervently she supported Russia, it was galling to lose a lifelong political affiliation merely to make a modest donation to the Soviet Medical Aid Fund. The People's Convention had represented Selina Cooper's last wave of political activity: she had taken its democratic aims and demands seriously. After this neither the Anglo-Soviet Committees nor the Communist Party itself could hold much attraction for her.[30]

Out of the Labour Party, and with her eightieth birthday drawing near, Selina Cooper felt politically isolated. She never joined the Communist Party – though whether this was because she felt it was too late in life to start again or because she was suspicious of communist manipulations, is unclear. 'She said, before she died,' Mary reported, 'if she had her time to do again she would join the Communist Party' – though doubtless Selina's feeling were more complex than her daughter's words suggest. Likewise, Mary never joined the Communist Party either, despite pressure from Elizabeth Stanworth and other friends. 'I said, "I will join the Communist Party, but I will not leave loose of this strength," ' Mary used to retort, for she valued the links Labour Party membership gave her to the broad trade union movement. Certainly, losing touch with ordinary Labour members was an anxiety which Selina shared with her daughter, and which in the end stopped either of them from taking the plunge.[31]

With the Second Front delayed, Russia continued to fight on unaided. Selina Cooper's interest in Russia grew, and she and Mary began to amass inexpensive pro-Russian propaganda booklets. One was *Russia Resists*, a half-crown paperback which tried to explain away the Nazi-Soviet Pact and uncritically celebrate the Red Army's bravery. Another, by Jennie Lee, one of Labour's first women MPs, was entitled *Our Ally Russia – the Truth!* Mary and Selina even put up a bust of Stalin on the mantelpiece in honour of their hero.[32]

Meanwhile the war dragged on. Japan's attack on Pearl Harbor brought America into the war. In Britain, call-up was extended, and Hitler continued his bombing raids. Not till 1944 did the 'Second Front' invasion eventually take place, followed soon after by a Russian offensive which took their army right into Poland. By spring 1945 the Russians had reached Berlin, an achievement followed with great excitement in the Cooper household. The full horrors of the Nazi concentration camps, whose early development Selina had glimpsed when she visited Germany a decade before, were now opened up by the Allies. Hitler committed suicide: the German army surrendered. The war in Europe was over. America bombed Hiroshima and Nagasaki: Japan surrendered. Selina Cooper, nearing her eightieth birthday but still alert to all developments, must have been stunned to learn of this genocide of innocent civilians.

While Stalin's armies drove back the Germans, enthusiasm for things Russian helped popularise socialist ideas. William Beveridge was commissioned to produce a report on social insurance provision, while the President of the Board of Education began to talk of exciting reforms to the school system. From Beveridge's proposals arose a plan for a National Health Service for everyone, there was also to be a uniform rate of unemployment benefit so that the 'out-relief' allocated by Guardians' Committees was gone forever. People who fell on hard times would no longer be stigmatised as harshly as they had been in the 1930s, and Guardians' meetings, which had been such a regular feature of Selina Cooper's life since 1901, now became a thing of the past.

The Labour Party was changing too and moving leftwards. It openly acknowledged its faith in widespread public ownership which Selina and other socialists had been advocating since the 1890s. It even readmitted Stafford Cripps, her old Popular Front hero, back into membership. Had Selina been sixty or seventy rather than eighty years old, she would doubtless have welcomed this radical change from the party's spineless behaviour during the 1930s. Yet for her generation it was all too slow, all too tragically late. She witnessed Labour's landslide victory at the 1945 general election when it won nearly twice the number of Tory seats. But neither Selina Cooper, nor Margaret Aldersley, nor Ada Nield Chew (who died in 1945) lived long enough to see the full flowering of the welfare state in 1948 through the new National Health Service and National Insurance scheme.

The welfare reforms were not only far too late to give help to working-class families like the Coopers, they also were far less radical than Selina would have liked. The system of family allowances, payable to the mother on a non-contributory basis, was a fitting end to her long campaign for women's economic independence; but, unlike the far-reaching plans that Selina had urged a quarter of a century earlier, the 1945 Act included neither an allowance for the mother nor for the first child. 'She'd have turned in her grave, would my mother,' Mary reported, 'if she'd known that the first child didn't get them.'[33]

Selina Cooper was approaching the end of her long lifetime. On her eightieth birthday, in December 1944, she asked to be transferred to the Retired List of magistrates.[34] Old age, poor health and failing eyesight made it difficult for her to take an active part in planning post-war Britain. She barely saw a year of Labour's new power. During 1946 her health deteriorated badly. It was clear she would never see the end result of the long and wearisome campaigns she and others of her generation had waged. Victory lay well in the future when their own daughters would be retired. Equal pay for women had to wait another thirty years, and even then the legislation offered was extremely weak. Access to birth-control advice came only in 1967, when local authorities' powers were widened in the way Selina had long sought. Likewise payment of child allowances to the first child was even slower. By then the daughters of Selina Cooper, Ada Nield Chew, Annot Robinson and the others were themselves elderly. The delay had been tragically long; but Selina, a pioneer of the first wave of the women's movement, would never have entertained any doubts that the second wave was well worth waiting for.

During 1946, as she grew increasingly infirm, Selina came to need constant care. Faithful Mary managed, with the help of two sympathetic local aldermen, to persuade the borough treasurer's department to allow her to work half-time. It was agreed she could look after her mother for part of each day, while two of her father's sisters came in during the other half. Mary had never been able to save from her wage during the harsh years she supported her parents. Now on half pay, she had to rely – ironically enough – on public assistance and appeal to the local Guardians to eke out her wage with out-relief payments. Perhaps only the older officials involved would remember that this infirm old lady had herself first been elected a socialist Guardian in the town in 1901 – before Nelson boasted either a Labour MP or Labour mayor.

Unlike Stafford Cripps, Aneurin Bevan and other Party rebels, Selina Cooper was never reconciled with the party she had helped form, though she still came under considerable pressure from local Labour officials who badly wanted her to rejoin, Mary recalls. To admit an erring pioneer back into the fold would have been a great symbolic triumph. But Selina would not relent: the wounds inflicted over the years by the right wing of the party had gone too deep:

> Before she died they were wanting to parade her round the town as though she'd come back to the Labour Party. But she had[n't].
> And it was only about six weeks before [she died]; and there was a delayed civic centenary for Nelson. And Willie John Throup said he'd come and take her round in an open car.
> She hadn't walked for three months. And the doctor said to me, 'If your mother goes out in that car, she'll die in it.' She died about a month after . . .

Before long Selina was being regularly dosed with morphia to ease her pain; yet Mary remembers that even during these last few weeks her mother still found ways of amusing herself:

> And my mother – for nine months she couldn't move. She was in a chair, sat in a chair . . . I used to say, 'Oh, aren't you bored, sitting in that chair, mother?' And she used to say, 'I'm about half way through my memories.'
> Her eyes were bad, but she could see everything going on in these back streets. And she said, 'Ee, I'm only about half way through my memories yet.'[35]

With the new luxury of time on her hands, Selina let her mind wander back over the packed years, from Callington to Keld, and from suffrage petitions to her trip to Nazi Germany. Her sight was fading but, using a thick indelible pencil, she still managed to scribble down a few notes on blank pages in her suffrage diary. She scribbled comments about the Beveridge proposals and about earlier events in her life that stood out dramatically: the Nelson Suffrage Society's trip to London, the women chainmakers of Cradley Heath, and about speaking in Central Hall on married women's rights. The memories came flooding back, and somehow found their way onto the page as near-illegible jottings. Then, when her eyesight was nearly gone and she could no longer read, Selina would ask Mary to sift through the piles of Education Committee papers, and to read aloud to her the recent minutes to bring her up to date on what was happening. All the while, Selina still kept in touch with people as best she could: the children in the neighbourhood would come round with bunches of flowers, and relatives and friends wrote to her to cheer her up.

Later still, Selina grew confused as the morphia took hold of her. Sometimes she would even forget who Mary was and mistake her for a long-forgotten relation. Only once at the very end did Selina's mind become momentarily clear again:

> My mother lost me entirely until the last day. And then she said, 'Don't give me any of that morphia.' She was in the ambulance, so she knew what she was getting . . . Anyhow, she says, 'Don't give me that stuff. I want to talk to you.' And she was as conscious and sane [as anyone]. And she says, 'I haven't a lot of breath to say a lot to you, but,' she says, 'I never –'. I never got spoilt, you see. And she says, 'I've said sharp things to you sometimes, but you know I've always loved you. Now give me the medicine,' she said.[36]

Selina Cooper died on Monday 11 November 1946, just weeks before her eighty-second birthday. The news of her death spread quickly round the town, and that evening the *Northern Daily Telegraph* carried an appreciative obituary. Among the first people who heard the news and sat down to write a letter of condolence to Mary was Nelson's Education Officer who knew Selina as a long-serving member of the Education Committee. By Tuesday others, including Selina's soldier brother Alf, had written. 'I am pleased she lived to see the Party in Power she spent her life supporting . . .', one of her Coombe relations wrote. 'For you know it must have been hard for an active woman like her to have stood up against it so long.'

By Wednesday the news had reached most of her friends. The Clerk to the Nelson bench wrote on behalf of the other magistrates, as did the Burnley Area Public Assistance officer on behalf of his committee. 'The world can ill afford to lose such stalwart champions of the working people,' wrote the secretary of a local guild.

Later on, after an obituary appeared in the local weekly papers, Mary received letters from local Labour Party Women's Sections; and from Jennie McCall of the Nelson Weavers' Committee and now a district nurse. Willie John Throup, burying the acrimonious past, sent a generous letter from the Nelson Labour Party. 'Though at the moment when clouds are low and all seems dark, I know you have this grand consolation – Your mother did not live in vain,' he wrote. 'In dark and difficult days she kept the truth aflame.' Indeed, many of the letters of condolence contain hints of a sense of guilt that Selina Cooper in her later years had been treated rather shabbily by the town. 'I loved her Mary as if she was my own . . .', one friend wrote. 'I wrote to the council telling them the least they could do was make her freeman [of the Borough] for the little time she would have here. I little thought it would be so soon. Now I wonder if they regretted not doing so.'[37]

Selina Cooper was cremated on Thursday 14 November. Beforehand, a memorial service was held for her in – symbolically enough – the Salem Methodist Chapel. The buildings had acted as cradle to Nelson's fledgling labour movement and provided Selina with the venue for so many of the public meetings that had marked her life. The service was conducted by two comrades who represented different facets of Selina Cooper's long life. One was Elizabeth Stanworth, Mary's friend who had worked hard, yet unsuccessfully, to persuade the Coopers to join her in the Communist Party; the other was one of Nelson's longest-serving Labour councillors who had sat with Selina on the Guardians' Committee, if not since 1901, at least during the 1930s.

The town turned out in full force to honour Mrs Selina Cooper JP. The mayor came along with a sprinkling of gentry and local dignitaries: 'Superintendent Pickering', noted the local paper, 'headed a posse of police.' Everyone was there: Alf, and Selina's Coombe nieces and nephews, plus some relations of Robert Cooper's; the Nelson Communist Party, and Labour Party with its Women's Sections; members of the Town Council, magistrates' bench, county police force, Public Assistance Committee, Education Committee, Women's Co-operative Guilds and members of the Town Hall treasurer's department who worked alongside Mary. Among the many friends and neighbours who crowded into Salem that day were one or two from the far off Edwardian days of the Nelson Women's Suffrage Society: Emily Murgatroyd and Margaret Aldersley's daughter.

Missing from the obituaries and submerged under layers of suffrage myth was, however, any real understanding of what Selina Cooper and her fellow radical suffragists had stood for. So many of the links between this generation of women had grown weak over the years and finally broken with old age and death. The only suffrage friends outside Nelson who apparently responded to Selina's death were Elizabeth Abbott of the Open Door Council and Kate Courtney, one-time secretary of the National Union of Women's Suffrage Societies, and a founder of the Women's International League for Peace and Freedom. 'I am sending your letter on to another of your mother's old friends, Margaret [Robertson] of whom I know she often spoke,' Kate Courtney told Mary, 'and will try and get in touch with some of her other old friends too, but the number is now dwindling rather rapidly.'

'In the old suffragette days,' commented the local obituary writers beneath their 'Suffragette Memories' headlines, 'Mrs Cooper took an active part that brought her into close relationship with many of the leaders of the movement, particularly members of the Pankhurst family and Eleanor Rathbone.' Deeply-felt differences of opinion with Mrs Pankhurst about militant tactics had seemingly long faded, forgotten into history. Arguments with Eleanor Rathbone about patriotism versus internationalism had apparently long had their day. So many of the radical suffragists – Annot Robinson and Margaret Aldersley, Ada Nield Chew and now Selina Cooper herself – had died in obscurity, mourned by few beyond their own circle of local friends.

It would take another generation and more, when their own daughters had grown elderly, before the causes they fought for, the methods they used and the lives they led, came to find a place in the histories of the women's movement they had helped build.[38]

AFTERWORD

═══════════════

Selina Cooper's life, pieced together here from a wide range of sources, reveals significant connections and continuities – suffragism and labourism, feminism and anti-fascism. But it is important to ask whether Selina's life story is unique or unusual in this respect. Would the memories and documents of other women of her generation shed equal light on this period of history?

In some respects the answer is no. There are sides to Selina Cooper's life which are rare. She lived within the same couple of square miles of Lancashire from the age of eighteen to her death at eighty-one. And from 1901 to 1946 she lived in the same small terraced house; and Mary continued to live there till 1982, a period stretching over eighty years. Not many ordinary families can claim such unbroken continuity. And in this respect the Cooper household offers the historian a rare chance to reflect upon the records of one particular family active in the labour movement since the late nineteenth century. In addition, Selina and Robert Cooper's one surviving child wholeheartedly supported her parents' political beliefs. After their deaths, Mary ensured that all important papers were kept and little thrown away. When Mary was approached by Jill Norris and myself years later, she did not query our arrival but immediately understood why feminist historians in the 1970s believed the story of her mother's life was worth telling. Such tidy-minded loyalty, spanning the first and second waves of the women's movement, is no longer commonplace.

There were other sides to Selina Cooper's life that were also unusual. Her formal schooling was perfunctory; and she never became a confident or prolific writer. The entries in her suffrage diary are extraordinarily curt, and her spelling remained idiosyncratic. Yet although Selina wrote little down herself, sufficient other written records have now come to light to reveal a good deal about her. The picture strongly emerges of a woman who was not only a talented organiser but who also had the rare ability of inspiring those she talked to. Her energy never flagged, and in this way she always stirred confidence and often affection in her listeners. Yet, for all her eloquence, she was conscious of her own lack of writing skills. So are historians; for so much of the development of women's history over the last dozen years has been based upon women's *writing*, whether autobiographies or journalism, pamphlets or correspondence. Because so few working women of Selina's generation had outlets for writing, or the confidence to write about themselves at length, we still know too little about their lives. Here then is a rare biography: the story of an unlettered woman.

In these ways *Respectable Rebel* presents an unusual tale. In other ways, though, Selina Cooper was typical of many other women of her generation. The cruel jolts she suffered in childhood, her brief schooling, the family pressures on her to keep house for her mother and brothers, her early socialism – all these find an immediate echo in, say, *A Hard Way Up*, the harsh autobiography of Selina's suffrage contemporary, Hannah Mitchell. There are parallels with other women too. In 1893–4 Selina helped organise her fellow women mill workers into one of the cotton trade unions; and also in 1894 Ada Nield Chew, shortly to become one of Selina's fellow suffrage organisers, helped expose tailoresses' appalling wages and conditions in a series of anonymous letters to the local paper, signing herself just 'Crewe Factory Girl'. Similarly, Selina's deep opposition to the 1914–18 War is closely mirrored in the lives of radical suffragists like Annot Robinson and Margaret Aldersley. Selina was never a lone voice; she always chose to work through democratic organisations, and, whenever she spoke, she spoke on behalf of the many, many people she worked beside.

What is particularly interesting about such women – Selina Cooper, Hannah Mitchell, Ada Nield Chew, Annot Robinson, Margaret Aldersley, Catherine Marshall and many others – is that only recently have they begun to emerge from obscurity. They had become, in Sheila Rowbotham's phrase, 'hidden from history'. Certainly, until the mid-1970s Selina's own life seemed destined to fade forever from the memory of all but those few older Nelson socialists who had known her. She figured in no local history and in no account of the labour movement or suffrage campaign. She left no memorial to her name. Yet again, such a 'disappearance' after death is typical of others' experience, even for those much more adept at writing than Selina.[1]

Hannah Mitchell long cherished a private ambition to become a writer; during the 1940s, by which time few of her contemporaries were still living, elderly Hannah began secretly to write the story of her humble life. But no publisher would accept such a seemingly ordinary tale, and the complete manuscript only came to light after Hannah's death in 1956. Eventually published in 1968, *The Hard Way Up* was reissued by Virago in 1977 and is now recognised as an invaluable source for those studying the social and political history of the period. Ada Nield Chew was another suffragist whose life seemed destined to slip away forgotten. She too had secretly written an autobiography towards the end of her life, only to have it rejected. Ada Nield Chew died in complete obscurity in 1945; only years later did her only daughter, Doris Nield Chew, determine that her mother's remarkable life should be remembered. She began patiently to piece together her mother's writings dating back to the 'Crewe Factory Girl' days. These were subsequently published in 1982, when Doris was eighty-four, and the following summer Ada's life was dramatised for television by Alan Plater.[2]

Annot Robinson, Margaret Aldersley, Catherine Marshall and others like them still remain little known, but are no less interesting for how their lives became hidden. Annot Robinson died in 1925; she was survived by two daughters who found it increasingly difficult to fit their talented, troubled mother – socialist, suffragist and pacifist – into the received wisdom about the suffragettes. Not till 1979, half a century after her death, were some of Annot's papers rediscovered and made available to Manchester Central Library. Similarly Catherine Marshall, one of the most outstanding suffrage and peace organisers of her day, died in obscurity in 1961. The following year the county council bought her Lake District house, and many of Catherine's papers were discovered chaotically jumbled in a hut in the garden. Luckily they are now deposited in the Cumbria Record Office, and so historians are now assured access to two important collections of papers that had lain forgotten for so long.[3]

During the difficult years of the 1950s and 1960s, when women seemed content with the limited freedoms won for them by an earlier generation and when feminist history had fallen from vogue, those few remaining suffragists (and their daughters) felt the world grow colder as each year passed. So it is perhaps hardly surprising that Mary Cooper found people increasingly sceptical when she told her tales about Cradley Heath chainmakers and delegations to Nazi Germany. Mary, nothing daunted, kept her faith in her mother undimmed.

Yet, since the early 1970s, there have been stirrings. The women's liberation movement generated in feminists an enthusiasm to search for a past, to trace the historical roots of the contemporary women's movement back over the last three or four generations. It became a compelling quest to discover and preserve the papers of those no longer living, and to record interviews with elderly women who could recall the great suffrage days and before. Over the last few years, the stirrings have swollen into a substantial gust. Women's history, once restricted to an obligatory nod in the direction of the suffragettes, now flowers magnificently. Women's history groups have sprung up around the country – first in London, then in Sheffield, Manchester, Birmingham, Liverpool, and more recently in West Yorkshire. Books which were long out of print, such as *The Hard Way Up*, or which were never published, like *Ada Nield Chew*, have been successfully reissued in popular editions. A handbook, *Discovering Women's History*, has recently been produced to help those wanting to find out about their own local past.[4] Television dramas like *God Speed Co-operation*, along with exhibitions and imaginative teaching material, introduce this new approach to history to an increasingly wide range of people. Women's history can no longer be shrugged off.

Among those now interested in women's history, debate continues about emphases and omissions. For the twentieth-century period, two particular debates focus on the suffrage campaign and the women's movement once the vote was won. I hope that *The Life and Times of a Respectable Rebel* adds to both.

Until about six years ago, suffrage narratives largely fell into two categories. One told the story through the eyes of the Pankhursts and the militant suffragettes, occasionally nodding in the direction of their poor cousins, the dowdy non-militants. Sylvia Pankhurst's *The Suffragette Movement* (1931) is now rightly recognised as a classic. Her meticulous research and moving descriptions of her own hunger and thirst strikes leave all historians in her debt. However Sylvia Pankhurst refers to the 'old non-militant societies' as if they were entirely peopled by decrepit and doddery old ladies – which was, of course, far from the truth.

The second category of suffrage narrative told of Mrs Fawcett and her non-militant suffragists in the National Union of Women's Suffrage Societies. Here the best known account is probably *The Cause* by Ray Strachey, a close friend of Mrs Fawcett and the National Union parliamentary secretary. However, both women belonged to the patriotic right wing of the National Union, and in their writings neither does justice to those National Union members who – like Selina Cooper, Annot Robinson, Margaret Aldersley, Kate Courtney, Catherine Marshall and many others – opposed the war and helped form the rebel Women's International League in 1915.[5]

Such was mainstream suffrage history till recently. Both categories of narrative told the truth – but not the whole truth. Suffragette accounts tended to sway the overall picture against the non-militants; and the main non-militant writers tended to gloss over the savage rift between the patriots and internationalists during the war.

Then in 1977–8 there began to appear accounts which adopted a different focus and began to challenge these sets of orthodoxies. They were often written by scholarly historians for an academic readership, which sadly left their excellent research inaccessible to the general reader. I was greatly reassured to read these new and detailed suffrage histories, for they helped place in context Selina Cooper's own experiences. This new suffrage history is particularly revealing for the years 1912 to 1918; here it describes in detail the story of the important pre-war labour-suffrage alliance and of the repudiation of war by so many of those suffragists who had earlier joined the fight for the vote.[6]

The third section of *Respectable Rebel* tells how the suffragists, who had devoted most of their adult life to the one campaign, coped with the complex post-war world. The story occurs against a backdrop of industrial decay, mounting unemployment and pressure to push married women out of jobs and back into the home. Unfortunately, few accounts of this period that are available give completely adequate descriptions of what these years felt like. Dora Russell's *Tamarisk Tree* and Vera Brittain's *Testament of Experience* are luckily now both available to the general reader; yet, written by educated women who survived the Depression in reasonable comfort, they shed little light on how the majority of ordinary women survived unemployment and the Means Test. The final chapter of *The Hard Way Up* provides one of the few biographical accounts available that seems to fill that gap; and hopefully Selina Cooper's story of the tumultuous events of north-east Lancashire will help flesh out the picture that Hannah Mitchell outlined nearly thirty years ago. The more such local stories come to light, the better the history of the inter-war women's movement can be understood.[7]

Selina Cooper has bequeathed historians a rich store of family papers and of oral testimony. It was stumbled across only by good fortune, and was just discovered in time: I met Mary only seven years before her death. The survival of other similar collections of records and of personal memories may be equally endangered by a move of house, by over-zealous spring cleaning, or by the death of the last surviving member of a family. Hopefully they too can be rescued and preserved in time, so that more pieces of the jigsaw can be filled in.

NOTES

ABBREVIATIONS

B Bd of Gs – Burnley Board of Guardians
B Co-op Record – Burnley Co-operative Record
B Gaz – Burnley Gazette
BWA – Burnley Weavers' Association
C&NT – Colne & Nelson Times
comm – committee
CC – Common Cause
CP – Communist Party
D Wker – Daily Worker
Exec – Executive
EFF – Election Fighting Fund
ILP – Independent Labour Party
Lab L – Labour Leader
Lab P – Labour Party
LRC – Labour Representation Committee
LCWToWRC – Lancashire & Cheshire Women Textile and other Workers' Representation Committee
LCC – Lancashire County Council
MG – Manchester Guardian
MNSWS – Manchester National Society for Women's Suffrage
mins – minutes
NEC – National Executive Committee
NUWSS – National Union of Women's Suffrage Societies
NUSEC – National Union of Societies for Equal Citizenship
N Chron – Nelson Chronicle
N Gaz – Nelson Gazette
N Lab P – Nelson Labour Party
NL – Nelson Leader
NWA – Nelson Weavers' Association
NESWS – North of England Society for Women's Suffrage
PLG – Poor Law Guardian

PAC – Public Assistance Committee
PRO – Public Record Office
SJC – Selina Jane Coombe/Cooper
SDF – Social Democratic Federation
UIL – United Irish League
WAWF – Women Against War and Fascism
WCG – Women's Co-operative Guild
WILPF – Women's International League for Peace and Freedom
WSPU – Women's Social and Political Union

PREFACE

1 See Liddington, J., 'Looking for Mrs Cooper', *Women and the Labour Movement*, North West Labour History Society *Bulletin*, no 7, 1980–1; also Liddington, J. 'Rediscovering Suffrage History', *History Workshop Journal*, No 4, 1977

2 Tape 915, p. 12.

3 Tapes 121 and 915; references to tape 121, pp 1, 2, 3, 13–4 and 21–2.

4 Deposits at the Lancashire Record Office made between 10.5.1977 and 28.2.1979 have been catalogued (DDX 1137); and I am grateful to Peter Taylor, then working at the Record Office, for the care with which he calendared the collection.

5 The Fawcett Library contains no record of SJC in its correspondence and biographical files; though the helpful librarian, David Doughan, has sent me copies of two portraits of SJC that are part of the Fawcett's postcard collection, recently catalogued.

Three dozen newspapers were circulated with the appeal in November 1979; appeal articles also appeared in *Lancashire Evening Telegraph* and *NL* 29, 11.1979 and 20.4.1979 respectively.

6 After Mary's funeral, Mary's cousin Jenny kindly forwarded to me another large bagful of 150 photographs, numerous letters, etc. These I have included in the final draft as far as possible; though, because the discovery was made only shortly before the manuscript was to be typeset it has not been possible to detail every new source.

7 Lord Fenner Brockway to author, 18.3.1982.

PART ONE: GROWING UP VICTORIAN

CHAPTER ONE: A WEST COUNTRY CHILDHOOD

1 Tape 835, pp. 11, 15–6 and tape B, p. 6. The 1871 census gives the Coombe family address as 1, West End, Callington, and this is the address

on Charles Coombe's death certificate five years later. Unfortunately the descriptions of the house and garden fit the house at the other end of the terrace (called Valentine Row) better than the house in the census, and it is difficult to unravel this confusion.

2 Information from 1871 census; Richard is missing, but oral evidence from his grandson (tape 914, p. 1) suggests he was apprenticed to a carpenter in Cornwall. Tape 900, p. 11 etc recalls Charles as very religious.

3 Tape 835, pp. 12–13, 17, tape 818, pp. 28–9, tape 896, pp. 1, 13, tape 900, p. 34, tape A, p. 5 are among Mary Cooper's many references to the trips in the jingle.

Rowse, A.L., *A Cornish Childhood*, Jonathan Cape, London 1944, pp. 70, 189 also refers to a donkey-and-jingle. Coleman, T., *The Railway Navvies*, Penguin, London, 1965, pp. 28, 151, 187 has useful information on navvy life.

A photograph of Charles Coombe's mistress was kept in the family for the best part of a century, but has now unfortunately been passed to distant relations.

4 1841 census for Rezare & Trekenner; unfortunately neither Charles nor Jane (aged 15 and 16 respectively) is listed, presumably because both were away learning a trade. The census lists Catherine Coombe with no occupation, but in the 1881 census she is listed as 'Formerly Lauderess' aged 78. Tape C, p. 4 for details of the Uren sisters' dressmaking.

Reference to John Littlejohn in *Nelson Leader* 12. and 19.9.1924 and tape 835, p. 27.

5 It is impossible to be precise about the date Charles Coombe left farm work and joined the navvies. Census data (1851 and 1861) along with birth certificates of his children (1851, 1853 and 1858) describe him as an agricultural labourer, suggesting he did not become a navvy until about 1859. However it is likely this is misleading and he left farming in the late 1840s. His marriage certificate (1850) listed him just as a 'labourer' which might refer to farming *or* railway building; also, photographs of him in his thirties (i.e. late 1850s) suggest he was by then a railway ganger in charge of a group of navvies; thirdly, photographs of him shortly before he died (i.e. early 1870s) suggest by then he had risen to become a sub-contractor. It seems unlikely a farm labourer could have been elevated to a sub-contractor in so short a space of time and more likely that the census enumerator's casual employment categories were too vague to document Charles Coombe's early changes of status.

This dating fits in with contemporary railway extension. Rolt, L.T.C., *Isambard Kingdom Brunel*, Penguin, London, 1970, chaps 7–9, describes how the London-Bristol extension to Exeter was opened in 1844, and thereafter the main work was in Devon and Cornwall.

6 Marriage certificate 22.9.1850; John Henry's birth certificate 23.2.1851;

1851 census for the parish of Lezant shows eight people squashed into the house of Simon Uren, tailor.

Steel, D., *Discovering your Family History*, BBC, London, 1980, for mid-century Devonport; also 1841 and 1851 census for Mount Street, Stoke Damerel.

7 Harry Edwin's birth certificate, Trekenner, 6.11.1852; William Uren's, Callington, 3.6.1858; Charles Alfred's, North Gate Callington, 24.9.1860. The 1861 census gives Jane Coombe's occupation as toll collector and the address as Launceston Road, i.e. the north road out of Callington. Keeping a tollgate was not an unusual job for a Victorian married woman, see Mitchell, H., *The Hard Way Up*, Faber, 1968, and Virago, London, 1977, p. 39.

It is difficult to be precise about which railway lines Charles Coombe was building when. In the *NL* 12.9.1924 interview, SJC is reported as saying that her father 'worked under the great Brunel, the famous engineer. He helped in the construction of the Devon line from Liscard to St Tossel' (surely a mistranscription of 'Liskeard' and 'St Austell'). Certainly Brunel did construct an impressive viaduct near Liskeard; and the Great Western Railway Company was contracting for line in West Cornwall (probably the Truro-St Austell stretch) in summer 1852; likewise the Liskeard-Saltash section (near Callington) was started around early 1853. So we may imagine Charles Coombe working in the Liskeard area, within easy travelling distance of his home, in the early 1850s. See MacDermot, E.T., *History of the Great Western Railway*, Great Western Railway Company, Paddington Station, London, 1931, p. 267.

8 I am grateful to the Cornwall Record Office and the Rector of Callington for help in searching for records of the birth, baptism and death of other infant Coombes; I could find no other infant deaths, prior to the burial of Selina 16.7.1864, aged one.

9 For details of the Cornish slump and its effects see Rowe, J., *Cornwall in the Age of the Industrial Revolution*, Liverpool University Press, Liverpool, 1953, pp. 317–27; Barton, R.M. (ed), *Life in Cornwall in the late Nineteenth century*, Bradford Barton, Truro, 1972, which is a selection of extracts from the *West Briton* newspaper 1855–75.

10 Details of relatives working for Charles Coombe, tape 896, pp. 1, 11–13 and tape 835, p. 13; Simon Uren is listed as a carpenter in the 1851 census; Thomas Williams is listed in the 1881 census as 'Lead Miner out of emp.''.

11 Tape 835, pp. 15–6, tape B, p. 6. It is interesting to note from the Register of Baptisms in the Parish of Callington that SJC was not baptised till she was nearly six (25.11.1870) in what appears to be a 'job lot' with three-year-old Alf (even though their brother Charles had been baptised aged three weeks); one possible explanation is that the rector would not teach her till she was baptised. Rowse, A.L., *A Cornish Childhood*, pp. 42–3 gives a

vivid account of Cornish dame schools in the 1860s.

12 Tape A, p. 3 and 835, p. 30.

13 Charles Coombe is referred to as a road contractor on his eldest son's marriage certificate (1891 and *NL* 12.9.1924).

It is difficult to date when the various sons left Cornwall. *The Book of Common Prayer*, Oxford University Press, Oxford, 1836 is inscribed 'R. Coombe Burnley Lancashire January 14 1875 etc'; since he was not living in the Coombe household in 1871, he may have already left Cornwall by then. The other brothers must have moved north some time after 1871; John, Charles, Dick and Alfred are listed in 1881 census living in Barnoldswick. Harry is more elusive and may have emigrated by 1881 (tapes 835, p. 2 and 907, p. 3). Oral evidence (tapes 835, pp. 1–2, p. 15, and 916, p. 18) is inevitably vague on this point.

14 Plans for the railway to Callington in *Cornish Times* 3.6.1876 etc; the little line, now overgrown, can still be seen at the bottom of Kit Hill.

15 It is difficult to be precise about Charles Coombe's death. His death certificate describes him as a 'labourer' who died at Valentine Row, Callington, of 'fever (typhoid) enteritis'. The witness is a Mary Ann Stead who put a cross, not a signature; since she gives her address as elsewhere in Callington, she is more likely to be a nurse than his mistress.

However, it is difficult to trace references in the *Cornish Times* that autumn to a typhoid epidemic. Oral evidence (tape 835, p. 13 and tape A, p. 4) suggests he died while working either in North Cornwall or on the South Devon coast. Perhaps he contracted the disease there and was rushed home: it is unlikely we shall ever know.

16 Tape 835, pp. 11 and 17. Strachey, R., *The Cause*, 1928 and Virago, London, 1978, pp. 275–6 for the legal delays regarding married women's rights.

17 It is difficult to know how soon after September 1876 they left Callington; I was unable to trace an advertisement selling the Coombes' house in the *Cornish Times*, and this might suggest that Mrs Coombe did a midnight flit to avoid creditors (also see tape 835, p. 17 and 896, p. 12). It is also uncertain whether, and how many of, the older Coombe brothers were then in Barnoldswick. Did the Williamses move to Barnoldswick because some Coombes were already there by 1876, or vice versa? It seems an odd choice of place to go to, for the 1881 census suggests there were only a handful of Cornish people in Barnoldswick, unlike, say, Burnley. I have been unable to find evidence of the major local employer, William Bracewell, recruiting labour from Cornwall.

CHAPTER TWO: THE SILENCE OF A
DUTIFUL DAUGHTER

1 Tape 835, pp. 10–11 and 18, tape 896, p. 2 and tape 900, p. 24; also 1881 census.

2 Half-timers were generally given a Labour Certificate to prove they could enter the factory. Oddly enough no such certificate has survived among the Cooper papers, although many other cotton workers still possess theirs. Perhaps her certificates were lost during one of her many moves of house.

3 Quoted from 'Little Things That Worry Us', handwritten BBC script, c. 21.9.1926. She also refers very briefly ('I was sent to the mill as a half-time creeler in the cardroom') in the interview, *NL* 12.9.1924.

. Liddington, J., and Norris, J., *One Hand Tied Behind Us*, Virago, London, 1978, chapter 5, gives a more comprehensive description of cotton mill processes.

4 For background to the half-timer question see *Colne & Nelson Times* 13.1.1899, which quotes the *Daily News*; *C & NT* 19.11.1897 records the Barnoldswick ballot of trade unionists on abolishing child labour as 0 votes to 81. Simon, B., *Education and the Labour Movement*, Lawrence and Wishart, London, 1965, pp. 138–9 emphasises how little criticism of the half-time system there was in the 1870s.

5 SJC's full-time certificate has not been preserved; references to her promotion in *NL* 12.9.1924. Cardroom wages from Wood, G.H., 'Statistics of Wages in the United Kingdom during the Nineteenth Century', *Journal of the Royal Statistical Society*, Jan & Mar 1910; no figures are specifically given for Barnoldswick, and the wages suggested are based on Manchester and district, and on Preston, Darwen, Blackburn, etc.

Information from 1881 Census for Barnoldswick.

6 Tape 916, pp. 2–3, tape 121, p. 17, tape 900, p. 3 etc; also *Burnley Express*, 26.3.1968 (nine years before first taped interview). The major interview with SJC (*NL* 12.9.1924) makes no reference to this period of her life, nor has any documentary evidence survived confirming SJC's years as nurse-cum-washerwoman.

7 For John Coombe, Barrett's *Directory*, 1896 and tape 818, p. 31, tape 907, pp. 13–14 etc; for Bill, marriage certificate 14.1.1899, and tape 896, p. 4, tape 907, p. 3 etc; for Charles, 1881 census and marriage certificate 10.9.1895. (Dick found a job as a skilled moulder at Dickett's, Burnley, which was currently developing a new model of water-closet; it is unclear whether he lived in Brierfield or Burnley; tape 896, pp. 2–3 and 914, p. 1)

It is difficult to date the move to Brierfield as the only source (*NL* 12.9.1924) is too inaccurate to be taken to be reliable on this detail.

8 Tape 835, pp. 3–4; also tape C, p. 4, tape 907, p. 9 and tape 896, p. 18.

9 Tape B, p. 4; tape 896, p. 18; tape D, p. 3; tape 835, p. 29; tape 900, p. 22; and *C & NT* 20.3.1896.

The Primitive Methodist Hymnal, compiled by a Committee appointed by the Conference of 1882, Joseph Toulson, London, 1887; quotation from Hymn 218 by I. Watts.

10 Jane Coombe's death certificate gives cause as 'Paraplegia Exhaustion'. The precise date of SJC's return to the mill is unclear, as I have been unable to locate contemporary records of Tunstills. However, interviews that she gave later indicate that it was shortly after her mother's death, see *Queen* 17.4.1909 and *Halifax Courier* 6.5.1905.

For winders see *One Hand* p. 92 and tape 916, p. 32. Wage figures from Wood, G.H., 'Statistics of Wages in the United Kingdom during the Nineteenth Century', *Journal of the Royal Statistical Society*, March 1910. Wood gives winders' wages as 15s 3d in 1886 and 18s in 1891; four-loom weavers' wages as 21s 5d (1886) and 24s (1891–3); tacklers' wages as 36s 3d (1886) & 40s (1891); these figures are for Burnley and district.

SJC may have acquired the Tunstills job through contacts established in the mill by her brothers, Bill and Charles. On the other hand, such family networks might not have been needed since the local cotton industry was expanding so rapidly that there were always jobs available.

11 Dating SJC's joining the BWA is difficult, as newspaper references are vague eg. *Queen* 17.4.1909 and *NL* 12.9.1924; also tape 672, p. 9–10.

On collectors, see BWA Mins 3.12.1894 etc; Foley, A., *A Bolton Childhood*, Manchester, University Extra-Mural Department and WEA, Manchester, 1973, p. 63; tape 900, p. 2 notes that union cards were kept in *The Christian Miscellany*. Women are largely absent from the union minutes except as complainants and Mrs Lord, the temporary cleaner, BWA Mins 25.6.1896. There are no references to women appearing at committee meetings; but there were also quarterly members' meetings held locally and SJC and other women might possibly have attended these.

12 I have so far been able to locate about eight photographs of Charles Coombe's gang of navvies; two portraits of Charles Coombe, including one with one of his sons; one of Jane Coombe and Alf; four of Alf Coombe as a soldier; one of Richard Coombe as a young man; at least one of Harry and his family in USA. However, the 150 photographs discovered after Mary's funeral may possibly include other early family portraits.

13 Ashby, M.K., *Joseph Ashby of Tysoe 1859–1919*, Merlin, London, 1974, pp. 98, 140 and 161–2.

For similar stories of Victorian women, see Mitchell, H., *The Hard Way Up*; Chew, D.N., *Ada Nield Chew: The Life and Writings of a Working Woman*, Virago, London, 1982; Davies, M.L. (ed), *Life As We Have Known It*, 1931 and Virago, London 1977; also Burnett. J. (ed), *Useful Toil*, 1974 and Pelican, London, 1977, the story of Lucy Luck, pp. 67–77.

CHAPTER THREE: FRONTIER TOWN

1 Farnie, D.A., *The English Cotton Industry & the World Market 1815–1896*, Oxford University Press, Oxford, 1979, chapter 8 for late developments in weaving. Population figures from Hawkes, G.I., *The Development of Public Education in Nelson*, Nelson Corporation, Nelson, 1966, p. 35.

Information about mill owners from obituaries eg. *N. Chron* 28.11.1902; 17.4.1903, *C & NT* 4.10.1912; 12.11.1915.

2 Most of the information about migration is taken from interviews with, or obituaries of, immigrants. The 1881 census is, of course, now available, but the 1891 census will be more valuable, as it was in the 1880s (when the population of Nelson more than doubled) that migration-can begin to be studied on a wide scale.

NL 13.10.1933 etc for Swaledalian reunions in Brierfield. Information about Cowling from Wood, A., (ed), *Cowling: A Moorland Parish*, Cowling Local History Society, Cowling, 1980, pp. 32, 35 etc.

3 Thompson, E.P., *The Making of the English Working Class*, 1963 and Pelican, London, 1968, p. 760; Bennett, W., *The History of Marsden and Nelson*, Nelson Corporation, Nelson, 1957, p. 168; Snowden, Viscount, P., *An Autobiography* vol I, 1864–1919, Ivor Nicholson & Watson, London, 1934, pp. 40–4.

4 Chapel figures from Bennett, W., *The History of Marsden and Nelson*, pp. 194–5; by contrast, only four Church of England, four Roman Catholic and four Baptist churches and chapels are noted.

For the Tunstills, see footnote 1 above, para. 2.

5 For William Rickard, *NL* 13–17.4.1934. Another Primitive Methodist was Clara Myers, Guildswoman and suffragist, but what role she played in her chapel is more obscure.

6 Tape 898, p. 11 tape 889, p. 4. *C & NT* 12.1.1894 & 18.1.1895 notes Salem classes on socialism, the new woman etc. Bealey, F., and Pelling, H., *Labour and Politics*, Macmillan, London, 1958, pp. 102–3 earlier drew attention to the importance of the Independent Methodist Connection.

7 Quoted by Cross, C., *Philip Snowden*, Barrie & Rockliff, London, 1966, p. 25.

The reasons for the radicalism of North-east Lancashire, and Nelson in particular, are complex and each given varying weight by different historians. The following accounts are helpful here: Weinroth, J., untitled paper, 1976 (based upon the research of the late Howard Weinroth), on the important link between local radicalism and the loom-and-power system, and the effect of this system of weakening paternalistic structures.

Fowler, A., *The History of the Nelson Weavers*, Nelson Weavers' Association, Nelson, 1984 forthcoming, explains Nelson's industrial militancy and political radicalism in the above terms, but also notes the late development of the Nelson Weavers (NWA) which put it in a strong bargaining position regarding the Uniform Wage List.

Joyce, P., *Work, Society & Politics*, Harvester, London, 1980, emphasises the similarities between North-east Lancashire and Yorkshire with regard to the above factors, noting the West Riding's late mechanisation, prevalence of small firms and relative social instability.

Bealey and Pelling, *Labour & Politics*, also note the loose federal structure of the cotton unions which gave considerable autonomy to local branches, plus emphasising the influence of Independent Methodism.

8 1901 Census figures for Burnley: of women over ten classified as occupied: unmarried 75.4 per cent, and married 33.8 per cent.

Interview with Deborah Smith, *NL* 28.11.1924.

9 For Burnley see Trodd, G., *Political Change and the Working Class in Blackburn and Burnley*, Ph. D. thesis, Lancaster, 1978, pp. 125, 177; the only working-class Tory councillor was not a cotton worker, but a miner. Amos Nelson was a Baptist and later became a Conservative.

For opposition to half-time laws, see BWA Mins 23.4.1894 etc and *C & NT* 19.11.1897; *Labour Prophet* Mar–April 1894.

10 Comment on Hyndman by Bruce Glasier quoted by Thompson, E.P., *William Morris: Romantic to Revolutionary*, Merlin, London, 1955 and 1977, p. 353; Thompson offers a fair picture of Hyndman although other writers have viewed him primarily through Marx's and Engels' critical perspective, and so found themselves unable to explain why Hyndman should be so popular among the workers in Burnley.

Quotation from tape 665, p. 29.

11 Membership figures from Watmough, P.A., 'The Membership of the Social Democratic Federation, 1885–1902', *Bulletin*, Society for the Study of Labour History, no 34, spring 1977, p. 38. Note also the difference between paid-up members and the much larger number of members claimed in *Justice*, who were sympathisers but not in membership.

Of the two councillors, the Miners' Secretary was John Sparling and the Twisters' official, John Tempest; see Trodd, G., *Political Change and the Working Class in Blackburn and Burnley*, pp. 292–4 and 341–2.

12 *Workman's Times* 12.8.1893. Copies of the *Socialist* 7.10.1893 – 22.12.1893 in Colindale; copies for 1.6.1894, 9.3.1894 and 10.8.1894 are in Burnley Library.

Burnley Weavers' vice-president was John Markham, see BWA mins 26.7.1892 and 25.7.1893. There seems some confusion over dating here, and some secondary sources suggest 1895.

13 ILP *Annual Report* 1893 notes only one Nelson delegate, Ernest Johnson; he was the first socialist on the Nelson School Board in 1894, and was selected that year as an SDF parliamentary candidate for Clitheroe but later withdrew. *C & NT* 13.1.1893 notes that C.W. Parratt went too (as represen-

tative of Padiham SDF), a weaver and long-standing SDF supporter. The *C & NT* also reports that S.R. Lowe JP went as Nelson ILP representative; for Lowe's obituary *NL* 15.10.1926.

It is difficult to give a precise date to the forming of the Nelson branch. *N. Chron* 27.1.1893 notes a meeting in the Weavers' Institute of various trade unionists who agree to form a branch, and this was apparently on 21 January. However, this meeting seems to represent the existing branch becoming public, for the Nelson ILP account book which has survived begins 1.1.1893 with the entry 'Subscriptions 11s', implying at least informal meetings of members at the end of 1892.

CHAPTER FOUR: ROBERT COOPER AND THE GREAT CRUSADE

1 John Cooper's story recounted in *NL* 2.9.1927. Primitive Methodist Scotland Road Leaders' Minute Book, 1.3.1894, 29.8.1895, 22.8.1896 etc. Tape 896, pp. 20–1 and tape 818, pp. 17–18; John Cooper's obituary, *NL* 27.5.1904.
2 Tape 835, pp. 19–20 and tape 896, pp. 15–19; Primitive Methodist Scotland Road Leaders' Minute Book, 26.8.1890.
3 Obituary, *NL* 18.5.1934. Certificate, 10.5.1899.
4 Tape 916, p. 16 and *NL* 18.5.1934.

Unfortunately, beyond oral reference and Robert Cooper's obituary, I have not yet been able to find contemporary confirmation of this incident; and indeed it is difficult to date exactly, though it seems to have occurred 1890–1. Clegg, H.A., Fox, A., & Thompson, A.F., *A History of British Trade Unions since 1889*, Clarendon Press, Oxford, 1964, pp. 215–17 notes the formation in 1889 in London of a General Postmen's Union; over the next few months postmen were fined or suspended if known to have taken part, and by about autumn 1890 the union had collapsed. A more moderate organisation, the Postmen's Federation, had been established by 1891 and proceeded circumspectly.

This suggests Robert Cooper's ill-fated union flourished not long after the London one, perhaps about 1890. This would coincide neatly with the formation of the short-lived Nelson Trades Council which aimed to support small struggling trade unions and which was socialist-minded. However I have not so far been able to trace reference in the Nelson Trades Council minutes, nor in local newspapers, to this incident (though note *N. Chron* 18.7.1890 editorial on the Leeds gasworkers, London postmen etc). (Ironically a Nelson branch of the Postmen's Federation was formed circa Feb 1892, and the secretary was Robert's elder brother John, *C & NT* 14.2.1896.) The absence so far of contemporary documentary confirmation of this incident might, perhaps, cast some doubt on these later references.

5 *N. Chron* 5.6.1891 and 12.6.1891; for Robert Cooper's involvement see *C & NT* 18.4.1934 and *NL* 18.5.1934 which notes 'he was one of the original members of the SDF'. This obituary is the only source for his attendance at this meeting.

6 *N. Chron* 14.4.1892 and 30.12.1892. Tape 896, p. 17.

The area of Massachusetts that Robert would be most likely to head for was the textile town of Fall River, on the Rhode Island border, fifty miles south of Boston. Fall River had developed close links with Burnley, for there Burnley people apparently had a good reputation and were often given jobs before others.

7 Tape B, pp. 2–3. Marriage certificate of John Coombe & Annie Stanton, 11.7.1891.

8 Clarke, A., *The Effects of the Factory System*, written and published serially 1895–8, J.M. Dent, London, 1913 (3rd edition), pp. 70–1.

BWA mins 8.6.1893 regarding sanitary accommodation at Brierfield, and 24.5.1894 for correspondence with sanitary inspector regarding closets and women winders. Also note *BGaz* 29.1.1896 etc.

9 *NL* 20.11.1924.

The Origin and Progress of the Nelson Weavers' Association, 1912, pp. 18–19. For analysis of this and similar incidents, see Lambertz, J.R., *Male-Female Violence in Late Victorian and Edwardian England*, BA thesis, Harvard, 1979, chap VII, 'Work-place sexual harassment and the Lancashire cotton industry'.

10 BWA mins 5.8.1892, 13.10.1982, 27.10.1892, 5.11.1892 etc. Burnley Federation of Textile Trade Union mins 23.2.1894, 2.3.1894; also note BWA mins 15.1.1894 & 23.4.1894. For further complaints from weavers at Tunstills, see BWA mins 7.1.1895, 18.6.1896.

11 Tape 916, pp. 29–30; see also tape 915, p. 8; it is difficult to place this incident in context, though stories about other kinds of myths concerning menstruation are not uncommon eg. McCrindle, J. and Rowbotham, S., *Dutiful Daughters*, Penguin, London, 1977, pp. 119 and 165; Davey, D., *A Sense of Adventure*, EE1 People's History Project, London, 1980, p. 16 about making towels; McCarthy, M., *Generation in Revolt*, Heinemann, London, 1953, pp. 19–20 notes of a later generation, 'We Lancashire working women are only a generation or two removed from the soil . . .'

Nevertheless, this particular piece of oral testimony still seems to hang in mid-air.

12 Tape 916, p. 1. St John Ambulance references include *C & NT* 11.5.1894 (the earliest newspaper reference to SJC I have been able to trace) and 20.3.1896; *BGaz* 10.1.1894 and 13.1.1894; BWA mins 13.4.1892, 28.7.1892 etc.

13 James, A., & Hills, N. (eds), *Mrs John Brown*, John Murray, London, 1937, p. 42, and see also pp. 37–41. Details of the Co-operative Society from

Bennett, W., *The History of Burnley from 1850*, p. 214.

14 *Burnley Co-operative Record*, June 1896, Feb and April 1897, March 1898. The last mentioned lecturer was a Miss Lanchester, possibly Edith Lanchester, a friend of Karl Marx's daughter Eleanor; she had scandalised people the previous year by practising 'free love'.

15 *NL* 12.9.1924 for SJC's meeting with Schreiner; James, A., and Hills, N., *Mrs John Brown* pp. 33, 39, 67 and 69.

It is difficult to date the meeting precisely. Schreiner was in Europe 1881–9 and visited the Browns in Burnley in April 1881; but at this time SJC was living away in Barnoldswick and was only sixteen, so a visit is unlikely. There are two more probable datings. Schreiner seems to have been in England from late May to early October 1893, and again from about February 1897 to late that year. Less seems to have been known about the 1897 visit; the meeting of the three women in Burnley seems more likely to have occurred in 1893, for we know that during her five months in England, Schreiner spent three months at Millthorpe (near Sheffield) where Edward Carpenter lived. Schreiner was certainly in touch by letter (15.9.1893) with Mary Brown at this time, and it seems not improbable that around September she travelled from Sheffield to Burnley to spend a few days at the Browns' house, and while there was introduced by her hostess to a young mill girl from Brierfield who was beginning to develop an interest in progressive ideas.

This remains speculative, for little is known of Schreiner's five months in England. For background see Meintjes, J., *Olive Schreiner: Portrait of a South African Woman*, Hugh Keartland, Johannesburg, 1965, pp. 122–4 and 133–66; First, R., and Scott, A., *Olive Schreiner*, Andre Deutsch, London, 1980, pp. 209–10; Cronwright-Schreiner, S.C. (ed), *The Letters of Olive Schreiner 1876–1920*, T. Fisher Unwin, London, 1924; Hobman, D.L., *Olive Schreiner: her friends and times*, Watts & Co, London, 1955, pp. 86–94; and James, A., and Hill, N., *Mrs John Brown*, p. 183.

16 Tape 915, p. 8. Precise dating here is also elusive. SJC's getting on the winders' committee can probably be dated to late 1893 or possibly early 1894. Oral testimony suggests this was 'soon' after her outspoken protest, suggesting the latter occurred in the summer or autumn 1893. But such testimony, handed down by word-of-mouth, is necessarily weak on the precise sequence of events, and so dating must remain tentative.

17 BWA mins 16.11.1893 – 6.8.1894 and *BGaz* for same period. The records of the BWA, including the minutes book for the period, have now been deposited at the Lancashire Record Office, but appear to include no handbills. There was a similar recruitment drive among beamers, who were to be paid at the same rate as four-loom weavers. Wood, G.H., 'Statistics of Wages in the United Kingdom during the Nineteenth Century', *Journal of the Royal Statistical Society*, Feb & Mar 1910 gives no evidence for winders' wages

in the Burnley district increasing due to the 1894 Winders' List: 18s (1891) and only 18 6d (1899).

18 Tape 121, p. 17.

Nelson, Colne, Brierfield & District Textile Trades Federation mins 22.2.1895; ironically the Federation's fourth (and last) choice of speakers was Annie Marland who worked for the Women's Trade Union League, see *One Hand* pp. 88–9 and 96–9.

Nelson and Burnley trade unions squabbled over Brierfield, clouding the question of local affiliation; for instance, Brierfield weavers and winders belonged to Burnley, but the tacklers belonged in the Nelson Overlookers' Association; additionally there were accusations from Burnley Weavers that Nelson had poached its Brierfield members.

19 The exact origins of SJC's research interest here remain unclear. There might be a link with WCG for, from at least 1894, the Guildswomen had been forwarding information about women's work in textile mills to the government; this may have been how SJC first came across Sarah Reddish.

20 The pamphlet was published by the *Clarion*. Margaret McMillan spoke at the Nelson ILP in October 1894 and to the Burnley WCG in January 1895 on 'Abolition of Half-time Child Labour in Factories', both of which lectures SJC might have attended. For further information, see Simon, B., *Education and the Labour Movement*, p. 157.

21 Tape 896, p. 17; *C & NT* 19.2.1897. Nelson etc District Textile Trades Federation mins 6.9.1895 etc; *Socialist* 9.3.1894; Nelson ILP account book 4.11.1895.

22 *Justice* 1.6.1895; see also *Justice* 29.6.1895, 20.7.1895 etc.

23 Hyndman, H.M., *Further Reminiscences*, Macmillan, London, 1912, pp. 66–9. However Hyndman fared better than the three other SDF candidates (George Lansbury won only 203 votes) and better than the majority of ILP candidates.

24 For the Literary & Debating Society, see *C & NT* 13.1.1893 – 9.3.1894; for Ben Smith, see *C & NT* 29.12.1893, 23.2.1893, 21.9.1894, also mins of Nelson etc Textile Trades Federation on which he was active; Smith was possibly a member of the SDF, for *Justice* 22.2.1896 notes he chaired an SDF debate in Rossendale.

For local labour representation, see Bennett, W., *The History of Marsden and Nelson*, pp. 212–13; BWA mins 1.8.1894; *C & NT* 21.9.1894 and 26.10.1894.

25 For SJC's involvement, *NL* 12.9.1924 and *NL* 27.5.1904.

For the Labour Electoral Association, *C & NT* 16.11.1894 etc; for Abel Latham, see obituary, *NL* 3.2.1928; he was perhaps more moderate than Smith. For the United Labour Party Club, see *C & NT* 15.11.1895, 3.4.1896 etc, and 1.10.1897 when it was disbanded.

26 Primitive Methodist Chapel Leaders' mins, 5.6.1896. SJC was listed by

her maiden name in the syllabus, although married, presumably because the list was printed during the summer before the marriage was agreed; *Justice* 1.2.1896.

CHAPTER FIVE: THE REVOLT OF THE DAUGHTERS

1 For Leonard, see *Justice* 7.1.1893 etc, *N. Chron* 13.1.1893, *C & NT* 9.3.1894 etc, tape 916, pp. 2–3 and tape 818, p. 16.

Wedding notices in *N. Chron* & *C & NT* 30.10.1896; oral evidence (tape 818, p. 13 and tape 900, p. 21) suggests a double wedding with another local SDF couple, but there seems no confirmation of this. If photographs were taken at the wedding, none seems to have survived. Thanks to Jenny Cranfield for information about Mrs Cooper.

2 Eleanor Rathbone to I. Newton, 5.3.1907 notes 'Mrs Cooper . . . was a worker in a cotton mill before marriage'. For other sources, see note 9 below.

3 Mitchell, H., *The Hard Way Up*, pp. 101–2.

4 For the formation of Brierfield SDF, see *C & NT* 15.1.1897 and 3.9.1897; it replaced the United Labour Party Club which was formally disbanded. The two pamphlets were published in September 1894 by the Labour Press, and 1896 by the *Clarion* respectively; Mann also came to speak at the Nelson ILP, 12.1.1895 and the Coopers may well have met him first then. The Nelson ILP Branch's Account Book; *C & NT* 25.6.1897 and 2.7.1897 for Mann meeting and SDF tussle with the police and magistrates.

5 Trodd, G., *Political Change and the Working Class*, p. 234 for poor housing in Burnley (twice the density per acre of Blackburn); and pp. 237–8 for infant mortality rates, noting the frequency of deaths of premature babies, baby deaths due to bronchitis and pneumonia, and deaths of babies of winders. The figures for Brierfield were less severe than for Burnley.

6 Tape 818, p. 31 and tape 896, p. 18, and also note tape 907, p. 12. Oral evidence here is understandably difficult to corroborate, especially as there appears to have been no inquest or coroner's report.

7 Tape B, p. 5–6. Ighamite Chapel, Wheatley Lane, receipt for 15s 6d for a new grave from Robert Cooper, 27.9.1897; death certificate dated 25.9.1897 of death previous day, mother present, due to 'acute bronchitic convulsions'. *N. Chron* 8.10.1897 for brief notice of death; it seems perhaps unusual that there should be no inquest if indeed the police *were* involved.

8 For discussion of 'maternal ignorance' and working mothers, see Lewis, J., *The Politics of Motherhood*, Croom Helm, London, 1980, pp. 78 and 90–108; also Davin, A., 'Imperialism and Motherhood', *History Workshop Journal*, spring 1978, especially p. 24.

9 Evidence on whether SJC returned to the mill is confusing. In an interview (*NL* 12.9.1924) SJC notes, 'before I came to Nelson in 1901 I was working for

Shaw & Hargreaves'; but her daughter (tape D, p. 4) doubts this. Another interview (*Queen* 17.4.1909) which is perhaps more reliable states that SJC worked in the factory for sixteen years; this would comprise six years at Barnoldswick (c. 1876–c. 1882), seven years at Tunstills (c. 1889–96), and, therefore, three more years at Brierfield (c. 1897–1900). Yet oral evidence remains vague here; tape 916, p. 4 notes, 'yes she went to the mill after she was married, yes, because she worked at a mill near where we lived . . .'; though later (tape 900, p. 32) Mary Cooper states quite definitely that her mother 'wasn't working then' – at the time of her brother's death. And the only oral evidence from a respondent who knew SJC at this period (tape 907, p. 12) states clearly 'No, no, she never worked in the mill while I was little. I can't remember her working in a mill, no . . .' So this aspect of SJC's life remains uncertain, unless other records from this period turn up; it is assumed that probably she worked in a Brierfield mill from late 1897 for about two and a half years.

10 Pearsall Smith, A.W., 'A Reply from the Daughters', *The Nineteenth Century*, Mar 1894, p. 450; the writer married Bertrand Russell later that year. James, A., and Hills, N., (eds) *Mrs John Brown*, p. 74. I have not yet traced the Fawcett article referred to, but am grateful to David Doughan at the Fawcett Library for his help here.

11 Cooper, S., 'The Lancashire Factory Girl', undated essay.

12 McLaren, A., *Birth Control in Nineteenth-Century England*, Croom Helm, London, 1978, pp. 108 and 178, which also discusses Besant's Malthusian links. The Coopers' copy of *The Law of Population* appears to have been published about 1888–9 by the Freethought Publishing Company, London.

Allinson, T.R., *A Book for Married Women*, L.N. Fowler, London, 1899, pp. 5 and 13; the earlier pamphlet was published by F. Pitman, London. McLaren notes the prosecution of Lambert, etc for sale of contraceptives and handbooks; and also of another Allinson's book which did inform his readers of a supplier.

13 For instance, Huxley, T.H., *Lessons in Elementary Physiology*, Macmillan, London, 1893. It is signed 'Emma Ashworth . . . Brierfield' and might be by a Mrs Ashworth who was a founder-member of the Burnley WCG.

14 For discussion of these fears of Malthusianism, see McLaren, A., *Birth Control in Nineteenth-Century England*, chap 9. Also, *Justice* 13.7.1895, 20.8.1895, 27.7.1895, etc.

15 For SJC's role in the Guild, *NL* 12.9.1924, and also *NL* 1.3.1901 and *N. Chron* 1.3.1901; for formation of the branch, *C & NT* 27.1.1893, *Burnley Co-operative Record* Dec 1898, *NL* 1.3.1901, *N. Chron* 28.10.1898 and 4.11.1898.

16 *C & NT* 10.2.1899, 10.3.1899, 6.10.1899 and 31.8.1900.

17 Bebel, A., *Woman in the Past, Present and Future*, W. Reeves, London, c. 1898, pp. 4–5.

18 *C & NT* 19.11.1897, 10.12.1897, 30.9.1898, 7.10.1898 and *N. Chron* 30.3.1899.

19 Mann, T., *Memoirs*, 1923, reprinted MacGibbon & Kee, London, 1967, p. 102; Nelson ILP Account Book, 5.11.1895 & 2.9.1896.

20 Her essay is discussed more fully in *One Hand*, pp. 130–1. *Socialist* 9.3.1894, Nelson ILP Account Book, 12.1.1897, 22.2.1897, etc; see also Tuckett, A., 'Enid Stacy', *Women and the Labour Movement*, North West Labour History Society *Bulletin* 7, 1980–81.
Another popular speaker was Katherine St John Conway, later Katherine Bruce Glasier; SJC became friendly with her later on.

21 Membership figures taken from ILP *Annual Report*; 1899, Nelson 57, Blackburn 76, West Ham 77; 1900, Nelson 74, Blackburn 75, West Ham 96; 1901, Nelson 72, Blackburn 75, Bradford 100; 1902, Nelson 72, Blackburn 82, West Ham 77, Bradford 340; Manchester also had very large branches.

22 Tape 907, p. 6 and tape 834, p. 24.

CHAPTER SIX: THE NEW LIFE

1 Thanks to Mark Bloomfield for supplementary information about the Union: while local Union branches stressed home study circles, others aimed to educate users of the public library system. There is no evidence to link the Coopers directly to NHRU, but significantly they attended classes run by the Education Department of the Co-operative Union c. 1904.
C & NT 28.1.1898, 2.9.1894, 14.9.1894 and *BGaz* 8.11.1893; tape 916, p. 30 for the Coopers and the *Clarion*, and *One Hand* pp. 120–4 for *Clarion* activities in Lancashire.

2 Leonard, T.A., *Adventures in Holiday-Making*, Holiday Fellowship, London, 1935, pp. 19 and 21.

3 *C & NT* 31.5.1895.

4 Leonard, T.A., *Adventures in Holiday-Making*, pp. 24–33.

5 Tape 915, pp. 7–8; *C & NT* 12.4.1899; dating is based largely on the autograph book referred to below.

6 Tape 818, pp. 19–20; *NL* 12.9.1924.

7 *C & NT* 15.12.1905.

8 Autograph book, p. 45, entry by G.R. Perrot, Sheffield, 11 (or 12).8.1899; pages numbered by author.

9 *NL* 12.9.1924; also *NL* 23.10.1908 and *N. Chron* 14.1.1898; autograph book pp. 24 and 74.

10 *NL* 12.9.1924; Leonard, T.A., *Adventures in Holiday-Making*, p. 34.

11 The street was called Coalpit Lane, but has been renamed Glen View; date of return from autograph book and tape 900, p. 12; tape D, p. 1. It is unclear which house the Coopers lived in after their marriage.

12 Tape D, p. 1; wage figures from Wood, G.H., 'Statistics of Wages in the United Kingdom during the Nineteenth Century', Journal of the *Royal Statistical Society*, Mar 1910 (unfortunately no figures are given specifically for Nelson).

PART TWO: VOTES FOR WOMEN

CHAPTER SEVEN: THE POWER OF THE BALLOT BOX

1 MNSWS *Annual Report* 1893–4 and *Burnley Co-operative Record* Dec 1897. It is difficult to unravel which of the many suffrage 'Phillips' Helen Phillip was (especially since printed annual reports may casually add and subtract an 's' at the end of a surname).

MNSWS *Annual Report* 1893–4 notes a Mrs Phillips and a Mrs Herbert Phillips on the General Committee; and a Mrs Arthur Phillip at the Accrington meeting; earlier MNSWS records note a Mrs Phillips on the Executive Committee from 1893, and a Mrs Phillips giving 5s in 1890; later NESWS records note a Mrs Phillip at a meeting in Wigan.

Because of this confusion, a letter appealing for further information about Helen Phillip was published in the *Manchester Evening News* July 1981; sadly this elicited no replies. However, a recently-discovered signed song-sheet suggests she kept in touch with the Coopers after Mary was born.

2 For further detail about the early suffrage movement, see *One Hand*, chap IV, or Strachey, R., *The Cause*, 1928 and Virago, London, 1978, chap VI. Other issues included the effects of the Corrupt Practices Act and the debates over the Contagious Diseases Act.

3 *Women's Suffrage Journal* Dec 1885.

4 BWA mins 27.6.1892.

5 *Justice* 2.11.1895, 26.10.1895, 4.1.1896, 11.1.1896 & 15.2.1896; such schemes were not always endorsed by the SDF; but, 'free maintenance' was one of the biggest campaigns organised officially by the SDF, and the SDF Women's Circles discussed the 'endowment of motherhood' as well.

6 *Justice* 10.8.1895, also 3.8.1895 and 24.8.1895. Whether 'L.B.' was a woman or man is not clear; the writer who provoked this response was, of course, Belfort Bax.

7 *Justice* 31.8.1895, also 29.6.1895, 2.9.1893 and 23.9.1893. One of the correspondents was Isabel Tiplady, an SDF activist from Blackburn, who noted that 'here in the North, our meetings are almost wholly attended by men . . . women fight shy of socialism . . .' For further discussion of the 'Sunday dinner' question, see Hunt, K., 'Women and the Social Democratic Federation: some notes on Lancashire', *Women and the Labour Movement*, North West Labour History Society *Bulletin* 7, 1980–1.

8 *Justice* 13.2.1897, also 2.11.1895; see also Kapp, Y., *Eleanor Marx* vol II, 1976 and Virago, London, 1979, pp. 558-9, and Harrison, B., *Separate Spheres: the Opposition to Women's Suffrage in Britain*, Croom Helm, London, 1978, p. 41.

9 *B Co-op Record* Oct 1896; also Aug 1894 and Jan 1898. For the national picture (and the Accrington and Darwin WCGs) see *One Hand*, pp. 141-2.

10 *B Co-op Record* Mar & Aug 1895.

11 James, A., and Hills, N., (eds), *Mrs John Brown*, pp. 91-4; also *C & NT* 4.1.1895. See also Chew, D.N., *Ada Nield Chew: the Life and Writings of a Working Woman*, p. 19.

12 *N. Chron* 4.1.1898 and 11.3.1898, *B Co-op Record* Feb 1897, and *C & NT* 18.1.1901; also Bennett, W., *The History of Burnley from 1850*, p. 201 and 214.

13 Mary Brown was a close friend of the Kay-Shuttleworths; she was sympathetic to socialist ideas, though not always to their methods. Mary Robb was active in the Women's Liberal Association, and as a Guardian, distinguished between the deserving poor and those whose 'own vicious habits' fitted them for detention colonies. Lady O'Hagan probably clung least tenaciously of the three to Liberalism; she stood in elections as a progressive candidate.

14 List of elected women from ILP *Conference Report* 1897, which also notes a woman on Keighley School Board. *One Hand*, pp. 126-7 details the attitude of Bruce Glasier, etc; conversations with Karen Hunt suggest *One Hand* was perhaps a little harsh towards the SDF here in comparison with the ILP.

15 ILP *Conference Report* 1893 and 1894. The 1894 Report included an article, 'To the Women of the ILP' which began, 'Of all the victims of our present industrial system none are so brutally enslaved as those wives and mothers who are compelled to go to the mills and the factories because their husband can't earn sufficient to keep their families in necessaries . . .'

16 ILP *Conference Report* 1902 (and a similar situation of dual resolutions being supported occurred at the 1904 ILP Conference). *One Hand*, pp. 168-9 was unintentionally unjust to Mrs Pankhurst in not noting her first intervention here; this was because we had not then located the *Conference Reports* and therefore relied over-much here on secondary sources. Oddly, Pankhurst, E.S., *The Suffragette Movement*, 1931 and Virago, London, 1977, does not appear to refer to her mother's 1902 motion, merely noting how Isabella Ford reported that the ILP leaders were 'no more than lukewarm on the subject of votes for women'. Pankhurst, E., *My Own Story*, 1914 and Virago, London, 1979, p. 37 refers to it only vaguely, implying it was a 'Labour Party' conference; pp. 40-1 note her 1904 resolution, of course.

17 The details of the Special Appeal are described in *One Hand*, pp. 76-80; see also MNSWS *Annual Report* 1894. The first organiser was a Mrs Wimbolt; little is known about Annie Heaton.

18 The *Queen* 17.4.1909; she expressed similar thoughts in *Halifax Courier* 6.5.1905. The annual reports of MNSWS/NESWS are lost 1896–9.

19 Reprinted in the *Englishwoman's Review* 15.4.1901.

20 Quoted from *NL* 12.9.1924. Many of the meetings are listed in NESWS *Annual Report* 1899–1900. The campaign is described in more detail, *One Hand*, pp. 145–7.

21 *N. Chron* 1.3.1901 and *NL* 22.3.1901 for signatures. NESWS *Annual Reports* notes, 1900–1 SJC subscribes 1s and collects 3s; 1901–2 subscribes 1s, collects 1s; 1903–4 subscribes 1s.

22 Esther Roper had already been down on 15 February for a conference of MPs and other suffrage sympathisers in the House of Commons, organised by the NUWSS. It decided to ballot for a women's suffrage bill, or failing that, a resolution; the former was unsuccessful and the day chosen for the latter (19 March) was taken up by government business. Thus the 18 March deputation must have arrived at Westminster with their hopes already low.

23 Quotation from *N. Chron* 22.3.1901, a sympathetic report headed 'The Franchise for Factory Women: A Nelson Textile Worker at Westminster'. *NL* 22.3.1901 also had a sympathetic report and editorial headed 'Lancashire Lasses in London'. *C & NT* 22.3.1901 was scathing, pointing out that 'women are . . . too indifferent to what happens outside their domestic life to take a too prominent and active part in public work', and marvelled at the likelihood of a lady Prime Minister. NESWS *Annual Report* 1900–01 also carried details.

24 The MP concerned was Charles Dilke; *Lab L* 23.3.1901. Pankhurst, E.S., *The Suffragette Movement*, p. 205 notes the rumour that Dilke behaved out of spite, following his divorce case.

CHAPTER EIGHT: SOCIALISM INTO LABOUR

1 Tape 900, pp. 10–2 and tape 900, pp. 12–14.

2 Tape 900, p. 12; it is unclear when Robert became secretary of the ward.

3 *N. Chron* 1.3.1901. An SDF woman from Colne, Lucy Patterson, stood for election in 1895, 1898 and 1901, unsuccessfully.

4 For Sarah Thomas, *NL* 24.12.1924.

5 *C & NT* 15.3.1901, 22.3.1901.

6 *N. Chron* 29.3.1901. *C & NT* 29.3.1901. Unfortunately the election photograph does not appear to have survived (though it may well be the same one printed in the *Nelson Workers' Guide* No. 3, March 1903 – for it would have been extravagant of the SDF-ILP to have paid for two separate portraits within the space of two years).

7 Thompson, L., *The Enthusiasts*, Gollancz, London, 1971, p. 70. John Veevers, the new chairman, was also a Freemason as was at least one other influential Tory Board member.

8 B. Bd of Gs mins 11.4.1901, 18.4.1901.

9 B. Bd of Gs mins 30.5.1901, 13.6.1901, 27.6.1901, 4.7.1901. The Guardians also supported the Thornton/Irving proposal that there should be a resident doctor in the Workhouse Infirmary.

10 B. Bd of Gs mins 11.7.1901. *N. Chron* 12.7.1901. *Burnley Labour Jubilee News* Feb 1950.

11 Tapes 121, p. 3; tape 916, p. 17; see also tape 121, p. 2.

12 *C & NT* 26.7.1901; B Bd of G mins 22.8.1901; 26.9.1901; on 28.11.1901 Irving & Thornton proposed SJC should be on the Out-relief Committee, but this was defeated by 12 to 6; 23.1.1902 on corn grinding; by 17.4.1902 SJC was on Visiting Committee, also Cottage Homes sub-committee, 31.3.1904.

13 However the militancy of the Nelson Weavers should not be under-estimated; it supported the notion of independent labour representation, sent delegates to the LRC founding conference – but then did not go on to affiliate, as the Colne Weavers did. See Bealey, F., & Pelling, H., *Labour and Politics*, chapter 5.

14 *C & NT* 6.4.1900; Nelson, Colne, Brierfield & District Textile Trades Federation mins 27.9.1901, 29.11.1901; tape 915, p. 19.

15 *N. Chron* 17.1.1902, 24.1.1902.

16 Nelson, Colne, Brierfield & District Textile Trades Federation mins 25.1.1902, 7.2.1902. *N. Chron* 7.3.1902. Hill. J., *Working Class Politics in Lancashire 1885–1906*, Ph. D., Keele, 1969, pp. 336–7 for individual mem bership structure of Clitheroe Division Labour Representation Association.

17 SJC had accompanied the second textile petition down to London in February 1902; for the success of this deputation, see *One Hand* pp. 152–3.

Esther Roper (NUWSS/NESWS) to Ramsay MacDonald (LRC) 15.5.1902, asking him to receive a deputation of herself, Eva Gore-Booth, and Christabel Pankhurst, a member of the Manchester Branch of the National Union of Shop Assistants; also 15.6.1902; this correspondence is housed in the Labour Party Archive, London.

18 Sarah Reddish to SJC, 20.11.1904; also among the Cooper papers is a blank form headed, 'Report on State of Employment in Textile Mills during the Month of October 1905 in the Nelson District. Please return . . . to Miss Reddish . . . Bolton'.

19 *The One and the Many*, Longmans, London, 1904; *Unseen Kings*, Longman, London, 1904; *The Three Resurrections and the Triumph of Maeve*, Longman, London, 1905; and possibly others.

20 *MG* 9.7.1902.

21 *N. Chron* 18.7.1902.

22 *NL* 1.8.1902.

23 For the problems of the local SDF see Hill, J., *Working Class Politics in*

Lancashire 1885-1906 p. 323 ff. For the links that SJC still retained with the SDF see Thomas Foster to SJC 14.1.1907 and Sarah Reddish to SJC 20.11.1904.

24 Thanks to Jo White for returning copies of the *Guide* to this country. The following copies have survived: No. 1, November 1902; No. 1 (presumably a re-start), January 1903; No. 2, February 1903; No. 3, March 1903, which included SJC's article and photograph; No. 5, May 1903; No. 9, October 1903; No. 11, December 1903; and No. 12, February 1904; and possibly others in private hands.

25 *Nelson Workers' Guide*, No. 1, November 1902. See also *NL* 23.10.1903, 18.3.1904; *C & NT* 25.3.1904.

26 *NL* 26.2.1904. For Harriette Beanland, tape 832, pp. 18 i-ii and tape 916, p. 18 and tape 900, p. 5.

27 Some of this argument must remain speculative for it is not clear how much of a hand Robert Cooper had in writing the first draft, at what stage Harriette Beanland intervened, nor what say the Labour Representation Committee had in their candidates' manifestos.

28 *NL* 4.3.1904 to 31.3.1904.

29 Of the forty-nine candidates standing in the Burnley township, none stood as Labour.

 B Bd of Gs mins 28.4.1904; *Halifax Courier* 6.5.1905; *NL* 27.5.1904; *C & NT* 12.5.1905, 19.5.1905.

30 *C & NT* 2.6.1905 and *NL* 28.6.1928.

31 ILP *Conference Reports* list ILP municipal successes; 1906: Nelson 6 ILP councillors, West Ham 6, Bradford 8, Woolwich 10; 1907: Nelson 6, West Ham 6, Bradford 9, Woolwich 10. Nelson ILP Account Book notes 72 members 1903, 84 in 1904 and 120 and 1906. For election results *NL* 26.1.1906 and 31.8.1906.

32 'Onward, Friends of Freedom' (with two other stanzas) taken from *The Socialist Sunday School Song Book* p. 30, with many thanks to Stan Iveson. Also *C & NT* 2.8.1907.

(Nelson ILP Account Book has as its last payment to Mrs Cooper 19s 6d on 3.4.1907; the 19s 6d seems to represent her quarterly travel expenses.)

33 Tape 898, pp. 17-8. Among the Cooper papers was preserved a copy of *Socialist Sunday Schools: A Manual*, National Council of British Socialist Sunday Schools, c. 1923, which sets out the syllabus for classes of different aged children, etc.

34 Tape 900, p. 6. See also *The Socialist Sunday School Hymn Book*, compiled by the National Council of British Socialist Sunday School Unions, 1910, inscribed by Mary Cooper and stamped by Nelson ILP; also *The Labour Church Hymn Book*, the Labour Church Union, Bradford c. 1906 inscribed by Mary Cooper 'Bought off the Labour Church'.

35 *NL* 3.4.1914. The incident had slipped from Mary Cooper's memory

over the intervening seventy years, and she was tickled to be shown a photocopy of the report.

CHAPTER NINE: WOMEN ORGANISE TOGETHER

1 Ramsay MacDonald seems to have handed over the correspondence from September to John McNeil; Esther Roper to McNeil 16.9.1902 and 15.10.1902.

2 Esther Roper to 'Sir' 29.10.1902. Unfortunately the LRC replies do not appear to have survived.

3 Tape 916, p. 27.

4 For further details of this campaign, see *One Hand*, p. 157 ff.

5 *Nelson Workers' Guide* March 1903 for SJC's role in collecting signatures; NESWS Annual Report 1902–3; *NL* 17.7.1903, 21.8.1903.

6 The fifth woman was Sarah Dickenson, involved with Eva Gore-Booth in running the Manchester and Salford Women's Trade Union Council.

7 Neither the precise date nor the exact motive for the founding of the Lancashire Women Textile Workers' Representation Committee is recorded; all that is known is that it was established before early October 1903. For further details see *One Hand*, p. 163 ff.

8 *NL* 15.4.1904. Pankhurst, C., *The Parliamentary Vote For Women*, published from 62 Nelson Street, Manchester by Abel Heywood, Manchester; it is undated but appears to be issued in spring 1903.

9 NESWS *Annual Report*, 1903–4; among the seventeen committees also listed were Blackburn, Accrington, Oldham, Hyde, Haslingden, Clitheroe, Manchester, Halifax, Elland, Colne Valley, Sowerby Bridge and Normanton. The NESWS also had its traditional 'affiliated societies' in big cities like Liverpool, Leeds, Newcastle, etc.

10 *C & NT* 16.11.1900; *NL* 6.11.1903.

11 *NL* 16.12.1904. NESWS *Annual Report* 1904–05.

12 The Manchester Women's Trades & Labour Council was also involved in the second survey. See the *Co-operative News* Jan 1905, p. 106; this concludes, 'the promoters of the Women's Enfranchisement Bill have undertaken to insert the words "married and single" in the text of the bill. The bill is supported by working women as the most practical step to Adult Suffrage', and was signed by Esther Roper, Sarah Reddish, Margaret Llewelyn-Davies and another leading Guildswomen, Eva Gore-Booth and Sarah Dickenson.

13 *C & NT* 2.6.1905; *Wigan Observer* 6.1.1906; see *One Hand*, pp. 197–200 for details. Among the Cooper papers is a postcard from Colne Weavers' Association to SJC 7.12.1905, noting its committee 'decided to bear the expenses of two of our women members to attend the demonstration'; this was presumably to Wigan, and suggests the Nelson Weavers might possibly have paid SJC's costs too.

14 For the meeting, see *NL* 15.6.1906; for Ula Blackburn, tape 832, p. 11. Less is known about Margaret Aldersley, and Mary could not recall much about her.

15 For Emily Murgatroyd, see *Burnley Express* 26.3.1968; for Nancy Shimbles, tape 900, pp. 28–9; for the Cooper/Coombe relations, tape 907, p. 14 and tape 896, pp. 6 and 8; for Florence Shuttleworth, tape 896, pp. 27–8.

16 Tape 121, p. 5; the only pre-war contribution that came to more than a shilling was 7s 6d given by Harriette Beanland and her sister, obviously the fruits of their successful dressmaking business; tape 915, p. 16.

17 For Clara Myers, obituary *NL* 11.7.1924; for Deborah Smith, *NL* 28.11.1924.

18 Tape 915, p. 16.

19 Manchester and District Federation *Annual Report* 28.10.1911. For further details of the national picture, see next chapter.

20 *C & NT* 21.5.1909 and SJC's diary 18.5.1909; this is the only meeting of the society for which a fragment of the minutes taken have survived (because Mary Cooper, when applying for a job 19.8.1916, used the back of a draft of the minutes to practise her application letter on).

21 See Linklater, A., *An Unhusbanded Life*, Hutchinson, London, 1980; unfortunately this valuable biography does not say which month in 1909 Mrs Despard and Gandhi met. The Women's Freedom League is introduced later on.

22 *C & NT* 6.8.1909; also SJC's diary 2.8.1909.

23 Tape C, p. 3 and tape C, pp. 3–4.

24 For Robert Cooper, tape 917, p. 2; tape 832, p. 26; tape 907, p. 7; tape 896, pp. 16 and 19; tape 818, p. 27. For contrast, note Mitchell, H., *The Hard Way Up*, p. 149 ff. Undated postcard.

25 *NL* 23.6.1911; the three dozen people in the photograph are presumably all society members (1911 membership: 35); people like Annie Coombe, who came just for the day, appear not to have been included, perhaps because they caught the train at Brierfield.

The eye-witness report, *NL* 30.6.1911, is anonymous; see also Manchester & District Federation *Annual Report* 1911.

26 SJC's diary, entry on page for 5th January 1908, but obviously written years later, probably in 1930s. For other details of the procession, see Pankhurst, E.S., *The Suffragette Movement* p. 353; MacKenzie, M., *Shoulder To Shoulder*, Penguin, London, 1975, p. 174 which quotes from Emmeline Pethick-Lawrence; also NUWSS *Annual Report* 1911, which notes that the NUWSS part of the procession, wearing its red, white & green suffrage colours and led by Mrs Fawcett, was estimated to form the largest section.

27 Tape 900, p. 28, and note also tape 121 p. 6; the Manchester Federation

Annual Report 1911 says the processionists got on the special train home without one single lost person.

CHAPTER TEN: THE LABOUR PARTY DESERTS WOMEN

1 The LRC was not renamed the Labour Party until 1906, but for convenience is referred to here by the latter name. Against Labour's conference decisions on women's suffrage should be set the voting of Labour MPs; Harrison, B., *Separate Spheres: the Opposition to Women's Suffrage in Britain*, p. 42 and Table 1, notes the PLP's consistent voting for suffrage bills.

2 For the absence of active adultist pressure, see Pugh, M.; *Electoral Reform in War and Peace 1906-18*, Routledge and Kegan Paul, London, 1978, pp. 29-30; and pp. 31-32 for the Liberals' concern to abolish plural voting and for the pressure regarding Ireland on the Liberals to retain the franchise *status quo*.

For details of the women's suffrage motion at the 1904 LRC Conference, see *One Hand*, pp. 159-60; it was seconded by Isabella Ford. Note also the success of adult suffrage motions at the TUC 1901-2, *One Hand*, pp. 149-51.

3 For the *Clarion* correspondence see *One Hand*, pp. 181-4; Ada Nield Chew had early travelled with the Clarion Van, and must have read the *Clarion*'s reservations about women's suffrage.

For the correspondence with the Coopers, see *NL* 30.12.1904 which criticizes Ethel Annakin; I have not yet found SJC's reply in *NL* 6.1.1905 which was reprinted from the *Co-operative News*; Ada Nield Chew, *NL* 13.1.1905; Robert Cooper *NL* 20.1.1905; Ada Nield Chew, *NL* 3.2.1905.

The WCG was obviously particularly keen to clarify the issue of the rights of married women; see Holton, S., *Feminism and Democracy: the Women's Suffrage Movement in Britain, with particular reference to the National Union of Women's Suffrage Societies*, Ph. D., Sterling, 1980, pp. 140-3.

4 Mrs Pankhurst to MacDonald, 15.1.1905, letter in the Labour Party Archive; Mrs Pankhurst adds, 'I cannot forgive myself for not having foreseen the present situation and drafted the resolution so as to forestall it', a reference presumably to the sudden adultist revival; she ends her letter with a generous plea for MacDonald not to judge the self-sacrificing Eva Gore-Booth too harshly.

5 LRC *Conference Report*, 1905; and *NL* 12.9.1924; and Snowden, Viscount P., *An Autobiography*, vol I p. 281-3.

6 E. Pankhurst to P. Snowden 2.2.1905, quoted in *An Autobiography*, p. 283; and E. Pankhurst to SJC 2.2.1905, Cooper papers.

7 Nelson ILP Account Book 12.5.1905; ILP *Conference Report* 1905.

8 *Halifax Courier* 6.5.1905; also *Halifax Guardian* 6.5.1905; they were supported by the local secretary of the WCG, the prospective Labour candidate

for Halifax and the president of the Women's Liberal Association.

9 *Manchester Evening Chronicle*, 20.10.1905, quoted in MacKenzie, M., *Shoulder to Shoulder*, p. 30. Christabel Pankhurst to Coopers, 24.10.1905, last page of letter missing. For reactions of other Manchester suffragists, see *One Hand*, p. 191 ff.

10 Isabella Ford to SJC 17 and 22.2. probably 1906, but no year given. *MG* 21.5.1906; *NL* 12.9.1924 and tape 916, p. 26 both suggest that SJC etc took down a petition of 85,000 signatures and presented them to Campbell-Bannerman, but the evidence and dates are very confusing; however the Cooper papers do include the billhead of one such suffrage petition, and recently a very large canvas-backed banner has come to light, possibly dating from May 1906. Most sources give 50 as the number of Lancashire textile delegates, yet the photograph shows only 40.

11 Report of meeting, *MG* 21.5.1906; other protest meetings were held by WSPU in Trafalgar Square and NUWSS in Exeter Hall.
SJC stayed down in London for a few days and she later gave a talk to the Nelson WCG on the slums of London.

12 Dora Montefiore to SJC 31.5.[1906]. It is not clear when SJC and Dora Montefiore first met; possibly SJC saw her while staying in London after the deputation. In her diary (page for July 2nd) she later wrote. 'Mrs Montefiore lived near William Morris Home at [Hammersmith] having street meeting I went into a Tailor shop to ask the loan of a chair for a platform A man with red hair come up through the floor from a trap door he kept me talking a long time he was annarkist and had a hand printing press he gave me a lot of books and ask me to come back after the meeting, but I was scared Mrs Montefiore said that I had not to go as he was a Russian Anarkist'.

13 *Manifesto*, undated, copy in Manchester Central Library; it is difficult to date this, but the date suggested seems most likely. It is clear that SJC did not entirely go along with the protests by the other Lancashire suffragists about the suffragettes during 1906; for this see *One Hand*, pp. 204–7.

14 *Huddersfield Daily Chronicle* 27.11.1906; also *Huddersfield Daily Examiner* 21.11.1906 etc. The Liberal majority over Labour was reduced from 489 votes to 340. Note also Mitchell, H., *The Hard Way Up*, pp. 163–4.

15 Ramsay MacDonald to SJC, undated letter; it was probably written in late-March 1905.

16 Francis Johnson, ILP, to SJC 17.1.1906 (in his haste, he forgot to put the new year, 1907, on his letter). Quotation from SJC's diary pages May 3rd and 5th; also note *NL* 12.9.1924.

17 Pankhurst, E.S., *The Suffragette Movement*, p. 246, which omits any reference to SJC. For Woolwich, see ILP *Annual Report* 1906, and McKibbin, R., *The Evolution of the Labour Party 1910–1924*, Oxford University Press, Oxford, 1927, p. 8 for details of its associate (ie individual) Labour Party membership. For SJC's speech and others, *C & NT* 1.2.1907, and also see Labour Party

Annual Conference Report, 1907 (though note that the former gives a fuller transcription).

18 *C & NT* 1.2.1907; Pankhurst, E.S., *The Suffragette Movement*, pp. 247–9, which notes that as a result of Hardie's outburst Labour MPs were allowed to vote as they pleased on suffrage.

For the League, see Rendel, M., 'The Contribution of the Women's Labour League' in Middleton, L. (ed), *Women in the Labour Movement*, Croom Helm, London, 1977, p. 63 which notes the influence of adultists in the League circa 1907; also *One Hand*, p. 235 for other resignations from the League.

For the Nelson League see *NL* 24.3.1905, 9.2.1906, 18.2.1906, and 2.3.1906; it appears to have been formed prior to the national League, and to have faded out 1906–7 until 1912–13.

19 Christabel Pankhurst to A.J. Balfour, 28.10.1907, quoted in Morgan, D., *Suffragists and Liberals*, Blackwell, Oxford, 1975, p. 46.

For the conference, see ILP *Annual Report* 1907 and Pankhurst, E.S., *The Suffragette Movement*, pp. 249–50. SJC attended 1908 ILP Conference (with Harriette Beanland), 1909 and 1912; in the 1908 Conference Report she is listed as an ILP· speaker competent in all three categories (indoor educational lectures, addressing trade union branches plus open air propaganda meetings).

20 For the LCWToWRC see *One Hand*, pp. 237–42.

CHAPTER ELEVEN: REFLECTIONS OF A SUFFRAGIST

1 Note particularly Mackenzie, M., *Shoulder to Shoulder*, Penguin, London 1975 and Raeburn, A., *The Suffragette View*, David & Charles, Newton Abbot 1976.

The self-effacement of NUWSS women is, by comparison, remarkable. For instance, Strachey, R., *The Cause*, contains no photograph of named NUWSS suffragists in action, but some specifically of militant suffragettes. Likewise in the Fawcett Library's albums of photographs, suffragette pictures appear to outnumber those of Mrs Fawcett's followers.

Why is this? Two major factors seem to be i) that although suffragists were more numerous, the dramatic suffragettes made more 'news worthy' pictures, and ii) suffragists, marginalized in suffragette accounts once women won the vote, lost confidence in themselves and destroyed or mislaid their photographs. It is difficult to generalize about this yet, but such appears to have been the case for Ada Nield Chew, who destroyed most of her own photographs before she died; Annot Robinson, who became a leading NUWSS activist, left few suffragist photographs; and the voluminous Catherine Marshall papers also contain suspiciously few; Jo Vellacott notes that Catherine's brother burnt many of her papers after her death. All this perhaps enhances the value of the Cooper papers.

2 For instance, twelve snapshots of Sarah Reddish and SJC were taken in Bristol 29 May – 5 June 1907.

Note also SJC's diary for 6.2.1909, 'Miss Gardner took a Snapshot of the deputation in the City Square Leeds.'

3 For the two portraits in the Fawcett Library Postcard Collection, thanks to David Doughan, who kindly sent me photocopies.

4 Isabella Ford to SJC 17.2.[no year].

5 'Mrs Selina Cooper in account with Bank of Liverpool Limited, Craven Bank Branch, Nelson', from 31.10.1908 to 7.11.1923. It is unclear whether this book records her National Union expenses, her salary, or whatever else. For instance, entries October–December 1908 appear to be a weekly salary of £1.12.6d, but thereafter are too irregular to bear this out.

6 Tape 915, p. 5 and Tape 916, p. 15.

7 Executive Committee of London Society, minutes 4.10.1906. The aspiring candidate was Vernon Hartshorn; for further details see Gregory, R., *The Miners and British Politics 1906–1914*, Oxford University·Press, 1968, pp. 125–7 and 141. Whether SJC got as far as Wales is not clear, for she was soon off to Tunbridge Wells for a National Union of Women Workers' conference.

8 For Liverpool see Grant, L., 'Women's Work and Trade Unionism in Liverpool, 1890–1914', *Women and the Labour Movement*, North West Labour History Society *Bulletin* no. 7, 1980–1.

9 Campaign details from NUWSS *Annual Report*, 1907; postcard to Mary Cooper, 7.11.1906; Eleanor Rathbone to Amalgamated Society of Carpenters and Joiners, 5.3.1907.

During the winter, SJC worked at the Huddersfield by-election and attended the Labour Party Conference in Belfast.

10 Entry in SJC's diary, pages April 21–22nd. Tape 915, p. 21. It is unclear what year this was, but 1907 is likely.

11 NUWSS *Annual Report* 1907 (but there is no indication that either candidate was sympathetic). Cole, G.D.H., *British Working Class Politics 1832–1914*, Labour Book Service, London, 1941, p. 288 etc indicates how closely Labour nipped at the Tory's heels.

12 NUWSS *Annual Report* 1910; it notes the Tory colonel and the Labour candidate, A.G. Cameron, were both favourable to women's suffrage but that because 'Mr Cameron gave promise of active support of Mr Shackleton's Bill', the NUWSS supported him.

It was only after Mary's death, that a copy of this particular photograph came to light among the Cooper papers. SJC's eldest nephew also had a print, and in the Fawcett Library Photograph Album no 23 is the identical photograph, with annotations by Cicely Leadley-Brown, the owner of the car.

13 NUWSS *Annual Report* 1907. Bertrand Russell's address 'To the Electors of the Wimbledon Division of Surrey', signed and dated 3.5.1907. Susan Power, Tunbridge Wells, to SJC, 28.10.1906.

14 The other suffragists working at Wimbledon included Bertha Mason, Margery Corbett (later Ashby), Mrs Stanbury; see Maud Arncliffe-Sennett Collection Volume I, though unfortunately the photographs in the cuttings are very blurred.

   Wimbledon Borough News 11.5.1907; Bertrand Russell typed letter to SJC, May 1907.

15 NUWSS *Annual Report* 1908; Maud Arncliffe-Sennett Collection Volume II; *Daily Mirror* 28.11.1907; the candidate was James Holmes, the man who had first proposed that the TUC should support the fledgling Labour Party. At West Hull, NUWSS policy was to oppose the unsympathetic Tory and give equal support to the Labour and Liberal candidates, but the photograph suggests on this occasion SJC found this 'non-party' stance particularly irksome.

16 The by-elections she worked at that year were Mid-Devon, Peckham, West Derby, North West Manchester, Wolverhampton, Pudsey, Pembroke (not certain), Newcastle-upon-Tyne and Chelmsford (Mid-Essex). Tape 915, p. 12, tape 818, p. 27, tape 900, p. 19. The second housekeeper was called Margaret Andrew, see tape 121, pp. 5 and 24, and SJC's diary pages January 22 and 26. It is not clear precisely how the housekeepers were paid, but note that SJC's account book opens 31.10.1908.

17 Pankhurst, E.S., *The Suffragette Movement*, pp. 272–3; Pankhurst, E., *My Own Story*, 1914 and Virago, London, 1979, pp. 90–93; *Western Daily Press* 8.1.1908.

18 Photograph etc from *Western Daily Mercury* 14.1.1908 is reproduced in *One Hand*; SJC's diary pages April 24–5th; caption from Maud Arncliffe-Sennett Collection Volume II. SJC kept both a press cutting and a photograph print.

19 NUWSS Quarterly Council Meeting, 14.7.1908. NUWSS *Annual Reports* give the following figures for salaries: 1907 £232, 1908 £467, 1910 £673, 1911 £750, 1912 £1,705 and 1913 £2,045 (excluding expenses).

20 For Margaret Robertson, see Brockway, F., *Inside the Left*, Allen and Unwin, London, 1942, p. 33; Swanwick, H.M., *I Have Been Young*, Victor Gollancz, London, 1935, p. 184; *CC* 26.9.1913; SJC's autograph book, 26.6.1910.

   For her appointment as NESWS organiser in May 1909, see NESWS *Annual Report* 1909, and note appointment of Kate Courtney as Secretary for the NESWS branches about the same time. After the resignation of many of the radical suffragists in late 1905 (see *One Hand*, pp. 195–6) the NESWS seems to have lain low during 1906–7; but by late 1908 it was revived, and its membership doubled to 509.

21 For Emilie Gardner, see *Queen* 17.4.1909. *CC* 3.6.1909.

22 NUWSS *Election Policy*, March 1908 and NUWSS *General Instructions for By-election Work*, March 1908.

For N-W Manchester by-election, SJC's diary for June 18th, and 22.4.1908. Gore-Booth, E., *Women's Right to Work*, Manchester and Salford Trade and Labour Council, Manchester, n.d. SJC had left Manchester to attend the ILP Conference with Harriette Beanland 19–21.4.1908, and returned afterwards.

23 SJC's diary 2.5.1908 and 20th April. NUWSS *Annual Report* 1907, both candidates favourable, propaganda only, Liberal won.

24 Emilie Gardner to SJC 21 and 28.6.1908. Whether she went to Pembroke or not is unclear; another possibility is that she went to help Vernon Hartshorn, the suffragist miner, who was currently campaigning in Mid-Glamorgan. For Pudsey, see *Pudsey District Advertiser* 21.5.1908, 28.5.1908, 4.6.1908 and 11.6.1908; Isabella Ford and Adela Pankhurst were also there.

CHAPTER TWELVE: CAPTAIN TREMAIN'S FOLLY

1 For Christabel, see Pankhurst, E.S., *The Suffragette Movement*, p. 221.

2 Rigby, E., to SJC, 4.2.1908, on behalf of Preston WSPU. Fawcett, M. G., *What I Remember*, Fisher Unwin, London, 1924, p. 192; also Strachey, R., *The Cause*, p. 313. Of course the division between WSPU and NUWSS was never so clear cut in practice, especially in grassroots suffrage societies; (and note Newcastle amendment at NUWSS quarterly Council Meeting 14.7.1908).

3 SJC's diary for April 22nd, 23rd and 24th.

Women's Franchise 1, 8 and 15.10.1908 suggests the rivalry between NUWSS and WSPU.

4 SJC's diary page April 18th and 22.1.1909; and NESWS *Annual Report*, 1908.

For mid-Essex, see Pankhurst, E.S., *The Suffragette Movement*, p. 298.

5 For anti-suffragist violence see Harrison, B., *Separate Spheres*, pp. 183–192. For the Glasgow by-election, SJC's diary 17 and 19.2.1909.

6 Pankhurst, E.S., *The Suffragette Movement*, p. 416. For details of the WSPU campaign, Rosen, A., *Rise Up, Women!* Routledge and Kegan Paul, London, 1974 pp. 139–181.

7 This incident at Great Harwood probably took place December 1910; see SJC's diary for May 12th.

8 Tape 915, p. 24; tape 916, p. 24 and tape 121, p. 18.

9 She left Leicester for a few days for the Croydon by-election. For MacDonald's relationship with the Coopers, and her visit to his family, see tape 121, p. 4 etc.

For SJC's Leicester campaign, see SJC's diary 15.3.1909 to 7.4.1909 also *Leicester Chronicle and Leicester Mercury*, 20 and 27.3.1909 and 3 and 10.4.1909.
10 Tape 915, pp. 12–13 and SJC diary 26.4.1909 to 28.4.1909, plus accounts listed at the end of the notebook. Mary kept the chains too; only after her death in July 1983 did they finally surface again among her possessions.
11 After she put the chainmakers on their train home, she hastened to Sheffield for the Attercliffe by-election; campaigned around Birmingham in June; took part in the Mid-Derby and High Peak by-elections in July; August and September were more leisurely with many days spent at home, though by mid-October she was working at the Bermondsey by-election; in mid-November she had an appendicitis and had to be rushed home in Margaret Ashton's car.
   SJC's diary pages 14–15th November; Page Arnot, R., *The Miners: Years of Struggle*, Allen and Unwin, London, 1953, pp. 29–30.
12 NUWSS *Annual Report* 1910; *MG* 11.7.1910; NUWSS programme of Mass Meeting, 9.7.1910; *Daily Sketch* 21.6.1910 (cutting in Mrs Fawcett's scrapbook). Membership etc figures from NUWSS *Annual Report*, 1911 and 1912; NUWSS Executive Mins 1.6.1911 and 4.1.1912; Manchester & District Federation *Annual Reports*, 1911 and 1912.
13 For Annot Robinson, see obituary by Ellen Wilkinson in *Woman's Leader* 6.11.1925; and interview with her daughter 4.10.1982 pp. 6–7; also ILP *Conference Report*, 1910 & 1911; and NUWSS Exec mins 13.4.1911. Annot Robinson was also a member of the Women's Labour League and spoke at its 1910 Conference on suffrage.
14 *CC* 16.2.1911.
15 NUWSS Exec mins, 13.4.1911 and 15.2.1912. It would be interesting to know more about Margaret Aldersley.
16 See Vernon, B.D., *Ellen Wilkinson*, Croom Helm, London, 1982, pp. 40–1; unfortunately this biography is sadly under-researched for the suffrage years. See also Davies, S., 'The Young Ellen Wilkinson', *Memoirs and Proceedings of the Manchester Literary and Philosophical Society*, 1964–5, vol 107, p. 4. Other NUWSS organisers included Helen Frazer, Mrs Cowmeadow, Mrs Dempster, Miss Grace Coleman, Miss Hilston, Mrs Chettle and Mrs Caulfield. Again it would be rewarding to know more of them.
17 Sylvia Pankhurst helped Keir Hardie prepare amendments to increase benefits, Pankhurst, E.S., *The Suffragette Movement*, p. 354; for SJC's appointment as lecturer, see National Health Insurance Commission to SJC, 24.12.1914; also SJC's diary for 19 and 24.2.1912, Margaret Llewelyn Davies to SJC, 5.3.1912 arranging for her to address a Guild conference in Lancashire, etc. For a critique of how the Act affected women, Wilson, E., *Women and the Welfare State*, Tavistock, London, 1977, p. 106. Quotation

from *Holmfirth Express* 15.6.1912.

18 *CC* 22.8.1913. See also McLeary, G.F., *The Early History of the Infant Welfare Movement*, Lewis, London, 1933, pp. 72–3; for the WCG visit to Ghent, see WCG MSS. vol II p. 7, LSE Library; Lewis, J., *The Politics of Motherhood*, Croom Helm, London, 1980, pp. 90 ff; NUWSS Annual Report 1913.

19 *NL* 26.9.1913. Recently discovered among the Cooper books is a copy of Martin, A., *The Mother and Social Reform*, NUWSS, Nov 1913.

Harriette Beanland's earlier letter (*NL* 19.9.1913) is also a strong and witty condemnation of male justice in handling the abortionist's case; women had apparently refused to move when asked to leave the court. 'Women of England, stand by and protect your fallen sisters', urged Harriette, 'copy the brave example of the women of Nelson!' All this coincided with SJC's interest in the Criminal Law Amendment Bill and the White Slave Trade.

20 H.M. Beanland to Labour Party, 2.10.1913, Labour Party Archive; *NL* 17. 10.1913; this was part of a wide campaign nationally e.g. see Reeves, M.P., *Round About A Pound A Week*, Bell, London, 1913 & Virago, 1979, produced by the Fabian Women's Group and supporting family allowances. See also Lewis, J., *The Politics of Motherhood*, p. 167 etc; Davin, A., 'Imperialism and Motherhood', *History Workshop Journal*, spring 1978; *NL* 27.3.1914 and 17.4.1914; the *exact* causes of the decline of infant mortality remain unclear.

21 Balfour, Lady F., *Ne Obliviscaris*, Hodder & Stoughton, London n.d., p. 169; SJC's diary, page January 12th; *NL* 21.2.1908; Chew quotation from *One Hand*, p. 225. The problem of splintering was most serious in the WSPU, and included the formation of the Women's Freedom League (1907), the Free Woman group (1911), the East London Federation of Suffragettes (1913), the United Suffragists (1914) and, during the war, the Independent WSPU. The Women's Freedom League also suffered similar problems of disunity, largely due to Mrs Despard's autocratic domination.

22 SJC's diary for 25.2.1909 and 3.3.1909 and pages April 30th- May 1st. For Lady St Helier, see *NL* 12.9.1924.

23 Lady Betty Balfour to SJC, 7.12.1911; NUWSS Executive Mins 7.3.1912 and 29.3.1912; SJC's diary, 25–27.2.1912, but the entries then peter out again; Nelson ILP branch mins, 25.3.1912; Mary St Helier to SJC 28.3.1912.

CHAPTER THIRTEEN: THE ELECTION FIGHTING FUND

1 It is not appropriate to the scope of this biography to offer a completely comprehensive review of suffrage literature to back the suggestion that accounts of the suffrage movement written before 1977–8 usually tell the

truth, but seem not to tell the whole truth. A brief discussion of this general point, with a note of the relevant historiography, can be found in the Afterword and its footnotes.

What follows here, then, is merely a compressed survey of suffrage historiography for these immediate pre-war years. Dangerfield, G., *The Strange Death of Liberal England 1910-1914*, (1935) is a brilliant and convincing account of this trinity of revolt, written in rollicking style. Published in the mid-1930s, Dangerfield's account could call upon two major emerging strands of suffrage history.

The first was the writings of the conservative non-militants, notably Fawcett, M.G., *What I Remember*, (1924), Strachey, R., *The Cause*, (1928), and Strachey, R., *Millicent Garrett Fawcett*, (1931). The second strand comprised the writings of the militants – most notably Pankhurst, E.S., *The Suffragette Movement*, (1931), a meticulous and moving personal history of the militant campaign. Dangerfield chose to notice the second strand but not the first, and his references to Mrs Fawcett are absurdly scanty. By concentrating on the militant campaign, Dangerfield therefore loses sight of the labour-suffrage alliance (which is referred to *briefly* in both *The Cause*, pp. 323-4, *Millicent Garrett Fawcett*, pp. 261-2, and *What I Remember*, pp. 202-16), rather in the way that Sylvia Pankhurst had, a few years earlier, disparagingly dismissed it in one icy paragraph (*The Suffragette Movement*, pp. 398-9).

Dangerfield's book was influential. It helped establish the centrality of the main strand of suffrage history which placed the Pankhursts firmly centre stage, which emphasized the 'revolutionary' quality of the suffragettes, and which marginalised the suffragists. By the same token, the general labour movement histories also ignore the labour-suffrage pact; here may be noted Gregory, R., *The Miners and British Politics 1906-1914*; and McKibbin, R., *The Evolution of the Labour Party 1910-1924*; the few exceptions to this labour history silence include Hamilton, M.A., *Arthur Henderson*, Heinemann, London, 1938, pp. 80-1, and Brockway, F., *Inside the Left*, Allen & Unwin, London, 1942, pp. 33-4.

As noted in the Afterword, recent scholarly accounts that note the labour-suffrage alliance have so far largely remained less accessible to a popular readership (and their influence less widespread) than earlier suffrage accounts. So, as a result, the interested general reader of the 1980s, trying to form a balanced opinion of all aspects of the suffrage campaign, may understandably still feel a little confused.

2 Later in November, Lloyd George announced that the Conciliation Bill had been 'torpedoed' by the Franchise Bill.

3 Frances Power Cobbe, quote by Holton, S., *Feminism and Democracy*, p. 138.

4 Strachey, R., *Millicent Garrett Fawcett*, pp. 255-6; NUWSS Exec mins, 9.11.1911.

5 ILP *Conference Reports* 1910, 1911, 1912.

6 Labour Party *Conference Report* 1912; also speaking in support of the motion was Philip Snowden MP of the ILP, and Millicent Murby of the Fabian Society. Mary MacArthur ended by appealing to the miners, 'in the memory of past battles, in the memory of past friendships, to withdraw their opposition to the resolution.'

For the reasoning of Henderson and other Labour leaders at this point, see Rover, C., *Woman's Suffrage and Party Politics in Britain 1866–1914*, pp. 152–5; also Hamilton, M.A., *Arthur Henderson*, pp. 80–1.

7 Holton, S., *Feminism and Democracy*, pp. 222. For MacDonald see Pankhurst, E.S., *The Suffragette Movement*, p. 372, and Brockway, F., *Inside the Left*, p. 34.

NUWSS *Programme*, 23.2.1912; also SJC's diary for 23.2.1912; Ethel Snowden was among the speakers.

8 SJC's diary 24.2.1912; NUWSS *Annual Report* 1912.

9 NUWSS *Annual Report* 1912; Strachey, R., *The Cause*, pp. 323–4 and *Millicent Garrett Fawcett*, p. 262, refers with diplomatic brevity to the problems of transition. Particularly revealing here is the Labour Party Archive (LP/WOM/12/1–18) which details the correspondence between Courtney and Henderson, and confirms the importance of H.N. Brailsford's role.

10 It is, of course, difficult to compare the structures of a multi-issue political party and a single-issue pressure group. For Labour Party figures (mainly 1909–10) see McKibbin, R., *The Evolution of the Labour Party 1910–1924*, pp. 2–11 and 24–5. For the National Union, see NUWSS *Annual Report* 1912 and Fawcett Library Catalogue. McKibbin pp. 18–20 notes that the Osborne Judgement forced many a frail local party to the wall.

11 For the setting up of EFF, see NUWSS *Annual Report* 1912 and LP/WOM/12/19–26, which notes Sylvia Pankhurst's opposition to this new alliance. Other members of the EFF Comm included Kate Courtney, Edith Palliser, Mrs Stanbury & Helena Swanwick.

12 For more on Catherine Marshall, see Vellacott Newberry, J., 'Anti-War Suffragists', *History* 1977 vol 62; she has skilfully catalogued the copious Marshall papers in the Cumbria Record Office and is working on a biography of Catherine Marshall.

For the early days of the EFF, see NUWSS *Annual Report* 1912; also EFF mins 14.6.1912 (£1,821), 20.9.1912 (£4,393) and 6.12.1912 (£5,819); EFF mins 5.7.1912 notes that Manchester and North East Federations were already preparing plans for EFF work in their areas. See also LP/WOM/12/27–28. Fenner Brockway, letter to author 18.3.1982, notes he was made Liaison Officer for Labour, with Margaret Robertson for women.

13 NUWSS Executive Mins, 11.5.1912, 6.6.1912; Pankhurst, E.S., *The Suffragette Movement*, p. 388, notes also the WSPU presence at Merthyr. ILP *Conference Report* 1912.

14 Manchester Federation *Annual Report* 1912. SJC does not appear to have been an EFF organiser at this early stage; but the NUWSS Exec mins 19.9.1912 note that the salary of certain organisers was to be raised, and that SJC was to be paid £2.50d a week 'in consideration of the fact that her work is not continuous and she is responsible for her own holiday arrangements'; and mins 7.11.1913 note that SJC is to be taken on for 6 months regular work, including 2 months non-election work in the Potteries.

This suggests that boundaries between the NUWSS salary fund and that of the EFF were flexible, and that SJC continued to be paid and employed by NUWSS, but to work regularly for EFF.

15 For the Holmfirth campaign, see NUWSS *Annual Report* 1912, which notes that the Liberal majority was reduced to less than half; Gregory, R., *The Miners and British Politics*, pp. 114–9 which sees the by-election as the final break between Miners and Liberals; EFF mins 14.6.1912 and 21.6.1912, (which note that the Labour agent thanked the NUWSS for its efficient help – though the £100 voted to go to Holmfirth remained with the NUWSS for a long time, suggesting Labour's suspicion of 'tainted money' from women) and 6.12.1912. See also NUWSS Exec mins 6.6.1912, 8.6.1912 and 10.6.1912 which note Catherine Marshall seeing Henderson about committee rooms; *Labour Leader* 20 and 27.6.1912; 13.6.1912; also *Holmfirth Express* 15.6.1912 and 22.6.1912; and LP/WOM/12/29.

16 For Platt Fields, see *MG* 20.6.1912, and Manchester Society *Annual Report* for 1912. For Margaret Ashton, see Manchester & District Federation *Annual Report* 1912; obituaries include *MG* 16.10.1937. See also LP/WOM/12/30-3.

Of the other EFF by-elections during the summer, the first was Hanley, a Potteries mining seat; here Labour actually lost its seat to the Liberals. At the second, Crewe, (also in the Midlands) the Liberals lost the seat – but Labour came third and it was, of course, the Tories who gained. At the third, Midlothian (Gladstone's old seat in Scotland), the Liberals were again toppled from power – but Labour still came third and once more the Tories gained the seat. For East Carmarthen see EFF mins 2.8.1912 and *LabL* 22.8.1912.

17 EFF mins 10.7.1912; 12.7.1912; see Pugh, M., *Electoral Reform in War and Peace*, pp. 38–9 for opposition from Lab P NEC to voting against Bill..

18 *C & NT* 2.8.1912, and Manchester and District *Annual Report* 1912; also present were Messrs Kershaw, Moser and Shuttleworth; noticeably absent was any representative of the Nelson Weavers' Association, or any textile union official.

19 EFF mins 19.7.1912 to 14.11.1912. NUWSS Exec mins 7.11.1912. The WSPU electioneering at Bromley and Bow was, it has been suggested, insensitive to the needs of the working-class electors, and Lansbury was badly defeated; at the EFF meeting 14.11.1912, Catherine Marshall

proposed NUWSS speakers should not speak from the same platform as the WSPU, but the EFF meeting 6.12.1912 notes that even this had annoyed Arthur Henderson and others.

20 EFF mins 20.12.1912; some of this work was to be paid out of the Transferable Fund; the meeting also revealed how closely EFF officials like Isabella Ford were working with ILP officials. For the 1913 Lab P Conference, see Snowden, P., *An Autobiography*, vol I, pp. 294–6; and *The Election Fighting Fund: What It Has Achieved*, NUWSS leaflet, n.d. [about May 1914].

CHAPTER FOURTEEN: WOMEN AND THE MIGHT OF THE MINERS

1 *The Election Fighting Fund: What It Has Achieved*; Robert Cooper to Catherine Marshall, [March 1913]; this and subsequent MSS quoted are from Box 9, Catherine Marshall papers, Cumbria Record Office; see also Gregory, R., *The Miners & British Politics*, p. 36ff.

Helena Renton, W. Riding Federation organiser, to Miss Mackenzie, 2.4.[1913]; Renton to Mackenzie, 4.4.[1913]; also (not quoted) postcard from Robert Cooper to Catherine Marshall, 4.4.1913. It is clear from Renton's letters that she was having difficulty launching EFF work in West Yorkshire, and felt isolated except for Isabella Ford. Renton to Marshall, 27.5.[1913]; *CC* 27.6.1913.

2 Jessie Bevan (Secretary, W. Lancashire, W. Cheshire and N. Wales Federation) to Marshall, 27.4.[1913]. Robertson to Marshall, 1.9.1913. *CC* 5.9.1913. West Riding Federation *Annual Report* April 1914 also noted SJC's work here; by then 16 Miners' Lodges had passed resolutions. Also, *CC* 2.6.1913 re SJC and Yorkshire miners.

For the 1913 TUC Congress see Pankhurst, E.S., *The Suffragette Movement*, p. 512; *Accrington Observer* 23.8.1913 for an eye-witness account by Ada Nield Chew; Robertson to (probably) Marshall, 18.9.1913. Miss G.W. Evans to Marshall [c. 16.9.1913]; *Trade Unions* report including 'Nottingham Miners Mrs Cooper's work' [1.10.1913]. Mansfield had 44% of its electorate miners, and a Liberal majority of over 7,000.

3 *CC* 3.10.1913; and 17.10.1913. For the demonstration, see reports in *CC* 17.10.1913, *The Election Fighting Fund: What It Has Achieved*, and NUWSS *Annual Report* 1913.

4 For N. Monmouth, see *CC* 10 and 24.10.1913; Pugh, M., *Electoral Reform in War and Peace*, p. 24 notes the success of this campaign; SJC's diary page April 17th.

5 Page Arnot, R., *The Miners*, pp. 51–3; *NL* 19.9.1924, SJC's diary for page March 13th; *CC* 2.10.1913; tape 916, p. 16.

6 Tape 916, p. 23; *Burnley Express* 26.3.1968; *CC* 11.7.1913; *NL* 11.7.1913, 8.8.1913.

7 The American suffragist was Mrs Chapman Catt; *CC* 1.8.1913. SJC was to be included in a post-pilgrimage deputation to Lord Lansdowne, but he chose not to make himself available.

8 There had been a hiatus in EFF elections between September 1912 (Midlothian) and November 1913 (Keighley); the only EFF election during these 14 months was Houghton-le-Spring; it seems that SJC was not among the organisers at Houghton, though it is unclear what she was doing that month.

Pugh, M., *Electoral Reform in War and Peace*, pp. 24 ff. gives details of the EFF constituency registration work e.g. in Mid-Durham the NUWSS organiser even went into the Revision Court as the Labour Agent.

Also present at Accrington was Hannah Mitchell, but SJC does not seem to have had much contact with her except here. For the campaign, see *MG* 21.10.1913 and 27.10.1913; *CC* 6.6.1913 (which notes a Mrs Tozer had set up a local EFF committee). 17.10.1913, and 31.10.1913 (Ada Nield Chew's account); *Accrington Observer* 26.8.1913 to 4.11.1913 etc. For these articles see Chew, D.N., *Ada Nield Chew*. Thanks to the Labour History Society in Accrington for asking me to speak at their inaugural meeting in 1978, and so firing me to look at the *Observer* in the local library.

Election Fighting Fund leaflet 15.7.1915 notes that James Bell of the United Textile Factory Workers' Association had agreed to stand against Baker; he had been adopted by the Labour Party and promised NUWSS support; an EFF organiser was currently working in the constituency.

9 Tape 121, p. 12; also tape 916, p. 24; and SJC's diary p. June 15. In contrast to this anecdote, the Keighley campaign was an unhappy affair; Buckmaster was a suffrage sympathizer, the NUWSS backed him rather than the ILP man standing for Labour, and the Labour Party was furious.

For the campaign, see *Keighley News* 1.11.1913 and 8.11.1913, also *CC* 7.11.1913 and 21.11.1913. Unfortunately I can find no reference to the SJC/Aldersley meeting at Howarth, and there might be some confusion with a by-election campaign there two years before.

10 Gregory, R., *The Miners and British Politics*, map on p. 103 shows the 13 ILP branches and isolated collieries that characterised the constituency; he includes Durham among his 'Front Runners' category, but within the county N.W. Durham lags; see p. 81.

CC 16.1.1914 to 6.2.1914. *Consett Guardian* 16.1.1914, 23.1.1914; *Consett and Stanley Chronicle* 16.1.1912 to 6.2.1914. Also present during the campaign were the Women's Liberal Federation and the WSPU.

11 Catherine Marshall papers, box 10, telegrams, transcribed by Jo Vellacott; *Election Fighting Fund* leaflet 15.7.1915 notes that James Winstone the Labour candidate was chosen by the local Party, but Miners' Federation sponsorship was still doubtful and his name had not yet been sanctioned by the national Labour Party; however the NUWSS had promised to support him.

What SJC did between N.W. Durham and the outbreak of war is not clear. In early February she was in Nelson; later in the month in Surrey; she had a programme for the London meeting to welcome the South African deported trade union leaders for 27th February; at the end of March she was again speaking in southern England.

She was at the Ipswich election in May, possibly going there straight from N. Monmouth; there is no sign that she went to the N.E. Derbyshire election; according to *CC* she was in N. Monmouth again in July, speaking at various small towns, and was still there a month later, according to *CC* EFF report 7.8.1914.

12 *Election Fighting Fund: What It Has Achieved*, p. 5; the ninth EFF by-election is discounted, because for purely localised reasons, Labour did very badly; for Keighley see ft nt 9. Catherine Marshall papers, box 10; see also Pugh, M., *Electoral Reform in War and Peace*, p. 17.

13 It is not clear when Margaret Ashton joined the Labour Party formally; nor is Catherine Marshall's biographer, Jo Vellacott, certain of the date *she* joined the ILP; quotation from Marshall papers Box 9, 5.6.1913. It would be interesting to know if Robertson & Gardner had been Liberals.

One of the fiercest critics of the Election Fighting Fund was Sylvia Pankhurst: too little and too late, she suggested. Involved at the time in her own courageous and horrific hunger and thirst strikes, she had scant patience for the slower propaganda of the NUWSS and the Lib-Lab compromises of the Labour Party. Even years afterwards, in *The Suffragette Movement*, she was disparaging about how 'in the hands of the National Union, the pro-Labour election policy attracted little attention: in those of the more efficient and active WSPU it might have proved a powerful weapon' (p. 251). 'The NUWSS never captured the interest of the multitude,' she continued (p. 485). 'It was so staid, so willing to wait, so incorrigibly leisurely.' Sylvia's feelings on this point are complex and demand a fuller study.

CHAPTER FIFTEEN: SUFFRAGISTS FACE WAR

1 *NL* 14.8.1914. Information about SJC's salary comes from NUWSS Exec Comm 27.8.1914 (Marshall papers Box 11) which includes a report of the EFF Comm where Catherine Marshall notes that two EFF organisers (unnamed) are staying at home with a retaining fee of £1, giving part of their time to relief work. EFF Comm Mins (Box 20) 29.1.1915, noting SJC was on half-time work for retaining fee of £1 per week, and this is confirmed by the EFF Mins 5.3.1915; and by EFF Mins 14.7.1915 (Manchester Central Library suffrage collection).

2 SJC's bankbook, 21.8.1914. *C & NT* 2.4.1915 and *NL* 1.4.1915. For her relief work, *CC* 30.7.1915 (anonymous) and EFF Comm Mins 5.3.1915;

SJC's report adds 'In the autumn I had several invitations to speak on Women's Suffrage to Labour and other organisations . . .'.

3 *C & NT* 22.6.1900, *NL* 5.2.1904 and 16.11.1906; ILP Branch Mins 25.5.1914, 12.5.1913 and 23.6.1913. For a local study of Passive Resisters, see *Gold Under The Hammer*, Cornholme WEA Branch, 1982.

4 Nelson ILP General Comm Mins 8.12.1913; *C & NT* 9.10.1914, 11.12.1914, 11.6.1915, 20.8.1915.

5 It is impossible to keep track of all members after 1914, but it seems as if the Society unanimously opposed the war. It seems that, at least for women like Harriette Beanland, relationships between the ILP and suffragists had already become strained. Harriette interrupted a Ramsay MacDonald ILP meeting accusing him of 'treachery' regarding women's suffrage, and was roughly ejected by the stewards. She publicly resigned from the ILP in disgust; see *NL* 6.2.1914, 27.2.1914 & 14.8.1914.

6 Harriette Beanland to SJC, 28.9.1916.

7 *NL* 18.2.1916 & 14.1.1916.

8 ILP Branch mins 21.6.1915; *NL* 26.11.1916 and 3.12.1915. The chairwoman was local novelist, Ethel Carnie.

9 *NL* 14.1.1916; ILP Branch mins 20.2.1916 and General Comm mins 8.5.1916 etc; *NL* 31.3.1916; Beanland to SJC 28.9.1916; *NL* 26.5.1916, 16.6.1916 and 24.6.1916.

10 Tape 918, p. 4; ILP General Comm mins 21.6.1916 and ILP Branch mins 2.6.1916 and 24.9.1916. Ingham, A. to SJC, n.d.

11 EFF Comm mins 29.1.1915 & 5.3.1915; *CC* 30.7.1915.

For Annot Robinson, see MISC/718/94 ff and interview recorded with her daughter, 4.10.1982. Other organisers included Mrs Townley (E. Bristol), Miss Hilston (Bradford), Miss Pressley Smith (Edinburgh), Miss Newton Harris (N. Monmouth, but returning home), Mrs Oldham (Rotherham), Miss Wilkinson (Stockport), Miss Tozer (Heywood), Mrs Smith, Miss Dring (North East), Miss Sheard (Gateshead), and Miss St John. Some of these resigned or were 'encouraged' to move to other jobs – Miss Dring to poultry farming, Mrs Oldham to secondary school teaching etc. See also Marshall papers, box 20.

12 NUWSS Exec Comm mins 4.3.1915 and EFF Comm mins 5.3.1915 & 14.7.1915; EFF leaflet 15.7.1915. Catherine Marshall papers, box 20; Brockway, F., *Inside the Left*, p. 49.

For discussion on this long-neglected aspect of women's history, see Vellacott Newberry, J., 'Anti-War Suffragists', *History*, vol 62, 1977; also Liddington, J., 'The Women's Peace Crusade: the history of a forgotten campaign', in Thompson, D., (ed) *Over Our Dead Bodies: women against the bomb*, Virago, London, 1983; also Pankhurst, E.S., *The Life of Emmeline Pankhurst*, Werner Laurie, London, 1935, pp. 152–3, which notes that 'Mrs Pankhurst & Christabel brought the WSPU to life again to oppose [the

Hague Congress]'; also Strachey, R., *Millicent Garrett Fawcett*, pp. 283–93, which notes 'the next six months which followed were in many ways the most difficult and painful of Mrs Fawcett's whole life . . . She gave them no place either in her published account of the movement or in her own reminiscences'.

The full WILPF title was not formally adopted till 1919.

13 Julie Tomlinson to SJC, 24.4.1915.

14 The first reference I noted to an Organisers' Union is *CC* 11.4.1913; it seems that suffrage organisers felt their position as employees was precarious and they needed to defend their jobs. In spring 1915 there was an organisers' deputation to Catherine Marshall to try and safeguard posts and wages, see EFF Comm mins 5.3.1915.

Marshall papers Box 20 contains a suggestion to separate NUWSS from the EFF, 6.5.1915, but apparently nothing came of this. Precisely how SJC reached her conclusion here is, inevitably, not recorded; for Margaret Aldersley and The Hague, see *NL* 7.8.1917.

15 R.W. Waterhouse, chief permit officer, to SJC, 28.9.15. SJC's original request has not yet been traced.

CHAPTER SIXTEEN: PACIFISTS AND MOTHERS

1 *CC* 28.8.1914, 2.10.1914 and 30.7.1915. Davies, M.Ll., *Maternity: Letters from Working Women*, Bell, London, 1915 and Virago, 1978, pp. 73 and 24; WCG Report 1915, pp. 7–9; printed invitation card (Oswaldtwistle), 22.6.1916. The Accrington poster is reprinted in Gaffin, J., and Thoms, D., *Caring and Sharing: the centenary history of the Co-operative Women's Guild*, Co-operative Union, Manchester, 1983. Also among the Cooper papers was a copy of *To Wives and Mothers: How to keep yourself and your children well and strong*, (pamphlet compiled by the Association of Infant Welfare and Maternity Centres), National League for Physical Education and Improvement, London 1916.

2 Harriette Beanland to SJC, 28.9.1916; tape 835, p. 20; Mary Cooper to Charles Brear, 19.8.1916. (SJC was also appointed as an assessor to the Local Munitions Tribunal; see W.H. Beveridge to SJC, March 1916.)

3 G.W. Evans to SJC, 20.1.1917, but implying that SJC had already been stepping up her activities in late-1916. Mrs Pankhurst quoted by Pugh, M., *Electoral Reform in War and Peace*, p. 143; Pankhurst, E.S., *The Suffragette Movement*, pp. 599–600, for Sylvia's differences with the other adultists. *NL* 25.8.1916.

4 Pugh, M., *Electoral Reform in War and Peace*, pp. 62–85 and 144 for a valuable analysis of the Speaker's Conference, on which this paragraph is based.

5 SJC's diary pages 3rd and 25th September. NUWSS Exec Mins, 4.1.1917; thanks to David Doughan for noting this reference for me.

6 Manchester and District Federation *Annual Report* 1917; it does not mention the names of those who organised the campaign, but it must have been Annot Robinson and SJC. *NL* 15.6.1917. Pankhurst, E.S., *The Suffragette Movement*, p. 604 for the ultra-adultists' isolation.

7 For Nancy Shimbles, *NL* 27.6.1917, 3.8.1917 and 27.7.1917.

8 *NL* 6.5.1917, 17.5.1917, 30.11.1917 and 27.3.1918. For other suffragists' (Catherine Marshall and Mrs Despard) reactions to Russia, see Newberry, J.V., 'Anti-War Suffragists', p. 423, and Linklater, A., *An Unhusbanded Life*, p. 193.
Women's Dreadnought 19.5.1917; *Workers' Dreadnought* 28.7.1917, 1.12.1917. Lucia Jones records that at the end of 1917 there were 24 provincial Federation branches and 17 London ones. But some of these may have been short-lived e.g. the Burnley branch faded out during 1917 as the Nelson branch appeared. One of the problems was perhaps the London-orientation of the *Workers' Dreadnought* which rarely covered provincial meetings unless Sylvia Pankhurst was there.

9 *NL* 3.8.1917 and *C & NT* 10.8.1917 and 17.8.1917. For Baby Week, see *NL* 10.8.1917, noting the mortality rate had increased during the war, and that the Nelson Baby Week was slightly later than the National Week.

10 *NL* 17.8.1917 and *C & NT* 17.8.1917.

11 *NL* 7.9.1917, and also *NL* 26.10.1917, 23.11.1917, 4.1.1918, 1.2.1918, 1.3.1918. Helena Swanwick to SJC, 20.9.1917; WILPF *Annual Report* 1917–18. Quotation from tape C, pp. 5–6.

12 Michila Seyd, Limpsfield, to SJC 18.12.1916. *Workers' Dreadnought* 28.7.1917 for American suffragists welcoming Russian envoys. Pankhurst, E.S., *The Suffragette Movement*, p. 607.

13 For more regarding the House of Lords, see Harrison, B., *Separate Spheres*, p. 220; also Pugh., M., *Electoral Reform in War and Peace*, p. 153, and noting Asquith's remarks about hopelessly ignorant women voters, p. 147. Strachey, R., *The Cause*, pp. 364–6 omits reference to Russia. Other valuable sources here are Holton., S., *Feminism and Democracy*, and Vellacott Newberry, J., 'Anti-War Suffragists'.

PART THREE: WOMEN BETWEEN THE WARS

CHAPTER SEVENTEEN: WHAT DO YOU DO ONCE YOU'VE WON THE VOTE?

1 Chew, D.N., *The Life and Writings of Ada Nield Chew*, pp. 62 and 67; Annot Robinson papers, MISC/718 99, 106 and 98.

Among the other organisers, Margaret Robertson (now Margaret Hills) left politics to bring up her children; Gwen Coleman went out to Rhodesia in 1919, married and started a Montessori school there.

2 Arthur Peters, Labour Party to SJC, 11.1.1918; Robert Smillie, Miners' Federation to Miss Gittins, Leicester, 23.9.1919.

3 NUWSS Exec, 1.11.1917; six organisers are listed, of whom two were temporary; included was Annot Robinson who was sent to Manchester, Sheffield and Leicester.

Minnie Lovat Owen, Swansea to SJC, 22.11.1917.

4 NUWSS Exec, 3.1.1918, organisational comm; the comm suggested that EFF work was ended (except in East Bristol), and that the EFF terminate the engagement of Annot Robinson, Miss Hilston and SJC; and that Hilston and SJC be re-engaged by the NUWSS as NUWSS organisers.

There then ensued a heated discussion about Annot Robinson. Eleanor Rathbone said Annot 'was heart and soul with the Labour Party and that it was impossible to expect her to work on non-party lines'. Why Annot lost her job because of her politics and not SJC is curious. However, within weeks Robinson had been taken on as Secretary to the Manchester branch of WILPF.

5 Minute Book of the Women's Citizens' Association (Nelson Parliamentary Division) 23.4.1918 to 3.8.1918; pinned at back, 3 receipts for SJC from Nelson Co-operative Society 24.4.1918 to 3.8.1918.

6 Ray Strachey (on NUWSS notepaper) to SJC, 5.6.1918. There was certainly friction between men and women workers locally e.g. *NL* 4.4.1919 about women mill clerks.

7 Phillips, Dr M. (ed) *Women and the Labour Party*, Headley, London, 1918, pp. 5 ff. Thanks to Sarah Perrigo for her help here.

8 Nelson ILP Branch mins, 30.12.1917; Nelson and Colne Parliamentary Borough (henceforth, constituency) Labour Party, inaugural conference 3.2.1918. Unfortunately I have not found a minute book for this Executive for the period 1918–1937.

To the Minute Book of the Women's Citizens' Association is appended a list of the names of twelve early members of the Women's Section.

9 SJC's diary, page for May 20th. Ray Strachey to SJG, 28.10.18 and

25.11.1918; these two letters only recently came to light among the Cooper papers. Bury, just north of Manchester, a textile constituency, was won by the Conservatives in 1918, the Labour candidate (H.W. Wallace) coming third. For an inkling into the Bury Labour Party and its likely prejudices, see Summerskill, E., *A Woman's World*, Heinemann, London, 1967, pp. 50–4. Tape 818, p. 27 in 1918.

10 The three named women Labour candidates selected stood in Manchester Rusholme, North Battersea, Stourbridge in Worcestershire respectively. The fourth, Mrs H.M. Mackenzie, stood for University of Wales. (And interestingly in 1922, Eleanor Rathbone stood as an Independent in East Toxteth, at the invitation of Liverpool Women's Citizens' Association and with the support of the local Liberal Party.)

Linklater, A., *An Unhusbanded Life*, pp. 200–1 describes how Charlotte Despard was selected. Pankhurst, E.S., *The Suffragette Movement*, p. 579 notes that Mary Richardson became a Labour candidate but was 'dropped when the seat became a promising one'. Gwen Coleman was chosen as candidate for Pudsey in Yorkshire, but being underage was ineligible, Sebestyen, A., '67 Years a Feminist', *Spare Rib* 23. Catherine Marshall considered standing in Cumberland about 1921.

11 Annot Robinson papers, MISC/718 98.

12 Nelson ILP Branch mins, 27.7.1919; also nominated by the ILP (for the ward Margaret Aldersley stood in) was a Mrs Spencer, a suffragist. *NL* 24.10.1919 and 7.11.1919.

13 J.W. Gradwell to SJC, 23.5.1922; Harriette Beanland to SJC, 9.5.1919 and 1.2.1920; Mitchell, H., *The Hard Way Up*, pp. 194–8; Annot Robinson papers MISC/718 110, 111 (also 69, when Annot Robinson stood again, in 1921); Vernon, B., *Ellen Wilkinson*, p. 65. However, in 1923–4 both Ellen Wilkinson and Hannah Mitchell were elected Manchester city councillors. And in an area such as Poplar there were almost half-a-dozen women councillors or aldermen from 1919.

14 *NL* 20.12.1918 on the death of two local COs in prison; *NL* 28.2.1919 Wilfred Wellock was courtmartialled for 3rd time & sentenced to 2 years hard labour; Nelson ILP Branch mins 30.3.1919 protests at treatment of COs, and 26.1.1919 affiliates to the Russian Literature Distribution Department.

15 *NL* 7.3.1919, 28.3.1919, 4.4.1919 and 23.5.1919; NWA mins 12.2.1919, 23.3.1919 and 16.4.1919.

16 NWA mins 16.4.1919; *NL* 17.4.1919, 6.6.1919; (however the Constituency Labour Party 23.6.1919 decided against supporting industrial action over political questions). Albert Smith MP took part in the Labour Demonstration (*NL* 22.8.1919) in which children marched with placards, 'Hail Free Russia' and 'Down with the Profiteers'. But Smith subsequently retired to the quieter waters of the Overlookers' Association. R. Graham

was elected MP at a by-election 17.6.1920.

For discussion of direct action at the TUC (September 1919) see Branson, N., *Britain in the Nineteen Twenties*, Weidenfeld & Nicolson, London, 1975, pp. 52–3.

17 For details, see Macfarlane, L.J., *The British Communist Party: its Origins and Development to 1929*, MacGibbon and Kee, London, 1966, p. 69; Frow, R. and E., *The Communist Party in Manchester 1920–1926*, North West History Group CPGB, Manchester, n.d., p. 8.

In Glasgow Helen Crawfurd, the suffragette who had addressed a Women's Peace Crusade meeting in Nelson in 1918, was secretary of the ILP Left Wing. In one of her reports (c. 1920) she claimed that Nelson was among ILP branches held to be strictly Communist; see Kendall, W., *The Revolutionary Movement in Britain 1900–21*, Weidenfeld and Nicolson, London, 1969, p. 423.

18 NWA mins 14.5.1920 to 8.9.1920; *NL* 3.9.1920; Constituency Labour Party mins, Special Conference on forming a local Council of Action, 5.9.1920.

Graubard, S.R., *British Labour and the Russian Revolution 1917–1924*, Oxford University Press, London, 1956, pp. 112–4 on the mythification of August 1920. Also see, Macfarlane, L.J., 'Hands off Russia', *Past & Present*, December 1967. For a less cynical assessment see Brockway, F., *Inside the Left*, pp. 132–3.

19 ILP Conference Report, 1921; *NL* 1.4.1921; Kendall, W., *The Revolutionary Movement in Britain*, pp. 273–7, which estimates around 500 recruits left the ILP; one of the strongest supporters of affiliation at Southport was Helen Crawfurd.

20 Tape A, p. 6. This interview, recorded 10.11.1980, is difficult to interpret, partly because Mary's memory had by then begun to grow hazy, and partly because what she describes cannot be easily checked against other sources. Her description of the pile of *Communists* (from 1923 called the *Workers' Weekly*) is sufficiently vivid and authoritative to sound accurate; however an unpublished autobiography of a founder-member of the Nelson Communist Party, *Seth Sagar's Memoirs*, makes no mention of this arrangement – though what he writes does not rule out the possibility that the Coopers could have been the main paper distributors at some point.

Later on in the same tape, after a discussion of SJC's childhood, Mary is asked 'With their selling the *Daily Worker*, I wonder why neither of them joined the Communist Party?' and replies 'Oh, they were members when they could be. You could be members then, at first, and then it was made that you couldn't . . . Oh, yes, they were in the Communist Party when they could be . . .' (Tape A, pp. 7–8).

This may well have been the case. Until 1925 joint Labour Party and Communist membership remained possible. But somehow I doubt it.

Firstly, it seems strange that Mary had not mentioned this in earlier interviews recorded regularly over the previous four and a half years; secondly, Mary's memory was no longer as clear as it had been during those earlier interviews; thirdly Mary, still a Labour Party activist but a regular supporter of *Morning Star* bazaars etc, might possibly have willed her parents to have closer links with the early CP branch than was actually the case; and fourthly, Seth Sagar mentions many of the 14 founding branch members in his *Memoirs* but does not refer to the Coopers. In short, I was unconvinced that they belonged to the Party, and so have left the statement out of the main text.

Seth Sagar's *Memoirs* refers to a branch minute book March 1924 – October 1928, but whether this has survived or not is unclear. Thanks to Andrew Bullen for letting me see a copy of the *Memoirs*.

21 See Rowbotham, S., *Hidden from History*, Plute Press, London, 1973, chapter 23 for an illuminating discussion of these tensions. For WILPF, see Bussey, G., and Tims, M., *Pioneers for Peace*, WILPF, London, 1965 and 1980, pp. 39–40.

22 Clitheroe Branch of NUWSS Treasurer's book, first entry 11th April 1912, last entry (to balance £1.5.2$\frac{1}{2}$d) 25th September 1921. M.G. Fawcett to Miss Murgatroyd and SJC, 12.1.1919.

23 Brockway, F., *Inside the Left* p. 49 notes how Brockway crossed swords with Eleanor Rathbone at a NUWSS annual conference over the war. Strachey, R., *Millicent Garrett Fawcett*, p. 335.

24 *Common Cause* from 27.2.1914 to 3.4.1914. For a discussion of these issues, see Land, H., 'The Family Wage', *Feminist Studies*, no 6, 1980; also Lewis, J., *The Politics of Motherhood*, Croom Helm, London, 1980, pp. 169–70; also Wilson, E., *Women and the Welfare State*, Tavistock, London, 1977, pp. 121–2. There was also debate on whether endowment of Motherhood would encourage thrifty, responsible parents to breed and so halt the threat of 'race suicide'; see next chapter.

25 Eleanor Rathbone to SJC [31.3.1918] and 10.12.[1918]. *NL* 23.11.1917; Nelson Women's Citizen Association mins, 21.5.1918 and 3.8.1918.

26 The NUSEC mins for 1919 are, according to the Fawcett Library, missing. However among the Cooper papers is a letter from the NUSEC Secretary (25.11.1919) which notes that the Exec Comm 'considered your offer to keep yourself free for the Union's work provided that the Union could guarantee you two days work a week', and that this the Committee was pleased to do. The NUSEC Finance Department calculated SJC's salary at 14s 4d per day. The letter asks SJC to respond to 'this proposed new arrangement', but there is no record of subsequent correspondence. Note also E. Macadam (NUSEC) to SJC, 26.9.1919.

On the evidence available (see footnote 4 re NUWSS 3.1.1918 decision) it seems that SJC worked for NUWSS up to circa June 1918, then worked for NUSEC from about March 1919 to about March 1920. (However her own account book records regular payments only until November 1919; the book finally closes 30.6.1923.)

Examples of the kind of work SJC did for NUSEC are contained in Edith Willis to SJC 27.3.1919 (to help a woman standing for council); and Elizabeth Wilson to SJC, 30.9.1919, concerning women boot and shoe trade unionists.

27 *NL* 10.10.1919 and 24.10.1919.
NUSEC Exec Comm mins reflect the transitory nature of many local branches eg. 14.10.20 four local societies affiliated, but five dissolved.

28 *NL* 23.1.1920 and 15.10.1920; NUSEC mins 11.11.1920. Tape 121, p. 26; also tape 915, p. 20; also tape 916, p. 26. *NL* 16.5.1919 & 19.3.1920.

29 Annot Robinson papers MISC/718 81, 108 and 111 etc.

30 NUSEC mins 11.11.1920; NUSEC reports (Box 342 in Fawcett Library) 17.11.1921.

31 Rathbone, E., 'Changes in Public Life', in Strachey, R., (ed), *Our Freedom and Its Results*, Hogarth Press, London, 1936, pp. 64–5. See also Doughan, D., *Lobbying for Liberation*, City of London Polytechnic, London, 1980. Eastman, C., *On Women and Revolution*, Oxford University Press, London, 1978, pp. 154–231 is an interesting (if partisan) account of these battles & deserves to be better known. Spender, D., *There's Always Been A Women's Movement This Century*, Pandora Press, London, 1983, gives a more optimistic picture of the inter-war years.

CHAPTER EIGHTEEN: THE UNITED IRISH LEAGUE AND THE BIRTH-CONTROL BATTLE

1 Conversation with Mary Cooper 9.3.1981. For the United Irish League (UIL) and Pat Quinn, see *NL* 14.1.1910 (UIL Exec. instructed its members to vote for Shackleton; Quinn presides); *NL* 31.10.1919 (UIL meeting; Quinn in chair, Irish people to support Labour); Nelson ILP branch mins, 15.2.1920, to support UIL nominee in Bradley ward; *NL* 3.11.1922 notes with surprise Quinn's victory. The balance on the Council now 9 Liberals, 8 Labour, 5 Conservative, 2 Independents. SJC probably was willing to support Quinn partly because of her interest in the Irish Self-Determination League c. 1921; among her papers is a League leaflet, 'War in Ireland', condemning the activities of the British army in Ireland, n.d.

2 Conversation with Mary Cooper, 9.3.1981. *C & NT* 21.9.1923, 26.10.1923 and 2.11.1923; *NL* 18.9.1924.

3 Nelson ILP branch mins, 28.4.1924. Joe Bates' interviews included *NL* 18.1.1924 (Wilfred Wellock 1879–1972, imprisoned 1917–19, became MP 1927); *NL* 16.5.1924 (Chartist father); *NL* 28.11.1924 (Deborah Smith);

NL 24.12.1924 (Sarah Thomas); *NL* 12 and 19th 9.1924 (Selina Cooper).

4 Tape 916, p. 28. After Mary's funeral, a copy turned up of Mrs N.J., *How We Are Born*, C.W. Daniel, London, 1906. Gould, Mr F.J., *Parents' Guide* Part I, a limited edition published privately by the author, London 1915, 7 pages.

5 Galton, Sir F., *Essays in Eugenics*, Eugenics Education Society, London 1909, pp. 2–3, p. 79 (quoting Professor Karl Pearson), 25–6 and 32. For the differences between the Malthusians' concern for quantity in population, and the eugenicists for quality, see McLaren, A., *Birth Control in Nineteenth Century England*, chapter 8.

6 Saleeby, C.W., *The Methods of Race-Regeneration*, Cassell, London, 1911, p. 35. For the response of feminists to eugenicist ideas, see McLaren, A., *Birth Control in Nineteenth Century England*, chapter 11. He notes that Galton was a supporter of the Anti-Suffrage Society.

7 Llewelyn Davies, M. (ed), *Maternity*, pp. 94, 115 and 13.

8 Hall, R., *Marie Stopes*, Andre Deutsch, 1977 and Virago, 1978, pp. 133–49 and 180–1.

9 *NL* 19.9.1924; tape 916, p. 1 and pp. 28–30.

SJC was of course by no means unique here. See Lewis, J., *The Politics of Motherhood*, chapter 7. For example she notes (p. 200) that feminists Eva Hubback and Edith How-Martyn joined the Malthusian League, and that later (p. 205) Maude Royden became interested.

10 Hall, R., *Marie Stopes*, pp. 186–98.

11 Hall, R., *Marie Stopes*, pp. 200–6 and 169–70; *NL* 15.12.1922. The replies to the questionnaire are to be found in the British Library Stopes Collection, and might conceivably include Greenwood's reply.

12 Rowbotham, S., *A New World for Women – Stella Browne: Socialist Feminist*, Pluto Press, London, 1977 pp. 49–51; also Russell, D., *The Tamarisk Tree: My Quest for Liberty and Love*, Elek Books, 1975 and Virago, London, 1977, pp. 168–70.

13 Rowbotham, S., *A New World for Women*, pp. 52 and 31; Hall, R., *Marie Stopes*, p. 239.

14 Tape 900, pp. 25–6; conversation, 21.1.1981.

NL 7.12.1923 and *C & NT* 7.12.1923; also Nelson Town Council mins 4.12.1923; the voting for the amendment that Minute No. 2 be referred back to the Health and Cleansing Committee was 10 to 9.

15 *NL* 11.1.1924; also Nelson Town Council mins, 8.1.1924. Conversation 9.3.1981; Mary was quite adamant that the quarrel, though partly about the jealousy of professional nurses on the committee, was largely about birth control and the Catholics' opposition to it.

16 *NL* 5.9.1924. It would be interesting to know if other local areas experienced such a change in spring 1924. Rowbotham, S., *A New World for Women*, p. 53 notes that Stella Browne made a tour of East Anglia then,

invited by Norwich Labour Party which had the newly-elected Dorothy Jewson as one of its two MPs.

17 *NL* 8.2.1924 and 29.2.1924; also Rowbotham, S., *A New World for Women*, p. 54; of the 13 Sections listed here, two-thirds were from in and around London, the others being Ipswich, Grimsby, North Edinburgh and of course Nelson.

18 Russell, D., *The Tamarisk Tree*, pp. 170–4; Rowbotham, S., *A New World for Women*, pp. 54–5.

Between 1923 and 1924 the votes cast for Arthur Greenwood increased (from 17,083 to 19,922) but his majority went right down; the reason for this is in 1922 and 1923 Labour was opposed by both Liberals and Conservatives; in 1924 no Conservative candidate was put up.

19 *NL* 7.11.1924; Nelson ILP branch mins, 31.8.1925; tape 907, p. 11, and tape 916, p. 19.

Edith Summerskill, when she stood in Bury in 1935 experienced similar Catholic pressure, see chapter 17, ft. nt. 9.

20 Quinn was a councillor 1922–45, Mayor 1936–7, and magistrate from 1932. *NL* 5.12.1924 & 27.3.1915.

Russell, D., *The Tamarisk Tree* Vol 1 p. 185 notes that by spring 1926, 18 local councils supported the campaign; Nelson significantly was not among them; and half of them were from the London area.

21 Russell, D., *Tamarisk Tree* p. 189. For the 1927 and 1928 Conferences, see Rowbotham, S., *A New World for Women* p. 58; information about Henderson from Sarah Perrigo.

Lewis, J., *The Politics of Motherhood*, pp. 197–8 notes that the following groups came out in support of birth control information: WCG (1923), Labour Party Women (1924), NUSEC (1925), Women's Liberal Association (1927), National Council of Women (1929).

22 Tape 916, pp. 27 and 14. *The New Generation*, June 1929.

23 One example of a birth-control pioneer was Dr Helena Wright (1887–1982) who joined a birth-control clinic in London in 1927.

24 *NL* 7.11.1924; tape 915, p. 9; NWA mins 27.8.1924 and 3.9.1924; unfortunately no minutes of the Labour Party Executive seem to have survived for this period.

Both NUWSS and NUSEC had urged from the earliest opportunity the appointment of women magistrates; in 1920 the first woman JP appointed for the borough (ie not county) bench in Nelson was the wife of a local doctor, Clara Myers, a suffragist and Guildswoman. Mrs Myers' death in summer 1924 prompted the Weavers to nominate SJC, so there would be at least one Labour woman on the bench.

25 Mitchell, H., *The Hard Way Up*, p. 229; tape 916, p. 27–8 (though Mary might possibly be confusing a minor case that came before her mother with the trial of a local abortionist at the assizes in 1913).

CHAPTER NINETEEN: POVERTY AND POWER

1 *NL* 7.10.1921, *C & NT* 27.7.1923.
Tape 900, p. 15.
2 Branson, N., *Britain in the Nineteen Twenties*, chapter 4 for further discussion of this complex issue. Unfortunately, this passport has not resurfaced among the other papers after Mary's death.
3 The writ was issued against the Poplar councillors, not for paying high rates of relief, but for refusing to levy rates against other London precepting bodies, e.g. Metropolitan Police.
NL 8.7.1921, 9.9.1921, 16.9.1921.
4 *NL* 21.10.1921 (notes Burnley Board paid out £3,868 per week in out-relief, compared to £255 for the corresponding week in 1920); *NL* 30.9.1921 and 27.2.1922; note also *NL* 28.10.1921 (a woman from Aberdare talks to the WCG on 'the unemployment problem').
NL 20.1.1922, 10.2.1922, 10.3.1922. The Relieving Officer had resigned; the clerk was sacked.
5 *NL* 24.2.1922; possibly she withdrew her name because she was planning to stand as councillor.
   Foot, M., *Aneurin Bevan*, Granada, London, 1975, vol I p. 68 (Bedwellty Union, January 1923); Macintyre, S., *Little Moscows*, Croom Helm, London, 1980, p. 96 (Vale of Leven, 1922); Scottish relief was administered differently from that of England and Wales.
6 *NL* 24.6.1926, 27.9.1926. James Hanna, President of Burnley Miners' Association, to SJC thanking her and others for parcel, 28.8.1926; Secretary of the Bolton branch of the Lancashire & Cheshire Miners' Federation to SJC, 9.9.1926, thanking the Nelson Women's Miners' Relief Committee for a bundle of clothes.
NL 17.9.1926.
7 E.M. [Hoskins], Abertillery, 18.8.1926, acknowledging receipt of parcel sent to head office; E.M. Hoskins, Abertillery [Newport] to SJC, 2.9.1926, thanking for parcel of clothes; G. Bayliss, Breconshire to SJC, as above, 4.3.1928; Cain Horn, [Hon. Sec. of the Abertillery Unemployed Distress Fund], 19.12.1928, as above; Opton Purnell [Secretary, South Wales Miners' Federation], Abertillery, 12.8.1926, as above; E.C. Noble, Tonypandy, Glamorgan, 8.9.1926 to Mary Cooper, thanking for parcel of clothes.
8 Unsigned letter from County Durham thanking SJC for parcel of clothes, 8.12.1926; Beatrice Hoyle, Leeds to SJC, as above, n.d.
Invitation printed on Kate Greenwood's monthly newsletter, October 1926.
9 *NL* 4.11.1927 to 25.11.1929. Andrew Smith became Nelson's 5th Labour Mayor.
Tape 832, pp. 23–4. About this point, SJC left the ILP.

10 *NL* 25.5.1928 to 28.6.1928 (the council voting was 23 to nil, with one abstention).

Tape 916, p. 17 (also tape 121, p. 22); unfortunately I have not been able to trace the film which Mary says was made of the march.

Dickinson, B., *James Rushton and his times 1886-1956*, published privately by author, Nelson n.d. (1970s), pp. 55–62, gives a valuable account of the lock-out. Macfarlane, L.J., *The British Communist Party*, p. 252.

11 *NL* 24.5.1929, 14.2.1930, 21.2.1930 (speech by James Rushton of Barnoldswick).

12 Public Assistance Committee (PAC), mins 25.11.1929; the clerk to the Lancashire County Council (LCC) notes the transference of certain local powers to the LCC, including Poor Law administration, infant life protection etc. The county was previously divided into 27 Poor Law Unions; it now consisted of 16 districts, each with its own Guardian Committee; these consisted of local councillors, three local county councillors, and other members appointed by the PAC (of whom at least 3 must be women). Nelson was represented on No. 6 Guardians' Committee by eight councillors, a Labour man and SJC.

The county councillors elected for Lancashire in 1928 were: Conservative (31), Labour (20), Liberal/Progressive (15), Independent/Others (9), Unknown (30), ie Labour was still therefore very much in the minority; see Marshall, J. (ed), *The History of Lancashire County Council*. Mitchell, H., *The Hard Way Up*, chapter 20, tells of her experiences on the Manchester PAC.

13 PAC mins 30.6.1930; *NL* 15.8.1930; *Nelson Gazette* (*NGaz*) 27.5.1930 and 12.8.1930. The particular problem was 'decontrolled' rents; privately rented accommodation was particularly expensive in Nelson because, in a boom town, demand for housing still exceeded supply.

14 PAC mins 29.9.1930 and 29.9.1930; *NL* 3.10.1930; *NGaz* 30.9.1930.

15 PAC mins 27.10.1930 and 24.11.1930; *NL* 7.11.1930; *NGaz* 16.12.1930 and 9.12.1930.

16 Pimlott, B., *Labour and the Left in the 1930s*, Cambridge University Press, Cambridge, 1977, pp. 25–6 for a brief biography of Greenwood. See also Arthur Greenwood to SJC, 2.1.1925; Kate Greenwood to SJC, n.d. (1926?); Kate Greenwood to Mary Cooper, n.d. (1926?).

NL 24.10.1930 for heckling by the Minority Movement, reported at length and with considerable glee by the conservative *Nelson Leader*. Greenwood was a particular target for Minority Movement and National Unemployed Workers' Movement anger; see for instance, Hannington, W., *Unemployment Struggles 1919–1936*, Lawrence & Wishart, London, 1936, p. 206–10.

17 This is a complex episode and needs further research. *NL* 6.3.1931 suggests that the inspector had not been helpful; *NGaz* 24.2.1931 says the inspector *was* putting people back on relief.

PRO material (MH 52/74) reveals Greenwood's concern about his constituents' complaints (eg. Greenwood's note about the deputation, 20.12.30.) The practical effects of his sympathy again need further research.
18 Throup, W.J., *Poverty and Power*, unpublished typescript (with added handwritten notes of actors). *NGaz* 24.2.1931 and 10.3.1931.
19 Nelson Co-operative Society, treasurer's book, kept by R. Cooper for the half year preceding 28.1.1928.
NL 10, 17 and 24.4.1931 for Robert Cooper's correspondence with Charlie Parratt (1866–1933), a pioneer socialist, and SDF activist, who remained a vocal opponent of the Labour Party on the non-Leninist left. Robert Cooper magnanimously attended his funeral, despite their previous arguments.
20 Tape 835, pp. 21–2, tape A, p. 2, tape 907, pp. 6–7.

CHAPTER TWENTY: A BENCH SWARMING WITH MANUFACTURERS

1 Tape 850, pp. 6–7; for further discussion see Branson, N., and Heinemann, M., *Britain in the Nineteen Thirties*, Panther, London, 1973, pp. 107 ff; also Hutt, A., *The Condition of the Working Class in Britain*, Laurence, London, 1933, chapter II; also Brockway, F., *Hungry England*, Victor Gollancz, London, 1932, chapter I (which gives a moving description of life in Great Harwood near Blackburn).
2 Tape 832, p. 10; *NL* 30.5.1930 (an incident known locally as 'Mucking Abaht the Garden', in honour of the tune the band played); *NL* 18.7.1930. Also, throughout 1930 a local weaver had been fighting in the law courts his employer's right to fine him for producing errors in the cloth he wove; shortly before Christmas the Court of Appeal eventually ruled that this kind of industrial fining *was* legal, *NL* 12.12.1930.
3 McCarthy, M., *Generation in Revolt*, Heinemann, London, 1953, pp. 155–6; she adds later that she was enraged when Party officials told them that, having stirred up local agitation, they should leave the More Looms struggle. McCarthy subsequently left the Party.
Bruley, S., *Socialism and Feminism in the Communist Party of Great Britain 1920–39*, Ph.D., London, 1980 includes valuable material on the role of Party women in the More Looms struggle, and notes that the Party's industrial strategy and its attacks on trade union leadership were not particularly appropriate to fighting what was essentially a defensive battle.
4 *NL* 2.1.1931, 23.1.1931; *NL* 6.2.1931 and 13.2.1931 for a 'Rebel Delegation' organised in defiance of the Weavers' Amalgamation leadership.
NL 13.2.1931 for Nelson Rank and File Strike Committee march to Preston; PAC mins 16.2.1931 (telegram dispatched 15.1.1931); *NL* 20.2.1931. It is difficult to gauge the effect Greenwood's decision had on the

lock-out. Hopwood, E., *The Lancashire Weavers' Story*, Amalgamated Weavers' Association, Manchester, 1969, p. 96 notes merely that during the fourth week of the lock-out 'it became evident there was weakness in the employers' camp' and they decided to terminate it on 14th February. This, however, still needs further research.

5 The employer was Vernon Haighton and his mill was Park Mill; the *Northern Daily Telegraph* 1.5.1931 ff. records the conflict which had built up between the NWA officials and local members of the Communist Party over the Haighton's dispute. *NL* 1.5.1931, 8.5.1931.

6 This account of the battle relies largely on the report in *NL* 15.5.1931; the report in *Northern Daily Telegraph* 12.5.1931 agreed with the *Leader* in all but small details. Note also 'Truncheon Charge at Nelson', *MG* 12.5.31. Another useful source is Foulds, H., 'The Disturbance in Pendle Street', Nelson Local History Notes, No. 1, March 1976; it alleges that pressure was put on Superintendent Linaker by local manufacturers to stop the march.

7 Tape 121, p. 14; Tape 832, pp. 4–5.

8 *Northern Daily Telegraph* 12.5.1931, 13.5.1931. NWA mins 12.5.1931. Nelson did not have its own police force because – unlike a big town such as Burnley – it was not a county borough and so was policed by the Lancashire Constabulary. The right to local policing had been lost to the county 1835–40, but resentment against 'foreign peelers' remained.

At the suggestion of Mayor Winterbottom, the Nelson Council therefore agreed that a sub-committee of the General Purposes Committee would be appointed to interview the Chief Constable of Lancashire, plus the Chairman of the Joint Standing Committee of the Lancashire County Council, and if they got no satisfaction they would take the matter to the Home Office.

9 *NL* 15.5.1931, 29.5.1931. NWA mins 13.5.1931 and 18.5.1931. It is difficult to be precise about the magistrates, because even though their names were published in the reports of the trial, information about them is usually only given when they are appointed (eg. *NL* 7.11.1924 and 13.7.1928) or in obituaries. The ninth magistrate was a freemason and Rotary member who, unusually, had links with the Labour Party; he seems to have held something of a casting vote here, but did not use it.

10 *NL* 12.6.1931 and *Northern Daily Telegraph* 10.6.1931.

11 The fourteen magistrates (with date of appointment if known) were:
i) Richard Winterbottom, Labour Mayor, nurseryman and jobbing gardener
ii) Selina Cooper, Labour (1924)
iii) Andrew Smith, Labour (1928) ex-Mayor
iv) James Helm, Labour (1924)
v) G.W. Hamilton, Co-operative (1924)
vi) Sir Amos Nelson, Conservative, (1907), ex-Mayor, mill-owner
vii) William Fell, Liberal Alderman (1920), ex-Mayor

viii) J. Roberts

ix) D.Tattersall, either Liberal or Conservative Alderman

x) Dr Jackson, anti-Labour possibly Independent (1905), ex-Mayor

xi) J.T. Dent

xii) W.E. Riley, Liberal Alderman (1920), ex-Mayor

xiii) C. Townsley, Liberal Alderman (1920), ex-Mayor

xiv) J. Ridehalgh, Conservative (1924), mill-owner

12 Tape 121, p. 14; *NL* 19.6.1931; *MG* 18.6.1931.

13 James Whitham JP was the same generation Labour stalwart as William Rickard, and was councillor 1901–1914.

Northern Daily Telegraph 20.6.1931 and 22.6.1931; *NL* 26.6.1931; *MG* 22.6.1931. Seth Sagar was expelled from NWA Comm 1929 for publicly discussing union business.

14 Tape 121, p. 14; presumably Sagar and Ratcliffe were not kept in police custody over the weekend, as they are referred to as 'defendants' not (like Butterfield) as 'prisoners'. There is no evidence that SJC got the 'objection in writing'. *Northern Daily Telegraph* 19.6.1931 for Anomalies Act plus 20 and 22.6.1931 for court case; also *NL* 26.6.1931.

15 Chief Constable of Lancashire to SJC, 30.6.31. Tape 121, p. 14. Sadly, I have not yet been able to trace this particular article; Mary refers to it appearing in the Saturday paper, whereas it would seem more likely to occur on Monday, after the case closed. The *Northern Daily Telegraph* (above) refers to her altercation with the lawyer, but not to her making a special statement.

16 Constituency Labour Party, conference mins, 1.5.1931. The *Nelson Gazette* which represented the official local Labour Party line seems little concerned about the Sagar-Ratcliffe trial; its line was that there was nothing wrong with the magistrates, but the law needed changing.

17 *NL* 17.7.1931. The point at which SJC had left the ILP, and the reason for this, remain unclear. Mary suggests her mother left the ILP because it was 'against Russia'. After the 1921 ILP Conference, she seems to have remained a locally active member till the mid-1920s. For details of the Anomalies Act, see chapter 21.

18 Tape 818, p. 6. Information about Greenwood from Mowat, C.L., *Britain Between the Wars 1918–1940*, Methuen, London, 1955, pp. 390–3 and 402.

Quotation from Branson, N., and Heinemann, M., *Britain in the Nineteen Thirties*, p. 19.

19 *NL* 11.9.1931; Constituency Labour Party, adoption conference mins, 11.10.1931; *NL* 2.10.1931, 23.10.1931.

20 Tape C, p. 7, tape 835, p. 22 and tape 818, p. 6. Mary's remarks presumably refer to the period 1931–4, but don't necessarily imply that her father was still registered as unemployed: he would have been able to apply to the Guardians because he was too sick to work.

21 PAC mins 26.1.1931, 28.9.1931, 26.10.1931, 5.11.1931, 30.11.1931. Branson, N., and Heinemann, M., *Britain in the Nineteen Thirties*, pp. 33–6.
22 *NL* 8.1.1932 to 12.8.1932; Guardians in nearby Colne had also refused to function. Nelson Labour Party, exec mins, 9.8.1932, which backed the Relief Committee's decision.
23 PAC mins, 30.5.1932 to 29.12.1932.
  NL 2.9.1932, 9.9.1932, 30.9.1932, 11.11.1932, 28.7.1933 (see also next chapter).
24 Tape 121, p. 13.

CHAPTER TWENTY-ONE: WHY CHAMPION MONEY-MAKING WIVES?

1 *C & NT* 1.11.1907; *CC* 22.8.1913 for SJC's letter on 'Married Women's Work and Infant Mortality' in reply to John Burns; Fawcett Library box 342 contains a draft of the Married Women (Employment) Bill 1926; Eva Hubback, NUSEC to SJC, 1.3.1926; anonymous to SJC, 25.2.1925.
2 1931 census; Jane McCall was elected to the NWA committee in June 1930, but by December 1930 had left Nelson to go to Ruskin; thanks to Allan Fowler for this information; another early member of the NWA committee, according to Seth Sagar's memoirs, was May Ainsworth.
3 Tape 679, pp. 28–30. Even after she had left Nelson for Ruskin, the Committee did not forget what happened; NWA mins 15.7.1931.
4 Eastman, C., *On Women and Revolution*, pp. 223–31.
  Tape 679, pp. 13–14 also *NL* 8.11.1929 (a report of the deputation).
5 *Manchester Guardian* 15.6.1928. Eastman, C., *On Women and Revolution*, p. 231 which notes that the 'equalitarian' feminists 'seem to attract the freshest, youngest and warmest personalities in the movement. Lady Balfour of Burleigh, who acted as spokesman for the eleven who resigned, belongs to the new order of feminists. She is, I should say, barely a voter, hardly over thirty, slim, tall and charming . . . Lady Balfour in her turn is some thirty years younger than Miss Rathbone . . .' The conflict between old & new feminism is clearly summarised in Delmar, R., 'Afterword' to Brittain, V., *Testament of Friendship*, Virago, London, 1980.
6 Wage figures from Utley, F., *Lancashire and the Far East*, Allen & Unwin, London, 1931, pp. 70–1.

I read the NWA mins book only from May 1931 to April 1932 and October–November 1933; it would repay someone to go through additional minute books. I have supplemented this Nelson information, with photocopies of Amalgamated Weavers' Association material (the originals are at the Lancashire Record Office) made by Alan Fowler.

The earliest that I noted was an Amalgamated Weavers' Association statement dated 1.12.1928 which noted of the 'more loom' experiment, that:

'You have a man and his wife, both weavers together. There is the possibility (though this is only in embryo yet) of the husband remaining on eight looms and the wife at home. The husband would get a good wage but not as good as two four-loom weavers between them . . .'

7 Amos Nelson, Valley Mills to Naesmith, Secretary of the Amalgamated Weavers' Association with a copy to Carey Hargreaves, Secretary of NWA, 22.4.1930; Sir Amos' proposal concerned the introduction of semi-automatic looms, mainly for new fabrics like artificial silk etc.

NL 29.5.1931; and in the same issue, was a letter suggesting that the crisis in the cotton industry was a 'disgrace to our manhood'. *NL* 8.8.1930, letter from 'Fed Up', criticizing NWA for opposing 'More Looms' and suggesting 'many married men would only be too glad to run eight looms and keep their wives at home . . . Why not take a ballot and let us have a say in the matter? Why not have a combing out of all married women who could afford to stay at home, and make room for others who need it?'

8 Nelson, D., *Memoir of Amos Nelson*, unpublished typescript, n.d., chapter 2 pp. 27-8; other local employers were resentful of Sir Amos' experiment, complaining that he could sell his cloth for shillings; but Burnley manufacturers, competing with the Japanese, had to sell at 3d or 4d a yard. For the question of ancillary labour at Valley Mills, see NWA mins 13.8.1931, 20.8.1931, 18.9.1931 etc.

Tape 850, pp. 4-5; also NWA mins 20.8.1931, 26.8.1931, 2.9.1931; the respondent says he was a fully paid-up union member, while the minutes state he was a non-member.

9 NWA mins 5.10.1931, 16.11.1931, 18.11.1931, 18.12.1931, 6.4.1932 etc. Nelson, D., *Memoir of Amos Nelson*, chapter 2, p. 30; Nelson adds that after months of negotiation a new six-loom system was agreed, with the older men in mind, and put into effect in November 1933. For wage differential between men and women weavers, see Gray, E.M., *The Weaver's Wage*, Manchester University Press, Manchester, 1937, pp. 10-19.

10 Anonymous, *Women and the More Looms System*, Textile Minority Movement, n.d.; Bruley, S., *Socialism and Feminism in the Communist Party of Great Britain*, gives further background and explains it was written by Bessie Dickinson and published in September 1931.

11 *NL* 12.12.1930; *Northern Daily Telegraph* 5.6.1931; anonymous, *Fight the Eight Looms*, Textile Minority Movement, n.d. (probably about August 1931).

12 *NL* 20.11.1931; *NGaz* 29.12.1931; *NL* 11.9.1931; Hutt, A., *The Condition of the Working Class*, p. 68.

13 *Cambridge Daily News* 7.12.1932, which also notes her opposition to protective legislation and her comparison between the current fight and the campaign for the vote.

14 Nelson Labour Party mins 16.5.1933. The way in which the Comintern line was a response to the rise of Nazism in Germany is discussed in Pimlott, B., *Labour and the Left in the 1930s*, pp. 80–2.

15 Rose Smith, Burnley to SJC, 16.7.1931; *NL* 27.8.1923; the hunger march did, of course, also receive Labour support from Willie John Throup etc.

The Nelson Labour Party Exec 18.7.1933 agreed to participate in the march, having rejected the United Front invitation two months before. Whether SJC had a part in this change of attitude remains speculation.

16 Tape 818, pp. 5 and 24; tape 896, pp. 9–10; Elizabeth Abbott to SJC 4.1.33.

17 NWA mins 9.10.1933 and 2.11.1933 (union acceptance of the proposals, which concerned 6-loom setts, was originally lost on the casting vote of the chairman).

Holtby, W., *Women in a Changing Civilisation*, Bodley Head, London, 1934, pp. 151–8 ff.

18 *C & NT* 20.10.1933; SJC may well have remembered Sir Stanley O. Buckmaster, as he then was, from the Keighley by-election of 1913.

The remaining speaker, Miss N.S. Parnell BA, I have not been able to trace, but she was quite probably speaking on behalf of white collar workers in education and government; Mrs Pethick-Lawrence was particularly active in fighting the London County Council's marriage bar for women.

19 Monica Whately, London to SJC, 1.11.1933 and 6.11.1933; *Daily Herald* 15.11.1933; Holtby, W., *Women in a Changing Civilisation* p. 113; *NL* 24.11.1933.

20 Diary, page Feb 21st and July 5th; Emmeline Pethick-Lawrence to SJC, 15.11.1933; Monica Whately to SJC, 16.11.1933; *John Bull* 25.11.1933; Elizabeth Abbott to SJC, 4.1.34. Viz News has a video recording of a film made of the meeting, showing SJC in cloche hat, coat with fur collar, and spectacles.

21 Women Against War and Fascism, *Bulletin* No. 2, Dec 1935; 'Report on the Life of Married Women Textile Workers', typescript, anon, n.d.; the substance of this report was published in Beauchamp, J., *Women Who Work*, Lawrence and Wishart, London, 1937, pp. 16–18; note also Joan Beauchamp to SJC, 2.12.36.

CHAPTER TWENTY-TWO: WOMEN AGAINST WAR AND FASCISM

1 *C & NT* 18.8.1934, *NT* 18.5.1934 and 25.5.1934.

2 *N & NT* 8.10.1920, 20.9.1924, 14.6.1926, 4.6.1926, 11.6.1926. The most probable contact between SJC and the Pilgrimage organisers was Kate Courtney who was involved in the Manchester area; she sent Mary a letter of

condolence after the death of SJC, 3.12.1946. However there is also among the Cooper letters one from A.E. Wilkinson (probably Ellen Wilkinson's sister, Annie) to Mrs Hall (probably Mrs Lucy Hall, then Secretary of the Women's Section) concerning the pilgrimage, 2.6.1926.

3 *NL* 24.6.1926 and 1.10.1926. See also Liddington, J., 'The Women's Peace Crusade, the history of a forgotten campaign' in *Over Our Dead Bodies*.

4 *NL* 5.2.1932; constituency Labour Party mins 29.4.1932 and 28.4.1933; Ceadel, M., *Pacifism in Britain 1914–1945*, Clarendon Press, Oxford, 1980, pp. 1–3 puts clearly the *ex post facto* rationalisation which has dogged historiography here. 'Attitudes and ideas which had seemed enlightened and even practical in the aftermath of the Great War, one of the most reviled wars in human history, were suddenly rendered obsolete and ludicrous by Hitler, whose behaviour rehabilitated warfare . . .' See also *Survey of Organisations in Manchester District Opposing War*, Manchester and District Anti-War Council Manchester, 1934.

The links between women and fascism are interesting; Nellie Driver a Nelson weaver became the BUF's local Women's Leader; she was among those who warmed to Mosley's appeal to the hard-pressed cotton workers. Also a letter appeared (*NL* 2.2.1934) from ex-suffragette Flora Drummond, Chief Organiser, Women's Guild of Empire, urging that 'one potential Drake or Clive is worth a hundred standardised products of elementary or higher education'. Martin Durham notes that other suffragettes also became involved in the BUF: Mary Richardson, Norah Elam, Mercedes Barrington (and later Mary Allen).

Quotation from Foot, M., *Aneurin Bevan*, vol I, pp. 198 and 209.

5 *NL* 10.8.1934; the date Elizabeth Stanworth joined the CP is not clear, and she may have joined after 1934; *C & NT* 10.8.1934.

6 *NL* 24.8.1934, *C & NT* 24.8.1934 and *DWker* 25.8.1934. The link between feminism and the Anti-War Movement needs further exploration, and the extent to which Nelson was unusual to be assessed. The Anti-War Movement was formed in 1932 and seems to have taken much of the steam out of the earlier No More War Movement formed in 1921; see footnote 4 for sources.

Nelson Labour Party mins, 14.8.1934, notes that the Party approved of the objects of the Women's Anti-War demonstration and sent official representatives.

7 Foot, M., *Aneurin Bevan*, vol I, pp. 174–5. Material about the WAWF is hard to come by as its London office was bombed in the War; some records exist in the Pankhurst Papers in Amsterdam, as well as in the Cooper papers; the Pankhurst material is revealing on the early days of WAWF and the friction that later developed between Sylvia and the organisers. For the Charter, see Maude Brown to Sylvia Pankhurst, 27.7.1934 and 2.8.1934; Maude Brown, of the National Unemployed Workers' Movement Women's

Department, was not in the CP but worked closely with Rose Smith etc; the Charter reflects Brown's concerns about maternal mortality etc. The 1934 WCG Conference also demanded imprisoned abortionists be released. The Charter idea seemed to disappear after mid-1934.

8 Roneod *Bulletin* No. 1, Women's World Congress Against War and Fascism, 4.8.1934; *C & NT* 19.10.1934; Women's World Committee Against War and Fascism, British section, leaflet, n.d. Significantly, the leaflet contained little of the broad feminism of the earlier Charter.

9 *Commission for Women's Delegation to Germany*, leaflet, WAWF, n.d.; it lists the hostages as Hertha Sturm (one year in prison), Mrs Beimler (14 months in prison, held hostage), and Else Steinfurth (one year in prison, husband arrested after Reichstag fire and murdered); the other delegate mentioned here was a Catherine Carswell. *DWker* 8.8.1934 also mentions Maude Royden as a possible delegate. *C & NT* 19.10.1934 gives Rose Smith as one of the delegates; why she dropped out is unclear; it might have been because of her direct connections with the Communist Party.

10 Tape 917, p. 1 (of partial transcript). Maggie Chapman was ninety-two when the interview was recorded, and understandably confused the German women hostages with the arrest of the Communist leader Thälmann shortly after the Reichstag fire; she also situates the visit in the First World War, which is misleading.

Tape 121, p. 16; in later interviews, Mary suggested 'it was connected with the World War from – against Fascism' (tape 818, p. 22); but she may possibly be confusing WAWF with her mother's later involvement with the People's Convention.

11 Katherine Cant, London to SJC, 14.9.1934; Enid Rossen to SJC, 10.10.1934; A. Naesmith, Amalgamated Weavers' Association, Accrington, to Whom It May Concern, 11.10.1934; Carey Hargreaves, Nelson, to Whom It May Concern, 12.10.1934; *C & NT* 12.10.1934; *C & NT* 2.11.1934; SJC carefully preserved her train reservation ticket; 'A Visit to Germany', International Women's Committee Against War & Fascism (British Section) n.d.

12 SJC to Mary Cooper, 17, 21 and 23.10.1934; tape 121, pp. 15–16; Mary claims Monica Whately was a stipendiary magistrate, and also refers to the *Times* Munich correspondent's making a secret code for them; *C & NT* 2.11.1934.

13 *Northern Daily Telegraph*, 'Nelson Woman's German Adventure – Agitation for Release of Political Prisoners – Story of a Great "Ordeal" '; *C & NT* 2.11.1934, 'My Visit to Germany'; *NL* 2.11.1934; *Daily Herald* 3.11.1934; *DWker* 9.11.1934 and 13.11.1934. Other speakers at the meeting in the London Playhouse Theatre included Dr Stella Churchill who had been a parliamentary Labour candidate and was pro-United Front; Gabrielle Duchene, who helped found WILPF in 1915 and was now a leader

of WAWF in France; Margery Fry, social reformer; two delegates from the Paris Congress; chair taken by Dorothy Evans of the Association of Women Clerks and Secretaries.

14 Monica Whately, London to SJC, 5.11.1934; Magda Gellan, Secretary WAWF, London to SJC, 20.11.1934; Magda Gellan, London, to SJC, 27.11.1934; tape C, p. 1.

15 'Report of My Impressions on the Women's Delegation by Mrs S.J. Cooper', handwritten draft; typed and signed version is almost identical; *A Visit to Germany* typescript (whether this was finally printed & distributed by WAWF is unclear).

16 Tape C, p. 1; tape 895, p. 6; possibly SJC objected to any sensationalising of the report, and certainly WAWF had an annoying habit of, for instance, exaggerating the extent of its non-Communist support e.g. SJC is referred to at least twice as 'Councillor Mrs Cooper JP', Stella Churchill (see footnote 13) is referred to as a Labour candidate whereas in fact she did not stand again in 1935; and the final report refers to the delegation as representing 'vast numbers of British women of all political parties' – a wishful exaggeration.

The Pankhurst papers reveal Sylvia Pankhurst's continuing connection with WAWF; 22.5.1935 she wrote to Magda Gellan, explaining that she was not able to attend Committee meetings, that she had not resigned but enquiring whether she was 'still Treasurer'.

17 Mowat, C.L., *Britain between the Wars 1918–1940*, pp. 565–6; *C & NT* 1.1.1935; *NL* 18.1.1935 and 8.2.1935 (letters from Elizabeth Stanworth about Mosley); Linklater, A., *An Unhusbanded Life*, p. 252.

18 The results of a Peace Ballot for Nelson were published, *NL* 21.12.1934; these showed that local people *overwhelmingly* wanted Britain to remain in the League of Nations; reduction of armaments by international agreement; abolition of national military and naval aircraft by international agreement; the manufacture and sale of arms for private profit to be prohibited by international agreement; and nations to take economic and non-military measures to compel one nation to stop attacking another. However on the last and most controversial question, only two thirds of the respondents said they would support *military* action to stop such an attack; one third (5,666 people out of about 18,500 replies) took a pacifist or socialist (opposing capitalist governments waging war) stance. These proportions were not dissimilar to the national results; see Branson, N. and Heinemann, M., *Britain in the Nineteen Thirties*, pp. 328–32.

In Nelson 379 people undertook the work for the Peace Ballot. Would Selina Cooper have been one of them? Possibly. The Cooper papers include a note of thanks (20.12.[34]) from the National Declaration Committee. However, people such as Elizabeth Stanworth opposed the ballot and asked people to add a footnote to their Ballot form that, 'I rely upon the organised strength of the working class of my own and other countries to prevent war, and recognise war as the great enemy of the workers since it intensifies all the vileness and degradation of existing capitalist conditions', *NL* 30.11.1934. For Mrs Despard's views, see Linklater, A., *An Unhusbanded Life*, pp. 193, 211-2 and 236-7.

19 *C & NT* 22.2.1935; at the meeting Bland talked of the international working class refusing to take up arms; at the Constituency Labour Party conference three months later he proposed, on behalf of the Nelson Weavers, a general strike in the event of war, and this was accepted. This position was not dissimilar to that of the Socialist League, but the League does not at this stage seem to have been in evidence in Nelson. For further discussion see Pimlott, B., *Labour and the Left in the 1930s*, pp. 90-1.

20 *NL* 22.2.1935; *NL* 22.3.1935; *C & NT* 17.5.1935.

Sylvia Pankhurst's links with WAWF seem to have become largely nominal by now; *DWker* 20.5.1935 for Caxton Hall meeting, which reports that Ellen Wilkinson was heckled for not giving the right line on the Soviet Union's peace policy.

21 *C & NT* 7.7.1935. There is an interesting parallel to SJC's problem in accepting Sylvia's account, with Annot Robinson's daughters' difficulties after their mother's death in 1925. Letters MISC/718 82-4 written autumn 1930 from the Suffragette Club to Helen Robinson, reveal that Helen had written asking what books she should read to understand better her mother's contribution, and is recommended to read accounts by Mrs Pankhurst, Annie Kenney, Sylvia Pankhurst, Ray Strachey, Constance Lytton and Mrs Fawcett. The confusions felt by the daughter of a radical suffragist would have been surely only increased by reading these books, and Helen was obviously very perplexed and discontinued the correspondence. For other examples, see the Afterword.

22 *C & NT* 9.8.1935. Bruley, S., *Socialism and Feminism in the Communist Party of Great Britain*, notes that WAWF was 'mysteriously' killed off at the time of the Nazi-Soviet Pact; in 1936 it had launched a monthly paper, *Woman Today*, edited first by Magda Gellan and later by Charlotte Haldane, and began to win wider support from such women as Eleanor Rathbone MP, Dr Edith Summerskill MP and Margery Corbett Ashby.

23 In the interests of my deteriorating eyesight and sanity, I stopped reading through the local newspapers after 1935, and for the last ten years of her life (1936-46), have traced SJC largely through the Cooper papers, Mary's oral testimony, and local Labour Party minutes. So possibly she *was* more active in the late 1930s than I suggest. However, neither in the Cooper MSS nor in interviews taped with Mary, was there a single reference to the Spanish Civil War. And since the Coopers' newspaper cuttings and letters for this period appear as a fairly reliable guide to SJC's activity, it seems likely she did not become actively involved in support for Republican

Spain – despite the position taken by the Socialist League and others.

The Labour Party records suggest something of SJC's feelings about war in the late 1930s. The Constituency Party (27.3.1936) approved unanimously a Nelson Weavers' motion critical of the 'imperialist' League of Nations, and calling for a strike in the event of war; however after the war in Spain broke out in the summer, the Party (30.4.1937) demanded the end of the non-intervention agreement and arms embargo, but also condemned the National Government's rearmament policy; by the next year (29.4.1938) the Party had swung round to support of the League of Nations; the call for a general strike against war became watered down (28.4.1939) merely to a strike against compulsory military conscription; by the following year (26.4.1940) Britain was of course at war, and a motion proposed by Alderman Bland of the Nelson Weavers calling for a halt to war was defeated by 50 votes to 28. So, despite some backtracking concerning opposition to military intervention (over Spain), it is clear that an important section of the local Party, doubtless including Selina Cooper, believed the British Government was not to be trusted to wage war. This is also borne out by the mins of the Nelson Labour Party, and of the Constituency Party Exec Comm mins (from January 1937). N.Lab.P. mins (11.8.1936) grants £2 to Spanish Workers' Fund; but (9.3.1937) decides not to support a N.E. Lancs (Spanish Workers' Aid Committee) ambulance, and its activities regarding Spain to be confined within the Party.

CHAPTER TWENTY-THREE: KBO AND THE PEOPLE'S CONVENTION

1 Membership of the Amalgamated Weavers' Association fell from its 1921 peak (224,000) to 163,000 (1930) to 101,000 (1935) to 87,000 (1939).
Tape 818, p. 6; Mrs Aldersley remained active in the Nelson Labour Party at least till the end of 1938, and died between 1939 and 1942.

2 Tape 832, p. 15; also tape 896, pp. 29–30 and tape 835, p. 29.

3 Tape 914, p. 1 (partial transcript); tape B, p. 3; tape 918, p. 1 (partial transcript); tape 898, p. 19.

4 Among the Cooper papers are: Borough of Nelson Municipal *Year Book* 1945–6; Lancashire County Council, Public Assistance Committee, Guardians' Committee Handbook, 1937. Letters include Unemployment Assistance Board, District Officer, Preston to SJC about Appeal Tribunal, 11.1.1935; Carey Hargreaves to Open Door Council about weavers' equal pay, 8.12.1936; Minister of Labour to SJC, thanking for help in Cost of Living enquiry, Sept 1938; Elizabeth Abbott, Open Door Council, to SJC about the Evershed Committee Report on the Cotton Spinning Industry, 2.12.1945 and 10.12.1945.

5 *Co-operative News* 6.8.1938, *NL* 12.8.1938 etc.

6 Constituency Lab P annual conference, 31.5.1936 and 27.3.1936.

7 Pimlott, B., *Labour & the Left in the 1930s*, Cambridge University Press, Cambridge, 1977, pp. 103–4.

8 Nelson Labour Party mins 16.3.1937; 18.3.1937 a general unity resolution was put and after long discussion, again defeated 58 votes to 27.

9 Constituency Party Exec Comm mins, 2.4.1937; Constituency Party Annual Conference, 30.4.1937.

10 Constituency Party Exec Comm mins, 21.4.1939; Nelson Labour Party mins 8.8.1939. The idea for a Popular Front was introduced in the mid-1930s, and inspired by events in Spain.

11 Tape 898, p. 23; tape 889, pp. 5–6; Foot, M., *Aneurin Bevan*, vol I p. 280. Bitter strife in Spain between the POUM and the CP exacerbated the bad relations.

12 Tape 818, p. 6; unfortunately there is some confusion between Cripps' Petition Campaign of 1939 and the People's Convention of 1940–1 described later in this chapter. However, Mary's frequent references to Cripps suggest how closely involved her mother was with groups like the Socialist League.

13 Nelson Labour Party mins, 16.2.1939; Constituency Party Exec Comm mins, 10.2.1939, voted similarly; Constituency Party Annual Conference 28.4.1939, with the motion seconded by J. Bracewell.

14 Constituency Party Exec Comm, mins 8.10.1939 and 19.11.1939; Nelson Labour Party Exec mins, 9.1.1940 and 13.2.1940; Constituency Party Annual Conference, 26.4.1940.

15 For Nellie Driver, see *NL* 13.12.1940; she died in 1981. City of Bradford Director Education to SJC, 19.9.1941 re Government Evacuation Scheme.

16 Pritt, D.N., *From Left to Right*, Lawrence and Wishart, London 1965, pp. 108, 110, 190, 221 and 227.

17 The original title was the People's Vigilance Committee; *NL* 20.9.1940.
   Bowes, N., *The People's Convention*, MA, Warwick 1976, which I have relied upon extensively for the general background of the People's Convention; p. 52 for Sydney Silverman's involvement, p. 62 for Lancashire activity.

18 Bowes, N., *The People's Convention*, pp. 45 and 93, which notes that by 18.12.1940 a 'Nelson Cotton Workers' Union' had agreed to support the People's Convention; see also *NL* 5.4.1940, 3.5.1940, 22.11.1940 etc.

19 *NL* 3.5.1940 which notes that the Constituency Executive had decided to prohibit Communists from taking Labour Party positions, having previously 'cast a blind eye . . . on the activities of Left-wingers'; this change was thought to be influenced 'by the action of a number of Communists and peace at any price people . . .'.

20 Organisational sub-comm of NEC, mins, 22.10.1940 and 22.11.1940; the latter concerns the National Agent's analysis of signatures to the Peo-

ple's Convention; signatories who were Lab P members would be asked whether they willingly signed, if they would be willing to withdraw their name – and, if not, steps would be taken to expel them. The Labour Party archivist (letter to author 17.11.1982) notes that the National Agents' MSS have not yet been deposited.

21 Bowes, N., *The People's Convention*, pp. 110–1; tape 818, pp. 6–7, and also tape 121, p. 21; see footnote 12 for confusion between the People's Convention and Stafford Cripps.

22 Tape 818, p. 7; it is difficult to be absolutely precise about the chronology of events here.

Constituency Labour Party Exec mins, 5.1.1941. *The People's Convention*, Free Trade Hall, Manchester, 12.1.1941, which adds to its manifesto, 'the work of the Labour Movement is paralysed because the leadership of the Labour Party is tied up with the Government'; the document then lists hundreds of names of supporters plus organisational designation, and these include: Cllr. Charlotte Haldane (St Pancras Borough Council); Wal Hannington (AEU, Organiser NUWM); Dr Hewlett Johnson (Dean of Cantèrbury); Harry Pollitt (Communist Party); D.N. Pritt, KC, MP; Michael Redgrave; Hilda Vernon (Nat. Council for Defence of Women & Children); Tom Mann (AEU); Rosamund Lehmann (Writers' Association for Intellectual Liberty); the Rev. Mervyn Stockwood (Bristol); Sylvia Townsend Warner; Edmund Frow (Manchester District Committee, AEU); Seth Sagar (EC Member, Management Committee, Nelson Co-op Society); H. Scanlon (Manchester District Committee, AEU); Sam Wild (Secretary, International Brigade Association); Arthur Horner (President SWMF); Mrs Helen Crawfurd (Secretary, Scottish Peace Council); William Gallacher, MP; and others.

23 Nelson Labour Party Exec mins, 14.2:1941. Thanks to James Hinton for drawing my attention to 'Party Membership and the National Convention', Labour Party National Exec Comm, 30.5.1941; the expulsions noted here were reported to the NEC on 26.2.1941; six Nelson and Colne members were expelled, along with 20 from Reading, 5 from Accrington, 4 from Sheffield etc. In Manchester, 8 people withdrew and 3 were expelled. The Nelson expulsions were listed under 'Action by Divisional Parties', suggesting local rather than head office initiative. Correspondence between constituency and regional officers would doubtless be revealing here. (Of course, Mary had said her mother cried over the 1931 crisis.)

24 Tape 900, p. 16; tape 818, p. 8; tape 818, p. 25; see also tape 121, p. 22. There is a possible confusion with women's suffrage here.

25 J. Bracewell to SJC, 25.5.1941. It is unclear precisely when the Nelson People's Convention group was formed; *NL* 24.1.1941 notes a local 'Labour Discussion' group's meeting on the People's Convention and refers to two delegates going to the Convention from the local group.

26 Quoted from Calder, A., *The People's War: Britain 1939–1945*, Panther, London, 1971, p. 300.

27 D.M. Heywood, Manchester to SJC, 24.6.1941; quoted Pritt, D.N., *From Right to Left*, p. 269. In practice, SJC may not have strayed far from the traditional People's Convention line so shortly after the invasion; Hinton, J., 'Killing the People's Convention: a letter from Palme Dutt to Harry Pollitt', Labour History *Bulletin* no 39 autumn 1979, p. 29 notes that the People's Convention hesitated to rethink its line to begin with, but had begun to change by July.

28 *The People's Convention Says . . .*, Manifesto issued by the National People's Convention, October 1941. Tape 818, pp. 6–8.

29 Pritt, D.N., *Right to Left*, p. 286; W.J.R. Squance, Honorary Secretary, the People's Convention, printed circular, 12.1.1942; J. Bracewell, Honorary Secretary, Nelson Committee (People's Convention) to SJC, 3.3.1942.

30 Hinton, J., 'Killing the People's Convention', cites a letter (13.11.1941) from Dutt to Pollitt, in which Dutt expresses his deep reluctance to 'kill' the Convention or replace it by other organisations. See also, Bowes, N., *The People's Convention*, pp. 136 ff, which notes that the Communist Party now saw the People's Convention as 'an inappropriate expression of mass activity'.

31 Tape 818, p. 4; tape A, p. 9. Other reasons may have included reservations about the CP's support for war; CP support for Tory candidates at by-elections; and the leftward swing of the Labour Party.

32 Sloan, P., *Russia Resists*, Frederick Muller, London, 1941; Lee, J., *Our Ally Russia – The Truth!*, W.H. Allen, London, August 1941; p. 5. Also Wainright, W., *Clear Out Hitler's Agents*, Communist Party, London, 1942, an anti-Trotskyist tuppenny pamplet; and others.

33 Tape 915, p. 20.

34 Chief Clerk, Duchy of Lancaster to SJC in reply to her request to retire, 13.12.1944; tape 818, p. 8.

35 Tape 916, p. 19 and tape A, p. 2; tape 916, p. 19.

36 Tape 916, p. 30; tape B, p. 5.

37 *Northern Daily Telegraph* 11.11.1946; W.H. Shepherd, Nelson Divisional Education Officer to Mary Cooper, 11.11.1946; I have so far been unable to trace a *Daily Herald* reference, though Mrs E. Cooper, Clevelys to MC 12.11.1946 notes 'I have read in the Daily Herald that your mother has passed away.'

   Mrs Ackroyd, Harle Syke Women's Co-operative Guild to MC 12.11.1946; Harry and May [Coombe], Redcar to MC, 12.11.1946; William Whittle, Clerk to the Nelson Borough Justice, 13.11.1946; Margaret Noon, St Joseph's R.C. School to MC 13.11.1946; Mrs Kirkbride, Secretary Albert Street Women's Co-operative Guild to MC (n.d.); Secretary Colne Labour Party Women's Section to MC 14.11.1946; Jane Summersgill (née McCall), Essex to MC (n.d.); W.J.Throup, agent Nelson Labour Party to MC 14.11.1946; Mrs E. Crowther, Nelson to MC (n.d.).

Altogether, about three dozen letters of condolence have been preserved. 38 *NL* 15.11.1946; the report lists in detail those who sent flowers, but only a few of the people who attended the memorial service. Ada Nield Chew died a year previously, 27.12.1945; Doris Nield Chew to MC 12.1.1946, thanking for letter of sympathy. Elizabeth Abbott, Hon. Sec. Open Door Council to MC, 1.1.1947; Kathleen Courtney to MC, 3.12.1946.

AFTERWORD

1 The scanty references made in passing to SJC consist of: Bennett, W., *The History of Marsden and Nelson*, Nelson Corporation, Nelson, 1957, p. 25; Makepeace, C., Lancashire, *Lancashire in the 20s and 30s from old photographs*, Batsford, London, 1977, photo 119; Ramelson, M., *The Petticoat Rebellion*, Lawrence and Wishart, London, 1972, p. 153; Rendel, M., 'The Contribution of the Women's Labour League to the Winning of the Franchise', in Middleton, L. (ed), *Women in the Labour Movement*, Croom Helm, London, 1977; and *The Lady's Who's Who* 1938–9.

However, some of Mary Cooper's photographs etc were apparently used for a national exhibition organised, according to Mary, by the Labour Party about 1968 to commemorate the suffrage victory.

Of course the local ILP Institute, though sadly growing delapidated, bears SJC's name on the foundation stone; also, Mary Cooper bequeathed a memorial seat to her mother, and this sits outside Nelson Library.

2 *Ada Nield Chew*, Virago, 1982; Plater, A., *The Clarion Van*, Granada TV 5.7.1983.

3 Oddly enough, the Robinson papers contain more material on the WSPU than on the NUWSS; the originals remain in the possession of Annot's daughter. Jo Vellacott, Catherine Marshall's biographer, notes that much of Marshall's later collection of papers was burnt by her brother, himself old and frail by then, after her death; letter to author, 22.1.1982.

Brief biographies of other forgotten Lancashire suffragists (for instance, Ethel Derbyshire of Blackburn who died in 1976 aged 97) are summarised in *One Hand*, pp. 288–92.

4 Beddoe, D., *Discovering Women's History: A Practical Manual*, Pandora Press, London, 1983.

5 Pankhurst, E.S., *The Suffragette Movement*, Lovat Dickson and Thompson, 1931 and Virago, London, 1977; Strachey, R., *The Cause: A Short History of the Women's Movement in Great Britain*, G. Bell, 1928 and Virago, London, 1978. Also note the slightly different approach taken by Morgan, D.,

Suffragists and Liberals: the Politics of Women's Suffrage in Britain, Basil Blackwell, Oxford, 1975; this, despite a misleading Sylvia Pankhurst photograph on the cover, consults the papers of Cabinet members to assess the attitude of the Liberal leadership to women's suffrage.

6 Pugh, M., *Electoral Reform in War and Peace 1906–18*, Routledge and Kegan Paul, London, 1978, pp. 17 and 22; Holton, S., *Feminism and Democracy: the Women's Suffrage Movement in Britain, with particular reference to the National Union of Women's Suffrage Societies 1897–1918*, Ph.D., Stirling 1980; (Holton p. vii ff. notes that recent historians' over-emphasis on the WSPU stems in part from the work of earlier historians who saw in women, Ulster and industrial militancy, a trinity of revolt, and this led them to see the WSPU as 'revolutionary'; Holton specifically cites George Dangerfield's *The Strange Death of Liberal England* as well as the more general English histories of E. Halevey and R.C.K. Ensor); Vellacott, Newberry J., 'Anti-war Suffragists', *History*, 1977 vol 62; Garner, L., *The Feminism of Mainstream Women's Suffrage in Early 20th Century England: An Evaluation*, Ph.D., Liverpool, 1980. Hume, L.P., *The National Union of Women's Suffrage Societies 1897–1914*, Garland Publishing Inc., New York & London, 1982; and others.

7 Russell, D., *The Tamarisk Tree: My Quest for Liberty and Love*, Elek Books, 1975 and Virago, London, 1977; Brittain, V., *Testament of Experience*, Victor Gollancz, 1957 and Virago, London, 1979.

Other inter-war accounts, though not always so vividly written, include McCarthy, M., *Generation in Revolt*, William Heinemann, London, 1953; Newitt, H., *Women Must Choose: The Position of Women in Europe Today*, Victor Gollancz, London, 1937; Holtby, W., *Women in a Changing Civilization*, Bodley Head, London, 1934; Eyles, L., *Women's Problems of Today*, Labour Publishing Co, London, 1926; Hamilton, M.A., *Remembering My Good Friends*, Jonathan Cape, London, 1944; Haldane, C., *Truth Will Out*, Weidenfeld and Nicolson, London, 1949; Manning, L., *A Life for Education*, Victor Gollancz, London, 1970; Utley, F., *Lost Illusion*, Allen and Unwin, London, 1949.

More recent brief biographical accounts include Callcott, M., 'The Organisation of Political Support for Labour in the North of England: the work of Margaret Gibb, 1929–57' in *Bulletin* of North East Labour History Group, no 11 1977; *Tough Annie: from Suffragette to Stepney Councillor*, Annie Barnes in conversation with Kate Harding and Caroline Gibbs, Stepney Books, London, 1980; and interviews in Rowbotham, S., *Dreams and Dilemmas*, Virago, London, 1983.

Since *Respectable Rebel* was completed, Oldfield, S., *Spinsters of this Parish: The Life and Times of F.M. Mayor and Mary Sheepshanks*, Virago, London, 1984 has begun to open up the history of the post-1915 women's peace movement.

LIST OF SOURCES

═══════════

PRIMARY SOURCES

1. Oral testimony
2. Collections of papers
3. Minutes and annual reports
4. Newspapers and periodicals
5. Other primary sources

SECONDARY SOURCES

1. Biographies and autobiographies
2. General histories
3. Local histories
4. Articles
5. Unpublished theses.

(Only major sources are referred to here; others are listed in the appropriate note.)

1. ORAL TESTIMONY

Interviews recorded with Mary Cooper:
29 March 1976 Tape no 121 (Interview includes Jill Norris and Bessie Dickinson)
21 June 1976 Tape no 915 (Interview includes Jill Norris)
2 May 1977 Tape no 916
1 Feb 1979 Tape no 835
26 Feb 1979 Tape no 818
22 July 1979 Tape no 896
20 Nov 1979 Tape no 900

Mini-interviews recorded with Mary Cooper:
10 Nov 1980 Tape A
28 Nov 1980 Tape B

15 Dec 1980 Tape C
4 June 1981 Tape D

Interviews recorded with other informants:
31 Mar 1980 Tape no 917 Maggie Chapman, born 1888, Burnley weaver
6 Dec 1979 Tape no 907 Billy Coombe, 1892–1982, Burnley weaver
21 Dec 1979 Tape no 914 Harold Coombe, born 1930s, Burnley decorator
26 Apr 1979 Tape no 832 Henry Foulds, 1907–81, Nelson weaver
14 Nov 1979 Tapes 889 and 898 Stan Iveson, born 1912, Nelson plumber
19 July 1979 Tape no 850 Robert Stansfield, born 1907, Nelson weaver
6 July 1978 Tape no 679 Jane Summersgill (née McCall), born 1900, Nelson weaver
4 Oct 1983 Tape E Helen Wilson, born 1911, Manchester

(Tape numbers refer to tapes deposited with Manchester Studies, Manchester Polytechnic; tape letters refer to cassettes in the author's possession.)

2. COLLECTIONS OF PAPERS

Cooper Papers, Lancashire Record Office, Preston (DDX 1137), series of
    deposits 1977–83
Fawcett Library MSS, City of London Polytechnic, London
Labour Party MSS, Labour Party Archive, London
Marshall Papers, Cumbria Record Office, Carlisle
Nelson Local History MSS, Nelson Library, Pendle
Pankhurst Papers, International Institute of Social History, Amsterdam
Robinson Papers, Central Reference Library Archives, Manchester
Suffrage MSS, Central Reference Library Archives, Manchester

3. MINUTES AND ANNUAL REPORTS

Burnley Board of Guardians, minutes
Burnley Federation of Textile Trades Unions, minutes
Burnley Weavers' Association, minutes
Independent Labour Party, Conference Reports
Labour Party, Conference Reports
Manchester and District (Women's Suffrage) Federation, annual reports
National Union of Women's Suffrage Societies, annual reports
National Union of Women's Suffrage Societies, Quarterly Council minutes
National Union of Women's Suffrage Societies, Executive Committee
    minutes

National Union of Women's Suffrage Societies, Election Fighting Fund, Committee minutes

National Union of Societies for Equal Citizenship, Executive Committee minutes

Nelson and Colne Parliamentary Borough Labour Party, Conference Reports

Nelson and Colne Parliamentary Borough Labour Party, Executive Committee minutes

Nelson, Colne, Brierfield and District Textile Trades Federation, minutes

Nelson Independent Labour Party, branch account book

Nelson Independent Labour Party, branch minutes

Nelson Independent Labour Party, General Committee minutes

Nelson Labour Party, minutes

Nelson Weavers' Association, minutes

Primitive Methodist Scotland Road (Nelson), Leaders' minutes

Public Assistance Committee (Lancashire), minutes

Women's Citizens' Association (Nelson Parliamentary Division), minutes

North of England Society for Women's Suffrage, annual reports.

4. NEWSPAPERS AND PERIODICALS

Accrington Observer; Burnley Co-operative Record; Burnley Express; Burnley Gazette; Colne and Nelson Times; Common Cause; Co-operative News; Daily Worker; Justice; Labour Leader; Manchester Guardian; Nelson Chronicle; Nelson Gazette; Nelson Leader; Nelson Workers' Guide; Northern Daily Telegraph; Socialist (Burnley); *Women's* (later, *Workers'*) *Dreadnought*

5. OTHER PRIMARY SOURCES

Baptism and burial church records

Birth, marriage and death certificates

Household census, 1841, 1851, 1861, 1871 and 1881

Throup, Willie J., *Poverty and Power*, unpublished playscript, 1931

Viznews, archive film

SECONDARY SOURCES

1. BIOGRAPHIES AND AUTOBIOGRAPHIES

Ashby, M.K., *Joseph Ashby of Tysoe 1859–1919*, Merlin, London, 1974

Brockway, F., *Inside the Left*, Allen and Unwin, London, 1942

Chew, D.N., *Ada Nield Chew: the Life and Writings of a Working Woman*, Virago, London, 1982.

Dickinson, B., *James Rushton and his Times 1886–1956*, privately published by the author, Nelson, n.d. (1970s)

Hall, R., *Marie Stopes*, Andre Deutsch, 1977 and Virago, London, 1978

James, A., and Hills, N., *Mrs John Brown*, John Murray, London, 1937

Linklater, A., *An Unhusbanded Life: Charlotte Despard, Suffragette, Socialist and Sinn Feiner*, Hutchinson, London, 1980

Mitchell, H., *The Hard Way Up*, Faber, 1968 and Virago, London, 1977

Pritt, D.N., *From Right to Left*, Lawrence and Wishart, London, 1965

Russell, D., *The Tamarisk Tree: My Quest for Liberty and Love*, Elek Books, 1975 and Virago, London, 1977

Vernon, B.D., *Ellen Wilkinson*, Croom Helm, London, 1982

2. LOCAL HISTORIES

Bennett, W., *The History of Burnley from 1850*, Burnley Corporation, Burnley, 1951.

Bennett, W., *The History of Marsden and Nelson*, Nelson Corporation, Nelson, 1957

Fowler, A., *The History of the Nelson Weavers*, Nelson Weavers' Association, Nelson, 1984 forthcoming

Hawkes, G.I., *The Development of Public Education in Nelson*, Nelson Corporation, Nelson, 1966

Leonard, T.A., *Adventures in Holiday-Making*, Holiday Fellowship, London, 1935

Wood, A. (ed), *Cowling: A Moorland Parish*, Cowling Local History Society, Cowling, 1980

3. GENERAL HISTORIES

Davies, M.Ll., *Maternity: Letters from Working Women*, G. Bell, 1915 and Virago, London, 1978

Gregory, R., *The Miners and British Politics 1906–1914*, Oxford University Press, Oxford, 1968

Harrison, B., *Separate Spheres: The Opposition to Women's Suffrage in Britain*, Croom Helm, London, 1978

Lewis, J., *The Politics of Motherhood*, Croom Helm, London, 1980

Liddington, J. and Norris, J., *One Hand Tied Behind Us: The Rise of the Women's Suffrage Movement*, Virago, London, 1978

McKibbin, R., *The Evolution of the Labour Party 1910–1924*, Oxford University Press, Oxford, 1974

McLaren, A., *Birth Control in Nineteenth Century England*, Croom Helm, London, 1978

Pankhurst, E.S., *The Suffragette Movement*, Lovat Dickson and Thompson, 1931 and Virago, London, 1977

Pugh, M., *Electoral Reform in War and Peace 1906–18*, Routledge and Kegan Paul, London, 1978

Strachey, R., *The Cause: A Short History of the Women's Movement in Great Britain*, G. Bell 1928 and Virago, London, 1978

4. ARTICLES

Davin, A., 'Imperialism and Motherhood', *History Workshop Journal*, spring 1978

Liddington, J., 'Looking for Mrs Cooper', *Women and the Labour Movement*, North West Labour History Society *Bulletin*, no 7, 1980–1

Liddington, J., 'The Women's Peace Crusade: the History of a Forgotten Campaign', Thompson, D. (ed), *Over Our Dead Bodies: Women Against the Bomb*, Virago, London, 1983

Vellacott, Newberry J., 'Anti-war Suffragists', *History*, 1977 vol 62

Wood, G.H., 'Statistics of Wages in the United Kingdom during the Nineteenth Century', *Journal of the Royal Statistical Society*, 1910

5. UNPUBLISHED THESES

Bowes, N., *The People's Convention*, MA, Warwick, 1976

Bruley, S., *Socialism and Feminism in the Communist Party of Great Britain, 1920–39*, Ph.D., London, 1980

Hill, J., *Working Class Politics in Lancashire 1885–1906*, Ph.D., Keele, 1969

Holton, S., *Feminism and Democracy: the Women's Suffrage Movement in Britain with particular reference to the National Union of Women's Suffrage Societies*, Ph.D., Sterling, 1980

Lambertz, J.R., *Male-Female Violence in Late Victorian and Edwardian England*, BA, Harvard, 1979

Trodd, G., *Political Change and the Working Class in Blackburn and Burnley*, Ph.D., Lancaster, 1978

INDEX